IMAGE AND REALITY IN ECONOMIC DEVELOPMENT

A Publication of the Economic Growth Center, Yale University

IMAGE AND REALITY
IN ECONOMIC DEVELOPMENT

LLOYD G. REYNOLDS

New Haven and London, Yale University Press, 1977

Designed by Sally Sullivan
and set in Monophoto Times Roman type
by Asco Trade Typesetting Limited, Hong Kong.
Printed in the United States of America by
The Murray Printing Company, Westford, Mass.

Published in Great Britain, Europe, Africa, and
Asia (except Japan) by Yale University Press,
Ltd., London. Distributed in Latin America by
Kaiman & Polon, Inc., New York City; in
Australia and New Zealand by Book & Film
Services, Artarmon, N.S.W., Australia; and in
Japan by Harper & Row, Publishers, Tokyo Office.

Library of Congress Cataloging in Publication Data

Reynolds, Lloyd George, 1910–
    Image and reality in economic development.

    (A publication of the Economic Growth Center,
Yale University)
    Bibliography: p.
    Includes index.
    1. Economic development.   I. Title.
II. Series: Yale University. Economic Growth
Center. Publications.
HD82.R44   338.9   77-76312
ISBN 0-300-02088-0

Contents

Foreword

This volume is one in a series of studies supported by the Economic Growth Center, an activity of the Yale Department of Economics since 1961. The Center is a research organization with worldwide activities and interests. Its purpose is to analyze, both theoretically and empirically, the process of economic growth in the developing nations and the economic relations between the developing and the economically advanced countries. The research program emphasizes the search for regularities in the process of growth and changes in economic structure by means of intercountry and intertemporal studies. Current projects include research on technology choice and transfer, income distribution, employment and unemployment, household behavior and demographic processes, agricultural research and productivity, and international economic relations, including monetary and trade policies, as well as a number of individual country studies. The Center research staff hold professorial appointments, mainly in the Department of Economics, and accordingly have teaching as well as research responsibilities.

The Center administers, jointly with the Department of Economics, the Yale master's degree training program in International and Foreign Economic Administration for economists in foreign central banks, finance ministries, and development agencies. It presents a regular series of seminar and workshop meetings and includes among its publications both book-length studies and journal reprints by staff members, the latter circulated as Center Papers.

Hugh Patrick, Director

Preface

"Nel mezzo del cammin di nostra vita," in Dante's phrase, I made a drastic shift of professional orientation. Having worked for twenty years on the economics of labor, I began to feel that I knew something about it, a frame of mind not conducive to future productivity. Several overseas missions—a summer in sub-Saharan Africa in 1952, a research study in Puerto Rico that I directed from 1953 to 1957, a 1956–57 visit to several Asian countries during a period of service with the Ford Foundation—persuaded me that the economic problems of developing countries were intriguing intellectually and also of urgent practical importance. At no one point did I sit down and decide to become a student of economic development; but I was led in this direction by small stages over a period of years.

Leaving the familiar for the unknown is a precarious, perhaps even a foolish, undertaking; but it does produce an intellectual rejuvenation, a feeling of growing up afresh in an area that requires rethinking and adaptation of familiar tools to new purposes. Over the past twenty years I have found it exciting to sift and appraise the rapidly growing development literature, discuss problems firsthand with economists and government officials in some thirty third-world countries, teach a graduate course in development economics, and help in the establishment and management of the Yale Economic Growth Center. In addition to the center's published research, there is an oral tradition and a custom of critical interchange within the research staff to which all of us associated with the center owe a deep intellectual debt.

This book is partly a mind-clearing exercise, an effort to think my way through problems that every development economist must face. It is also an effort to outline the present structure of the subject. One difficulty in studying and teaching development economics has been an uncertainty about the content of the subject and about how it relates to more traditional branches of economics. This book defines the core of the subject as I see it; and although no one will take it as the final word, it may stimulate discussion of fundamentals.

The book might have been written earlier, but it would have been a thinner and poorer book. For the subject has moved forward through continued interaction of intellectual analysis and development experience, and we have more insights today than we had in 1950. We have become inured to changing intellectual fashions—the takeoff, the magical operation of the Incremental Capital-Output Ratio (ICOR), the population bomb, the green revolution, the new international economic order—and to waves of optimism and pessimism about development prospects. The shortsighted projections of rapid and universal development that were fashionable in the 1950s have yielded to a more realistic appreciation of the wide diversity among third-world countries with regard to economic structure, political organization, past growth rates, and outlook for the future.

The "development boom," as indicated by volume of public discussion, level of foreign aid appropriations, or graduate course enrollments, peaked in the mid-1960s and has since been declining. But like Everest, the third-world countries are still there, and we now know a good deal more about them. The growing economies have been sorting themselves out from the nongrowing, and there are more and more monographs analyzing these diverse experiences. Further, in addition to efforts to analyze economies *in toto* or to build comprehensive growth models, there is a growing body of research by specialists in various branches of applied economics—international economics, agricultural economics, demography, public finance, and so forth—who have turned their expertise toward third-world problems.

The development literature, indeed, is now so voluminous that sorting it out is a major task. "What must I read and what can I forget about?" asks the harried graduate student. In addition to the signposts in successive chapters of this book, I hope that the selected bibliography may prove useful in answering this question. If the list of suggested readings seems oppressively long, you should see the ones that got away. The bibliography certainly does not include more than 10 percent of the titles that I have examined, often with more disappointment than profit, over the past twenty years.

No book satisfies everybody, and this one will be no exception. I can already anticipate two kinds of criticism. Some will say that, in trying to touch on every important issue in development economics, I have ended up with a superficial treatment of each. There is no doubt a tradeoff between coverage and depth, and I have deliberately opted for the former. It seemed to me more useful at this stage to define the broad contours of the development landscape than to dig into particular ravines or craters. On most points, those who want to dig deep will find pointers in the bibliography.

A second reaction may be that I have raised many questions but provided few answers. This is partly in the nature of the subject. It is still a young subject, and we do not really know very much—certainly not as much as we should know a generation from now. The discussion may also reflect a teacher's wariness about taking strong positions on disputed issues. I have thought it more important to raise the right questions, and to sort out pros and cons, than to assert my own conclusions. As James Thurber remarked, "It is better to know some of the questions than all of the answers."

Lloyd G. Reynolds

Big Cedar Lake
West Bend, Wisconsin

Acknowledgments

It is impossible to recognize individually the hundreds of people who have contributed in one way or another to this book—colleagues and graduate students at Yale, economists and government officials in the developing countries, development economists in the United States and Europe, foundations that have helped finance leaves of absence and research support. But the problem of listing them does not reduce my gratitude for their aid, and my feeling that in large measure I am riding their intellectual coattails.

Friends who read and commented on semifinal versions of the manuscript include Samuel Ho, University of British Columbia; Frederick Pryor, Swarthmore College; Henry Bruton, Williams College; Paul Clark, Williams College; Carlos Diaz Alejandro, Yale University; and Gustav Ranis, Yale University. Hugh Patrick of Yale reviewed the discussion of Japanese growth experience in chapter 9, and Bruce Reynolds of Union College reviewed the comments on China in chapter 15. These comments were invaluable in the final revision, but any blame for remaining deficiencies is entirely my own.

The statistical tables in chapters 10–14 were prepared by Mahmood Ayub, Nantanee Vacharasiridham, and Christine Wallich, without whom this work could not have been completed. Once more, my greatest single debt is to Gail Ross, who typed, edited, and proofread the manuscript with her usual speed and precision.

L.G.R.

PART 1   CONCEPTS

1

The Content of Development Economics

If one asked ten economists, What is public finance about? there would be a strong similarity in the answers. Course syllabi and reading lists from different universities would also show a family resemblance. The reason is that economists have been trying to systematize the subject for a century or more.

Although reasoning about economic development can be traced back to the classical economists, the modern revival of interest in the subject dates only from about 1950. This is one reason why courses and texts in economic development are more diverse than those dealing with older branches of applied economics. Another reason is the vastness of the empirical terrain that the subject professes to cover. Economic development relates to a hundred or so economies of Asia, Africa, and Latin America; and, since the effort is to understand the growth of these economies in its totality, the discipline includes, in principle, interests in agriculture, population, industrial organization, public finance, international economic relations, and so on. It is evident that no one can know everything about the economies of all those countries. So, what is a "development economist" anyway?

One purpose of this book is to move the subject a step forward by projecting a clearer image of its content. Even if the specifications outlined here do not win full agreement, the effort to formulate and rationalize disagreement will serve a constructive purpose.

SOME QUESTIONS OF LANGUAGE

Definitions are tedious but necessary. We begin with them because our subject has been afflicted by confusion over terminology and because words have a profound influence on our thinking. When we coin a descriptive label, we are making a statement about the economic world.

The subject itself should be called *not* economic development but development economics. Economic development is an activity, an art—something that politicians and entrepreneurs try to accomplish. It connotes the battleground of action. Development economics is a branch of applied economics in which theorizing, research, and policy applications are blended in about the normal proportions. Its habitats are the university and the research institute. A scholar can also be a practitioner; but the roles are distinct.

Is it useful to distinguish between *growth* and *development*? Economic growth is defined conventionally as a sustained rise in per capita output; and research has tended to focus on the mechanism of such a sustained upward movement. Some find this focus too narrow, because it does not include other valid policy objectives—fuller employment, more equal distribution of income—or because a single measure cannot capture the richness of events during a period of economic and political modernization.

If, however, one observes a sustained rise in per capita output, one can infer a number of other structural changes, including growing commercialization of production, gradual improvement of markets, shifts in the composition of output by sector of origin, and a rise in savings and investment as a percentage of gross national product (GNP). The significance of rising per capita output is not just that it connotes the possibility of a rise in living standards but also that it stands as a proxy for many associated aspects of economic change. For the countries whose growth accelerated at various points in the nineteenth century, the pattern of associated changes has been documented by the massive investigations of Simon Kuznets. It is reasonable to assume that similar changes can be observed in countries whose (conventionally defined) growth has accelerated since 1940.

The fact that an economy is growing does not mean that its performance is necessarily satisfactory on all counts. There is evidence that in today's third-world countries growth is often accompanied by rising underemployment, increasing regional disparities, and growing inequality of personal incomes. But this should not lead one to deny the reality or twist the definition of growth to encompass these other criteria. Rather, one should seek the sources of the observed trends in distribution and employment and explore the feasibility of growth paths that would not have these undesirable side effects.

One might give a distinctive meaning to "development" by saying that, in addition to measured growth and associated structural changes, it connotes systematic change of economic and political institutions in a growth-promoting direction. Historical observation suggests, however, that (conventionally defined) economic growth and institutional change are closely intertwined. Some minimal framework of politico-economic organization may be a "precondition" for growth acceleration. But institutional modernization can also be regarded as an accompaniment or side-product of sustained growth, both stemming perhaps from vigorous political leadership, as in the classic case of Japan. Thus, the measured growth rate does not lose its significance as a proxy for a complex process of change.

For these reasons, we shall use the terms *growth* and *development* interchangeably. But this is not meant to imply that output *per se* is the sole objective of policy, or that the changes accompanying aggregate growth are simple, or that a growing economy meets all the normative standards of good performance.

A national economy need not grow. Over the long course of history, economic stagnation has been by far the most common situation. But in some countries, at a certain point, time series that have hitherto been fluctuating about an almost horizontal trend line begin to turn upward. Typically, a number of series—population, food production, total output and output per capita, exports and imports, rates of saving and capital formation—turn up almost simultaneously within a short span of years. This seems to have happened in England in the 1740s, in several of the continental countries in the 1820s and 1830s in Japan in the 1880s, and in several Latin American countries in the 1940s.

One upturn does not make a growth saga. There are many cases in which a country took off and then landed again. But in the success cases, the higher growth rate continues decade after decade. Eventually, after a period that may be a half-century in length, one can conclude that sustained growth is built into the economy. But such a judgment can only be reached after the fact. The predictions of future success that abounded in the 1950s proved notoriously fallible.

What are we to call this period between the initial inflection point and the point of arrival at sustained growth? "Takeoff" is unsatisfactory because it connotes a *very* short period, because of the implication of invariable success, and because Rostow's description of what happens during takeoff did not stand up well against the historical evidence.[1] Kuznets calls it the period of *transition* to modern economic growth. We prefer to call it the period of *growth acceleration*. Analysis of events during this period is the central concern of development economics. The focus is not on economic growth in general, but on *early* economic growth.

Once growth has become routine, the economy becomes, from our standpoint, uninteresting. It continues to have growth problems, but these are problems that it is nice to be able to afford: problems of economic stability, income distribution, government action to repair deficiencies in the market mechanism.

This leads to a word on classification of economies. A common procedure is to array countries in order of per capita income and then draw a line dividing "developed" from "less developed" countries. Or, one can make a finer classification into "high-income," "medium-income," "low-income," and "poorest" categories. The statistical hazards of such a procedure are well known: the large probable error in national income measurements for many countries, the inaccuracy of exchange rate conversions, and the fact that in some soil- or mineral-rich economies the per capita average gives a misleading impression of both economic structure and living standards for the bulk of the population.

These measurement difficulties, which in principle might be overcome, are still not the heart of the matter. The key problem is that cross-sectional comparisons at a particular point in time do not reveal the growth characteristics in which we are mainly interested. They do not tell us which countries are essentially stationary, which are experiencing growth acceleration, and which have reached the stage of built-in growth capacity. This can be judged only from time series extending over a long period.

I suggest, then, that the most significant classification involves: (1) *stagnant economies*—countries in which per capita output is not rising, or is rising so slowly or erratically that the persistence of growth is uncertain. While a rich country could fall into this group, most members of the group are relatively poor; (2) countries that are experiencing growth acceleration as defined earlier. These I shall call *developing economies*, avoiding the misleading euphemism by which this term is applied indiscriminately to almost all of Asia, Africa,

---

1. See papers by Kuznets, Deane and Habbakuk, and others in W. W. Rostow, ed., *The Economics of the Takeoff* (New York: St. Martin's Press, for the International Economic Association, 1964).

and Latin America. Most of these countries are also relatively poor, but they are moving upward in the world league and ranked higher in 1975 than they did in 1950; (3) countries that have passed through the acceleration phase and are now in the phase of sustained growth. These include the "OECD club," plus the Soviet Union and a few others. These I shall call *mature economies.*[2]

Note that this growth classification cuts across the lines of an economic systems classification. There are mature socialist as well as capitalist economies; and, along with the developing capitalist (or precapitalist) economies, there are developing socialist economies such as China, Yugoslavia, and Rumania.

The central concern of development economics is with the countries is group 2, those experiencing growth acceleration. The stagnant economies of group 1 are of some interest because they suggest possible barriers or obstacles to growth, but I do not propose to explore that theme here. As for the countries of group 3, the development economist is interested, not in their current economic performance, but in what occurred during their period of growth acceleration—in England from 1740 to 1800, in France from 1815 to 1860, in Japan from 1880 to 1920.

In sum, the key terms in my suggested vocabulary are: *development economics; economic growth; growth acceleration;* and *stagnant, developing,* and *mature economies.* Occasionally, when I wish to refer to third-world countries in general, whether developing or stationary, I shall use the conventional term *less developed countries* (LDCs).

THE LIMITS OF GROWTH THEORY

A preliminary puzzle is why there is any need for a special theory of early economic growth in poor countries. After all, growth theory is now a standard component of graduate curricula in economics. Students learn about natural and warranted rates of growth, about Cobb-Douglas and other aggregate production functions, about embodied and disembodied technical progress, and about optimal capital accumulation over time. Is there anything more to be said?

---

2. This is not to say that every country fits neatly into such a schema. There are anomalies such as Argentina and Chile, middle-income countries that experienced sustained growth for quite a long time but recently have managed to stagnate. Israel, whose per capita income would now put it with the mature economies, still has significantly different characteristics. The classification of some countries would depend on *how long* a period of growth one requires as evidence of sustained advance. Most countries, however, could usefully be classified in this way.

Formally, of course, the standard models are sufficiently general to embrace any economy at any stage of development. In an accounting sense, the growth rate of output can always be decomposed into rates of increase in factor quantities, rates of factor augmentation, disembodied technical change, and other possible components of the famous "residual." But accounting is not the same as explanation. The analytical models used in modern growth theory are often completely aggregative. Even in two-sector models, which distinguish capital-goods from consumer-goods production, growth theorists are primarily concerned with the existence and stability of equilibrium and with the problem of optimal capital accumulation. But these are not the most important questions to the development economist. Development economics, in a sense, is concerned with *disequilibrium*, with how an essentially stagnant situation is disrupted, and with the somewhat disorderly course of sectoral development during the growth-acceleration period.

In commenting briefly on the limitations of growth theory, we assume that the reader is familiar with the structure of the models under discussion so that we can go directly to an appraisal of their usefulness for developing economies.

Demand-oriented Models

These post-Keynesian models, developed mainly in the 1940s by Harrod, Domar, Duesenberry, and others, were oriented toward mature industrial economies with an aggregate demand problem. For such an economy, the models tried to answer the question: What are the requirements for sustained growth with full employment over an extended time period?

It is ironic that early writers on economic development seized on the Harrod-Domar model and converted it from the original demand orientation to an emphasis on the growth of output capacity under highly simplified assumptions. But it is understandable in the sense that, as of 1950, this was the *only* model of long-term growth lying ready at hand. Further, it appeared to provide a convenient planning instrument and a way of rationalizing foreign aid requests. Consider the following arithmetic: country X wishes to increase its GNP at, say, 5 percent per year. Assume that the incremental capital-output ratio is constant at, say, 3:1 (which somehow emerged as a magic ratio in the 1950s). Thus, gross investment must amount to 15 percent of GNP if the growth target is to be attained. Unfortunately, the average gross domestic savings rate is only 10 percent of GNP. So, dear AID or IBRD, please supply the difference.

This approach was often combined with the Rostow hypothesis of a quick "takeoff" into self-sustained growth. If, with the aid of foreign capital transfers, the investment rate could be held at the required level for a decade or so, the growth of output would raise the domestic savings rate (via a Keynesian savings function) to a level at which foreign aid would no longer be necessary. Paul Rosenstein-Rodan, in a remarkable tour de force, used this mixture of Harrod-Domar, Rostow, and Keynes to predict the amount of foreign aid required to launch all the world's LDCs into self-sustained growth.[3]

With the benefit of hindsight, the superficiality of this reasoning is apparent. It is now well established that the ICOR varies widely, among industries and economic sectors, among national economies, and over time. If a country somehow succeeds in growing rapidly, an ex post calculation will reveal a low ICOR; conversely, if the growth rate is zero, the ICOR will be infinite. But such calculations have no explanatory or predictive value. Asking Why was the ICOR unusually low? is equivalent to asking Why was the growth rate unusually high? It does not bring us any closer to an answer.

This kind of model also conveys the misleading implication that the main, or even the only, constraint on growth is ability to produce or import conventionally defined capital goods. This diverts attention from the complexity of actual growth requirements.

Supply-oriented Models

Although capital accumulation (human as well as physical) is important to the growth of output capacity, also important are labor supply, natural resource availability, possibilities of factor substitution, technical progress, and intersector shifts in the composition of output. The Meade-Tobin-Solow line of theorizing has developed complex production functions to explain capacity growth.[4] There has been a parallel stream of econometric work designed to decompose a country's output growth into its constituent elements. This research

3. P. N. Rosenstein-Rodan, "International Aid for Underdeveloped Countries," *Review of Economics and Statistics* (May 1961): 107–38.

4. For a review of this and other branches of growth theory, see F. H. Hahn and R. C. O. Matthews, "The Theory of Economic Growth: A Survey," published originally in the *Economic Journal*, reprinted in *Surveys of Economic Theory*, vol. 2 (New York: St. Martin's Press, 1965), pp. 1–124.

provides useful background for economists interested in long-term growth in any kind of economy. But for the student of growth acceleration, is it any more than background? Its limitations revolve around the twin facts that it relates to *a certain kind of economy* and that it asks *a limited range of questions* about such an economy.

A supply-oriented model normally depicts a one-sector economy producing a single output, which can serve either as a consumption good or a capital good (not unlike the "corn" of the classical wages fund). The factors of production are labor and capital. A Cobb-Douglas production function is usually assumed, though the more flexible CES (constant elasticity of substitution) function has come into increasing use. Factors are fully and continuously employed (though some models permit initial unemployment of labor, which is absorbed gradually over time). Pure competition prevails throughout the economy, and factor prices and income shares are determined in competitive markets. Technical progress usually enters the model, but it can be specified in a variety of ways.

Within this framework, growth theory asks two main questions. First, given certain rates of increase in labor and capital inputs, plus (usually) a certain rate and direction of technical progress, what will be the "steady-state" growth rate of output? How will this growth rate be affected by changes in the parameters? This *comparative dynamics* is logically similar to the comparative statics used in other branches of economics. Second, if the economy is not initially on a steady-state growth path, will it converge toward such a path or move farther away from it? This is a problem in the stability of equilibrium.

These are important issues for a developed country; but they are *not* the most important questions to be asked about a less developed economy. And the framework of assumptions is highly unrealistic. Particularly damaging is the assumption of a single product and a single production function. The essence of underdevelopment is the existence of a small "modern" sector, monetized and operated on commercial principles, alongside a larger "traditional" sector. Nor can one get around this by saying: "We will apply standard growth theory only to growth within the modern sector," treating the traditional sector as a residual. For the behavior of the traditional sector as factor supplier and product demander, including its gradual shrinkage and annexation to the modern sector, constitutes an integral part of early economic growth. The notion of a growing modern sector embedded in a static environment is self-contradictory. Any theory of early growth must deal explicitly with sectoral interaction.

Related to this is the neglect of land and the primacy of capital in modern growth theory, which stamps such theory as industrially oriented. In the LDCs, however, agriculture is usually the largest sector at the beginning of growth acceleration, and for a long time it continues to expand absolutely while declining in relative terms. Therefore, the characteristics of agricultural production functions, the initial land-labor ratio, the rate of population growth, and the speed and factor bias of technical progress in agriculture must be brought into any usable growth model.

Modern growth theory also bypasses what for the LDCs is the most important single question: How does a stagnant economy change into a slowly growing economy? How does economic growth begin? In the standard growth models, progress is already underway before the curtain rises. Some positive growth rate is taken for granted, and the only problem is how high this rate will be.

Put differently, in modern growth theory the determinants of the national growth rate are taken as given, with no effort to explain why they have one value rather than another. Population growth rates, savings propensities, production technology, and rate and direction of technical progress are all exogenous. But in the LDCs, these parameters are changing—indeed, the main object of policy is to ensure that they do change. The givens of the standard growth problem become variables in the LDC setting.

Normative Growth Theory

Modern growth theory comes also in a normative variant, which is concerned with defining optimal growth paths. This line of inquiry was initiated by the mathematician John Von Neumann, and subsequent work has been carried on mainly by mathematicians or by economists with strong mathematical interests. The problem is usually to maximize the discounted value of consumption over an infinite time period—or alternatively to maximize discounted consumption over a finite period subject to the requirement of a terminal capital stock. The early models were completely aggregative. The Von Neumann model involved a single "Shmoo-type" good, which could either be eaten or used as a tool. More recent work, however, usually specifies separate capital-good and consumer-good sectors. Capital is the sole source of output increases. Indeed, these are essentially models of optimal capital accumulation over time. Consumption is often taken as freely adjustable, though some models specify a minimum consumption level as a constraint.

It is not clear that the results of such exercises can be given a useful economic interpretation even for mature economies, let alone for the LDCs. The myopic concentration on capital and the single-good assumption are major defects when dealing with disaggregated and natural-resource-based economies.

The LDCs also lack either a market mechanism or a political mechanism capable of indicating the "social rate of time preference," which is crucial to optimizing models. Even if this rate were known, governments of LDCs typically lack the control instruments required to enforce a target rate of saving and capital formation. In virtually every LDC, the domestic savings rate is below what would be desirable. To raise the gross savings rate from, say, 10 percent to 15 percent is a difficult and important problem. But a finance minister who has studied the turnpike theorem will not be any farther ahead in meeting this problem.

DEVELOPMENT ECONOMICS: CORE CONTENT

We turn now to the positive task of specifying what development economics is about. The core of the subject is longitudinal analysis of growth and structural change in developing economies, that is, economies that have entered the phase of growth acceleration. There are twenty or so sizable economies whose growth has accelerated since 1940. This is our empirical universe. The majority of LDCs, which are still essentially stationary, are of less interest, since explanation of nongrowth is a dubious undertaking.[5]

Within this universe of developing nations, the development economist tries to grapple with an entire economy in what John Fei terms a "whole-istic" way. A national economy is more than a collection of sectors. These sectors interact in ways that we can theorize about and try to measure. Analysis of this interaction involves, as usual, a blend of theorizing and research. At a theoretical level, one needs models with an much sector detail as is feasible without making

---

5. This is not to deny that the plight of these countries is of humanitarian concern. One would like to see more of them moving forward into the growth acceleration phase. But how-to-do-it prescriptions for policy cannot be the main focus for development economics, any more than for other branches of applied economics. Further, the chances of a particular country moving forward depend largely on political and social changes internal to the country. Foreign countries—and economic advisers from those countries—have less influence than has sometimes been imagined.

the model unmanageable. The goal is to strip away secondary complications, schematize the essential features of what is going on, and go for the jugular. At the empirical level, a comprehensive system of national income and product accounts provides the best assurance that one is looking at the total system.

Models conceived in this spirit, of which the best-known are the Lewis and Fei-Ranis models, usually relate to a closed economy. They are multisector, though the number of sectors and their specification varies from case to case. The earliest models placed modern industry in the center of the stage, leaving agriculture as a rather shadowy residual; but the recent tendency has been to specify the structure of agriculture in more detail and to incorporate technical progress and capital accumulation in agriculture as well as in industry. They are usually "surplus labor" models, though the content of this elusive concept differs somewhat among theorists. The "success criterion" in such models runs in terms of employment as well as of output. A key question is whether, given an exogenous rate of population increase and other parameter values, the initial labor surplus will tend to increase or diminish over time.

While closed-economy models are a necessary first step, actual developing economies are involved in international trade. Most of them, being small in economic size, are heavily involved; and so any relevant development model must incorporate a foreign sector. At this point, development theory merges imperceptibly into trade theory, and it is no accident that some of the most penetrating work on developing economies has been done by people who would regard themselves as primarily international economists. Work on this trade-growth borderland should, we believe, be included in the central core of development economics; and "trade" should be viewed broadly as including not only merchandise flows but flows of people, capital, and technology.

Using these closed- and open-economy models, plus concepts from microeconomics and other branches of theory, the development economist tries to understand the growth of a particular developing country over an extended period of time. He tries to test growth hypotheses against data on sector performance, intersectoral flows, international economic transactions, and associated institutional change. It is not inaccurate to regard such work as analytical economic history (which all economic history is increasingly becoming). The small number of good country monographs produced to date testifies to the difficulty of the task and to the special kinds of insight and expertise required.[6]

When enough such studies have been completed, one would hope to proceed to a further stage of comparative analysis. How similar, or how different, have been the growth patterns of different developing countries? To what extent can one see resemblances to one or another analytical model? We are not really able to make such comparisons at present, however, because of the shortage of good country-specific material.

Since economic time series for individual countries are fragmentary, and often available only for a brief recent period, many researchers have employed the shortcut of cross-section analysis, using current data that are in more ample supply. Although such work is not without interest, and may sometimes be dictated by data considerations, there are several reasons why it is not a fully satisfactory substitute for time series analysis. First, most cross-section studies, in an effort to maximize the number of observations, include the whole universe of national economies, or at least of nonsocialist economies. Thus, the analysis includes a hodgepodge of stagnant economies, economies in the phase of growth acceleration, and middle-to-high-income economies undergoing sustained growth. It is hard to say what such a mixture can tell us about the limited number of poor-but-growing economies in which we are mainly interested.

Second, the figure of per capita income in U.S. dollars, which is usually relied on as a key explanatory variable, is highly fallible. In addition to the crudeness of GNP estimates for many LDCs and the conceptual difficulties of comparing high-income and low-income economies, the exchange-rate conversion procedure is notoriously unreliable. A recent study calculated, first, Gross Domestic Product (GDP) per capita for each of a number of countries as a percentage of U.S. GDP per capita, using official exchange rates; and second, GDP per capita for each country as a percentage of U.S. GDP, using

6. On this point the writer can testify from hard experience. In the early 1960s, the Yale Economic Growth Center launched a Country Analysis Program, which involved sending young economists to some twenty-five LDCs for one to two years of field work. Because of the formative state of the subject, the advice and instructions we could give them were limited. The hope was that they would devise their own methodology and would come back with an analytical "story" of the economy's growth over as long a period as feasible. The fact that only about half of these potential country monographs were actually completed resulted partly from turnover of personnel, but also from the fact that the task itself proved extraordinarily difficult and time-consuming.

international prices reflecting the actual purchasing power of national currencies.[7] Dividing the second percentage by the first yielded an index of "exchange rate deviation." This was in all cases greater than 1, *that is*, relative per capita income in other countries was always *understated.* Moreover, the degree of understatement varied inversely with the income level of the country concerned, the deviation being greatest for the poorest countries. For example, the exchange rate deviation index for selected countries was as follows: West Germany, 1.16; United Kingdom, 1.35; Japan, 1.47; Kenya, 1.91; Colombia, 2.32; India, 3.49.

Third, in order to interpret cross-section results as equivalent to change over time, we must assume that the observations are drawn from the same universe. Such an assumption may be valid for regressions of investment behavior by U.S. manufacturing companies. But it is more dubious when applied to the treacherous terrain of cross-national comparisons.

A different kind of problem in growth analysis arises from the fact that economic growth occurs in a political and social setting and that economic, political, and social variables are interacting in a complex way over time. The question is what can be done about it. The economist can, of course, draw about him the cloak of professional modesty and underline that he is depicting only one aspect of a complex social system. But this leads to the abandonment of any effort to explain how and why growth acceleration occurs at some times and places and not at others.

A different tactic, beloved of foundations and research organizers, involves the setting up of interdisciplinary teams including political scientists and students of social relations as well as economists. This has not worked very well either. The reason seems to be that other social sciences have their own kind of narrow-mindedness, their own conceptual schema, which fail to make effective contact with that of the economist. The political scientist does not want to work for the economist by accepting, on subcontract, the task of determining what political situation is or is not conducive to growth acceleration. Rather, he wants to be like the economist, to build his own abstract models of power relations and political behavior. But these models often do not bear on the questions that the economist wants answered.

7. Irving Kravis and others, *A System of International Comparisons of Gross Product and Purchasing Power* (Baltimore: Johns Hopkins University Press, for the World Bank, 1975).

The moral seems to be that the economist, if he seriously wants to reach beyond his usual framework, must himself try to acquire expertise in related skills. One can point to a growing number of economists, such as Gunnar Myrdal, Simon Kuznets, Everett Hagen, C. E. Lindblom, Irma Adelman, and Cynthia Taft Morris, who have made this sort of effort.

DEVELOPMENT ECONOMICS: SECTOR PROBLEMS

An across-the-board analysis of a developing economy is the most complex task confronting a development economist. But even a cursory glance at the literature reveals a wide array of more specialized activities. Developing countries, like any others, have labor markets, product markets, money markets, fiscal systems, international economic relations, and producing sectors, which can be analyzed by those trained in specialized branches of applied economics. Thus, anyone can become a "development economist" in the sense of deploying his analytical skills abroad rather than at home. A corollary is that to come out of graduate school proclaiming oneself a development economist pure and simple is a bit like setting up as a general medical practitioner. It is preferable to come out as a development economist *and* something else—monetary economist, public finance specialist, labor economist, or whatever.

The idea that sectoral specialists work only on domestic problems is purely conventional and, in an interdependent world with rapid communications, increasingly obsolete. There is no reason why public finance people should confine their attention to the American fiscal system. They can equally well work on problems of public revenue and public output in Thailand or Kenya. This will, to be sure, require some rethinking and reshaping of conceptual tools to adapt them to a new empirical context; but it is a challenging task that will make better economists of those who attempt it.

Over the past twenty years, there has already been an encouraging movement in this direction. The movement has been strongest among agricultural and international economists, and there are natural reasons for this. Agriculture is the largest economic sector in most LDCs—and a sector whose modernization is unusually difficult. This has challenged Western agricultural economists to work on such matters as the economics of tenure systems, farmers' responsiveness to price incentives, and the generation and diffusion of technical change. Most LDCs are also deeply involved in the network of world trade and capital movements, and so international economists have paid increasing attention to the interaction of more- and less-developed economies. A valuable side effect has been a substantial broadening and dynamizing of trade theory.

The advantages of such a redeployment of effort by sectoral specialists toward the LDCs are self-evident. There is the scientific consideration that hypothesis building and hypothesis testing should rest on as wide a range of observations as possible. If forty or fifty countries have data on a particular problem, this provides the equivalent of forty or fifty independent experiments. Unless we take advantage of these other laboratories, we cannot tell whether conclusions drawn from mature-economy experience are generally valid.

There is also an efficiency consideration. The prospective returns from economic research are higher abroad than at home. As research projects and doctoral dissertations on the American economy proliferate, and as we push harder on the intensive margin of scientific cultivation, we find ourselves dealing increasingly with trivia. The anatomy and physiology of the less-developed economies, on the other hands, is imperfectly understood. The basic research that could lead to such understanding has scarcely begun. On this extensive margin of research, yields are higher than at home; and economists, above all people, should appreciate the advantage of reallocating resources toward high-yield areas.

Careful research by sectoral specialists can also provide a basis for improved economic policies. The policy problems that arise in the LDCs are mainly micro problems; and to the extent that Western economic analysis is transferable to these economies, it is mainly our microeconomics rather than our macroeconomics that is relevant.[8] This is not to deny the potential contribution of macroplanning; but given the small size of the public sector, and the limited effectiveness of controls on the private sector, the potential is still limited. Most of the economic decisions that government is capable of executing involve action in particular markets, affecting specific prices and quantities. It is here that microeconomic reasoning and research can be especially helpful.

8. Some will find this statement controversial, and space does not permit full discussion at this point. I have developed this theme at some length in *The Three Worlds of Economics* (New Haven: Yale University Press, 1971), chaps. 8–9, "The Usefulness of Western Economics."

Sequence of the Book

The chapters that follow are, in one sense, a series of essays on distinct themes. But these themes are so interrelated as to lend unity to the undertaking.

Chapter 2 reviews the tradition of development theory, with main emphasis on the closed-economy, labor-surplus family of growth models. I conclude, not surprisingly, that the last word has not yet been said and that progress requires, among other things, a clearer specification of the agricultural sector. In chapters 3 and 4, therefore, I examine what is now known about the structure and dynamics of low-income agriculture. The focus is on owner-operated or "peasant" farming and on the response of owner-operators to such exogenous changes as population growth, changes in relative prices, and new technical opportunities. The object is to develop assumptions about agricultural behavior that can plausibly be incorporated into multi-sector models.

Building on this foundation, I develop in chapters 5 and 6 a closed-economy model rather different from others in current use. The model highlights what I regard as the strategic variables in early economic growth and permits a qualitative appraisal of their impact. The model could also be used for simulation experiments, which I did not find time to undertake but which I urge others to do if they find the approach intriguing.

Any closed-economy model is admittedly only a first step toward a more realistic analysis of open economies. In chapters 7 and 8 I try to sort out the voluminous literature on trade, aid, and growth and to assess the present state of knowledge in the area.

I emerge from the analytical discussion in part 1 with many hypotheses about how an economy might be expected to behave during the period of growth acceleration. How well do these hypotheses stand up in the light of historical experience? The review of development experience in part 2, in addition to being interesting in its own right, is intended to serve as a means of testing and improving development theory.

I begin with the case of Japan (chapter 9), the first non-Western country to experience growth acceleration. This involves no assumption that Japanese experience closely resembles contemporary growth patterns. But it seemed a useful exercise to focus the relatively abundant Japanese economic data on the kinds of questions that development theorists have been raising since 1950.

In chapters 10–14 I raise the same questions for fifteen economies whose growth has accelerated noticeably since World War II. The list includes most, though perhaps not all, of today's developing economies. It is too early to predict that all of these countries will reach the stage of sustained growth; but even in today's disturbed world economy, their prospects appear good. After a review of their overall economic performance since 1950, I engage in a comparative sector-by-sector analysis, with a view to testing hypotheses about what "should" be happening in a developing economy. I consider also the much-debated question of whether or not countries can be classified into a limited number of distinct "growth patterns"—the "typology problem."

The economies examined in chapters 10–14 are mixed economies; but there are also a number of socialist developing economies. It is interesting to ask whether their growth pattern is distinctively different and whether, or in what respects, it can be regarded as "more successful." Chapter 15 examines these questions with respect to China and several of the less developed Balkan countries.

In the body of the book, I have made a determined effort to stick to positive economics; but this does not mean that I regard policy as unimportant. On the contrary, issues of economic policy are even more urgent in developing than in mature economies, and it would not be proper to conclude without some reference to them. In the final chapter, therefore, I sort out some high priority issues and comment briefly on them.

2

The Tradition of Development Theory

Although there is an element of autonomous scientific development in economic theory, there are also cycles of interest induced by exogenous economic and political events. Thus, it is not surprising that the first wave of interest in economic development occurred in countries that were experiencing growth acceleration. In England, this acceleration occurred in the decades following 1740; in France and the predecessor German states, in the decades following the end of the Napoleonic Wars in 1815; and by the 1850s, several other European countries had been drawn into the broadening current of economic growth. The classical economists, most of whose work was published between the appearance of *Tableau Économique* in 1758 and Mill's *Principles* in 1848, set out to explore the principles underlying long-term growth, including the question of whether such growth could be expected to continue indefinitely in the future.

We should not, therefore, approach the classical writers as relics of a bygone era, whose work is no longer of interest. Rather, we should view them as having faced issues that still confront economists in India, Nigeria, or Brazil. I must assume, as I shall throughout this book, that the reader is familiar with the body of literature under discussion. With this understanding, let me underline briefly what each of the major writers accomplished.[1]

The Physiocrats

The members of this group, whose leading spirit was François Quesnay, were the first to view the economy as a general equilibrium

1. For a fuller statement, see L. G. Reynolds, "Development Theory: The Classics," in *Essays in Honor of William Fellner*, ed. Bela Balassa and Richard Nelson. (forthcoming). See also Lionel Robbins, *The Theory of Economic Development in the History of Economic Thought* (New York: St. Martin's Press, 1968).

system, involving a circular flow of income and product among a few major sectors (the Tableau Économique). The sectors they distinguished were: *landowners; farmers*, whom they though of as large, well-capitalized tenants renting land from the landowners; and *everyone else*—artisans, traders, soldiers, servants. Broadly, the division is between agriculture and nonagriculture.

The distinctive feature of agriculture is that it is the only economic activity that produces a *net product*. In a regime of laissez-faire or pure competition, which they took as both an analytic model and a policy objective, the total amount that manufacturers and other nonagriculturalists receive for their product is distributed as wages of labor or interest on capital. There is nothing left over. But in agriculture, there is something left over. The farmer, after covering his labor and capital costs, has a surplus, which he pays as rent to the landowner. This net product, attributable to land, is the only true surplus in the economy. The physiocratic policy prescriptions follow directly from this doctrine. First, agricultural development should be promoted in order to make the net product as large as possible. Second, some unspecified part of the agricultural surplus should be transferred out of agriculture by a single tax on land rent.

Adam Smith: The National Income of Nations

Despite its precursors, Smith's great work is rightly regarded as the first systematic treatise on economic development. By the *wealth* of nations Smith meant the *income* or, as we would say today, the GNP of nations. Smith sets forth clearly, and for the first time, the concept of *income per capita* as the criterion of economic progress.[2] He shows that national income and output must be equal, distinguishes gross from net concepts, and separates out the main components of capital. Indeed, his treatment of capital, is in some ways superior to later practice. He explicitly includes "the acquired and useful abilities of all the inhabitants," which have recently been rediscovered as "human capital"; and he excludes housing, treating it as a consumer durable.

---

2. The first paragraph of *The Wealth of Nations* begins as follows: "The annual labor of every nation is the fund which originally supplies it with all the necessaries and conveniences of life which it annually consumes.... Accordingly, therefore, as this produce ... bears a greater or smaller proportion to the number of those who are to consume it, the nation will be better or worse supplied with all the necessaries and conveniences for which it has occasion."

Smith agreed with the physiocrats that the basic sectoral division is between agriculture and nonagriculture and that the interchange of commodities between them is of central importance.[3] Regarding the agriculture-industry terms of trade, he thought that urban producers typically have an advantage because, being fewer in number, they can more readily conspire to fix the prices of their products. They also have disproportionate political influence and can secure restrictions on entrance to industry, tariffs against competing imports, and other measures that benefit them at the expense of the farm population. Smith also estimated, however, that the "corn price" of wool cloth and other key manufactures had fallen considerably in England over the previous century, suggesting that the machinations of industrialists might not be sufficient to avert declining terms of trade.

Smith also shared the physiocratic view that agriculture should be preferred over other sectors. He felt it to be particularly productive because "nature labors along with man." He believed that the capital-labor ratio is lower in agriculture than in manufacturing, while the output-labor ratio is higher.[4] It follows that the output-capital ratio must also be higher in agriculture. Further, agriculture is the basic industry, on whose growth all others must depend. The city depends on the country for subsistence, raw materials, and a market for its products.[5] The functions of the agricultural sector in a developing economy have never been more clearly expressed.

The growth of national output depends on capital accumulation, on growth of the "stock" that can be advanced to productive laborers.

3. "The great commerce of every civilized society is that carried on between the inhabitants of the town and those of the country. . . . The country supplies the town with the means of subsistence, and the materials of manufacture. The town repays this supply by sending back a part of the manufactured products to the inhabitants of the country." (Book 3, chap. 1.)

4. "The capital employed in agriculture, therefore, not only puts into motion a greater quantity of productive labor than any equal capital employed in manufacture, but in proportion too to the quantity of productive labor which it employs, it adds a much greater value to the annual produce of the land and labor of the country, to the real wealth and revenue of its inhabitants. Of all the ways in which a capital can be employed, it is by far the most advantageous to the society." (Book 2, chap. 5.)

5. "It is this commerce which supplies the inhabitants of the town both with the materials of their work, and the means of their subsistence. The quantity of the finished work which they sell to the inhabitants of the country, necessarily regulates the quantity of the materials and provisions which they buy. Neither their employment nor subsistence, therefore, can augment but in proportion to the augmentation of the demand from the country for finished work; and this demand can augment only in proportion to the extension and improvement of cultivation." (Book 3, chap. 1.)

The classical writers tended to regard landowners as a prodigal class, spending their income on retainers and high living. In this view, the real savers are the capitalists in both the agricultural and nonagricultural sectors. The savings rate thus depends on the size of the profit share of income and on how this is divided between saving and employment of unproductive laborers. Capital accumulates through reinvested profits, as in Arthur Lewis's model, which, as Lewis himself emphasized, is a revival and elaboration of classical thought.

Growth also depends on correct allocation of capital, which, we must remember, includes circulating as well as fixed capital. This issue, prominent in contemporary development theory, is also a central theme in the *Wealth of Nations*, developed in a chapter on "the natural progress of opulence." Smith was, of course, premarginal, and the concept of equating yields at the margin was foreign to him. Rather, he regarded some sectors as superior to others in an absolute sense. One should pour capital into the socially most profitable sector until that is, as it were, "filled up." Then capital should spill over into the second-best sector until it is full; and so on.

His ranking of sectors is based on the amount of labor that will be employed by a unit of capital. The "best" sector is that with the highest L-K ratio—which, if one assumes no intersectoral difference in output per worker, would also mean the highest Y-K ratio. The use of capital that contributes most to output will also contribute most to capital accumulation, and hence to continued increase of output in the future. The criterion is not employment per se but rather the contribution that a particular use of capital makes to future growth.

In this view, the best sector, as already noted, is agriculture. Manufacturing ranks next in labor-absorbing capacity (one must remember that English manufacturing at this stage was still almost entirely handicraft production, with a high labor-capital ratio). Wholesale and retail trade, which use little labor relative to the capital employed, are least advantageous. Smith believed that this ranking, based on social profitability, corresponded to the ranking in terms of private profit and that, if government did not intervene unwisely, capital owners would be led "as by an invisible hand" to allocate capital in the proper sequence.

He observed, however, that in France and England the historical sequence of development had been almost the reverse of that which he prescribed. The low level of investment and productivity in agriculture he blamed mainly on faulty tenure arrangements—large landholdings owned by unprogressive landlords, share rentals amounting to as much as half the total produce, insecurity of tenure—as well as on heavy and erratic government levies on agriculture.

To return to the central theme: As the capital stock grows, more labor is employed. Where does this labor come from? There is no clear concept of "surplus labor" in Smith, though British economic historians seem agreed that there was in Smith's time a labor surplus in both town and country. Smith, however, relied on population growth as the main source of additional labor.

Smith shared with his classical followers an essentially cost-of-production theory of labor supply. In a stationary state, the worker earns only a subsistence wage, defined as one that will enable him to rear enough children to maintain the labor force intact. If the demand for labor rises through capital accumulation, the market rate of wages will rise above this "natural" level, and the labor supply will respond. Population will grow, mainly through fewer children dying prematurely. If and when the labor supply begins to rise as rapidly as the capital stock, wages will level off; and if the labor supply should rise faster, wages would be driven down again toward subsistence level, retarding the rate of population increase.[6] In Smith's model, population cannot rise more rapidly than capital stock over the long run; and the capital-labor ratio in production is fixed, a natural assumption given the interpretation of capital as primarily circulating capital.

But with capital and labor increasing proportionately, how can output per capita grow? Part of the answer is that, as total output rises, there is increasing opportunity for specialization and exchange, that is, "the division of labor is limited by the extent of the market." Increases in labor productivity arising from greater specialization are a key force raising per capita income.

A second source of higher labor productivity is greater mechanization of production. This also stems from division of labor because, as tasks become more finely subdivided, they are also more readily mechanized. Finally, Smith believed that a higher real wage would by

---

6. The market wage level thus depends, not on the *size* of the capital stock, but on its *rate of increase*. "It is not, accordingly, in the richest countries, but in the most thriving, or in those which are growing rich the fastest, that the wages of labor are highest. England is certainly, in the present times, a much richer country than any part of North America. The wages of labor, however, are much higher in North America. . . ." (Book 1, chap. 8.)

itself raise the productivity of labor,[7] leading to a "virtuous circle" of cumulative upward progress. The hypothesis of a backward-bending supply curve of labor was firmly rejected.[8]

Formally, then, Smith's model includes output as an increasing function of capital and labor inputs, capital as (implicitly) a function of output, and employment as a function of capital stock. These three equations are sufficient to determine the three variables Y, K, and L. But Smith's insights are more important than the technical completeness of his model.[9]

What is the long-run tendency of the system? Smith believed that the rate of profit tends to fall over time, though his explanation of this is not very convincing. (His most explicit statement is that, as more and more capital crowds into the same industry, competition will reduce the level of prices and profits. But this is surely not adequate at a macroeconomic level.) Eventually, profit will fall to a level that discourages further net saving. The concept of the "fully stocked" economy in which accumulation has ceased—China is the favorite illustration—recurs at several points in the book. When an economy has been in this situation for some time, population growth must eventually reduce wages to a subsistence level, after which population growth will also cease.[10] There is no clear picture of the stationary state in Smith, however, and he obviously regarded it as a distant prospect.

7. "A plentiful subsistence increases the bodily strength of the laborer, and the comfortable hope of bettering his condition, and of ending his days perhaps in ease and plenty, animates him to exert that strength to the utmost. Where wages are high, accordingly, we shall always find the workmen more active, diligent, and expeditious than where they are low; in England, for example, than in Scotland...." (Book 1, chap. 8.)

8. "That a little more plenty than ordinary may render some workmen idle, cannot well be doubted; but that it should have this effect upon the greater part, or that men in general should work better when they are ill fed than when they are well fed ... seems not very probable." (Book 1, chap. 8.)

9. For an effort to formalize Smith and other classical models, see Irma Adelman, *Theories of Economic Growth and Development* (Stanford: Stanford University Press, 1961).

10. "... It is in the progressive state, while the society is advancing to the further acquisition, rather than when it has acquired its full complement of riches, that the condition of the laboring poor, of the great body of the people, seems to be the happiest and most comfortable. It is hard in the stationary, and miserable in the declining state." (Book 1, chap. 8.) "Progressive," "stationary," and "declining" are to be interpreted in terms of the size of the capital stock.

Another line of analysis involves the interrelation of economic growth and foreign trade. Smith's views on this subject have been analyzed by Hla Myint,[11] and little need be added here. Smith believed that a nation benefits from international trade in two ways, which differ from each other and also from the classical theory of comparative costs. First, trade enables an industry to expand beyond the confines of the domestic market, which makes possible a finer division of labor with a resulting gain in productivity. This is different from the gain posited by comparative cost theory, which results entirely from resource reallocation after the opening of trade, with *given* production functions.

Second and more novel is Smith's "vent for surplus" doctrine, which views trade as providing an outlet for goods that otherwise could not find a market.[12] In order for such an output surplus (potential) to exist, there must be a surplus of productive resources not presently in use. If these can be mobilized to meet a foreign demand, the imports received in return are a net gain to the economy. (This calls to mind recent writings on mobilization of "surplus labor" for economic development. The modern tendency, however, is to urge mobilization of this labor, not to produce export products, but to produce manufactures for domestic use. It is these manufactures, which under rather extreme assumptions can be viewed as costless, that then result in a net gain to the economy).

David Ricardo: Food Bottleneck and the Stationary State

If Smith impresses with his wide historical knowledge and sharp policy insights, Ricardo impresses with the tightness of his analytical system. Ricardo professed little interest in the *size* of national income,[13]

11. "The 'Classical Theory' of International Trade and the Under-developed Countries," *Economic Journal 68* (June 1958): 317–37, reprinted in H. Myint, *Economic Theory and the Underdeveloped Countries* (London and New York: Oxford University Press, 1971).

12. "It carries out that surplus part of the produce of their land and labor for which there is no demand among them, and brings back in return for it something else for which there is a demand. It gives a value to their superfluities, by exchanging them for something else, which may satisfy a part of their wants. . . ." (Myint, *Economic Theory*, p. 119.)

13. In a letter to Malthus, cited by Robbins, he says: "Political Economy you think is an enquiry into the nature and causes of wealth—I think it should rather be called an enquiry into the laws which determine the division of the produce of industry among the classes who concur in its formation. No law can be laid down respecting quantity, but a tolerably correct one can be laid down respecting proportions. Every day I am more satisfied that the former enquiry is vain and delusive, and the latter only the true object of the science."

asserting that the central problem is what determines the *distribution* of that income among "the three classes of the community"—landowners, capitalists, and wage earners. But "distribution" here must be interpreted in a historical sense. The problem is how factor returns tend to *change over time* and whether their projected movement is consistent with continued economic progress. This is clearly a problem in growth theory.

We must assume that the reader is familiar with the main outlines of the Ricardian system: the theory of *value* (or relative prices) as dependent on the amount of labor, direct and indirect, required to produce a good; the concept of *diminishing returns* from land; and the theory of *rent* as the return to the original and indestructible powers of the soil.

Technical progress, including technical progress in agriculture, is absent from Ricardo as it was from Smith. The evolution of rent is then readily explained. As population grows, agricultural production is pushed harder on both the intensive and extensive margins of cultivation. Because of diminishing returns, the amount of labor needed to produce an additional bushel of corn rises steadily. Since there has been no change in the amount of labor required to produce industrial products, the relative price of corn must rise. The internal terms of trade move against industry. Rent per acre of land, and the rent share of national income, rise continuously over time.

The wage rate is the price of labor and, like any price, depends on the amount of labor required to produce the article in question—in this case, the amount of labor required to grow enough food to support a worker at subsistence level. This Ricardo defines as the *natural* level of wages.

There is also a *market* level of wages that depends, as in Smith, on the relative rates of increase in the labor supply and in the stock of (circulating) capital that governs the demand for labor. If capital is growing more rapidly, the market wage rate will diverge above the natural rate. According to Malthusian reasoning, however, the rate of population growth will in time overtake and exceed that of capital accumulation, and the market wage will then fall toward the natural level.

If the natural rate is of dominant importance, the crucial question is how this rate changes over time. In real terms, it does not change, that is, the amount of food required for the worker's subsistence is constant. But the money wage required to buy this amount of food rises over time. The reason, already noted, is that the relative price of food is rising because of the operation of the principle of diminishing returns in agriculture.

This tendency, usually termed "the Ricardian food bottleneck," puts a squeeze on industrial profits. Consider a cloth manufacturer. He is faced with a rising wage bill for the reason just noted. But the value of his cloth has not increased, because there has been no change in the amount of labor required to make it. Rising labor costs with no increase in product prices must reduce the profit share of value added.[14] Here is the basis for a secular decline in profit, which Smith forecast but did not adequately explain. Moreover, since competition must lead to the same profit rate in all industries, this decline will extend throughout the economy.

Profit could conceivably fall to zero. But at some point before this, the incentive to net saving will vanish and the capital stock will become constant. With the lag necessary for population to catch up, the market rate of (real) wages will fall to the natural rate, after which population (as well as output and output per capita) will also remain constant. This is the Ricardian stationary state. Ricardo recognized the possibility of technical progress as a counteracting tendency; but he thought that it could do no more than slow down the eventual arrival at the stationary state.

Until recently, the Ricardian system seemed interesting merely in antiquarian terms. But in today's less-developed economies, the Ricardian food bottleneck is no historical figment. The agriculture-industry terms of trade are central to contemporary development models. The pressure of rapidly growing population on food supplies has already turned the domestic terms of trade in favor of agriculture in some countries—and threatens to do so in others; and, as Ricardo predicted, this tends to choke off industrial development.

John Stuart Mill: The Dawn of Victorian Optimism

Mill was the first great systematizer of economics, the first textbook writer to break the 900-page barrier. His *Principles*, published in 1848, remained the standard text for British and American students until well after 1900.

14. To repeat, the worker's "corn wage" has not risen—he eats no more than before. But to provide him with this fixed amount of corn, the employer must give up more and more cloth, since corn prices have risen relative to cloth prices. The worker's "cloth wage," his share of value added, has risen. The essence of the matter is that the terms of trade turn increasingly against industry on account of diminishing returns.

While Mill built upon Ricardo's theoretical system, he made important new contributions. He anticipated Marshall in using the *ceteris paribus* technique. His chaper[15] on the effect of economic growth on factor prices first analyzes the consequences of population growth in isolation from any other change in the economy, then the effect of capital accumulation acting alone, and finally the effect of technical progress by itself. This is about what we have been doing ever since. Mill distinguishes nicely between the effect of land-saving improvements and labor-saving improvements in agriculture. And he distinguishes between cost reductions in the production of goods consumed by workers ("wage goods," as we would now say) and "luxuries" consumed by the population at large. The latter benefit consumers generally but do not affect income distribution. Improvements in producing wage goods, however, influence the behavior of Ricardo's natural rate of wages and so influence distribution.

By 1848 Britain had clearly entered the phase of sustained growth. Thus, it is not surprising that Mill's book is more optimistic than Ricardo's a generation earlier. Mill is impressed with the importance of technical progress and other dynamic changes, which postpone the consequences of the Ricardian model. We are always within sight of the stationary state, but the horizon recedes as we approach it. Nor would eventual arrival at the stationary state necessarily be undesirable. In an interesting chapter,[16] Mill argues that a (high-level) stationary state would probably be more pleasant than any other. The sight of people trampling over each other in the race for progress, the intense concentration on money-grubbing (to which he considered Americans particularly addicted), was not edifying to a man who at heart was a moralist and a political philosopher. The tone resembles that of some of today's antigrowth arguments.

Karl Marx: The Great Dissenter

It is currently fashionable to urge social scientists not to be "narrow specialists" but broad-ranging, multidisciplinary scholars. The classical economists certainly followed this pattern. Adam Smith was a moral philosopher. John Stuart Mill was a political theorist. The outstanding example, however, was Karl Marx—philosopher, historian, political

15. Mill, *Principles*, book 4, chap. 3. This book contains most of Mill's systematic reasoning on long-term growth.
16. Book 4, chap. 6.

theorist, and Old Testament prophet. Marx's technical economics was by no means the most consequential part of his total system.

Post-Marxian controversy has focused mainly on his prognosis of the eventual breakdown of capitalism. But this is not the part of Marx that is relevant for our present purpose. A country in an advanced stage of capitalist development is scarcely a less-developed country. Our concern here is with how growth acceleration occurs in a pre-industrial, primarily agricultural economy, that is, with the emergence of industrial capitalism rather than its eventual fate. The relevant part of Marx's schema, therefore, is his analysis of the transition from the feudal to the capitalist stage of development.[17]

Where did the capitalists come from, and how did they accumulate the capital needed to launch large undertakings? Some of them were initially small artisans who gradually took on employees and expanded their scale of operation.[18] Large initial capital, however, was usually accumulated either through money lending or commerce ("primitive accumulation"). Once such capital has been converted to employment of industrial workers, further capital accumulation presents no problem. It occurs naturally and cumulatively through reinvestment of profit ("surplus value") extracted from the laborers. Along with other classical writers, Marx believed that industrialists have a natural passion for accumulation and will not waste their income in prodigal living. He joined the other classical writers, too, in the conviction that continued accumulation drives down the rate of profit, so that the capitalists must accumulate ever more frantically to maintain the same *total profit*.

Where will the new class of industrial workers come from? Since agriculture is the dominant industry, they will come mainly from agriculture. In contemporary development models, this rural-urban flow of labor is a voluntary movement induced by a substantial wage gap. According to Marx, on the other hand, small farmers are forcibly evicted by large landowners, with the cooperation of government, and turned into landless proletarians against their will. His description of this process doubtless reflects elements of reality. The large landhold-

17. The fullest statement of his views is in part 8, volume I, of Karl Marx, *Capital*, which should properly be read as the introductory rather than the concluding part of that volume.

18. "Doubtless many small guild-masters, and yet more independent small artisans, or even wage-laborers, transformed themselves into small capitalists, and (by gradually extending exploitation of wage-labor and corresponding accumulation) into full-blown capitalists." (Vol. 1, chap. 31.)

ings that had developed in England by the eighteenth century were achieved partly through land consolidation and displacement of small farmers and cottagers. Enclosure of the old common lands, depriving individuals of living space and rights to fuel and pasturage, contributed to this enforced movement. Marx does appear, however, to overstate the conscious malevolence with which landlords and government collaborated to drive the dispossessed into the arms of the waiting capitalists. Nor does this "English model" have much relevance to the small peasant producers who dominate the agriculture of contemporary Nigeria or Thailand.

A secondary source of labor supply is the extinction of the artisans, who are displaced by the more productive capitalist enterprises. The small handicraft producer is separated from direct contact with the means of production and is forced to sell his labor power to the capitalist who now owns those means. Marx regarded this process as inevitable and even desirable. Small workshops do not permit the division of labor and the mechanization required for high productivity. Modern technology *requires* large-scale enterprises, and history, ever responsive to technological imperatives, obligingly brings them into being.[19]

It cannot be overemphasized that, in Marx's view, the capitalist stage of development serves a necessary historical purpose. It concentrates capital in fewer, larger production units through competition among capitalists ("one capitalist kills off many"), which permits a steady increase in specialization, mechanization, and productivity.

---

19. "...This petty mode of production...attains its adequate classical form only where the laborer is the private owner of his own means of labor set in action by himself; the peasant of the land which he cultivates, the artisan of the tool which he handles as a virtuoso. This mode of production presupposes parcelling of the soil, and scattering of the other means of production. As it excludes the concentration of these means of production, so also it excludes co-operation, division of labor ... and the free development of the social productive powers. It is compatible only with a system of production, and a society, moving within narrow and more or less primitive bounds. To perpetuate it would be, as Pecqueur rightly says, 'to decree universal mediocrity.' At a certain stage of development it brings forth the material agencies for its own dissolution. From that moment new forces and new passions spring up in the bosom of society; but the old social organization fetters them and keeps them down. It must be annihilated; it is annihilated. Its annihilation, the transformation of the individualized and scattered means of production into socially concentrated ones, of the pygmy property of the many into the huge property of the few, the expropriation of the great mass of the people from the soil, from the means of subsistence, and from the means of labor, this fearful and painful expropriation of the mass of the people forms the prelude to the history of capital." (Vol. 1, chap. 32.)

These enterprises eventually reach a scale at which their socialization is technically easy and, indeed, essential for further progress. Capitalist resistance to socialization provokes a revolutionary struggle, in which the capitalists are overthrown and socialism is ushered in. Marx would have been quite surprised to see countries like China, Cuba, and Vietnam attempting to move directly from an agrarian economy to full-blown socialism, skipping the industrial capitalist stage.

Yesterday and Today: The Contribution of Classical Thought

On rereading the classics, the dominant impression is not of what they overlooked but of how much they anticipated. They dealt with most of what are now regarded as leading issues in development economics. Most, but not all. They underrated technical change—and particularly the potential of technology as an offset to diminishing returns in agriculture. They would have been surprised to hear that, in the United States over the past several decades, output per man-hour has risen faster in agriculture than in any other sector except electric power production. They could scarcely foresee the decolonization of most of Asia and Africa, the emergence of new centers of political and economic power, the increased volume and changed pattern of international trade, or the marked increase of "official" capital flows relative to private capital movements. They would have been surprised, too, to see some of today's poor countries attempting to skip the capitalist stage of development.

Nevertheless, one is impressed by how many of today's central issues were central also in classical economics. A brief listing of these may serve to summarize the preceding discussion:
—The determinants of population growth, and the importance of relative rates of increase in population and food supply
—The functions of the agricultural sector in a growing economy, as food supplier to the towns and as a market for industrial products.
—The importance of the intersectoral terms of trade, and the possibility that a continued movement of the terms of trade in favor of agriculture may choke off industrial development
—The delineation of forces governing long-term trends in relative factor prices and in the functional distribution of national income
—The reinvestment of capitalist profits as the dominant mechanism for capital accumulation
—The issue of optimal allocation of capital among economic sectors
—The potential contribution to domestic growth of participation in international trade

—The importance of government economic policies in stimulating (or possibly impeding) economic development.

These issues are perhaps discussed more precisely in contemporary development theory. But the increasingly narrow and technical character of modern economics has involved loss as well as gain. The classical writers worked close to the earth. They had a rich understanding of the economic process. But they did not hesitate to talk demography, psychology, politics, and ethics. Instead of worrying about how far they could go before transgressing the boundaries of their discipline, they asked how far they must go to reach the boundaries of a problem. In this, as in other respects, we can still learn from them.

INTERLUDE AND REVIVAL

After 1850, growth vanished from the mainstream of economic thought for almost a century. The reason may be partly that during this long period only one non-Western country, Japan, was drawn into the current of modern economic growth. Most parts of Asia and Africa were colonies, which by definition could have no *national* growth objectives. The Latin American countries, although politically independent, were economic satellites of western Europe and the United States. In the countries where economics flourished (Britain, France, Germany, the United States), economic success was already assured, and attention could be turned to the ills of a successful economy—cyclical fluctuations, maldistribution of income, market power and market failure, and trade and monetary relations "within the club."

Marshall and Schumpeter might be regarded as partial exceptions to the general tendency. Marshall was old-fashioned in that he was interested in the sources of capital accumulation and in the qualitative as well as quantitative growth of the labor force, rather than simply in the allocation of *given* resources. But writing in the heyday of Victorian optimism, he believed that the tendency toward increasing returns in manufacturing would readily outweigh diminishing returns in agriculture, and he foresaw no barriers to long-term economic growth.

Schumpeter was also concerned with dynamic problems, and his concepts of innovation and the entrepreneur have proven highly useful. But his *Theory of Economic Development* did not mean what this term connotes today. His book is primarily an explanation of economic fluctuations in an industrialized economy with a developed financial system. The empirical reference is to Britain or Germany, not to Thailand or Nigeria.

The recent revival of interest in development economics was prompted by the decolonization movement, which peaked between 1945 and 1960. Scores of newly independent countries, as well as the older countries of Latin America, found themselves in a position to pursue national growth objectives. The richer countries also became interested in these economies due to a mixture of humanitarian concern, an interest in export promotion, and big-power rivalries. International organizations, of which the World Bank has emerged as the most important, were established to promote growth in the poorer countries.

Both national and international agencies looked to economists for policy analysis and, because of the scarcity of economists in the less developed countries, the main impact was felt in Europe and North America. This was flattering to economists but also embarrassing, for hardly any of them had thought seriously about economic development in several generations. Thus, hundreds of economists who had hitherto pursued domestic specialties found themselves retreaded as development economists; and thousands of young people, even more responsive than their elders to emerging policy issues, flocked into undergraduate and graduate courses for training as "second-generation" development specialists.

We shall not try to review the vast output of policy-oriented, or "how to develop," literature over the past generation. We propose rather to examine the smaller stream of analytical writing.

This theoretical work is of three kinds: (1) "partial theories" of a microeconomic sort, which analyze behavior in particular sectors or markets. Examples are theories of peasant behavior, rural-urban migration, and technology transfer in manufacturing. Quantitatively, such work comprises the bulk of the analytical writing in development economics, and, while it lacks the grand sweep of macroeconomic models, it may turn out to be at least equally important; (2) macroeconomic, closed-economy models analyzing interaction of major sectors in the growth process; (3) open-economy models that examine the interactions between growth and trade. This branch of the literature is sufficiently distinctive and important that we will defer examination of it until chapters 7 and 8, after closed-economy problems have been explored.

MICROANALYSIS OF DEVELOPING ECONOMIES

We argued in chapter 1 that any economist can become a "development economist" by deploying his skills in a developing economy and conversely, that anyone professing to be a development economist is well advised to acquire depth in other branches of applied economics. Many economists have taken this lesson to heart over the past generation; and the totality of their work is impressive. To look only at total-economy models is greatly to underestimate the richness of the development literature.

A brief review can suggest only the general thrust of this work, leaving detailed references to the bibliography. We shall not distinguish sharply between pure theory and research, since they are blended in varying proportions in the material under review. Indeed, one virtue of this microeconomic theorizing is that it leads rather directly to possibilities of testing and tends to be accompanied by a parallel stream of statistical investigation.

Population Growth

An initial task here is to explore the mechanics of accelerated population growth in the LDCs, that is, to trace changes in age-specific fertility and mortality rates over the past several decades. We know that there has been an unusually rapid decline of mortality rates resulting from disease control and other public health programs; but less is known about fertility rates, which may also have changed significantly. A number of economists and demographers have been working to straighten out the historical record and to project population growth rates for the decades ahead.

A second research frontier is the analysis of household decisions about numbers of children. In the United States, where most births are intended, models of fertility behavior incorporating economic variables have stood up well to statistical tests. In the LDCs, the percentage of unintended births is certainly higher, but we do not know how much higher. As regards intended births, it is commonly hypothesized that desired family sizes are larger in the LDCs than in the mature economies because of differences in the incentive structure. But there is need for more testing of this hypothesis through microanalysis of household samples.

As knowledge of fertility behavior improves, there may be important applications to the design of family planning programs. Most LDCs now have such programs, but their apparent impact varies from country to country. How far is this due to differences in the amount of resources committed to the program, and how far to differences in program design? How far does the limited response to family planning reflect large *desired* family sizes, rather than lack of information and techniques? Considerable research effort is going into follow-up studies of family planning programs in order to answer these questions.

Another well-known hypothesis is that industrialization, urbanization, and rising per capita incomes tend by themselves to reduce age-specific fertility rates. Thus, if a developing country can manage to outrace population growth for several decades, it can hope that the population tide will begin to recede. A number of developing countries already show declining fertility rates, and investigation of just how this has occurred is an important research priority. This work has also stimulated a reexamination of what happened in the older industrial countries during their periods of "demographic transition" to lower rates of population growth. The results thus far suggest that the picture of a uniform and almost automatic decline of birthrates consequent on economic development is considerably oversimplified.

Underemployment, Migration, Wage Determination

Because of the common assumption of "surplus labor" in the rural sector, there have been numerous efforts to define this concept more precisely and test its existence statistically. These efforts have led to a more detailed examination of rural labor markets—utilization of family labor time, hiring-in and hiring-out of labor, variations in the degree of underemployment by region and by season of the year, and the question of whether the pattern of rural wage rates is susceptible to economic explanation.

In most LDCs there is a strong current of migration from rural to urban areas. This phenomenon has stimulated several lines of research: the creation of models of migration, incorporating expectations of the probability of urban employment as well as rural-urban earnings differences; the examination of who migrates, and whether the incidence of migration can be interpreted on economic grounds; and the investigation of how unemployed urban populations can subsist in countries without public support systems. Measures of open un-employment in the cities typically show a secular increase since 1950;

and underemployment in traditional activities is also believed to be widely prevalent.

Urban labor markets are notably imperfect, and earnings differentials are wide. There have been numerous efforts to interpret the phenomena of an apparently "abnormal" gap between earnings in modern and traditional activities and an upward trend of real wages in the modern sector despite substantial unemployment. There has also been considerable analysis of earnings differentials among occupational levels.

Economic Responses in Agriculture

The wealth of interesting problems in this sector has drawn the attention of both full-time agricultural economists and development economists with a secondary interest in agriculture. We shall pass over this work lightly, since it will be examined more thoroughly in chapters 3 and 4.

Broadly, work in this area can be divided into: (1) tests of the economic rationality of farmers' resource allocation and of their response to changes in prices and other exogenous variables. Interest in such work is declining, however, because the results come back with monotonous regularity: Even small peasant farmers *are* economically rational. Their responses to changing incentives are predictable on economic grounds; (2) the use of farm families' labor time, on and off the farm, and the extent of underemployment. Related to this is the policy issue of what can be done to absorb more labor time in productive activity within the rural sector—a clear necessity if rapid population growth is not to lead to a secular rise in underemployment; (3) a variety of issues in the area of technical change: how new agricultural technology is generated and diffused, nationally and internationally; why there continues to be a wide gap between experiment station results and actual farm practice; which farmers adopt new technology most rapidly; and what the economic and other constraints on more rapid adoption are.

Economic Issues in Industrialization.

In this sector, too, there is a wide range of research and policy issues. These issues include:

1. The actual (and optimal) sequence in the introduction of new manufacturing industries. There has been much analysis of the "natural" sequence of industrialization, from the earlier work of

Walther Hoffman to that of Hollis Chenery and others in recent times. To the extent that government undertakes to guide the sequence via allocations of capital, foreign exchange, licensing, and other devices, there is a question about what criteria should be used for such allocations. This has often been approached through the concept of "linkages," involving explicit or implicit use of input-output analysis. There has also been extended debate over the use of shadow prices for inputs and outputs in estimating economic profitability.

2. Choice of technology by new manufacturing enterprises. How is technology transferred from more to less developed countries, and how are choices actually made in the LDC setting? To what extent can imported technology be modified in a labor-using, capital-stretching direction?

3. Competition between large, "modern," relatively capital-intensive plants and traditional small-scale industries with a lower wage level and a much lower capital-labor ratio. Given the relative factor endowments in developing countries, one way of stretching capital and absorbing labor is to slow down the elimination of small-scale producers. Does this make economic sense, and how might it be done?

4. What are the sources of new industrial "entrepreneurs," whose absence has sometimes been cited as an important barrier to economic modernization? Speculative reasoning on this issue is gradually being replaced by investigation of the origins and characteristics of large and small businessmen in the industrial sector.

5. Analysis of productivity and unit production costs for relatively standardized products. Intracountry analysis is relevant to the large business-small business issue. Intercountry analysis can indicate the international competitiveness of LDC manufactures in the world market, which has a bearing on both the possible loss from import-substitution policies and the problem of developing export capacity.

Saving and Capital Supply

A well-documented feature of successfully developing eonomies is a sustained rise in saving and investment as a percentage of GNP. There are several potential sources of increased saving, some of which have been investigated more fully than others:

1. Household saving. The relatively few studies in this area suggest substantial savings potential, even in low-income households. Realization of the potential seems to depend importantly on the existence of outlets for saving, either in financial intermediaries offering security and an attractive rate of return, or more directly in household pro-

duction activities. Investments in farming and in small-scale business are financed largely from household saving by the owner of the business.

2. Private corporate saving. The importance of this source depends on profit rates, usually high in the early stages of growth acceleration, on the proportion taken in taxes, and on the disposition of after-tax profits between reinvestment and consumption.

3. Saving by public corporations. These corporations presumably could set prices, wages, and so forth at levels profitable enough to cover their own expansion needs and even make a contribution to the general government budget. But there are obvious political pressures for overpayment and underpricing, plus the economic argument that cheap power, transport, and other infrastructure services encourages investment in "directly productive activities." Fragmentary evidence suggests that saving by public enterprises is zero or negative overall—and quite variable by country and type of enterprises. But the reasons call for further analysis.

4. Savings from the general government budget. This source, too, which sometimes looms important in planning projections, has proven disappointing in practice. Countries have often been quite successful in raising government revenue as a percentage of GNP; but current expenditures tend to rise at least as rapidly, leaving little room for capital expenditures. The political pressures and budget procedures that produce this result have been little investigated.

In general, the financial structure of developing economies has received less attention than the "real" (or production) structure. A number of economists have emphasized, however, that mobilization and efficient allocation of investment funds requires modernization of financial institutions and development of a rational interest rate structure. Under conditions of severe inflation, this implies indexation or some other technique for avoiding negative real rates of interest. McKinnon, Gurley, Shaw, Goldsmith, Tun Wai, and others have made contributions in this area.

Income Distribution

The conventional hypothesis is that the distribution of household incomes tends to become increasingly unequal during the period of growth acceleration, with a reverse tendency toward greater equality setting in only at an advanced stage of development. On one hand, this has stimulated a search for alternative growth paths that might have less serious disequalizing consequences; and on the other hand, it has led to efforts to trace actual changes in distribution over time. As yet, however, few countries have the recurrent, comparable surveys of urban and rural households needed for this purpose. The limited evidence to date does suggest growing inequality in most developing countries, though there are a few counterexamples.

MACROECONOMIC, CLOSED-ECONOMY MODELS

Here we shall focus primarily on labor surplus models, exemplified by the work of Lewis, Fei and Ranis, and Ishikawa. The intuitive appeal of these models, and their continued prominence in the literature, springs from the fact that they incorporate a key "stylized fact" of low-income economies. Although different authors define surplus labor somewhat differently, they agree on its existence and importance. New economic activities can activate additional man-hours of employment simply by opening up opportunities—labor demand, as it were, creating its own supply. This phenomenon is not confined to such densely populated areas as Egypt, India, or Java. Surplus labor can perfectly well coexist with surplus land, as seems to have been true in West Africa and much of Southeast Asia a century ago. In both areas, the development of export crops, and the concomitant opportunity to consume imported manufactures, called forth additional man-hours of labor and the cultivation of additional land, with no reduction in food-growing and other traditional activites. This can be viewed as a Smithian "vent for surplus."

In short, labor surplus is not a special characteristic of one category of LDC but a virtually universal phenomenon in the preacceleration period. Let us examine briefly how this phenomenon is incorporated into the work of different model builders.

The Lewis Model

Lewis[20] sets out to portray how a capitalist economy expands through reinvestment of industrial profits. The purpose is "to provide a mechanism explaining the rapid growth of the proportion of domestic savings in the national income in the early stages of an economy whose growth is due to the expansion of capitalist forms of produc-

20. W. Arthur Lewis, "Economic Development with Unlimited Supplies of Labor," *Manchester School* (1954); "Unlimited Labor: Further notes," *Manchester School* (1958); "Reflections on Unlimited Labor," in W. Arthur Lewis *International Economics and Development* (New York and London: Academic Press, Inc., 1972).

tion."[21] Thus, it is not specifically an LDC model. It is perhaps better regarded as a model of early capitalist development in Britain. It is "stylized history" on a grand scale, covering by implication a period of a century or more.

The focus on capitalist profits as a source of saving dictates the division of the economy into a *capitalist* sector, in which employees work for wages and generate profits, and a *noncapitalist* or subsistence sector characterized by self-employment. The subsistence sector (and the surplus labor it contains) is *not* coterminous with agriculture. It includes handicraft workers, petty traders, domestic servants, and others as well as farmers.

The capitalist sector is neoclassical, with employers equating the marginal productivity of labor to the market wage. Neither wage earners nor subsistence workers save; all saving comes from capitalist profits (though it is not necessary to assume that *all* profit is saved). The increase in capital stock raises the demand schedule for labor; technical progress may also raise labor demand, though this is not explored in detail.

The noncapitalist sector, which functions mainly as a source of labor, is less clearly outlined. Implicitly, agriculture is *peasant-* or owner-operated agriculture. Farmers earn a subsistence wage, apparently equal to their average rather than their marginal productivity. And, again by implication, traders, artisans, and other noncapitalist workers earn the agricultural wage. The marginal productivity of *man-hours* in the noncapitalist sector is normally positive. But the marginal productivity of *workers* is assumed to be zero, that is, as workers are withdrawn for industrial employment, those remaining do enough additional work so that output does not fall.[22] One can readily visualize how this might occur in an occupation such as petty trade. But in the case of agriculture, Lewis does not explain clearly why those remaining on the land would put in additional man-hours or what incentive would be required to induce them to do so.

There is a "wage gap" between the subsistence wage and the market wage in the capitalist sector, a gap large enough to induce workers to transfer as rapidly as there are jobs for them. The labor supply curve to

---

21. Lewis, "Reflections."

22. "I do not believe that the productivity of a manhour is zero in agriculture, domestic service, petty retailing, handicrafts, or any other part of the non-capitalist reservoir. Nevertheless, I have seen nothing in the now vast literature of under-employment to alter my belief that in India or Egypt one could mobilize a group equal to (say) ten percent of the unskilled noncapitalist labor force without reducing significantly the output of the noncapitalist sectors from which they were withdrawn." (Ibid., p. 12.)

the capitalist sector is infinitely elastic at the market wage. Lewis recognizes the possibility, however, that this schedule may shift upward over time. There are several possible reasons: (1) productivity increases in the subsistence sector may raise real wages there and, given the need for a certain "wage gap" to induce labor transfer, the capitalist wage level would have to rise correspondingly; (2) the mere drain of labor from the subsistence sector raises the average earnings of those remaining, which again forces up the capitalist wage; (3) if agricultural output does not expand at an appropriate rate, the internal terms of trade will turn against industry, and workers will have to be paid a higher money wage to ensure the same real wage; (4) finally, industrial workers may simply demand higher wages—and succeed in getting them!

For these reasons, Lewis does not assert that the capitalist wage level *will* in fact remain constant. Normatively, it is desirable that the wage level *should* remain constant, because this maximizes the rate of increase in capitalist employment, output, and profits. Eventually, if capitalist expansion is rapid enough, the surplus labor reservoir will run dry and employers will face a normal forward-rising labor supply schedule.

Lewis points out that his model can come in either closed-economy or open-economy versions. In a closed economy, the noncapitalist sector would trade food and other agricultural products for manufactures. In order for the intersectoral terms of trade to remain constant, the relative rates of output increase in the two sectors must be the inverse of the relative income elasticities of demand. Lewis notes, however, that such a model would be relevant only to a few very large countries. Normally, undesirable shifts in the internal terms of trade can be corrected through imports. Realistically, then, the constraint on growth is usually an export constraint rather than a food constraint.

Since economic growth is propelled by reinvestment of profits, the behavior of the growth rate over time is closely related to profit behavior. With a constant money wage and an upward-shifting labor demand curve (because of technical progress as well as capital accumulation), the profit share of value added in the capitalist sector will necessarily rise.[23] Indeed, even if money wages are rising, pro-

23. "If we assume technical progress in agriculture, no hoarding, and unlimited labor at a constant wage, the rate of profit on capital cannot fall. On the contrary it must increase, since all the benefit of technical progress in the capitalist sector accrues to the capitalists." (Lewis, "Economic Development," p. 154.)

ductivity may well be rising faster, so that the "product wage" (ratio of wages to value added) will fall. Moreover, capitalist output is increasing as a percentage of GNP. So, if a constant percentage (not necessarily 100 percent) of profit is saved, the saving-GNP ratio must rise over time. It follows that the growth rate of GNP will also be rising.

Eventually, however, wages will begin to rise. If this does not happen for the reasons suggested earlier, it must happen when the surplus labor in the noncapitalist sector is exhausted—a point that Lewis labels *the turning point*. The rise of wages checks the rise in the rate of profit on capital, tends to stabilize this rate, or may even reduce it. In the later stages of growth, Lewis seems to visualize a situation in which the product wage and the labor and capital shares remain roughly constant. This would tend also to stabilize the growth rate of output.

The Lewis model is not a "tight" model in the sense of predicting the time path of every variable. There are many loose ends. But his system captures major features of reality: the initial labor slack in a preindustrial economy, the agriculture-industry wage gap, the lag of real wages in the early decades of industrial growth, the profit share of output rising at first and later stabilizing or declining. To be sure, the wage lag and the snowballing of profits may be more characteristic of nineteenth-century development than of contemporary LDCs, which tend to be "prematurely welfaristic" with regard to wage legislation and profit taxation. But if theory is the artful simplification of reality to get at fundamentals, the Lewis model deserves the high repute it has enjoyed in the literature. Rarely has a hundred pages of writing by one scholar produced so many thousands of pages by others.

The Fei-Ranis Model

This is a Lewis-type model in the sense that it focuses on the existence and absorption of an initial labor surplus; but it elaborates and enriches the Lewis schema in several directions. The determinants of labor transfer are set forth more fully and formally. The internal structure of agriculture is described in greater detail. The criteria of "success" in development are more thoroughly explored. The model is "tighter" in that it is formulated algebraically and yields quantitative predictions. At the same time, there is a strong emphasis on policy implications. The empirical illustrations are mainly from the Japan of 1868–1920.

The sectoral division is between agriculture and nonagriculture, which are regarded as operating on different economic principles. Agriculture is organized by landlords who employ wage earners, paying them a constant institutional wage (CIW).[24] Nonagricultural production is organized in capitalist firms, which pay a wage somewhat above the CIW in agriculture and which maximize profit by equating labor's marginal product to that wage. Because of the existence of redundant labor in agriculture (workers who can be withdrawn with no decrease in agricultural output), the supply schedule of labor to industry is infinitely elastic at a constant real wage. As in Lewis, saving out of profits is a major source of capital accumulation; but it is no longer the only source, since landlords are also assumed to save.

There are two tests of successful development—an employment test and an output or "balanced growth" test. The rate of increase in industrial employment is governed by several variables: the rate of increase in capital stock, the rate of technical change, the factor bias of technical change, the steepness of labor's marginal productivity schedule, and the rate of increase in the wage level (which, as Lewis noted, may not remain constant in practice). A critical test of successful development is whether the rate of labor absorption in nonagriculture exceeds the rate of population growth. If it does, the industrial share of total employment will rise—and the economy's "center of gravity" will shift toward nonagriculture.

Assuming that this criterion is met, labor transfer will continue until all redundant labor has been withdrawn from agriculture. Beyond this point, termed the "shortage point," withdrawal of additional labor would by definition reduce agricultural output. This would shift the internal terms of trade against industry, raise the industrial wage in terms of industrial goods, reduce profits, and choke off development as in the Ricardian system. To avoid this, technical progress in agriculture becomes necessary, which enlarges the supply of redundant labor and postpones the shortage point. Balanced growth can continue

24. At the outset, the CIW equals the average product of labor, and wages exhaust the total output. As some farm workers are withdrawn to industry, the remaining workers put in more hours per year. Output remains unchanged, but, since there are fewer workers to share it, average output per worker rises. Each worker, however, receives no more food than before—the CIW remains unchanged. (How the landlords persuade them to put in the extra hours is not explained.) The food formerly consumed by the departed workers thus becomes an "agricultural surplus." This belongs in the first instance to the landlord, who presumably markets it (so that surplus food follows surplus labor to the city) and keeps the proceeds. How the landlord's growing revenue is divided between consumption, agricultural investment, and industrial investment is important to the chances of successful development.

as long as the number of workers displaced from agriculture by technical progress just equals the number required in industry, as determined by the labor absorption equation. Continued success in improving agricultural technology can postpone the shortage point until it coincides with Lewis's turning point.

In output terms, the condition for balanced growth is that agricultural and industrial output should increase at rates that will avert any marked shift in the internal terms of trade. If markets are working properly, any such shift will tend to be self-correcting. If one sector's terms of trade are improving, and it is thus becoming more profitable, investment funds will be allocated more heavily toward that sector; and this, by increasing the rate of output growth in the sector, will tend to reverse the terms-of-trade movement. A major agent in this reallocation is the "dualistic landlord," who is portrayed as a heavy saver and a shrewd investor, willing to invest in agriculture or industry on the basis of its relative profitability.

Discussion of the Fei-Ranis model has turned heavily on the concept of "redundant labor" and the associated notion that, as redundant workers are withdrawn from agriculture, the employing landlords can require the remaining wage earners to work longer hours with no increase in their daily compensation, so that man-hour input and agricultural output remain unchanged. This result seems to depend on the landlord-wage earner relationship. Models that start from family farming, such as those of Sen and Ishikawa, usually conclude that additional man-hours of effort will be forthcoming only if they yield at least the same hourly return as earlier hours, that is, an increased daily return.

Realistically, a substantial body of opinion holds that withdrawal of workers from agriculture under strict *ceteris paribus* conditions will normally reduce output. To the extent that this is true, technical progress in agriculture becomes important from the beginning of economic development rather than at some later stage. But controversy over this feature of the model should not detract from its contribution toward moving the subject forward and encouraging investigation by others.

The Ishikawa Model

Ishikawa is concerned with the economies, lying in an arc from India to Japan, in which irrigated rice cultivation is prominent. His model has more variables than those of Lewis or Fei-Ranis, and it is designed for simulation experiments rather than deterministic solutions. The agricultural sector is central, and the problem of absorbing additional amounts of labor in agriculture is faced explicitly. Agriculture is organized into peasant farms of equal size, whose production function includes only land and labor. The industrial sector is divided into consumer-goods and capital-goods subsectors. Government enters the scene only to allocate new capital among three uses: expansion of consumer-goods capacity, expansion of capital-goods capacity, and construction of irrigation works and other agricultural infrastructure. There is no price system. Thus, although agriculture and industry are assumed to be privately owned, there is a strong "physical planning" tone to the model.

Figure 1. Determinants of Labor Utilization

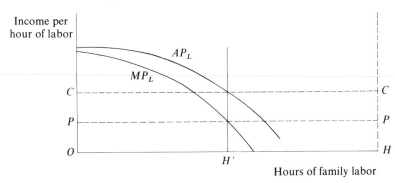

On the peasant farms, there is a positive, constant, minimum supply price for a man-hour of labor. Additional inputs of labor, Ishikawa believes, require additional food consumption plus some psychological reward. This minimum supply price is shown by the line *PP* in figure 1. It remains constant over the whole range from zero hours to "normal full-time" hours for all family members, indicated by point *H*.

The number of hours actually worked, *H'*, is determined by the intersection of labor's marginal productivity schedule with the supply schedule *PP*. Family consumption is determined by the *average* productivity of labor with this labor input, shown by *OC*. The difference between actual and potential man-hours, H–H', is defined as "surplus labor" or "unemployment." All surplus labor is located in the agricultural sector, and a key question in the simulation experiments is what combinations of parameter values will permit this surplus to shrink over time.

It the rate at which labor is transferred to industry exceeds the growth rate of the agricultural labor force, *H* will move to the left and surplus labor will decline, with no change in labor inputs or agricultural output. This is "costless labor transfer" à la Lewis or Fei-Ranis. In the more likely situation of a secular increase in the farm labor force, *H* moves to the right over time and surplus labor will increase, *unless H'* can be moved to the right at least as fast by shifts in the productivity schedules. How might such shifts occur?

Land is assumed to be fully occupied, and it cannot be increased in amount. It can be *improved*, however, by investments in rural infrastructure. Ishikawa emphasizes improved water-control systems, where the technological possibilities range from drought avoidance through modest supplementing of rainfall to multiple cropping with optimal water supply. A move from one water-control level to the next higher level makes possible the use of improved input "packages," particularly heavier fertilizer applications, which shift the productivity schedules upward. The marginal productivity schedule now intersects the labor supply schedule farther to the right, and labor input per acre increases.

A further key assumption is that government, by means of expenditure on major irrigation works and other projects, can induce farmers to put in additional man-hours on complementary improvements. The ratio of *total* investment to direct government expenditure, σ, plays an important role in the simulations. (Labor's marginal productivity schedule, and farm labor inputs *H'*, includes labor spent *both* in direct production and on land improvement. Farmers are assumed to allocate their labor time efficiently, that is, to equate marginal productivity in these two activities.)

Government also taxes agriculture in order to finance its agricultural investments or for other purposes. Ishikawa assumes, however, that government must leave the peasant some fixed share, ϕ, of any increment of output in order to induce him to produce it. This parameter is not just a psychological fact of life; it is influenced by institutional conditions, and notably by tenancy arrangements, and thus is alterable within limits by government action.

Increments to agricultural output are divided, then, between tax payments, marketings, and farm consumption. Tax payments are specified as $1 - \phi$. Marketings are whatever is required to feed the growing industrial labor force at a constant per capita level. Farm food consumption per capita is a residual, which may either rise or fall. In the simulation runs that yield a "successful" growth path, it typically falls for an initial five years or so, then rises indefinitely. In the "failure" cases, it falls from the start and declines indefinitely.

Employment increases in the two industrial sectors at a rate proportionate to the increase in their output, the necessary labor being transferred from agriculture. But rural employment also increases because government hires workers for agricultural improvement, because this induces farmers to devote more man-hours to agricultural improvement, and because the consequent upward shift of agricultural productivity schedules results in larger labor inputs to current crop production. In the early years of development, employment increases in agriculture exceed those in industry; and their magnitude, in conjunction with the rate of population growth, has a decisive effect on whether the labor surplus will grow or shrink.

Farmers neither save nor invest, except through investment of labor time in farm improvement. The only intersectoral flows of finance, then, are the tax flow from agriculture to government and the reverse flow of government expenditures on agricultural improvement. The net flow can be in either direction. In a later and more realistic chapter,[25] Ishikawa argues that, in the early stages of "successful" development, the net flow will typically be *toward* agriculture rather than away from it. The cases of Taiwan and Meiji Japan, where net transfers *from* agriculture occurred, he regards as exceptional.

Intersectoral commodity flows are balanced out endogenously within the model, without use of a price mechanism. A lag of agricultural output, for example, would not lead to inadequate marketings and a relative rise of agricultural prices. Rather, marketings would continue at the level necessary to feed the industrial labor force, whose growth rate is independently determined, and the slack would be taken up by a decline of per capita food consumption on the farm. (This is reminiscent of Soviet policy in the Stalin era.)

Growth in this model depends basically on the rate of capital accumulation and on the allocation of new capital by sectors. The "success" cases typically involve an initial absolute decline in per capita consumption, a high proportion of new capital goods assigned to the capital-goods sector, and an eventual payoff in accelerated increase of output and employment. Investment in agricultural improvement, however, also plays a prominent role. Technical change is present, too, though its nature is not clearly spelled out. In agriculture, it is assumed that there is always a shelf of known and superior technology, requiring

25. Shigeru Ishikawa, *Economic Development in Asian Perspective* (Tokyo: Kinokuniya Bookstore, Ltd., 1967), chap. 4.

only improved water control to permit its application. In industry, there are known techniques that permit an indefinite increase in the capital stock without depressing the marginal yield of capital.

Like any simulation model, this one can yield a variety of outcomes. The system may manage to outrace population growth—or it may not. Unemployment may diminish, or it may rise at an accelerating rate. The chances of success rest critically on *two initial conditions*, the rate of population growth and the capital-output ratio in agriculture (assumed constant over time); on *two policy variables*, the allocation of new capital to capital-goods industries and to agriculture; and on *two institutional parameters*, which, however, can to some extent be manipulated by government—the maximum feasible tax rate in agriculture and the inducement ratio reflecting farmers' response to government investment in agriculture. The direction of effect of these variables is obvious. Thus of the six simulation runs that Ishikawa presents for illustration, one of the two most successful cases involved a combination of low population growth rate (1.5 percent), low K/O ratio in agriculture (1:1), strong inducement effect in farmers' investment (1.5), and a high (50 percent) allocation of new capital to capital-goods production. It is easy to visualize alternative combinations leading to steady deterioration.

The Mellor-Lele Model[26]

John Mellor and Uma Lele also approach development theory from the side of agriculture. Earlier labor surplus models, they believe, seriously understate both the need for and the difficulty of achieving a sustained increase in foodgrain production. Their empirical reference is largely toward India, where they have done extensive work on agricultural development.

Briefly, Mellor and Lele reason as follows: The notion that farm laborers can be made to work longer hours with no increase in compensation is unrealistic. Some increase in compensation is necessary; and so a growth model should incorporate a rising level of per capita income in agriculture. Since the flow of labor to the nonagricultural sector is influenced by relative earnings, one must assume that urban

26. A formal model is presented in John W. Mellor and Uma J. Lele, "A Labor Supply Theory of Economic Development" (Cornell Agricultural Economics Staff Paper No. 34, June 1971). Related writings include Uma J. Lele and John W. Mellor, "Technological Change and Distributive Bias in a Dual Economy" (Cornell Department of Agricultural Economics, Occasional Paper No. 43, October 1972); and John W. Mellor, "Modernizing Agriculture and Theories of Economic Growth," mimeographed, April 1973.

real wages will also be rising. Further, since poor people's income elasticity of demand for food is high, much of the increase in rural and urban incomes will be translated into higher food demand. This would be true even in the absence of population growth; but population pressure intensifies the food supply problem.

How can increased food supplies be obtained? *Aggregate* food production, they believe, is quite unresponsive to changes in the internal terms of trade. To balance demand and supply by this route would require such a sharp rise in the relative price of food as to choke off industrial growth. Nor can much be achieved simply by larger labor inputs in a fixed land area. In the absence of technical change, labor's marginal productivity schedule slopes downward quite steeply. Mere growth in the agricultural labor force is thus an immiserizing process leading to falling per capita incomes.

This leads to a conclusion that technical change in agriculture is essential from the outset—and that it should be a central feature of any growth model. The *rate* of technical progress and the *factor bias* of progress are both important. In a fully settled economy with rapid population growth, a land-saving and labor-using bias is desirable. The nature of technical change is important also for *income distribution* in the rural sector. Welfare considerations apart, income distribution matters because high-income landowners and low-income laborers have different demand patterns. Increments of income to landowners will be spent mainly on nonfoods as opposed to foodstuffs, on factory-produced goods as opposed to handicrafts, and on imported rather than domestic manufactures. Thus, the growth path of the economy will differ from what it would be if additional income were to go mainly to the laborers.

By way of illustration, Mellor and Lele outline a two-sector model. The model is of interest because of the treatment of agriculture (the nonagricultural sector being quite conventional). Agricultural output is a function of land, labor, and technology. In traditional agriculture, capital can be regarded as essentially a direct embodiment of labor. Under conditions of technical change, it takes the form of circulating capital, that is, an increase in current production inputs. These inputs are purchased from the nonagricultural sector and financed from the higher income generated by technical change. The agricultural population consists of "landowners" and "laborers."[27] Laborers are paid

27. "The sharp dichotomy between landowners and laborers is a very helpful simplifying assumption which distinguishes between those cultivators who predominantly produce for the market as against those whose produce is mostly consumed domestically.

their (positive) marginal product, and, depending on the characteristics of technical change, their share of agricultural output may increase or decrease over time. The significance of this lies, as noted earlier, in the different demand elasticities assumed for the two groups.

There is no intersectoral transfer of finance in the model. Landowners save only to finance increased purchases of current production inputs, and they do not invest in nonagriculture. There is a transfer of labor sufficient to equate laborers' real earnings in the two sectors.[28] There is a flow of foodstuffs to nonagriculture and a return flow of manufactures and agricultural inputs. The model focuses on two markets, the food market and the labor market, which are regarded as central and interdependent. Thus, after deriving equilibrium conditions for each market, the two sets of conditions are combined to define a general equilibrium.

An interesting feature of the discussion is the use of sensitivity analysis to explore the impact of several kinds of exogenous change. First, *capital accumulation* in the nonagricultural sector tends to raise the relative price of food, the marketed supply of food, and the real wage in nonagriculture, but it lowers the percentage of the labor force remaining in agriculture. Second, *population growth* tends to raise the percent of the labor force in agriculture and the relative price of food while lowering the marketed supply of food and the real wage in nonagriculture. Finally, *technical changes that raise agricultural output* have a variable effect, depending on what happens to labor's share of output. If labor's share remains *unchanged*, the effect is to lower the percent of the labor force in agriculture and the relative price of food and raise the marketed supply of food and the real wage in nonagriculture. In general, these results are reinforced if labor's share of output *declines*. But if labor's share *increases*, the effects may go in either direction, depending on the extent of the increase.

The behavior of the distributive shares in agriculture thus affects

The real world of peasant agriculture and gradation in size of farm is accommodated by viewing intermediate situations as appropriately weighted averages of landowners and laborers with a consequent weighted average set of demand elasticities." (Mellor and Lele, "A Labor Supply Theory," p. 8.)

28. There is thus a marked neoclassical tone to the analysis. All labor is apparently employed, workers in both sectors are paid their marginal productivity, the supply curve of labor of industry is forward-rising. But there is a little ambiguity about this, because at one point the existence of surplus labor in agriculture is also suggested: "It also seems apparent that with some reorganization of traditional agriculture, involving little additional capital input and marginal changes in techniques, it would be possible to withdraw a substantial amount of labor from agriculture without reducing per capita output." (Mellor and Lele, "A Labor Supply Theory," p. 10.)

development in the nonagricultural sector. The faster the increase in labor's share, the larger the increase in farm workers' per capita income and hence in the industrial wage level, which will retard the growth of industrial employment. There can, therefore, be a conflict between growth objectives and distributional objectives.

Where Do We Come Out?

It seems fair to conclude that no one has said the last word in development models and that there is room for further experiments. A prime requisite in such experiments is a convincing specification of the agricultural sector. The race between technical progress in agriculture and population growth, which poses some of the most difficult problems in development policy, should also be the main axis of development theory. This is not to minimize the importance of capital accumulation and technology in the industrial sector. But industry is easier to handle with conventional theoretical tools; and in policy terms, it is easier to build new factories than to double yields per acre in agriculture.

The importance of agriculture consists in its potential contribution to employment as well as to output. Under conditions of rapid population growth, accompanied by capital-intensive technology in manufacturing and public utilities, industry cannot be expected to absorb more than a small proportion of annual increments to the labor force. The question of attracting additional labor to the industrial sector is really a nonproblem, as industrial managers in developing countries can testify. The actual problem is how to absorb additional man-hours of labor in agriculture without depressing marginal productivity. Without this, underemployment of labor will necessarily increase.

Another basic issue is whether a two-sector schema is really adequate. A considerable part of the labor force is employed (or under employed) neither in agriculture nor in "modern" industry—but in what I have elsewhere termed[29] the *urban traditional* sector, whose existence Lewis also clearly recognized. Further, government is an important producer, employer, and channel for financial transfers; and a model without government is seriously deficient.

It would be logical to go directly from these critical comments to the positive suggestions for model construction in chapters 5 and 6.

29. L. G. Reynolds, "Development with Surplus Labor: Some Complications," *Oxford Economic Papers* 21 (March 1969): 89–103.

Thus, the discussion of agriculture in chapters 3 and 4 may appear to be a detour, but it is not really so. Development of plausible assumptions about the agricultural sector requires closer examination of agricultural structure and behavior. In addition, the richness of the agricultural literature is often not appreciated by development economists who have not specialized in that direction. Therefore, a brief review of this literature will serve an educational purpose and will also provide building blocks for our later discussion.

3

The Agricultural Production Unit

There are several reasons why a discussion of development theory should begin with agriculture. First, agriculture is usually the largest single sector in terms of output—and much the largest in terms of employment. Second, a multisector model of early economic growth necessarily embodies assumptions about agricultural structure and behavior. The range of possible assumptions is wide; and an economist unfamiliar with agriculture may inadvertently choose assumptions that are so far from reality as to limit the predictive power of the model.

Third, agricultural economists from both developed and less developed countries have devoted much effort to developing and testing hypotheses about low-income agriculture. But they tend to work in a separate orbit, with their own faculties, associations, journals, sources of research support, and ties to operating agencies such as the Department of Agriculture (U.S.D.A.) and the UN's Food and Agriculture Organization (F.A.O.). Many development economists are not fully familiar with the richness of the agricultural literature. Thus, it seems useful to make a survey (necessarily brief and incomplete) of the issues with which agricultural specialists are wrestling.

I begin by outlining some of the production characteristics of agriculture that differentiate it from other producing sectors, and then I look briefly at the way in which commercial farming emerges from an initial condition of pure subsistence production. After these preliminaries, I come to the main theme of the chapter: the static equilibrium, and the comparative static adjustment, of farm production units with market contacts. I consider the way in which such units have been specified by previous writers, and I describe the kind of specification that I believe to have widest real-world applicability. I then outline the static equilibrium conditions under assumptions of perfect certainty and perfect markets. This leads to a discussion of how such equilibrium may be modified by yield and price uncertainties, market imperfections, and other institutional constraints.

The comparative static discussion that follows examines the impact of a change in the price of a single farm output or input, a change in the overall agriculture-industry terms of trade, a change in the market wage for rural labor, a change in tax rates, and a change in the man-land ratio resulting from population growth. I defer discussing one major type of change—technical progress in agriculture—until chapter 4 to avoid making the present chapter unduly long.

SPECIAL FEATURES OF AGRICULTURAL PRODUCTION

At an abstract level, all production functions are brothers. But a farm is not like a factory, and it is worthwhile to remind ourselves of the special characteristics of agricultural production. Although the discussion is oriented toward low-income agriculture, much of it is applicable also to agriculture in the developed countries.

A Family-based Enterprise

In factory-style manufacturing, the clear employer-employee division lends sharpness to such concepts as "the wage rate," "labor force participation," "employment," and "unemployment." In agriculture, where self-employment is the general rule, these concepts are less precise. Most labor inputs are provided by family members, under arrangements rooted in custom and necessity. Much of family output is consumed at home rather than marketed. Decisions about factor supplies, products and production methods, and consumption patterns, though they can be separated analytically, are in fact interwoven in the family's life style.

Specificity of Production Functions

Agricultural production is rooted in soil and climate, which vary geographically. Thus, production functions are specific not only to a particular crop and state of technology but also to a specific region and even a particular farm. What is optimal for one farm will not be so for the next. This makes it difficult to draw conclusions from aggregate data on farm output and inputs. Meaningful research normally involves a particular crop in a particular region,[1] using micro data from individual farms.

1. For an illustration of the variety of production behavior in a large country, see Vahid Nowshirvani, "The regional and crop-wise pattern of the growth of per acre output in India," *Bulletin of the Oxford Institute of Economics and Statistics* (February 1970).

Land a Key Factor

In LDC agriculture, land and labor are the basic inputs to production. Machinery is typically unimportant, though seed, fertilizer, and other forms of "circulating capital" often are important. The production problem is how much labor and other variable factors to apply to the "fixed factor," land.

But this misstates the problem in two respects. First, land is to some extent "manufactured," that is, improved by past investment; and this investment component becomes more important as the level of technology rises. Thus, there is a problem of resource allocation between current production and land improvements for the future.

Second, although total land in the nation may be fixed, the land available to a particular farm operator is not fixed. He can rent or buy additional land, or conversely he can lease out part of his present holdings. It may thus be more appropriate to regard the farm family and its labor power as the "fixed" factor. One can then ask, for a particular crop and technology, how much land and capital it pays to combine with this amount of labor.

Complementarity among Nonland Inputs

In LDC agriculture, there is a substitute relation between land on one hand and nonland inputs *as a group* on the other. A larger package of nonland inputs can raise output per acre and thus is land-saving.

Within the group of nonland inputs, however, there is a high degree of complementarity. Movement from a lower to a higher level of technology normally involves a *simultaneous* increase in inputs; and the proportions in which they increase is critically important. A correctly proportioned "package" of improved inputs has an output effect greater than the sum of the effects that each input would produce if varied in isolation. This is usually termed the *synergistic* nature of production relations in agriculture.

One of the best-documented cases is that of rice production. Here the first requisite for technical advance is movement to a more sophisticated system of *water control*. This makes it feasible to use larger amounts of chemical *fertilizer* without damaging soil and plant roots. It then pays to introduce improved *seed varieties* having fertilizer-response curves that peak higher and farther to the right. Careful *weeding* and use of *pesticides* is necessary for optimal results. All this requires larger inputs of *labor*—for construction and maintenance of irrigation works, for weeding and pest control, for harvesting and marketing.[2]

Another aspect of complementarity is that among labor inputs at different times of year. A certain input in soil preparation and planting necessitates an appropriate input at harvest time. Otherwise, the earlier inputs will be unproductive. Again, the advance to a higher level of technology involves a balanced increase of labor inputs in the annual production cycle *and* labor inputs of an investment character in irrigation systems and land improvement. Since these latter activities can be carried on during off-peak periods, the increased labor inputs are accompanied by some reduction in seasonal fluctuations of employment. At best, however, farming activity is strongly seasonal. This is important for production decision making, the operation of the rural labor market, and the definition of such concepts as "under-employment" and "surplus labor."

Inputs Divisible, Scale Economies Small

Large machinery units are much less prevalent in the LDCs than in more developed countries. There is some indivisibility in the use of animal power—for example, bullock teams; but this can be ameliorated by sharing and leasing arrangements. Fertilizer, seed, pesticides, and other current inputs are highly divisible.

The main indivisibility is in the farm family itself. On the basis of some arbitrary definition of a "standard" work year, the family possesses a certain potential labor input. A farm can be "too small" in the sense that application of this potential input would force down the marginal productivity of labor to a very low level. The "family-sized farm" might be defined as the acreage that the operator would choose to cultivate given his preference system, the size and labor potential of his family, and the possibility of buying or renting additional land in a competitive market.

Although the median size of LDC farms is small, most countries show a considerable dispersion of farm sizes. But the possible existence of economies of scale is difficult to test statistically, because large and small farms seem to differ in ways that destroy comparability—in choice of crops, in production techniques, in intensity of cultivation,

---

2. For a detailed discussion of different levels of rice technology, see S. Ishikawa, *Economic Development in Asian Perspective* (Tokyo: Kinokuniya Bookstore, Ltd., 1967), especially chap. 2.

in proportions of family and hired labor used, in access to financial resources. One cannot assume that farms of differing size are operating on the *same* production function. One can say, however, that nothing in the research literature to date refutes the hypothesis that (always for a specific crop, region, technology), over a considerable range of farm sizes, scale economies are insignificant.

Nature of Technical Progress

In manufacturing, technical change is usually generated within the industry in question through expenditure on research and development. But this is not always true. In some industries—coal mining, textiles, printing—manufacturers of the machinery used in the industry have been the main source of inventions.

In agriculture, technical change comes almost entirely from outside the industry. This is not to minimize the gradual learning process by which traditional farmers have adapted to their soil and climatic environment, passing on their accumulated knowledge to succeeding generations. But the rapid shifts in technique that are now occurring in some countries result from work in research laboratories and experiment stations, usually maintained by government, whose results are then disseminated among farmers through field agents. Further, technical change is usually *embodied* in new or improved inputs of water, fertilizer, seed, pesticides, and so on.

Activities Supporting Agriculture Have Large Optimum Scale

We noted earlier that the optimum scale of agricultural production units is typically small. But this does not mean that a multitude of such units, left to themselves, will add up to an efficient agricultural sector. Even pure subsistence farmers can benefit from improved input supplies, water control systems, and research and informational facilities. As production for market increases in importance, these needs grow and new needs, for marketing and processing facilities, transport networks, and sources of finance, arise. The optimum scale of these ancillary activities is usually large. Small-scale production units can attain optimal efficiency only when embedded in a framework of supporting activities organized on a much larger scale. Development of these supporting activities is primarily a government responsibility.

Wide Productivity Gap Between Agriculture and Nonagriculture

Output per worker in "modern" manufacturing and infrastructure activities is usually several times the output per worker in agriculture. The true gap may be less than that suggested by official statistics because of omission or undervaluation of goods produced by the farm household for its own consumption. But even with adequate correction, the productivity gap between agriculture and industry would still be puzzlingly wide. Especially interesting is the fact that the gap appears to be a function of national income per capita. In some LDCs, output per worker in agriculture is only 0.10 to 0.20 of that in nonagriculture. In the developed countries, on the other hand, the ratio is commonly in the range of 0.50 to 0.70. In most of these countries, too, the ratio has risen appreciably over the past century as income per capita has risen.[3] Why the income gap between agriculture and nonagriculture should tend to shrink, but not disappear, over the long course of economic development is an intriguing question about which I shall have more to say later.

FROM SUBSISTENCE FARMING TO MARKET CONTACTS

Before examining the owner-operated farm with market contacts, let us consider briefly how such farms emerge from an initial condition of pure subsistence production.

As polar types, one can visualize "fully closed" and "fully open" farm units. The fully closed unit uses only home-produced inputs and consumes all output but nothing else. This is "subsistence agriculture" in its purest form. A fully open unit purchases all inputs other than family-owned land and labor, markets all output, and buys all consumption requirements.

At any point in time, the farm units in a country are distributed in one fashion or another over this continuum. Over time, in a developing economy, there is a gradual displacement of farm units toward the open end of the range. Thus, the open and closed types are not merely analytical constructs but represent a *historical sequence*. The percentage of units of the open type and the *degree* of their openness—that is,

---

3. Paul W. Kuznets, *Economic Growth and Structure in the Republic of Korea*. A Publication of the Economic Growth Center, Yale University. (New Haven: Yale University Press, 1977) table 3.4, p. 117.

the percentage of inputs and outputs passing through markets—are significant development indexes.

Visualize an economy (still approximated in some remote regions of the world) consisting entirely of closed units. In what sense, or under what conditions, can these units be regarded as containing a "surplus" or "reserve" of unutilized labor time? Consider a simple model developed by E. K. Fisk and R. T. Shand on the basis of experience in Papua New Guinea.[4] Members of a village produce only food and consume all they produce. They have a certain labor potential, defined as "the quantity of labor input that could be sustained by the subsistence unit if the incentive to work full time were present." It is assumed that the efficiency of work increases with the level of nutrition. This is indicated by the upward slope of the labor supply curve, *EN*. Beyond *N*, additional food intake does not add to efficiency, and labor potential is constant at the above definition of full-time work. *OT* is the total product curve relating labor input to food output.

An assumption that is critical but (under conditions where sweet potatoes provide up to 90 percent of the caloric intake) not implausible is that there is a fixed food consumption ceiling, indicated by *D*. Fisk terms this the "fully belly" (*FB*) point. Point *E* is the starvation level below which work and life would become impossible.

Under these conditions, food production will be carried to point *A*. Thus, there is a virtual food surplus of *PS*, the difference between actual output and potential output if labor were fully employed. There is an actual labor surplus of *AP*, the difference between actual and potential labor input. Work will presumably be shared among members of the village, each working considerably less than full time. This kind of situation, in which the full-belly point can be reached with a few hours' work per day, Fisk terms *subsistence affluence*. There is a strong resemblance to the underutilization of resources implied in Adam Smith's "vent for surplus."

Even without market contacts, the size of these surpluses may be altered by exogenous change. Population increase will raise the *D* line and also shift the labor potential line, *NS*, to the right. Beyond some

4. E. K. Fisk and R. T. Shand, "The Early Stages of Development in a Primitive Economy: The Evolution from Subsistence to Trade and Specialization," *Subsistence Agriculture and Economic Development*, ed. Clifford Wharton (Chicago: Aldine Publishing Co., 1969), pp. 257–74. See also E. K. Fisk, "The Response of Nonmonetary Production Units to Contact with the Exchange Economy," *Agriculture in Development Theory*, ed. L. G. Reynolds (New Haven: Yale University Press, 1975), pp. 53–83.

Figure 1. Economic Surplus in Subsistence Agriculture

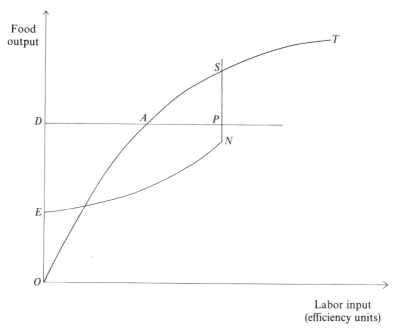

population density, the actual labor (and potential food) surplus will decline and eventually disappear. Exogenous technical change, which may go on slowly even in a primitive community, will tend to increase both surpluses, the exact effect depending on whether the changes are mainly labor-saving or land-saving.

More interesting, however, is the question of how such unused productive potential can be "unlocked" by opening these closed production units to market contacts. What are the main ways in which this opening may occur? What determines the speed of the process? Myint, Fisk and Shand, Helleiner, and others have contributed to the analysis of these questions.

One can visualize a development process along the following lines. Assume a large island with towns scattered along the coast, in which simple consumer goods are fabricated for sale. Subsistence farmers live in the mountainous interior, initially having no contact with the towns. Development of market linkages depends on a combination of (1) growth of facilities for processing, transporting, and marketing saleable farm products; and (2) growth in the availability and variety of consumer goods imported from the towns and reduction in their cost through improved transport and marketing facilities. The first line of development raises the farmer's cash return for a given effort, and the second increases the goods available for a given amount of cash.

Both the "exporting" and "importing" facilities can be developed to several levels of sophistication. Consumer goods from the towns may be distributed initially by itinerant peddlers in the rural areas. Later on, small shops may be established in permanent locations, perhaps as a sideline to agricultural activities. With growing trade volume, retail outlets increase in number, size, and efficiency, with a consequent lowering of retail margins. Similar stages of development exist on the "exporting" side. An improvement on one side tends to stimulate improvement on the other. Reduction of processing and marketing costs for farm products increases commerical sales and raises farmers' cash incomes, which provides a broader market for consumer goods, which stimulates growth of retailing facilities and a reduction in prices. This, in turn, further increases the real return on farmers' effort, calling forth still more commercial production. Thus, the rural economy moves upward hand-over-hand to higher income levels and higher degrees of commercialization.

Broadening of the rural market for consumer goods reduces costs not only in retailing but also in manufacturing, through the process described by Adam Smith when he stated that "the division of labor depends on the extent of the market."

Several footnotes should be added to this cheerful picture. First, the process is "natural" only in a limited sense. Government can readily block development along the lines indicated by imposing (or failing to remove) impediments to internal trade or by failing to make appropriate investments in transport and other infrastructure facilities.

Second, the public and private investments required for market development are somewhat lumpy, introducing the possibility of discontinuities in development. An economy may reach a point at which commercial output from farms is not *quite* large enough to induce investment that would yield a major reduction in processing or transportation costs; or retail volume may not be *quite* large enough to warrant more modern retail facilities and lower consumer goods prices. Getting the economy over such "stagnation points" may require temporary government subsidies.

Third, the potential gains from internal market improvement may eventually be exhausted. To keep the process going beyond that point may require calling in a *deus ex machina* from outside.

Historically, the most important *deus ex machina* has been the foreign trader appearing in coastal ports, offering, on one hand, a demand for exports of rice, cocoa, palm oil, coffee and other agricultural goods and, on the other, a supply of low-cost, factory-produced consumer goods from the industrial countries. In many parts of the world, notably tropical Africa and Southeast Asia, such a development impinged on a thinly spread population living in subsistence affluence. The new goods—cotton cloth, other clothing items, trinkets and ornaments, and, more recently, radios and bicycles—quickly became conventional necessities and induced the farmers, without reducing their food output, to put in additional labor time on marketable products. This could often be done with no increase in land acreage— for example, by interplanting cocoa trees and subsistence crops in West Africa. But to the extent that additional land was required, it was usually available.

In terms of figure 1, this development can be interpreted as a simultaneous upward shift of the productivity schedule, OT, resulting from the addition of new crops and frequently new acreage, and of the minimum consumption level, D, to incorporate the new conventional necessities. In the new equilibrium, each farmer was producing and consuming more, working longer hours, and having less surplus labor time. The labor surplus was tapped by an increase in effective demand for output.

In most countries, this was part of a larger colonial pattern in which one of the European powers assumed military control and governmental responsibilities. The colonial government then proceeded to "open up" the interior by means of transport investments and maintenance of law and order to the extent necessary to enable traders from the home country to tap potential export supplies and market imported consumer goods. Public investment served mainly to facilitate business activities and was financed mainly by import and export levies.[5]

While the initial induction of peasant producers into the money economy came from foreign sources, a secondary effect was substantial growth of a domestic money economy. Some peasants began to

5. See in this connection Thomas Birnberg and Stephen Resnick, *Colonial Development* (New Haven: Yale University Press, 1975).

specialize entirely in export crop production, buying their food from others; this led to the development of a cash market for foodstuffs. Income earned from cash crops was spent on domestic goods as well as on imports. Both the retailing of imported goods and the initial purchasing of cash crops from farmers were carried on largely by local traders, with foreign businessmen confining themselves mainly to wholesale trade and provision of finance.

An alternative, though still foreign-induced, path of development involved the appearance of mining and plantation enterprises hiring wage labor. Occasionally, as on the Ceylon tea plantations, even the labor was imported, so that interaction between the foreign enclave and the domestic economy was minimal. But more commonly, local labor was employed. The preexisting labor surplus was tapped, not by increasing labor inputs to agriculture, but by withdrawing some villagers for full-time employment elsewhere. In tropical Africa this was facilitated by a customary division of labor, under which planting and harvesting of crops was done mainly by women. Men did the heavier work of clearing new land, an intermittent activity that permitted them to be absent from the village for extended periods. Thus developed the African system of migrant labor, in which men traveled to the areas of wage employment without their families, worked for a year or two until they had earned a target amount of money, then returned home and were replaced by new migrants.

A concomitant of this system was a low-wage, low-productivity policy on the part of employers. This was rationalized on the grounds that the initial productivity of workers fresh from the bush was low, with constant turnover it did not pay to invest in training to raise productivity, and because of fixed consumption patterns the only effect of higher wages would be to reduce labor supply—the celebrated "backward-bending supply curve of labor." Migrants were willing to accept low wages because the opportunity cost of their labor was also low. There was no reduction in agricultural output, and anything saved out of the cash wage was a net addition to income.

The cash earnings provided the laborers with a means of buying both imported consumer goods and domestic products and a way of paying poll taxes imposed by the colonial governments (who were also substantial employers of labor for roadbuilding and other public works). Thus, there was some increase in monetization of the economy. The impact on the total economy was more superficial, however, and the growth stimulus smaller than in the case of expanded peasant production. Because of the low-wage policy, the amount of cash income generated remained modest. There was little improvement in labor productivity. The agricultural system continued virtually unchanged, with little movement toward cash-crop production. Indeed, the colonial authorities often discouraged introduction of cash crops, which, it was thought, would dry up the supply of migrant labor by offering alternative sources of income.

STATIC EQUILIBRIUM: NO UNCERTAINTY, PERFECT MARKETS

We turn now to an analysis of farm units that have been opened to market participation; and we continue to focus on the owner-operated farm, leaving other tenure farms to chapter 4.

Modeling the Production Unit

Models of farm units are by no means lacking in the literature. Table 1 gives a schematic description of ten such models. They differ substantially in structure, partly because of the differing purposes outlined in the final column of the table. About half the models focus entirely on the internal dynamics of agriculture, treating all developments in nonagriculture as exogenous. Several models (1, 4, 10) grew directly out of the controversies over the existence and meaning of "surplus labor" in agriculture and over whether the supply curve of labor to nonagriculture can be regarded as horizontal. But in other cases (2, 5, 6, 8), the assumptions about agriculture are embedded in a larger model of the economy, and the focus is on intersectoral relations over time.

A further characteristic of most of the models in table 1 is a high degree of simplification: one tenure form, two inputs, one food output, often only one form of market participation. They understate the complexity of the actual environment. A model incorporating more of reality, while harder to work with, has greater explanatory potential. Let us suggest some desirable features of an enriched production model.

1. Tenure form. The choice of assumptions on this point is decisive for all that follows. Predictions derived from one tenure system cannot be generalized to others. The advantage of starting from an owner-operator framework has already been suggested; and we shall follow this course throughout the present chapter.

Table 1. Models of the Agricultural Production Unit

Author	Tenure Form	Inputs	Outputs	Market Participation	Behavioral Principle	Purpose of Model
Berry-Soligo[a]	Owner-operator Tenancy Landlord-laborer	Labor Land	Food	Labor market only	Max U	Derive labor supply curve to nonagriculture
Fei-Ranis[b]	Landlord-laborer	Labor Land	Food	Food market Labor market	Landlord: max. surplus Laborer: subsistence wage	Analyze transfer of food, labor, savings to nonagriculture
Fisk-Shand[c]	Village unit	Labor Land	Food	Food market only	Conventional consumption ceiling, shiftable	Analyze transition from subsistence to market economy
Hymer-Resnick[d]	Owner-operator	Labor Land	Food Z-goods	Food market only	Max U	Analyze resource reallocation in agriculture when trade opened up with nonagriculture
Ishikawa[e]	Owner-operator	Labor Land Capital (= land improvements)	Food	Food market Government taxes and invests	Complex	Develop intersectoral model oriented toward Asian rice cultivation
Kelley-Williamson-Cheatham[f]	Capitalist-wage earner	Labor, Capital, Technology	Food	Food market Labor market	Max profit	Develop two-sector simulation model to trace long-term growth paths

Krishna[g]	Owner-operator	Labor Land	Food	Food market Labor market	Max U	Analyze response of farm units to exogenous change
Mellor-Lele[h]	Landowner-laborer	Labor Land Technology	Food	Food market Labor market	Landowners: max profit Laborers: max U	Develop general equilibrium model of food and labor markets, to trace change in employment and other variables over time
Nakajima[i]	Owner-operator	Labor Land	One, unspecified	Product market only	Max U	Analyze response of farm units to exogenous change
Sen[j]	Owner-operator	Labor Land	Food	Food market Labor market	Max U	Explore existence of "surplus labor" in agriculture

a "Rural-urban migration, agricultural output, and the supply-price of labor in a labor surplus economy" *Oxford Economic Papers* (July 1968).

b *Development of the Labor Surplus Economy* (Homewood, Ill.: Richard D. Irwin, Inc., 1964).

c "The early stages of development in a subsistence economy", in C. Wharton, ed., *Subsistence Agriculture and Economic Development* (Chicago: Aldine Publishing Co., 1969).

d "A model of an agrarian economy with nonagricultural activities", *American Economic Review*, (September 1969).

e *Economic Development in Asian Perspective* (Tokyo: Kinokuniya Bookstore, Ltd. 1967).

f *Dualistic Economic Development* (Chicago: University of Chicago Press 1972).

g "Models of the family farm", in Wharton, ed., *Subsistence Agriculture*.

h "A labor supply theory of economic development", Cornell Ag. Econ. Staff Paper 34, June 1971.

i "Subsistence and commercial family farms: some theoretical models of subjective equilibrium", in Wharton, ed., *Subsistence Agriculture*.

j "Peasants and dualism, with and without surplus labor", *Journal of Political Economy* (October 1966). pp. 425–50.

2. Inputs. Although family members normally provide the bulk of *labor* inputs, there is no need to assume that all farms and all families are of the same size and that only family labor is used in production. It is more reasonable to posit a labor market in which farmers can buy additional labor as required or can sell surpluses of family labor to other farmers or to nonagricultural employers.

Land available to the family at any moment is fixed in area and quality. But it is important to specify, as Ishikawa does, that land quality can be raised over time by investments of labor; and that decisions about how much labor time should be spent in this way are part of the family's allocation problem.

Capital can reasonably be restricted to circulating capital in the form of seed, fertilizers, and other inputs purchased from the non-agricultural sector. *Technology* is a given element at any moment, though it is susceptible to improvement over time.

3. Outputs. One should recognize at least three, and possibly four, types of output: (a) *investment goods* in the form of land improvements. In the developed countries, the initial land endowment has been much improved, mainly through investments of labor time, though this is usually not included in estimates of national capital formation. Such nonmonetized and unrecorded capital formation is important also in the LDCs; (b) *nonagricultural consumer goods*, often labeled *Z-goods*, for family use. On farms toward the subsistence end of the subsistence-commercial spectrum, most of the clothing, housing, furniture, fuels, entertainment, personal care, and other services are home-produced; (c) *food output* is recognized in all models, and in fact is usually specified as the only output. This form of output, unlike the two previous ones, can be either consumed or marketed; (d) for completeness, one should probably include a *nonfood crop*, which can only be marketed. A combination of food and nonfood production is common in many parts of the world; and there is evidence that farmers' behavior toward the two types of crop is significantly different.

4. Production functions. The production functions for crop outputs should assume complementarity of variable inputs, including labor time. Increases in the size of the input "package" applied to a given land area yield average and marginal productivity curves of the usual shape. These curves can be shifted upward by land improvement or by technical change, which can be regarded as embodied in the variable inputs, including labor (human capital). Scale economies can be assumed to be absent.

5. Market participation. From what has been said, it follows that farmers should be assumed to participate in both product and labor markets, and on both sides of these markets. In the labor market they can either sell family labor time or hire outside labor at a cash wage. In product markets they can sell food and nonfood crops and can buy food, other consumer goods, and agricultural inputs.

6. Household preference functions. Shall we go seriously astray by using the conventional apparatus of income-leisure preferences, preferences among consumer goods, price and income elasticities, and the rest? It is sometimes assumed that low-income families in the LDCs have fixed consumption standards and that they will work only the number of hours needed to achieve the conventional consumption bundle. It is true that people can consume only the goods they know and that consumption habits are rather fixed in the short run. But the real question is whether people are responsive to the appearance of new, improved, or lower-cost products and interested in the income needed to buy them. There is much evidence of such responsiveness in the LDCs and conventional consumption levels appear to shift upward over time as they do in developed countries.

Static Equilibrium

Given the production structure outlined above, and also given perfect markets and absence of uncertainty, it is a straightforward task to deduce the static equilibrium conditions for the farm family.[6] Without going through the formal exercise, we may note the general nature of these conditions.

In *production*, there should be efficient choice of inputs (with marginal productivities of all inputs proportionate to their relative prices), and efficient choice of outputs (with the price of each output equal to its marginal cost). For home-consumed outputs that do not pass through markets, an imputed price must be used; and this is a substantial obstacle to statistical tests of allocative efficiency. In *consumption*, the usual role of marginal utility proportional to price applies. Where home-produced and purchased consumer goods are in competition, the marginal utility they yield should be proportional to the marginal outlay of labor required to obtain them.

---

6. For a good illustration, see Chihiro Nakajima, "Subsistence and Commercial Family Farms: Some Theoretical Models of Subjective Equilibrium," in *Subsistence Agriculture*, ed. Wharton, pp. 165–84.

Labor time has to be allocated among several competing uses: land improvement, food for home consumption, Z-goods for home consumption, production of crops for market, wage employment, and leisure. In equilibrium, time should be allocated so that its marginal return is equal for all uses and also equals the marginal disutility of labor. The marginal productivity of labor in agriculture should also equal the market wage.

What is the likelihood that all these marginal yields of labor will be zero, as has sometimes been assumed in development models? This could happen in three situations:

1. "Subsistence affluence," as defined earlier. But this relates, properly speaking, to closed household or village units without market options, which is not the situation being considered here.

2. Leisure satiation, extending over a considerable range before the marginal disutility of effort becomes positive. The marginal-productivity-of-labor schedule could conceivably reach zero *within* this range; but this case is probably not important in practice.

3. Grinding poverty, in which the last bit of output is essential to subsistence. Thus, the utility yielded by the last hour of labor is very high even though its physical productivity is low.

In the normal case, however, one would expect a positive marginal productivity of labor, and virtually all statistical studies confirm this expectation. True, this marginal productivity is low by Western standards; but this is simply because we are discussing a less-developed economy. It follows that, if man-hours are withdrawn from agriculture with no other change, output will fall. It is odd that this should ever have been denied, at least with regard to *family* farming.

This by no means disposes of the labor surplus issue, to which we shall return in chapter 6. A low, positive marginal productivity of labor is not necessarily inconsistent with the existence of a labor surplus, in a meaningful sense, within the agricultural sector.

CONSTRAINTS ON ADJUSTMENT: UNCERTAINTY AND MARKET IMPERFECTION

The above picture of internal equilibrium in the family farm unit is sometimes dismissed as highly unrealistic. Some degree of unrealism must be conceded. But it is important to distinguish between valid and invalid lines of criticism.

A traditional line of attack runs in terms of the motivation of farm operators. The "inert peasant," bound by custom and tradition, unresponsive to new production and consumption possibilities, is a stock figure in the literature. So is the "satisficing peasant," who will put forth only the effort needed to achieve some target income. These concepts have been advanced energetically by colonial administrators, low-wage employers in the LDCs, and even some social scientists.

In contrast, Schultz and others have defended the "optimizing peasant," a shrewd fellow who has learned through experience to allocate efficiently and who is responsive to economic opportunities within his perceived opportunity set. The weight of recent research evidence supports this view. There is evidence of substantial allocative efficiency in input and output choices. When production functions are fitted to cross-section data, there is a marked relation between the marginal productivities of inputs and their prices, and also between marginal costs and prices of outputs. True, one finds marked efficiency differences among farms in the same region of a developing nation. But these differences do not seem to be any greater than those among farms in the United States.[7]

Behavior differences between farm operators in the LDCs and those in mature economies, then, are not to be explained by differences in motivation. They stem rather from a variety of institutional and other *constraints* on economic behavior. These can retard or even prevent movement toward a hypothetical equilibrium position. Or they may cause adjustment to stop at "peculiar" values of one or more variables. The more important constraints involve the inherent uncertainty of agricultural production, peculiarities of land as an asset, nonhomogeneity of home labor and market labor, and characteristics of rural capital markets.

Uncertainty of Yield and Prices

Variations in rainfall and temperature, plus the uncertain incidence of pests and plant disease, produce substantial variations in yields from year to year. For marketed outputs, price fluctuations are also important. Thus, the farm producer has to calculate in terms of probabilities rather than certainties; and producers may respond differently to the same expected values, depending on their degree of

7. Some evidence on this point is presented in Y. Hayami and V. W. Ruttan, *Agricultural Development: an International Perspective* (Baltimore: Johns Hopkins Press, 1971), pp. 276–77.

risk aversion. The existence of uncertainty does not prevent efforts at utility maximization; but it changes the concrete form of maximization.[8]

First, it produces a concern for security, for making sure that family subsistence needs are covered. Some basic amount of subsistence production may be virtually removed from the marginal calculus. Resources above those needed for this purpose are then allocated on efficiency grounds.

Uncertainty also produces a certain anticommercialization bias. Returns from market sales may appear high, but they are also risky. Uncertainty is increased by uncertainty of purchased food prices, seasonal fluctuation of these prices, and wide spreads between farm and retail prices. These uncertainties may prevent specialization in cash-crop production, even when this would otherwise appear profitable.

There are various ways of hedging against uncertainty. The most obvious is to select crops with lower but more certain expected returns. Another is to interplant several crops, not all of which are likely to fail simultaneously. Still another, used in West Africa, is to plant manioc and tubers, which, although they are not preferred as foods, are regarded as an essential reserve against failure of the preferred food crops.

Uncertainty is a serious obstacle to the adoption of new seeds, which are perceived by farmers to be more risky and actually are more risky. Traditional plant varieties have acquired immunity to drought, rust, insect pests, and so on over many generations. New varieties, though higher-yielding under optimal conditions, will show greater variance because they have not yet become fully adapted.

Risk aversion is particularly strong among very small farmers, whose low inventories of food and cash make them particularly vulnerable to disaster. Crop failure can lead to a crushing burden of debt, possible loss of land, and, conceivably, starvation. Larger farms with more income and assets, where subsistence is not in question, can afford to be more venturesome. Thus, in a situation where innovation, though risky, does pay off on balance, income distribution within the rural community may become increasingly unequal.

8. For elaboration of this point, see Michael Lipton, "The Theory of the Optimising Peasant," *Review of Development Studies* (April 1968); and Vahid Nowshirvani, "Land Allocation Under Uncertainty in Subsistence Agriculture," *Oxford Economic Papers* 23 (November 1971): 445–55.

Land as an Asset

Even in developed countries, farmers do not regard their land as they would regard a stock or a bond. Land is the family's patrimony. It is an object of affection. It is a prestige symbol. It is to be preserved and protected, even when to sell it might seem obviously profitable. In short, it is a consumption good as well as a capital good.

This consideration, plus legal constraints on transfer of land and poorly developed capital markets, may prevent adjustment of acreage to differences in family size, work preferences, and productivity. Families for whom purchase of additional land would pay off may be unable to bid it away from its owners, though leasing provides an important adjustment mechanism in such cases.

The practice of inheritance in equal shares by surviving children, where it exists, tends to produce fragmentation of farm units over time. It can also lead to inefficiency in current land use—for example, through subdivision of land into many small plots assigned to different children, which leads to waste of land in boundaries and footpaths. Even though the behavior of each cultivator may be optimal, utilization of the total land area is not.

The Rural Labor Market

The stones that have been cast at rural labor markets in the LDCs are not entirely deserved. There is much evidence that wage rates in these countries are genuine market rates, varying by season and region and reflecting degrees of labor scarcity at a particular time and place.[9]

It remains true, however, that "home labor" and "marketed labor" are not freely interchangeable and are not valued at the same rate. People will usually work at home for an hourly return that is less than the market wage. The market rate must be adequate to sustain life. No such minimum applies to family labor. The farm family's subsistence is an overhead cost and, up to the limit set by disutility, it pays to "spread" this overhead by additional labor inputs.

There may also be impediments to the marketing of family labor. For example, the farm may be located far from sources of off-farm employment. And the labor of women and children, usually important in farm operations, may not be marketable off the farm. Moreover,

9. On this, see Bent Hansen, "Employment and Wages in Rural Egypt," *American Economic Review* 59 (June 1969): 298–313; and R. Albert Berry, *Agriculture in Colombia* (New Haven: Yale University Press, forthcoming).

working for others—or even just working—may carry a social stigma. Thus, in West Bengal many small farmers hire outside labor even though family labor is far from fully utilized. More broadly, employment relations are also social class relations. The landless laborer is not interchangeable with the owner-operator.

Capital Formation and Financing

Commercial banking facilities are usually concentrated in urban areas. Farmers, particularly small farmers, are dependent on rural moneylenders who charge high rates of interest. Much of this borrowing is for consumption rather than for productive purposes. People with low and intermittent incomes resort to it on occasion as an act of desperation, and many remain in debt year after year. One effect is to strengthen the security drive of the farmer, the urge toward enough subsistence output to prevent falling into the moneylender's hands.

The tools and circulating capital that can be used in traditional agriculture are simple and largely home-produced. This kind of capital formation is within the capacity of even poor households. The level of capital formation is low because, with existing techniques, the marginal productivity of capital is low.

But with the appearance of new agricultural technology requiring larger material inputs, the scarcity and the high cost of capital become serious constraints that bias the adoption of new techniques toward large farmers with greater saving capacity.

In sum, those who seek to explain LDC farmers' behavior in terms of limited economic aspirations are on the wrong track. Farmers *are* interested in income and wealth, and their pursuit of these goals becomes increasingly informed and effective as development proceeds. What may at first glance appear to be uneconomic behavior usually turns out to be quite economic under the circumstances. But it takes effort and imagination to reconstruct the economic milieu as seen through the farmers' eyes.

COMPARATIVE STATICS: CHANGES IN PRICE PARAMETERS

Farmers are subject to several types of exogenous change—in price parameters, in man-land ratios (as a result of population growth), and in technical possibilities. The direction of change can often, although not always—be predicted from the kind of model outlined earlier. Not always, because in some cases a conflict of substitution and income effects produces an ambiguous result. Much research effort has been devoted to testing such predictions and thus deriving inferences about the economic rationality of LDC farmers.

Hypothesis testing in this area is difficult. The variables being measured usually do not correspond exactly to the concepts being tested. Actual situations usually involve simultaneous change in several variables, so that *ceteris paribus* conditions do not apply. It is easier to test specific predictions—for example, reallocation of acreage devoted to competing crops in response to a change in their relative prices—than it is to test broader propositions—for example, reallocation of time between work and leisure. In view of these difficulties, it is not surprising that results on many points remain inconclusive. It will nevertheless be useful to examine briefly the contours of the research literature.[10] We consider changes in price parameters in this section and changes in the man-land ratio in the next. Response to new technology we leave until chapter 4, since it seems efficient to collect everything we have to say about technical change at one point.

A Relative Price Increase for a Single Output

Consider a farmer growing two or more crops. The farm price of one of these crops rises relative to prices of the others. This is the kind of case on which most research has been done, perhaps because the predictions of theory are unambiguous and because the situation occurs frequently in practice.

Economic reasoning predicts both an *acreage response* and a *yield response*. Acreage will be transferred from other crops to the one whose price has risen. In addition, the price increase raises the marginal value product of variable inputs applied to that crop so, assuming no change (or a less than proportionate change) in input prices, more inputs should be applied and yield per acre should rise.

Many research studies have confirmed the prediction of a positive acreage response.[11] Elasticity coefficients are positive, significant, and of the same order of magnitude as in developed countries. The size of

10. Two surveys that provide extensive bibliographies are Gerald Helleiner, "Small-holder Decisionmaking: Tropical African Evidence," in *Agriculture*, ed. Reynolds; and J. N. Bhagwati and S. Chakravarty, "Contributions to Indian Economic Analysis: A Survey," *American Economic Review* 59 (September 1969): 2–73.

11. See, for example, Edwin R. Dean, "Economic Analysis and African Responses to Price," *Journal of Farm Economics* (May 1965); Raj Krishna, "Farm Supply Responses in India-Pakistan: A Case Study of the Punjab Region," *Economic Journal* 73 (September 1963): 477–87; Walter Falcon, "Farmer Response to Price in a Subsistence Economy: The Case of West Pakistan," *American Economic Review* 54 (May 1964): 580–91; Bhagwati and Chakravarty, "Contributions to Indian Economic Analysis."

the coefficient, however, varies with the kind of crop in question. It is low for basic subsistence crops, somewhat higher for crops (such as rice or wheat) grown both for home consumption and for sale, highest of all for straight cash crops such as cotton, jute, or sugarcane. This can be explained on the ground that, where a large part of the crop is earmarked for home consumption, the "shiftable" acreage is a smaller part of total acreage than in the case of a cash crop.

The positive price response applies to investment decisions as well as to current output decisions. For example, Peter Ady obtained a good explanation for the number of cocoa trees, planted in Africa in terms of the existing stock of trees and expected prices. "The Uganda results support those for Ghana and Nigeria as to the relatively sophisticated character of peasant producers' investment decisions. Contrary to widely held beliefs that perverse supply responses are common form in African countries, results in all four regions indicated a strongly positive reaction of plantings to real prices. They also indicate that peasants base investment decisions upon a calculus similar to that of entrepreneurs in developed market economies . . . the capital stock factor . . . turns out to be significant in all the equations."[12]

There is less evidence of a significant yield response to a price change. This may be partly because fluctuation of yields is dominated by weather and other natural hazards; and partly because use of inputs is influenced by traditional cultivation practices and by physical availability of inputs as well as by their profitability.

Improvement in the Agriculture-Industry Terms of Trade

More complicated, ambiguous, and interesting are the questions raised by a general shift in the terms of trade between agriculture and nonagriculture. Here, the income effect, which may be regarded as minor for a single crop, can no longer be neglected. All dimensions of the family's economic equilibrium are likely to be affected. One must distinguish even more carefully between effects on food crop and cash crop production—and also between the effect on output and on marketed surplus, which need not run in the same direction.

Consider first farms on which only food crops are grown and output can either be consumed or marketed. Let us call these type I farms. There is now a general price increase for these crops, relative to prices

12. Peter Ady, "Supply Functions in Tropical Agriculture," *Bulletin of the Oxford Institute of Economics and Statistics* (May 1968): 157–88.

Table 2. Predicted Responses to an Improvement in
Agriculture-Industry Terms of Trade

	I: *Only Food Crops Marketed*	II: *Only Cash Crops Marketed*
Total labor input	+ or −	+ or −
Labor input to:		
Food production	prob. +	+ or −
Cash crop production	n.r.	+
Z-goods production	−	−
Capital input to:		
Food production	prob. +	+ or −
Cash-crop production	n.r.	+
Output:		
Food crops	prob. +	+ or −
Cash crops	n.r.	+
Marketed surplus	+ or −	+
Farm income	+	+
Farm consumption of:		
Food	+	+
Purchased goods	+	+
Z-goods	−	−

n.r. = not relevant.

of purchased consumer goods. The predicted signs of the response for major farm variables are listed in the first column of table 2. Comment is required only for those variables where the outcome is uncertain or where the reason for the predicted response may not be obvious.

Whether the family's total labor inputs will rise or fall as the real return to an hour of effort rises depends on (1) the relative strength of income and substitution effects, and (2) whether increases in income are readily translatable into purchased consumer goods. The greater the variety, accessibility, and quality of goods available from the industrial sector, the more likely is it that total labor input will rise.

Because purchased consumer goods that compete with Z-goods are now relatively cheaper and also because, with rising incomes, Z-goods may be treated as inferior, there will be a reallocation of labor time away from the production of Z-goods and toward the growing of food crops. This makes it probable, though not certain, that labor inputs to food crops will increase. If they do, complementary capital inputs should also increase, and total food output should rise.

It is important to recall, however, that units of family labor time are not homogeneous and interchangeable. Z-goods may be produced mainly by women and children while agricultural operations are done mainly by men, so that labor time is not freely transferable among outputs. Or Z-goods production may be concentrated in the slack season, when the opportunity cost of labor is low. These circumstances will tend to retard the displacement of Z-goods by factory products.

The sign of a change in "marketed" surplus has been much debated in the literature because, under closed-economy conditions, an increasing flow of foodstuffs to nonagriculture is a basic condition of sustained economic growth. The question of whether improving agriculture's terms of trade will increase the size of the food transfer thus becomes important for economic policy.

This is unfortunately one of the questions that cannot yet be answered with certainty. Theoretical efforts to prove that the food transfer *must* increase (or decrease) in size have not been very successful. If farmers' income elasticity of demand for food is high, and if the output response is small, food consumption on the farm could rise more than output, leading to a decline in marketings. But under other conditions this result need not follow.[13]

It is difficult to estimate farmers' income elasticity of demand for food because of the difficulty of measuring their real income, most of which may be in noncash form. It is possible, however, to measure the elasticity of marketed surplus with respect to output, and this usually turns out to be positive. If, then, the elasticity of output with response to price is also positive, one can multiply the two coefficients, and this will necessarily yield a positive elasticity of marketings. Thus, although the theoretical prediction is ambiguous, agricultural specialists tend to think that an improvement in the agriculture-industry price ratio will draw forth larger food marketings. Agricultural price policies, which in some countries have aimed mainly at securing low-cost food for the urban consumer, need to take account of this (probable) supply response. It should be added, however, that technical change

13. It is important here to distinguish between responses within a single season and responses over a number of seasons. Within a season, where the size of the crop is already determined and the only question is how much should be marketed, a negative relation between price and marketings seems entirely possible. Over a period of years, during which output can be raised and farmers can learn to make effective use of additional cash, a negative response seems less likely. One experienced observer, Raj Krishna, has expressed the view that, over several seasons, the elasticity of marketed surplus will be negative only under "very special conditions."

offers a possibility of much larger increases in food marketings than could be achieved by manipulation of relative prices under technically stagnant conditions.

An interesting result of farm sample surveys, particularly in India, is that the percentage of food output marketed seems to be related systematically to the size of the farms; but the nature of the relation is not entirely clear. Some studies report a linear relationship, with the percentage of food marketings rising steadily with increased farm size.[14] But other studies find a U-shaped curve, with the percentage of output marketed falling as one goes from very small to medium-sized farms, then rising again and reaching its highest value in the largest farm-size classes.[15] A possible explanation of such behavior might be that the small farms have some minimum need for cash (for taxes, interest and debt repayment, purchased agricultural inputs). To meet this need, they often specialize in high-price, labor-intensive crops such as vegetables, of which a high percentage is marketed.

Continuing down column 1 of table 2, if food output and food prices both rise, farm income must rise. Hence family consumption will increase, but unevenly for different types of goods. Much depends on the availability of purchased consumer goods and whether these are close substitutes for home-produced goods. If they are acceptable substitutes, then, as income rises, many Z-goods may turn out to be inferior, and they will be replaced increasingly by purchased goods. Note also that, because of the relative increase in food prices, the cost of purchased goods in terms of *effort* has fallen, whereas for Z-goods this cost has remained unchanged. The substitution effect will thus make for a shift in consumption patterns. In a number of countries, scholars have noted a gradual displacement of home production (and also of village handicrafts) by factory goods as commercialization and monetization proceed.[16]

Now consider farms that produce (1) a food crop, all of which is consumed at home, and (2) a cash crop, all of which is marketed. Let

14. For example, Carl C. Malone, "Some Responses of Rice Farmers to the Package Program in Tanjore District, India," *Journal of Farm Economics* (May 1965); and Raj Krishna, "The Marketable Surplus Function for a Subsistence Crop: an Analysis with Indian Data," *The Economic Weekly*, February 1965.

15. Dharam Narain, *Distribution of the Marketed Surplus of Agricultural Produce by Size-level of Holdings in India: 1950–51* (Bombay: 1962).

16. See Stephen A. Resnick, "The Decline of Rural Industry Under Export Expansion: A Comparison Among Burma, Philippines, and Thailand, 1870–1938," *Journal of Economic History* (March 1970): 51–73.

us call these type II farms. The price of the cash crop rises relative to the price of purchased consumer goods. The predicted directions of response are shown in the second column of table 2. Out of the total fixed farm acreage, more land will now be allocated to the cash crop. Labor inputs, capital inputs, and output of the cash crop will all rise. Since all output of this crop is marketed, the marketed surplus rises by definition.

As before, farm income and farm consumption increase. Purchased consumer goods will tend to displace Z-goods on substitution grounds, and possibly because of the inferior-good effect as well. Food consumption will rise, since at this level income elasticity of demand for food remains high.

Where will this additional food come from? It could conceivably come from these same farms, the reduced acreage devoted to food crops being more than outweighed by larger labor and capital inputs per acre. But it need not do so. If we specify that the economy also includes some type I farms, which produce and market only food, then the type II farms could increase their good consumption through market purchases, while keeping their own food output unchanged or even reducing it. Whether the type II farms will actually find it efficient to specialize increasingly in cash crops while increasing their food purchases will depend on market price relations, on the steepness of the declining AP_L and MP_L curves for food production on their own farms, on the risks involved in dependence on market purchases of food, and on the farmers' attitudes toward these risks. The outcome can go in either direction, which explains the ambiguous sign for the food output variables in table 2.

To the extent that market demand for food increases, food prices will tend to rise, helping call forth larger marketed surpluses for transfer to cash-crop producers. Thus, even though the improvement in agriculture's terms of trade began in the cash-crop sector, it will tend to be generalized to food output as well.

Price Decline for Purchased Agricultural Inputs

This category includes water, fertilizer, seed, pesticides, and tools. A decline in the prices of these items, with farm output prices unchanged, means an increase in the profitability of agricultural operations. So, one should observe effects similar to those analyzed above: a probable increase in total labor inputs, both for current crop production and land improvement; a concurrent increase in complementary purchased inputs; an increase in yields per acre, in farm output, and (probably) in marketed surplus; a rise in real farm income and consumption; and (probably) a decline in Z-goods production, with the qualification noted above.

An important issue, which has been much studied, is the relationship between farm output prices and fertilizer prices. In rice cultivation, for example, the fertilizer-rice price ratio differs widely among countries. It has also varied over time, the well-documented Japanese case showing a long secular decline of fertilizer costs relative to rice prices. Falcon and Timmer have shown that a lower fertilizer-rice price ratio is associated with larger fertilizer inputs and a consequent increase in rice yields per acre.[17]

A Rise in the Market Wage

The use of some hired labor is a normal feature of agricultural systems. Those working large farms hire to supplement their inadequate supply of family labor. Part of the hired labor is supplied by small farmers who cannot efficiently apply all their time to their own holdings. Cross-section studies typically show that amount of time worked off the farm rises as farm size diminishes. There are also some landless laborers who must work, and, in densely populated countries such as India, these form a substantial part of the farm labor force.

Studies of rural labor markets[18] suggest that they are quite flexible, with wage differentials adjusting to the supply-demand balance. Wage rates typically rise toward seasonal peaks of activity and fall in the slack season. They vary regionally, reflecting the local supply-demand situation. Women and children earn less than adult males. There is no indication, however, that the marginal productivity of hired workers is less than their wage. On the contrary, a common criticism of large landholders is that they underutilize their land, failing to hire enough labor to bring labor's marginal product down to equality with the wage rate.

Usually, there are also opportunities for nonagricultural employment. This may be in nearby towns or more distant cities. It may be seasonal, short-term (as in the one- or two-year contracts offered by South African mining companies), or permanent. The response of

17. C. Peter Timmer and Walter P. Falcon, "The Political Economy of Rice Production and Trade in Asia," in ed. Reynolds, *Agriculture*, pp. 373–408.
18. See, for example, Hansen, "Employment and Wages in Rural Egypt," 298–313.

agricultural workers will naturally vary with the nature of the opportunity. For example, studies of the utilization of farm labor time in the Zaria region of northern Nigeria indicate that many workers take up part of the seasonal slack by moving to Zaria for work in construction, service, and other industries—and that the propensity to do this decreases as the distance of the home village from Zaria increases.[19]

In the case of long-term or permanent migration, one would expect this to be a function of the earnings gap between agricultural work and urban employment. There is a good deal of research evidence supporting this hypothesis. The percentage of the male population in Zambia and Rhodesia that migrated to find employment during the 1940s and 1950s was inversely related to the cash-crop potential of their home region.[20] A study of interregional migration in Ghana, using 1960 census data, found that the propensity to migrate varied directly with the income differential and inversely with distance.[21] Similar results have been obtained by Berry for Colombia, migration to Bogotá varying inversely with the level of agricultural earnings in the home district, and by Sahota for internal migration in Brazil.[22] In a study aimed more directly at response to wage *changes*, Dean found that the time spent on cash-crop production by Malawi tobacco farmers was inversely and significantly related to wage rates in the Rhodesian and South African labor markets where migrants could find work.[23]

An important consideration in migration decisions is that urban areas provide both relatively high-wage jobs in the "modern" sector and self-employment at substantially lower earnings in traditional activities; and that there is normally a surplus of applicants for the high-wage jobs. On this ground, Todaro developed a well-known model[24] in which the migration decision depends first on the gap

19. D. W. Norman, "Labor Inputs of Farmers: A Case Study of the Zaria Province of the North-Central State of Nigeria," *Nigerian Journal of Economic and Social Studies* 11 (1969): 3–14.

20. William J. Barber, "Economic Rationality and Behavior Patterns in an Underdeveloped Area," *Economic Development and Cultural Change* (April 1960).

21. L. N. Moses, R. E. Beals, and M. B. Levy, "Rationality and Migration in Ghana," *Review of Economics and Statistics* (November 1967).

22. Gian S. Sahota, "An Economic Analysis of Internal Migration in Brazil," *Journal of Political Economy* (March/April 1968): 218–45.

23. E. R. Dean, "Economic Analysis and African Response to Price," *Journal of Farm Economics* (May 1965).

24. Michael P. Todaro, "A Model of Labor Migration and Urban Unemployment in Less Developed Countries," *American Economic Review* 1969, *59* (1), pp. 138–48; also idem, "Income Expectations, Rural-Urban Migration and Employment in Africa," *International Labour Review* 104 (1971): 387–414.

between the agricultural wage and the modern-sector urban wage and secondly on the probability of getting a job in the modern sector, for which the existing level of urban unemployment might serve as a proxy. Either an increase in the modern-sector wage or an increase in the probability of employment will induce additional migration.

We may note, finally, a number of production-function studies[25] that show a reasonably close relation between the marginal value product of labor in agriculture and the opportunity cost of labor as indicated by potential off-farm earnings. Thus, in the labor market areas, as in others, there are strong indications of economic rationality in farmers' decision making.

An Increase in Taxation

Until now, we have considered only changes affecting farm incomes in a favorable direction. Let us now consider an adverse change—imposition of a new tax or an increase in the rate of taxation. Here one must distinguish among types of taxes, specifically among:

1. Commodity taxes that alter the internal terms of trade. There are a great variety of such taxes, which as a group dominate the tax structure of most LDCs. The prices that farmers pay for nonfarm goods can be raised by tariff protection and excise and sales taxes. Receipts from the sale of farm products can be reduced by marketing board operations, export taxes, and exchange control systems.

A tax change that reduces real farm income will have disincentive effects opposite to those examined in an earlier section. One would predict a drop in labor inputs and farm output and a shift in the output pattern toward home-consumed outputs where the return to labor has not changed. We have little evidence, however, about the probable magnitude of these effects. Existing evidence relates mainly to situations in which the tax "take" has been reduced significantly and a favorable response of farm output has been observed.[26] Schultz and other experienced observers have expressed the view that government

25. See, for example, H. A. Luning, *Economic Aspects of Low Labor Income Farming* (Wageningen, Netherlands: Center for Agricultural Publications and Documentation, Research Report No. 699, 1967); and D. W. Norman, "Dry Land Farming Among the Hausa in the North of Nigeria" (Draft paper, Rural Economy Research Unit, Ahmadu Bello University, 1971).

26. See the literature summarized in T. W. Schultz, *Agriculture and Economic Growth.* See also the discussion of the Philippines case in Y. Hayami and V. W. Ruttan, *Agricultural Development: An International Perspective.*

price and tax policies in the LDCs, which in many countries have been strongly exploitative of argiculture, have had a strong discouraging effect on farm marketings of export as well as domestic products.

This discouraging effect seems particularly likely in the technically stagnant type of agriculture that we have been discussing implicitly up to this point. Where farm incomes are being raised by technical progress, it may well be possible to draw off part of the income increment through taxation without an adverse effect on production. But again, we know little about possible magnitudes.

2. A land tax. This can be of various types. A favorite proposal of tax reformers in the LDCs is a tax based on potential output, designed to put pressure on large landowners either to utilize their land more intensively or to sell it to those who will. This avoids the possible disincentive effect of heavier types on existing levels of output. Such proposals are rarely adopted, however, because of the political power of the groups at which they are aimed.

Consider rather a conventional tax on land area, unrelated to output. This is presumably non-shiftable. The income effect should favor increased farm output, in an effort to restore the previous income position. The positive effect on marketings may be even greater, because of the need for cash to meet tax payments. A further possibility, historically important in the United States and Canada, is that the tax may in effect be collected in labor time, that is the farmer may work on roads or other local improvements until he has earned enough cash to pay his taxes. If these labor inputs are timed to occur in off-peak agricultural periods, they need not mean any decrease in labor inputs to agriculture.

3. Income tax. Even in developed countries, we do not know whether income taxation has a positive or a negative effect on labor supply. A similar degree of uncertainty must be admitted for the LDCs. In LDC agriculture, there is a further uncertainty arising from the fact that much of farm output is consumed at home. This is neither valued nor included in the tax base. The fact that cash income from marketings is taxed might be expected to produce a shift away from marketed outputs toward home production.

Tax experts have nevertheless viewed income taxation favorably as a means of capturing part of the income of large landowners, and they do not seem to regard the disincentive effects as serious. Stephen Lewis, for example, concludes that "income and personal taxes can have incentive effects similar to those discussed for land taxes, though generally not as powerful, provided that all income from agricultural pursuits is included in the tax base."[27] It is, of course, difficult (even in the United States) to get an accurate accounting and reporting of farm income. But this difficulty can be overcome by the use of assessments based on estimated "normal" income from a given acreage.[28]

COMPARATIVE STATICS: CHANGES IN THE MAN-LAND RATIO

There has been a lively discussion in the literature over the effect on agricultural output of a net reduction in the farm labor force. Schultz and others have argued that such a reduction must, *ceteris paribus*, mean a drop in output. Fei and Ranis and others have developed models in which no such drop occurs.

While this discussion may be of intellectual interest, it cannot be of any practical significance in the near future. In most LDCs the rural labor force is increasing absolutely and clearly will continue to increase for decades to come. The policy problem is not whether labor can be withdrawn costlessly from agriculture for industrial employment. Rather, the problem is how increased labor inputs can be absorbed within agriculture without unduly depressing the marginal productivity of labor.

This point can be demonstrated with simple arithmetic. If the agricultural population is to remain stable, the nonagricultural population must increase by the rate of population growth multiplied by the inverse of the *initial* fraction of the labor force in nonagriculture. For example, suppose that population is growing at 3 percent per year and that one-fourth of the labor force is employed initially in nonagriculture. For the agricultural labor force to remain constant, nonagricultural employment would have to increase by 4 × 3 percent or 12 percent per year. In actuality, few LDCs have been able to raise nonagricultural employment at more than 4 percent per year.

In most LDCs rural population is continuing to rise at 1 to 2 percent per year. Using plausible parameters, Folke Dovring projects that agricultural population in these countries will still be rising fifty years from now, though more slowly as the nonagricultural share of the

27. Stephen R. Lewis, Jr., "Agricultural Taxation in a Developing Economy," in *Agricultural Development and Economic Growth*, ed. Herman M. Southworth and Bruce F. Johnston, (Ithaca: Cornell University Press, 1967), p. 468.
28. This system is used, for example, in Uganda and has been refined to include other farm characteristics (such as livestock holdings) that affect its income-earning capacity.

labor force gradually rises and takes on greater weight in the labor transfer equation.[29] This projection is supported by historical experience in the developed countries. Although their population growth rates were low—typically around 1 percent per year—their agricultural populations continued to rise for something like a century after the beginning of rapid industrialization. Although the agricultural labor force declined relatively, absolute declines in the labor force are very recent—occurring after 1920 in most Western countries, after 1950 in Japan. In semideveloped regions such as southern Italy, Spain, and Portugal, the agricultural population is still rising.

In a country with supplies of cultivable land equal in quality to that already under cultivation, this presents no problem. Additional workers can settle additional land, with no change in the average or marginal productivity of labor. Indeed, if there are increasing returns to a national economy as it grows in size, such a process of extensive growth can raise per capita output. This situation of land surplus is still common in Africa, Latin America, and some parts of Southeast Asia (though the limits of cultivation are being approached quite rapidly there).

But let us consider a situation, which some LDCs face already and more will face eventually, in which all cultivable land is already occupied and further growth can occur only on the intensive margin. A rising rural labor force then means a rising man-land ratio. (I assume also for simplicity that rural population and labor force are rising at the same rate, that is, I overlook the lag effects that occur during transition from one population growth rate to another). There is no change in agricultural technology. It is intuitively obvious that under these conditions the situation of the rural population must deteriorate. But it will be useful to spell this out in some detail.

The Process of Immiserization

The rising man-land ratio can be visualized either as more people per farm of unchanged size or as fragmentation of land into smaller farm units. If there are no economies of scale, this does not matter. What consequences will follow?

1. Food availability per capita will decrease, which will raise the

29. Folke Dovring, "The Share of Agriculture in a Growing Population," in *Agriculture in Economic Development*, ed. Eicher and Witt (New York: McGraw-Hill, 1964) pp. 78–98.

marginal utility of food and hence the value of output relative to leisure.

2. It will thus pay to apply more man-hours of labor to each acre of land. (But since there are also more workers, the number of man-hours per worker may or may not increase. This depends on the shape of productivity and utility schedules.) This prediction is consistent with cross-section evidence from a number of countries, which shows labor inputs per acre, complementary capital inputs per acre, and output per acre all rising as farm size decreases. Small farms also supply more labor for off-farm employment than do larger farms. Even so, the *utilization ratio* of farm family labor tends to decline with decreasing farm size. Increased labor inputs per acre and increased sales of off-farm labor fail fully to absorb the increasing labor available.

3. Increased labor inputs must, with unchanged technology, reduce the marginal and average productivity of labor. Output per capita falls toward the subsistence level, and the concept of what constitutes subsistence may also be revised downward. The severity of this effect depends on how steeply the productivity curves slope downward. There is considerable consensus among agricultural economists that the decline is quite steep under strict *ceteris paribus* conditions.[30]

4. Additional labor will be applied not only in current farm production, but at all the other margins noted in my discussion of static equilibrium. It will pay to apply more labor to farm investments designed to raise future output. More labor will also be offered on the off-farm market, and the wage rate in this market will fall in step with declining productivity in agriculture.

5. With the decrease in food availability per capita, food will rise in value relative to purchased consumer goods. There will thus be a reallocation of labor time toward food for subsistence and away from cash marketings. The marketed surplus will shrink and eventually disappear. This is an antidevelopmental sequence, which will gradually choke off growth in the nonagricultural sector. Matters may become even worse if overcultivation of land produces a deterioration in its quality through erosion and loss of soil nutrients.

---

30. This is confirmed by experience in what is now Bangladesh, where a combination of rapid population growth and slow technical progress has produced almost a laboratory experiment on this point. Between 1951 and 1961, cropped acreage rose only 5 percent while the farm labor force rose more than 30 percent. The man-land ratio rose from 0.41 to 0.51 workers per acre. In consequence, average productivity per worker (in constant prices) fell from 514 rupees to 452 rupees per year. See Warren C. Robinson, "Disguised Unemployment Once Again: East Pakistan, 1951–1961," *American Journal of Agricultural Economics* (August 1969): 592–604.

Stages of Deterioration

With the aid of a conventional productivity diagram (figure 2), we can trace several stages in this hypothetical downward path. MP_L and AP_L are the marginal and average productivity schedules in agricultural production. S is the subsistence level of per capita consumption.

Figure 2. Productivity Schedules in Agriculture

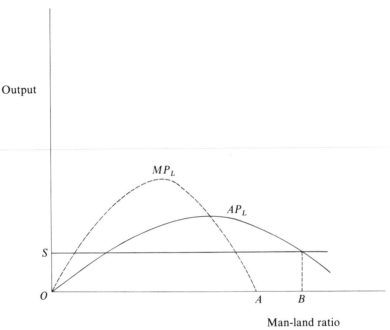

Man-land ratio

As labor inputs are increased to counter the growing food scarcity, the farm slides down the MP_L schedule toward point A, at which the marginal productivity of additional man-hours is zero. The wage rate in the off-farm market, of course, cannot fall to zero. It will retain some positive value, perhaps related to the subsistence minimum OS. But as more and more labor spills over into this market from farm activities, a point is reached at which employers are not willing to hire any additional labor at the prevailing wage.

The number of workers available, however, continues to increase. As this happens, the fixed total of available employment is shared among more and more people. The input of hours per worker declines. The decline in the number of hours worked is accompanied, and in a sense checked, by a decline in the quality of these hours. This results partly from a decline in nutritional levels, making workers less energetic and more disease-prone. The intensity of work declines also because each worker makes a rational calculation that, if he works harder and accomplishes more, the only result will be less work for others. This attitude gets built into the culture of densely populated countries. It resembles the "ca'canny" outlook of many industrial workers—that there is only so much to be done, so let's not do it too quickly—but with considerably more justification.

Eventually, when the man-land ratio rises to B, the average productivity of labor falls to subsistence. The definition of subsistence may then be forced downward, but this must stop at some rock-bottom level. At this point, the convention that everyone is entitled to remain on the farm and to share equally in output may break down, and people will be pushed off the land. The supply of landless laborers increases, putting downward pressure on the market wage and spreading the misery of the countryside to the towns.

At some point, rarely reached in modern times, Malthusian positive checks on population growth would become operative.

Brakes on Deterioration?

The reason why this gloomy picture seems somewhat unreal is the offsetting force of technical progress. But continuing to leave this on one side, let us ask whether there are any natural brakes on the process of deterioration outlined above. Are there any reasons to expect a self-correcting process rather than a cumulative downward spiral?

A drain of rural labor into nonagricultural employment will retard the rise of the man-land ratio; and the more rapid the drain, the more beneficial the result. But given present population growth rates and the limited absorptive capacity of other sectors, this drain can only postpone the day of reckoning, not avert it. Nevertheless, it can win additional breathing space during which other remedial measures can be brought to bear.

Increased inputs of labor at the *capital formation* margin will shift the AP_L and MP_L curves for current crop production upward, retarding the decline in physical productivity. In rice cultivation, for example, increasing sophistication of water-control systems can bring substantial yield increases. Even so, with no technical change in other directions,

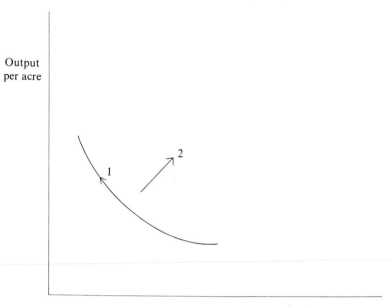

Figure 3. Two Types of Productivity Change

the point of zero marginal productivity seems certain to be reached.

Adversity could conceivably induce corrective action. Obvious and growing overpopulation could lead to a spontaneous or a government-induced spread of family planning. Adoption of population control by the government of China, for example, seems already to have had considerable effect on urban birth rates. In most other LDCs, however, government action has been feeble and public response slight.

Population pressure may also lead, as Ester Boserup has argued, to growing intensity of cultivation. As farmers slide down the existing set of productivity schedules, this pressure induces a change in the agricultural regime which leads to a new and higher set of curves. As evidence, Boserup cites the gradual change in some parts of the world from forest fallow → bush fallow → short fallow → annual cropping → multiple cropping.

With no modernization of inputs or production practices, however, such increasing intensity of cultivation is unlikely to raise per capita output and, at best, may hope to maintain it unchanged. The rural economy would tend to move leftward along the rectangular hyperbola in figure 3, with the area under the hyperbola (output per man) remaining the same. (Interestingly enough, a scatter diagram of rice yields in various Asian countries, with the axes defined this way, is fitted quite well by a hyperbolic function.)[31]

What this means is that the farmer can hold his own in terms of subsistence only at the cost of larger labor inputs per worker. Mrs. Boserup argues that this is the real deterioration that traditional peasant producers suffer over the course of time. They have to work harder and harder simply to keep afloat. True progress, on the other hand, would consist in moving away from the hyperbola in the direction of arrow 2, as countries like Japan and the United States have been doing.[32] This requires the kinds of technical change that we shall examine in chapter 4.

---

31. See Ishikawa, *Economic Development*, p. 78.
32. Ester Boserup, *The Conditions of Agricultural Growth* (London: Allen and Unwin; Chicago: Aldine Publishing Co., 1965).

4

The Agricultural Sector

In chapter 3 we assumed an owner-operator framework and asked how the individual farmer adjusts to the economic circumstances confronting him. When we look at the agricultural sector as a whole, however, we must recognize that:

1. There is usually a variety of tenure forms, including share tenancy and leasehold. Will a tenant allocate resources and adjust to change in the same way as an owner-operator? Is tenancy inherently inferior to family farming?

2. Even among owner-operators, there may be wide differences in farm size. Particularly in Latin America, but also in other countries, there exists a "dualistic" structure of large, commercially oriented farms operating alongside small units producing mainly for family use. Apart from income inequality, is this structure inefficient in production terms? Could output be raised substantially by subdividing the large units into family-sized farms?

3. Technical progress in agriculture is rightly regarded as the main hope for offsetting diminishing returns, absorbing the growing rural labor force, and feeding a growing population at improving nutritional levels. Where does new technology come from? What is required to ensure its generation, diffusion, and adoption? What has been the impact of recent breakthroughs in wheat and rice technology on output, employment, and rural income distribution?

THE ECONOMICS OF SHARE TENANCY

The proportion of agricultural land operated under different tenure forms as of 1960 is shown in table 1. The designation *holdings operated under more than one tenure form* refers usually to a situation in which the farmer owns part of the acreage he cultivates and rents the rest. Only about 11 percent of all land is operated by tenants without ownership rights; but in Asia the proportion rises to 22 percent. The

Table 1. Area of Holdings by Tenure Form, 1960
(Percent)

	All holdings	Holdings operated under one tenure form			Holdings Operated Under More Than One Tenure Form
		Owner-Operator	Landlord-Tenant	Other	
Europe	100	60	13	7	20
North & Central America	100	39	11	16	33
South America	100	80	9	5	6
Asia	100	54	22	4	20
Africa	100	64	7	20	9
Total	100	56	11	12	21

Source: FAO, *Report on the 1960 World Census of Agriculture,* Rome: 1971, vol. 5, pp. 92–97.

most frequent tenancy arrangement is cropsharing, and we shall concentrate on that form here, with only minor reference to cash leases.

There is a long literature on share tenancy. The discussion has usually assumed a simple contract specifying only the percentage of the crop to be delivered to the landlord. The tenant is assumed to provide all inputs and to be responsible for all production decisions. Theorists have usually concluded that resource allocation under such a contract will be inferior to that attained under owner operation.

Consider a tenant with a fixed land area deciding how much labor and other inputs to apply to this area. His share of output is 50 percent. Therefore, by the usual reasoning, he will apply each variable input to the point at which its marginal cost equals half its marginal value product. Variable inputs are underapplied and land is underutilized—compared with family farming. The higher the landlord's rent share, the stronger the disincentive effect.

During the past decade, however, students of LDC agriculture have taken a fresh look at share tenancy[1] and this discussion differs in

1. See, for example, Anthony Bottomley, *Factor Pricing and Economic Growth in Underdeveloped Rural Areas* (London: Crosby, Lockwood and Son, 1971); Steven N. S. Cheung, *The Theory of Share Tenancy* (Chicago: University of Chicago Press, 1969); P. K. Bardhan and T. N. Srinavasan, "Cropsharing Tenancy in Agriculture: A Theoretical and Empirical Analysis," *American Economic Review* 61 (March 1971): 48–64; David M. G. Newbery, "The Choice of Rental Contract in Peasant Agriculture," and Mahar Mangahas, "An Economic Theory of Tenant and Landlord Based on a Philippine Case," in *Agriculture in Development Theory,* ed. L. G. Reynolds, (New Haven: Yale University Press, 1975), pp. 109–37 and 138–64.

several respects from earlier writings. They have recognized, first, that the rental contract can be quite complex, covering such matters as:

1. Landlord and tenant shares of output. Here the shares may differ with the crop. A common arrangement is for the landlord to receive, say, 50 percent of the major crop, while the tenant is free, within limits, to produce minor products and keep the proceeds. The share ratios may apply to gross output or to net output after the deduction of specified types of operating expanses. The shares may be set for a period of years, or they may be subject to annual renegotiation.

2. It is common for the landlord to share in the *financing of variable inputs*. His share may range from zero to 100 percent and may vary among inputs. Typically, these advances must be repaid in kind before the sharing of the remaining output; and the repayment terms include an implicit rate of interest. The landlord thus earns interest as well as rent, and this will affect his maximizing behavior.

3. Control of production practices. At one pole, the landlord may be a passive absentee who simply collects his rents. At the other pole, he may manage his tenants' farms in detail, specifying allocation of acreage among crops, amount of inputs to be used, and major cultivation practices. In the latter case, he may specify the same inputs that would be applied by an owner-operator.

Consider the following excerpt from a pre-1949 cropsharing lease in Honan Province, China:

> Tenant A agrees to cultivate (so many *mow*) of land for landowner B. We hereby stipulate that tenant A provides (so many head) of water buffalo, (so many) men; and every year the tenant must cultivate wheat once, Indian corn three times, and soybeans twice. Fertilizer expenses are to be shared (in certain proportions). The yields of all crops are to be shared (in certain proportions). The lease may terminate only after the autumn harvest.[2]

4. Length of tenure. A longer lease provides a longer time horizon for the tenant and may make him more willing to invest in farm improvements. On the other hand, it may weaken the landlord's hand in controlling production practices, since the sanction of terminating the agreement is less available. Even with a short-term lease, of course,

---

2. Cited in Steven N. S. Cheung, "Transaction Costs, Risk Aversion, and the Choice of Contractual Arrangements," *Journal of Law and Economics* (April 1969): 34.

the landlord can protect himself to some extent by writing in a provision that the tenant must return the land in as good condition as he received it.

Not only are there numerous dimensions of the rental contract, but different items are tradeable against each other. The Mangahas paper cited earlier provides interesting detail on rental arrangements in the Philippines. Sample surveys show the landlord's share varying from 25 percent to as much as 55 percent. The higher rental rates, however, tend to be offset by concessions to the tenant in other directions: a reduction in the proportion of output subject to cropsharing, an increase in the landlord's contribution to operating expenses, and an increase in the "agad" (produce that the farm family is allowed to harvest for its own consumption before the general harvest with hired workers takes place).

Second, the recent literature attempts to explain existing tenure systems rather than simply taking them as exogenous. The problem is set up by first defining utility schedules for would-be landlords and tenants and then permitting market negotiation of rental terms. The result varies with the degree of population pressure, greater land scarcity increasing the landowner's return. It is influenced by market structure. Tenants do better in a fully competitive market than they do where landowners have monopoly or oligopoly power. The outcome also depends on whether the model incorporates uncertainty and risk aversion by the contracting parties. It can be shown that, with static technology, certainty of yields and prices, and a competitive market for rentals, the landlord's return under share tenancy will be identical with that under cash rental; but under uncertainty this will no longer be true.

The upshot is that it no longer seems possible to draw general conclusions about the allocative efficiency of share tenancy. Anything can happen, depending on the specific terms of a potentially complex agreement. One can specify a share-tenancy agreement that will yield input-output results identical with those of owner operation. One can also construct a hypothetical market in which bidding by tenants and landlords will lead to such an agreement. For example, Bottomley has constructed a model in which the variables to be determined are the total acreage it pays a landlord to bring under cultivation, the division of this acreage among tenants (acres per family), and the rental shares. He assumes a competitive market in which tenants can bid for land and landlords can compete for tenants, and he demonstrates that this will yield optimal resource allocation.[3]

The hypothesis of allocative inefficiency under share tenancy has also been undermined by research studies, which often reveal no systematic difference in factor productivity between tenancy and owner operation. As regards the Philippines, Mangahas observes that "productivity on share tenant farms is very often no different from that on owner-operated or leasehold farms, and, where different, is almost always greater. Neither have share tenants lagged behind with respect to adoption of high-yielding varieties of rice."[4] Strict *ceteris paribus* conditions, of course, are difficult to establish. Tenant- and owner-operated farms may not be comparable in regard to land quality, farm size, crop mix, and access to credit and modern inputs. But the absence of striking productivity differences cast doubt on the older criticisms of share tenancy.

In any event, comparisons of static efficiency may be less important than the question of how the tenure system affects the speed of adoption of new agricultural technology. Again, it may not be possible to reach general conclusions. The extent to which landowners have entrepreneurial ability and motivation, the extent to which they specify production practices, and the extent to which they finance inputs may vary widely within the same nominal tenure form. Research evidence in this area is still limited. Tenancy also involves inequality in the distribution of wealth, income, economic opportunity, and political influence. One could well argue against it on these grounds, even if no adverse output effects could be shown.

FARM SIZE AND FACTOR PRODUCTIVITY

Farms differ widely in size. Skewness of the size-distribution is greatest in Latin America, where less than 10 percent of the holdings typically contain more than 90 percent of the acreage. It is at a minimum in Africa, where tribal assignment of land in family-sized plots acts as a check on inequality. In most of the Asian countries, inequality is substantial. In India, for example, about one-third of the agricultural labor force are landless laborers and one-third occupy farms of less

---

3. Bottomley, *Factor Pricing and Economic Growth.*
4. Mangahas, "An Economic Theory," in *Agriculture,* ed. Reynolds, p. 138.

Table 2. On-farm, Off-farm, and Total Mandays Worked Per Year by Operators, India

Farm Size (acres)	*Days Worked Per Year*		
	On-farm	*Off-farm*	*Total*
<1.25	80	195	275
1.25–2.5	106	173	279
2.5–5.0	159	86	245
5.0–7.5 } 7.5–10.0 }	220	48	268
10–15	231	21	252
15–20	247	31	278
>20	241	9	250

than five acres, while the remaining one-third have farms ranging from five to hundreds of acres.

The farm family is a relatively fixed factor of production. When this factor is combined with a small land area, the family adapts by working the land intensively and also by selling labor in the market. Even so, the family's labor time is often underutilized. As farm size increases, man-hours worked on the farm per family member increase and off-farm work diminishes. The evidence from Indian sample surveys reproduced in table 2 is probably typical.[5] In this case, the larger operators did not work more total days per year. But other studies have found the utilization of family labor time rising with increasing farm size. In Taiwan, for example, Koo found that the utilization ratio rose from 42 percent in the smallest size class to 77 percent for farms of 8–9 acres.[6]

Beyond the point at which family labor time is fully utilized, hiring of outside labor becomes necessary. With increasing size, the owner-operated farm shades over gradually into a landowner-wage earner system. The hired workers may be landless laborers or small farmers whose full time cannot be used on their own farms. Hired labor is used both to cover seasonal peaks and to relieve family members of arduous, disagreeable, or hot-weather tasks. Mellor comments that "in many areas more permanent and temporary hired labor is used than in high-income countries ... [due to] ... a combination of low levels of wages relative to peasant incomes and a relative paucity of

5. A. M. Khusro, "Farm Size and Land Tenure in India," *Indian Economic Review* (1969).

6. Anthony Y. C. Koo, *The Role of Land Reform in Economic Development* (New York: Frederick A. Praeger, 1968), p. 94.

attractive consumer goods. Low wage rates favor expenditure on labor by providing a relatively attractive situation for buying leisure and social position."[7]

There has been much research on the relation between farm size and partial and total factor productivity,[8] but the results are not easy to interpret. The data usually measure output rather than value added and average rather than marginal productivity. It is not possible to control for land quality, which may differ between large and small farms. There may be differences in the quality of farm management. There are usually differences in output mix. In Colombia, for example, an important reason why value product per acre tends to decrease with farm size is that the larger farms devote more acreage to livestock rather than to crop cultivation. In India, too, farm management surveys suggest that smallholders tend to produce more labor-intensive crops, invest more time in digging irrigation channels, and have higher multiple-cropping ratios.

Another complication is that it is difficult statistically to separate differences in total factor productivity from possible economies of scale. While a few studies seem to show modest economies of scale, the weight of the evidence is that such economies are of negligible importance in traditional agriculture. This situation may be changing, however, with increasing use of tractors and other large machine units (though the resulting indivisibilities can be reduced by leasing arrangements).

The crude data on factor inputs and productivities are quite consistent for countries as diverse as India, Colombia, and Brazil. Labor inputs per acre on large farms are normally less than 50 percent, and often only 20 or 25 percent, of those on the smallest farms. The result is that the large farms show higher output per worker but the small farms show higher output per acre. Berry's results for Colombia (table 3) illustrate the general pattern.[9] The term *effective hectare* is an attempt to adjust for land quality, which is substantially lower on the larger farms. Even after such adjustment, land productivity is

7. John W. Mellor, *The Economics of Agricultural Development* (Ithaca: Cornell University Press, 1966), chap. 8.

8. For a summary of such work, see R. A. Berry, "Cross-Country Evidence on Farm Size/Productivity Relationships," mimeographed (New Haven: Yale Economic Growth Center.

9. R. Albert Berry, "Farm Size Distribution, Income Distribution, and the Efficiency of Agricultural Production: Colombia," *American Economic Review* 62 (May 1972): 403–08.

Table 3. Factor Productivity and Farm Size in Colombia, 1960
(Values in thousands of 1960 pesos)

Farm Size (hectares)	Manyears of Labor/ Effective Hectare	Value Added/ Worker	Value Added/ Effective Hectare	Value Added/ Hectare	Value Added/ Value of Land and Capital
0–3	.45	1.67	.75	1.37	.35
3–5	.38	2.08	.79	.86	.36
5–10	.19	2.71	.73	.73	.33
10–50	.16	3.47	.57	.44	.25
50–500	.06	6.18	.38	.23	.16
> 500	.023	15.07	.35	.13	.14

twice as high on the smallest farms as on the largest, while labor productivity varies in the opposite direction.

What explains this pattern of input use? A common hypothesis is that the cost of labor differs between large and small farms. The large farmer hires labor at a wage that cannot fall below some conventional minimum, and so he will—at most—hire only up to the point at which labor's marginal value product equals this wage. We say "at most" to take account of an argument, heard particularly often in Latin America, that large landowners are satisficers rather than maximizers. They hold land as a portfolio item and a source of prestige, often live in the city, entrust farm operations to a hired manager, and demand only that the farm produce some customary income flow. They would prefer to hire fewer workers rather than more, because workers are not only difficult to manage but are potential claimants to the land. Thus, employment may well fall short of the profit-maximizing point.

The small farmer, on the other hand, uses mainly family labor and applies this labor to the point at which its marginal value product equals the marginal disutility of effort. But given an outside labor market, why does he not value family labor at the market wage? Perhaps partly because off-farm jobs are somewhat undependable and seasonal, partly because the labor of women and children may not be readily (or customarily) marketable, and partly because his total return on the farm includes a return to land and capital ownership. Total return is larger than the return to labor alone; but it can be realized only through the application of labor time. There is also a convention that the family should grow enough to eat; and the smaller the farm, the more labor input per acre this will require.

Differences in partial factor productivity, although they suggest

Table 4. Relative Social Efficiency and Implicit Returns to Capital (including Land) by Farm Size:
Varying Assumptions re the Opportunity Cost of Labor
(Product Prices Assumed to Equal Marginal Social Benefit)

Farm Size	Case 1 Nonwhite-Collar Labor: 1,400 White-Collar Labor: 8,000		Case 2 Nonwhite-Collar Labor: 700 White-Collar Labor: 8,000		Case 3 Opportunity Cost of All Labor = 0	
	Coefficient of Efficiency	Social Rate of Return to Cap.	Coefficient of Efficiency	Social Rate of Return to Cap.	Coefficient of Efficiency	Social Rate of Return to Cap.
0–3	.85	5.69	1.16	20.48	1.73	35.3
3–5	1.00	11.84	1.30	24.11	1.79	36.4
5–10	1.14	15.92	1.36	24.45	1.62	33.0
10–50	1.10	14.05	1.16	19.04	1.21	25.0
50–100	0.98	11.46	0.87	13.27	0.78	16.0
>500	1.00	11.82	0.81	12.47	0.69	14.0
Total	1.00	11.98	1.00	15.82	1.00	20.4

misallocation, are not conclusive evidence of differences in total factor productivity. Conclusions on this point are quite sensitive to factor prices. Some studies have found that, using market prices of the factors, there is little variation in efficiency by farm size. If, however, the price of labor is lowered to its estimated social opportunity cost, there is a decisive advantage for the smaller farms. This is illustrated in table 4, which shows Berry's estimates for Colombia. He comments:

> For almost all plausible assumptions about social opportunity cost of factors, total factor productivity emerges higher for relatively small farms. . . . When labor's annual opportunity cost is based on the recorded average wage rate (and assuming 250 days as a typical working year), the larger farms' productivity is about equal to the smaller ones. . . . The use of other assumptions . . . cases 2 and 3 . . . gives the smaller farms (especially those of 3–10 hectares) a clear-cut efficiency advantage, the relation being monotonic from at least the size group 5–10 hectares upward. That size group stands out as the most efficient over the full range of plausible assumptions. A more detailed breakdown by size . . . suggests that the smallest farms (those below two hectares) are dominated.

This situation, often termed *agricultural dualism*, raises questions of both dynamic and static efficiency. Dynamic considerations we defer to the next section. With regard to static efficiency, the research results suggest that reorganization of large farms into smaller units would increase both output and employment. It would also reduce inequalities of income and wealth, though this depends on the compensation scheme used. If landowners were compensated at full market value, income distribution would initially be little affected. But a government capable of mounting an effective land reform program would probably be capable also of squeezing the landlords, particularly through payment in fixed-income securities whose value is eroded through subsequent inflation.

The output effect can be analyzed on either an ex ante or an ex post basis. Ex ante, one can take the productivity data used by Berry, Cline,[10] and others and ask what would be the *ceteris paribus* effect of a given reorganization scheme. Even if *ceteris paribus* conditions cannot in fact be realized, this is an interesting exercise. Using Brazilian

10. William R. Cline, *Economic Consequences of a Land Reform in Brazil* (Amsterdam: North-Holland Publishing Co., 1970).

data, Cline predicted that farm output would increase by 20 to 25 percent under a "total redistribution," which would scale down all farms to the socially optimum size. On the other hand, output would rise only 5 percent under a conservative reform exempting intermediate-size farms.

Even if output rose, the marketed surplus might decline, since the new smallholders would have larger incomes and a high income elasticity of demand for food. Technical progress might be slowed, though this would depend on government policy. It is sometimes argued that agricultural savings would decline; but this argument is questionable. Research to date does not indicate that the savings-income ratio varies appreciably by farm size.

Ex post, one can examine what happened to output and productivity in countries where substantial land reforms have occurred—Mexico, Egypt, Iraq, Japan, Taiwan, and others. Though the ex ante predictions are clear, the ex post evidence is uneven. In some countries the output effect has clearly been favorable, but in others it has not. To explore the reasons would require a case-by-case analysis.[11] Broadly, the outcome seems to depend on how rapidly and decisively the redistribution program is carried out. The "announcement effect" is bound to be unfavorable; and if it is followed by a long lag, which creates uncertainty and withdrawal of investment by landowners, the new system will have to pick up from a low base. The other question involves *what else* government does in addition to redistributing land. The new smallholders stand in need of technical information, credit, marketing facilities, and input supplies in order to function effectively. This point, of major importance in practice, will be illustrated in our discussion of agricultural development experience in chapter 11.

TECHNICAL CHANGE IN AGRICULTURE

In earlier sections of chapters 3 and 4 we have explored the possibility of securing increases in farm output by improving farmers' terms of trade, altering tenancy arrangements, and reorganizing large

11. In addition to Koo's study of Taiwan cited earlier, see Solon L. Barraclough, "Agricultural Policy and Land Reform" *Journal of Political Economy* 78 (July–August 1970): 906–47; R. P. Dore, *Land Reform in Japan* (London: Oxford University Press, 1959); Folke Dovring, "Land Reform and Productivity in Mexico," *Land Economics* 46 (August 1970): 264–74; Doreen Warriner, "Employment and Income Aspects of Recent Agrarian Reforms in the Middle East," *International Labor Review* 101 (June 1970): 605–26; and E. Eshag and M. A. Kamal, "Agrarian Reform in the United Arab Republic," *Bulletin of the Oxford Institute of Statistics* (May 1968): 73–104.

landholdings into family-sized units. With traditional technology, these possibilities appear quite limited. Only technical progress holds out the prospect of large increases in farm employment, output, and marketings. It is desirable, therefore, to examine the nature of technical change in agriculture and to explore the impact of recent advances in wheat and rice technology.

Innovations in agriculture are of two main kinds: (1) mechanical innovations, such as the long series of developments in American grain growing from the horse-drawn reaper to the tractor and combine harvester. These innovations are labor-saving and tend to reduce the man-land ratio; (2) biological-chemical innovations, such as those involved in the recent advances in rice and wheat production or in the earlier development of hybrid corn in the United States. These are yield-increasing and land-saving. They typically require increased labor inputs per acre—and so increase employment as well as output.

Hayami and Ruttan argue[12] that the direction of technical change can be regarded as endogenous, as a response to relative resource availabilities and resource prices. Technical change is oriented toward saving resources whose relative price is rising. Not only is this profitable to farmers and input suppliers, but the concept of induced innovation can be applied also to the public sector. Farmers will urge government research organizations to innovate in directions indicated by resource scarcities, and these agencies will respond. Hayami and Ruttan believe that this approach adequately explains the dominance of mechanical innovations in American agriculture and the dominance of biological-chemical innovations in Japan. Given the resource availabilities of most LDCs, the biological-chemical type of innovation is the more important; and whenever we speak of "technical change" without qualification, this is what we mean.

Generating and Diffusing Technical Change

Technical progress in agriculture differs from progress in manufacturing in two respects. In manufacturing, it is mainly the producers themselves who invent and innovate. Government and university laboratories are of some importance, and so is the "lone wolf" inventor. To a large extent, however, innovation occurs *within* the producing unit, or at any rate within the manufacturing sector. For example,

---

12. Yujiro Hayami and Vernon W. Ruttan, *Agricultural Development: An International Perspective* (Baltimore: Johns Hopkins Press, 1971).

machinery manufacturers are an important source of inventions for the industries they supply.

In agriculture, on the other hand, technical progress comes mainly from *outside* the industry. The individual producing unit is too small to support inventive activity. Discoveries made by one farmer cannot be appropriated and kept secret from others. Further, because of the competitive structure of the industry, productivity improvements tend to be reflected in lower prices and bring no permanent benefit to producers. These qualities of economies of scale in producing inventions, nonappropriability of results, and major external effects give agricultural research the properties of a public good. In some countries, to be sure, producers of machinery, fertilizer, and other inputs are an important source of invention. For the most part, however, agricultural research, experimentation, and dissemination are a government responsibility. Governments in the LDCs differ widely in their recognition of this need and their willingness to allocate resources to it; and this is an important reason for differing productivity trends in their agricultural sectors.

A second difference is in the difficulties attending international and interregional transfers of technology. In assembling electronic equipment, a plant in Singapore need not look very different from a plant in Osaka, San Juan, or São Paolo. Technology flows readily from more developed to less developed countries through consulting engineers, machinery exports, turnkey plants, and branches of multinational companies. True, this technology may not be appropriate to local factor proportions; but it is at least usable with little modification. In agriculture, however, this is not true. The reason is that plants are sensitive to differences in rainfall, soil, sunlight, length of the growing season, and other local circumstances. Thus, successful innovation is locality-specific. International and interregional diffusion of technology requires investment in research and experimental facilities to adapt new seed or animal strains to local conditions. Without such adaptive research, technological borrowing is not feasible.

A case that has been studied intensively is that of hybrid corn development in the United States. This was not a once-and-for-all invention of new varieties that could be disseminated throughout the Corn Belt. Rather, it was "invention of a method of invention," which could be used to develop a large number of differing hybrids suited to different localities. Studies have found a significant relation between state expenditures on research and experimentation and increases in crop yields.

Robert Evenson and Yoav Kislev have analyzed the relation between agricultural research activity in a country and international transfer of wheat and corn technology among countries in the same climatic zone.[13] The contribution flowing from a country's research activity was divided into (1) the direct earnings stream associated with the indigenous research activity, (2) the transfer acceleration (the "borrowing from others" effect), and (3) the contribution to other countries in the region that were in a position to borrow from this country. Although all three contributions were substantial, the borrowing effect was the largest. Where no indigenous research was undertaken, the intercountry transfer was virtually zero. Costless transfer apparently does not exist.

In another study, Evenson used data from India to analyze the growth of total factor productivity in agriculture over the period 1953–1971.[14] Again, he found that a state's rate of productivity increase is associated significantly with its expenditure on both research and extension. He concluded that "the regional disparity in productivity change is quite consistent with the hypothesis that the research program in India has been the major determinant of change."

Vernon Ruttan distinguishes three stages or levels of agricultural technology transfer:

Material transfer is characterized by the simple transfer or importation of new materials such as seeds, plants, animals, machines.... Local adaptation ... is not highly institutionalized ... and tends to occur primarily as a result of trial and error by farmers.

Design transfer is characterized by the transfer of information in the form of blue prints, formulas, journals and books.... New plants and animals are subject to systematic tests, propagation, and selection.

Capacity transfer occurs primarily through the transfer of scientific and technical knowledge and capacity.... Increasingly plant and animal varieties are developed locally to adapt them to local ecological conditions.[15]

13. Yoav Kislev and Robert Evenson, "Research and Productivity in Wheat and Maize," *Journal of Political Economy* (April 1974).
14. Robert Evenson, "Technology Generation in Agriculture," in *Agriculture*, ed. Reynolds, pp. 192–223.
15. Vernon W. Ruttan, "Technology Transfer, Institutional Transfer, and Induced Technical and Institutional Change in Agricultural Development," in *Agriculture*, ed. Reynolds, pp. 165–91.

Only at this third stage is a country capable of sustained, built-in growth of agricultural productivity.

A network of research laboratories and experiment stations, though necessary, is not a sufficient condition for progress. There is need also for an extension service capable of spreading knowledge of any new technology to millions of farmers. There is by now much evidence that even small, illiterate farmers are responsive to profit opportunities. If a new technology actually works, it will be accepted rapidly. The most convincing thing to a small, insecure, hesitant farmer is the fact that his neighbor has tried new methods and has made money by so doing. On the other hand, unless the extension agent has something to sell in the form of research-based proposals with a high probability of payoff, his efforts may be counterproductive. The literature abounds in tales of extension agents' suggestions that, for lack of a research-experimental base, were not actually suited to local conditions and were wisely rejected by farmers.

Differentials in Farmer Response

A frequent observation in the LDCs is that agricultural scientists profess to know how yields can be doubled or tripled, but farmers are not achieving these higher yields. True, the "technology gap" may be smaller than it appears. The resource constraints pertinent to a scientist in an experimental station differ from those facing the farmer. High experimental yields may be attained partly by raising variable inputs per acre to a level that would be quite uneconomic for the farm operator. But even after adjusting for this difference, there is a substantial lag between new technical developments and their general incorporation in farm practice.

Looking at the matter cross-sectionally, one observes that at any given time some farmers are taking fuller advantage of new technology than others. Who innovates and who does not? What determines the speed of response to technical opportunities? Intuitively, one might expect speed of response to be influenced by:

1. Personal characteristics of the farm operator. For example, one might expect the propensity to innovate to vary directly with education and inversely with age. "Modernity" of outlook and other cultural characteristics might be important.

Research evidence is still limited and in some respects surprising— for example, education does not seem to be as important as might be expected a priori. Helleiner, after a survey of African evidence, notes that characteristics positively related to adoption of innovations include:

... farm size, wealth, tenure status, extension contact, participation in local organizations, use of communications media, degree of full-time commitment to farming, commercial experience, and 'modernity.' Among the factors tested but found to be unrelated to adoption were age, educational attainment, religion, sex, work or farming experience;[16]

2. Tenure form. One might expect owner-operators to innovate more rapidly than tenant farmers. A few studies have found this to be true, but most show little difference in response by tenure form. The reason may be that, as noted in an earlier section, tenancy systems are multidimensional and can be structured to resemble owner operation. One interesting tendency, noted by Ishikawa for the Philippines,[17] is for landowners to dispense with tenants and go over to directly managed farming, since recent technical advances have made this highly profitable;

3. Size of farm, which is large measure serves as a proxy for differences in income and wealth. Farmers with larger asset holdings and annual incomes are in a better position to bear risk and finance purchases of modern inputs. One would hypothesize, therefore, that they would take advantage of new technology faster than farmers with smaller resources. Although the results of some studies run counter to this hypothesis,[18] the general drift of the evidence favors it. Particularly in the Asian countries where improved wheat and rice strains were introduced from 1965 onward, productivity levels on large farms have tended to rise faster than those on small farms.

Do these research findings run counter to what was said earlier about the tendency of large farm units to have lower output per acre than small units and about the possible tendency of large landholders to behave as satisficers rather than as maximizers? Several comments are in order. First, the earlier observations were based on cross-section

16. Gerald K. Helleiner, "Smallholder Decision Making: Tropical African Evidence," in *Agriculture*, ed. Reynolds, p. 49.

17. Shigeru Ishikawa, *Agricultural Development Strategies in Asia* (Manila: Asian Development Bank, 1970).

18. For example, Carl C. Malone, "Some Responses of Rice Farmers to the Package Program in Tanjore District, India," *Journal of Farm Economics* (May 1965).

results, while the present hypothesis involves relative rates of improvement over time. It would be quite possible for large farmers to raise yields per acre for a particular crop faster than small farmers without closing the productivity gap. Second, the differences in productivity behavior between large and small units result partly from a different output mix. Third, the agricultural systems of the world are very diverse. Much of the writing about satisficing landlords and low productivity on large estates comes from Latin America, whereas much of the research on differential response to new technology comes from South and Southeast Asia. Cultural, legal, and other differences among countries must be borne in mind in weighing the research evidence.

Suppose further research confirms the hypothesis that, *ceteris paribus*, large farmers tend to pick up new technology faster than small farmers. What might explain this behavior? One important consideration is the small savings capacity of the small farmer and his limited access to credit, which limit his ability to buy inputs embodying the new technology. Mellor cites a study of the combined impact of high-yielding seed varieties, increased fertilizer applications, and irrigation on farm costs and revenues in Madhya Pradesh, India.[19] For a two-acre farm, the amount of cash needed to buy current inputs more than doubled, from 80 to 167 rupees. The increase in cash needs was about 14 percent of the previous level of net income. Moreover, a diesel-driven tube well to provide irrigation water cost about 9,000 rupees, or fourteen times the previous annual net income.

Large farmers have a greater capacity to invest from their own resources and better access to commercial credit. They also tend to dominate the boards of credit cooperatives, where these exist, and make loans mainly to themselves, with the small farmer coming at the end of the queue. Moreover, as Mellor notes in the case of India, there is often excess demand for fertilizer and other modern inputs at prevailing prices. Again, the large farmers tend to corner the market and block off supplies from the small man.

The other important consideration is the lower risk-bearing ability of the small farmer. Introduction of new high-yielding seed varieties, even assuming proper domestication through experiment, is *inherently* risky. It involves greater risk of failure through inadequate water supply, lodging from excessive weight of heads, and destruction by

19. John W. Mellor, *The New Economics of Growth* (Ithaca: Cornell University Press, 1976), chap. 4.

local pests and diseases—dangers against which traditional varieties have become immunized over many generations. The new varieties will in time become immunized in a similar way, so that inherent risk decreases with time, a consideration that alone would warrant a model of gradual rather than instantaneous adoption.

Not only is there genuine risk, but the risk may be perceived as larger than it actually is. Nor is it comforting to point out that the uncertain yield can be reduced to a certainty equivalent by a probability calculus. For a small farmer living near the subsistence level with low inventories of food and cash, for whom crop failure could have consequences ranging from heavy indebtedness to loss of land and even death, even a low probability of failure may be intolerable. The large landowner with ample reserves is obviously in a better position.

The importance of risk is underlined by Indian studies which "show small farmers as particularly laggard relative to large farmers where yield variability is large, as for bajra in unirrigated areas compared to rice; or rice in unirrigated areas as compared to rice in irrigated areas; or rice grown in the low sunlight more pest ridden rainy season compared with the dry season . . . or in unirrigated areas generally."[20]

Interestingly enough, other Indian studies show that small farmers who do adopt the new varieties and associated cultivation practices appear to perform better than the large farmers. They use more labor but less fertilizer per acre, achieve higher crop yields, make larger cash profits per acre (partly because they use family rather than hired labor), and devote a larger percentage of their cultivated acreage to the high-yielding varieties.[21] This suggests that, apart from the problem of financing tube wells where these are needed for water supply, there are no important indivisibilities involved in use of the new technology. It also suggests that removal of the credit and other obstacles to small-farmer innovation by appropriate government action can increase total output as well as reduce income differentials.

Impact of Improved Wheat-Rice Technology

In 1969 I sent to a senior development economist a draft manuscript expressing doubt about future food adequacy in many LDCs. He

20. Mellor, *Economics of Agricultural Development*, chap. 4. Later references to Mellor in this chapter are from the same source.
21. Government of India, Directorate of Economics and Statistics, *Report on High-Yielding Varieties Programme, Kharif, 1967–68* (New Delhi, 1969).

replied that I was living in the past. Hadn't I heard about the "revolution" in LDC agriculture? The danger for the future was food surpluses and low prices resulting from export competition. This was a common view in the late 1960s. But in development economics, fashions change rapidly. The literature is once more full of foreboding about food shortages and world hunger. So perhaps I was, after all, living in the future.

It is still only a decade since the improved wheat and rice strains began to be introduced in several Asian countries; and it is too early for a definitive assessment of the consequences. But there has already been considerable research into the initial impact on output, employment, and income distribution.

The penetration of the new technology has been quite uneven, by crop, by country, and by region. In India, wheat has been affected in the first instance much more than rice. New rice varieties have made a substantial impact in the Philippines but not in Thailand. A major reason for this uneven incidence is that the heavy fertilizer use needed to actualize the yield potential of the new seed varieties requires a controlled water supply. Thus, the new varieties have been introduced mainly in areas with river-fed irrigation systems or with the possibility of tube-well irrigation at moderate cost. On rain-fed land, yield increases are both lower and more variable.

Where water supply conditions are favorable, the potential yield increase is substantial. It is not as large as might be suggested by experimental yields free of cost restrictions; but to speak of a doubling of yields over a short period is not unrealistic. Mellor summarizes upwards of a dozen recent Indian studies that show increases in gross value of output per acre ranging from 33 percent to 208 percent, and averaging 97 percent. A report from a large experimental tract in Mexico indicates a doubling of corn yields by smallholders simply through the use of improved traditional varieties and associated improvements in cultivation practices.[22] A Philippines study reports a large increase in rice yields, particularly on irrigated land.[23]

The new technology, which shifts labor's marginal productivity

22. Leobardo Jiménez Sánchez, "Strategies for Increasing Agricultural Production on Small Holdings: The Puebla Project," mimeographed (Paper prepared for Stanford Food Research Institute Conference, 1971).

23. Randolph Barker, Mahar Mangahas, and William H. Meyers, "The Probable Impact of the Seed-Fertilizer Revolution on Grain Production and on Farm Labor Requirements," mimeographed (Paper prepared for Stanford Food Research Institute Conference, 1971).

curve upward so that more labor is demanded, typically involves a substantial increase in labor inputs per acre. More is used for soil preparation, sowing, or (in the case of rice) transplanting of seedlings. Labor is needed also for more careful weeding and for fertilizer and pesticide applications. To the extent that yields are increased, more labor is needed for harvesting, threshing, and marketing the crop.

Studies to date suggest that man-hour inputs rise considerably less than yields per acre, that is, that there is a substantial increase in man-hour productivity. The AP_L and MP_L curves are shifted upward sufficiently so that, even with larger labor inputs, one ends up at a higher point on the productivity schedules. This raises the demand schedule for hired labor and also the supply price of labor for work outside the home farm. One would thus expect an increase in the agricultural wage level. This is supported by Evenson's finding that, although rural wage levels fell in five out of seventeen districts in India over the decade 1960–1970, they rose rapidly in the states of Punjab and Haryana, where the new wheat strains had been adopted most widely. Between 1966 and 1970, the money wage rate for farm labor in these states rose by 80 percent, compared with a 13-percent rise in the consumer price index.[24] This suggests also that interstate labor mobility is not sufficient, at least in the short run, to prevent such differential wage movements.

Estimates of the elasticity of employment with respect to output vary considerably, partly because of differences among crops and regions, and partly because of estimation difficulties. The Indian studies surveyed by Mellor show elasticities falling mainly in the range of 0.2 to 0.5. The Barker-Mangahas-Meyers paper on the Philippines estimates the employment elasticity at 0.7 for the agricultural sector as a whole (compared with 0.5 in manufacturing and 1.2–1.3 in trade and services).

The increase in employment may be reduced by a rising agricultural wage level, which leads farm operators to economize on hired labor. The outcome also depends on whether adoption of the new technology is accompanied by mechanization of farm operations. This has been an important tendency in the Punjab of India and Pakistan, in the Philippines, and in many parts of Latin America. The controversy over the merit of farm mechanization will be examined below.

24. Robert Evenson, "Employment in Indian Agriculture," mimeographed (New Haven: Yale Economic Growth Center, 1972).

The direct increase in labor inputs to agriculture, of course, is only part of the total increase in employment associated with agricultural progress. Production of larger supplies of fertilizer, tube wells, and other modern inputs means increased employment in the industrial sector. Higher farm incomes provide a larger market for consumer goods and services. Increased supplies of raw materials from agriculture stimulate the growth of processing industries. These increases in industrial employment further raises final demand for goods and services. Experimental calculations[25] with input-output data suggest that these indirect effects probably exceed the direct increase in employment. To the extent that output increases in agriculture relax the "foreign exchange bottleneck," either by increasing exports or by reducing food imports, the overall impact on output and employment may be even greater.

The initial effect of the new technology may often be to increase income inequality (though this has not been true everywhere, as will become clear in part 2). This would follow if large farmers adopt the new technology faster than small farmers. A further consideration is that, where labor is very cheap, most of the value of agricultural output (and hence of increments to output) is imputed to land and capital. Thus, the unequal distribution of land and capital ownership results in a skewed distribution of the gains from technical progress.

Dixit and Singh have estimated the division of the increased income resulting from introduction of high-yielding wheat varieties in Aligarh District, Uttar Pradesh, India. Before the change, 12 percent of the value of output was attributable to labor (including family labor), 32 percent went for other input costs, and 56 percent was a return on the family's ownership of land and capital. The introduction of high-yielding varieties increased gross value of output by 71 percent, actual or imputed payments to labor by 59 percent, and net returns to land and capital by 82 percent. When one looks at the sharing of the *increase* in output, labor's share is only 10 percent because of its low initial base, while 67 percent goes to land and capital.[26]

The dozen or so surveys summarized by Mellor show a similar result. The increase in payments to labor is substantial, averaging 35

25. For example, Raj Krishna, "Measurement of the Direct and Indirect Employment Effects of Agricultural Growth with Technical Change," in *Agriculture*, ed. Reynolds, pp. 297–326.
26. R. S. Dixit and P. P. Singh, "Impact of High Yielding Varieties on Human Labor Inputs," *Agricultural Situation in India* 24 (March 1970).

percent. The proportion of the increment to output received by labor, however, averages only 9 percent.

The increase in employment that results from technical change depends partly on whether there is a concurrent increase in farm mechanization. On the larger farms in Pakistan, northwestern India, and the Philippines, there has been a substantial increase in the use of tractors for plowing, harvesting, threshing, and other farm operations.[27] In Mexico, Colombia, and other parts of Latin America, too, the larger, commercially oriented farms show a strong tendency toward mechanization. This has provoked considerable discussion of whether mechanization is or is not socially efficient under labor surplus conditions.

There are obvious reasons why mechanization may be privately profitable. Mechanization can be yield-increasing as well as cost-reducing. By enabling the critical operations of sowing and harvesting to be compressed into a shorter, optimal time period, mechanization reduces the risk of crop loss from adverse weather conditions. The time reduction also facilitates double-cropping (and in this respect, of course, it may increase labor use). On some soils, the deeper plowing made possible by tractors also increases yields. Yield effects, however, are less important than cost reductions. Where tractor power replaces bullock power, the land previously used to grow fodder for the bullocks can now be used for cash crops. Machinery saves labor throughout the year, and this becomes particularly important at the seasonal peak, when labor is often scarce, even in densely populated regions. In addition to reducing money costs, machinery reduces the burden of supervising labor. In some cases, too, mechanization enables the landowner to dispense with tenants and operate the farm himself.

The key criticism of mechanization is that its private profitability stems from price distortions. In the Pakistani case, support prices for wheat raised its price above the world level during the 1960s. At the same time, duty-free import of tractors at an overvalued exchange rate made the machines artificially cheap. In the late 1960s the tractor-wheat ratio at domestic prices was only about half that at world prices.

Loans for machinery purchase are available, mainly to the larger farmers, at rates below the shadow price of capital—sometimes even at negative real interest rates. On the other hand, the market wage

27. In India, the number of tractors rose from about 21,000 in 1955–56 to 54,000 in 1965–66 and 98,000 in 1969–70, an annual growth rate of about 15 percent.

rate, which the farmer necessarily uses in his calculations, is above the shadow price of labor. Although the individual farmer can dispense with laborers or tenants, the economy must still support them. Displacing them through mechanization intensifies the overall labor absorption problem.

A related criticism is that, since mechanization pays off only above a certain farm size, its benefits flow mainly to farmers who are already at the top of the rural income distribution. As these increasingly profitable farms expand output, the depressing effect on product prices worsens the situation of the small farmers who cannot mechanize. Landless laborers are harmed through reduced demand for their services and a continuing downward pressure on wages.[28]

Two policy recommendations typically emerge from these discussions: (1) that government should not subsidize mechanization through artificially low interest rates and machinery prices. In principle, the market-shadow wage gap should also be eliminated, but as a practical matter less can be done in this area; (2) that mechanization, to the extent that it is socially profitable, should be extended to the smaller farmers. One possibility is an emphasis on small machine units— Japanese tractors rather than American tractors—which are also easier to produce in local facilities. Another possibility is leasing arrangements, whereby machine use can be shared among a number of small-farm operators. Such arrangements tend to develop in any event as a market response to farmer demand.

28. For discussions of mechanization with particular reference to Pakistan, see B. F. Johnston and J. Cownie, "The Seed-Fertilizer Revolution and the Labor Force Absorption Problem," *American Economic Review* (September 1969); H. Kaneda, "Economic Implications of the 'Green Revolution' and the Strategy of Economic Development in West Pakistan," *Pakistan Development Review* (Summer 1969); and Swadesh R. Bose and Edwin H. Clark, II, "Some Basic Considerations on Agricultural Mechanization in West Pakistan," *Pakistan Development Review* (Autumn 1969). See also R. Albert Berry's forthcoming volume on Colombian agriculture and chapter 4 of John Mellor's study of India (*New Economics*).

5

Building a Closed-Economy Model: Economic Sectors

After the detour into agricultural behavior in chapters 3 and 4, we pick up the discussion where we left it at the end of chapter 2. The detour was necessary because of the size of the agricultural sector and the fact that its characteristics are not always understood by those who are not agricultural specialists. But I must now bring in industry, trade, services, government, and other branches of the economy. In an economy experiencing growth acceleration, all these sectors expand at varying rates. They also become more interconnected through intersectoral flows of goods, labor, and finance. To develop simplified models of this process is the central task of development theory.

I begin with a critique of the urban-industrial orientation of most closed-economy models and their tendency to treat agriculture as simply a resource reservoir; and with a consideration of the "typology problem"—the view that LDCs can be classified into distinct "types," each requiring a different analytical model. I then proceed to positive suggestions for an improved closed-economy model.

AGRICULTURE AS A RESOURCE RESERVOIR

Until quite recently, analytical and policy discussion had a strong urban-industrial bias. The dynamic role was seen as played by expansion of factory-style manufacturing and associated infrastructure industries, and the key problem was to mobilize resources for this expansion. Agriculture was treated as a sluggish sector, serving mainly as a resource reservoir, that is, a sector that could be milked for supplies of food, labor, and finance to fuel the growth of urban activities. It was argued that this was both a logical necessity and a valid generalization of historical experience, illustrated particularly by the case of Japan.

Because this outlook has been so prominent in the theoretical tradition, and because I dissent from it in important respects, a few comments are in order—partly to emphasize conceptual distinctions that are frequently ignored. For example, it is one thing to assert that, in an economy that has not yet entered the phase of growth acceleration, the agricultural sector already contains surpluses of labor time, food output, and saving capacity requiring only appropriate public policies for their release. It is quite a different thing to assert that agriculture is *potentially* capable of generating such surpluses through technical progress and other changes within the agricultural sector. The latter statement is more plausible than the former and carries different policy implications. The concept of "surplus labor" is also quite ambiguous, and some interpretations of this phenomenon are more persuasive than others.

Surplus Labor

The question of whether, or in what sense, traditional agriculture contains a labor surplus has perhaps occupied more space in the literature than it really deserves. It is a remarkably confused discussion. There is often confusion as to whether the discussion involves laborers or man-hours of labor. Yet the question of what happens when more man-hours are applied to a given land area is quite different from the question of what happens when people are added to or withdrawn from the agricultural labor force.

Further, the supposed surplus has been defined in a variety of ways, some of which are not readily testable, and which in any case would require different kinds of tests. At least six variants of the concept can be distinguished.

1. Ishikawa surplus. Members of farm families are working fewer hours than they would be willing to work, at the existing rate of hourly earnings, if the demand for labor were higher. This concept, developed by both Shigeru Ishikawa and Amartya Sen, assumes that, when hours are short, the schedule of the disutility of labor may be flat over a considerable range. How far people work out into this range depends on the level of demand. The implication is that, if some people are withdrawn from agriculture, those remaining can be persuaded to work more (for the same hourly return, which means an increased return *per worker*), so that total man-hour input need not fall.

This contention is difficult to test empirically. Efforts to compare available man-hours with man-hours actually worked raise difficult problems. Time worked should include time spent by family members on all productive activities, including Z-goods production, trade, transport, off-farm employment, and land improvement. Time not spent in field work is not necessarily leisure time. The definition of "availability," that is, of a normal work day and week, is necessarily arbitrary. Hours that appear short to the observer may partly reflect deficiencies of nutrition, health care, and physical strength, plus the fact that heavy physical labor does have disutility. Much depends on the point in the seasonal cycle at which the measurements are taken. Even in such densely populated countries as Egypt, the rural labor force seems to be fully employed at the seasonal peak.

2. Lewis surplus. Labor supply to the industrial sector is perfectly elastic at a constant real wage. This is what Arthur Lewis calls "unlimited supplies of labor." This view seems to be supported by the fact that manufacturers and other "modern" employers in the LDCs rarely have any difficulty recruiting a labor force. But this does not demonstrate that the labor supply curve is horizontal. It is quite possible that employers, for one reason or another, are paying more than the supply price of labor. If industrial wages are being forced upward by minimum wage legislation, trade union pressure, and other institutional forces, then their movement over time does not necessarily say anything about labor supply conditions, or about labor's productivity in agriculture.

3. Fei-Ranis redundant labor. The private marginal productivity of labor in agriculture is zero. This concept can scarcely apply to people, if there is efficient work sharing within the family, but must apply rather to the last man-hour of labor input. Marginal productivity in this sense could be zero only if, over a certain range, increased hours of work had zero disutility that is, if leisure had zero value. This is conceivable; but research studies in which production functions are fitted to cross-section farm data typically show a significantly positive marginal productivity of labor.

4. Fei-Ranis disguised unemployment. The private marginal productivity of a man-hour of labor, though positive, is below the hourly return to labor. This could readily happen in family farming, where each family member's share of output reflects the average rather than the marginal product of labor. A corollary is that the supply price of labor for work away from the home farm, and hence the rural wage level, will reflect average productivity on the farm.

For employers of hired labor, however, marginal productivity cannot fall below the wage rate unless the employer ignores profitability or unless he is obliged to hire a fixed number of workers at a fixed daily wage. In the latter case, the worker's daily earnings become an overhead cost and, if the employer can set the hours of work, it will pay to lengthen those hours until marginal productivity approaches zero. This is also essentially the situation on a Chinese commune, where subsistence for members of the commune is overhead, and it consequently pays to use additional man-hours even on work of very low productivity.

This use of the term *disguised unemployment* differs somewhat from the way in which it was originally used. The concept was developed in the 1930s with respect to depression conditions in developed countries. In such periods, many workers are forced downward on the skill ladder. Although they are still employed, their productivity in their current employment is below their *potential* productivity on their regular job. There is thus a hidden labor potential that can be activated as demand rises during recovery.

One could argue that the LDCs exhibit disguished unemployment in this original sense because of the productivity gap between agricultural and nonagricultural workers. When a worker is transferred from agriculture to "modern" employment, his marginal and average productivity rise substantially. He must, therefore, have been disguisedly unemployed in his previous activity. A difficulty with this argument is that virtually all economies, mature as well as developing, show a gap between the marginal productivity and earnings of labor in agriculture and in other economic sectors. To conclude, therefore, that agricultural workers are always and everywhere disguisedly unemployed may not be very meaningful.

The productivity gap is unusually wide in the LDCs, however, and it does tend to narrow in the course of economic growth, particularly after the Lewis turning point is reached. The reason is not that farm workers mysteriously become more efficient but rather that they become fewer in number. Continued suction of labor out of agriculture shrinks the denominator in the agricultural output-agricultural labor force ratio; at the same time, labor scarcity induces labor-saving innovations that may also be yield-increasing.

5. Zero social productivity. Another conceivable situation is one in which, given the social objective of maximizing the value of current income, the combination of techniques and resources is such that the

shadow wage and hence the *marginal social productivity* of labor is zero. The existence of surplus labor in this sense does not necessarily imply its existence in the other senses listed. To test the existence of this situation would require use of programming techniques, and the assumptions used in constructing a programming model are so restrictive that little practical importance can be attached to the results.

6. Costless labor transfer. Finally, it is said that surplus labor exists if workers can be withdrawn from the agricultural sector without reducing agricultural output. This must mean that, as workers are withdrawn, the remaining workers put in enough additional hours to keep total man-hour input as high as before. This would imply the kinds of assumptions about disutility of labor that were made in cases 1 and 3 above, and so it is not really a distinct definition.

The realism of such labor transfers has been strongly denied by T. W. Schultz. It is difficult to put the argument to an empirical test because one observes an absolute decline of the farm labor force only at an advanced stage of economic development or under atypical conditions of plague or famine. However, it is intuitively plausible to think that, *if* the rural labor force shrank absolutely, and *if* there were no other change in the situation, agricultural output would also decline.

In sum, there has been a tendency to confuse several different concepts of labor surplus. One of these does not necessarily imply the others. One or more of them can be true without all being true. For example, it is not inconsistent to maintain that labor surplus does not exist in sense 3—the marginal productivity of man-hours worked in agriculture is significantly positive—while at the same time insisting that labor surplus does exist in sense 2—elastic supply of labor to the industrial sector.

However one rationalizes it, there seems to be substantial labor force *slack* in most LDCs—low labor force participation rates of female and even prime-age male workers, short hours per week and per year, low intensity of work, low output per man-hour, plus a good deal of open unemployment. This slack is not confined to agriculture. It pervades all traditional, self-employed activities and even penetrates the modern sector through such devices as compulsory overstaffing.

Mobilization of this unused labor potential requires mainly an intensification of demand. But two caveats are in order. First, within the agricultural sector, intensification of demand *means* mainly technical changes that shift labor productivity curves upward. Second, technical change would be needed in any event to compensate workers who are being asked to work harder and who will demand a reward in terms of higher consumption, including higher food consumption. The notion of a costless labor transfer from agriculture and the accompanying notion that technical progress in agriculture is required only at some later stage of development seem misguided. A development process that does not incorporate technical change in agriculture from the beginning must, under closed-economy assumptions, quickly grind to a halt. Even when the possibility of trade is admitted, few countries have sufficiently dependable nonfood exports to sustain a growing food deficit.

Surplus Food

Most of what might be said under this heading has already been implied. If the static argument for a costless labor transfer is implausible, the notion of a costless food transfer is equally suspect. There is normally a potential food surplus in the sense that, with improved modern inputs, improved rural infrastructure, and perhaps reform of landholding, agricultural output could be substantially increased. Progress in some countries since the mid-1960s suggests that a doubling of agricultural output within twenty years is not unrealistic.

But this is quite different from saying that a growing urban population can be fed simply by diverting food output from the countryside, in a context of static technology and slow output growth. Even in socialist countries with their powerful institutional controls, the frequent policy of treating agriculture as a low-priority, exploitable sector has not been very successful. In the nonsocialist world, the success stories of post-1945 development have usually involved substantial modernization of and investment in agriculture.

Surplus Saving

Development models usually incorporate an increase in industrial and infrastructure investment, financed partly by an increase in the amount of agricultural savings transferred for urban use. Institutionally, the transfer is viewed as occurring through some combination of private capital markets and the fiscal system. The implication is that agricultural investment is not required—or that investment possibilities within agriculture have already been pushed to the margin of profitability.

From a dynamic view, however, there is a need for rising agricultural productivity requiring changes in techniques. These changes require substantial investment: public investment in transportation, irrigation facilities, fertilizer factories, and agricultural research and development; and private investment by farmers in land improvement, tools, and improved inputs. Thus, private saving, tax levies, private investment, and public investment should be viewed as going on simultaneously in both agriculture and nonagriculture. Financial flows are going in both directions, with the gross flows substantially larger than the net flow.

One should not assume a priori that the net flow will be from agriculture to industry. Clearly, one could construct assumptions that would produce the opposite result. Historically, this is a matter for empirical investigation. As for policy, allocation of investment funds should presumably be guided by relative returns rather than by doctrinaire notions of the absolute superiority of industry (or agriculture). R. A. Berry's analysis of Colombian agriculture concludes that, as of 1970, prospective returns to agricultural investment considerably exceeded returns to manufacturing. But this is something to be investigated on a country-by-country basis.

To the extent that net transfers are expected from agriculture, these will clearly be facilitated by rising agricultural incomes. Marginal savings rates are typically higher than average rates. With regard to fiscal transfers, it is obviously easier to tax away part of the increment to a rising income than it is to cut into a stationary income without adverse incentive effects.

In sum, the conception of agriculture as a reservoir for development is correct in one sense but incorrect in another. It is correct to regard the agricultural sector as one containing a large economic potential—underutilized labor, unused saving capacity, land that is considerably less productive than it could be. It is also correct to say that, in an economy that is experiencing growth acceleration, the agricultural sector will show an increased outflow of marketed produce, labor (probably), and finance (possibly).

It is incorrect, however, to suppose that an expanding industrial sector can be fueled for more than a short time by resource transfers from a static agricultural sector. The economic potential of agriculture must be mobilized before it can be used. The requirements for such mobilization lie at the core of development theory and policy.

The moral for model builders is that the internal structure of the agricultural sector needs to be specified and that technical change should be built into the model from the outset. Under closed-economy assumptions, the growth of other sectors must, at a minimum, be sustained by an appropriate rate of increase in agricultural output and productivity. Nor should the possibility of an *agriculture-led* growth process be ruled out of consideration.

THE TYPOLOGY PROBLEM: ONE MODEL OR SEVERAL?

A second basic question involves the scope of development models. Given the obvious heterogeneity of the LDCs, can any one model have a wide range of application?

The feasibility of a single model is sometimes asserted by implication. Thus, when one runs cross-section regressions covering scores of economies, one implies that different countries are at different points along a standard growth path. What one observes in higher-income countries today will occur eventually in (presently) low-income countries as they move up the income ladder. A similar universalism was implicit in Rostow's "stages of growth" schema—that is, that all countries pass through definable stages in a unique sequence.

An alternative view is that LDCs can be classified into types, each of which needs to be modeled separately. But although the idea of such a typology is widely accepted and various bases of classification have been suggested, no classification scheme commands general agreement. The bases most frequently urged in the literature are *economic size, factor endowments*, and *development strategy*. These are offered either singly or in what are regarded as typical combinations (such as small economic size, ample labor supply, poor natural resource base, leading to a strategy of growth through industrial exports à la Taiwan). Let us explore briefly each of these criteria.

Economic Size

Chenery and others have demonstrated that a country's population and GNP have a major influence on its production structure and its participation in foreign trade. The growth of a city-state such as Hong Kong or Singapore is necessarily dependent on trade. In a large country such as India or Brazil, on the other hand, output and consumption patterns are more closely linked, and the domestic market is of primary importance.

The difficulty is that size is a continuous variable, with no obvious breaking points. Once we have set aside the city-states as special cases, there is no clear basis for dividing the remaining LDCs into two, four, or any other number of categories. Trade ratio is inversely related to size, but this is a continuous function. At no single point does a "small economy" suddenly become a "large economy." Even the nations largest in area and population—India, Indonesia, Pakistan, Brazil— are not very large in total market (GNP) terms; and even these countries have a substantial trade ratio.

One implication is that only an open-economy model is relevant to actual developing economies. What, then, is the point of the closed-economy models on which so much effort has been expended? One possible answer is that, for a few large countries where exports are 10 percent or less of GNP, the closed-economy model is a reasonable simplification of reality. Indeed, it has sometimes been termed *the Indian model.*

A more persuasive answer is that, for any economy, an applicable model can best be developed by stages. All economies have an internal structure, a response mechanism, and a large volume of internal transactions. As a first step, these can be modeled as they might exist in isolation from outside contacts. The foreign sector can then be built into the model at a later stage. This is the traditional procedure in international trade theory. We set up two economies in isolation, define their characteristics, then "open" them to trade and explore the effects on resource allocation and productivity.

The pattern of participation in international commodity and capital flows cannot, however, be used as a basis for classifying closed-economy models, where such flows are excluded by definition. Whether open-economy behavior can be fitted into a meaningful typology is a different question.

Relative Factor Endowments

This seems a plausible basis for classification, since factor endowments will strongly influence a country's growth possibilities. Capital is normally scarce relative to other factors and has a high marginal productivity and shadow price. As is well known, capital becomes relatively more abundant as development proceeds (which does not imply that increased capital availability *causes* output growth in a mechanical sense), and its yield tends to fall. To classify economies by capital availability, then, would not be very profitable, since this would correspond closely with a classification by per capita income—in which Brazil and Mexico would rank high, Uganda and Ghana low.

Unskilled labor, on the other hand, is normally in surplus, in both the Lewis and Ishikawa senses. Even in lightly populated countries, there are typically unutilized man-hours that can be activated by an increase in demand. Labor scarcity sets in only at an advanced stage of development. This means that models incorporating an initial labor surplus have a wide range of applicability. Indeed, it can be said that any useful model should be a labor surplus model. On this score, then, there seems no basis for a type classification.

We come down, then, to land and other natural resources as possible differentiating characteristics. A country well endowed with oil or mineral resources has an initial advantage, which will show up in a relatively high export-GNP ratio, an easy balance of payments position, price and exchange-rate stability, and the possibility of simultaneous increases in domestic investment and consumption. For the time being, at least, the oil-exporting countries have unlimited supplies of capital. Among other things, this relieves them of any immediate need to raise agricultural productivity, since food can readily be imported.

A more important resource for most countries is *cultivable land*; and Helleiner has used land availability as the basis for a type classification.[1] In his schema, countries with differing land-labor ratios are represented as different points on a common metaproduction surface. If we draw an isoquant for agricultural production, with land no the vertical axis and labor on the horizontal axis, this must logically have a vertical section on which land is redundant, a curvilinear section on which both factors are scarce, and a horizontal section on which labor is redundant. Different countries are located at different points on such an isoquant. Given a positive rate of population growth, a particular economy moves to the right along the isoquant over time. What was once a land surplus economy may, a century later, have become a labor surplus economy.

In this view, economies would be classified into those in which: (1) labor is scarce and land redundant; (2) both factors are scarce; and (3) land is scarce and labor redundant. But, as we have already noted, surplus labor time seems to exist in virtually all less-developed eco-

1. Gerald K. Helleiner, "Typology in Development Theory: The Land Surplus Economy (Nigeria)," *Food Research Institute Studies* 6 (1966), reprinted as Yale Economic Growth Center Paper No. 102.

nomies, including those with ample land reserves. In the case of Nigeria, from which the Helleiner model derives, there seems to have been a surplus of both land and labor time in 1900, which enabled cocoa and other export-crop production to expand with no reduction in food-crop production.

With regard to land, it seems at first glance that one could distinguish between frontier economies and fully settled economies. In frontier economies, additional land is still available for settlement, making possible a pattern of extensive growth that relieves pressure to raise land productivity on the intensive margin of cultivation. Note, however, that the new land is not costless, since its settlement requires land clearing and improvement as well as road building and other infrastructure investments. Thus, land is scarce in the sense of having a positive supply price. In fully settled economies, all cultivable land is already in use. Even here, additional land can usually be created by reclamation, but at a cost. Multiple cropping can be extended. Yields can be raised by land-saving innovations—improved irrigation and water-control systems, better cultivation practices, improved seed varieties, heavier fertilizer applications, and so on. Output increases obtained in these ways are logically on the same footing as those obtained through land settlement Each involves a balancing of costs and returns. Even in a country with unsettled land, such as Colombia or Venezuela, an efficient output-increasing program requires weighing costs and returns on both the intensive and extensive margins.

Instead of a dichotomy between land surplus economies and land scarce economies, then, one could think in terms of a single model in which the land in use at any moment is fixed—but in which additional land can be created, at a cost, through either land settlement or land saving. The model to be suggested later incorporates this characteristic, along with the labor surplus characteristic, which we regard as universal.

Development Strategy

A different basis for classifying LDCs is in terms of the development strategy that their governments appear to be following, and particularly their strategy in the foreign sector. Thus, Hla Myint speaks of the "inward-looking" and "outward-looking" countries of southeast Asia, concluding that the outward-looking countries have been considerably more successful.[2] John Fei and Douglas Paauw distinguish among strategies of *import substitution* (Philippines, Taiwan up to 1960), *export substitution* (Taiwan since 1960), and primary export promotion or *neocolonialism* (Thailand and Malaysia).[3] Hollis Chenery and colleagues at the IBRD have developed a rather similar classification based on deviations from the trade ratios and production proportions that cross-section analysis reveals as normal for a country of given size and per capita income.[4] Their categories are: *primary specialization*, *balanced production and trade*, *import substitution*, and *industry specialization*.

These schema will be discussed at some length in chapter 14, after a review of recent development experience. But even at this stage, it may be noted that they involve several difficulties. First, they emphasize performance in the foreign sector and thus say little about a useful typology of closed economies. Second, the concept of strategy implies purposeful direction over an extended period. But actual economic policies are short-run and changeable, as are the governments that devise them; and a country may change course frequently over time. Thus, Taiwan appears in one of the Fei-Paauw boxes from 1950 to 1960, but in another from 1960 onward.

Even in the short run, one cannot assume that government is pursuing a coherent development strategy. What one observes more frequently is a mixture of partly contradictory measures, often accompanied by weak administration. To determine how far government action has actually altered economic events is a difficult task.

Third, differing strategies can be viewed, not as alternatives confronting a country at a given moment in time, but rather as stages in a temporal sequence. Any LDC must rely on primary exports in the first instance, since these are the only exports available. As the economy grows in size, import substitution in manufactures sets in naturally, following a well-documented sequence. Government can accelerate this process by protectionist measures, but differing degrees of pro-

2. Hla Myint, "The Inward and Outward-Looking Countries of Southeast Asia," *The Malayan Economic Review* 12 (April 1967): pp. 1–13, reprinted in Hla Myint, *Economic Theory and the Underdeveloped Countries* (Oxford: Oxford University Press, 1971).

3. Douglas Paauw and John C. H. Fei, *The Transition in Open Dualistic Economies* (New Haven: Yale University Press, 1973).

4. Hollis Chenery and Moises Syrquin, *Patterns of Development, 1950–1970* (New York: Oxford University Press, 1975). This interesting study, which bears mainly on development experience, will be discussed at greater length in part two.

tection do not seem to warrant a "type" classification. In any event, accelerated import substitution has only a short-run effect on the growth rate of industrial output. Export substitution, in the sense of a rising percentage of manufactured goods in the export total, occurs at a still later stage of the game, attainable only when some of a country's industries are mature and efficient enough to meet world price levels.

A Suggested View

If we set aside the city-states and the oil sheikdoms as special cases, the remaining LDCs resemble each other closely enough to warrant our treating them as a single category and trying to develop a growth model adapted to their structure. What are some of these common features?

1. They all contain labor surplus—in the sense of some combination of open unemployment, low labor-force participation rates, low annual hours of work, and low productivity of the hours that are worked.

2. Population is increasing at 2 to 3 percent per year.

3. Land is scarce, in the sense that either yield improvement or the extension of the frontier of settlement involves costs, through the severity of this scarcity no doubt differs substantially among countries.

4. The per capita capital stock, consisting of both material and human capital, is much lower than in the developed countries.

5. A large proportion of the labor force is locked up in agriculture, but, even so, there is usually a precarious balance between food supplies and food requirements.

6. The public sector is relatively small and so is the modern manufacturing-public utilities sector.

7. Output per worker in traditional activities, nonagricultural as well as agricultural, is low relative to that in the modern sector, the gap being substantially wider than in mature economies.

The major Latin American economies have a relatively large modern sector and a moderately high per capita income. But this reflects mainly a longer history of postcolonial development, a rich resource base, relatively large economic size, and (especially in the case of Mexico) strong interaction with the American economy. These economies are best regarded, not as different in kind from other LDCs, but as farther along a broadly similar road.

In addition to this argument based on empirical resemblances, one can argue also that "economics is just economics." What we are trying to do in development economics is to apply the tools of our trade in order to understand a developing economy. The fact that the economy may be more or less well endowed with a particular factor does not call for a different theory. A development model incorporates behavioral and technological assumptions, which can be varied from case to case; but this does not mean that the model structure depends on which input is plentiful, what development policies are being followed, and so on.

Although I thus argue for a unified approach, this does not preclude country-specific models tailored to the circumstances of a particular economy.[5] These are useful, perhaps even necessary, if study of a country's growth over time is to go beyond mere description. Further, my advocacy of a single, closed-economy model does not exclude the possibility of a useful typology when we move to the open-economy level of discussion. To the extent that a type classification makes sense, the classification scheme should probably run in terms of foreign sector performance. I return to this point in chapter 14.

STRATEGIC ISSUES IN MODEL CONSTRUCTION

In the remainder of this chapter I begin, and in chapter 6 I complete, the exercise of constructing a closed-economy model that takes account of the stylized facts that are characteristic of the great majority of

---

5. For example, Taiwan is said to have been characterized as of the early 1950s by "(1) open dualism characterized by the existence of a large food producing agricultural sector, a small externally oriented agricultural sector (mainly sugar), and a small non-agricultural sector; (2) a situation of labor surplus, *i.e.*, excess supply of labor at given institutionally determined wages, especially in traditional agriculture; (3) a shortage of natural resources, *i.e.*, land and exportable raw materials for the long run; (4) a relatively favorable rural infrastructure as a consequence of the rural emphasis of Japanese colonial rule; and (5) a relatively favorable human resources endowment traceable once again partly to Japanese colonial education policy and partly to the post-war influx of entrepreneurial talent from the Mainland. These background conditions gave Taiwan a peculiar set of initial conditions . . . admittedly shared by relatively few contemporary LDC's." John C. H. Fei and Gustav Ranis, "The Role of Agriculture in Development," in *Agriculture in Development Theory*, ed. L. G. Reynolds (New Haven: Yale University Press, 1975), pp. 355–72.

One might perhaps add to this list extensive contact with U.S. economic advisers and a large capital inflow from the United States after 1949. The only other country sharing a number of these characteristics, including Japanese colonial rule before World War II and strong U.S. influence since World War II, is South Korea.

LDCs. The model is reasonably complex and is intended for simulation use rather than for deterministic solutions. I have not actually run any simulations, however, and this may leave the reader feeling a bit let down. Indeed, some of those who commented on early drafts of this book raised the question, "Why bother to construct a model that you aren't going to use?"

There are several possible answers to this question. First, the exercise has a certain pedagogic usefulness. Anyone else setting out to build a development model would have to face and answer essentially the same questions that I have confronted. It is useful to set forth these questions clearly and systematically. A reader who finds any of my answers implausible may thereby be stimulated to seek better ones.

Further, anyone who does find my model plausible can run his own simulations. And even without numerical results, the model permits qualitative conclusions of considerable importance for economic policy. I shall use it for this purpose toward the end of chapter 6.

Any would-be model builder has to face a variety of strategic issues. Should population growth be taken as exogenous or endogenous? Along what lines is it useful to sector the economy? What should one assume about production functions in each sector? What intersectoral flows of resources and products should be distinguished? I proceed to explore these questions and to suggest ways of handling them.[6]

The Demographic Base

Most theorists have considered the rate of population growth to be exogenous and equal to the rate of growth of the labor force. I shall do the same, but the rationale for doing so requires brief comment.

Some theorists (Nelson, Leibenstein, Jorgenson) have treated population growth as endogenous by making it a positive function of per capita income or per capita food consumption. Thus, a temporary increase in per capita income may readily be swamped by a propor-tionate increase in the population growth rate, leaving the economy caught in a "low level equilibrium trap."

This approach is not in accord with the stylized facts. The population spurt in the LDCs over the past several decades has little to do with the course of per capita income. Population growth has been as rapid

6. The model presented here is in part an elaboration of suggestions that I advanced in "Development with Surplus Labor: Some Complications," *Oxford Economic Papers* (March 1969): 89–103.

in stationary as in developing economies. Fertility in most LDCs remains high. But mortality rates have been reduced rapidly, partly through technical assistance programs mounted by the World Health Organization and other bodies. Thus, the earlier situation in which birth rates of, say, 45 per thousand were largely offset by a mortality rate of 40 has shifted to a 45–15 relation, permitting population to grow at 3 percent per year. To take population growth as exogenous, then, seems realistic, and it simplifies the model.

Population growth is not identical with labor force growth. There is a lag between an increase in the number of surviving children and the entrance of these children into the labor force. Although this initial rise in the dependency ratio has short-run effects, it seems legitimate to ignore these in a model oriented toward long-term growth. So I postulate a population in which the exogenously given growth rate has lasted long enough for the system to attain a "steady state."

Labor force growth may be affected also by changes in labor force participation rates. In the United States and other developed countries, age- and sex-specific participation rates are influenced by such things as: legal school attendance requirements, legal and informal retirement provisions, educational levels, economic and social status of women, and level of demand for labor. The determinants of labor force participation in the LDCs have been little investigated. A recent study of Pakistan presents results that resemble those of U.S. studies on many points.[7] The aggregate labor force participation rate in any LDC will doubtless change over the course of time; but the rate of change is likely to be slow. It seems reasonable, then, to assume a constant participation rate as a first approximation.

Sectoring the Economy

Previous models have usually specified two sectors: capitalist employers versus the self-employed in Lewis, agriculture versus non-agriculture in Fei and Ranis, rural-agricultural versus urban-industrial in Kelley, Williamson, and Cheatham (K-W-C).

Considerations of realism suggest that a finer subdivision of the economy would be useful. But adding sectors complicates the algebra and the computation. At what point does growing complexity of the model outweigh any gains in predictive power?

An important consideration is that I am interested in employment

7. Ghazi M. Farooq, "An Aggregative Model of Labor Force Participation in Pakistan," *The Developing Economics* (September 1972): 267–89.

and income distribution as well as in output. Thus, I regard a branch
of economic activity as a separate sector if it (1) employs a substantial
proportion of the labor force and (2) is distinctive with regard to the
other factors that are combined with labor, or with regard to the
criterion for employment decisions, or both. These considerations
suggest a minimum of four sectors, which I define as follows:

1. Agriculture. This comprises all activity within farm production
units, including investment of time in land improvement and production of consumption goods for home use (Z-goods). Land is fixed
in amount at any time, and all farms are owner-operated.

Some writers distinguish subsectors within agriculture, such as
subsistence agriculture producing for home use, commercial agriculture
producing for the domestic market, and, in open-economy models,
export agriculture. But a classification of farm output by destination
does not correspond to a classification of production units. The same
farm is usually engaged, in varying degrees, in both subsistence and
commercial production. If the commercial product is a food crop,
part of which is exported, then the farm may be engaged in export
production as well.

One occasionally finds a clear dichotomy between large, export-
oriented plantations and small farms producing mainly for family
use; but this is scarcely the standard case. As a first approximation,
therefore, it is reasonable to assume a homogeneous sector of owner-
operated farms.

2. Traditional Nonagriculture. This includes a wide range of small-
scale manufacturing activities—baking, spinning and weaving, mat
making, tailoring, shoemaking and shoe repair, woodcarving, carpen-
try, and fabrication of metal products. In most African and many
Asian countries, the number of persons employed in these activities is
much larger than the number employed in modern factories. The
sector also includes traders, porters, and service workers of every sort.

This is not solely, or even primarily, an urban sector. Most LDC
residents live in the countryside and depend on nearby artisans and
traders. The number of such people in small towns and villages may
exceed the number in larger urban centers.[8] The sector is characterized

8. An enumeration of small-scale industry (less than 20 workers) in Sierra Leone
revealed that 89 percent of the establishments and 78 percent of the employment were
in "rural enumeration areas," with no town larger than 2,000 people. See Enyinna
Chuta and Carl Liedholm, "The Role of Small Scale Industry in Employment Generation
and Rural Development: Initial Research Results from Sierra Leone" (Michigan State
University, Department of Agricultural Economics, African Rural Employment Paper
no. 11, 1975).

by self-employment and minimal use of capital. Like agriculture, it is a "spongy" sector, capable of absorbing an indefinite amount of labor at a declining level of average output per worker. In most LDCs, employment in this sector is considerably larger than in the so-called modern activities.

3. Industry. This includes factory-style manufacturing; air, road, and rail transport; electric power production; modern communications systems; organized large-scale construction; banking and finance; and other "modern" activities in the urban centers. It does not matter for present purposes whether the production facilities are privately or publicly owned. Public corporations are included in this sector along with private businesses. The sector's distinctive production characteristics are use of hired labor, a relatively high capital-labor ratio, relatively high output per worker, and employment decisions based on an economic calculus.

There is often a distinct dualism within the industrial sector. Large, capital-intensive, high-wage and high-productivity firms coexist with smaller, less capital-intensive firms with lower output per worker and a lower wage level. Sometimes, these are directly competitive forms of organizations. But they can also be symbiotic, as in the Japanese subcontracting system; or they may produce different types or qualities of product. Small units are usually dominant in the early decades of accelerated growth, with large firms growing in relative importance over time.

One could thus argue for distinguishing two industrial subsectors, the small-scale one and the large-scale one. But much of what might be accomplished by a sectoral subdivision can also be accomplished by recognizing that the value of a particular variable is an average of the values for different firm sizes. For example, a shift toward larger-scale production units means, among other things, a secular increase in the capital-labor ratio and in output per worker. It is legitimate to build such features into the model independently of what is happening within each production unit.

4. Government. Many models omit government. In others, it is lumped with industry into a single modern sector. This glosses over the different production functions, demand characteristics, and employment behavior in the public sector. It also ignores the role of government in mobilizing and allocating financial resources through the fiscal system.

By government, I mean general government, as distinct from

publicly owned utilities or industrial enterprises. It includes general administration, defense and policing, health and education, roads and other public works, and a variety of services to agriculture and industry. In production terms, it can be regarded as employing labor only, capital inputs being of minor importance. The level of employment, however, is not decided on the maximizing basis used in the industrial sector. Rather, it depends on government revenue and on the wage level of public employees. If the latter rises more rapidly than the former, one can have (and some countries have had) the curious phenomenon of public employment shrinking in a growing economy.

THE FOUR SECTORS: PRODUCTION CHARACTERISTICS

Having defined our four sectors, the next step is to specify their production characteristics.

Sector 1: Industry

I need not say much about this sector, because its treatment by model builders is standard and noncontroversial. Neoclassical rules of the game prevail. Production is organized in business enterprises (private and public), employing wage labor and aiming at maximum profit.[9] The production function includes labor and capital, and each factor is paid its marginal product. All after-tax profit is saved; no wage income is saved. There is no unemployment or underemployment. Surplus labor is confined to the two traditional sector, to be drawn on as needed.

The production function is Cobb-Douglas, with unit elasticity of factor substitution. We recognize that planning models typically work with fixed coefficients. But there seems no reason why factor proportions should be more rigid in the LDCs than in mature economies. Studies of manufacturing industries in the United States and elsewhere typically estimate the elasticity of capital-labor substitution to be in the range of 0.8 to 1.2. The Cobb-Douglas form thus appears satisfactory as a first approximation.

---

9. This involves some degree of unrealism about public enterprises, which typically give less weight to profit objectives than private corporations do, and which often fail even to cover operating costs. It can still be argued, however, that they are more nearly analogous to private industries than to general government.

Technical progress is factor-augmenting, reducing capital and labor requirements per unit of output at a constant annual rate (though not necessarily at the *same* rate for the two factors.) The diffusion mechanism for technical change remains obscure, in industry as well as in agriculture. It can be interpreted in vintage terms as a steady increase in factor quality over time. It can also be visualized as a steady increase in managerial capacity, which does seem to rise markedly during the early stages of industrialization. Or it can be interpreted as resulting partly from the shift from smaller-scale to larger-scale production units within the industrial sector.

The industrial wage rate, defined as the real wage in terms of agricultural goods, I take to be institutionally determined rather than determined by supply. It is farther above the agricultural wage level than would be necessary to recruit the desired number of workers. In other words, employers are operating "off the supply curve." As this wage, the supply of labor to sector 1 is infinitely elastic. I also take the rate of wage increase over time to be exogenous. The industrial wage does not necessarily rise faster than the agricultural wage, but it may do so. It does not necessarily rise faster than output per worker, but again it may do so. Since employers equate labor's marginal productivity with the wage rate, the rate of employment increase is inversely related to the rate of wage increase.

I do not subdivide the industrial sector into capital-goods and consumer-goods subsectors, as is often done in planning models. Mine is a market model, in which the behavior of investment demand and consumption demand, reflected in price movements, brings about an appropriate division of productive capacity.

An important input to industry is raw materials produced in the agricultural sector: cotton, wool, jute, flax, and other nonfoods—as well as foodstuffs for primary processing. In a closed-economy model, there is no other source of these materials; and the growth rate of light manufacturing is heavily dependent upon them. (The importance of this constraint is illustrated by Chinese experience, where the marked decline in agricultural output after the "Great Leap Forward" campaign of 1958 was followed, with a lag of about one year, by a parallel downturn in industrial production.) I assume a fixed-coefficient relation between industrial output and required agricultural inputs, though material-saving innovations are doubtless of some importance in practice.

Sector 2: Agriculture

I have already suggested some of the difficulties in modeling agricultural production. The variable treatment of agriculture by development theorists, contrasting sharply with the standard treatment of industry, stems partly from these difficulties and also from the variability of actual agricultural systems. My assumptions for this sector, which draw heavily on the work of Ishikawa, are most directly relevant to agriculture in South and East Asia, though I believe them to have considerable applicability elsewhere. I assume that:

1. The area under cultivation at any time is fixed and is divided into family farms. (Tenancy is ignored.) All labor input comes from family members. Since families differ in size, there is room for corresponding differences in farm acreage. Here one could resort to the useful Marshallian expedient of the "representative farm."

If one wanted to complicate the model, one could permit wider variation of farm sizes and introduce an agricultural labor market, in which large farmers hire labor time from smaller farmers or landless laborers. This would introduce the wage for hired agricultural labor as an additional variable. But one would expect this wage to move closely with per capita income of family members on their own land; and it does not seem that this addition would yield sufficient results to warrant the work involved.

2. The production function includes land and labor. It can be shifted through land reclamation or improvements, as explained in point 5 below.

3. The marginal productivity of man-hour inputs to agriculture is positive. But there is also, at the outset, a labor surplus in the Ishikawa sense. More man-hours would be forthcoming if productivity schedules were shifted so that these man-hours could be worked without reducing marginal productivity below the initial level. In other words, there is a horizontal supply curve of man-hours over a considerable range.

I ignore the seasonal variation in farm employment, and consequently in the degree of labor surplus, which is an important feature of reality. There seems no ready way of incorporating this into the model. One should bear in mind, however, that, in practice, this is an important constraint on transfer of labor to nonfarm uses.

4. Population is increasing at a contant exogenous rate, which I take to be the same in the country as in the city. (One could assume a

lower urban rate, but the effect would be minor). Under any plausible set of parameters, the agricultural labor force will also be rising; but, if labor demand in other sectors is high enough, it may rise less rapidly than the population.

5. Government invests in agricultural improvement. This can take either or both of two forms. The first is extension of the acreage under cultivation, through land reclamation or through extending the frontier of settlement. This involves government investment in such things as drainage, land clearance, road building, and construction of public buildings in new communities. Such government investment call forth complementary private investment by farmers in land improvement, fencing, terracing, ditching, construction of farm buildings, and so on. As farmers are withdrawn from older areas for settlement on the new land, the labor surplus in those older areas will decline. I assume that the productivity schedules on new land are the same as on old land and that there is continuous adjustment that equates the marginal productivity of labor in old and new areas. This feature of the model, I believe, makes it applicable to so-called land surplus economies with unoccupied land as well as to fully settled economies.

6. The second possibility involves government investment designed to raise productivity schedules on land already under cultivation. Where the settlement frontier is being extended at the same time, I assume that government investment funds are allocated so as to equate their marginal yield in the two uses.

Concretely, this kind of investment could include providing for major irrigation works, pumping stations, and other water-control facilities. It could also include the construction of feeder roads and the building of warehouses and other marketing facilities. Very importantly, it includes the establishment of agricultural research centers, experiment stations, and staffs of extension workers. In accord with my general treatment of the government sector, I assume that these government-financed improvements (as well as those noted under point 5) are produced *by labor only*.

I assume further that this government expenditure induces farmers to invest additional man-hours in complementary improvements—for example, in land terracing and small irrigation channels to link up with larger irrigation canals. Why will the farmers do this? They presumably calculate in terms of expected future returns. We could rationalize their behavior by saying that they have found in the past that government-financed improvements, when complemented by additions of their own labor, have yielded a marginal return above the minimum required level. If they have never been disappointed in this respect, it is reasonable to hold the same expectations for the future.

7. These improvements permit movement to a higher level of agricultural technology, as explained in chapter 4. As productivity schedules shift northeastward for this reason, it becomes profitable to use more man-hours of labor in current-crop production.

Additional rural labor is thus called forth and absorbed in three complementary ways: (a) government hires workers for agricultural improvement; (b) this leads farmers to invest additional man-hours; and (c) these improvements make it profitable to apply more labor in current production. In my model, b is a function of a, and c is a function of a + b. The size of the government allocation for agricultural investment is thus of critical importance.

Movement to a higher technical level also involves an increase in nonlabor inputs purchased from the industrial sector: fertilizers, pesticides, and possibly tools and machinery. To bring this factor into the model would mean adding one commodity flow—industrial goods used as agricultural inputs—and one financial flow—allocation of part of farmers' income to input purchases. In an effort at simplification, I have not separated out these two flows; but anyone who disagrees with this decision can readily elaborate the model in this direction. In any event, this backward linkage should be recognized as an important channel by which agricultural progress interacts with industrial development.

8. A word should be added on the meaning of underemployment and "the agricultural wage." I assume that underemployment is confined to sectors 2 and 4 (agriculture and traditional nonagriculture). All workers attached to industry and government are fully employed. There is no room in the model for open unemployment, though this does occur in reality.

Following Ishikawa, I define available labor supply to sectors 2 and 4 as the maximum number of man-hours that would be offered in response to increases in demand, with no change in the hourly rate of return. Underemployment is the gap between available man-hours and hours actually worked; it is spread evenly over the sector 2–sector 4 labor force. The model is designed to explore the conditions under which this gap will narrow or widen over time.

The agricultural "wage" (really, agriculturalists' per capita income) equals agricultural output, minus tax payments, divided by the agricultural labor force, that is, it is based on the *average* rather than the *marginal* product of labor. It may rise or fall over time, depending on the values of the variables (especially technical progress and population growth rate) that influence it. Normally, a combination of variables that reduces underemployment will also produce a rise in the agricultural wage.

Sector 3: Government

The significance of government is that, on one hand, it employs labor to produce public and quasi-public goods and, on the other hand, the fiscal system serves to channel funds into capital formation. On the output side, I assume that: (1) public goods are produced by labor only; (2) there is no technical progress; and (3) the government wage is the same as the industrial wage and rises exogenously at the same annual percentage rate. The level of employment, then, is computed by dividing government revenue by the wage rate. As in the case of industry, though for different reasons, the more rapid the rise in wage rates, the slower the growth of employment.

Government revenue is derived from three sources: (1) an excise or sales tax on all industrial products; (2) a corporate profits tax at a fixed percentage rate; and (3) a tax that takes a fixed percentage of agricultural income. Export and import taxes, an important LDC revenue source in practice, are excluded by the closed-economy assumption.

On the expenditure side, I single out one item for special attention. I assume that a fixed percentage of government revenue is allocated to agricultural improvement. Government employment is thus not synonymous with urban employment because some government workers are employed in rural areas.

Since public goods are not marketed, there is no demand schedule for them. (Recall that output of public utilities and other government enterprises is included in the industry sector.) Government output apart from agricultural improvements is a residual, obtained by first calculating public revenue and then deducting the agricultural investment share.

Sector 4: Traditional Nonagriculture

In addition to trade and service workers, this sector includes manufacturing workers producing consumer goods by traditional handicraft methods. These artisans are of special interest because they compete with both household production and modern factory production. Historically, production of nonfood consumer goods (Z-goods) is at first centered largely in farm households. With the growth of a money economy, trade, and specialization, much of this production is turned over to specialized artisans. At a later stage, these artisans are in turn eliminated by factory production. But they survive for a long time because, being self-employed, they can offset their low productivity by accepting low incomes.

This sector is defined by its production characteristics rather than by geographic location. Many of its members are found in larger towns and cities; but others are distributed throughout the countryside in small towns and villages. They are self-employed. I assume that they work without capital, labor being the only production input. They sell their products to both agricultural and nonagricultural workers. It is plausible to assume that there is no technical progress in this sector, since the absence of capital removes a major source of such progress.

Because of self-employment and the absence of any capital require-ment, entrance to the sector is completely open. If the inflow of workers exceeds the rate of increase in demand, output and income per worker will fall. But workers always have the option of remaining in or return-ing to agriculture. I assume that, in equilibrium, the real wage per man-hour is the same in agriculture and in traditional nonagriculture. But this specific value for the real wage is not crucial to the argument. We could just as easily set it 10 percent above or 10 percent below the agricultural wage; all we need is some regulator of the migration flow.

Why do I not consolidate sectors 2 and 4 into a single traditional sector? The answer is partly because of their differing production functions and demand schedules and partly because of the substantial labor absorption possibilities of traditional nonagriculture. In a grow-ing economy, the influx of people into this sector is not an immiserizing process. There is a genuine increase in labor demand and employment which, if we ignore them, will lead to an unduly pessimistic view of the employment outlook.

The next step in the argument is to outline the intersectoral flows in the model, which I shall do in chapter 6.

6

Building a Closed-Economy Model: Intersectoral Relations and Economic Growth

I have outlined a four-sector closed-economy model, which is described more formally in the appendix.* I will proceed now to examine the intersectoral flows of goods, labor, and finance in the model and to consider the exogenous and policy variables that determine the growth of output and employment.

THE FLOW OF GOODS

Producers in one sector supply outputs to workers in each of the other three sectors, as well as to themselves. The production functions on the supply side have already been outlined, but I must now say a word about demand.

Not all demands in the system come from consumers. Industry demand agricultural raw materials. If we assume fixed material-input coefficients, this demand grows at the same rate as output grows. Industry also has a demand for capital goods, which is determined by the after-tax profits available for reinvestment.

For consumers, I use a Stone-Geary set of demand equations. Some minimum amount of foodstuffs, essential to survival, is a first charge on consumer budgets in all sectors. "Supernumerary income" above this level is allocated according to fixed Engels coefficients. I assume that these coefficients differ between "low-wage people" in sectors 2 and 4 and "high-wage people" in sectors 1 and 3. At given relative prices, low-wage people consume relatively more food and traditional products and relatively less factory-produced consumer goods. This

* The algebraic formulation of the model in the appendix was prepared by Dr. James A. M. Elliott, Assistant Professor of Economics, Georgetown University. In addition to preparing the appendix, Dr. Elliott made many helpful suggestions on the substance of the model.

can be interpreted as resulting from some combination of differing income-level and differing preference systems. Negative price elasticity of demand is also assumed.

Government output is not determined by demand as is output in the other three sectors. Rather, it depends on government employment, which equals current revenue divided by the government wage level. Current revenue, of course, is influenced by tax rates, which are policy variables. The government wage level, here assumed to be equal to the industrial wage level and rising at the same exogenous rate, could also be a policy variable.

Demand and supply for the output of the other three sectors are equilibrated through the price system. Thus, given the parameters of the model, one can deduce the rate of increase in agricultural output that is required for stability of the industry-agriculture terms of trade. Reasonable stability of the internal terms of trade is usually regarded as desirable.[1]

Stability should be defined in terms of price movements over an extended period. Because of weather-induced fluctuations in crop yields, year-to-year stability is not to be expected. We should also recall that deterioration in the commodity terms of trade for a sector does not necessarily mean deterioration in its factoral terms of trade, since the reason for the former may be an unusually rapid rate of technical progress (as in U.S. agriculture in recent decades). The Ricardian system, in which rising food prices squeezed industrial profits inexorably, achieved this result by ignoring not only the possibility of international trade but also the likelihood of technical progress.

THE FLOW OF LABOR

On this front, our four-sector model reduces to a two-sector model. Industry and government are high-wage sectors without underemployment and with an infinitely elastic supply schedule of labor at the going wage. Agriculture and traditional nonagriculture are low-wage

1. For example, John Mellor, using what he considers characteristic values for population growth, demand elasticities, and so on, estimates that a 5-percent annual increase in output would produce terms-of-trade stability. A 3-percent increase, on the other hand, accompanied by a 3-percent rate of population growth, would raise relative food prices about 1 percent per year. See Mellor, "Toward a Theory of Agricultural Development," in *Agricultural Development and Economic Growth*, ed. Herman M. Southworth and Bruce F. Johnston (Ithaca: Cornell University Press, 1967), pp. 21–61.

sectors from which labor can be extracted as needed; they are characterized by underemployment.

The growth rate of demand for labor in the high-wage sectors depends on the parameters specified earlier. Part of this demand will be met from the natural increase in the urban population. In a "success case," however, the rate of increase in "modern" labor demand will exceed the rate of population growth, leading to transfer of labor from the low-wage sectors. This intersectoral labor transfer will be accompanied by rural-urban migration. If we suppose that the expanding modern sectors draw in the first instance on urban workers engaged in traditional nonagriculture, we can see that the average income of those remaining in that sector will tend to go up. This will, in turn, induce enough migration from agriculture to restore equality of per capita income in the two low-income sectors.

Even if intersectoral labor transfer is occurring, there is likely to be a continuing increase in the absolute number of workers attached to the two traditional sectors. At the beginning of growth acceleration, the annual rate of increase in modern employment would have to be unrealistically high—in the range of 10 to 15 percent—in order for this not to happen.

But while the labor supply in the traditional sectors is likely to be increasing, labor demand in those sectors is also going to increase: in agriculture, because of the process of agricultural improvement described earlier; and in traditional nonagriculture, because of rising demand for that sector's output as per capita income rises. With no capital and no technical progress, labor inputs in traditional nonagriculture will increase at the same rate as output. In the early decades of development, when employment in industry and government is a small part of the total employment, it is mainly the rate of increase in demand for labor in the two traditional sectors that determines whether underemployment will increase or diminish.

It is worth noting that rural employment is not synonymous with agricultural employment. Some of those engaged in traditional nonagriculture, and also government employees working on agricultural improvement, are located in rural areas. Thus, migration out of agriculture is not identical with rural-urban migration, though there is a large overlap. Under favorable conditions, rural employment will rise faster than agricultural employment, and part of the agricultural labor surplus will be absorbed in rural locations. I shall have occasion to note in chapter 9 that the substantial increase in the incomes of

Japanese farm families from 1880 onward, with little increase in hourly rates of return, resulted partly from increased man-hour inputs into small-scale, rural-based industrial activities.

There is no place in our schema for open unemployment. In actuality, the larger cities in most LDCs do have a considerable (and often increasing) number of unemployed people. There are indications, however, that many of these unemployed are not among the most impoverished of the urban population. It is not facetious to say that, in a country without public support systems, "you have to be well-off to be unemployed." Many of the unemployed are relatively well-educated young people, with high job aspirations, who are willing to wait and search for high-wage jobs rather than accept lower incomes in traditional activities. They can afford to wait because they have parents or relatives who do have jobs and who are under a social obligation to support them. Eventually, if the search proves fruitless, they lower their aspirations and squeeze into some traditional activity in the city or return to the countryside. Thus, the unemployed, though numerous at any one time, are in large measure a transient and changing group, as is true also in the mature economies.

THE FLOW OF FINANCE

Although demand and supply for each type of output must be balanced, there is no need for commodity exports from agriculture to equal commodity imports to agriculture. But if they do not, agriculture is either making a net resource transfer to, or receiving a net resource transfer from, other sectors; and this must be reflected in a corresponding flow of payments. It is usually assumed, explicitly or implicitly, that the net resource transfer will be away from agriculture. But this is not logically necessary, and whether it is a valid empirical generalization is a matter for quantitative research.

The resource transfer can be viewed in three ways, which are equivalent in national accounting terms: (1) the difference between exports of goods and services from the agricultural sector and imports to that sector $(E_A - M_A)$; (2) the difference between investment in agriculture and savings generated in agriculture $(S_A - I_A)$; and (3) net financial transfers from agriculture on current account (V) plus net financial transfers from agriculture on capital account (K). If we call the net resource transfer R, then

$$R = E_A - M_A = S_A - I_A = V + K$$

where R can be either positive or negative.[2]

Looking first at the *export-import formulation*, two points should be noted. First, E_A and M_A are defined in current value terms. A change in the net resource transfer, then, can come about either through a change in the physical quantities exchanged or through a change in the terms of trade. If agriculture's terms of trade deteriorate, for example, there is an invisible resource transfer to nonagriculture, even though the export surplus does not change in physical terms. Second, agriculture's exports to nonagriculture include labor services as well as commodities. In addition to farm workers who migrate permanently to towns or cities, those remaining on the farm often work in non-agriculture during the off-season. Although this flow of services does not appear in our model, in practice it provides an important addition to total farm income.

In *savings-investment terms*, the direction of the net flow depends on: (1) prospective rates of return to investment in agriculture, which in turn are related to the rate of technical progress; (2) the development of banks and financial intermediaries that permit farmers to borrow for agricultural investment or, alternatively, to direct part of their savings to nonagricultural investments; (3) whether nonagriculturalists are able to invest in agriculture, which depends partly on the farm tenure system; and (4) whether government investment in agriculture exceeds the tax drain from agriculture.

Finally, a word about the $V + K$ formulation, which involves financial flows among agriculture, industry, and government. Following Ishikawa, we can distinguish the following major flows:

	To Agriculture $(-)$	From Agriculture $(+)$
Current (V)	Current government services to agriculture	Tax payments, net of subsidies; interest payments
Capital (K)	Government capital expenditures and subsidies to agriculture	Investment by farmers in nonagriculture
	Borrowings by farmers from nonagriculture	Loan repayments

2. For a searching analysis of the transfer problem, see Shigeru Ishikawa, *Economic Development in Asian Perspective* chap. 4. For a detailed case study of Taiwan, see T. H. Lee, *Intersectoral Capital Flows in the Economic Development of Taiwan, 1895–1960* (Ithaca: Cornell University Press, 1971).

Investment in agriculture by nonagriculturalists is excluded by our assumption of owner-operated farming. But farmers can borrow and so are involved in interest and loan repayments. They also have transactions with government, in which they may pay either more or less than they receive.

Clearly, then, the balance can be either positive or negative. Consider, for example, the following set of circumstances: (1) agriculture is lightly taxed; (2) agriculture receives substantial allocations from government on both current and capital account; (3) agriculture, being expanding and prosperous, is a good credit risk, and farmers' borrowings exceed interest and loan repayments; (4) security markets and other institutions permitting farmers to invest in nonagriculture are poorly developed. Such a combination could result in a net resource flow to agriculture rather than away from it.

Two side comments may be added. First, in this schema the magnitude and direction of resource transfer depends (apart from the governmental budget) on voluntary private decisions. But prices and incomes in the rural sector are affected by a variety of government policies, including use of price supports or price ceilings for farm output, pricing of fertilizer and other farm imputs, and (in an open economy) tariff and exchange-rate policies. Not uncommonly, such policies have been used to exploit agriculture and bring about an enforced resource transfer that would not have been forthcoming otherwise.

Second, a word on the much-disputed question of the desirable direction of resource transfer. The early tendency in development discussion was to emphasize expansion of factory industry and economic infrastructure—and to take it for granted that this expansion should be fueled by resource transfers from agriculture. More recently, economists impressed with the key role of food output and the investment requirements of a progressive agricultural sector have suggested that a net inflow of resources to agriculture may be desirable at the outset of growth acceleration.

But why is it necessary to take an a priori position on this matter? Why not follow the usual allocation criterion of relative rates of return? Depending on a country's resource base, land tenure system, and agricultural technology at a particular time, the rate of return to agricultural investment may be low or high. Investment decisions should presumably aim to equate this rate to that in other sectors of the economy.

A very important consideration is whether factor productivity in agriculture is stationary or rising. If the agricultural sector is sluggish, a net transfer of resources to agriculture, which Mellor thinks has been the tendency in India since independence,[3] may be undesirable. By the same token, a sluggish agriculture cannot contribute substantial resources to other sectors. Thus, the question of the desirable direction of resource transfer becomes moot. But an agricultural sector with a high rate of productivity may generate a sufficient surplus to both cover its own investment needs and permit a substantial resource outflow, as in Japanese and Taiwanese experience.

GROWTH RATE AND GROWTH CHARACTERISTICS

The purpose of growth models is to generate a hypothetical growth path that will somewhat resemble historical experience. The model should answer such questions as: What are the determinants of growth in per capita output? What is the predicted time path of the growth rate? For example, does it rise during the early decades and eventually taper off to a stable level? How does the pattern of employment growth differ from that of output growth? Is growth continuous and incremental, or can one distinguish "stages" of growth in which the rules of the game become different? In the course of exploring what my model has to say on these points, I shall remind the reader occasionally of how these questions were answered by earlier models.

Determinants of the Growth Rate

At the most general level, increases in per capita output must come from capital accumulation or technical progress; and these processes may be going on in industry, agriculture, or both. It may be interesting to tabulate the sources on which earlier models have relied. The bracketed entry in the lower right-hand box reflects the fact that, in the Fei-Ranis system, technical change in agriculture becomes necessary only beyond the "labor shortage point," that is, the point at which all labor of zero marginal productivity has been transferred to industry.

Some models draw on more sources of growth than others. Lewis emphasized a single source—capital accumulation in industry. The only previous model that drew on all four potential growth sources

---

3. John W. Mellor, *The New Economics of Growth* (Ithaca: Cornell University Press, 1976).

	Capital Accumulation	*Technical Change*
Industry	Fei-Ranis Ishikawa Kelley-Williamson Lewis Mellor-Lele	Fei-Ranis Kelley-Williamson
Agriculture	Kelley-Williamson	[Fei-Ranis] Ishikawa Kelley-Williamson Mellor-Lele

was K-W-C. The reason is that, in their system, agriculture is just another industry. The industrial orientation of most models is clear. Further, within industry the main emphasis has been on capital accumulation. In agriculture, on the other hand, there has been a tendency to emphasize technical change, since, in most models, capital is not used in agriculture and hence cannot accumulate.

In my model, the growth rate of output depends on: (1) the rate of capital accumulation in industry, which, in turn, depends on capital's share of output and the rate of profit taxation; (2) the assumed exogenous rate of technical progress in industry; (3) government expenditure on agricultural improvements; (4) the two-stage response to this expenditure, involving induced investment of farmers' time in agricultural improvements, which, in turn, raises productivity schedules in current production.

In the early decades of growth, agricultural progress is especially important because of the heavy weight of agriculture in total output. It involves "capital accumulation" in a special sense, comprising changes in land surface (such as terracing), drainage, and water supply; social overhead capital in the form of major irrigation works, feeder roads, and storage facilities; and improvement of farmers' production knowledge through agricultural research, experimentation, and extension. (Capital in the conventional sense of tools and current inputs will also be increasing, but this is a side product rather than a prime mover.) It involves "technical change" in the sense that these things enable farmers to draw on the world stockpile of agricultural technology, which is assumed to be expanding continuously in advance of actual utilization. So, although agricultural progress can be reduced formally to the same two components as industrial progress, its concrete form is distinctively different.

Nothing in the structure of my model guarantees a positive growth rate. The parameter values could be such as to produce stagnation or even deterioration, that is, an output growth rate below the rate of population growth. But by choosing more optimistic values, one can derive "success cases" with a positive growth rate.

On what does this growth rate depend? The following adjustments would raise the rate of increase in per capita output:

1. A lower rate of population growth.

2. A lower rate of wage increase in the industrial sector. Given the exogenous rate of productivity increase, this will raise the profit share of output and hence the rate of capital accumulation.[4]

3. A higher rate of exogenous technical progress in industry. This is a "wild card" in the system, which can be manipulated to produce any desired outcome. A conscientious experimenter, however, would hold it within the range of observed values in actual developing economies. There is also a built-in check, since a higher rate of increase in industrial output will reduce the relative price of that output, thus reducing profits and checking capital accumulation.

4. A lower tax rate on business profits. Unless compensated by an increase in some other tax, this will reduce government revenue that can be used for agricultural improvement and other public sector purposes; but this effect is probably outweighed by the stimulus to industrial investment (assuming full reinvestment of after-tax profits).

5. A larger real investment by government in agricultural improvements. This is a complex variable whose size depends on: (a) the three tax rates in the model, which together determine government revenue; (b) the proportion of revenue allocated to agriculture; (c) the number of man-hours of labor that can be purchased with this revenue, which depends on the government wage level. Note that, under my assumptions, a lower rate of increase in the industrial wage level is doubly beneficial. In addition to raising the profit share in industry, it lowers

4. This involves an assumption that the level of workers' consumption does not affect the rate of productivity increase. In practice, there probably is some relation; and thus the gain from a lower rate of wage increase is somewhat overstated. It also implies that the goods market will always adjust appropriately—if there is less worker demand for consumer goods, there will be more demand for "machines to make machines."

the government wage level and thus makes possible larger public-sector output from the same revenue.

6. A higher response coefficient of farmers to government-financed improvements.

7. A larger shift of productivity schedules in response to government-plus-farmer investment in land improvement. Technical progress in this sense is land-saving and labor-using, or "biological-chemical" in the Hayami-Ruttan classification.

8. A lower tax rate on agricultural output. Depending on the relative strength of the income and substitution effects, this may lead to an increase in farm labor inputs[5] and hence in farm output. Unless the positive effect is large, however, government revenue will fall.

9. In addition to these direct effects of individual variables, there are important *interaction effects*. For example, higher values of the coefficients listed in points 4, 5, or 6 will increase agricultural output and reduce the relative price of foodstuffs. This change in the terms of trade and in farm incomes affects consumer demand in all four sectors.

These results are unsurprising and in general accord with those of earlier models. Thus, a low rate of population growth, stability of the industrial wage level, full reinvestment of industrial profits, and rapid technical progress in industry and agriculture are all beneficial in terms of their effect on the growth rate.

Time Pattern of the Growth Rate

I shall restrict myself now to success cases, those yielding a positive growth rate. An interesting question is whether this rate will remain constant or whether it will rise to a higher level. Does the model predict steady-state growth or growth acceleration?

Some earlier models provide no specific prediction on this point. In those models anything can happen, depending on parameter values. Where there is a prediction, it is typically one of growth acceleration. In the Lewis model, the growth rate rises because industrial profits, which are entirely reinvested, form a growing share of national output. But eventually, when surplus labor is exhausted, the profit share

---

5. Ishikawa, it will be recalled, assumes a discontinuous function under which government can tax increments of output up to a certain level with zero effect on labor input; but if the tax percentage rises above this level, there is a 100-percent effect—the output will not be produced. On the more reasonable assumption of a continuous relation between tax rate and effort, one can still define a tax rate that is optimal in output terms.

stabilizes and so does the growth rate. In Ishikawa's success cases, the growth rate not only rises but continues to do so indefinitely, mainly because of the cumulative effect of reinvestment in the capital goods sector. In the K-W-C model, the parameter values that they consider plausible lead to a very gradual rise in the growth rate over time. The growth rate of output per capita is about 0.75 percent per year at the beginning of their fifty "periods" and about 1.5 percent at the end; and this increase presumably continues indefinitely.

It appears that my model also predicts acceleration during the early decades of growth. In my system as in most others, the weight of the industrial sector will increase gradually because of income elasticities of demand. Thus, even if the profit share of industrial output remains constant, reinvested profits will form a rising share of GNP over time. Further, to the extent that government revenue is drawn from profit taxes, government revenue will rise faster than GNP. This will mean a relative increase in agricultural investment by government, which will raise the growth rate of agricultural output. For these reasons, one would expect acceleration in the rate of increase in output per capita.

Although this acceleration may continue for some decades, it cannot continue forever. When the growth rate reaches some critical value, the rate of underemployment of labor will begin to diminish, eventually reaching zero. The Lewis effect will then set in. That is, as surplus labor is exhausted, the rate of wage increase will rise, and this will cut into industrial profits and reinvestment. This is likely to be reinforced by the Kuznets effect—a secular decline in labor inputs per worker because of normal income-leisure preferences.

Output Growth and Employment Growth

Does success in output terms also imply success in employment terms? Is there a conflict between output and employment objectives?

Under my assumptions, there can be no such conflict in the agricultural sector because land improvements are produced solely by additional labor inputs, which in turn make it possible to absorb more labor in current production. In actuality, of course, government could use bulldozers rather than men with shovels; but under labor surplus conditions this would be wasteful. In a later chapter I shall point out that the much-discussed full employment of labor in China has been accomplished partly by rural public-works projects executed by very labor-intensive methods.

In traditional nonagriculture, too, there can by definition be no conflict of objectives. With no capital and no technical progress, output and employment necessarily grow at the same rate.

Thus, it is mainly in the industrial sector that a conflict may arise. The time path of industrial employment depends not only on the growth rate of industrial output but also on the initial capital-labor ratio and on whether there is any trend in this ratio over time. Under labor surplus conditions it would be preferable, as Fei and Ranis argue, to have a "capital-shallowing" bias in technical change, so that increments of capital absorb progressively larger amounts of labor. Such a bias can be built into the model by the values assigned to the labor- and capital-augmentation coefficients. But is it plausible to do this? A labor-using bias would have to result from some combination of (1) capital stretching within individual production units;[6] (2) a shift in the industry mix toward industries with a higher labor-capital ratio; and (3) within each industry, a rising proportion of output coming from smaller, more labor-intensive plants. Each of these things can be influenced by public policy, though the influence is often inadvertent rather than deliberate. Thus, assuming an upward trend in the labor-capital ratio perhaps amounts to assuming a policy stance weighted toward employment objectives.

The rate of increase in the industrial wage level will also affect the growth of employment. Because of the technical-change assumption, real returns per unit of labor (and capital) can rise at the technical-progress rate without disturbing product prices or factor shares. But suppose we assume a higher rate of wage increase, which means a secular increases in unit labor costs of production. Then the relative price of industrial goods will tend to rise and their relative output will fall. Further, the squeeze on profits will tend to reduce the rate of capital accumulation. These effects, plus the increased incentive to substitute capital for labor in production, will reduce the growth rate of industrial employment.

To the extent that my model can project changes in the pattern of employment, it also has something to say about income distribution. Since the labor forces engaged in the modern and traditional sectors

6. For example, by running machinery faster, by using multiple-shift operation, or by employing labor-intensive methods in materials handling and other supplementary operations. For a review of historical and current experience in this connection, see Gustav Ranis, "Industrial Sector Labor Absorption," *Economics Development and Cultural Change* 21 (April 1973): 387–408.

typically have different average incomes, employment shifts among sectors affect overall income distribution. In the early decades of development, this may be a more important influence on distribution than changes in factor shares within the industrial sector.

Continuity or "Stages"?

Some models have viewed economic development as a continuous process, involving no change in the rules of the game. Others have viewed development as separable into distinct stages, with discontinuities or "turning points" marking the transition from one stage to the next.

If we set aside Rostow's ill-fated stages of growth, which were not rigorously formulated and did not stand up well to historical tests, the leading representatives of stage theories are the Lewis and Fei-Ranis systems. Lewis's "commercialization point" occurs because, as more and more surplus labor is transferred from agriculture to industry, labor's marginal product in agriculture begins to rise and eventually reaches equality with that in industry. It marks the transition between an early growth period, in which the labor supply schedule to industry is horizontal and real wages are stable, and a later period, in which the supply schedule is upward-sloping and real wages are rising (and equal) in both industry and agriculture.

There are two potential turning points in the Fei-Ranis system. The first is the "shortage point" at which redundant labor, that is, workers of zero marginal productivity, is exhausted. As I noted earlier, however, and as Fei and Ranis emphasize, the shortage point can be postponed by technical progress in agriculture until it coincides with Lewis's commercialization point. Thus, their system, like his, can be interpreted as involving only one major turning point.

The K-W-C model makes a special point of rejecting stage hypotheses and proceeds to generate a gently accelerating growth path with no sharp turning points. The Mellor-Lele and Ishikawa models are simply unconcerned with stage concepts. In Ishikawa's success cases, the surplus-labor reservoir would eventually run dry. Indeed, since in these cases the growth rate is accelerating over time, the system would slam hard into the labor-shortage barrier. But Ishikawa is interested in the initial acceleration period and does not analyze the long-run consequences of success.

In any historical case of development, there must have been a major turning point at the beginning of the growth process, that is, a point at which an economy with essentially stationary per capita output turned into a gradually growing economy. Kuznets designates this point (more correctly, this period) as that of *transition* to modern economic growth. I call it the beginning of *growth acceleration.*

None of the development models analyzed in chapter 2 professes to explain this initial turning point; nor do I attempt to do so here. An initial growth rate is built into the model by definition.

Once this initial point has been passed, economic growth is best regarded as a continuous process without sharp breaking points; and this supposition is embodied in our model. Without having run simulation experiments, one cannot be sure what kind of growth path the model would yield. It seems intuitively plausible that the model, given favorable values of the parameters, would yield a mildly accelerating growth rate. Of particular interest is the feature that real wages in both agriculture and industry rise from the outset, despite a continuing labor surplus. Formally, this results from the model structure; but I believe the result is realistic in terms of recent historical experience. In contemporary developing economies, austerity growth à la Lewis does not seem likely except under a very repressive political system.

There is, to be sure, an eventual second turning point. This is Lewis's commercialization point—the point at which surplus labor is exhausted, labor becomes "scarce" in all sectors, the rate of real wage increase accelerates, and the rural-urban wage gap shrinks or disappears. It should be emphasized, however, that this occurs at a very late stage of the game, only after an economy is so far along that it has passed into the mature category. Japan reached this point only in the 1950s, after almost a century of unusually successful development. One of the most successful cases of contemporary development, Puerto Rico, is not in sight of this point after thirty years of rapid growth and large net emigration to the U.S. mainland.

I conclude that, of the two genuine turning points in economic development, the first is (presently) inexplicable on economic grounds, and the second comes so late as to be essentially uninteresting. In between these points, both theoretical analysis and historical evidence suggest a growth process that is continuous, not in the sense of an absence of short-term fluctuations. but in the sense of no change in the rules of the game.

Policy Implications of the Model

In conclusion, it is useful to check over the exogenous and policy variables (listed in the appendix) and to inquire what government can do about them. The distinction between policy and exogenous variables is artificial, in the following sense. By a *policy* variable I mean one that government can alter directly and immediately—and that is thus relevant to policy formation within the time period. The *exogenous* variables are taken as constant within the period; but they, too, are amenable to government influence over a longer time span. They might more properly be termed *semi-exogenous* or *indirect policy* variables.

If I wanted to complicate the model, I could treat these indirect policy variables as alterable within the period by manipulation of policy variables proper. For example, the farmers' investment response function (M) could be taken as a function of the agricultural tax rate (t_2), if it depends on anticipated net returns to increments of output.

There are only four policy variables proper: the three tax variables and the percentage of government revenue allocated to agricultural improvement. But looking only at these variables gives too restricted a view of the potential for government action. As already suggested, variables that are taken as exogenous in the short run can also be regarded as amenable to gradual change over time. Specifically, these variables are: (1) the rate of natural increase in population. While this has proven stubbornly resistant to simplistic approaches, a few countries have been quite successful in speeding the decline of fertility; (2) the rate of increase in the modern sector wage rate. Since government employment is usually a sizable percentage of all modern employment, government's own wage policy is influential. Government can also influence the policies of large private employers and the institutional framework for industrial wage determination; (3) the labor technical progress variable, which is mainly a proxy for human capital formation. The size and strategy of government allocations to formal education and job training are important here; (4) the capital technical progress variable. Both the rate and factor bias of technical progress in the industrial sector can be affected by stimulation of scientific and technological research, the rate of capital accumulation permitted by the tax system, and policies affecting the viability of small-scale industry; (5) the farmers' investment response coefficient to agricultural investment by government. This can be influenced by the agricultural tax rate and also by farm price policies, tenure reforms, and other measures that affect farm operators' expected returns on investment; (6) the responsiveness of current productivity schedules in agriculture to government-plus-farmer investment. This can be influenced by government allocations to agricultural research and extension, by the encouragment of production and distribution of modern inputs, and by the development of adequate credit facilities.

The interesting thing about each of these areas is that, with the exception of education, they do not require a large commitment of resources. They require mainly a clear policy orientation and effective organization. A review of what a particular country is doing in these areas provides a good test of its government's seriousness about development and competence to achieve it.

The rate of capital accumulation in industry, dependent on the profit share of output and the rate of profit taxation, is important in the model; but we have not emphasized it as a policy variable. This reflects a view that capital accumulation is one of the easier things for a well-organized government to accomplish. In the private sector, capital accumulation through reinvestment of after-tax profits occurs almost automatically. Government investment in infrastructure is also fairly easily financed by internal or external borrowing. Recall the famous definition that "social overhead capital is anything for which the World Bank will make a loan." This assumes, of course, that the government in question is competent and creditworthy.

Two other policy areas, important in practice, are excluded by the structure of the model. First, being a closed-economy model, it cannot accommodate policies affecting foreign trade, exchange rates, and capital movements. These issues will be explored in chapters 7 and 8. Second, although the existence of a monetary and financial system is implied, the model does not highlight its operation. In practice, government action in developing and managing financial institutions, and in serving as a financial intermediary, is undoubtedly important.

My model does have the merit of placing government explicitly in the center of the picture. The picture of a private economy developing without government, implied in some previous models, is archaic. I consider it a merit also that the model is agriculture-oriented. This implies that success in development depends heavily on the effectiveness of government action in that difficult sector.

7

The Open Economy: Growth and Trade

When we shift from closed- to open-economy assumptions, the possibilities of economic transformation are obviously much enlarged. Resources can be transformed into products indirectly via trade as well as directly via domestic production. The link between domestic consumption and production patterns is broken. A low-income, densely populated country can export manufactures and import food. Machinery and other requirements for industrialization can be imported rather than home-produced. Technology and education can also be imported. The cost of imported resources may be reduced by grants or borrowing at subsidized rates of interest.

But does admission of trade involve any new analytical difficulties? When country A becomes part of a world trading system, can we not predict what will happen in that country from a general equilibrium model reflecting comparative advantage? Can the development economist add anything to the skills of the specialist in international economics?

There is indeed a long tradition of trade theory. One might better say that there are two traditions—one of highly simplified analytical models, and one of ad hoc policy advice with a strong protrade bias. This mainstream reasoning, however, has never been universally accepted. The names of Hamilton, List, Manoilescu, Myrdal, Baran, and Prebisch suggest the countercurrent of opposition to received doctrine.

Before embarking on a positive discussion of trade and growth, then, some ground clearing is in order. In particular, we must take account of the literature of colonialism and neocolonialism and also of the doctrine of "export pessimism" advanced by Prebisch and others.

THE ECONOMICS OF COLONIALISM

Trade theory, like economic theory in general, tends to abstract from power relations. The trading nations are assumed to be fully independent. But a colony is by definition not independent. Its government is responsible to authorities in the colonizing power (hereafter called the "home" country) rather than to the indigenous population. It is reasonable to assume that government policy will aim at maximizing economic benefit to the home country.

Consider first a pure enclave case, which we can later modify in certain respects. Mining or plantation enterprises are set up in the colony to exploit local resources. Management and capital goods are brought in from the home country. Assume for the moment that labor is also imported (as it has been in some cases, such as for Ceylon tea plantations). All output is exported to the home country. Export proceeds are divided among repatriated profits, imports of consumer goods for residents of the enclave, and (in periods of active demand) imports of capital goods for expansion of production.

The colonial government can be regarded as supported entirely by import and export taxes—and as spending only on infrastructure facilities for the export industry. Under these assumptions, there is no economic interaction between the enclave and the indigenous economy, which continues to operate as before. The enclave is an integral part of the economy of the home country, however. Its geographic location in the colony is irrelevant.

The money flows in such an economy are outlined in figure 1. The

Figure 1. Payment Flows in a Colonial Economy

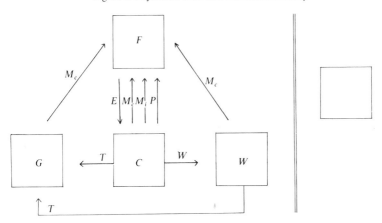

Enclave economy   Indigenous economy

hub of the system is the interchange between the home country (F) and capitalist producers (C) in the colony. Wage earners (W) receive a wage bill from C, which is spent on consumption imports (M_c). Government employees (G) also consume imported goods. Government is supported by export and import taxes (T) whose incidence is divided between capitalists and wage earners. Value added in the enclave, all of which is exported, is $E - W$. The proceeds are divided between consumption imports (M_c), investment imports (M_i), and repatriated profits (P).

How does the enclave grow under these circumstances? The prime mover is the growth of GNP in the home country, which raises demand for the colony's exports. By itself, this would tend to raise export prices; and the colony's capacity to import would rise both because of rising export volume and the favorable price shift. But as this happens, government revenue from import and export taxes also rises; and as these revenues are spent in export-promoting ways, the supply curve of exports shifts to the right, braking the tendency toward improvement in the colony's terms of trade. Even apart from government action, the supply of export products may be quite elastic for reasons noted by Lewis, Myint, and others.

Birnberg and Resnick have shown[1] that a model incorporating these features can simulate quite closely the changes in exports, imports, and terms of trade for ten colonial countries over the period 1900–45. These colonies were attached to countries as diverse as the United Kingdom, the United States, and Japan. Variations in the rate of export growth among these countries are well explained by the GNP growth rate of the home country; the resulting rate of growth of export demand, which differs from one commodity to another because of differing income elasticities; the effectiveness of colonial government expenditure in raising export capacity ("the reflection ratio"); and dummy variables for major shifts in the home country's trade policies.

The home country gains from this process through enlargement of its domestic economy (of which the enclave is part) and through increased opportunities for profitable investment. Such gains help

1. Thomas Birnberg and Stephen Resnick, "A Model of the Trade and Government Sectors in Colonial Economies," *American Economic Review* (September 1973): 572–87; idem, *Colonial Development: An Econometric Study* (New Haven: Yale University Press, 1975).

sustain returns on capital, and so the benefit may go mainly to capital owners. Wage earners in the home country may also gain—or they may not. Members of the educated class in the home country gain through increased opportunities for government and managerial employment in the colony.

The question of whether these gains are *at the expense* of the indigenous population outside the enclave is largely speculative. To argue that colonialism blocked development assumes that, without the enclave and the colonial regime, the indigenous economy would have grown more rapidly. This counterfactual hypothesis is difficult to test. The growth of economies that did not become colonies, such as Thailand and Ethiopia, was far from spectacular.

Let us now modify this simple model and consider the possibility of spillovers from the enclave to the indigenous economy. These spillovers can be positive or negative, and both are usually present.

There are several ways in which enclave development may stimulate the indigenous economy. Suppose, first, that the foreign enterprises hire local labor rather than imported labor, as in the Kenya tea plantations or the South African mines. The *W* box in figure 1 is moved over, if you like, into the traditional sector. Part of the wage income will be spent on imported consumer goods, whose availability provides an incentive to take modern sector jobs. But part of it will go into increased demand for locally produced food, handicrafts, housing, and services.

Historically, however, this stimulus was limited by a low-wage policy, characteristic especially of European employers in Africa. The policy was made possible by a low supply price of labor. But it was rationalized on the basis of a supposed backward-bending (individual) labor supply curve. Research studies offer little support for this hypothesis; but it persisted in colonial times as a convenient explanation for low wages. Foreign-owned enterprises thus became locked into a circular situation. The cost of labor per unit of *time* was very low; labor being so "cheap," it did not pay to train, stabilize, and supervise the labor force effectively; so productivity remained low and labor was not "cheap" in terms of cost per unit of *output*; so employers could argue that workers were getting all they were worth and that wage increases were impossible.

The European enterprises tended also to employ local labor predominantly for low-skilled work. Management remained entirely

European; and in Africa, skilled and clerical jobs were often assigned to Indians or some other intermediate group. Thus, Africans were barred from occupational progress, and creation of "modern" jobs did not have the educative effect that might otherwise have been expected.

The effects on the indigenous economy are greater when the primary export is produced, not by foreign-owned enterprises, but by local peasant producers. Classic examples are the growth of cocoa exports from Ghana and Nigeria and rice exports from Burma, Thailand, Taiwan, and Korea. This may be visualized by moving most of the *C* box in figure 1 over into the indigenous sector, while the *W* box disappears. Those remaining in the enclave, then, are largely merchants, bankers, and government officials.

The growth of peasant-produced exports was mainly a net addition to previous output rather than a substitute for it. In these thinly populated countries there were, as of 1900, ample reserves of unused land. There were also unused reserves of labor time. Peasants could reach the "fully-belly point" in a few hours a day, and they had no incentive to go beyond that. The appearance of imported consumer goods, purchasable with money income, induced them to work longer hours, cultivate more land, and produce an exportable surplus in addition to the normal food supply. Thus, per capital output and per capita consumption rose at a moderate but sustained rate.

This process also, as Myint has emphasized,[2] led to increased specialization and monetization of the economy. Some peasants came to specialize mainly or entirely in exports, while others concentrated on producing a marketable food surplus. The volume of food traded on local markets rose. Part of the increased money income also went into purchases of local handicrafts and services. The network of local traders and artisans expanded, and so did the transport network, which was needed to reach the thousands of scattered small producers. Under this pattern of export expansion, a higher percentage of the additional income generated remained *within* the colony than occurred in the case of the mining and plantation enterprises.

Although export expansion thus contributed to long-term growth, there were also negative effects of the colonial experience. The flood of low-cost, factory-produced imports tended to undercut local handi-

2. Hla Myint, *The Economics of the Developing Countries* (London: Hutchinson and Co., 1964), esp. chap. 3.

craft production. Resnick has traced the decline of handicrafts in Burma, Thailand, and the Philippines under colonial rule;[3] and the experience in India is said to have been similar. One could argue that it is natural for low-productivity handicraft techniques to be super-seded by high-productivity factory methods. But here the handicrafts were local, the factories foreign. Thus, there was a destruction of skills that would have been useful at a later stage of independent development.

Recent discussion suggests that, given the factor proportions and (shadow) factor prices characteristic of most LDCs, relatively small-scale, labor-intensive manufacturing techniques usually have lower social costs than highly capitalized methods. Even where small enter-prises cannot be justified as the dominant method of production, they can fill in the interstices of the economy as subcontractors on the Japanese pattern. Countries that now want to encourage small-scale industry would be in a better position to do so had they not suffered an attrition of handicraft skills in colonial days.

Further, although peasant incomes rose in the course of export expansion, they rose less than they would have under competitive market conditions. Part of the increase was appropriated by the foreigners who enjoyed monopoly power as employers of local labor, wholesalers of imported goods, purchasers and shippers of export crops, and bankers. Residents of the colony were exploited, not in the sense of an absolute decline in living standards, but in the sense of a transfer of real income through the exercise of market power.

Perhaps most harmful, however, was the development of an occupa-tional ladder of which the indigenous population occupied only the lowest rungs as farmers and laborers. First- and second-echelon jobs in business and government were reserved for Europeans. Clerical and skilled manual jobs were often filled by immigrant groups—the Indians in many parts of Africa, the Chinese in Southeast Asia. This intermediate group provided an effective buffer between rulers and natives, sealing off the latter from any progress in skills, status, and income. There is much to support Myint's view that the central problem of the LDCs after 1945 was not underdevelopment of resources but

3. Stephen A. Resnick, "The Decline of Rural Industry Under Export Expansion: A Comparison Among Burma, Philippines, and Thailand, 1870–1938," *Journal of Economic History* 30 (March 1970): 51–73.

backwardness of people, a backwardness that was accentuated rather than alleviated under colonial rule.[4]

The development of an educational infrastructure, like the development of a physical infrastructure, served mainly the administrative needs of the governing group. There had to be clerks and record-keepers, people capable of reading and following simple instructions. So a minority of the population, drawn mainly from the "middlemen" rather than from the indigenous group, had to be educated through the primary level. Secondary education was much more restricted and often on a fee basis. University education, except in India, was virtually unknown. Natives of the Belgian Congo, for example, were not allowed to go to Belgium for higher education. Natives of Indonesia could study medicine, but nothing else. Thus, some LDCs arrived at independence with virtually no indigenous administrative or professional personnel and with a staggering educational deficiency at the lower levels.

It is not feasible in a few pages to evaluate the entire colonial era. The research base for such an evaluation is fragmentary; and the ideological tone of much of the literature hampers dispassoniate analysis. Moreover, it may not be sensible to attempt generalization for all colonies at all times. Colonial policy and outlook differed substantially among British, French, Spanish, and other territories. Even within the British sphere, conclusions about Kenya might differ from those about India.

Further, different questions can be asked about the colonial experience, and the analysis and results will differ correspondingly. Did the colonial powers exploit the colonies in the sense that consumption levels for the mass of the population declined absolutely? This would probably be hard to demonstrate; and in any case the question is of only historical interest. A different and more interesting question is whether colonial policies left the countries that achieved independence from 1945 onward in a good situation to embark on sustained growth.

On this point, appraisal of colonialism has to be mixed if not negative. The new countries inherited a certain amount of physical infrastructure and possibly a wider range of human skills than they

4. Hla Myint, "An Interpretation of Economic Backwardness," *Oxford Economic Papers* (1954), reprinted in idem, *Economic Theory and the Underdeveloped Countries* (London, New York, Toronto: Oxford University Press, 1971).

might otherwise have had. On the other hand, they were left with an export pattern including a limited range of primary products and directed mainly toward a single foreign market, a pattern reflecting political relations rather than economic advantage; dramatic shortages of (indigenous) human capital, which are less easily remedied than physical capital shortages; and fragile political institutions and administrative services. The starting point would have been quite different had preparation of the colonies for economic progress as independent entities, rather than for economic aggrandizement of the home country, been the objective of colonial policy from the beginning.

Colonialism now belongs to history. Or does it? Political independence has been achieved almost everywhere. But an important current of thought contends that the economic independence of the former colonies is still severely limited. Terms commonly used in this connection are *neocolonialism* and *the dependence effect*. Dependence means something more than mere involvement in the world network of trade and capital flows. It means involvement on *unfavorable* terms. These terms, it is said, are dictated by the economic power of the rich countries, which have undue influence over the volume and prices of primary exports from the LDCs, the prices of manufactures imported by the LDCs, and the size and cost of long-term capital flows. Current LDC proposals for "a new international economic order" involve a demand that these decisions should be shifted from the market to political forums and determined by multilateral negotiations in which rich and poor countries would have an equal voice.

The meaning of neocolonialism varies somewhat from one writer to the next. It is sometimes applied to countries that have not broken sharply with the colonial trade pattern, that continue to rely heavily on primary exports, and that follow a relatively open-economy policy.[5] The underlying issues here are whether primary exports can provide a sustained stimulus to overall development and whether attainment of economic independence requires a sharp shift toward import substitution.

Perhaps more commonly, "neocolonialism" is applied to the activi-

---

5. On this ground, Fei and Paauw term the postwar growth of Thailand and Malayisa *neocolonial*, in contrast to that of Taiwan and the Philippines, which have followed a policy of "economic nationalism" involving trade and exchange controls designed to further impart substitution. Douglas Paauw and John C. H. Fei, *The Transition in Open Dualistic Economies* (New Haven: Yale University Press, 1973).

ties of multinational corporations, particularly those engaged in oil or mineral extraction. Where foreign-owned companies export materials that provide both the bulk of a country's foreign exchange earnings and a large share of government revenue, one can argue that the country's economic (and even political) independence is precarious. A local subsidiary of Alcan, Kennecott, Unilever, or Shell is part of the economy of that company rather than the economy of the country in which it is located. Its policies, dictated from London, Paris, or New York, are designed to promote the growth and profitability of the company rather than the welfare of the host nation.

These charges raise substantial issues, which will be examined later in this chapter and in chapter 8.

EXPORT PESSIMISM: PREBISCH, MYRDAL, AND OTHERS

This line of argument, which peaked in the 1950s, has been seriously weakened by the good LDC export performance of the 1960s and, for oil-producing countries, by the great increase in export proceeds since 1973. But it still deserves brief examination. In good measure it reflects colonial experience plus the impact of the Great Depression. Primary production for export is what the colonial rulers encouraged —and what must therefore have been beneficial to *them*. So how can it be beneficial to *us*? Should we not rather do what they *did* (not what they *said*) and shift the economy as rapidly as possible to an industrial base? Is not anyone who advises to the contrary a secret colonialist, working against our best interest?

Associated with this outlook is an attack on conventional trade theory which, it is thought, tends to rationalize and justify existing trade patterns. This involves some misconception (in a sense, an overestimate) of how much the Heckscher-Ohlin apparatus actually says. It does not say that real-world trade flows, under conditions of market imperfection and trade restrictions, necessarily reflect comparative advantage. It certainly does not deny that comparative advantage changes over time. Nor does it say that the opening of trade between a poor and a rich country will always accelerate the growth rate of the former or reduce the income gap among nations.

It is not necessary to depart from conventional reasoning to reach pessimistic conclusions. Consider an LDC exporting a single primary product. GNP in the mature economies is growing at 6 percent a year, and income elasticity of demand for the product in question is

0.5. Overlooking capital movements, then, the LDCs capacity to import will grow at only 3 percent a year, a rate too low to support an ambitious development program. If price elasticity of demand is also low, efforts to raise export volume to more than 3 percent will lead to deteriorating terms of trade and a shrinkage of export value. No one would deny that such a combination of circumstances is possible—or that it has sometimes occurred in actuality.

Confusion arises, however, when one tries to prove too much, to demonstrate that exchange of primary products for manufactures must have adverse effects. An example is Prebisch's theory of the effect of differing market structures in the trading nations. Primary products, it is said, are produced under competitive conditions, so that improvements in productivity are quickly reflected in lower prices. Manufactured goods in the mature economies, however, are produced under conditions of oligopoly and controlled pricing. Productivity improvements, then, are not passed on to the buyer but are appropriated in higher profit margins (or, in another variant of the argument, are appropriated partly by strong trade unions through higher wage rates). This combination of rigid prices for manufactures and downward flexibility in primary product prices must, according to this theory, lead to secular deterioration of the terms of trade.

Let us waive the dubious empirical assumptions of this argument. (Controlled pricing of primary products—oil, coffee, cocoa, rubber —is certainly not unknown; and oligopolistic manufacturers in country A may be subject to effective competition from oligopolists in countries B, C, and D.) The analysis itself is clearly defective. A maximizing monopolist does not hold prices unchanged when costs fall. Studies of U.S. manufacturing show a strong inverse relation between rates of productivity improvement and rates of price change, with no visible effect of market structure. There may be a tendency for seller concentration to be associated with higher wage levels; but the tendency is not strong, and its existence is still being debated.

A second example is Myrdal's argument about the (possible) disequalizing effects of exchange between areas at different levels of development. This argument was developed initially with respect to regions of a particular country. There is a "center" and a "periphery." The center has higher factor productivity and factor returns and a higher growth rate. Growth at the center stimulates growth at the periphery by generating a demand for raw materials and labor and by providing manufactures at progressively lower prices. Both the price decline for purchased goods and the price increases for factors will tend to raise real income at the periphery. But against these "spread effects," Myrdal argues, must be set adverse or "backwash effects," which may cancel out the spread effects or even reverse them. Suppose, for example, that the best-educated and most talented people from the periphery migrate to the center in response to the greater opportunities available there. Suppose also that savings from the periphery flow toward the center in response to higher investment returns. Then the periphery may be left so stripped of resources that it cannot respond to favorable impulses from the outside, it cannot organize and sustain new economic activities.[6]

To explore how far this hypothesis is valid within national economies would lead us far afield. The northeast of Brazil is often cited as a region whose union with the rest of Brazil has led to economic deterioration. If true, this could not be taken as an inevitable result of economic processes; rather it must partly reflect government policy. In the United States, twentieth-century growth clearly has had marked equalizing effects among regions. But, Myrdal might reply, disequalizing tendencies may prevail at an early stage of development, even though they tend to be reversed at a later stage.

In any event, it is questionable how far this essentially interregional argument can be internationalized. It rests heavily on flows of factors rather than of products; and factor movements among countries are severely restricted. It seems unlikely that trade will lower the real income of an LDC, that is, that the combination of circumstances required for "immiserizing growth" will occur frequently in practice. Trade is compatible with unequal rates of growth and with growing income inequality between less-developed and more-developed countries. But this is a different matter and is readily explainable without the kind of reasoning on which Myrdal relies.

The central issues involved here—whether market structures are systematically biased against the LDCs, whether primary exports face

6. In Myrdal's intellectual schema, this forms part of a larger thesis that economic intercourse between unequals can lead to cumulative and self-reinforcing movement away from equality rather than toward it, a "vicious" rather than a "virtuous" spiral. This was developed initially in his massive study of the American Negro. Here, he argued, economic and educational discrimination has led to a lower income level, consumption level, and pattern of life, all of which then become the bases for justifying and continuing the initial discrimination. This approach, which, he believes, contrasts strongly with the equilibrating assumptions of "orthodox" economics, was later extended to regional and international economic relations.

a sluggish world demand, and whether the terms of trade are destined to move in one direction or the other—are ultimately empirical questions, about which we shall have something to say in later sections.

GROWTH IN THE TRADE LITERATURE

Turning to mainstream work, there has been a growing interpenetration of work in international economics and in economic development over the past generation. This rapprochement has gone on from both sides: through work on "growth and trade," the subject of this section; and through work on "trade and growth," examined in the following section.

Trade theory in its Heckscher-Ohlin version has two obvious limitations. The first inheres in the specification of the trading countries, including the determinants of trade flows. The second concerns the static character of the model. Let me comment first on the second aspect, since much of the recent theoretical work involves an examination of the effects of economic change.

Assume two isolated economies, each with two factors and two industries, which use these factors in differing proportions. Production functions are identical in the two countries. Full resource mobility and competitive pricing are assumed. These economies are now opened to trade. Each economy undergoes changes in outputs and in factor and product prices. Given demand patterns as well as resource supplies, we can predict the new prices and outputs, the terms of trade, and the division of the gains from trade. In the new equilibrium, there is a once-and-for-all gain in real income but no growth in any other sense.

Suppose that we now introduce a change in income or resource supplies and ask how (in a comparative static sense) this will affect the volume and terms of trade. Suppose that, for whatever reason, national income rises in one country but not in the other—or that income rises in both but at differing rates. This will affect output, trade, and relative prices via demand elasticities. Or suppose that, in country A, the supply of one factor rises but that of the other does not, or that both rise at differing rates. If one knows whether A's export industry or its import-competing industry is more intensive in the rapidly accumulating factor, one can (usually) predict the effect on the volume and terms of trade. Finally, technical change can be brought into the picture. Here the impact depends on the nature (labor-saving, capital-saving, or neutral) of the change and on whether it occurs in the export or the import-competing sector. In more complex models, all three types of change can be combined to predict the "total growth impact" of a specified growth pattern for one or both economies.

The results of such taxonomic work are summarized in a number of convenient sources.[7] As one might expect, "anything can happen." Country A's exports may rise or fall; its terms of trade may improve or deteriorate. Everything depends on the assumptions. The results are useful to the extent that one knows what kinds of change are characteristic (historically) of the LDCs or what changes can plausibly be assumed for the future. They are useful also for casting doubt on assertions that certain developments *must* occur in the future—for example, that the terms of trade must move in favor of or against primary products. There is no a priori basis for such general statements. One can specify conditions that would produce a particular result; but the question of whether these conditions are likely to exist is a matter for research and judgment.

Whether changes in income, factor supplies, and technology will have a marked effect on the terms of trade depends on elasticities of factor supply and product demand. The higher these elasticities are, the more readily economic change can be accommodated without large shifts in the terms of trade. Thus, the supposedly limited resource transferability in some LDCs, combined with low price and income elasticities of demand for some primary products, presents a danger (though not a certainty) of adverse price shifts.

One can specify conditions under which trade will reduce a country's real income instead of increasing it. An increase in output and exports is accompanied by a sufficient deterioration in the terms of trade so that real income is lower than before. The conditions required for such "immiserizing growth" are stringent and unlikely to occur frequently; but the possibility of a loss through trade cannot be denied.

Developments in welfare economics have led to more careful qualification of the traditional propositions that "some trade is better than no trade," and "more trade is better than less trade." Suppose that one or more of the conditions usually assumed in trade theory do not exist. For example, suppose there are imperfections in one or more

---

7. For example, Gerald Meier, *The International Economics of Development* (New York: Harper and Row, 1968); and Bo Södersten, *International Economics* (New York: Harper and Row, 1970).

factor markets. Then one can no longer assert that a reduction in trade barriers will invariably increase welfare. Rather, one has to work out specific cases in a second-best world.

A further development in trade theory has been deeper analysis of the bases of comparative advantage. The discussion initiated by the "Leontief paradox" has suggested that natural resources should be admitted as a factor along with labor and capital and that to identify capital with physical equipment is a serious misspecification. Rather, capital formation should be defined in such a way that it encompasses all expenditures aimed at raising productive capacity, including expenditures for education, research, and development.

The development and diffusion of technology has emerged as a central issue. Some countries devote more resources to innovation than do others. Product innovations appearing in one country will be oriented in the first instance toward domestic use. Exporting develops as a spillover from satisfactory performance (and learning) in the home market, and the innovating country for the time being enjoys a comparative advantage. As the new technology is diffused to other countries, however, this advantage diminishes and eventually disappears, completing the "product cycle."

The focus of interest has thus shifted from the determinants of comparative advantage at a specific moment to the determinants of shifts in comparative advantage over time. Trade theory has become more historical, if not more dynamic in a technical sense.

These developments have tended to reduce trade theory to a series of special cases and at the same time to undercut the traditional presumption against government intervention. As Diaz Alejandro remarks,

> By now any bright graduate student, by choosing his assumptions regarding distortions and policy instruments carefully, can produce a consistent model yielding just about any policy recommendation he favored at the start. . . . Good algebra and consistent models can prove nothing about the real world, but perhaps the major contribution of these models . . . is to force the discussion of the realism of different assumptions which are crucial for determining under what conditions more trade benefits whom, and by how much.[8]

8. Carlos Diaz Alejandro, "Trade Policies and Economic Development," in Peter B. Kenen, ed., *International Trade and Finance* (New York: Cambridge University Press, 1975).

THE FOREIGN SECTOR IN DEVELOPMENT MODELS

Looking now at the trade-development interaction from the development side, how does the introduction of a foreign sector alter the
closed-economy model? Suppose I want to build a foreign sector
into the model outlined in chapters 5 and 6. Does this mean that I
must redefine the domestic boxes in the model? What external flows
of commodities and finance must be distinguished? Should foreign
demand for the country's exports be taken as exogenous? What
changes occur in agriculture's role in development?

The answer to the first question seems to be no. True, the LDC
is now exporting and importing. Thus, there has to be some place for
exports to come from. But this does not require any change in the
number of domestic sectors or in their rules of behavior. To the extent
that exports consist of minerals, petroleum, timber, etc., these come
from the modern industrial sector. If and when a country reaches the
stage in which it exports manufactures, these also come from the
industrial sector. To the extent that exports consist of agricultural
products, they can be regarded as coming from the agricultural sector
as defined earlier, that is, from farmers who are also producing for
the domestic market and for home consumption. There are situations
in which export crops come mainly from foreign-owned plantations
or from specialized, relatively large-scale commercial farms. But exports as an overspill from peasant production are more common, as
in the cases of Thai rice, Bangladesh jute, Nigerian cocoa, Colombian
coffee. Thus, I see no need to distinguish, as Paauw and Fei do,[9]
between export agriculture and so-called traditional agriculture.

The addition of foreign trade solves one awkward problem in the
industrial sector. A closed economy must produce its own capital
goods as well as consumer goods. Thus, manufacturing should logically
be subdivided into capital-good and consumer-good subsectors.
Models of optimal capital accumulation usually do make such a
separation. Many other models do not, assuming a single good that
can either be eaten or used as a tool. Admission of trade removes the
necessity for this odd assumption, since capital goods can now be
imported.

As regards commodity flows, then, I assume that exports are divided
in some proportion between agricultural exports and modern-sector

9. See particularly diagram 1.1, p. 4, Paauw and Fei, *The Transition*.

exports. These two export streams have different internal effects, but there is no need to assume either of them out of existence.

The import flow should probably be divided into four components: manufactured consumer goods, capital goods, fuels and other intermediate products, and foodstuffs. Each of these has different demand determinants. These four categories can be reduced to two by assuming that the country feeds itself and by lumping capital goods and intermediate products; but there is some loss in such a simplification.

Corresponding to these commodity flows are flows of payments for imports and exports. There are also capital movements: foreign "official" loans and grants, foreign private investment, debt service payments, profit repatriation. In practice, these are interrelated with the trade flows; but I adopt the common device of setting them aside for separate treatment in the next chapter.

Another financial flow arising from the introduction of foreign trade is government revenue from open or implicit taxes on exports and imports. This is a major revenue source and an important policy variable in early economic growth.

Foreign demand for the country's exports is often taken as exogenous, rising at a certain percentage rate per year. This implies that the rate depends only on the growth of world demand. But in actuality, export growth is influenced substantially by what the country itself does. Large differences in export performance by countries in apparently similar circumstances are a familiar fact of life, as we shall see in a later section. Thus, it is best to regard the export growth rate as a policy variable, which by appropriate policies can be raised above the growth rate of both foreign demand and domestic output.

My earlier analysis of the interaction of agriculture and non-agriculture in development needs to be rethought in an open-economy setting. As Myint points out,[10] agriculture is usually expected to promote development by (1) increasing food supply for domestic consumption; (2) enlarging the domestic market for manufactures; (3) increasing the supply of domestic saving; and (4) earning more foreign exchange through agricultural exports. It is assumed that these objectives are mutually consistent; and the question of whether we are discussing a closed or an open economy is often glossed over.

10. Hla Myint, "Agriculture and Economic Development in the Open Economy," in *Agriculture in Development Theory*, ed. L. G. Reynolds (New Haven: Yale University Press, 1975), pp. 327–54.

In a closed-economy model, function 4 does not exist by definition. On the other hand an open-economy model, taken seriously, raises many new possibilities and policy issues. For example, an increase in agricultural income need not increase the domestic market for manufactures, since the additional income may be spent on imports. In policy terms, promotion of objective 3 involves siphoning income out of agriculture through private or governmental channels. But this conflicts with promotion of objectives 1 and 4, which might require net investment *in* agriculture.

Investment allocations should follow lines of (potential) comparative advantage. This is obviously difficult to predict in advance. But there seems no general ground for assuming that the advantage will always lie in labor-intensive manufacturing. If this were true in a particular case, policies to promote objectives 1 and 4 would be counterproductive. The country should presumably import food, earning the necessary exchange by nonfood exports. But if the potential comparative advantage is in food production, a different allocation of resources is indicated. Myint surmises that agriculture will often turn out to be the true "infant industry" in the economy.

From these preliminary comments, I turn to an examination of alternative growth paths: primary export expansion, import substitution, and development of manufactured exports. What are the possibilities and limitations of these strategies? How far are they competitive in resource use? Should they be regarded, not as logical alternatives at a given moment in time, but as steps in a historical sequence, with import substitution providing a bridge from reliance on primary exports to development of a strong manufacturing sector?

GROWTH THROUGH PRIMARY EXPORTS

I am concerned here, not with the "engine of growth" controversy in general, but with the narrower question of how much reliance can be placed on primary exports as a source of import capacity. Views on this point have fluctuated greatly over time. To the classical economists, it seemed self-evident that primary products, whose supply is limited by scarce land and other natural resources, would become steadily more expensive relative to manufactures. A century later the sharp decline in primary product prices during the Great Depression produced a wave of "export pessimism" that lasted into the 1960s. By 1970 the "limits of growth" prophets were once more proclaiming the inevitable exhaustion of resource supplies. These models, developed mainly by natural scientists rather than by economists, usually contain no price system; but the implication is that primary products must become relatively more expensive, giving the whip hand to primary exporters. The success of the OPEC countries in raising crude oil prices fivefold seems to lend weight to this view.

Can continuing economic growth be sustained by reliance on primary exports? In this general form, the question is doubtless unanswerable. "It depends."

It depends, first, on the products in question. It is wrong to treat all primary products as a homogeneous category, just as it would be wrong to treat all manufactures in this way. Although some primary products face a low income elasticity of demand in the developed world, this is not equally true of all of them. Oil and mineral products are more hopeful than agricultural goods; and among the latter, livestock, poultry, feed grains, and temperate-zone cereals have better prospects than traditional tropical crops such as tea, coffee, and cocoa. But even tropical products have not done badly. Lewis notes that from 1955 to 1965 the physical volume of exports from tropical countries grew at the rate of 4.5 percent per year, about the same as the average growth rate of the OECD countries excluding Japan, and well above the 3.6 percent rate of export increase achieved in the "golden age" of 1883–1913. Over the whole period 1883–1965, a linear relation between the log of (tropical) agricultural exports and the log of (developed-country) industrial production, both measured in quantity terms, has a slope of 0.84. Agricultural exports did not grow as fast, but almost as fast.[11]

Moreover, export performance is not independent of what a country itself does. A recent GATT study[12] analyzing the export performance of fifty-eight LDCs from 1959 to 1965 divides them into "superior," "middle," and "inferior" groups. For each group they calculated (1) a *world market* factor, showing what each country's exports would have been had its exports changed only in response to changes in the world demand for its traditional exports; (2) a *competitiveness* factor, based on increases or decreases in each country's share of world

11. W. A. Lewis, *Aspects of Tropical Trade, 1883–1965* (Stockholm: Almquist and Wiksell, 1969).

12. Reported in Irving Kravis, "Trade as a Handmaiden of Growth: Similarities Between the Nineteenth and Twentieth Century," *Economic Journal* (December 1970): 850–72.

demand for its traditional exports; and (3) a *diversification* factor, equivalent to the ratio of the share of traditional exports in the country's total exports in the initial period to the share of the same products in the terminal period.

The performance of the "superior" exporters is interesting. Their world market factor rose 23 percent over the period (virtually the same as for the middle and inferior groups); but their export earnings rose 78 percent. The explanation lies in rises of 33 points in the competitiveness factor and 13 points in the diversification factor, compared with declines in these factors for the "inferior" group. Changes in the country's own performance, in other words, explained about two-thirds of the export growth of the "superior" countries. A country that is adept at moving out of unpromising and into more promising export products, and at lowering costs and improving competitiveness in those products, will do better than a less-innovative country. This is something that depends on oneself, not on the outside world.

Even if physical export volume rises at a good rate, may this not be partly or wholly offset by declining terms of trade? The classical view that the terms of trade must inevitably turn against manufactures persisted well into modern times. Commenting on the deterioration of Britain's terms of trade from 1900 to 1910, Keynes remarked:

> The deterioration—from the point of view of this country. . . is due, of course, to the operation of the law of diminishing returns for raw products which, after a temporary lull, has been setting in sharply in quite recent years. There is now again a steady tendency for a given unit of manufactured product to purchase year by year a diminishing quantity of raw product. The comparative advantage is moving sharply against the industrial countries.[13]

One may doubt whether recent arguments by Prebisch and others that the terms of trade must move in favor of the industrial countries are any more prescient than Keynes's earlier remark. One can, to be sure, find periods of a few years that show a marked movement in one direction or the other. But these periods may only constitute the kind of "temporary lull" to which Keynes referred. Over periods of fifty to a hundred years, statistical studies have found no evidence of a secular deterioration in commodity terms of trade for primary products.[14]

13. J. M. Keynes, *Economic Journal* 22 (1912): 630.
14. See Charles Kindleberger, *The Terms of Trade* (New York: John Wiley & Sons, 1956).

Even if such a tendency could be shown, deterioration of the commodity terms of trade is not necessarily an unfavorable development if it reflects productivity increases in the export industries. There may still have been an improvement in the factoral terms of trade and in real income.

The kind of primary product in question affects not only market prospects but also employment and income distribution in the export industry. Baldwin has noted the striking differences in numbers of workers employed per thousand dollars of annual product, ranging from 6.0 in tea (Ceylon) and 2.6 in rubber (Malaya) to 0.13 in copper (Zambia) and 0.03 in oil (Venezuela).[15] Agricultural export crops employ relatively large amounts of labor and use other imputs that can be produced mainly within the country. Thus, a large share of the money proceeds remain within the country, increasing the demand for locally produced food and for local as well as imported manufactures. Minerals, on the other hand, use mainly imported capital goods and (in the first instance) imported skilled labor, so that the contribution to domestic income may be small.

The amount of *returned value*, in Clark Reynolds's term, contributed to the local economy is also a function of government policy. In the Chilean copper case, Reynolds found that returned value as a percentage of output value rose from 30–35 percent in the 1920s to about 60 percent in the late 1950s.[16] This resulted partly from government-sponsored increases in wage levels but more importantly from direct and indirect government levies on the foreign-owned mining companies.

Much depends, also, on what proportion of the returned value is used for private and public investment. And this depends on the strength of the "internal engine of growth"—the existence of local entrepreneurship, capital markets, and a competent and growth-oriented government. Without these elements, the potential stimulus from export proceeds may run to waste.

So, it depends on the resource base, which may permit or severely hamper diversification of exports; on actual progress in diversification and cost reduction; on the organization and ownership of export

15. R. E. Baldwin, "Export Technology and Development from a Subsistence Level," *Economic Journal* (March 1963): 80–92.

16. Clark Reynolds and Markos Mamalakis, *Essays on the Chilean Economy*. A Publication of the Economic Growth Center, Yale University (Homewood, Ill.: Richard D. Irwin, Inc., 1965).

production; on the size of returned value and who appropriates this in the first instance; and on the capacity of government and the strength of the internal engine of growth.

Figure 2. Major Payments Flows in a Primary-export Economy

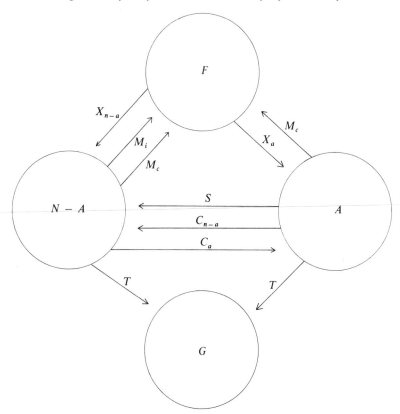

The main intersectoral-payments flows in a primary exporting economy are sketched in figure 2. (Commodity flows move in the opposite direction from the payments flows.) For simplicity, I have consolidated the industrial and traditional trade-service sectors into a single nonagricultural sector ($N - A$). Receipts from exports ($X_a + X_{n-a}$) are spent on imports of consumer goods, M_c, and capital goods, M_i. I show all imports of capital goods as going to the nonagricultural sector, but this is not important to the argument.

The two domestic sectors exchange food supplied by the agricultural sector, C_a, for goods and services from the nonagricultural sector, C_{n-a}. I assume that there is a net financial transfer, S, from agriculture to nonagriculture and that both sectors pay taxes, T, to government. The S flow does, and the T flow may, contribute to domestic capital formation.

In simulating with this sort of model, the growth rate of export receipts is very important. This rate depends, as noted earlier, not only on growth of world demand, but on developments within the exporting country. The higher the export growth rate, *ceteris paribus*, the higher the overall growth rate generated by the model. The pattern of growth will also be influenced by the composition of the export flow. For example, if exports are mainly agricultural products, the growth rate of total agricultural output would be expected to diverge above that of food output for domestic use.

Rising domestic income will induce expansion of domestic manufacturing capacity, as more and more industries reach the point at which the market will sustain at least one efficient-sized plant. The logic of this natural import substitution has been explained by Hirschman; and there is a sizable statistical literature on the sequence in which new industries appear on the domestic scene. Under outward-looking and nonprotectionist policies, however, the appearance and survival of new industries depends on their ability to meet world price levels plus transportation costs. This cannot be taken for granted. Effective competition depends on a supply of local or imported entrepreneurship, effective borrowing of technology, and fairly rapid development of labor skills.

The domestic industrial sector expands, not only through displacement of imports, but also through encroachment on handicrafts and on household production of Z-goods. Thus, one would expect that factory-produced goods would constitute a rising share of consumer-goods consumption and that, within factory production, the domestic proportion would be rising and the proportion of imports falling.

A contrary conclusion is reached in the Fei-Paauw analysis of Southeast Asian development, which treats Malaysia and Thailand as exemplifying a neocolonial pattern of dependence on primary exports. They argue that, even if export income is rising, inducing investment in expansion of domestic industry, imports of manufactured goods will rise even faster and will form a growing proportion of total consumption of manufactures. This result they regard as a "reversion to enclavism," a dead end in terms of domestic development.

Industrialization will founder whether or not primary product exports expand. This dilemma is easy to explain; for, after all, neo-colonialism is merely a new variant of the old colonial systems which we know from experience was not a growth type conducive to industrialization. . . .

The major disadvantage of neo-colonialism is that it does not offer a significant departure from colonial land-based growth nor the prospect of rapid labor-based industrialization. Even where primary product exports grow at a satisfactory rate, momentum toward industrialization is impeded by import competition and freedom for capital flight.[17]

These results are achieved, however, within a highly simplified model. The economy consists solely of a primary exporting sector and a factory-type manufacturing sector. Manufacturing output grows in strict proportion to the capital stock—no learning by doing, no technical progress. Manufacturing output, moreover, consists of a single good, with a single demand schedule, domestic price, and world price. At the outset, the price of the domestically produced good is well below the world price level. As domestic income rises because of rising export proceeds, domestic industrial output does *not* rise for the time being. Instead, the price level of domestic manufactures rises until it hits a ceiling set by the world price. At this point, imports come flooding in. Although domestic output continues to rise at a rate governed by domestic investment, imports rise even faster.

This discouraging result, however, arises from the peculiar features of the model, and there is no reason to take it as characteristic of real-world conditions. Even in the two neocolonial cases studied by Fei and Paauw, the proportion of industrial goods consumption supplied by domestic production rose quite sharply in Malaysia from 1962 onward, from less than 40 percent in 1962 to more than 50 percent in 1967. In Thailand the ratio, after stagnating at around 60 percent through the 1950s and early 1960s, turned sharply upward in 1965.

Under this growth path, it is probably true that, at least for a time, factory industry will grow more slowly than it would under import substitution policies. But this does not necessarily mean that the

17. Paauw and Fei, *The Transition*, pp. 70–71.

growth of total output will be slower. Nor is it clear how far import substitution and primary export expansion are conflicting or competitive policies.

Competition might exist with regard to *resource use* or *income incentives*. As for the former, export expansion does not necessarily take resources away from industrial development. In a labor surplus situation, there need be no competition for labor supply. Nor does expansion of agricultural exports typically require large amounts of private capital. There is competition within the governmental budget, since money spent on agricultural research and extension and on rural infrastructure is not available for other purposes. There may also be competition for the attention of government. Administration is a scarce resource, and a focus on the export sector may interfere with effectiveness in other directions.

The two lines of policy clearly are competitive with regard to income distribution. The essence of import substitution policy is to make manufacturing profitable by turning the internal terms of trade against agriculture. But a reduction in the farmers' real return per unit of output will also reduce their incentive to expand production for the market. The strength of this effect is uncertain, but its direction is not.

GROWTH THROUGH IMPORT SUBSTITUTION

The idea that the route to economic independence and progress lies through accelerated industrialization behind a protective wall has a long history in economic thought and practice. The United States was a highly protectionist country from the early nineteenth century until the 1930s; and most of the other mature economies were also protectionist during the early stages of their industrialization. (They are not, therefore, on strong ground in urging free trade on today's LDCs!)

An initial question, then, is: What's new about import substitution? Is it simply another name for traditional infant industry arguments? Or are there new pros and cons to be considered?

While there are traditional elements in contemporary protectionist thought, there are also new arguments related both to differences in the economic situation of today's LDCs and to recent developments in economic theory. Let me outline five such arguments.[18]

---

18. For a good review of this area, see Myint, *Economic Theory* chap. 6, "Infant Industry Arguments for Assistance to Industry in the Setting of Dynamic Trade Theory."

1. Assume a labor surplus economy in which workers can be employed in new industries without reducing output in other sectors. Assume also that capital goods are freely available from abroad through government-to-government grants. Under these conditions industrialization is costless to the domestic economy, and the value added by the new industries is a net addition to national output. (It does not follow, of course, that the new products need to be consumed domestically. They can be exported.)

These conditions, to be sure, are never realized completely. Rural workers are at the outset unskilled in factory work. The education and training needed to produce a stable, efficient factory labor force and provision of the housing and other amenities required to transplant workers from country to city involve resource costs. Thus, the shadow price of factory labor is not zero, though it may be below the private wage. Again, there may be a substantial grant element in government-to-government loans, but this is rarely 100 percent. These considerations weaken the force of the "costless industrialization" argument.

2. A closely related argument involves the discrepancy between the private and social cost of factory wage earners. Although the marginal product of agricultural laborers may be low, what they actually receive —in a family farm setting—is the (higher) *average* productivity of labor. Further, to induce them to transfer to industry, the industrial wage must be substantially above what they receive in agriculture; and maximizing employers will hire only up to the point at which the marginal productivity of industrial labor equals the wage. The resulting gap between labor's marginal productivity in the two sectors reflects a misallocation of labor, which can be corrected by subsidizing the disadvantaged industrial sector.

Three comments should be made on this argument. First, it presumably applies to densely populated countries. In the rather thinly populated countries that still constitute most of the LDCs, one cannot presume a low MP_L in agriculture and a large intersectoral wage gap. In the African case, it has been argued that the effect of a large subsistence sector was to lower rather than raise the supply price of labor to the mines and plantations. Migrant laborers attracted to these "modern" employments still had a foothold in the tribal village and could accept a low money wage because it was not their primary source of income.

Second, labor is not the only factor of production. It is usually thought that capital markets are distorted in the opposite direction from labor markets, interest rates to industry being held artificially low while rural interest rates remain high. Thus, it is not necessarily true that industry is disadvantaged in terms of total costs.

Third, it is now accepted in trade theory that tariff protection is an inefficient method of offsetting factor market distortions and that the preferred method is to correct such distortions at the point where they occur—for example, by subsidizing "unduly" high industrial wage rates. There are obvious political difficulties in applying this prescription, however, and so second- or third-best methods may continue to be used.

3. A third line of reasoning involves the minimum efficient scale of production and the input-output relations among industries. The unit costs of, say, a proposed steel mill will depend on the size of the prospective market. But the size of the market depends on how many steel-using industries will be established in the near future. Thus, investment in a mill geared to the present known market might appear unprofitable. But simultaneous investment in a complex of, say, a power plant, an iron-ore mining enterprise, a steel mill, and two machinery factories might pay off.

The importance of interindustry linkages has been emphasized by Hirschman as well as by Chenery and other writers on development programming. In the writings of Chenery, this idea appears mainly as an argument for government initiative and planning in the industrial sector, to overcome the myopia of private investment decisions.

4. The previous point stresses external effects in production, but another line of reasoning stresses external effects in demand. This is the "balanced growth" argument, stated forcefully a generation ago by Ragnar Nurkse. If, in a small and stationary economy, one sets up an efficient-sized shoe factory, the market may prove too small to absorb the output. But, if one could set up simultaneously a wide range of consumer-goods industries, the workers in one plant would buy the products of the others—that is, supply would create its own demand, in Say's Law fashion.

There are several difficulties with this argument. First, it does not explain where the resources are to come from for a massive burst of investment on all fronts. As Hirschman pointed out, it amounts to saying, "If we could suddenly create a new economy on top of the old one, the new structure would be self-sustaining." But this is a utopian vision rather than a feasible program. Second, there seems no reason why growth should be balanced only within the manufacturing sector.

Indeed, a viable growth path must involve an appropriate expansion of agricultural output, economic infrastructure, and government services. The problem of efficient resource allocation among these competing uses still remains. Third, the "balanced growth" concept makes sense only under closed-economy assumptions and is thus relevant to only a few very large countries. For most economies, unbalanced growth, in the sense of a divergence between output and consumption patterns, is both characteristic and (potentially) efficient.

5. A final argument, invoked particularly in Latin America, involves balance-of-payments considerations. The typical LDC, it is said, can expand primary exports at only a moderate rate, say 4 percent a year. But the government wishes the economy to grow at 5 percent, and this may involve an even higher rate of increase in imports. The propensity to import consumer goods is high and, in addition, an industrializing economy must import large amounts of capital goods, fuels, raw materials, and intermediate products. Thus, a balance-of-payments gap develops, which can be closed only by import restrictions. These serve the further purpose of sheltering the growth of domestic industries and gradually reducing the need for consumer-goods imports.[19]

How much these arguments add to traditional reasoning is not clear. At bottom, the urge toward import substitution still rests largely on infant industry considerations, the natural desire of nascent industrialists to invoke protection as a source of profits, and the notion that manufacturing is somehow superior to agriculture as an economic activity. Because, however, many countries will continue to employ protectionist policies, let us look briefly at the techniques used and at their economic consequences.

The essence of import substitution policy is to make domestic manufacturing profitable. The available instruments are *exchange rate policy*, *inflation*, and *import restriction* (which we shall interpret as tariff protection, since import quotas can be converted to a tariff equivalent.) As a matter of arithmetic, these can be substituted for each other—that is, the same degree of profit transfer to industry can be achieved via different policy packages.[20] The economic effects are not identical, however, and there may also be political reasons for preferring one package over another.

19. It is now familiar, however, that the saving in foreign exchange is less than appears on the surface because of increased imports of capital goods, fuels, and intermediate products for the enlarged manufacturing sector. On this point, see Carlos Diaz Alejandro, "On the Import-Intensity of Import Substitution," *Kyklos* 17 (1965): 495–509.

20. This is thoroughly analyzed in Paauw and Fei, *The Transition*, chap. 3.

Maintenance of an overvalued exchange rate taxes exporters for the benefit of importers. Because there is excess demand for foreign exchange at the official rate, exchange rationing becomes necessary; and those who receive allocations of exchange enjoy a windfall profit. To be extent that domestic manufacturers are able to buy capital goods and intermediate inputs at (in terms of local currency) artificially low prices, their profit margins are raised. To the extent that consumer goods imports are allowed, trading profits are raised.

Domestic inflation, with a fixed exchange rate, increases the squeeze on exporters and the profit transfer to importers. It is apt to be attractive partly because the mechanism is less obvious than if the exchange rate itself were adjusted to be unfavorable to exports.

Tariff protection, by raising domestic prices of manufactures relative to world prices, further increases the opportunity for profit. Its effects are additive to those of an overvalued exchange rate. It differs from the latter, however, in two respects. First, it is easier to use such protection differentially, to offer more encouragement to some industries than to others (though exchange quotas could also be manipulated for this purpose). Further, it brings in revenue to government. (The exchange control system could also do this via differential buying and selling rates or via an exchange auction; but to the extent that this is done, the profit transfer to industry is reduced.)

The fact that different policy packages may be close economic (but not political) substitutes for each other has been emphasized by Soligo.[21] "A system of offsetting export subsidies and import tariffs is a substitute, in the sense of producing the same trade effects, for a change in the official exchange rate. In fact, there exists an infinite set of combinations of official exchange rates, coupled with tariffs and subsidies, which can produce the same effective exchange rate." He then demonstrates that, as the official value of the Pakistan rupee is reduced (combined with an offsetting adjustment of taxes and subsidies), there is a reduction in: (1) government revenue; (2) the (nominal) national savings rate; and (3) the percentage of domestic capital formation apparently financed from domestic sources rather than from foreign aid.

The highly overvalued exchange rate is politically attractive precisely because it inflates the government budget and the national savings rate, reduces the country's apparent dependence on foreign aid, and

21. Ronald Soligo, "Real and Illusory Aspects of an Overvalued Exchange Rate: The Pakistan Case," *Oxford Economic Papers* (March 1971): 90–109.

veils the real resource transfer from agriculture. The disadvantage is that it also conceals and confuses the policy alternatives. The policy makers end up deceiving themselves along with the public!

Especially in a country of substantial size, import substitution can cause industries to appear earlier than they would under the "normal" sequence of industrialization; and it can (at least temporarily) accelerate the growth rate of manufacturing output. But this does not mean that it raises resource productivity in the country or increases the aggregate growth rate. Most research studies have been quite critical of import substitution. The criticisms are partly of the policy itself, partly of the ways in which it is commonly applied.

A common defect is that protection, investment allocations, and other forms of encouragement are provided, not to a limited number of the most promising "infants," but to any and all branches of manufacturing. Studies of Argentina, for example, show little relation between indicators of comparative advantage for a particular industry and the degree of governmental stimulus it received. Similar results have been obtained by Krueger for Turkey and by Lewis and others for Pakistan. At the extreme, one finds cases of "negative value added," that is, cases in which the value of inputs exceeds that of outputs at world prices.

Analysis of international productivity differences in manufacturing is only in the early stages. But such work as has been done—by Diaz for Argentina, by Nelson and others for Colombia—indicates that the productivity gap between developed and less developed countries varies greatly among branches of manufacturing. To ignore such differences through indiscriminate industrialization is to court serious inefficiency. As Balassa points out,

> We cannot accept as a criterion of success the fact that the structure of manufacturing industry in countries following an inward-looking strategy approaches that of the industrial nations. . . . The industries in question generally use backward technical methods, manufacture products of low quality, and have not achieved the degree of intra-industry specialization that is desirable under modern condition. . . . One may say that countries pursuing inward-looking policies have built up an industrial structure which is "prematurely old" in the sense that it is based on small-scale production with inadequate specialization and outdated machinery.[22]

22. Bela Balassa, "Growth Strategies in Semi-Industrial Countries," *Quarterly Journal of Economics* 84 (February 1970): 45.

The exchange control system is often operated in a way that encourages additional inefficiency. Emphasis on plant expansion can lead to a situation in which foreign exchange availabilities do not permit importation of enough inputs to operate these plants at capacity. If allocations of import permits for materials are based on installed capacity, overconstruction of capacity is encouraged. There is evidence from some LDCs that industrial capacity is operated less intensively than in the MDCs (single-shift operation, for example, is widely prevalent), whereas one would expect capital scarcity to produce the opposite result.

Even if the control system were more rational than it is, the import substitution approach has inherent limitations. The benefits conferred on industrial producers are mainly at the expense of exporters, who are penalized by the overvalued exchange rate and by the high domestic price of protected manufactures. This discourages production of export goods. Thus, apart from any limitations of foreign demand, export expansion may be slowed down from the supply side. Export pessimism, often urged as a reason for import substitution, can readily become self-fulfilling.

Over the long run, of course, these disadvantages may be ameliorated by improvements in industrial efficiency that bring costs and prices down to the level of world competition. But the hothouse atmosphere of protection, where profit margins are guaranteed, reduces the incentive for efficiency improvements. Experience suggests that efficiency improves only when profit margins are threatened by a lessening of protection or in some other way.[23]

Finally, import substitution necessarily comes to an end. The extent of import substitution achieved at any time can be measured in either of two ways: by the percentage of foreign exchange allocated to the purchase of capital and intermediate goods as against consumer goods, or by imports of manufactured consumer goods as a percentage of domestic consumption of manufactures. The former percentage cannot

23. A case that has been analyzed extensively is that concerning the expansion of manufacturing in Puerto Rico since about 1950. Wage rates were initially far below the U.S. level and permitted large profits with little managerial effort. The stimulus to efficiency improvements in this case came from a rapid forcing up of wage levels under the minimum wage system. The main response was not capital-labor substitution but greater managerial effort, which raised man-hour output in line with the wage increases and came close to maintaining previous profit rates (on equity capital). For a detailed discussion, see L. G. Reynolds and Peter Gregory, *Wages, Productivity, and Industrialization in Puerto Rico* (Homewood, Ill.: Richard D. Irwin, Inc., 1965).

rise above 100, nor can the latter fall below zero.[24] So, although domestic output of manufactures can for a time rise faster than domestic consumption, this growth rate must eventually fall to that of the domestic market—unless the country can shift to an export position in manufactures, a possibility to be considered below.

The extent to which the possibilities of import substitution have been exhausted varies widely from country to country. Lewis asserts that a number of countries—Pakistan, Egypt, several Latin American countries—have about reached the limit with regard to light manufactures.[25] Overall, however, he estimates that about $4 billion a year in LDC imports of light manufactures, or about 55 percent of total imports in this category, are still substitutable. Moreover, the LDCs spend about $7 billion a year to import machinery and other heavy industry products, much of which money could be saved by moving further into heavy manufacturing.

Although import substitution still presents physical possibilities, and on occasion some economic advantage, the tone of discussion in the past decade has become increasingly critical.[26] There is now much agreement that inward-looking policies have often been applied too strongly and too indiscriminately, to a degree that has hampered economic progress instead of promoting it, and that countries pursuing less restrictive trade policies have in general fared better.

GROWTH THROUGH MANUFACTURED EXPORTS

A key indicator of successful development is the ability to compete in the world market for at least some types of manufactures, evidenced by a rising share of manufactures in the country's export total. This gradual replacement of primary exports by manufactures has been termed *export substitution*. A country that has reached this stage,

24. The rate at which the domestic market for manufactures will be used up and the limits of import substitution reached is analyzed for a simple model in Fei and Paauw, *The Transition*, chap. 3.

25. Lewis, *Aspects of Tropical Trade*.

26. See, for example, Ian Little, Tibor Scitovsky, and Maurice Scott, *Industry and Trade in Some Developing Countries* (New York: Oxford University Press, for the OECD, 1970) and the supporting country monographs; Myint, *Economic Theory*, chap. 12, "The Inward and the Outwrd-Looking Countries of Southeast Asia"; Bela Balassa, "Growth Strategies in Semi-Industrialized Countries, *Quarterly Journal of Economics* 84 (February 1970); and Balassa, "Trade Policies in Developing Countries," *American Economic Review* 61 (May 1971); also Henry Bruton, "Productivity Growth in Latin America," *American Economic Review* (December 1967).

whatever its per capita income level, is well on the way to mature-economy status.

It is often said that it is difficult to break into the world market for manufactures in competition with well-established industries in the more developed countries. But this is how the world looked to the French in 1825, when Britain's domination of textile and iron exports seemed unchallengeable. In 1880 Japan faced a half dozen major manufacturing nations, yet within a few decades she had managed to join this select group. No developing country, with the possible exception of Britain from 1750 to 1800, has ever had the field to itself.

Further, the European latecomers and Japan did not develop export capacity by forcing their way into the home markets of other major exporters. France and Germany did not invade the British market on a significant scale, nor did Japanese manufactures find their way mainly to Europe and the United States. Rather, new exporters competed with earlier ones mainly in third markets; and this route remains open. LDC exports of manufactures may in the first instance find their way mainly to other less developed or semideveloped countries rather than to the OECD group.

The export substitution stage might be regarded as following logically from a prior stage of import substitution, during which industrial capacity was developed to serve the domestic market. Except for the atypical city-states, such as Singapore or Hong Kong, one would not expect export industries to appear suddenly in a previously nonindustrial setting. Rather, as Linder suggests, exports develop normally as a spillover from successful domestic performance.

But there is a contradiction here. I noted earlier that the protectionist atmosphere of import substitution is unfavorable to efficiency. More-over, the measures used penalize *all* exports, manufactures as well as primary products. How can industries that have been developed in such an atmosphere become internationally competitive? It is feasible to make the transition from an inward-looking to an outward-looking industrial sector?

That the transition is not easy is evidenced by the small number of countries that have succeeded in making it. Looking at such documented cases as Taiwan, South Korea, and Spain, one notes several favorable background circumstances: (1) a good supply of indigenous entrepreneurs, without the racial cleavages found in many LDCs; (2) a ready supply of potential industrial workers (from the rural sector in Taiwan and Korea, from returning emigrant workers in the case of

Spain); (3) geographic and economic proximity to major export markets (Japan and the United States in the cases of Taiwan and Korea, the E.E.C. countries in the case of Spain); (4) an easy balance-of-payments position (large agricultural exports from Taiwan, large foreign capital inflows to Korea, a booming tourist industry in Spain).

A major catalytic agent in these cases was a new policy package designed to remove penalties on exports and introduce new export incentives. This happened in 1958 in Spain, around 1960 in Taiwan, and around 1965 in South Korea. The main steps taken were: (1) a substantial currency devaluation and substitution of a unified for a multiple exchange rate; (2) liberalization of import quotas and reduction of tariff rates; and (3) a variety of export incentives. In Taiwan, for example, these included creation of duty-free zones; rebate of customs duties and indirect taxes on imported inputs for export products; reduction of the corporate income tax on export earnings; loans at low interest rates; export insurance; a government institute for market research; and a direct subsidy to some industries, administered through manufacturers' associations.

The response of industrialists to these incentives was strong and rapid. Manufacturing output, exports, and productivity rose at spectacular rates during the 1960s.[27] One cautionary note, however, should be added. Export promotion, like import substitution, can be inefficient when applied across a wide range of industries that differ markedly in potential comparative advantage. The accepted principle is that the marginal domestic resource cost of earning a dollar of foreign exchange should be equated across industries and also to the marginal resource cost of saving a dollar of foreign exchange. This principle, often violated on the import substitution side, is now being violated in varying degree on the export promotion side. In South Korea, in particular, the domestic resource cost of some export products is unreasonably high.

It is perhaps a truism to say that, in a developing world economy, one should expect a gradual diffusion of manufacturing—and parti-

---

27. For documentation, see J. B. Donges, "From an Autarchic Toward a Cautiously Outward-looking Industrialization Policy; The Case of Spain," *Welwirtschaftliches Archiv* 107 (1971): 33–72; Bela Balassa, "Industrial Policies in Taiwan and Korea," *W. W. Archiv* 106 (1971): 55–76; chapter on Taiwan in Paauw and Fei, *The Transition*; and John C. H. Fei and Gustav Ranis, "A Model of Growth and Employment in the Open Dualistic Economy: The Cases of Korea and Taiwan," mimeographed (New Haven: Yale Economic Growth Center, 1972).

cularly of labor-intensive manufacturing—throughout the world. As Harry Johnson has suggested:

> To the extent that techniques of production can be taken to be either the same or potentially similar in the different countries, ... industries can be ranked globally by their average labor productivities, and the results will show those industries—the high labor-productivity industries—in which the capital-rich labor-scarce economies will have a comparative advantage, and those—the low-labor productivity industries—in which the labor-abundant capital-scarce economies will have a comparative advantage; and hence the results of the ranking of labor productivities by industry can be used as a predictor of and guide to policy for the evolution of trade patterns in a developing world.[28]

Johnson argues further that comparative advantage changes systematically over time in the following manner. In the more developed countries, the cost of labor time is rising, both absolutely and relative to the cost of capital. This stimulates labor-saving innovations. In addition, rising income levels stimulate development of new products adapted to higher incomes. These new products—both consumer and capital goods—will tend to be produced initially in the country of innovation and exported to other countries. But as the world market develops, and as production methods become standardized and routinized, there will be a tendency for production to shift to lower-cost locations. The wide and growing difference between rich and poor countries in the unit value of labor time provides a continuing incentive for such transfer. "The process of transfer will be associated with the 'maturation' of the innovated product, as actual or potential competition increases the elasticity of demand facing the producer and makes low production cost increasingly important, and as the routinization of production techniques reduces the necessity of close contact with specialist suppliers and consultants."[29]

The barriers to transfer are of two kinds. First, there are the impediments posed by restrictive trade policies in the developed countries, where effective tariff rates are typically highest on the most labor-intensive products. (This is also true of LDC tariff structures, ham-

28. Harry Johnson, "Comparative Cost and Commercial Policy Theory in a Developing World Economy," *Pakistan Development Review* (Spring 1969): 18 (Wicksell Lectures, 1968).
29. Ibid., p. 23.

pering their trade with each other.) Such barriers are understandable in political terms, since industries employing large numbers of workers have correspondingly large political influence (witness the southern textile case in the United States). But economic considerations suggest a policy of redeploying labor out of such industries in the developed countries.

Difficulties within the LDCs include shortage of managerial skills, institutional obstacles to enterprise, and inward-looking policies that penalize trade. Despite these difficulties, exports of manufactures from the LDCs have been growing much faster than those of primary products—and even a bit faster than exports of manufactures from developed countries.[30] The growth is on a small base, however, and is heavily concentrated by countries and by product lines. Just as in the case of primary products, there is a danger that pressing more of the same goods on reluctant buyers may depress prices and encounter political resistance. There is a need for diversification out of textiles and clothing into electronics, machinery, and other labor-intensive products. There are also substantial possibilities for trade among countries outside the OECD group.

The possibilities in this direction are suggested by the Spanish success story. Of thirty-five export commodities analyzed by Donges, eleven were bought mainly by the LDCs, including machinery and equipment. He concludes that semi-industrialized countries have a large potential for exporting capital goods to still less industrialized countries *and* entering the markets of the MDCs with goods that are in an advanced stage of the product cycle.

30. Lewis, *Aspects of Tropical Trade*; Hal Lary, *Imports of Manufactures from Less Developed Countries* (New York: National Bureau of Economic Research, 1968); Carlos Diaz Alejandro, "Some Characteristics of Recent Export Expansion in Latin America," in *The International Division of Labour: Problems and Perspectives*, ed. Herbert Giersch (Kiel: Institut für Weltwirtschaft, 1974).

8

The Open Economy:
Transfer of Capital and Technology

There is a long tradition of writing on international capital movements as well as on international trade. In the peaceful period between 1815 and 1915, such flows were substantial, occurring mainly through private capital markets. These capital transfers were regarded as a normal response to profit opportunities, requiring no special explanation. Expected profit rates, adjusted for risk, were high enough in the new areas relative to the European countries to call forth substantial private investment.

At the macro level, attention was concentrated on two questions. The first, the so-called transfer problem, asked how financial flows could lead to a real resource transfer to the borrowing country. The second involved the eventual need for repayment of principal and interest through a real resource transfer in the opposite direction. In this connection, there developed a "historical life-cycle hypothesis," portraying how a successfully developing country may move from "early debtor" to "mature debtor" to eventual creditor status.

All this was familiar doctrine before the World War II era, when decolonization created a large number of new potential borrowers. One might have expected that the borrowing problems of the new countries could have been readily assimilated into the existing body of thought. Instead, there has developed a large literature on the "economics of foreign aid." This differs substantially from earlier writings and has been associated with new institutional developments and policy issues.

INSTITUTIONAL DEVELOPMENTS BEARING ON CAPITAL TRANSFERS

Most basic is the different politico-economic situation of the new borrowers. The old borrowers (the United States, the British dominions, Argentina) were countries of substantial size, rich resources, literate populations of mainly European origin, stable governments—countries, in short, whose economic progress was never seriously in doubt. Income levels in these countries were from the outset well above the level of those in contemporary Africa and Asia. The new debtors, with few exceptions, are small in economic size, with a limited resource base, largely illiterate populations, low income levels, unstable governments, and uncertain development prospects, Capital is scarce and potential returns to investment may be high, but these returns are also highly uncertain and, after adjustment for risk, are not adequate to induce private capital transfers on the nineteenth-century scale.

The other side of the coin is the appearance in the mature economies of governmental and intergovernmental lending agencies willing to lend on concessional terms and assume risks that would deter private lenders—the appearance, in short, of the "aid business." Countries like Britain and France have ties of sentiment as well as economic interest to their former colonies, and they have made grants and low-cost loans on a substantial scale. The United States has a few quasi-colonies and has made loans and grants to many other countries either in the hope of achieving political influence or to finance American exports. Japan, Canada, China, the Soviet Union, and most of the European countries have also been substantial lenders. The United Nations makes grants for preinvestment surveys and technical assistance. The World Bank group has "soft-loan" as well as "hard-loan" windows and is now the largest single source of capital transfers.

Exports are still by far the largest source of foreign exchange for the LDCs; but capital transfers are also substantial. Until quite recently, "official" capital transfers from developed-country governments and multilateral agencies exceeded the private capital flow. But private capital has been growing in relative importance and is now about equal to official capital. To illustrate, in 1973 total LDC exports were about $108 billion, net loans and grants from official sources totaled about $12 billion, and the net flow of private capital was about $13 billion. Since 1973, the export proceeds of the LDCs have more than doubled, but this mainly reflects oil revenues flowing to a limited number of countries.

Official capital transfers are often referred to as *aid*; but this is a misnomer. Much of the government-to-government flow is on terms approximating those in the capital markets of developed countries. There are grants, however, and also loans that are "soft" with respect to grace period, repayment period, interest rate, or repayment in local currency rather than "hard" currency. (On the other hand, bilateral loans are usually tied to the purchase of products from the lending country, which prevents borrowers from shopping for lowest prices in the world market and thus reduces the real value of the loan.) Considerable effort has been spent on defining and estimating the grant proportion in particular loan transactions.[1] From these estimates it appears that the grant element in the public capital flow is of the order of one-third to one-half. It varies substantially from one lender to another. Horvath, for example, estimates the grant proportion for selected countries as follows: Austria 0.12; Switzerland, 0.12; France, 0.26; Japan, 0.26; Germany, 0.32; United Kingdom, 0.46; U.S.S.R., 0.52; Canada, 0.58; United States, 0.68; Australia, 0.90.

The size of the public capital flow, and the substantial grant element it often contains, raises problems of economic rationale for both borrowers and lenders.[2] A lending government has a budget constraint and, under full employment, a real resource constraint. A criterion is required to decide how much of a nation's resources should be diverted to foreign borrowers. Further, on the reasonable assumption of an excess demand for loans, there is a problem of allocation among potential borrowers. Political considerations apart, these criteria must run in productivity terms. This has stimulated research on why public capital transfers are productive to the borrower and how their productivity can be estimated.

The borrowing country also has an economizing problem. There are many potential lenders offering a spectrum of terms and conditions. So the borrowing country has a problem of efficient "debtmanship," of trying to minimize the discounted repayment cost of a given amount of capital. This problem does not bulk large in the literature, perhaps because most of the writing has been done by economists in the lending countries; but it must bulk fairly large in the internal memoranda of borrowing governments. The borrower must also estimate how much it can afford to borrow. This involves weighing the additions to

---

1. John A. Pincus, *Economic Aid and International Cost-Sharing* (Baltimore: John Hopkins Press, 1965); idem, "The Cost of Foreign Aid," *Review of Economics and Statistics* (November 1963): 360–67; Janos Horvath, "Foreign Economic Aid in the International Encyclopedia of the Social Sciences: A Review Article," *Journal of Economic Literature* (June 1971): 432–41; Göran Ohlin, *Foreign Aid Policies Reconsidered* (Paris: OECD, 1966).

2. See in this connection Wilson E. Schmidt, "The Economics of Charity: Loans *Versus* Grants," *Journal of Political Economy* (August 1964): 387–95.

national output against eventual repayment obligations and projecting the export earnings out of which these obligations must be met.

In loan negotiations, the borrowing country is usually required to demonstrate that the funds requested will in fact be used productively and that the prospects of repayment are good. Lending agencies have rules of thumb about the percentage of export earnings that can safely be precommitted to debt service; as the actual percentage rises above this norm, the country's chances of additional credit decline. Further, they often ask the borrowing country to submit an overall development program for, say, five years ahead, with particular emphasis on invest- ment allocations and the extent to which these require foreign financing.

All this has given a strong programmatic twist to post-1945 work on capital transfers. The object of earlier work was to explain capital movements ex post. Recent work has been largely ex ante, aimed at developing estimates of future capital needs that can be deployed to influence actual allocations.

This is related to the emphasis in development theory on capital goods as the prime requisite for economic growth. Capital, it is argued, is crucially important; but domestic sources of capital formation are insufficient to achieve a desirable growth rate. The argument sometimes goes that domestic saving is insufficient to finance the desired rate of capital formation, so that foreign finance is needed to close a *S-I* gap. Alternatively, it may be argued that the capital goods and intermediate inputs essential to industrial growth must be imported, and that export proceeds are insufficient to pay for these imports. Here, foreign aid serves to close an *M-E* gap. Let us look more closely into this reasoning.

THE "GAP" APPROACH TO FOREIGN AID

Consider first the simple macro model often used in national economic plans. In its most aggregative form, there are seven variables: Y, C, S, I, M, E, and A, where A is foreign aid and the other symbols have the conventional meanings.

The *accounting* or *balance* equations are as follows:

Total resource balance	$Y + M = I + C + E$
Income distribution balance	$Y = C + S$
Foreign exchange balance	$M = E + A$
Financial balance	$I = A + S$

This provides three independant equations, so four behavioral equa- tions are needed to determine the system. Some of these equations can simply be lifted from developed-country economics. Thus, a Keynesian savings function is usually assumed. Output is assumed, in the Harrod-Domar tradition, to increase in strict proportion to the capital stock. Other relations, however, appear *de novo* in the development literature. For example, it is usually assumed that it is politically necessary to achieve some target growth rate of total and per capita output. "Absorptive capacity" (for investment) is a similar concept, summarizing a variety of intuitive judgments about the economy and society. Interestingly, this is a total rather than a marginal concept. The marginal productivity of capital, instead of continuing to decline gradually, drops suddenly to zero when the limit of absorptive capacity is reached.

The number of possible behavioral relations exceeds the four that are required, so a choice is necessary, and this is a matter of judgment. Despite its appearance of precision, development planning remains an art.

The best way to see what judgments a planner is making is to examine which variables he treats as exogenous and which as endogenous. The key issue for present purposes is the treatment of the aid variable. Consider the following two cases.

Case 1 ("Needed-aid" model)

    Exogenous variables are : C, I, M, E

    Endogenous variables are: Y, S, A

Given the exogenous values, the system can be solved in three stage:

$$Y = C + I + (E-M)$$
$$S = Y - C$$
$$A = I - S$$

The exogenous variables are those regarded as "hard" or intractable:

A minimum rate of increase in consumption (C) is necessary for political reasons.

Investment requirements (I) are set by the assumption of a fixed capital coefficient.

Import propensities, which determine M, are fixed and unchangeable.

Export possibilities (E) are also fixed and unchangeable.

The endogenous variables, on the other hand, are judged to be "soft" or adaptable. Specifically, it is judged that the amount of foreign aid can be adjusted to needs. This is the generic type of all aid-getting models.

Case 2 ("Available-aid" model)

Exogenous variables are: C, I, E, A.

Endogenous variables are: Y, S, M.

The system is then solved as follows for the endogenous variables:

$$M = E + A$$
$$Y = C + I + (E-M)$$
$$S = Y - C$$

Here C, I, and E are intractable for the reasons given earlier. But in addition, the amount of aid is taken as fixed. So something else has to adjust. In this example, the adjustment comes through M, which assumes that import coefficients can be reduced as needed. Alternatively, one could treat E as endogenous, which implies that exports can be raised by policy measures.

Planning models, then, can be classified as needed-aid or available-aid models.[3] Most actual models are of the former type, since a major objective is to persuade potential lenders that some minimum level of foreign capital is essential.

These illustrative cases are helpful in understanding the more complex two-gap models developed by Hollis Chenery and others.[4] Let us look briefly at the kind of economy visualized in these models as well as the meaning of the two gaps and the "gap between the gaps."

The economy assumed in these models bears a strong family resemblance to our needed-aid economy in case 1. There is a politically determined target growth rate, treated as exogenous. There is a fixed incremental capital-output ratio. There is a minimum level of imports required to sustain a given level of GNP, set mainly by the need for imports of capital and intermediate goods. There is a maximum feasible rate of increase in exports. The economy is by implication a (largely) private economy, with an institutional structure favorable to growth acceleration.

3. For more detailed discussion of this point, with illustrations from the Pakistan experience, see John C. H. Fei and Gustav Ranis, *Planning Methodology with Special Reference to Pakistan's Five-Year Plan* (Karachi: P.I.D.E. Monograph no. 1, June 1960).

4. See particularly Hollis Chenery and Michael Bruno, "Development Alternatives in an Open Economy: The Case of Israel," *Economic Journal* (March 1972); R. W. McKinnon, "Foreign Exchange Constraints in Development and Efficient Aid," *Economic Journal* (June 1964); Hollis Chenery and Alan Strout, "Foreign Assistance and Economic Development," *American Economic Review* (September 1966); John C. H. Fei and Gustav Ranis, "Foreign Assistance and Economic Development: Comment," *American Economic Review* (September 1968).

The growth rate of the economy may be constrained in either of two ways: (1) a *savings constraint.* The level of domestic saving is below the investment level required, given the fixed capital coefficient, to attain the target rate of growth. There is an *I–S* gap; (2) a *trade constraint.* The target growth rate of GNP requires imports in excess of the assumed level of export earnings. There is an *M–E* gap.

Ex ante, there is no reason why these gaps need be equal. There will usually be a "gap between the gaps." The amount of foreign aid needed at a particular time is the amount required to close the larger of the two gaps. The function of foreign aid is to relax whichever of the constraints—the domestic savings constraint or the foreign exchange constraint—is binding at a particular time.

Although the gaps need not be equal ex ante, they must by the rules of national accounting be equal ex post. How is this equality achieved? Suppose, first, that the savings constraint is binding and that foreign aid is set at the level needed to close the *I–S* gap. This is more aid than would be required to close the *M–E* gap. This is a comfortable trade situation. The country can afford to admit nonessential imports, or it can relax on export promotion. Suppose, on the other hand, that the foreign exchange constraint is binding. Aid, set at the level needed to close the *M–E* gap, is more than sufficient to close the *I–S* gap. The practical implication is that savings efforts can be relaxed.

Chenery and Strout hypothesize that these distinctions are not merely typological but represent a chronological sequence of development. This is not asserted as a logical necessity but rather as a strong empirical tendency. A country's progress from the beginning of sustained growth until the happy day on which foreign aid is no longer required can be divided into three phases.

Phase 1. In the earliest period of development, the limit on growth is set by the country's "absorptive capacity," its ability to invest. Raising the investment rate involves improvements in managerial capacity and labor skills, which take time. As these improvements occur, the feasible level of investment rises, and the amount of foreign aid that can be used effectively rises with it. This phase ends when the investment rate reaches a level sufficient to sustain the target growth rate of GNP (say, a 15-percent investment rate, an ICOR of 3.0, and a 5-percent GNP growth rate). The target growth rate is thus a ceiling as well as a floor.

Phase 2. By the end of phase 1, the investment rate has been raised well above the domestic savings rate. The *I–S* gap will typically be larger than the $M-E$ gap, and the function of foreign aid is to fill the savings gap. The time path of aid requirements, then, depends on the marginal rate of domestic saving. Since the investment rate does not increase further, a marginal savings rate higher than the average rate will gradually reduce the $I-S$ gap and with it the aid requirement. Eventually, this gap falls below the trade gap, bringing phase 2 to an end.

Phase 3. In this phase, the trade constraint is binding, and the function of aid is to fill the $M-E$ gap. The problem arises from limited flexibility in the production structure of the LDCs. Both development of (new) export products and reduction of import requirements through import substitution take time. The trade constraint would not have to arise if countries could anticipate the necessary changes in their production structure and take timely action. But in practice, this seems to be even harder than raising the national savings rate; and this is why Chenery and Strout regard the trade constraint as the ultimate bottleneck on the way to sustained growth. Whether a country can achieve independence of foreign aid, and how long this will take, depends on the rate of increase in exports and on the marginal import coefficient. In order for the trade gap to be eliminated, either export growth must exceed the target growth rate of GNP or the marginal import ratio must be substantially less than the average ratio.

Before criticizing this schema, let us consider its potential uses. Suppose one could estimate the parameters for a particular country— particularly the marginal savings rate, the marginal import coefficient, and the rate of export growth—and could assume that these would remain unchanged over time. Then, one could determine whether the country would eventually become independent of foreign capital and could estimate how long this would take.[5] For countries not in the "hopeless" category, one could calculate the cumulative amount of foreign capital required up to the date of self-sustained growth. Doing this for all potential aid recipients would provide a check on the estimates of the need for foreign aid that have been made by UN agencies and private scholars.

The cumulative aid requirement of a particular country is positively related to its target growth rate. Therefore, choosing alternative growth

5. A trial run by Chenery and Strout for twenty-six countries, based on data for 1957–62, indicated that twelve countries met *both* the trade and savings criteria for eventual independence, nine met one of these criteria but failed on the other, and five failed both tests.

rates and calculating the cumulative aid required for each will provide an estimate of the marginal productivity of foreign capital.

One can then go on to solve a variety of optimizing problems. Suppose a lending country wants to allocate its aid budget so as to achieve the greatest increment in world output. Calculations for all potential recipients will indicate what allocation would equate the productivity of aid at the margin. Or, one can ask how aid can be timed to enable a country to reach self-sufficiency with the smallest cumulative aid bill. A "peaking" of aid in the early years is efficient, because the rapid growth of per capita income raises domestic savings, which reduces the aid bill later on. If one imposes a constraint on the annual aid bill, instead, it takes longer to achieve self-sufficiency, and the cumulative aid total is higher.

Thus, in addition to the growth paths outlined in chapter 7, there is a fourth such path, which might be labeled *foreign-aid dominated growth*. This is relevant mainly to small LDCs, where the inflow of foreign capital can be large enough to have a significant impact on the economy. Taiwan, South Korea, and Israel, for example, received large transfers from the United States during the 1950s and 1960s. Studies of the country distribution of aid indicate a strong negative relation between size of population and foreign aid per capita.[6]

The real-world applicability of the gap models, however, is less than may appear at first glance. In addition to data difficulties, which are serious, the assumptions used are far from reality. Particularly dubious are:

1. The concept of absorptive capacity, and the assumption that this capacity will rise steadily if foreign capital is available. This sweeps under the rug at the outset most of the sociopolitical problems of growth acceleration. Absorptive capacity resembles Rostow's "preconditions for growth" in that it can only be determined ex post and so lacks predictive power.

2. The assumption that capital formation is the key to development and that GNP grows in proportion to the capital stock. There is no empirical basis for this assumption. Incremental capital-output ratios in fact vary widely, by countries, by sectors within a country, and over

---

6. Benjamin Cohen, "The International Development of India and Pakistan," in *Economic Development in South Asia*, ed. E. H. G. Robinson and M. Kidrin (New York: St. Martin's Press, 1970); Thomas Birnberg, *Foreign Assistance and Economic Growth* (Berkeley: Institute for International Studies, University of California, 1968), Technical Report no. 10.

time. This is simply to say that the productivity of new capital is highly variable, depending on how it is allocated and managed. One can find cases in which a modest capital formation rate was accompanied by a high growth rate and other cases in which large capital transfers vanished like water in sand.

3. The concept of a savings gap, with investment tugging at the leash and being restrained only by the propensity to save. It is pertinent to note that this does not appear to have been true during the growth-acceleration phase of today's mature economies. The prevailing opinion among economic historians is that capital shortage was not a major bottleneck at this stage. Rather, the appearance of new opportunities for profitable investment called forth the necessary saving, much of which came from reinvestment of earnings. Some documentation of this point from British and Japanese experience will be presented in part 2.

I would hypothesize that in today's LDCs, too, the effective restraint on investment is weakness of profit incentives rather than insufficiency of finance. Public-sector saving, to be sure, is more important than it used to be and differs from private saving in important respects. Two serious defects of the gap models are their failure to draw any public-private distinction—or indeed any sectoral distinctions at all—and their treatment of total savings as fungible.

4. The implication that imported capital goods are necessarily a major component of total investment. It is noteworthy that more than half of all investment normally consists of physical structures—roads, dams, irrigation channels, housing, and commercial and industrial buildings. These embody local labor and (largely) local materials. Although bulldozers and other imported equipment can be used, the same results can usually be achieved by labor-intensive techniques. So the need for imported capital goods comes down largely to transportation equipment, power-generating equipment, and industrial machine tools.

5. The assumed constancy of the key parameters: the ICOR, the target growth rate, the marginal savings rate, the rate of increase in exports, the marginal propensity to import. But a central objective of development policy is surely to change these parameters in a favorable direction. Instead of saying, "Given these values of the parameters, so much aid is indispensable," one could equally well say, "Given a certain amount of aid, what changes in parameter values can the *country itself* make, and what will be the resulting growth rate?" The

Chenery-Strout analysis, indeed, does consider investment in trade-improving activities, which could alter initial parameters in a favorable direction.

6. Finally, the target growth rate, on which everything else in the model depends, is pulled out of the air. Popular pressure for higher consumption levels is doubtless operative, to a greater or lesser degree, even under authoritarian governments; but it is hazardous to specify a particular growth rate as necessary and sufficient to contain this pressure.

None of this is meant to deny the usefulness of capital transfers from mature to developing economies. Our objection is simply to mechanistic, aggregative models that purport to determine that a certain amount of foreign capital is essential and try to specify its productivity independently of local effort. Lending agencies in practice use, and are wise to use, more conventional criteria. Project loans are based increasingly on cost-benefit analysis, which has been considerably refined over the past generation. Broader program loans require an experienced banker's judgment of the would-be borrower's past performance and credit worthiness, which involves, among other things, a judgment of the economic competence of government. Such judgments will doubtless warrant a continuing flow of bilateral and multilateral loans and grants.

DIRECT FOREIGN INVESTMENT

Private capital flows to the LDC through a variety of channels. Short-term suppliers' credit is of substantial importance, and so is short-term lending by commercial banks. In particular, LDC borrowings in the Eurocurrency market have increased rapidly during the 1970s. Longer-term portfolio investment, the dominant type before 1930, has not entirely disappeared. Governments and public corporations in some LDCs are sufficiently creditworthy to market securities in New York and elsewhere.

The largest component of the private long-term capital flow, however, is direct investment by multinational corporations. We shall focus on this type of capital transfer, both because of its size and because of the controversies surrounding it.

What are the pros and cons of direct private investment from the standpoint of the *host* government? Assuming that private companies will act in their own interests, what should an LDC government do in its national interest?

We may begin by distinguishing between politically sensitive areas, such as public utilities or natural-resource industries, and less sensitive areas, such as manufacturing. One cannot expect that an independent country will allow public utilities and natural-resource industries to remain indefinitely in foreign hands. Public utilities are central to the economy, and almost everywhere outside the United States they are operated by public corporations. Oil and mineral extraction involve such major issues as the optimal rate of resource depletion, pricing and marketing strategy, and distribution of the foreign exchange proceeds. Company decisions are unlikely to coincide with national interest. A host government can regulate private activity, but it can do more if it is in full control. In such industries, then, nationalization of existing foreign holdings is only a matter of time. The main policy issue is the optimal technique of nationalization and the appropriate compensation for foreign owners.

Because of the limited market for manufactures in most LDCs, foreign private investment in that area is still small. Subsidiaries of U.S. manufacturing companies are found mainly in Britain, Europe, Canada, South Africa, and Australia, which offer large and relatively risk-free markets. But investment in the larger Latin American countries is growing quite rapidly; and as the markets of other LDCs increase in size, foreign investment in those nations will also become profitable. Even countries whose domestic markets are not large, such as Taiwan, can provide a base for export-oriented industries.

The tendency of private capital to flow toward areas of potential profit can be accelerated, retarded, or even prevented by LDC governments; the question is what such governments should do in their own interest. Proponents of private investment emphasize the following supposed advantages:

1. Transfer of capital, that is, of the ability to import capital goods and productive inputs. The impact on domestic investment, indeed, may be larger than the initial capital transfer. Raymond Vernon has estimated that "for every dollar transferred across the exchanges, another has been ploughed back from local earnings and two more have been raised from local capital sources."[7] How far this constitutes a net gain to the economy depends, however, on the assumed alternative. Would local entrepreneurs have been able to establish the same

7. Raymond Vernon, "U.S. Enterprise in the Less Developed Countries: Evaluation of Costs and Benefits," in *The Gap Between Rich and Poor Nations*, ed. Gustav Ranis (New York: St. Martin's Press, 1972), p. 216.

production facilities if the foreign company had not done so? Would the LDC government have been able to devote foreign borrowings to this purpose? Such questions can be answered only on a case-by-case basis.

2. Transfer of technology. The subsidiary is part of a worldwide organization with an accumulated stock of production know-how, which can now be used in the local market. The outcome depends on how far the company is able to retain the rents attributable to its superior technology and whether use of the technology leads to lower product prices, higher factor prices, or larger tax revenues to government. Moreover, as Harry Johnson points out, this is not the only possible form of technology transfer, and it may not be the most efficient form from the standpoint of the host country. It might be better to buy the know-how for a lump-sum payment and then place this knowledge—which has "public good" properties—at the disposal of all producers, domestic and foreign.[8] Institutional arrangements for such purchase are poorly developed, however, and transfer within a corporate organization may be better than no transfer at all.

3. Transfer of managerial skills. The management hierarchy is usually provided in the first instance by the parent company. Over the longer run, government can require training of local personnel in the relevant skills, so that foreign managers can be phased out over the course of time. This is not, however, the only possible technique of skill transfer. Managers and engineers can be sent abroad for training, as was done to facilitate the expansion of India's basic-steel capacity. Or foreign management consulting firms can be hired to advise on the installation of modern management systems.

Introduction into an economy of new enterprises with superior management has an indirect impact on management practices, even in unrelated industries, through informal diffusion of know-how, hiring away of management trainees in the new enterprise by other industries, and so on.

4. Transfer of labor skills. All employees of the new enterprise, from "common labor" upward, learn new job skills as well as the general routine of factory life. How far the company actually bears the cost of this training depends, as Becker and others have shown, on the nature of competition in the labor market and on whether the skills

8. See Harry G. Johnson, "The Efficiency and Welfare Implications of the International Corporation," in *The International Corporation*, ed. Charles Kindleberger (Cambridge: M.I.T. Press, 1970).

in question are specific to the enterprise or are transferable to other enterprises. Under LDC conditions, where a single firm often constitutes "the industry" and where opportunities for skill transfer among enterprises are limited, companies probably bear a larger share of training costs than would be true in a developed industrial economy.

5. Prices, profits, taxes. Why does a multinational corporation decide to invest in country X, instead of producing at home and exporting to country X? High tariffs, encouraging construction of "tariff factories" may be a sufficient answer. Even without protection, there may be important advantages in proximity to the local market. Richard Caves argues that foreign investment is particularly likely by large, oligopolistic concerns selling a differentiated product.[9] Such concerns have scarce knowledge about product characteristics and production and marketing techniques which, because of the differentiation feature, can be employed most effectively in close conjunction with the local market.

What one oligopolist can do, another can do equally. So the oligopolistic market structure prevailing for, say, U.S. drug production will tend to be reproduced abroad; and there, as here, it will lead to profits above the competitive level. Caves argues that the multinational oligopoly will tend to equate its rates of return in various countries (just as a national corporation within the United States will do for regional submarkets). Thus, there is a tendency for profit rates to be equalized among countries for the same industry—but not among industries in the same country.

How far the foreign concern is allowed to retain the profit thus acquired depends on tax policy. Through profit taxation, the host government can appropriate a share of the addition to real national output generated by the foreign company. Against this must be offset any tax concessions to the company, such as rebate of import duties on materials, postponement of income tax liabilities during a "tax holiday" period, low-interest loans, and other subsidies. It is quite possible for a country, in its eagerness to attract foreign capital, to make deals that involve a net revenue loss to the government.

Let us turn now to possible negative effects that have been advanced as reasons why foreign private investment should be discouraged or restricted.

---

9. Richard E. Caves, "The Industrial Economics of Foreign Investment," *Economica* (February 1971): 1–27.

1. Under very simple assumptions, it can be shown that capital inflow to a country will reduce the rate of return to domestic owners of capital and increase the rate of return to labor.[10] Such a redistribution of income might tend to discourage domestic saving and capital formation. If, however, the supply of industrial labor increases *pari passu* with the capital stock, this result need not follow. This might occur through immigration (in Macdougall's Australian case) or, in a typical LDC case, through labor transfer from the traditional sector.

2. To the extent that repatriation of profits is permitted, there is an adverse balance-of-payments effect. Particularly if foreign investment is channeled toward products of low international tradeability, it may be hard for the host country to increase foreign-exchange earning sufficiently to finance the remittances. Whether the balance-of-payments position is worse than if the foreign investment had never occurred, however, depends on what one assumes about alternatives. If the foreign investment displaces an equivalent amount of home investment that would otherwise have been made, the balance-of-payment effect may be negative. But if one assumes that, in lieu of the investment, the parent company would have continued to serve the LDC market by exporting, the balance-of-payments effect is certainly favorable.

3. Circumstances may arise in which the operation of the foreign concern produces an income transfer from nationals to foreigners rather than vice versa.[11] For example, in economies with chronic inflation, real interest rates are frequently negative. A foreign concern that borrows locally at such rates is receiving a subsidy. Moreover, "more capital" is better than "less capital" only if the additional capital is well allocated. With high tariff protection, activities can exist that *reduce* GNP, measured at world prices; and when profits of the foreigners are subtracted, GNP is reduced even more! Finally, in natural resource industries, the large foreign corporation may have a bargaining advantage over resource owners in the LDC and may be able to appropriate an unduly large share of the rents. Footloose

10. This argument was developed initially by Macdougall with reference to Australia. See G. D. A. Macdougall, "The Benefits and Costs of Private Investment from Abroad: A Theoretical Approach," in *Readings in International Economics*, ed. Richard Caves and Harry Johnson (Homewood, Ill.: Richard D. Irwin, Inc., for the American Economic Association, 1968).

11. See Carlos F. Diaz Alejandro, "Direct Foreign Investment in Latin America," in *International Corporation*, ed. Kindleberger.

manufacturing industries may also bargain for and receive excessive subsidies.

4. The foreign producer may tend to set up capital-intensive plants similar to those it operates in the home country. The effect may be to displace local small-scale and cottage industries with higher labor-capital and lower capital-output ratios, which are better adapted to local factor proportions.

5. The incursion of large, relatively efficient, foreign concerns may inhibit the appearance of local entrepreneurs. A process of locally based industrialization, though slower, might be preferable on political and social grounds. This involves questions of fact—whether the local entrepreneurs are real or mythical, how the tempo of industrialization would compare in the two cases, and so on—the answers to which will differ from country to country.

6. Finally, there is the argument that foreign investment produces a pattern of economic dependence, so that the nominally independent LDC is not actually so. Suppression of foreign investment is regarded as necessary to achieve genuine independence. It might be more reasonable to say that politicoeconomic independence in the world community depends on the achievement of high productive capacity, however this is accomplished. A poor country is necessarily dependent —on trade, aid, private capital, or something else—though it has some latitude in choosing its *pattern* of dependence.

These pro and con arguments do not dictate any general conclusion. They leave room for the possibility that direct foreign investment will injure the host country in some cases and benefit it in others. The outcome depends on what one assumes would have happened in the absence of the foreign investment and also on the policies of the LDC government. Some of the difficulties noted above—negative interest rates, inefficient tariff structures, unduly generous tax concessions, poor bargains over rents of natural resources—are not facts of nature. A competent, maximizing government may be able to secure gains from foreign investment. An incompetent or corrupt government may well allow its citizens to be exploited.

TRANSFER OF KNOWLEDGE AND TECHNOLOGY

Economic interaction between more and less developed economies is not limited to flows of commodities and finance. The mature economies have an accumulated stock of scientific, technical, and managerial knowledge; and, through research laboratories and universities, they have facilities for producing and disseminating additions to knowledge. There is a "technology shelf" embodied partly in physical capital goods, partly in the minds of production managers. It is often said that the possibility of borrowing technology gives latecomers to the development process an advantage that the pioneers of industrialization did not possess. But the problems involved in borrowing and adapting technology have not yet been thoroughly explored.

Transfer of Industrial Technology

The problems involved in the international transfer of agricultural technology were examined in chapter 4. We confine ourselves here to the rather different problems encountered in manufacturing and other branches of industry.

In industry, new technology is embodied partly in machinery and equipment—but also in scale of enterprise and in managerial methods. Diffusion of technology consists in the gradual superseding of small production units using traditional methods by new, larger-scale enterprises with modern equipment and methods.[12] The new enterprises may be branch plants of multinational corporations, but they may also be indigenous enterprises under private or public management. In the multinational case, diffusion of technology occurs within the corporate organization. In the other case, there are a variety of possible techniques: "turnkey projects," built and operated for an initial learning period by a foreign producer; use of visiting teams of engineering and management consultants; sending indigenous management personnel abroad for training; developing local training capacity for engineers and managers. The relative effectiveness of these techniques is an important question, on which there must by now be a good deal of accumulated experience, but which has been little discussed in the economic literature.

In semi-industrialized countries, the old and the new are usually in active competition. The population of manufacturing plants contains two subgroups: older craft enterprises and newer modern factories. The craft enterprises are relatively small, with employment in the

12. For a convincing argument on this point, illustrated by data from Colombia, see Richard R. Nelson, T. Paul Schultz, and Robert L. Slighton, *Structural Change in a Developing Economy* (Princeton: Princeton University Press, 1971), chap. 4.

range of 0–50, which may be near optimum scale for their technology. They have markedly lower capital-labor ratios, value added per worker, and wage levels. In Colombia, Nelson found that wage rates in the smallest enterprises in an industry were typically only 50 to 60 percent of wages in large factories. This situation, reminiscent of the Japanese "dual wage" system, arises partly because unionism and minimum wage legislation do not effectively cover the small plants.

How do the small enterprises survive? Partly by producing a different range of products from the factories, products in which labor-intensive techniques are more appropriate; partly by paying lower wages; and partly by being willing to accept less than the high profit margins that accrue to the large producers in a protectionist system. But over the years, they do not all survive. The percentage of manufacturing output coming from modern plants gradually rises; and technical progress occurs mainly through extrusion of the old by the new, rather than through progress *within* each size-class.

A problem much discussed in the development literature is how far industrial technology can be twisted in a labor-using direction, adapted to LDC factor endowments. Some degree of adaptation is usually desirable. But is it actually feasible? What do production isoquants look like? To what extent are new, more labor-using techniques discoverable by industrial research?

It is a reasonable surmise that, in most industries, the possibilities are limited and lie mainly in three directions: (1) use of additional labor in materials handling and other supporting operations, as against the central processing activities; (2) use of relatively old-fashioned equipment, perhaps through purchase of secondhand rather than new machines. An interesting example is the suggestion that LDCs should normally buy secondhand rather than new trucks and automobiles. Repair costs would be higher, and it would be necessary to train a corps of repair mechanics. But this would create employment, and the higher repair cost would be more than offset by the lower initial cost of equipment; (3) multiple-shift operation, which is not as widely used as labor surplus conditions might warrant.

A substantial impact on factor proportions can also be achieved through: (1) attention to the industrial mix in the economy, since, even within manufacturing, different industries have very different capital-labor ratios; and (2) retarding the elimination of smaller, more labor-intensive establishments within each line of production. This need not mean subsidization; but it usually does mean improved access to credit, technical information, and government regulatory agencies.

Optimal Educational Borrowing

In a developing economy, the demand for "high-level manpower" rises. There is a need for more doctors, scientists, engineers, teachers, business managers, public administrators, and technicians. The supply can be expanded by importing these skills or by training more indigenous practitioners. Training may involve either sending students abroad for training or expanding local training institutions. In the latter case, the supply of teachers is the critical bottleneck, and again there are the alternatives of borrowing teachers from the MDC's or of sending the LDC nationals abroad for training. Thus, in a specific case—say, agronomists—the import possibilities include import of agronomists for service in the country, import of educational capacity by sending students abroad to be trained as agronomists, import of foreign teachers of agronomy to permit enlargement of local training capacity, and the sending of local agronomists abroad for post-graduate training that will enable them to serve as teachers when they return.

These possibilities are not mutually exclusive. The problem is in what proportion they should be combined. There is also a problem of phasing. At the outset, it may be cheapest to rely heavily on educational imports, particularly if the mature economies are willing to make these available at low cost. But over the long run, any country will want to work its way toward educational independence through a program of import substitution. Given the long production period for professional and technical skills, this implies a long-term educational strategy.

Optimal strategy will naturally differ among countries and among types of skill. The economic considerations are the relative productivity of local as against foreign training, the relative costs of the two types of training, and the extent to which the mature economies are willing to share these costs.

It is natural for an American observer to think that training in his own country is more effective than that in the typical LDC. There is a larger corps of experienced teachers, a lower student-teacher ratio, better library and laboratory facilities, perhaps more rigorous standards of academic performance, and the advantage of mingling with American students accustomed to such standards. But there are considerations on the other side. The risks involved in selection of students are increased, since it is usually harder to evaluate foreign than domestic applications. Curricula adjusted to American institutions and skill demands may be less than optimal for LDC students (witness the chronic complaints about the irrelevance of training in Western economics.) Students lose the support of a familiar culture and family environment, which are favorable to good academic performance. They may also after some years become alienated from their country and decide to join the "brain drain."

The training cost per student-year will usually be substantially lower in the LDC setting. Students' living costs are much lower. Teachers' salaries will be lower (though this depends on whether imported teachers are a large component of the total). Student-teacher ratios are higher and, in a warm climate, there is less expense for physical structures and heating. Laboratory equipment and books will usually have to be imported and will be more expensive than in Europe or the United States; but overall, unit training costs will certainly be lower in the LDC.

A further consideration is the extent to which the more-developed countries are willing to share the costs of educational interchange. It makes a difference whether students coming from an LDC for training are supported on MDC scholarships, or whether the LDC must provide their tuition and maintenance out of foreign-exchange earnings. Again, it makes a difference whether MDC teachers and other professionals working in an LDC are supported by their home government or the host government. Thus, the strategy that involves the least cumulative cost to the LDC may differ from that which would involve the least cost from a global standpoint.

The LDC's strategy problem has a mirror-image on the MDC side. Suppose an MDC decides to grant a certain amount of aid to an LDC free of charge. How should this be allocated between contributions of physical capital and contributions of human capital? This involves estimating the real resource costs involved (for example, if some parts of the MDC educational system have excess capacity, the marginal cost of additional LDC students may be low) and also estimating prospective rates of return to the two types of capital formation.

This kind of problem has been less investigated than its intrinsic importance warrants. It is a reasonable surmise that there is under-allocation to human capital as against physical capital transfers, and that there is wide variance in the benefit-cost ratio for different educational programs. But we have no solid basis of information.

Economists have a responsibility here to their own profession. In most LDCs, there are far from enough economists to meet the combined needs of teaching institutions and government agencies. Domestic facilities for training and research in economics are inadequate, there is undue dependence on foreign economics texts that do not reflect LDC institutions and policy priorities, and so on. How can the economic expertise of the mature economies be deployed most efficiently to aid in repairing these deficiencies? Private groups such as the Ford and Rockefeller foundations have wrestled with this problem within their resource constraints. The U.S. government, with its much larger resources, has done relatively little. But do we know what ought to be done? We need more economic analysis of the problem of import substitution in economics.

The LDCs are exporters as well as importers of educated manpower via the brain drain of professional and technical people to North America and Europe. This is a complex phenomenon.[13] Salary differentials are only one of numerous stimuli to migration. The higher-education structures of some LDCs are not well adjusted to the nations' manpower requirements and may turn out graduates with little chance of employment. The maladjustment of the educational structure involves economic loss, but emigration of the educated unemployed does not. In scientific fields, the much better research facilities available in the MDCs may be as important as income differentials. Too, some of the educated migrants move rather than face political repression or victimization by their home governments.

It is not self-evident that the brain drain constitutes a problem. When an individual moves to a more highly paid job, there is a prima facie case that his productivity is also higher on the new job and that world output is increased. One can set up conditions, involving mainly deviations of private from social productivity, in which this would not be true; but it is unlikely that these conditions exist on a broad scale. There may, to be sure, be a loss to the country through emigration, but even this is not invariably true—witness the case of the unemployed Indian engineer. In this case, the loss arises from a maladjustment of educational capacity and can be corrected by action within the LDC itself. Where a scarce and valuable skill is lost, on the other hand, the LDC has a case for compensation by employers or government in the recipient country.

Discussions of this issue should probably focus on specific skills.

13. See the penetrating analysis of Harry Johnson, Hla Myint, and others in *The Brain Drain*, ed. Walter Adams (New York: The Macmillan Company, 1968).

The largest single flow, for example, and the one that has focused attention on the issue, is that of medical practitioners. In view of the very high population-doctor ratio in most LDCs, this undoubtedly does involve a welfare loss. The inflow of doctors to the United States has been stimulated by the relatively low domestic output of doctors and by the growing tendency toward specialization as opposed to general practice. This has had quantity as well as price effects: a rapid rise in doctors' incomes and many unfilled vacancies for hospital interns and residents as well as for general practitioners, especially in the smaller communities. The remedy, to the extent that a remedy is needed, lies in accelerated output of doctors in the United States and some reorientation toward family practice as opposed to surgery and other specialties. These trends are in fact underway, and it seems likely that the volume of medical migration will diminish along with the controvery surrounding it.

PART 2   EXPERIENCE

9

Growth Acceleration in Japan, 1868–1905

Among the countries that experienced growth acceleration before 1900, two are of particular interest: England, which was the first country to embark on modern economic growth during the period 1740–1800; and Japan, the only non-European country to be drawn into the nineteenth-century growth current. Because of its non-Western culture, its initial very low income level, and its early entry into modern economic growth, Japan is often regarded as a model for other developing countries.

Before looking very briefly at English experience, and more thoroughly at Japanese experience, we must ask what we are looking *for*. What are the central features of the acceleration phase that we should expect to show up in country time series? What are the main hypotheses suggested by the models examined in part 2? What, in short, is the linkage between the world of development theory and the world of historical experience? The amount of factual information that is available on a national economy—and especially on an older economy that has been extensively investigated—is so large that, without principles of selection stemming from analytical hypotheses, the investigator must sink beneath the sea of data.

INITIAL HYPOTHESES

The hypotheses outlined below are precisely that. The reader is asked to accept them, not as truths, but as guides to investigation. How far they are warranted by country experience will be reexamined at the end of chapter 14.

1. *Growth acceleration does not start from zero*. Close scrutiny, though usually dependent on fragmentary data, suggests that population, total output, and output per capita have all been growing at low rates for some time before the acceleration period.

2. *The initial conditions on which growth acceleration depends are mainly political.* They include a sense of national unity, effective maintenance of law and order, continuity of political leadership, an economic orientation of leadership, and some minimal development of administrative staffs. Most countries already have untapped resources of labor time, saving capacity, and business initiative. To mobilize and energize these resources requires mainly a favorable political environment.

3. *Growth acceleration is attended by systematic changes in the composition of output.* The hypotheses developed by Kuznets from mature-economy experience are generally familiar. In terms of output composition by sector of origin, the main changes are a secular decline in agriculture's share and a rise in the manufacturing-construction-public-utilities share. Changes in the composition of output by end uses include gradual rises in capital formation and in public consumption, with a corresponding decline in personal consumption.

4. *Sustained growth requires successful performance in the agricultural sector,* that is, a rate of increase in food output sufficient to accommodate population growth plus increased food demand per capita resulting from rising incomes. Under land-surplus conditions, this may be accomplished mainly by extension of cultivated acreage. But in some countries, and increasingly in all countries, it implies an increase in yields accomplished through land-saving innovations. The behavior of the rural-urban terms of trade is an important indicator of whether the demands on the agricultural sector are being met. Absence of persistent movements of the terms of trade in one direction is significant also as an indication of the economy's ability to reallocate resources in response to changing price signals.

5. *Manufacturing output grows in relative importance, and its composition changes in a predictable way.* Hoffman, Chenery, and others have identified a "normal" sequence of industrialization, dominated initially by industries processing agricultural raw materials and by consumer-goods industries of small optimum scale, with heavy industry growing in relative importance at a later stage. But how far and how fast a country moves through this sequence is influenced by the size of the national market; and the sequence can also be altered or accelerated by government policy. Small-scale production units predominate in the early stages of manufacturing growth and are only gradually superseded by modern factory units.

6. *There are systematic changes also in public revenue and expendi-*

ture. These include diversification of tax sources, a rise in total tax collections as a percentage of national income, a shift in expenditure allocations toward growth-promoting activities, and (particularly in modern times) a rise in public-sector capital formation as a percentage of total capital formation and of GNP.

7. *Sustained growth is accompanied by good export performance.* Exports become more diversified and will often rise faster than GNP. There are also systematic changes in the commodity composition of exports and imports. Although some foreign borrowing is normal during the growth-acceleration phase, large capital inflows are not a prerequisite for successful development. This is partly because capital itself is not as important a constraint as has sometimes been supposed.

8. *The main basis for a "growth typology" is to be found in foreign-sector performance.* There has been much discussion of whether developing economies can usefully be classified into distinct "types," and a variety of criteria for such a classification have been suggested. The most promising of these, we believe, involves differences in the size and importance of the foreign sector.

The main purpose of part 2 is to test these hypotheses against the experience of fifteen LDCs that have undergone growth acceleration since 1945. Hypotheses 1, 2, and 3 are examined in chapter 10, number 4 in chapter 11, number 5 in chapter 12, numbers 6 and 7 in chapter 13, and number 8 in chapter 14. Before setting out on this exploration, however, I propose in this chapter to look at these hypotheses in the light of Japanese experience and to comment on the issue of a "Japanese development model."

A WORD ON BRITISH EXPERIENCE, 1740–1800

The first draft of this book included a long chapter on the British experience. This chapter has been deleted in the interest of holding the book to reasonable length; but we include its summary comments, which are perforce presented here without adequate documentation. Those who wish to examine the British case more thoroughly will find the key references listed in the bibliography.

The directions of structural change in the British economy between 1740 and 1800 are summarized in table 1. These estimates, of course, are based on fragmentary and imperfect data, but they are probably of the right order of magnitude.

Between 1740 and 1800 the rural sector changed from a majority to a minority role in the economy, although growing substantially in absolute size. Note that, as late as 1800, about three-quarters of food output was what would today be called "subsistence production." The apparently anomalous decline of food marketings as a percentage of GNP is explained by the fact that, as of 1740, Britain was still a substantial food exporter. By 1800, however, the country had shifted to a net import position. Note also the continued prominence of cottage industry, which, partly because of widespread use of the "putting-out system," grew in absolute size throughout the growth-acceleration period.

In the urban sector, industry expanded substantially in relative terms and even more substantially in absolute terms; but handicraft production still overshadowed factory production. The private trade and services sector also grew in relative importance. Government output, always small, declined a bit in relative terms, contradicting our hypothesis on this point. The foreign sector, not shown explicitly in table 1, roughly doubled in importance, mainly because of a rapid growth of manufactured exports. The overall picture is one of gradual change, with an output composition in 1800 that was still almost half rural and contained only a small component of factory industry.

In sum, growth acceleration in Britain can be characterized as: (1) gradual, in terms of aggregate output growth, population growth, capital formation rates, and other structural changes; (2) balanced, in the sense of parallel expansion of economic sectors, with agricultural output running not too far behind domestic food requirements; (3) based on small-scale production, which dominated the economy throughout the acceleration period, with factory industry becoming

Table 1. Sector Composition of Output in Britain, 1974 and 1800
(Percent)

	1740	1800
Rural sector	(58)	(44)
Food for home use	32	24
Food marketings	10	8
Cottage industry	16	12
Urban sector	(42)	(56)
Factory industry	0	5
Small-scale industry	8	12
Government	6	5
Private trade and services	28	34
Total	100	100

important only when economic success was already assured; (4) capitalistic, in the sense of almost unfettered private enterprise, low tax rates, and small output of public goods; (5) unaustere, in the sense that savings rates were relatively low and per capita consumption was probably rising gradually from 1740 onward; and (6) internally generated.

This last characterization may seem dubious in view of the traditional emphasis on Britain's prowess as an exporter. But consider that Britain depended very little on capital-goods imports; that she was never dependent on foreign finance, and was on the contrary an early capital exporter; that the major innovations in power, transport, and manufacturing were home-produced; and that, even in the late eighteenth century, the domestic market was large enough to make these innovations highly profitable. Being first in factory production of textiles, and later of iron and steel products, was clearly an important advantage. But this is different from saying that growth was induced from abroad.

TRANSITION TO JAPAN

Japan provides an unusually interesting case of growth acceleration. Its initial conditions—income level, factor endowment, institutional structure—were closer to those of contemporary Asian countries than were the corresponding conditions in the European countries. The data on early modern growth in Japan have been analyzed by both Japanese and Western scholars, and the literature is richer than for any other non-Western economy.

It is necessary first to erase from our minds the image of contemporary Japan: the rapid tempo of growth, the very high capital formation rate, the widespread development of heavy industry, the flooding of the world with manufactured exports. These features were not present in the late nineteenth century. Our interest is in the years from the Meiji Restoration of 1868 to about 1905, by which time Japan had emerged triumphant in wars with China and Russia and was embarked on sustained growth. At some points we shall extend the story to include the years 1905–20, capped by the World War I boom, during which Japan profited from neutrality. After 1920, Japan was so clearly a growing, modern economy that the story loses interest from a development standpoint.

The evidence of growth acceleration between 1868 and 1905 is convincing. Ohkawa and Rosovsky divide this era into two subperiods: (1) 1868–85, a period of transition, beginning with the 1868 Restoration and the adoption of economic growth as a national objective and ending at the point at which accelerated growth is clearly visible. This period is dominated by institutional reform. Although statistical data are fragmentary, informed opinion is that income per capita was rising only slowly. (2) 1885–1905, the first of the "long swings" or "Kuznets cycles" that have characterized Japanese economic growth. The growth rate in this period is higher and better documented. Ohkawa and Rosovsky estimate that on the upswing of this cycle, from 1885 to 1898, real GNP rose at an annual rate of 4.3 percent. On the downswing, from 1898 to 1905, this dropped to 2.3 percent. (On the subsequent upswing, which peaked in 1919, the rate of GNP increase rose again to 4.2 percent).[1] With population growing at about 1 percent a year, the growth rate of per capita income was about 1 percentage point lower in each period.

The reality of growth acceleration is confirmed by other kinds of evidence. Population growth accelerated along with output growth. Agricultural output rose faster than population. Exports rose more rapidly than GNP, permitting the imports needed for industrialization. The composition of national output changed along Kuznetsian lines.

INITIAL CONDITIONS

Japan in 1868 was a traditional society, but it was an *advanced* traditional society.[2] It had a long experience of national unity and subordination to political authority, a well-developed system of roads and communications, a rather advanced agricultural technology (combined with considerable commercialization and habituation of the peasants to turning over a large part of their output as tribute), a relatively high literacy rate, effective methods of population control, handicraft workers turning out a wide array of consumer goods, and

1. Kazushi Ohkawa and Henry Rosovsky, "Postwar Japanese Growth in Historical Perspective," in *Economic Growth: The Japanese Experience Since the Meiji Era*, ed. Lawrence Klein and Kazushi Ohkawa. A Publication of the Economic Growth Center, Yale University. (Homewood, Ill.: Richard D. Irwin, Inc., 1968), p. 9.

2. The comments of this section draw heavily on Henry Rosovsky, "Japan's Transition to Modern Economic Growth, 1868–1885," in *Industrialization in Two Systems*, ed. Henry Rosovsky (New York: John Wiley & Sons, 1966); and E. Sydney Crawcour, "The Tokugawa Heritage," in *The State and Economic Enterprise in Japan*, ed. W. W. Lockwood (Princeton: Princeton University Press, 1965).

a rich literary and artistic tradition. In Rosovsky's terms," . . . society was more advanced than the economy, and this permitted rapid and efficient change preparatory to the massive induction of Western technology and organizations in the twentieth century."[3]

Growth at a modest rate had already been underway for several decades before 1868. Population was beginning to inch upward. Output was rising at perhaps 1 percent a year. Agricultural infrastructure, particularly in the area of irrigation facilities, was being strengthened. Progress was also occurring through selection of improved seed by expert farmers; but because of barriers to internal movement, these advances remained confined to the areas in which they occurred. The manufacturing monopoly of craftsmen attached to the Japanese court and the feudal lords was already weakening, and there was a diffusion of handicrafts throughout the countryside, providing considerable side employment for farm families. About 80 percent of the population in 1868 could be classified as (mainly) agricultural, and agriculture provided 60 to 65 percent of national output.

Japan's per capita income in 1868 was below that of the western European countries at the time of their growth acceleration. This can be inferred from the fact that, in the European countries, the agricultural population had by this time been reduced to between 50 and 60 percent of the total, so that the higher-productivity secondary and tertiary sectors carried greater weight in national output. Kuznets estimates that per capita income in Japan in 1868 was one-third to one-half that of the western European countries at a comparable stage of development.[4]

With somewhat less assurance, one can say that Japanese per capita income in 1868 was above that of Asian and African LDCs in 1950. Foreign travelers' accounts of a prosperous and contented peasantry, and of the wide array of consumer goods available in village stores, support such an inference. Japan thus embarked on modern growth from an "in-between position," neither as well off as the European precursors nor as poor as contemporary Asian-African economies.

The economy was already productive enough to provide a surplus over current consumption, which was potentially available for eco-

3. Henry Rosovsky, "What are the 'Lessons' of Japanese Economic History?" in *Economic Development in the Long Run*, ed. A. J. Youngson (London: Allen and Unwin, 1972), p. 233.

4. Simon Kuznets, "Notes on Japan's Economic Growth," in *Economic Growth*, ed. Klein and Ohkawa.

nomic development. Tsuru estimates that in the 1860s about 37 percent of the gross product of agriculture went to the feudal lords and
their retainers, about 25 percent to landowners, and only 38 percent
to the actual cultivators.[5] Crawcour estimates that 25 to 27 percent
of total national product went to the feudal lords and the court. Thus,
development strategy required not so much an enlargement of the
surplus as its redirection to productive purposes.

Commercialization was well advanced. Yamaguchi estimates that as
early as 1870 some 25 to 30 percent of farm output was marketed.
To be sure, the degree of commercialization varied considerably
among regions. In some remote prefectures, the marketed proportion
of output may have been as low as 10 percent, while in others it was
50 percent or more. Thus, farmers as well as villagers were no strangers
to the money economy.

Primary education in 1868 was more advanced than in the European
countries at a comparable stage of development. Education was
largely a private industry, provided by teachers on a fee basis. Demand
for education was high enough so that an estimated 40 to 50 percent of
boys, though only 15 percent of girls, received some formal education
outside the home. This education was of a relatively practical character,
including not only basic literacy but arithmetic, measurement systems,
and elements of bookkeeping and accountancy.

Japan had long been a unified country with a clear structure of
authority running from the shogun to the 300 or so feudal lords, and
from them to lesser retainers in their fiefdoms. So the Meiji Restoration,
although it changed the superstructure of government, involved no
problem of nationbuilding. The periodic migration of the feudal lords
to and from Tokyo, prescribed by the shogunate with a view to checking
local separatism, had already resulted in the establishment of trunk
highways and a communications system.

It can even be argued that the intrusion of foreigners after Perry's
1853 visit was favorable to Japan's future development. The establishment of foreign traders in the treaty ports helped change Japan from
an autarchic to a semiopen economy. The treaty of 1865, which
provided that Japanese tariff rates could not exceed 5 percent, also
stimulated growth of the foreign sector. Perhaps most important, the
foreign intrusion presented Japan with a choice between continued

5. S. Tsuru, "The Takeoff in Japan, 1868–1900," in *The Economics of the Takeoff*,
ed. W. W. Rostow (New York: St. Martin's Press, for the International Economic
Association, 1964).

dependence on more-advanced economies or development of independent economic and military power. Given Japanese traditions of nationalism and xenophobia, there was only one possible decision.

Why is 1868 usually taken as a turning point? Because it was a year of revolution. Formally, power passed from the Tokugawa shogun to the restored Meiji emperor. More importantly, power passed from feudal lords, oriented toward passive enjoyment of surplus from the land, to a more fluid and openended ruling class, including some remarkably able young administrators with a commercial and industrial orientation and a strong commitment to economic growth.

The growth-promoting actions of government during the first two decades of the new era have been well described by Rosovsky, Patrick, Lockwood, and others, and there is no need to repeat their analysis. Several points, however, should be underlined. First, the Japan of this era was not a democracy. Control rested with an interlocking, intermarried oligarchy of political, business, and military leaders. Most of the population consisted of docile peasants. The growing class of industrial workers accepted managerial authority with little question. This lack of popular pressure on government permitted development through austerity, with per capita output rising considerably faster than per capita consumption, yielding a growing margin for capital formation and military expenditure.

Second, the path of the new government was not entirely smooth. There was a major rebellion in 1877, led by samurai resentful of their reduced status and income. The cost of crushing this revolt and paying off the former samurai with interest-bearing bonds, plus rising government expenditures to finance model factories and mines, produced large budget deficits and a 65 percent price rise between 1877 and 1881. Only after a strong finance minister stopped the issuance of inconvertible paper currency, overbalanced the government budget, and brought the price level under control in the years 1881–85 was the stage set for the first long upswing in national product.

Third, the main thrust of policy was toward institutional reforms that would create a favorable setting for private enterprise. These included abolition of the rigid system of five social classes, membership in which was determined by birth and each of which was limited to prescribed economic activities, and substitution of a more fluid class structure open to men of talent from diverse social origins; abolition of barriers to internal movement of goods and people and dissolution of the restrictive craft guilds; displacement of the former feudal lords who, in lieu of their former revenues from agriculture, received initially a government pension, commuted in 1876 to an allotment of interest-bearing bonds; replacement of farmers' payments in kind to the feudal lords by a land tax payable in cash to the government, and simultaneous abolition of the Tokugawa prohibition against the purchase and sale of land; creation of a modern banking system under the National Bank Act of 1872, accompanied by the retirement of the many varieties of Tokugawa paper money and their replacement by a single currency; and development of an efficient budgetary system, which, for the first time, permitted forecasting and control of the revenue-expenditure balance.

This list of accomplishments is thoroughly in the spirit of classical economics and would certainly have been applauded by Adam Smith and John Stuart Mill.

OVERALL PERFORMANCE: POPULATION AND PRODUCTION

In the decades immediately before 1868, the GNP growth rate was probably not above 1 percent per year. Between 1868 and 1885, the economy made the transition to a markedly higher growth rate. By the 1890s, we find GNP rising at about 3 percent per year. In interpreting the record, and especially in choosing beginning and end years for comparison, it is important to recognize the presence of long swings—Kuznets cycles—in the growth rate. It is thus desirable, as Ohkawa and Rosovsky point out, to measure from peak to peak or trough to trough of a long cycle. Comparing 1887 with 1917, both peak years, shows a growth rate over the intervening period of 2.73 percent per year in GNP and 1.52 percent in GNP per capita.

It is interesting, though it does not form part of our story, that this stepping-up of the growth rate continued during the twentieth century. Between the 1917 and 1937 peaks, GNP rose at an average rate of 3.68 percent per year, and the post-World War II growth rate is once more substantially higher. This is the phenomenon that Ohkawa and Rosovsky term *trend acceleration*.[6]

Growth between 1868 and 1905 was largely growth of agriculture and other traditional industries by traditional methods. Modern large-scale industry had scarcely made an appearance in 1905, and its first major expansion occurred during the 1920s and 1930s.

6. See in particular Kazushi Ohkawa and Henry Rosovsky, *Japanese Economic Growth* (Stanford: Stanford University Press, 1973) and Ohkawa and Rosovsky, "Postwar Japanese Growth," in *Economic Growth*, ed. Klein and Ohkawa.

Population growth accelerated almost simultaneously with output growth. Population was growing slowly, probably at not more than 0.5 percent per year, in the last Tokugawa decades. A faster rate of growth set in around 1875.[7] This came about mainly through a rise in birth rates rather than a decline in death rates. Data cited by Umemura show the crude death rate fluctuating around a level of twenty per thousand, with no perceptible trend, from 1870 to 1920. The crude birth rate, on the other hand, rose from about twenty-five to thirty-five per thousand over this period. The rate of natural increase peaked at 1.4 percent in 1920, after which there began the gradual decline characteristic of the developed countries. A chart of the rise and decline of Japan's population growth rate resembles a chart for Britain with a shift of one century in the dates on the horizontal axis.

The increase in fertility may have been due partly to improved health and nutrition of potential mothers. Rising family incomes, permitting maintenance of larger numbers of children, also produced a reduction in earlier practices of abortion and infanticide. Infanticide had been particularly common for girl children and, as a consequence, during the eighteenth century the number of females in the population was less than 90 percent of the number of males. During the nineteenth century, however, the female-male ratio rose gradually, attaining virtual equality by 1900. This improved sex balance in the population also tended to raise crude birth rates.

Although the rate of natural increase was never high, it provided a growing labor supply for new economic activities. The number of people engaged in agriculture remained virtually unchanged throughout the period we are considering. Thus, the whole of the increase in population was available for employment in manufacturing, construction, government service, and other expanding sectors.

When we turn from growth of output to its composition, we encounter measurement difficulties. Much of the manufacturing output in the early years came from farm households, and this output is not easy to estimate. There is a considerable difference between estimates in current and constant prices. For the early decades, both output and price data are fragmentary.

Different estimates, however, show the same general trends. During

7. See the data in Kazushi Ohkawa, *The Growth Rate of the Japanese Economy Since 1878* (Tokyo: Kinokuniya Bookstore, 1957), pp. 140–41; and M. Umemura, "Agriculture and Labor Supply in the Meiji Era," in *Agriculture and Economic Growth: Japan's Experience*, ed. K. Ohkawa, B. F. Johnston, and H. Kaneda (Tokyo: Tokyo University Press, and Princeton: Princeton University Press, 1969).

the crucial years 1885–1902, the rate of structural adjustment was moderate. Agriculture's share of net domestic product fell from about 41 to 35 percent, while the share of manufacturing and public utilities rose from 9 to 14 percent. In the two decades 1903–22, structural change accelerated somewhat. Agriculture's share fell from 35 to 24 percent, while the industry share rose from 14 to 27 percent.[8] But even in 1920, after a half century of accelerated growth and industrialization, agriculture still provided one-quarter of the national output and employed more than half of the labor force. Secondary industry employed only 17 percent of the labor force, and most of this employment was in small-scale, labor-intensive units.

Looking at the uses of national output, gross fixed capital formation rose from about 9 percent of GNP in 1887 to 12 percent in 1900, 15 percent in 1910, and 19 percent in 1920.[9] The increase in capital formation was largely offset by a drop in the proportion of output going to private consumption. Government consumption, as a percentage of output, rose only slightly in these early decades, from 9.5 percent in the 1890s to 10.3 percent in the 1920s. Government was active in the development process, but this activity did not take the form of a relative increase in government output.

In view of recent high capital-formation rates in Japan, the moderate rates of earlier decades are striking. Even in the 1920s and early 1930s, the gross national capital-formation rate was only about 16 percent. One of the puzzles about Japanese development is how a high rate of output growth could be accompanied by a modest rate of capital formation. The implication is that the incremental capital-output ratio must have been unusually low and must have remained low during the first fifty years of modern growth. Ohkawa estimates that the capital-output ratio in the nonprimary sector was 1.90 in 1885 and had risen to only 2.33 in 1919.[10] Indeed, Kuznets finds that, even in the postwar period, the capital-output ratio has been no higher than it was in the 1920s and 1930s.[11] The explanation seems to lie partly in a large initial

8. K. Ohkawa et al., eds., *Estimates of Long-Term Economic Statistics of Japan Since 1868*, vol. 1 (Tokyo: Keizai Shinposha, 1974), table 36 (hereafter cited as *LTES*). The table referred to uses a seven-year moving average centered on each year, a desirable feature in view of fluctuations in agricultural output, and is in constant prices.

9. *LTES*, table 35. These estimates are also seven-year moving averages, in constant prices.

10. K. Ohkawa, "Agricultural Development and Economic Growth," in *Agriculture and Economic Growth*, ed. Ohkawa, Johnston, and Kaneda, p. 25.

11. Kuznets, "Notes on Japan's Economic Growth," in *Economic Growth*, ed. Klein and Ohkawa.

labor surplus and partly in an unusually labor-using path of development in both agriculture and industry.

THE AGRICULTURAL SECTOR

Initial Conditions

A pervasive fact of life in Japan is land scarcity. In 1880 Japan had 0.61 hectares of arable land per farm worker (compared, for example, with 10 hectares in the United States at that time). A natural consequence was relatively high land prices. In Japan in 1880, the value of a hectare of arable land was almost 1,600 times the daily farm wage rate. The corresponding ratio in the United States was 180 times. Moreover, the Japanese ratio rose from 1,600 times in 1880 to 2,800 times in 1920, while the U.S. ratio fell from 180 to 107 over this same period.[12] Hayami and Ruttan argue convincingly that these differing factor endowments and factor price ratios induced different paths of technical change: biological, land-saving innovations in Japan and mechancial, labor-saving innovations in the United States.

Japan in 1880 had already reached a relatively high level of agricultural productivity, well above that of some Asian LDCs today. The rice yield in 1880 is estimated to have been 2.36 tons of paddy per hectare. During 1953–62, Asian rice yields ranged from 1.17 tons per hectare in the Philippines, 1.36 in India, and 1.38 in Thailand to 2.75 tons in South Korea and 2.93 in Taiwan.[13] Productivity was high enough to both support the rural population at more than a bare subsistence level and feed the growing urban population. The substantial commercialization of agriculture has already been noted.

The major land reform of 1873 among other things, replaced the former payments to the feudal lords with a tax payment to government. Tsuru estimates that before the reform about 37 percent of agricultural output went to the feudal lords and their retainers. Immediately after the reform, about 34 percent of output was going to government in the form of taxes.[14] The lords, to be sure, were not simply expropriated. They were paid off with government pensions, soon commuted to a lump-sum payment of interest-bearing bonds. As of 1878, 42 percent of government expenditures consisted of interest on these bonds.

12. Data are from Y. Hayami and V. W. Ruttan, *Agricultural Development: An International Perspective* (Baltimore: Johns Hopkins Press, 1971), p. 113.

13. Y. Hayami and S. Yamada, "Agricultural Productivity at the Beginning of Industrialization," in *Agriculture and Economic Growth*, ed. Ohkawa, Johnston, and Kaneda, p. 108.

14. Tsuru, "The Takeoff in Japan," in *The Economics of the Takeoff*, ed. Rostow.

It might seem, then, that nothing had changed except that the lords' income now flowed through government channels. The sharp inflation of the late 1870s, however, reduced the real value of the interest payments, which continued to shrink with the moderate but persistent inflation of later decades.

The new agricultural regime was mainly one of peasant proprietorships, though about 40 percent of the land area was rented to tenants rather than operated by owners. The new agricultural tax was based on land value rather than output, and it was collected in money rather than kind. With assessments remaining fixed for considerable periods of time, increases in agricultural productivity and prices gradually lightened the tax burden. Ranis estimates that during 1878–82 total taxes on agriculture (including excises and other taxes as well as the land tax) amounted to 16.9 percent of net agricultural income. By 1918–22, this had fallen to 9.2 percent.[15] Agriculture continued, however, to be taxed more heavily than nonagriculture. The percentage of nonagricultural income taken in taxes was 2.2 percent during 1878–82, 5.4 percent during 1918–22. Since agriculture received little in the way of government subsidies during this period, there was a financial transfer from agriculture through the fiscal system.

Reduction of the agricultural tax burden benefited mainly the new landowners, who were left with a growing income surplus. Japanese landowners being thrifty, most of this surplus was reinvested in agricultural improvements, agricultural side occupations such as silk production, or securities issued by the nonagricultural sector. Tenant farmers did not benefit equally, since their rents were paid in kind, and gains in productivity or prices were thus shared with the landlord. But Ranis's estimates suggest that even tenants benefited somewhat, their share of net agricultural output rising from about 22 percent during 1878–82 to 32 percent during 1918–22. These income gains provided both an incentive and a means of financing continued agricultural improvement.

The population classified as agricultural in 1880 was not engaged only in agriculture. Much of the output of manufactures and services came from farm households. Although comprehensive data are not available, a study of one prefecture found that, along with 26,418 workers who regarded manufacturing as their primary occupation in

15. Gustav Ranis, "The Financing of Japanese Agricultural Development," in *Agriculture and Economic Growth*, ed. Ohkawa, Johnston, and Kaneda.

1879, there were 21,375 who were employed in manufacturing as a side occupation. Again, 14,498 were employed in services as a main occupation, 15,035 as a side occupation. It is a reasonable surmise that the great majority of these side workers came from farm households. Further, there were 29,238 who worked at agriculture as a side occupation, along with 194,164 who considered it their primary job.[16] This interpenetration of agricultural and nonagricultural activities within the rural areas continued throughout the period we are discussing, and it accounts for some of the most interesting features of subsequent development.

Output, Inputs, and Productivity

The rate at which Japan's agricultural output rose between 1880 and 1920 has been much disputed. An early estimate by Bruce Johnston set the average annual increase at 1.9 percent, and Kazushi Ohkawa made an estimate of 2.4 percent. These estimates were criticized by James Nakamura on the ground that the output level during 1878–82 was substantially higher than indicated by official statistics derived from tax returns.[17] By raising the base-period figure substantially, he concluded that the true rate of increase in subsequent decades was about 1.0 percent.

Nakamura's paper failed, on the whole, to persuade other scholars, but it did stimulate data revisions and additional estimates. Recent estimates appear to converge in the neighborhood of a 2-percent growth rate. The Long Term Economic Statistics of Japan (LTES) study estimates output growth at 1.9 percent per year from 1888 to 1900 and 2.0 percent from 1900 to 1920.[18] Hayami and Ruttan estimate output growth at 2.1 percent from 1880 to 1900 and 2.2 percent from 1900 to 1920.[19]

In terms of contemporary LDC needs and objectives, this growth rate appears very low. Yet, it did enable Japan to avoid a food bottleneck. The explanations are, first, that the population growth rate was

16. Arlon R. Tussing, "The Labor Force in Meiji Economic Growth," in *Agriculture and Economic Growth*, ed. Ohkawa, Johnston, and Kaneda; see also in the same volume Umemura, "Agriculture and Labor Supply."

17. James I. Nakamura, "Growth of Japanese Agriculture, 1875–1920," in *The State and Economic Enterprise in Japan*, ed. Lockwood.

18. *LTES*, table 39. These estimates, like those cited previously, are based on seven-year moving averages of output, in constant prices.

19. Hayami and Ruttan, *Agricultural Development*, p. 114.

only about 1 percent a year and, second, that Japan had by 1880 reached a level of nutrition at which the income elasticity of demand for additional food was quite low. Estimates by Yamada and others suggest that, for the period 1878–1922, the income elasticity of demand for food products in general was 0.39 and for rice only 0.21.[20] Finally, Japan was not a closed economy. Rice imports, mainly from the new colonial areas of Taiwan and Korea, rose steadily from 1905 onward. Without this, Japan might well have encountered a food constraint.

The sources of agricultural output growth have been analyzed in detail by Ohkawa, Hayami, Ruttan, and others. From 1880 to 1905, the growth was almost entirely in productivity rather than in inputs. After 1905, fertilizer and other capital inputs became more important. But over the whole period 1880–1920, only about one-quarter of the output growth is traceable to inputs, while three-quarters must be attributed to technical change.

It is worth looking briefly at labor, land, and capital inputs. The number of agricultural workers remained virtually constant over this period, the rural population increase being about offset by emigration to urban areas. But the amount of time spent by farm household members on silk reeling, handicrafts, and other sideline activities grew substantially, so that their labor inputs to agriculture must have declined. As an offset, many of the young women and others who shifted to factory work remained household members and came home when laid off in recessions or when needed to cover harvesting peaks. This interpenetration of agricultural and industrial activities complicates the estimation of labor inputs to agriculture. But it is a reasonable surmise that labor inputs fell more than is indicated by the data on workers "attached" to various sectors.

The amount of land under cultivation grew at a modest rate and was 26 percent larger in 1920 than in 1880. With labor declining slightly, arable land per male farm worker increased by 30 percent. There is no indication, however, of an increase in average farm size. The increased acreage took the form of more rather than larger farms.

Most difficult to estimate are capital inputs. Ohkawa's estimates exclude water-control facilities and other infrastructure improvements. Although these had already reached an advanced stage by 1868, there must have been substantial further development. This is implied by

20. These and other estimates are summarized and evaluated in H. Kaneda, "Long-Term Changes in Food Consumption Patterns in Japan," in *Agriculture and Economic Growth*, ed. Ohkawa, Johnston, and Kaneda.

the extension of cultivated acreage and by the rising use of fertilizer, which requires an assured water supply. The other important form of early capital formation was the planting of mulberry trees for silkworm production.

The years around 1905 mark a turning point, after which input increases became more important and productivity growth relatively less important (though equally rapid). The number of farm livestock grew at 0.26 percent per year from 1894 to 1905 but at 0.84 percent from 1905 to 1919. The amount of farm equipment grew at 1.26 percent per year from 1894 to 1905 but at 2.10 percent per year from 1905 to 1919. Fertilizer inputs turned upward even more sharply around 1900, increasing almost five times between 1900 and 1920. The growth of a modern chemical industry during this period provided growing supplies at declining prices.

Ohkawa estimates the average annual percentage rates of change as follows:

Period	Output	Inputs	Productivity
1877–85	2.18	0.03	2.03
1885–94	1.67	0.05	1.50
1894–1905	1.85	0.19	1.43
1905–19	2.24	0.74	1.48

What was the nature of technical progress? Until 1920 it involved mainly improved seed varieties, combined with complementary improvements in water supply, fertilizer application, and cultivation practices. Under the Tokugawa restrictions on movement, improved seed varieties developed by farmers in one part of the country did not spread readily to other areas, and there was wide variation in regional productivity levels. In the Meiji era there was a systematic effort to discover, transfer, and domesticate these already-known varieties through a network of government research and experiment stations. Hayami and Ruttan estimate that the percentage of rice area planted with improved varieties was only 0.2 in 1880 and 4.1 in 1895. But an acceleration then set in which raised the figure to 42.0 percent by 1920. As a consequence, rice yields rose from an average of about 2.4 tons per hectare in 1880 to 3.5 tons in 1920. This was accomplished within a traditional framework of small farms and with no mechanization beyond simple hand tools.

Agricultural progress was stimulated by improving terms of trade. An index of the ratio of agricultural prices to prices of manufactured goods (1934–36 = 100) rose from 81.4 in 1886 to 107.1 in 1919.[21] This suggests that output was not quite keeping up with demand. (As rice imports from the colonies came flooding in during the 1920s and 1930s, agriculture's terms of trade turned down again and by 1938 had returned almost to the 1886 level.)

Even more dramatic was the improvement of farm prices relative to the prices of purchased agricultural inputs. Between 1880 and 1920, fertilizer and machinery prices doubled; but the price index for all farm crops increased four times. Thus, farmers had a strong incentive to increase output through larger input purchases, and they also had the income to finance such purchases.

A word should be added on relative productivity levels in agriculture and industry. The conventional picture of early economic development implies transfers of agricultural labor to manufacturing and other modern activities with much higher productivity levels. Shifting sector weights thus produce an automatic increase in national output per capita. Although there is something to this in the case of Japan, there is less than one might have anticipated. Estimates by Ohkawa and Kuznets[22] indicate that:

1. Output per worker in 1880 was about half as high in agriculture as in manufacturing (compared with one-tenth to one-fifth in most contemporary LDCs).

2. This ratio did not change materially between 1880 and 1920, that is, output per worker grew as rapidly in agriculture as in manufacturing. This partly reflects the fact that, as late as 1920, Japanese manufacturing was still quite small-scale, labor-intensive, and traditional.

3. The Japanese agriculture-manufacturing productivity ratio during this period was almost the same as in the United States. This raises questions about describing the Japanese economy as *dualistic* without a similar characterization of our own economy.

THE INDUSTRIAL SECTOR

One tends to think of "industry" as meaning large factories and of labor transfer as involving movement of people from country to city.

21. Ohkawa and Rosovsky, "Postwar Japanese Growth," in *Economic Growth*, ed. Klein and Ohkawa, p. 16.
22. Ohkawa, "Phases of Agricultural Development and Economic Growth," in *Agriculture and Economic Growth*, ed. Ohkawa, Johnston, and Kaneda; Kuznets, "Notes on Japan's Economic Growth," in *Economic Growth*, ed. Klein and Ohkawa.

This does not fit the facts of Japanese experience, particularly in the crucial years before 1905. Much of the expansion of manufacturing occurred through a redirection of effort *within* the farm household. The case study of Yamanashi Prefecture mentioned earlier shows the proportion of agricultural workers reporting side employments rising from 33 percent in 1879 to 63 percent in 1920. In Yamagata Prefecture, the proportion rose from 23 percent in 1887 to 42 percent in 1920.[23]

The remaining growth occurred mainly in small-scale workshops producing traditional consumer goods by labor-intensive methods and was closely associated with agriculture through rural location, use of agricultural raw materials, and employment of single (usually female) workers who retained their connection with the farm household. This is what Ohkawa has aptly termed *the semimodern sector*.

There were also a few large establishments, usually promoted by government. A shipyard to produce warships was established as early as 1863. Several power-driven cotton-spinning mills were built between 1878 and 1882, including two model plants financed by the government. The Yawata steel mill, financed from Sino-Japanese war reparations, was built in 1901. But these were isolated islands in a sea of small-scale activity. In 1900 factory output—defined generously to include establishments with five or more employees and thus including much handicraft production—accounted for only about 40 percent of manufacturing output and only 6 percent of national output. Even within the factory sphere, the representative unit was small. In food processing, 68 percent of the workers were in establishments with fewer than fifty employees; for textiles the proportion was 37 percent, and for heavy industry, 43 percent.[24]

The story after 1905 is rather different.[25] Except for the early cotton mills, the growth of a truly modern industrial sector in Japan dates from the long upswing of 1905 to 1919. During this period the capital stock in manufacturing grew at about 7 percent a year, outdistancing the 3-percent-a-year increase in labor force. The result was an accelerated rise of labor productivity. Factory production rose to about 61 percent of total manufacturing production and 11 percent of net domestic product. The proportion of workers in plants with less than fifty workers fell by about 10 percentage points.

The growth rate of manufacturing output was never high by modern

23. Umemura, "Agriculture and Labor Supply," in *Agriculture and Economic Growth,* ed. Ohkawa, Johnston, and Kaneda, p. 191.
24. Ohkawa and Rosovsky, *Japanese Economic Growth,* p. 15.
25. And also better documented. See in particular ibid., chaps. 3, 4.

Table 2. Composition of Manufacturing Output, Selected Industries and Periods

Industry	Share of Gross Value of Manufacturing Output (percent)			Annual Growth Rate of Gross Output (percent per year)		Relative Contribution of Growth of Manufacturing Output (percent)	
	1881–85	1900–04	1919–23	1881–85 to 1900–04	1900–04 to 1919–23	1881–85 to 1900–04	1900–04 to 1919–23
Food products	32.8	31.3	22.5	4.1	3.8	33.2	21.0
Textile products	23.1	31.7	35.4	8.7	6.9	29.1	29.9
Chemicals	11.3	9.6	10.1	4.7	5.7	11.0	11.4
Metals	3.9	5.0	6.6	7.4	10.1	4.6	10.4
Machinery	3.1	5.1	11.3	9.1	12.7	5.3	17.4
All manufacturing	100.0	100.0	100.0	5.0	5.7	100.0	100.0

standards, and it fluctuated with the long swings in general economic growth. Starting at about 2 percent a year in 1880, it rose to a peak of 8 percent during the 1885–98 upswing, dropped to about 2 percent at the 1902 trough, then rose to a peak of 9 percent in the long upswing of 1905–19. Overall, the average annual rate of growth from 1888 to 1920 was about 6 percent.[26] Since this was higher than the growth rate of output in general, the weight of the manufacturing sector in the economy gradually increased—from about 8 percent of net domestic product in 1887 to almost 20 percent in 1920.

Changes in the composition of manufacturing output were also gradual. Table 2, derived from Shionoya,[27] shows in the first three columns the share of selected light and heavy industries in total manufacturing output at three points in time. The next two columns show the average annual growth rate of each industry over the intervening periods, and the final two columns show the percentage of manufacturing-output growth that came from each industry in each period.

The predominance of light industry throughout the period is clear. Food and textiles alone formed 56 percent of manufacturing output in the early 1880s and 58 percent of output around 1920. Food-processing industries shrank moderately in relative size, as would be expected in view of income elasticities of demand. But this was more than offset by the rapid and prolonged expansion of the silk and cotton textile industries, based partly on penetration of foreign markets.

Chemicals grew at about the same rate as manufacturing in general. Metals and machinery grew at a high percentage rate—but from a very small base. There was some acceleration in heavy-industry growth rates after 1905. Even in 1920, however, these industries yielded less than 30 percent of manufacturing output. A beginning had been made, but the great expansion of heavy industry did not come until the armaments boom of the 1930s.

We turn now to the sources of inputs for manufacturing, beginning with labor. The common (and basically correct) view is that there was a plentiful labor supply to nonagriculture. This may at first appear puzzling. Population was growing at only about 1 percent. The labor force was growing even less rapidly, because of declining labor-force

---

26. *LTES*, table 39.
27. Yuichi Shionoya, "Patterns of Industrial Development," in *Economic Growth*, ed. Klein and Ohkawa, pp. 74–75.

participation rates associated with urbanization and the spread of education. Ohkawa estimates that the rate of labor-force growth declined from 1.4 percent per year during 1883–87 to only 0.4 percent per year during 1908–17.[28] How, then, can one speak of an ample labor supply?

The explanation lies partly in the fact that in 1880 there was substantial labor slack within the rural households. As labor demand rose, this slack was taken up in two main ways: (1) an expansion of side employment in silk reeling and other handicrafts within the household; (2) the release of some family members, particularly single women, for employment in textile mills and other factories. Since these were supplementary family wage earners, their supply price was low. The scattered data suggest that daily earnings of female textile operatives were below the average daily income per worker in agriculture.[29] Recruitment of these workers, without permanent detachment from the household, was facilitated by the rural location of most of the early factories. In the early 1880s, 77 percent of all Japanese factories were located in rural districts, only 23 percent in urban areas.[30] By 1900, however, the urban proportion had risen above 50 percent.

The other part of the story is the substantial rate of productivity increase in agriculture. From 1880 to 1920, output per male worker rose at the rate of 2.2 percent per year. This enabled agricultural output to keep pace with demand without requiring net additions to the farm labor force. All the natural increase in rural population was available for transfer to nonagriculture. The outflow from agriculture was consistently in the neighborhood of 150,000 workers a year, or about 1 percent of those remaining in agriculture. Only a minority of these went into manufacturing, however, since the service sector was a much larger proportion of the economy at this time.[31]

Labor surplus models ordinarily assume a rural-urban differential in real wages, which keeps the migration current going. They also assume that the industrial wage level will not rise so long as the rural

28. Kazushi Ohkawa, *Differential Structure and Agriculture* (Tokyo: Kinokuniya Bookstore, 1972), chap. 1.

29. See in particular Tussing, "The Labor Force," in *Agriculture and Economic Growth*, ed. Ohkawa, Johnston, and Kaneda.

30. Umemura "Agriculture and Labor Supply," in *Agriculture and Economic Growth*, ed. Ohkawa, Johnston, and Kaneda.

31. Ohkawa (*Differential Structure and Agriculture*, chap. 1) estimates that migration out of agriculture between 1872 and 1920 totaled 8,000,000 workers. But in 1920, employment in factories with more than five workers was only 2,000,000. So most of the migrants must have gone elsewhere!

labor surplus persists. The Japanese story is not easy to untangle, partly because of deficiencies in the wage and price data, partly because the results vary with the kind of labor in question. In the rural sector, hired wage laborers are a small proportion of the labor force, and their wages may not compare closely with the average earnings of family members. In the industrial sector, it makes a difference whether one is talking about female textile operatives, unskilled male laborers, or skilled workers. It appears that skilled industrial workers were never in surplus and that, particularly after 1905, they commanded a growing premium over the unskilled.

There is also a difference between wage *rates* and *earnings*. For example, Tussing reports that in Yamanashi Prefecture the real hourly wage of female employees in silk-reeling factories did not rise between 1885 and 1910. Their annual earnings, however, almost doubled because of a much higher rate of capacity utilization. During 1908–11 these factories averaged 251 days operation per year, compared with only 143 days during 1883–87. Thus, without any increase in real hourly wages in either industry or agriculture, the real incomes of rural households could have risen substantially through fuller utilization of the family's labor time.

For such reasons, the wage story remains one of the more obscure parts of Japanese economic history; but several tentative observations can be made:

1. The average wage rate in manufacturing was substantially above that for hired agricultural labor, and this differential did not change appreciably over the period we are considering. Ohkawa and Rosovsky report the agricultural-manufacturing wage ratio as about 70 percent in 1886 and 74 percent in 1919.[32] There were fluctuations, however, related to the long swings of economic growth. During an upswing, the accelerated demand for industrial labor and the increased suction out of agriculture raised agricultural wages relative to industrial wages. On the downswing, the pressure was relaxed, the agricultural labor surplus rose, and agricultural wages suffered a relative decline. Thus, the agricultural-manufacturing ratio stood at 69.9 percent in 1886, 76.5 percent at the 1898 peak, 69.6 percent at the 1905 trough, and 73.7 percent in the peak year of 1919.

2. The behavior of the real wage level in manufacturing is not en-

---

32. Ohkawa and Rosovsky, "Postwar Japanese Growth in Historical Perspective: A Second Look," in *Economic Growth*, ed. Klein and Ohkawa. Their more recent book, *Japanese Economic Growth* (p. 126) reports somewhat higher ratios for agriculture but again without any noticeable time trend.

tirely clear. Estimates of real wages[33] suggest little increase until the turn of the century but a sustained rise beginning around 1905, which marked the first substantial growth of modern industry. Gleason's index of real wages in manufacturing shows gains of 30 percent between 1905 and 1919, or almost 2 percent per year. Consumption studies by Gleason and Kuznets, however, find that real per capita consumption rose from the very beginning of economic growth. This casts considerable doubt, in Kuznets's view, on the alleged constancy of real wages even in the period 1880–1905.[34]

3. The evidence of rising consumption levels is conclusive. The GNP after 1885 was rising at around 4 percent per year. The percentage share of personal consumption in GNP fell only from 77 percent during 1889–98 to 72 percent during 1919–28. It follows that consumption rose almost as fast as GNP. Kuznets's index of personal consumption expenditures rises from 34.3 during 1879–83 to 54.4 during 1904–08 and 81.6 during 1919–23. This impression of a strong uptrend in consumption levels is confirmed by data on food availability. Rice availability per capita is estimated to have risen from 137 kilos per year during 1878–82 to 162 kilos during 1903–07 and 173 kilos during 1918–22. An index of total agricultural products available per capita rises from 39 during 1878–82 to 55 during 1903–07 and 68 during 1918–22.

One possibility is that, particularly in the years before 1905, rising per capita income came mainly from increased hours of work rather than from higher real returns per hour. We have already noted the probable importance of this in the dominant rural sector. But it also seems likely that after 1905, and possibly even earlier, the growth of modern industry was accompanied by a rising real-wage level. One way of reconciling this with a continuing labor surplus is to note that the surplus consisted largely of young, untrained, and mobile farm family members (not unlike the situation in some of today's LDCs). As Ohkawa and Rosovsky point out, "Modern enterprise increasingly

33. See in particular Tussing, "The Labor Force," in *Agriculture and Economic Growth*, ed. Ohkawa, Johnston, and Kaneda; and Alan H. Gleason, "Economic Growth and Consumption in Japan," in *The State and Economic Enterprise in Japan*, ed. Lockwood.

34. Simon Kuznets, "Trends in Level and Structure of Consumption," in *Economic Growth*, ed. Klein and Ohkawa. Data in the following paragraph are from this source. In support of Kuznets's position, the LTES estimates (table 42) show real personal consumption expenditure rising at 2.8 percent per year from 1887 to 1900, which would mean an increase of almost 2 percent per year in per capita terms.

needs a reliable, committed, and above all trained labor force,"[35] and the effort to create such a force could explain some bidding up of wages.

4. The rise in real wages, however, did lag behind the growth of productivity. This is suggested, though not fully demonstrated, by a decline in labor's share of output. Ohkawa and Rosovsky estimate that earnings per worker in agriculture were 67 percent of output per worker in 1886 but only 52 percent of output by 1917. More strikingly, wages per worker in the industrial sector were only 35 percent of output per worker in 1886, and by 1917 this had fallen to 25 percent.

Profit rates in industry were very high, and reinvested earnings provided most of the finance for industrial capital formation. Wages lagged sufficiently that large surpluses accrued to businessmen and landowners, who reinvested most of it in classical fashion. This was supplemented by forced saving imposed on the mass of the population by government, partly through the tax structure and partly through tolerance of secular inflation.

Japan also got remarkably good results from its capital. The capital-output ratio in the early years seems to have been below 2.0 and, though it rose a little between 1880 and 1920, it remained remarkably low in comparison with Western industrial countries.[36]

The explanation is that output was increased by very labor-using methods, which gradually absorbed the preexisting labor slack in the rural economy while economizing on scarce capital. In agriculture, output was increased by vigorous dissemination of improved seed varieties, continued effort on water-control systems and other land improvements, increased application of (primarily organic) fertilizer, the planting of mulberry trees, and diversification into silkworm production. All this involved mainly education plus increased labor inputs, with little capital outlay. Although there was a gradual improvement of hand tools, there was no mechanization in the modern sense.

In manufacturing, too, the pre-1900 output increases were accomplished mainly within the farm household or in small, rural-based workshops drawing on farm family labor. Cotton spinning, to be sure, was mechanized from the outset; but the capital-output ratio was held

---

35. In *Economic Growth*, ed. Klein and Ohkawa, p. 30.

36. Ohkawa and Rosovsky estimate the capital-output ratio in nonagriculture, in 1934–36 yen, as 1.27 in 1897, 1.76 in 1917, and 1.91 in 1964! The corresponding estimates for agriculture are 2.00 in 1897, 2.02 in 1917, and 4.29 in 1964. Ohkawa and Rosovsky, *Japanese Economic Growth*, p. 36.

down by three-shift operation, higher machine speeds, and other methods. By the time of the 1905–19 upswing, factories were appearing in considerable numbers. But there was a striking persistence of the small, labor-intensive workshop—Ohkawa's "semimodern sector"— alongside the large factory as a distinctive feature of Japanese industrial organization. The reasons for this—the labor surplus that permitted a two-tier wage structure, the development of subcontracting and other symbiotic relations between large and small enterprises, the continued consumption of traditional products that could be produced efficiently on a small scale—are too complex to be explored here. But this is clearly one of the most important features of the Japanese experience.

Entrepreneurs came mainly from the wealthier landowning and mercantile families.[37] Former samurai, members of the traditional, educated ruling class, were an especially important source of talent. The new business class was given wholehearted support by government. Cabinet ministers and top civil servants came from the same social background as the industrialists, and they shared the same outlook. There was much movement back and forth between the two groups. No one doubted that development of profitable and powerful private enterprises was good for Japan.

In technology, Japan has always been a heavy borrower from other countries. The technology borrowed in the period 1880–1920, partly in the form of large machinery imports, was not well adapted to Japanese factor proportions—a situation comparable to that of today's LDCs. Faced with capital-intensive technology, Japan's adjustment to its own labor surplus situation took three main forms: (1) a choice of industries that emphasized those with relatively high labor content per unit of output. This meant mainly textiles in the period we are considering, machinery and electronics at a later stage; (2) persistence within each industry of a wide range of plant sizes, including many very small establishments. These small plants often used secondhand machinery, had a higher labor-capital ratio than the large plants, and often developed a symbiotic rather than a competitive relationship with the latter through subcontracting; (3) inten-

37. For sketches of the origins and careers of some early industrial leaders, see Y. Horie, "Modern Entrepreneurship in Meiji Japan," and J. Hirschmeier, "Shibusawa Eichi: Industrial Pioneer," in *The State and Economic Enterprise in Japan*, ed. Lockwood. See also Johannes Hirschmeier, *The Origins of Entrepreneurship in Modern Japan* (Cambridge: Harvard University Press, 1964); and Kozo Yamamura, "A Re-examination of Entrepreneurship in Meiji Japan," *Economic History Review*, 2d series, 21, no. 1 (1968).

sive use of capital through multishift operation, which was characteristic of Japanese industry from the beginning.

This was still insufficient, however, to generate a high rate of increase in manufacturing employment or to reduce the absolute size of the agricultural labor force. The agricultural reservoir did not begin to run dry until the 1950s, long after the end of the early growth period.

THE PUBLIC SECTOR

The public sector is not very well documented; but the evidence suggests a highly capitalistic development path—a small public sector, a regressive tax structure with gentle treatment of high incomes and profits, and strong encouragement of private industry through loans and subsidies.

The LTES estimates[38] show government consumption as a percentage of GNP fluctuating in the range of 6 to 8 percent from 1885 to 1920, with brief wartime spurts but no long-term uptrend. Emi shows (civilian) central government employment rising from 19,542 in 1880 to 27,263 in 1920, or only 1.13 percent of the gainfully occupied population at that date.[39] Even if one added military personnel, local government employees, and employees of public corporations, the public sector would remain relatively small.

The largest item of current expenditure was military costs. During war periods, this rose to well over half the central government's budget. For the period 1879–1912, Oshima estimates military expenses at about one-third of central plus local government expenditures.[40] The second-largest budget item was interest payments on the public debt.

Promotion of economic activity, however, was a significant part of the total. Oshima shows the following percentages of central plus local expenditures going for this purpose:

	Average 1873–77	1920
Transport and communications	7.7	11.9
Agriculture	1.9	2.6
Secondary and tertiary industries	1.8	7.9
Total	11.4	22.4

38. *LTES*, table 33.

39. Koichi Emi, *Government Fiscal Activity and Economic Growth in Japan, 1868–1960* (Tokyo: Kinokuniya Bookstore, 1963), p. 5.

40. Harry T. Oshima, "Meiji Fiscal Policy and Economic Progress," in *The State and Economic Enterprise in Japan*, ed. Lockwood.

Education was a relatively small item, rising from 3.9 percent of the total budget during 1873–77 to 9.6 percent in 1920. Primary education was made compulsory at an early stage, but the schools continued for a long time to be fee-charging institutions. Health and other social expenditures were insignificant in the early decades.

The tax system by which these activities were supported was highly regressive.[41] We have already noted the relatively heavy taxation of agriculture. A major revenue source was excises or government monopoly profits on such items as sake, soya, sugar, textiles, tobacco, and salt. Although income taxes were instituted as early as 1887, exemptions were high and tax rates were low, so that these taxes yielded only a small proportion of public revenue. Business taxes were negligible. Interestingly, import and export duties formed only a minor part of government revenue because of the low-tariff policy imposed on Japan by the foreign treaties of the 1860s.

Government's contribution to capital formation was more substantial than its contribution to current output. Contrary to U.S. practice, the Japanese data include military structures and equipment as part of capital formation. (Without this item, Japanese gross capital-formation rates would be quite low—less than 10 percent of GNP up to 1910, less than 15 percent in the 1920s.) Counting military items, the government's share of total capital formation rose from one-third during 1887–96 to one-half during 1902–11, and it remained at this level for several decades thereafter.[42] In only one other capitalist country, Australia, has government's share of capital formation been so large over such a long period.

What forms did government investment take? The military proportion varied widely over time, reaching peaks of about 80 percent in the Sino-Japanese and Russo-Japanese war periods. On the average, over the years 1887–1921, it ran between 30 and 40 percent of government fixed investment. The great bulk of this investment was in durable equipment—warships, guns, tanks, and motorized vehicles. Government orders for these items stimulated the growth of heavy industry during the early decades of development. Much of the output was

41. See in particular Gustav Ranis, "The Financing of Japanese Economic Development," in *Agriculture and Economic Growth*, ed. Ohkawa, Johnston, and Kaneda. This article appeared originally in substantially the same form in *The Economic History Review* 11 (1959).

42. The classic source in this area is Henry Rosovsky, *Capital Formation in Japan, 1868–1940* (New York: The Free Press, 1961).

produced in army arsenals and navy shipyards, which remained in government hands after most other government-initiated factories had been sold off to private enterprise.

Government's nonmilitary investment, on the other hand, was predominantly (70 to 80 percent) in the form of construction rather than in producers' durables. Much the largest item was railroad construction. In the years 1894–1920, railroad investment averaged 45 percent of total nonmilitary investment by the central government. The fact that public construction could be carried on by traditional, labor-intensive methods was helpful both in absorbing labor surplus and in raising the capital-formation rate.

Government investment was financed in several ways. Most of the military outlay was simply "expensed," that is, treated as part of the current budget. There was substantial government borrowing from households, facilitated by a high propensity to save among even the lower-income groups, which led by the 1920s to a national debt about half as large as Japanese GNP. Revenues of the railroads and other government enterprises made some contribution. Finally, there was the possibility of monetary expansion. Japanese development has been moderately inflationary. Between 1885 and 1915, the general price level tripled, an average annual increase of about 5 percent.[43]

Government was active also as a financial intermediary—borrowing through its own bond issues and relending to private industry, extending credit through a network of government banks, and so on. The conventional image of an activist, growth-conscious government from the 1870s onward is correct. It is the combination of this high activity with (in production terms) a small public sector that is extraordinarily interesting.

THE FOREIGN SECTOR

Japan has shown a consistently strong export performance. From the opening of the country in 1859, exports rose considerably faster than GNP and formed an increasing share of national output. Exports plus imports were about 10 percent of GNP in the 1870s but had risen to 30 percent during 1910–13. Japanese exports also grew about twice as fast as world exports over the period 1880–1914. Thus, Japan was steadily increasing her share of world markets.

43. *LTES*, table 30.

This performance is largely the story of two industries: raw silk, which was preeminent before 1900 and continued to contribute heavily to foreign exchange earnings thereafter; and cotton textiles, which became increasingly important from 1900 onward.

Japan's initial export products were raw silk and tea. Raw silk alone (including silkworm eggs and cocoons) formed 61 percent of the country's exports from 1868 to 1875. This fell gradually to around 40 percent at the turn of the century and then stabilized near that level through the 1920s. Since total export volume was growing rapidly, this stable share meant a rapid growth of silk exports in absolute terms.

Raw silk is a semifinished product derived from cocoons of the silkworm by a process known as reeling. The basis of the industry was a rapid expansion of mulberry-tree planting and cocoon production by farmers. Sericulture as a percentage of total agricultural production rose from 5 percent in the 1870s to 10 percent by 1900 to 16 percent in the 1920s. Sericulture, carried out on dryland fields, was a relatively profitable activity. In 1899 the farm value of sericultural products per *tan* (about one-tenth of a hectare) was 30 yen. The value of wheat or barley output (the main competitiors for dryland areas) was 8 or 9 yen, and of rice, 14 yen.[44]

Although increases in grain prices after 1900 reduced the price advantage of cocoons, the profitability of the industry was sustained by rapid technical progress. Actively promoted by government, this progress resulted in such things as heavier yields of mulberry leaves through fertilizer application and improved cultural practices; improved strains of silkworms, obtained by egg selection and cross breeding; and the discovery that it was possible to obtain both a spring and a fall "crop" of cocoons, instead of just a spring crop. Thus, though the index of mulberry area (1881–90 = 100) rose to 371 in 1921–30, the index of cocoon production rose from 100 to 714.

Sericulture absorbed surplus family labor. Cocoon gathering has to be completed within a week, so that it does not interfere continuously with other agricultural activities. Reeling can be done in the home by simple hand methods, thus using additional labor time. As late as 1890, about 60 percent of all raw silk was reeled at home. But silk-reeling factories also sprang up early, typically in rural areas, using waterpower and hiring farm girls as workers. From 1886 through 1914, the

---

44. Kenzo Hemmi, "Primary Product Exports and Economic Development: The Case of Silk," in *Agriculture and Economic Growth*, ed. Ohkawa, Johnston, and Kaneda, p. 318.

silk industry provided about one-quarter of the total employment in factories employing ten or more workers.[45]

In addition to elastic supply conditions, silk had a high income elasticity of foreign demand. Baba and Tatemoto[46] estimate the income elasticity of demand for Japanese exports in the period 1879–96 at 2.95; and silk has a heavy role in this estimate. The main market was the United States, which, after discovering that sericulture was impracticable, abandoned efforts to protect raw silk but maintained protection on silk fabrics. The main rival exporters were Italy and China. Italian silk was somewhat better but also more expensive, and Chinese silk was cheaper but poorer. Japan had a combination of price, quality, and ability to increase output that enabled it to take over a growing share of the market.

Factory production of textiles was domesticated in Japan by systematic government effort. Two model silk-reeling factories using French equipment were established in 1871 and 1874. In woolens, a government mill using German technology was established in 1874 to provide army and navy uniforms. In cotton spinning, the government set up two model factories using British equipment and also financed the import of British machinery by private spinners. The government cotton mills, however, were notably unsuccessful, and it was really the establishment of private mills after 1880 that set the pattern for the cotton-spinning industry.

During the 1880s and 1890s, cotton textile production increased rapidly, following the typical sequence from yarn through cloth to eventual production of domestic spinning machinery. Imports of cotton yarn turned downward in the late 1880s and by 1897 Japan was already a net exporter of yarn. A net export position in cotton cloth was achieved by 1910, after which the export surplus widened rapidly. Production of spinning machinery on a substantial scale began during World War I, and by 1930 Japan was a net exporter in this area as well.

The upsurge of manufactured exports stands out clearly in the statistics. The percentage of finished manufactures going into exports rose from less than 10 percent in the 1870s to 20 percent around 1900 and almost 30 percent by 1920.[47] Viewed from another angle, Japanese

45. Ibid., p. 309.
46. Masao Baba and Masahirv Tatemoto, "Foreign Trade and Economic Growth in Japan: 1858–1937," in *Economic Growth*, ed. Klein and Ohkawa.
47. Shionoya, "Patterns of Industrial Development," in *Economic Growth*, ed. Klein and Ohkawa, p. 89.

exports rose at 9.4 percent a year over the period 1901–17, compared with a 2.9 percent rate of increase in GNP.[48] Although this figure includes large exports of raw silk as well as a variety of manufactures, cotton textiles were a major part of the total. From 1881–85 to 1919–23, textile output grew at more than 7 percent per year, much above any conceivable increase in domestic demand.

Income elasticity of demand for Japanese exports continued high. Baba and Tatemoto's estimate for the period 1897–1913 is 1.42. Another important consideration, emphasized by Ohkawa and Rosovsky,[49] was the price competitiveness of Japanese goods in world markets. This rested on a combination of: (1) rapid increases in output per man-hour in manufacturing, stemming from a combination of imports of advanced technology, increases in average scale of establishment, and rapid growth of aggregate output; and (2) a labor-supply situation that held the rate of wage increase well below the rate of productivity advance, with a consequent reduction of unit costs and prices. Taking the year 1906 as 100, the index of agricultural prices in 1938 stood at 95.3. But the index for manufacturing was 74.2; for textile products, 50.0; and for all Japanese exports, 43.5.[50]

An interesting feature of Japan's exports of manufactures was its differing behavior during the long upswings and downswings of economic growth. On the upswing, the percentage of manufacturing output exported tended to fall, as active domestic demand diverted supplies to the home market. On the downswing, the percentage of manufactures exported rose as domestic demand slackened. Manufacturing exports thus served as a balance wheel in the economy.

Despite Japan's notable success as an exporter, Ohkawa and Rosovsky conclude that it is not accurate to speak of "export-led growth" in the sense that foreign demand propelled the economy forward. Rather, one should emphasize the internal dynamics of the economy, with export growth appearing as a by-product of successful domestic performance.

Our position is that Japan's rate of growth of exports has been high and well above world averages because the rate of growth of

48. Ohkawa and Rosovsky, *Japanese Economic Growth*, p. 34.
49. Ibid., chap. 7.
50. Ibid., p. 179.

Table 3. Percentage Composition of Japanese Trade

	Food	Materials	Semimanufactures	Finished Manufactures
A. *Exports*				
1876–80	38.1	11.1	41.6	4.7
1894–98	15.1	10.7	44.3	26.5
1895–99	14.3	10.7	45.9	26.0
1911–15	10.8	7.9	49.5	30.4
1921–25	6.4	6.0	47.8	38.6
B. *Imports*				
1876–80	13.5	3.7	27.2	52.1
1894–98	23.2	22.5	18.2	34.1
1895–99	22.5	25.9	17.8	32.0
1911–15	11.7	52.2	18.3	17.1
1921–25	14.1	49.3	18.0	17.9

Source: Baba and Tatemoto, in *Economic Growth: the Japanese Experience Since the Meiji Era,* ed. Klein and Ohkawa, p. 177.

Table 4. Import Ratio by Demand Category in Manufacturing
(Percent of total supply, current prices)

	Consumer Goods	Producers Durables	Construction Materials	Intermediate Products
1874–83	10.5	25.1	27.3	12.9
1877–86	8.8	26.9	27.5	12.0
1882–91	7.5	25.6	38.3	13.0
1887–96	8.2	24.2	34.4	13.7
1892–01	7.9	38.9	31.5	14.5
1897–06	7.9	47.2	36.5	15.2
1902–11	6.9	37.3	39.5	14.6
1907–16	4.9	21.8	32.7	12.6
1912–21	3.4	11.3	25.8	11.1
1917–26	4.2	16.7	25.7	12.1

Source: Shionoya, in *Economic Growth: The Japanese Experience Since the Meiji Era,* ed. Klein and Ohkawa, p. 87.

its economy and especially of its industry has been high and well above world averages, and not vice versa. . . . Even though manufactured exports frequently grew at rates that exceeded those of manufacturing output . . . this was primarily due to a decline in the relative price of these products as a result of productivity gains in manufacturing. The emphasis is on the side of supply, and it is our contention that, in a long-term sense, the most important fact has been the shift of the domestic supply curve.[51]

Tables 3 and 4 show long-term trends in the composition of Japan's trade. After what has been said, the changes in table 3 are unsurprising. On the export side, note the growing importance of finished manufactures and the continuing great importance of semimanufactures (primarily raw silk). On the import side, note the decline of manufactured imports as domestic manufacturing capacity rose and the rapid increase in the importance of materials (raw cotton, wool, fuels) to supply the growing manufacturing sector.

Table 4 shows the proportion of the total supply of each category of manufactured good that came from foreign sources. It is interesting to note that Japan never depended heavily on imports of finished consumer goods. Japanese consumption patterns remained substantially unchanged throughout this period, with a strong preference for traditional goods from domestic sources. On the other hand, a high proportion of investment goods, both producers' durables and construction materials, was obtained from abroad. Import substitution in these products was very gradual and did not set in seriously until 1910. This gradualism has been commended by Tsuru, [52] who argues that, if Japan had tried to achieve self-sufficiency in machinery too soon, she could not have expanded plant capacity in textiles and other manufacturing industries so rapidly. As it was, the rapid growth of foreign-exchange receipts from silk and textiles helped finance the large imports of investment goods. In addition, foreign machinery imports were a major channel of technology transfer.

Despite the good export performance, there was recurrent pressure on the balance of payments. The need for large imports of cotton and wool fiber, fuels in which Japan is deficient, and machinery and construction materials produced a tendency toward deficit in the current balance most of the time. These deficits were handled by a variety of expedients: in the late 1870s by gold and silver shipments from existing reserves; in the late 1890s by Chinese reparation payments after the Sino-Japanese war; during 1904–13 by large foreign borrowings, mainly of a portfolio type; and in the early 1920s from reserves accumulated during the export boom of 1914 to 1918, when other major exporters were out of the market.

51. Ibid., pp. 173–74.
52. Tsuru, "The Takeoff in Japan," in *The Economic of the Takeoff*, ed. Rostow.

Apart from reparations payments, plus limited and temporary borrowing by the Japanese government, the economic expansion was carried out without reliance on foreign capital. Foreign private investment was contrary to policy and insignificant in amount, which is still true today.

THE JAPANESE GROWTH PATTERN

The Japanese economy in 1880 was overwhelmingly rural. More than 80 percent of the population lived in the countryside, and three-quarters of the national output was produced there. Even manufacturing was basically a rural activity, carried on in the home and in small, scattered workshops.

Over the next forty years the center of gravity shifted gradually toward urban activity. Although the farm population did not decline, neither did it increase, the net increase in population being entirely in urban areas. Agricultural output grew absolutely but shrank relatively. By 1920 the rural population was only 55 percent, and rural output perhaps 45 percent, of the national total.

The most striking structural changes were: (1) a large relative expansion of the private-trade-and-services sector, from about 17 to 31 percent of national output. Production of government services, on the other hand, grew only slightly as a percentage of output; (2) a similar relative expansion of industry, including manufacturing, infrastructure, and construction. Factory manufacturing increased in

Table 5. Sectoral Composition of Output in Japan, 1880 and 1920
(Percent)

	1880	1920
Agriculture:		
Subsistence	48	14
Marketed	16	20
Handicrafts:		
Rural	9	8
Urban	2	5
Factory industry	0	12
Government	8	10
Private trade and services	17	31
Total	100	100
Exports/GNP	5	15

relative importance from the 1890s onward and by 1920 was producing half of all manufacturing output. It should be remembered, however, that "factory" is defined to include any establishment with five or more workers. The average size of each establishment was small, and much of the manufacturing activity was still dispersed throughout the countryside; (3) a rough maintenance of its share of GNP by the rural cottage and handicraft sector, partly because of the booming raw silk industry, which meant a rapid growth in absolute terms. The proportion of farm family labor time devoted to manufacturing as a side activity probably doubled between 1880 and 1920; (4) growth of the foreign sector with disproportionate speed, with exports rising from about 5 to 15 percent of GNP over the period.

In sum, the Japanese pattern of growth acceleration can be characterized as *moderately rapid*—faster than in Britain and western Europe, slower than in some countries since 1945; *balanced*, in the sense that agriculture expanded simultaneously with industry and commerce and at a rate that avoided any marked shift in the internal terms of trade; based heavily on *small-scale production* from cottage and handicraft industries, with factories becoming important only after the economy was over the hump; *capitalist* in the sense of unfettered private enterprise, high profit rates, low tax rates, and a small public sector, but with government playing a very active facilitating role; *moderately austere*, in that consumption levels lagged considerably behind the growth of per capita output; and *internally generated*, in the sense of the nation's virtual independence of foreign capital or entrepreneurship. Trade linkages were important, however, in broadening markets for domestic output, in removing food-supply constraints, and in facilitating borrowing of technology via machinery imports.

Japanese experience suggests that a capitalist growth path, initiated under favorable conditions and intelligently pursued, was as viable in the Asia of 1880 as in the Britain of 1750. This is not to say that countries attempting growth acceleration today can or should repeat the Japanese experience. Japan started with an unusual combination of advantages: a large capital stock of roads, irrigation facilities, and paddy land development in agriculture; a relatively high level of agricultural productivity and per capita consumption, achieved over centuries of gradual growth; a relatively high level of popular education; a strong central government, strong nationalist sentiment, and a cultural tradition of obedience to constituted authority; and a position of "first comer" in the world's most populous continent.

Few of today's LDCs have such a favorable set of internal characteristics; and there are more strong competitors in world markets than there were a century ago. It is doubtful in any event that the growth experience of one successful economy is directly transferable to others. Each nation develops on its own historical track. Although it can learn something from others, it cannot become exactly like them; and economic success, if it comes, will not duplicate previous patterns.

I have tried to show what Japan did—and that what Japan did worked. The reader must judge to what extent this constitutes a development model.

10

Contemporary Developing Economies:
An Overview

In this and the next four chapters I shall examine the growth experience of fifteen developing countries over the period 1950–73. I chose 1973 as a terminal year partly because the statistical data from national and international sources end at that point as this is written. The year 1973 is appropriate also in that it marks at least a temporary halt in the worldwide economic boom that began in 1945. Most of the mature economies turned downward into recession during 1973–74, curtailing export markets for the less developed countries; in addition, many of the LDCs were afflicted by food shortages, sharply higher prices for petroleum imports, and consequent foreign-exchange difficulties.

Throughout chapters 10–14, we should bear in mind the weakness of the underlying quantitative information. The data reprinted by international organizations cannot be any better than the national sources from which they are drawn. Foreign trade, government revenue and expendture, and the output of large-scale industry can be measured with some accuracy. Estimates for agriculture, trade, services, and traditional small-scale production are much cruder; and since these are the major part of GNP, the GNP estimate necessarily contains a large probable error.

In addition to this margin of error, GNP estimates for the LDCs have several sources of upward bias. Two biases emphasized by Kuznets[1] are: (1) that the ratio of industrial to agricultural prices is substantially higher in the LDCs than in developed countries, and that this leads to overweighting of the fast-growing industrial sector; (2) that the estimated growth of service outputs is partly spurious, since it contains the "regrettable necessities" arising from urbanization,

---

1. Simon Kuznets, "Problems in Comparing Recent Growth Rates for Developed and Less Developed Countries," *Economic Development and Cultural Change* 20 (January 1972): 185–209.

industrialization, and (in some cases) militarization. These things, as Kuznets has long maintained, are intermediate goods rather than final output—a qualification that applies equally, of course, to the developed countries. One might add that the faster-growing activities in the LDCs are overweighted simply because they are more visible and easier to measure. As the chief national-income economist of Burma once explained to this writer, "Anything that happens in Rangoon I can measure. What happens outside Rangoon, I cannot."

How can one get a general view of growth acceleration in the post-1945 era? Most satisfying in many ways are thorough case studies of particular countries. But even if information were available, space would not permit us to examine each economy in the same detail as we did for Japan. Further, it is not easy to go from a series of country vignettes to generally applicable conclusions.

At the opposite pole from country case studies is cross-section analysis of a large number of countries, in which institutional detail and historical evolution tend to disappear. A recent study by Hollis Chenery and Moises Syrquin attempts a comparative quantitative analysis of 101 economies,[2] comprising the great majority of countries with the exception of the Communist group. Although there is limited use of time series, most of the analysis involves cross-section comparisons of economic structure as of about 1965. In these comparisons the structure of economies at different current income levels is taken as indicative of change through time. Such work is useful, just as Simon Kuznets's earlier work was useful, in clarifying the structural differences between rich and poor countries. But it has the limitations that we noted in chapter 1. To treat stagnant economies, developing economies, and mature economies as comprising a universe with homogeneous properties raises many questions. Nor do static comparisons at a particular point in time really illuminate the nature of economic change (or lack of change) over the course of time.

The approach used here involves several methodological principles. First, we believe that the relevant universe consists of countries where there is strong evidence of growth acceleration since 1945. Within this group, the most interesting are countries of substantial size that are not heavily dependent on a single export product—oil, copper, bananas, or whatever. This at once brings the universe down from a hundred countries to perhaps fifteen to twenty.

2. Hollis Chenery and Moises Syrquin, *Patterns of Development, 1950–1970* (New York: Oxford University Press, for the World Bank, 1975).

Second, we believe that analysis should focus on the behavior of country time series, that is, on a comparative view of time-series experience. Actually, instead of continuous series, we shall rely mainly on beginning and end comparisons, usually comparisons of 1950–52 with 1971–73. We shall also use decade rates of change, that is, average annual rates of change in a particular variable over the years 1950–60, 1960–70, and 1965–73.

Third, in interpreting the observed behavior, we shall draw on related quantitative material and institutional detail from country monographs and other sources. This is an effort to get behind the performance of highly aggregated variables and gain insight into the dynamics of change rather than simply look at the end result. Our work is more nearly in the spirit of the quantitative economic historian than in that of the econometrician. Those of econometric bent will doubtless regard it as methodologically crude, even naive. It is crude, but it should be viewed as a preliminary fishing expedition in an area where both models and data are themselves crude and fragmentary.

THE SELECTION OF COUNTRIES

To select countries that meet the tests suggested above is not easy, and no selection will satisfy everyone. Given our objective of focusing on clearly developing economies, and given the probable error plus the upward bias in the GNP data, we decided first to exclude countries whose *reported growth rate of GNP per capita* over this period was below 2 percent per year. Some of these countries may have experienced sustained growth since 1950; but we cannot be sure. Some of the largest LDCs, including India and Indonesia, drop off the list on this score.

The other criteria used in our selection were:

1. Economic size. There are about sixty LDCs with populations of less than ten million. Some of these, such as Hong Kong, Singapore, and Puerto Rico, have had high GNP growth rates; but the growth pattern is trade-dominated and easily explainable. The only country we include from this size category is the Ivory Coast, with a population of about six million, which has had a high growth rate and serves also to give some representation of African experience.

2. Capitalist or socialist structure. By "socialist" we mean socialist in the Soviet or Chinese sense, that is, countries with a Communist government. Rather than lumping socialist LDCs with the non-

socialist countries, it seemed better to devote a separate chapter (chapter 15) to the socialist growth pattern. Our present sample, then, includes only countries following a mixed-economy growth path.

3. Oil-mineral economies. In general, we have excluded these economies, where growth is heavily concentrated in one or two export products and where increases in income may not be widely disseminated among the population. Thus, we exclude the small Persian Gulf oil states, along with Iraq, Saudi Arabia, Libya, Algeria, Zambia, and Zaire. We do, however, include three important oil producers—Iran, Nigeria, and Venezuela—whose production structure is more diversified and where oil revenues have helped activate a general growth process.

Among the countries remaining after these exclusions, we gave some weight to availability of secondary sources. Countries for which there is some research literature in English were preferred over countries without such a literature. The outcome was a list of fifteen countries, distributed as follows:

Asia	South Korea	*Africa*	Kenya
	Taiwan		Nigeria
	Philippines		Ivory Coast
	Thailand	*Latin America*	Brazil
	Malaysia		Colombia
	Pakistan		Mexico
	Iran		Venezuela
	Turkey		

Several comments may help avoid misunderstandings. First, this is not intended as a complete roster of post-1950 "success cases," though we believe that it includes most such cases. Second, we do not assert that all these countries have "taken off" into sustained growth. The indications are favorable; but twenty-five years is too short a period to warrant a final judgment. Finally, we have considered the objections that might be raised against one or another country on the list. Several —Colombia, Venezuela, Philippines—have had relatively low and precarious growth rates. It may be said that Taiwan is not a country but a province of China. It has, however, been politically and economically separate from the mainland for almost a century. Pakistan, for present purposes, means "old Pakistan," and the growth outlook for "new Pakistan" is not entirely clear. Nigeria has had a turbulent political history, including a major civil war, and its future also contains uncertainties. In each of these cases, however, we judged that the balance of considerations favored inclusion of the country. The resulting list, we believe, is large and diversified enough to test hypotheses about growth acceleration.

It may be useful to compare our selection of countries with an earlier ranking by Irma Adelman and Cynthia Taft Morris.[3] On the basis of the growth rate of real per capita GNP from 1950–51 to 1963–64, they divided countries into A, B, C, and D groups. Two of our countries, Thailand and Taiwan, received an A grade from Adelman-Morris. The remainder of their A group comprised Japan, South Africa, Greece, and Israel (regarded by us as mature economies); Jamaica, Trinidad, Jordan, and Nicaragua (excluded here on grounds of size); and Iraq and Libya (excluded here as oil economies).

The thirteen remaining countries on our list received a B, or better-than-average rating, in the Adelman-Morris classification. Indeed, our list, though arrived at independently, is almost identical with their B list. This encourages us to believe that we have identified economies with above-average growth rates.

This chapter is concerned with preliminaries, with the circumstances surrounding growth acceleration, and with the evidence on aggregate economic performance; and we propose to proceed as follows. First, we want to ask what economic, political, and social characteristics have been associated with the strong economic performance of these countries. What distinguishes them in the universe of LDCs? Second, we shall look at specific historical events—wars, revolutions, national independence—that might be regarded as having some bearing on growth acceleration. Third, we shall comment briefly on demographic trends. During nineteenth-century growth acceleration in today's mature economies, there was a nearly simultaneous rise in the growth rate of population, output, and output per capita. How similar, or how different, are today's developing countries in this respect?

Fourth, we shall present data on the growth rate of output and output per capita in these economies since 1950. Finally, we shall test the reality of growth in these countries by looking at changes in the composition of national output and other indicators such as growth rates of food output and per capita food availability. The point of

---

3. Irma Adelman and Cynthia Taft Morris, *Society, Politics, and Economic Development: A Quantitative Approach* (Baltimore: The Johns Hopkins Press, 1967). This basic source will be cited hereafter as Adelman-Morris.

such cross-checking is as follows. Suppose we did not know the growth rate of GNP. Or suppose we did not entirely believe the estimates we had. Would we still conclude, after surveying these other types of evidence, that the economies on our list are high-growth economies?

SOCIAL, POLITICAL, AND ECONOMIC CHARACTERISTICS

Here, we are fortunate in being able to draw on a valuable body of material assembled by Adelman and Morris.[4] Having selected a sample of seventy-four underdeveloped countries, they developed a list of forty-one social, political, and economic 'indicators' that may be related significantly to economic growth. With respect to each indicator, the countries in the sample were classified usually, though not invariably, into A, B, C, and D groups. The classification work was laborious and involved scanning a variety of social-science materials as well as consulting authorities on each country. The procedures used should be consulted in the original source. Except for a few mechanical adjustments, we have simply accepted the Adelman-Morris ratings as valid.[5]

The information summarized in tables 1, 2, and 3 will warrant careful study. On the assumption that the reader will do just that, we limit ourselves to comments on points of particular interest. For each indicator, an A rating signifies a situation hypothesized to be most favorable to economic growth, while a D rating is least favorable.

4. Adelman-Morris, chap. 2, "Social, Political, and Economic Indicators." This 120-page chapter is a small monograph by itself.

5. In developing tables 1, 2, and 3, we have departed from Adelman-Morris in three respects:

(1) We discarded some of their indicators, whose rationale did not seem entirely persuasive, thus reducing the list from 41 to 27.

(2) In a few cases, Adelman-Morris used an A–C ranking, or occasionally an A–F ranking, instead of the standard A–D. In these cases, we reclassified the countries concerned into four groups to achieve a standard format, which was facilitated by the generous use of pluses and minuses by Adelman-Morris to indicate finer ratings.

(3) In a few cases, we *inverted* the rank order, making our A correspond to the Adelman-Morris D. For example, "political strength of the traditional elite" was rated by them in descending order of strength, so that an A rating represented a situation *least* favorable to development. We inverted this ranking so that, in our tabulations, an A rating is always "good."

Note also that one of our countries, Malaysia, which came into existence relatively late, was not included in the Adelman-Morris study and so does not appear in tables 1–3.

It should be emphasized that Professors Adelman and Morris are in no way responsible for our adaptation of their material.

The numerical equivalents used in calculating group scores were A = 3, B = 2, C = 1, D = 0. Thus, a country score of 1.5 on a particular set of indicators means average performance (half Bs, half Cs) relative to the entire Adelman-Morris sample of seventy-four countries.

We approach the data with the following hypotheses: (1) that the countries on our list will score substantially better than 1.5, that is, that they are superior with respect to the chosen indicators; (2) that the faster-growing countries on the list will score higher than the slower-growing countries; and (3) that each indicator will also score appreciably above 1.5. Where this is not so, that is, where this "superior" group of countries scores only average or below on a particular indicator, the hypothesized relation of that indicator to economic growth is called into question.

Social Indicators

These indicators, listed at the bottom of table 1, are rather a mixed bag. Some of them, such as size of the traditional subsistence sector (1) and extent of urbanization (3), appear more closely related to past development and present income level than to prospects for future growth. Thus, it is not surprising that the relatively high-income Latin American countries score high, while the African countries score low.

There is probably the clearest rationale for hypothesizing a relation to economic growth in the case of indicator 4 (size of the indigenous middle class), which is related to the supply of both entrepreneurs and civil servants, and indicator 5 (extent of social mobility), which permits recruitment of able individuals to high-level positions. The prevalence of As and Bs in these columns, and the relatively high overall score at the bottom, suggests that our group of countries is indeed superior in these respects. Indicator 2 (extent of dualism) also appears significant, all but one of our countries being in the upper half of the LDC distribution on this count. On the other hand, with regard to the extent of literacy (6) and the extent of mass communications (7), there is marked dispersion in the country ratings, and the overall score is only average—that is, our countries are no better or worse in these respects than the LDC world in general. This suggests that the degree of literacy may be less closely related to growth rates than has sometimes been supposed.

Table 1. Social Indicators

Country	1	2	3	4	5	6	7	Country Score
Brazil	B	B	B	B	A	B	B	2.1
Colombia	B	B	A	B	A	B	B	2.3
Iran	C	C	C	B	B	D	B	1.3
Ivory Coast	C	B	D	C	C	D	D	0.7
Kenya	C	B	D	D	C	C	C	0.9
Korea, South	C	B	B	B	A	A	A	2.3
Mexico	B	B	A	A	A	B	A	2.6
Nigeria	C	B	D	B	B	D	D	1.0
Pakistan	C	B	D	B	C	D	D	0.7
Philippines	B	B	A	B	A	A	C	2.3
Taiwan	B	A	B	A	A	B	B	2.4
Thailand	C	B	C	C	B	A	C	1.7
Turkey	B	B	B	B	A	B	B	2.1
Venezuela	A	B	A	A	A	B	A	2.7
Indicator score	1.6	2.0	1.6	1.9	2.4	1.6	1.6	1.8

Code:
1   Size of the traditional subsistence sector (A = smallest size)
2   Extent of dualism (A = smallest degree of dualism)
3   Extent of urbanization
4   Size of the indigenous middle class
5   Extent of social mobility
6   Extent of literacy
7   Extent of mass communications

Looking across the table at the country scores, it does not appear that the social indicators discriminate successfully between fast-growing and slow-growing economies. Some high-growth economies (South Korea, Mexico, Taiwan) achieve a high overall score, but so do some slower-growing economies (Colombia, Philippines); and some countries with a high growth rate (Iran, Ivory Coast) have scores well below average. There is a clearer relation to geographic location. Latin American countries tend to have the highest scores, Asian countries lower scores, and African countries the lowest scores.[6]

6. This parallels a finding by Adelman and Morris. On the basis of consolidated scores on political and social variables, they divided their seventy-four countries into: (1) those with the highest level of socioeconomic development. Almost all the South American countries are in this group; (2) those with an intermediate level of socioeconomic development. A majority of this group are Asian countries; (3) those with the lowest level of socioeconomic development. This list is dominated by African countries. See their table 5, p. 170.

Experience

Table 2. Political Indicators

Country	1	2	3	4	5	6	7	8	9	Country Score
Brazil	B	C	A	C	B	C	C	B	C	1.6
Colombia	A	C	A	A	C	A	A	B	B	2.3
Iran	C	A	B	D	D	B	C	C	C	1.2
Ivory Coast	D	D	C	D	B	A	C	B	A	1.4
Kenya	D	A	A	C	A	B	A	C	C	1.9
Korea, South	B	A	A	D	B	C	C	D	C	1.4
Mexico	A	C	B	B	A	A	A	A	A	2.6
Nigeria	D	C	A	B	B	A	B	B	A	2.0
Pakistan	C	B	D	C	B	D	C	A	B	1.3
Philippines	C	C	A	A	B	A	B	C	A	2.1
Taiwan	A	A	B	D	A	B	A	B	A	2.3
Thailand	C	A	D	D	C	D	C	B	B	1.1
Turkey	A	B	A	C	A	C	A	B	B	2.2
Venezuela	A	C	A	B	A	C	A	A	C	2.2
Indicator score	1.7	1.8	2.2	1.1	2.1	1.8	2.0	1.9	2.0	1.8

Code:

1 Degree of national integration and sense of national unity
2 Degree of centralization of political power
3 Degree of competitiveness of political parties
4 Strength of democratic institutions
5 Political strength of the traditional elite (A = smallest political strength)
6 Political strength of the military (A = smallest political strength)
7 Degree of administrative efficiency
8 Extent of leadership commitment to economic development
9 Extent of political stability

Political Indicators

Turning to the political indicators in table 2, we face the same difficulty—that is, that some political characteristics may be related mainly to income level rather than to rate of change. Further, association says nothing about causation. For example, at a higher level of development one might expect the political influence of traditional elite groups (indicator 5) to be weakened by the rise of a modernized middle class. But this may be largely a *consequence* of development rather than a prerequisite for it.

A further difficulty is that, on some points, there is no clear a priori basis for a hypothesis. Who can say whether strength of democratic institutions is, on balance, a help or a hindrance to economic growth? Is military government more or less favorable to development than civilian rule? (And countries keep changing their status! Since 1964, when the Adelman-Morris ratings were made, Nigeria and the Philippines have passed from civilian to military rule, while Thailand has passed from military to civilian and then back to military government.)

Several positive suggestions nevertheless emerge from table 2. Our list of successful economies is clearly superior to LDCs in general with regard to degree of administrative efficiency (7), extent of leadership commitment to economic development (8), and extent of political stability (9). The usual hypotheses on these points are confirmed. Indeed, the score for "leadership commitment" should probably be higher than it is, because the Adelman-Morris ratings for Iran, Kenya, and South Korea seem too low in the light of post-1964 developments.

It is interesting also that, in our list of countries, the political strength of traditional elites is below average—and so is the political influence of the military. Only one-third of these countries have had extended periods of military rule, while the proportion for LDCs in general is probably above one-half. Interesting in a different sense are the low scores achieved by degree of national integration (1) and strength of democratic institutions (4). In this last respect, our countries are below average, even for the less developed world.

Looking across the table at the country scores, the continental differences noted with respect to social indicators are no longer in evidence. Latin American countries do not score consistently high, nor are African countries consistently low. The results resemble those of table 1, however, in that the fast-growing countries on our list do not score higher than the slower-growing countries. Indeed, a crude scatter diagram suggests a negative relation. Nigeria and Colombia, with "political scores" of 2.0–2.3, have grown rather slowly. Iran, South Korea, and Thailand, with below-average scores of 1.1–1.4, have grown more rapidly. Only Mexico and Taiwan show a high growth rate *and* a high score oń political structure.

Economic Indicators

The Adelman-Morris economic indicators fall into two categories. Items 1–4 are measures of *economic performance:* rate of increase in GNP per capita, gross capital formation rate, diversification of industrial output and extent of shift from handicraft to factory production, and rate of increase in industrial output. The Adelman-Morris ratings, of course, are based on performance from 1950 to 1964, while our

Table 3. Economic Indicators

Country	1	2	3	4	5	6	7	8	9	10	11	Country Score 5–11
Brazil	B	B	A	A	A	B	B	B	A	A	B	2.4
Columbia	C	A	B	B	B	B	B	B	B	B	B	2.0
Iran	B	C	B	A	A	D	C	C	D	B	C	1.1
Ivory Coast	B	C	D	C	C	C	D	C	C	C	D	0.7
Kenya	C	C	C	C	C	D	C	C	B	B	D	1.0
Korea, South	B	C	B	A	C	C	C	C	A	C	A	1.6
Mexico	B	B	A	B	A	A	B	A	B	A	B	2.6
Nigeria	C	C	C	A	B	C	C	C	B	C	D	1.1
Pakistan	C	D	C	A	D	C	C	C	C	B	B	1.1
Philippines	B	D	B	A	C	C	B	B	C	B	A	1.7
Taiwan	A	A	A	A	D	A	A	A	B	B	A	2.3
Thailand	A	C	C	A	C	C	C	C	B	B	B	1.4
Turkey	B	C	B	A	A	A	B	B	C	B	B	2.1
Venezuela	A	A	A	A	A	B	A	A	A	A	A	2.9
Indicator score	1.9	1.4	1.9	2.6	1.7	1.5	1.6	1.7	1.8	2.0	1.8	1.7

Code:

1 Rate of growth of GNP per capita, 1950/51–1963/64
2 Gross investment rate
3 Level of modernization of industry
4 Growth rate of real industrial output
5 Abundance of natural resources
6 Character of agricultural organization (point on commercial-subsistence spectrum)
7 Level of modernization of techniques in agriculture; degree of improvement in agricultural productivity since 1950
8 Level of adequacy of physical overhead capital
9 Level of effectiveness of the tax system; degree of improvement in the tax system since 1950
10 Level of effectiveness of financial institutions; degree of improvement of financial institutions since 1950
11 Rate of improvement in human resources

selection of these countries was based on their record over a longer period, 1950 to 1973. Several countries (Taiwan, South Korea, Pakistan, Malaysia, Iran) did substantially better in the 1960s than in the 1950s, one (Nigeria) did less well.

Since our selection of countries was based on economic performance, those countries should do well on the performance indicators. And they do fare relatively well, particularly with regard to the growth rate of industrial output, where they scored 2.6 out of a possible 3.0.

There is a possible bias in our perceptions here. A high growth rate of industrial output may tend to be overweighted, both in the national accounts and in our general impression of the country, leading us to classify as success cases those countries in which industry has done unusually well. One surprising result is that for indicator 2, which shows the gross capital-formation rate in our countries to be slightly below that for all LDCs. This runs counter to the conventional wisdom on economic development, though it is not inconsistent with the historical experience in Britain and Japan.

The remaining indicators, 5–11, bear more directly on *development potential.* Some of them relate to resource endowments (natural resources, physical overhead capital, human capital), others relate to institutional structures that might be considered conducive to growth. It is a plausible hypothesis that our success cases should have been above average in these respects. Unfortunately, this expectation is not borne out by the data. Our countries turn out to be only about average on most of the resource variables. Our sample does seem to have some advantage with regard to the adequacy of financial institutions. Moreover, most of the country ratings are above average with regard to the adequacy of tax structures and the rate of improvement in human resources.

Looking across the table at the country scores on indicators of economic potential, we observe little relation to realized growth rates. But there are once more distinct continental differences, apparently related to levels of development. All the Latin American countries score 2.0 or above and are joined in that range by Turkey (a semi-European country) and Taiwan (which shows up as a superachiever in most of our tabulations). But the 1960–70 GNP growth rate for this group ranges from Colombia's 4.9 to Taiwan's 10.0 percent. At the bottom, the African countries score in the range of 0.7–1.1 and are joined at that low level by Iran and Pakistan. But again, realized 1960–70 growth rates within this group range from Nigeria's 3.0 to Iran's 8.3 percent.

A Summary Word

The hypothesis that our sample of developing economies is superior in socioeconomic structure to the universe of LDCs is in general supported by the evidence. On about two-thirds of the indicators, these countries score better than average, sometimes decidedly better. In-

Table 4. Indicator Scores, Per Capita Income, and GNP Growth Rates

Country	Per Capita Income, 1970 (U.S. dollars)	Average Indicator Score	Average Annual Increase in GNP, 1960–73 (percent)
Venezuela	980	2.6	5.7
Mexico	670	2.6	6.9
Brazil	420	2.0	6.6
Taiwan	390	2.3	10.1
Iran	380	1.2	9.8
Malaysia	380	n.a.	6.1
Colombia	340	2.2	5.3
Turkey	310	2.1	6.6
Ivory Coast	310	0.9	7.0
Korea, South	250	1.8	9.4
Philippines	210	2.0	5.4
Thailand	200	1.4	7.8
Kenya	150	1.3	6.9
Nigeria	120	1.4	4.8
Pakistan	100	1.0	6.5

teresting examples are: (limited) extent of dualism, size of the indigenous middle class, degree of social mobility, (low) political strength of the traditional elite, (low) political strength of the military, degree of administrative efficiency, extent of leadership commitment to economic development, level of effectiveness of tax systems and financial institutions, and rate of improvement in human resources. On the whole, our sample countries score somewhat better on political than on economic indicators. This suggests that their superiority may consist more largely in political organization than in economic resources.

On the negative side, several plausible expectations are disappointed. Thus, our group scores only average or below on extent of literacy, degree of national integration, strength of democratic institutions, gross investment rate, level of modernization of techniques in agriculture, and level of adequacy of physical overhead capital. This does not demonstrate that these variables are unrelated to economic growth; but neither is their importance confirmed by the procedure used here.

Since the countries in our sample differ widely in income level and growth rate, it is interesting to make comparisons within the sample as well as between it and LDCs in general. The clearest relationship that appears in table 4 is that between a country's indicator scores and its level of per capita income. The relatively high-income Latin American countries score consistently in the B+ –A – range. The low-income African countries, on the other hand, score C–C– on the social and economic indicators, though doing somewhat better in political terms. This suggests a hypothesis that development becomes progressively easier as per capita income rises. Countries that are already relatively well-off tend to have political and social structures favorable to further growth. This association, of course, does not explain *why* this should be so.

There is little association, on the other hand, between country test scores and recent growth experience. The ratings are of little help in solving the puzzle of why some countries in the group grew much faster than others or in making short-range projections for the future.

All this raises questions about the concept of socioeconomic prerequisites for economic development. Some of the indicators strike out on our tests, suggesting that their relation to growth is less clear than a priori reasoning might suggest. Moreover, the fact that indicator scores seem more clearly related to income level than to growth rate raises questions about causation. Instead of the one-way relationship implied by the prerequisites concept, more complex feedback relations seem to be involved. Some of the structural characteristics of high-income economies and societies are doubtless results as well as sources of sustained growth.

GROWTH ACCELERATION: TIMING AND CIRCUMSTANCES

Let us now ask about these countries several questions raised earlier about Britain and Japan. At what point in time did growth acceleration begin? Did growth begin suddenly from a position of near stagnation? Or was there a prolonged period of gradual growth before the recent speedup? Can growth acceleration be associated with specific events—wars, revolutions, national independence, world prosperity?

Some of the relevant information is summarized in table 5. In the four Latin American countries, which benefitted from war demands without being directly involved in World War II, growth acceleration can be dated from the 1940s. The diversion of productive capacity in the industrialized countries to war purposes reduced the availability of manufactures to the LDCs, thus enlarging the market for domestic industries. The drop in import availabilities, combined with strong demand for primary exports, also enabled the Latin American countries to accumulate large foreign exchange reserves, which permitted large imports of capital goods and industrial materials in the years after 1945.

Table 5. The Timing of Growth Acceleration

Country	Beginning of Growth Acceleration	Preceding Period of Gradual Growth	Attendant Circumstances
Brazil	1940	1890–1940	Great Depression; W.W.II.
Colombia	1940	1920–40	Great Depression; W.W.II; suppression of domestic violence.
Iran	1950	1925–40	Oil nationalization, 1950.
Ivory Coast	1960	1920–60	Independence, 1960; French financial and technical assistance.
Kenya	1960	1900–40	Independence, 1964; U.K. finance.
Korea, South	1953	1910–40	Independence, 1945; Korean War, 1950–53; U.S. finance.
Malaysia	1960	1920–60	End of civil war, 1956; Independence, 1957; U.K. finance.
Mexico	1940	1870–1910	Revolution, 1910–20; Great Depression; World War II.
Nigeria	1950	1900–40	Independence, 1960; petroleum expansion, 1965; end of civil war, 1970.
Pakistan	1960	none	Independence, 1947; wars with India; U.K. finance.
Philippines	1950	1900–40	Independence, 1946.
Taiwan	1950	1900–40	Independence, 1945; occupation by mainland Chinese forces, 1949–50; U.S. finance.
Thailand	1950	1870–1940	Decline of foreign influence after 1945.
Turkey	1950	1923–50	Dissolution of the Ottoman Empire; establishment of the Turkish Republic, 1923.
Venezuela	1950	1920–50	Beginning of petroleum boom, 1950; overthrow of Perez Jiménez regime, 1958.

Most of the other countries on our list, however, did not exist as independent countries in 1940; and on most of them the impact of World War II was unfavorable. Some areas, such as Malaya and the Philippines, were ravaged by combat and military occupation. Return to normal economic conditions required some years after 1945. For most of these countries, then, growth acceleration set in around 1950, aided by widespread preparation for national independence and by the raw materials boom of the Korean War period, which swelled foreign-exchange earnings.

In a few cases, accelerated growth set in only around 1960. Pakistan, starting with an unusually meager resource base, did not accomplish much in the 1950s. Kenya and Malaya achieved independence relatively late, and Malaya in addition had a virulent guerrilla war that was not brought under control until the late 1950s.

Growth acceleration did *not* usually begin from a stationary situation. Most countries on our list had a record of from fifty to seventy-five years of gradual growth before 1940. This was often growth under colonial auspices (eight of the fifteen countries were colonies before 1945). It was typically export-led growth—rice from Thailand, tin and rubber from Malaya, cocoa and palm oil from Nigeria, coffee from Brazil. It was primarily extensive rather than intensive growth. Most of these countries had large reserves of unutilized land. Cultivated area, population, output, and exports expanded together. There are also indicators, in most countries, of a modest rise in per capita output and consumption. In Nigeria, for example, consumption of imported manufactures rose without consumption of anything else falling, the imports being paid for by additional expenditure of labor time on export crops.

In general, then, the time profile resembles that of the British and Japanese cases. Growth had typically been going on for several decades before the acceleration point. The one area where growth had to be generated almost from scratch is the Indian subcontinent. True, the colonial authorities had established a transport and communications network. Population had been growing slowly since at least 1900, and output must have been growing proportionately, since there is little evidence of immiserization. But neither is there evidence of a rise in living standards or of a marked structural change in the economy. Indeed, the proportion of the Indian population working as farmers or farm laborers was slightly *higher* in 1961 than in 1901. The growth problems of independent India and Pakistan are thus rooted deep in history and were bound to be more difficult than those of countries that had gotten a running start before 1945. The partition of the subcontinent was also disruptive, especially for Pakistan, which inherited only a minor part of the accumulated physical and human capital.

What economic and political circumstances attended growth acceleration in these countries? The most important, so pervasive that we have not listed it explicitly in table 5, was the unprecedented expansion of world output and trade from the late 1940s to the early 1970s. Output in the Western industrial countries grew at 5 to 6 percent a year, a substantially higher rate than in any earlier period of comparable length. The Soviet and East European economies grew at roughly the same rate. The developing countries were riding the tide of this long upswing, and it is not surprising that those on our list managed to keep up with or exceed the world average. At this writing, however, with a sharp redistribution of income toward the oil-producing countries and with the major industrial countries emerging only slowly from the first serious post-1945 recession, the buoyant atmosphere of 1945–73 cannot be projected into the future. If the tempo of world economic growth should slow down, as seems quite possible, the prospects of the developing economies will be correspondingly dampened.

The second dominant circumstance was the spread of national independence. Of the fifteen countries on our list, four are former colonies of Britain, two of Japan, one of France, and one of the United States. Between the late 1940s and the early 1960s, all these areas became self-governing countries. The new governments, in addition to being relieved of exactions by the "mother country," were able to levy taxes (on foreign businesses as well as on local citizens), impose import tariffs and exchange controls, and aim at building a national economy in lieu of the satellite economies of the colonial era.

Even in countries that were not colonies in 1945, there was often an upsurge of nationalistic spirit that served somewhat the same purpose. Examples include the liquidation in Mexico of the last important foreign public-utility holdings during the early 1950s; the Iranian nationalization of foreign oil properties in 1950, which led to a great increase in the share of oil revenue flowing into government channels; and the displacement of the British treasury representative in Thailand, who previously had something of a veto power over foreign economic policy. Inspired by the widespread decolonization movement, the LDCs became noticeably less responsive to advice and pressure from the major powers and more insistent on pursuing national objectives.

Foreign aid was important in some countries, mainly the smaller ones where a given amount of aid bulked larger as a percentage of GNP. In the immediate pre- and postindependence periods, the British and French governments made substantial grants to many of their African colonies. U.S. finance was important in Taiwan, South Korea, and

Pakistan. Taiwan, indeed, became a classic case of aid-assisted takeoff, signaled by impressive "graduation ceremonies" in 1965. Other LDCs, however, which also received substantial amounts of aid, do not appear on our list of success cases. It seems clear that success has depended mainly on the effectiveness of domestic economic management.

A WORD ON POPULATION

In the older industrial countries, population was often growing slowly for some time before the onset of modern economic growth; and this was frequently accompanied by a very gradual increase in output per capita. When the growth rate of output per capita accelerated, however, the rate of population increase also accelerated. This was due primarily to a reduction in death rates, arising from improved transport of food and elimination of famines, improved nutrition, improved sanitation and health conditions, and a reduction in infant mortality. In some countries, there was also a moderate increase in fertility, possibly arising from increased social mobility, earlier and more frequent marriages, improved health and nutrition of potential mothers, and rising incomes, which made a large family appear less burdensome.

The combination of falling death rates and stable or rising birth rates produced a population bulge, which in some countries lasted for fifty to seventy-five years. Eventually, as is well known, birth rates followed death rates downward, and these countries completed the demographic transition to a new equilibrium with a low birth rate, low death rate, and low rate of natural increase.

In the LDCs, too, population was often growing gradually well before the modern period. This was true particularly in countries with large reserves of arable land, where extensive growth could continue unchecked. Clark Reynolds reports that from 1877 to 1900 the population of Mexico grew 1.6 percent per year. Population was doubtless growing also in the other Latin American countries. The population of Thailand was growing in the late nineteenth century, though probably at less than 1 percent per year. In the Philippines, population grew at 1.9 percent per year during 1902–18. In Kenya, population is estimated to have been growing as early as 1900 by about 0.7 percent per year. For most countries, however, we have little information from before the 1920s. In some countries, including Iran and Nigeria, informed observers judge that population was virtually stationary until around 1925.

The limited information available suggests that, in most LDCs, the population growth rate accelerated in advance of any appreciable rise in per capita output. This was observable in many countries in the 1910s and 1920s and was apparent almost everywhere by the 1930s. During the 1930s the typical population growth rate for the countries in our sample was about 2 percent a year, the rates ranging from as low as 0.6 percent in Nigeria and 1.4 percent in India to as high as 2.5 percent in Korea. The acceleration was due almost entirely to a decline in death rates, traceable partly to the public health activities of the colonial authorities. Thus, the death rate in Taiwan and Korea began to fall almost immediately after the Japanese takeover around 1900, as did the death rate in the Philippines after the American occupation in 1898. But the same trend also appears in the independent countries. In Iran, for example, road improvements and importation of trucks during the 1920s virtually eliminated local famines and turned a static population into one that began growing at about 1.5 percent per year.

It is apparent from table 6 that a further acceleration has occurred since the 1940s, from a typical growth rate of 2 percent a year in 1940 to about 3 percent a year in 1970. The reason, again, is a continuing decline in death rates. National governments, aided by technical

Table 6. Crude Birth Rate, Death Rate, and Rate of
Natural Increase (Per thousand)

Country	1950			1960			1965–70		
	B	*D*	*N.I.*	*B*	*D*	*N.I.*	*B*	*D*	*N.I.*
Brazil	43.0	n.a.	n.a.	42.0	12.0	30.0	37.8	9.5	28.3
Colombia	36.7	14.2	22.5	42.4	13.0	29.4	40.2	9.8	30.4
Iran	27.9	(8.1)	(19.8)	39.3	24.5	14.8	41.5	16.6	24.9
Ivory Coast	53.0	n.a.	n.a.	52.5	30.0	22.5	46.0	22.7	23.3
Kenya	n.a.	n.a.	n.a.	n.a.	n.a.	n.a.	47.8	17.5	30.3
Korea, South	45.0	n.a.	n.a.	44.7	8.4	36.3	35.6	11.0	24.6
Malaysia	44.0	15.8	28.2	40.9	9.5	31.4	33.8	7.3	26.5
Mexico	45.7	16.2	29.5	45.0	11.4	33.6	44.0	9.1	34.9
Nigeria	56.0	16.3	39.7	49.2	12.8	36.4	49.6	n.a.	n.a.
Pakistan	49.0	12.2	36.8	49.0	16.17	32.5	50.9	18.4	32.5
Philippines	(50.0)	(8.2)	(42.8)	n.a.	n.a.	n.a.	44.7	12.0	32.3
Taiwan	49.3	11.3	32.0	39.5	6.9	32.6	33.1	15.3	17.8
Thailand	28.4	10.0	18.4	34.7	(8.4)	(25.7)	33.7	6.7	27.0
Turkey	43.0	15.2	27.8	n.a.	n.a.	n.a.	40.1	13.6	26.5
Venezuela	42.6	10.9	31.7	45.1	(7.5)	(37.6)	37.2	6.5	30.7

Source: UN, *Demographic Yearbook*, 1973, pp. 225, 279.

assistance from the World Health Organization, have been remarkably successful in curbing infectious diseases and improving health conditions. Thus, in half the countries on our list, crude death rates[7] have now fallen to the "mature economy range" of 8.0–12.0 per thousand, and in the remaining countries they are approaching this range. In a few countries (Colombia, Iran, Thailand), a rise in fertility has contributed to the population bulge; but in general, the behavior of death rates is dominant.

Only a few LDCs have entered the later stages of the demographic transition, with birth rates falling toward a new low-population-growth equilibrium. The clearest cases are South Korea, Taiwan, and Malaysia. The only other country on our list that shows a significant decline in fertility is Brazil, a relatively urbanized and industrialized country with a rapid growth of per capita income.

Table 7. Average Annual Growth Rates of
Population, GNP, and GNP Per Capita, 1950–1973
(Percent)

Country	*Population*			*GNP*			*GNP Per Capita*		
	1950– 60	*1960– 70*	*1965– 73*	*1950– 60*	*1960– 70*	*1965– 73*	*1950– 60*	*1960– 70*	*1965– 73*
Brazil	3.0	2.9	2.9	6.8	5.3	9.0	3.8	2.4	6.1
Colombia	3.3	3.2	3.2	4.7	4.9	6.0	1.4	1.7	2.8
Iran	2.8	2.9	3.2	6.2	8.3	10.9	3.4	5.4	7.7
Ivory Coast	3.7	3.0	3.3	n.a.	7.5	7.4	n.a.	4.5	4.1
Kenya	3.0	3.1	3.3	4.0	6.7	7.3	1.0	3.6	4.0
Korea, South	2.8	2.6	1.9	6.0	9.4	10.7	3.2	6.8	8.8
Malaysia	2.9	3.1	2.8	n.a.	6.2	5.9	n.a.	3.1	3.1
Mexico	3.2	3.5	3.5	5.8	7.2	6.3	2.6	3.7	2.8
Nigeria	1.9	2.9	2.5	4.1	3.0	8.3	2.2	0.1	2.8
Pakistan	n.a.	2.6	3.3	2.6	5.0	5.6	n.a.	2.4	2.3
Philippines	3.0	3.0	3.0	6.6	5.9	5.8	3.6	2.9	2.8
Taiwan	3.4	2.9	2.8	8.1	10.0	10.4	4.7	7.1	7.6
Thailand	3.0	3.1	3.0	6.4	8.0	7.3	3.4	4.9	4.3
Turkey	2.7	2.5	2.5	6.3	6.4	7.1	3.6	3.9	4.6
Venezuela	3.7	3.5	3.6	7.7	5.8	5.0	4.0	2.3	1.3

Source: IBRD, *World Data Book*, 1975.

7. It should be remembered that these are crude rates rather than age-specific rates. If the age-specific rates were the same in LDCs and MDCs, one would expect the crude rate to be lower in the LDCs because of high fertility leading to a high concentration of population in the lower age groups. Further, the recording of births and deaths in most LDCs is quite imperfect, so that changes of a few percentage points in table 6 are not necessarily indicative of trends.

There would be little dissent from the proposition that most developing economies stand to gain from a decline in fertility; but how far this decline can be accelerated by public policy is a complex question, the pursuit of which would carry me beyond my expertise as well as space limitations. I will comment on the issue briefly in chapter 16.

THE GROWTH AND STRUCTURE OF OUTPUT

The basic data on growth of output and output per capita are assembled in table 7. The rates of GNP increase are impressively high—high enough to outweigh any reasonable margin of error in the data and to outrace population growth. There is evidence, too, of growth acceleration over time. In almost every country, GNP rose faster from 1960 to 1970 than from 1950 to 1960; and in two-thirds of the countries the 1965–73 growth rate was still higher. From 1965 to 1973, the median rate of increase of per capita income in these countries was 4.0 percent. This is in line with the performance of the mature economies over this period. These success cases, in short, kept up with the pace of world economic growth, though the LDCs in general did not.

We now want to cross-check the reality of this aggregate growth by looking at changes in the composition of output. Here the Chenery-Syrquin cross-section results[8] may serve as a reference point. Comparing poor countries (annual per capita income below $100) with rich countries (annual per capita income above $1,000), they find the following differences in the percentage composition of output:

	Poor Countries	*Rich Countries*
Private consumption	.779	.624
Government consumption	.119	.141
Investment	.136	.234
Exports—Imports	− .033	− .001

Regarding output by sector of origin, they find the following differences:

	Poor Countries	*Rich Countries*
Primary production	.522	.127
Industry and utilities	.178	.488
Services	.300	.386

8. Chenery and Syrquin, *Patterns of Development*, pp. 20–21.

One would expect, then, that the composition of output in our sample countries has shifted perceptibly in a rich-country direction since 1950 and that in some cases it may be approaching the proportion characteristic of mature economies. Let us look first at data on the sector composition of output and then at the composition of output by end uses.

Output by Sector of Origin

Table 8 divides output into the familiar Kuznets categories of agriculture, industry (in the broad sense, including mining, public utilities, and construction), and services; and it compares three-year averages for an initial and a terminal period, typically 1950–52 and 1971–73. Three-year averages are advisable because of weather-induced variations in agricultural output, which could seriously distort the results for a particular year.

In all but two countries, the sectoral shifts are large enough to confirm the reality of overall growth. The agricultural share of national

Table 8. Gross Domestic Product by Industrial Origin,
Period 1 (1950–1952) and Period 2 (1971–1973)
(Percent)

Country	Agriculture		Industry		Services	
	1	2	1	2	1	2
Brazil[c]	28.9	17.6	30.4	34.4	40.7	47.0
Colombia	40.5	29.0	26.8	33.7	32.7	37.2
Iran[a,b]	33.1	14.3	33.6	56.3	33.3	29.0
Ivory Coast	57.6	27.0	17.1	32.2	25.3	40.1
Kenya	44.7	31.6	23.7	28.2	31.6	40.1
Korea, South	51.2	30.0	12.6	35.6	36.2	34.4
Malaysia	39.4	29.2	22.1	31.6	38.5	39.2
Mexico	22.4	10.4	35.4	36.5	38.5	53.0
Nigeria[b]	70.2	40.2	11.5	39.2	18.3	20.5
Pakistan	59.7	36.0	10.7	28.5	29.6	35.4
Philippines[c]	39.0	36.6	23.8	28.9	37.2	34.3
Taiwan	35.8	16.4	22.0	41.8	42.2	41.7
Thailand	57.4	33.3	15.2	30.9	27.4	35.5
Turkey	50.0	27.9	21.7	35.6	28.3	35.0
Venezuela[b]	8.0	6.2	51.5	54.0	39.5	39.8

Source: IBRD, *World Data Book*, 1975.
[a] Period 1 is 1959–60.
[b] "Industry" includes petroleum.
[c] Net domestic product rather than gross domestic product.

output typically falls by 10 percent or more. The exceptions are Venezuela, where oil (included in the industrial sector) dominates the output mix, and where the agricultural percentage in 1950 was already so low that it could not fall much farther; and the Philippines, where the small sectoral shifts raise a question about whether the aggregate growth rate was actually as high as reported.

Part of the decline in agriculture's share is normally picked up by the industrial sector. This is a standard and unsurprising result. But there are some surprises in the behavior of the services sector. We tend to think of a relative expansion of services production as a characteristic of late development in countries that are already relatively rich. But table 8 suggests that it may also, at least under contemporary conditions, be a characteristic of early development. In all but four countries, the services share of output rose between the initial and terminal periods. In several countries, the percentage point increase in the services share was larger than that in the industry share. By 1968–70 the median share of the services share in this group of countries was 39 percent, compared with Kuznets's figure of 37 percent in a sample of mature economies.[9]

Why does the services sector bulk so large in these economies? Two hypotheses may be suggested. First, in the LDCs, white-collar workers (civil servants, professional people, businessmen, even bank tellers and typists) earn a good deal more relative to manual workers than is true in more-developed countries. These white-collar people are employed predominantly in service production, and their relatively high wages swell the value of output in that sector. In addition, a high population-growth rate and large rural-to-urban migration increases the number of people available for porterage, petty trade, and personal services. If service output is estimated on the assumption that these people must be earning some conventional amount, the service sector may be inflated beyond its true dimensions.

Note that, although the countries in our group have moved in the expected direction, most of them remain well short of mature-economy proportions. The median share of primary production is still close to 30 percent. Industrial output still averages only about one-third of GNP rather than one-half. Only in the services share do our countries come close to the Chenery rich-country pattern.

---

9. Simon Kuznets, *Modern Economic Growth*. A Publication of the Economic Growth Center, Yale University (New Haven: Yale University Press, 1966), p. 144.

Output by End Use

In a growing economy, one would expect the percentage share of capital formation, and possibly also that of government consumption, to be rising. This should be offset by a decline in the share of private consumption. The experience of our sample countries, summarized in table 9, generally follows this pattern; but there are exceptions. The percentage shifts in Brazil, Venezuela, and Pakistan are quite small. In these countries, too, the percentage of output going to private consumption rose slightly, instead of declining as expected.

Production of current government services rose relatively in most countries. The exceptions were Venezuela, Kenya, and South Korea (this case being explained mainly by a relative decline in military expenditures after the end of the Korean War.) The gross capital formation rose in all but two countries (Brazil and Venezuela), typically by more than 5 percent, and in a few cases (South Korea, Taiwan, the Philippines, and Thailand) by 10 points or more.

Since these are open economies, the total of goods available for

Table 9. Gross National Product by End Use, Current Market Prices,
Period 1 (1950–1952 and Period 2 (1971–1973)
(Percent)

Country	Private Consumption		Central Government Consumption		Gross Domestic Capital Formation		Exports-Imports	
	1	*2*	*1*	*2*	*1*	*2*	*1*	*2*
Brazil	71.0	72.9	11.0	10.3	17.0	19.2	−3.2	−1.5
Colombia	77.6	73.7	6.2	8.2	15.6	21.0	0.2	−0.7
Iran	70.5	51.8	10.0	19.5	15.5	22.7	4.5	+8.9
Ivory Coast	n.a.	64.9	n.a.	18.3	n.a.	22.6	n.a.	+0.9
Kenya	69.0	62.5	22.2	17.7	14.4	24.9	2.6	−3.4
Korea, South	87.7	71.4	14.6	10.6	8.6	24.3	−7.9	−5.9
Malaysia	67.2	59.5	8.5	20.9	7.7	19.2	16.5	+0.2
Mexico	81.8	74.2	4.4	8.4	11.7	20.0	2.9	−0.9
Nigeria	86.2	65.6	3.4	11.4	7.5	22.8	2.1	+6.8
Pakistan	83.4	76.9	6.3	11.2	11.7	14.7	−2.8	−3.4
Philippines	84.5	71.3	7.5	8.7	6.8	20.1	−0.2	+0.9
Taiwan	68.0	51.9	17.2	16.6	12.5	25.0	−4.1	+6.3
Thailand	77.1	67.3	10.1	11.1	13.5	23.7	−1.7	−2.0
Turkey	74.8	67.0	10.8	13.0	10.2	19.2	−0.5	−3.0
Venezuela	53.9	53.9	13.5	14.5	23.3	30.1	8.3	+9.9

Source: IBRD, *World Data Book*, 1975.

Note: Figures do not add to 100.0 because of omission of net factor income from abroad.

Table 10. Average Annual Growth Rates of GNP Components,
1960–1973 and 1965–1973, at Constant Market Prices
(Percent)

	1960–73					*1965–73*				
	C	G	I	X	M	C	G	I	X	M
Brazil	6.5	6.0	8.5	7.4	9.3	8.5	10.4	13.6	11.6	19.6
Colombia	5.8	6.3	5.1	3.8	5.4	6.4	7.5	6.6	4.1	6.6
Iran[a]	7.3	18.2	13.5	13.2	14.4	7.7	20.7	14.3	14.3	16.9
Ivory Coast	6.0	11.0	10.5	6.8	7.5	5.7	9.9	9.2	7.2	6.3
Kenya	6.2	9.0	7.8	4.5	5.6	6.1	11.3	11.2	3.6	5.5
Korea, South	7.7	6.6	19.8	32.0	20.9	9.0	8.3	18.4	34.4	25.6
Malaysia	4.2	7.3	7.4	5.3	3.6	4.0	6.0	7.1	6.2	4.1
Mexico	6.8	8.1	7.4	5.7	5.9	6.3	7.3	7.6	6.9	8.0
Nigeria	3.5	12.9	8.3	11.6	8.0	7.0	18.6	9.9	13.2	12.4
Pakistan	6.3	6.6	4.6	6.7	3.2	5.8	4.7	−0.0	5.6	0.3
Philippines	5.1	4.3	6.2	6.2	4.5	6.0	4.8	3.9	4.1	2.0
Taiwan	7.9	5.8	15.2	23.7	18.6	7.3	6.8	13.5	26.0	21.2
Thailand	7.3	9.2	11.4	9.0	11.2	7.5	9.3	6.5	8.3	7.9
Turkey	5.0	9.0	9.5	8.2	7.2	5.7	9.9	8.0	8.9	9.6
Venezuela	4.9	6.9	4.7	6.7	6.4	4.2	7.6	2.8	7.1	8.0

Source: IBRD, *World Data Book*, 1975.
[a] 1960–72 and 1965–72.

domestic use differs from domestic output by the size of the merchandise trade balance. In some countries, a relative increase in imports cushioned the decline of private consumption. As of the early 1970s, about half the countries in our sample had a negative balance in their merchandise account. The only countries with sizable export surpluses were Taiwan and the three oil economies—Iran, Nigeria, and Venezuela.

Information on output composition from a different point of view appears in table 10, which shows annual percentage growth rates for each GNP component during the periods 1960–70 and 1965–73. Note that consumer-goods output was typically rising at better than 5 percent a year, indicating an improvement in *average* living standards, though not necessarily for every group in the population. In most countries, however, output of public goods and capital goods was rising at still higher rates. Exports rose at a median rate of 7 percent during 1965–73, though rapid export growth tended to be accompanied by rapid import growth as well.

By 1973 the distribution of output in this group of countries was very close to the Chenery-Syrquin rich-country pattern and also to the

distribution found by Kuznets in his sample of mature economies.[10]
The average distributions compared as follows:

	Mature Economies (Kuznets)	*Rich Countries* (Chenery-Syrquin)	*Developing Economies* (Table 9)
Private consumption	65%	62%	65%
Government consumption	13	14	13
Gross capital formation	22	23	22

There was, of course, considerable dispersion within the LDC group,
the private-consumption share varying from 52 percent in Taiwan and
Iran to 77 percent in Pakistan. For the group as a whole, however,
one is impressed with the strong resemblance to mature-economy
proportions.

The fact that our sample of developing countries has achieved
mature-economy proportions in this respect, but not in regard to the
sector origin of output, presents a paradox for which we have no ready
explanation. It is apparently easier, under modern conditions, to raise
the investment and government-consumption levels than it is to
achieve an equally rapid change in the structure of production.

Additional Growth Indicators

In addition to national accounting estimates, data are available on
such things as urban housing space, supply of radios and bicycles,
miles of improved road, educational enrollments, literacy rates,
hospital beds, doctors per capita, food availability per capita, and
morbidity and mortality rates. Although we have not attempted to
review this mass of evidence, we can comment briefly on health care
and food availability.

Increased life expectancy, reduced incidence of infectious and
chronic diseases, and improved medical and hospital care are among
the important improvements in welfare that accompany economic
growth. The crude death rate can serve as a rough proxy for this kind
of improvement. Evidence on the behavior of mortality rates was
presented in an earlier section of this chapter (see table 6). Though the
data are not completely dependable, for most countries they show a
fall of several points in the death rate between 1950 and 1970. By 1970

10. Ibid., table 3, pp. 236–38.

the median crude death rate for the countries in our sample was twelve per thousand, which is not much above the median for the mature economies.

On the food front, we have two kinds of information: estimates from the FAO on the growth rate of food output and total agricultural output; and FAO estimates of calorie and protein availability per capita. The relevant tables are presented in chapter 11, where we examine agricultural sector performance. Briefly, they show satisfactory rates of increase in food output, rates that, for most countries, were higher in the 1960s than the 1950s. The median annual rate of increase in food output from 1959–61 to 1969–71 was 6 percent. Country rates varied from a bit under 4 percent in Turkey, Iran, and the Philippines to better than 7 percent in Thailand, Malaysia, Venezuela, and South Korea. These rates were generally sufficient to accommodate population growth plus the marked rise of per capita incomes.

The tables on calorie availability, on the other hand, show little evidence of dietary improvement in a number of countries. These data, in fact, show some marked inconsistencies with the production data. For example, Malaysia, South Korea, and Colombia have high rates of food-production increase during the 1960s but no increase in per capita food availability. On the other hand, the Philippines, with one of the lowest rates of production increase in the 1960s, shows a marked rise in consumption. Although some discrepancy could arise through food exports and imports, the size of these differences suggests unreliability in the underlying data, probably mainly in the consumption estimates.

Altogether, then, we have four tests of whether the aggregate data on GNP growth are believable: a sector composition-of-output test, an end uses-of-output test, a health-improvement test, and a food-availability test. Eleven of the fifteen countries in our group pass all these tests without difficulty. But Iran and Venezuela emerge as atypical, oil-dominated economies in which income increases may not have been widely distributed throughout the population. Venezuela shows little structural change in the composition of output either by sector of origin or by end use. Iran has a low growth rate in agricultural output in the 1960s and no evidence of dietary improvement.

Some doubt is also cast on the growth record of Pakistan and the Philippines. In both countries, food output grew at less than 4.5 percent during the 1960s. The Philippines shows little change since

1950 in the sector composition of output; Pakistan shows little change in the end uses of output. The crude death rate in Pakistan, too, is the second highest in table 10 and seems not to have fallen since 1950. So, although we continue to include these four countries, there is more question about them than about the others on our list.

11

The Agricultural Sector

In a closed-economy model, if economic growth is to proceed smoothly over the long run, the supply of foodstuffs must rise at an appropriate rate. This rate depends on, among other things, the growth rate of the population, the rate of increase in per capita income and its distribution by income level, and the income elasticity of demand for foodstuffs at different income levels.

How can one tell whether food output is keeping pace with demand? A significant indicator is the behavior of the internal terms of trade. A relative increase in food prices suggests an inadequate rate of output increase. A decline in agriculture's gross barter terms of trade, however, is not necessarily an unfavorable symptom. If it reflects a rate of productivity increase in agriculture higher than that in other sectors, it could be accompanied by an increase in farmers' real income.

Opening the economy to foreign trade breaks the linkage of domestic production and domestic output; and this is as true of food supply as of other sectors. If a country has comparative advantage in certain nonfood products, it will tend to shift resources toward those products and exchange them for food in the world market. The most obvious examples are city-states such as Hong Kong or Singapore. The product with comparative advantage may be an agricultural export crop; and it may then be reasonable to divert land from, say, rice to sugar. Or the export crop may also be the main domestic food crop, as in the case of Thai rice. In such cases, a rate of demand increase that exceeds the rate of output increase can be met for a time by eating into the export surplus.

Where do output increases come from? Closed-economy models tend also to be closed-frontier models, in which output can increase only through rising yields per acre. But in actuality, extensive growth through expansion of cultivated acreage is still quite important. Even in a country that appears fully settled, cultivated acreage can often be enlarged by land reclamation, irrigation, and encroachment on pasture and forest land. As this potential is used up, however, the frontier gradually closes, and one is forced back on yield increases as the main source of growth. A sustained increase in yields per acre typically involves some combination of improved water control and other land improvements; technical progres in seed varieties and cultivation methods; application of larger amounts of modern inputs, notably fertilizer; larger labor inputs per acre; and possibly a shift in composition of output toward more labor-intensive and yield-responsive crops.

My discussion will focus on the behavior of agricultural output, but several related questions deserve attention.

1. What has been the rate of increase in the agricultural labor force? Has underemployment in agriculture been increasing or decreasing?

2. Development models usually embody a transfer of finance as well as labor from agriculture to the urban sectors. Has this been the typical pattern in our group of economies? Are there important counterexamples?

3. Some governments have paid more attention than others to agricultural development. What are the main ingredients of a pro-agriculture policy? Can one trace a relation within our sample between the policy stance of government and the rate of increase in agricultural output?

FOOD OUTPUT AND FOOD AVAILABILITY

Space limitations force me to deal in aggregates; and so it is important to underline the limitations of any summary measure of agricultural performance. In most countries the structure of agricultural output is complex. There are dozens of separate products—for export, for domestic industrial use, and for domestic food consumption —whose relative importance is shifting over time. Whether one is speaking of acreage increases, yield increases, price trends, or demand elasticities, statements that are true of some products will not be true of others. I shall illustrate this diversity occasionally from country data; but for the most part, I must stick to aggregative measures.

The data summarized in table 1 permit several generalizations. For most countries in our sample, agricultural output rose more rapidly during the 1960s than during the 1950s, and this is an important

Table 1. Growth of Agricultural and Food Production
(Average annual percentage rate)

Country	Agricultural Production		Food Production	
	1949–51 to 1959–61	1959–61 to 1969–71	1949–51 to 1959–61	1959–61 to 1969–71
Brazil	4.24	3.65	4.90	6.11
Colombia	0.57	5.35	3.76	5.36
Iran	n.a.	3.54	n.a.	3.63
Ivory Coast	n.a.	n.a.	n.a.	n.a.
Kenya	n.a.	n.a.	n.a.	4.30[a]
Korea, South	n.a.	3.54	n.a.	8.67
Malaysia	0.63	6.37	5.94	7.86
Mexico	3.35	1.63	13.22	6.69
Nigeria				
Pakistan	3.96	5.48	5.56	4.43
Philippines	7.08	2.84	12.33	3.84
Taiwan	n.a.	4.69	n.a.	5.74
Thailand	2.22	3.73	3.84	7.37
Turkey	1.69	4.13	13.06	3.97
Venezuela	n.a.	6.26	n.a.	11.97

Source: FAO, *Production Yearbooks*, 1952, 1962, 1972.
[a] IBRD agricultural sector survey estimate for 1964–71.

reason why overall GNP growth rates were higher in the 1960s. Further, in most countries, the growth rate of food production was above that of agricultural output in general. In the countries for which data are available, the median annual growth rate during the 1960s was about 4 percent for agricultural output but close to 6 percent for food output. The discrepancy arises from the fact that, in some countries, there was a relative decline in the production of export crops. The cases of coffee in Brazil, sugar in the Philippines, and jute in Pakistan are particularly well known. From one standpoint, the large acreage devoted to export production in some countries provides a reserve that can be drawn on to meet the food needs of a growing population. But on the other side, diversion of acreage to food production weakens the country's export position.

How adequate were these rates of increase to meet the rising demand for food? The answer doubtless differs from country to country. We should recall that, in the open economies, a shortfall of domestic output can be compensated for by food imports; and some countries in our sample took advantage of this possibility. Several of these countries—Malaysia, Ivory Coast, Iran, South Korea—were in a strong export position and could import food without cutting seriously into imports of capital goods and industrial materials. The proportion of all imports that consisted of foodstuffs was running in the early 1970s at about 20 percent in Iran, Ivory Coast, and Malaysia and about 15 percent in South Korea. Two other countries—Pakistan and the Philippines—were in the less-happy position of spending about 15 percent of their foreign exchange on foodstuffs despite a weak balance-of-payments position.

What can we say about the behavior of the internal terms of trade? There are several possible indicators here: the "parity ratio" of prices received and paid by farmers, which the FAO calculates for some countries; wholesale price indexes for farm products and manufactures; and behavior of the food and nonfood components of the consumer price index. Not all these data are available for every country; and the underlying price series are not highly reliable. We have nevertheless assembled and examined the series that are available.

Two differing predictions about terms-of-trade behavior appear in the literature, one reflecting closed-economy and the other open-economy assumptions. In a closed economy, a divergence between the rates of increase in food demand and food availability must cause a shift in the internal terms of trade. In a completely open economy, on the other hand, the price of food (and other tradeable goods) depends solely on world price levels; and a discrepancy between domestic output and demand is absorbed entirely in the export balance.

Our economies are best described as *semiopen*. They carry on substantial trade, including trade in agricultural goods; but trade is by no means free, and an overall import constraint is usually operative. Thus, it is quite possible for the closed-economy effect and the open-economy effect to occur together, and a recent study by Philip Burstein suggests that this typically occurs in practice.[1] A shortfall of food output relative to demand tends to be reflected in both a relative price increase for agricultural products and a reduction in net exports of such products.

The data for our fifteen countries show short-term fluctuations in the rural-urban terms of trade combined with reasonable stability over

1. Philip L. Burstein, "Problems of Labor Allocation and Absorption in Developing Countries" (Ph.D. diss., Yale University, 1976), chap. 6. This analysis covered eleven LDCs, including five of those in our sample, over a period of sixteen years.

the long run. This stability reflects varying combinations of good agricultural performance and use of the export-adjustment mechanism, the mix often changing over time for the same country. In South Korea, for example, the terms of trade moved in favor of foodstuffs from 1959 to 1965; but as food imports rose in response to this, the terms of trade stabilized from 1965 onward.

Even though the terms of trade have tended to remain stable on the average, there have been differential price movements for particular products, and particularly between foodgrains and animal products. The latter have a much higher income elasticity of demand and a longer production cycle. Thus, when per capita income is rising rapidly, supplies tend to lag behind demand, putting upward pressure on prices. In Brazil, for example, Nicholls reports that the "real price" of all vegetable foods, with 1948–52 = 100, had fallen by 1968–69 to 84. The index had risen, however, to 132 for beef, 107 for pork, and 120 for mutton.[2] In Turkey, the price index for all cereals rose from 100 in 1964 to 159 in 1972. But over this same period, the index rose to 274 for sheep, 317 for goats, and 398 for cattle.[3] The overall agriculture-industry relative price index, however, has remained rather stable since 1950.

Scattered data from other countries show a similar divergence between crop and livestock prices. One would expect this to lead to an accelerated increase of livestock output, which in some countries could be accomplished by converting more land into permanent pasture. But insofar as an increase in livestock output means increased use of cereals for animal rather than human consumption, this puts increased pressure on crop production. Thus some countries which have managed in the past to raise food output at an adequate rate will face increasing difficulties as diets shift from cereals toward meat products with the continued rise of per capita income.

The only country for which there is evidence of serious food diffi-culties is the Philippines. During the 1960s the country began to run into a food bottleneck because of a diversion of acreage from food production to export crops, accompanied by high population growth and a moderate growth of per capita income. Rice output grew at only 2.3 percent per year between 1958–60 and 1967–69. The terms of trade turned sharply in favor of agriculture after 1965. In addition

2. William H. Nicholls, "The Brazilian Agricultural Economy," in *The Economy of Brazil*, ed. Howard S. Ellis (Berkeley: University of California Press, 1969).
3. Turkey, State Institute of Statistics, *Summary of Agricultural Statistics, 1971*.

to stimulating food imports, this put a Ricardian squeeze on industry via higher money wages (though not real wages), which rose faster than the selling price of manufactures.

At the other pole, two countries show a substantial terms-of-trade movement *against* agriculture. In Pakistan, a combination of price ceilings on farm products, an overvalued exchange rate, and import-substitution policies that raised the relative price of manufactures turned the terms of trade sharply against agriculture during the 1950s; and it is not surprising that farm output was sluggish. During the 1960s, however, price controls were relaxed, export taxes lowered, and fertilizer inputs subsidized. While farmers' terms of trade were still well below what they would have been at world prices, they did improve, and this was partly responsible for stronger agricultural performance after 1960.

In Kenya, too, there are price ceilings on many farm products and much of the produce is sold through state marketing boards. This system, combined with import-substitution policies, has turned the terms of trade decidedly against agriculture from 1960 to the present.

A different indicator of food adequacy is provided by FAO estimates of food availability per capita (table 2). These are derived from "food balance sheets," which take into account exports, imports, and inventory changes as well as annual output. We have selected for each country the data corresponding most closely to the 1950, 1960, and 1970 calendar years. There are some gaps, particularly for 1950, as well as considerable imprecision in the estimates; but the data are still worth examining.

Let us look first at absolute consumption levels in 1970 and then at time trends. Consumption levels in North America and western Europe can be used as a standard of comparison. Per capita calorie consumption in most of those countries runs between 2,900 and 3,100 per day. The averages for our fifteen developing countries, on the other hand, lie mainly in the range of 2,100 to 2,700. This represents a moderate level of nutrition—not as good as in the richest countries, not as poor as in the most overpopulated and stagnant economies. One must remember, of course, that in most of these countries income is quite unequally distributed. Thus an average per capita consumption of, say, 2,400 calories means that a sizable percentage of the population is below the 2,000 level, which is regarded by nutritionists as a bare minimum.

A scatter diagram of the caloric consumption shown in table 2

Table 2. Food Availability per Capita Circa 1950, 1960, and 1970

Country	Net Food Supply Calories/Day			Total Protein Grams/Day			Animal Protein Grams/Day		
	1	*2*	*3*	*1*	*2*	*3*	*1*	*2*	*3*
Brazil	2,240	2,720	2,620	55	66	65	16	18	22
Colombia	2,200	2,370	2,120	46	50	53	21	25	26
Iran	n.a.	2,050	2,030	n.a.	60	55	n.a.	13	12
Ivory Coast	n.a.	n.a.	n.a.	n.a.	n.a.	n.a.	n.a.	n.a.	n.a.
Kenya	n.a.	2,290	2,330	n.a.	72	69	n.a.	16	16
Korea, South	n.a.	2,485	2,437	n.a.	64	67	n.a.	7	8
Malaysia	n.a.	2,400	2,350	n.a.	54	52	n.a.	16	17
Mexico	2,370	2,500	2,620	63	65	66	17	16	14
Nigeria	n.a.	2,440	2,140	n.a.	66	56	n.a.	10	9
Pakistan	2,000	2,090	2,410	47	48	55	8	10	10
Philippines	1,750	1,880	2,010	45	48	52	18	18	20
Taiwan	1,980	2,350	2,500	43	59	65	8	15	20
Thailand	n.a.	n.a.	2,210	n.a.	n.a.	51	n.a.	n.a.	12
Turkey	2,510	3,110	2,760	81	98	71	15	16	15
Venezuela	2,030	2,180	2,390	53	55	59	19	26	26

Source: FAO, *Production Yearbooks,* 1952, 1962, 1972.
Note: Period 1 = year closest to 1950; period 2 = year closest to 1960; period 3 = year closest to 1970.

against reported GNP per capita in U.S. dollars shows no apparent relation. The lowest country in terms of per capita income, Pakistan, has a per capita calorie consumption equal to that of Venezuela, whose per capita income is ten times as high. We have not tried to untangle this puzzle; but it reinforces the skepticism we expressed earlier about the meaningfulness of intercountry comparisons of absolute per capita income.

An indicator of *quality* of diet is protein intake—more especially, the proportion of protein from animal sources.[4] We may note for comparison that, in western Europe and North America, per capita protein intake runs in the range of eighty to a hundred grams per day and intake of animal protein in the range of fifty-five to sixty-five grams, or about two-thirds of the total.

4. The high proportion of animal foods in the diets of the richest countries is undoubtedly partly a matter of taste and is higher than required for adequate nutrition. At the same time, animal proteins are "superior" in that they are very similar in structure to human proteins and are thus almost immediately assimilable by the body, while vegetable proteins have to be broken down and reassembled into appropriate forms. Research on structural improvement of vegetable proteins has made considerable headway, but for the time being a moderate amount of animal protein does improve dietary adequacy.

In the countries of our sample, on the other hand, protein intake rarely reaches the level of sixty-five grams per day that is recommended as a minimum by nutritionists; and of this intake, only one-third to one-fifth consists of animal protein. Again, a scatter diagram shows no visible relation between a country's per capita income and its per capita protein intake. With regard to animal protein, however, a marked relationship is apparent. The seven highest-income countries in table 2 average twenty grams of animal protein per day, compared with thirteen grams for the seven lowest-income countries. Diets do shift toward a higher proportion of food from animal sources as per capita income rises.

When we look across the rows in table 2 to observe changes over the period 1950–70, the most striking observation is that, for some countries, the data seem inconsistent with the output data in table 1. In particular, Colombia, Malaysia, and South Korea show quite high rates of increase in food output. But table 2 indicates that calorie intake declined between 1960 and 1970 in all three countries and that only Colombia showed improvement in protein intake. Several other countries show a decline in calorie intake between 1960 and 1970, despite increases in agricultural output and rapid GNP growth. Possible explanations might be: (1) differing commodity composition of the food output and food availability series; (2) use of single years in table 2 rather than the three-year averages used in table 1, which may have introduced some effect of weather variations; (3) inaccuracy in one or both sets of measurements.

SOURCES OF OUTPUT INCREASE: ACREAGE VERSUS YIELDS

An increase in agricultural output must come about through some combination of the following factors.

1. An increase in cultivated acreage (or, for livestock, an increase in acres of pasture or intensity of pasture use). Table 3 gives FAO data on arable land plus land under permanent crops (such as vines or tree crops), for years around 1950, 1960, and 1970. In most countries, acreage in use has been rising, often quite rapidly. Cultivated acreage expands by encroachment on pastures, meadowlands, and forests; and in many countries the possibilities in this direction are far from exhausted. Another important fact, not revealed by table 3, is that in many countries *cropped* acreage has expanded faster than cultivated acreage through extension of double and triple cropping. This requires

Table 3. Amount of Arable Land plus Land Under Permanent Crops
(In thousands of hectares)

Country	Year	Acreage	Year	Acreage	Year	Acreage
Brazil	1947	18,835	1957	19,095	1960	29,760
Colombia	1950	2,440	1960	5,062	1970	5,054
Iran	1950	16,760	1960	16,850	1971	16,727
Ivory Coast		n.a.		n.a.	1971	8,887
Kenya	1948	1,600	1960	1,670		n.a.
Korea, South	1950	1,954	1961	2,095	1969	2,311
Malaya	1951	2,091	1958	2,186	1970	2,856[a]
Mexico	1950	19.928	1960	23,817		n.a.
Nigeria	1951	22,317[b]	1961	21,795		n.a.
Pakistan	1948	20,720		n.a.	1969	19,235
Philippines	1951	6,690	1961	6,780	1971	11,145
Taiwan	1951	875	1960	869	1970	905
Thailand	1949	4,750	1960	6,381	1965	11,415
Turkey	1949	15,260	1961	25,167	1970	27,378
Venezuela	1951	2,700	1956	5,220	1961	5,214

Source: FAO, *Production Yearbooks*, 1952, 1962, 1972; table 1, *Land Use*.
[a] West Malaysia.
[b] Including British Cameroons.

a mild climate and assured water control and has been important particularly in the rice-growing areas of South Korea, Taiwan, the Philippines, Thailand, and Malaya. But there has also been widespread irrigation development in Mexico and, on a lesser scale, in Pakistan, Iran, and Turkey.

2. An increase in yields per acre for individual crops. Detailed yield data on individual crops are collected from national sources and published annually by the FAO. These data would be cumbersome to present in tabular form, since in most countries there are many crops and the yield trends differ substantially from one crop to the next. But we can say that, on the average, the yield increases in some countries have been small; in others, moderate; and in still others, quite substantial.

3. A shift in the composition of output toward products with higher value added per acre, usually accompanied by larger labor inputs per acre. Such products include most fruits and vegetables, sugarbeets, oilseeds, poultry, eggs, and milk. Since these products have higher income elasticities than cereal foods, a shift in this direction is natural as per capita income rises, and it can be an important source of both yield increase and labor absorption.

We have not attempted to break down the output increase in each country into these three components, which would be a large statistical job. We have made judgments as to whether yield increases have been substantial, moderate, or slight and corresponding judgments for acreage increases. These judgments are summarized in table 4. In general, "substantial" means in excess of 3 percent per year; "moderate," in the range of 1 to 3 percent; and "slight," less than 1 percent. A few countries, in which food crops have behaved quite differently from industrial or export crops, appear in two boxes of the table.

To anyone reared on the India model, the extent to which the output increases of the past generation have been obtained from acreage increases is surprising. This has been almost the exclusive source of output growth in five of our fifteen countries and a major source in six additional countries. Only Taiwan, South Korea, and Pakistan approximate closed-frontier conditions. Kenya is difficult to classify because, although total farm acreage has changed little, there has been an intensification of use through subdivision of the large farms in the former "White Highlands" among African smallholders.

In most of these countries, too, the possibilities of expanding cultivated acreage are far from exhausted,[5] and extension of the margin of cultivation will continue for decades to come. Tentatively, one can hypothesize that the presence of a land frontier is one reason why these economies rather than others appear on our list of success cases.

It is clear also from table 4 that country performance in the yield dimension is not unrelated to performance in the acreage dimension. The four countries in the northwest box, which have had no difficulty in expanding acreage, have shown little increase in crop yields. Toward the shoutheast corner of the table, on the other hand, land scarcity has forced yield improvements, which have been large in Taiwan and South Korea, moderately large in Pakistan and Kenya. A number of

5. Until recently, the FAO land-use tables published in the *Production Yearbook* contained estimates of potentially cultivable land not yet in use. For many countries, however, these figures are too large to be entirely credible, nor do they provide any indication of land quality. For these reasons it did not seem useful to tabulate them here, and the fact that they do not appear in the most recent *Production Yearbook* suggests that the FAO statisticians also doubt their reliability. More careful estimates for particular countries, however, can sometimes be found in secondary sources. Thus, Julian Chacel estimated that, as of 1965, only 49 percent of usable agricultural land in Brazil was actually in use. This was distributed as follows: crops, 9.6 percent; livestock, 31.6 percent; forests, 8.2 percent. *Economy of Brazil*, ed. Ellis, chap. 4.

Table 4. Sources of Output Increase, 1950–1970

| | Increase in Cultivated Acreage | | |
	Substantial	Moderate	Slight
Increase in Crop Yields — Slight	Brazil Ivory Coast Nigeria Venezuela: food crops	Iran	
Increase in Crop Yields — Moderate	Malaysia: food crops Mexico Turkey: food crops	Colombia Philippines Venezuela: industrial crops Thailand: rice	Kenya Pakistan

Increase in Crop Yields — Substantial	Turkey: industrial
	    crops
	Thailand: export and
	    other nonrice crops
			South Korea
			Malaysia: rubber
			Taiwan

countries, finally, have been able to both expand acreage and raise yields. This accounts for the fact that Malaysia, Mexico, and Thailand show unusually high rates of output growth and are, for the time being, in a comfortable food situation.

From a policy standpoint, the yield dimension is the more interesting of the two. An increase in yields requires systematic effort, including promotion and support by government. This leads one to ask whether the more rapid increase in yields in some countries can be related to more active government policies and, if so, just what government did in these cases.

A careful reading of the country evidence suggests that agriculture has indeed been most successful where government has given high priority to agricultural development. From this standpoint, our sample falls into three groups: (1) countries whose governmental policies have been most strongly proagriculture, that is, Taiwan, South Korea, Mexico, Malaysia, and Thailand. A glance at table 4 indicates that these countries have also performed well with regard to yield increases; (2) countries that have acted to stimulate agricultural output, although less forcefully than those in the first group, but that have also taken some counterproductive actions. This group would include Pakistan, Turkey, the Philippines, Kenya, and Colombia. These countries have in general made less rapid progress than those in the first group; (3)

finally, countries in which government has been relatively inactive on the agricultural front, such as Brazil, Venezuela, Nigeria, the Ivory Coast, and Iran. To be sure, Brazil has encouraged movement to the frontier, there has been some colonization of new lands in Venezuela, both Nigeria and the Ivory Coast have built roads into the interior to tap new resources, and Iran has carried out a substantial land reform. But for the most part, these countries have coasted on their still ample land reserves, reinforced in some cases by a strong export position.

What has happened in the five countries that have been most active in promoting agricultural development? In interpreting the experience of South Korea and Taiwan, one must recall their pre-1945 status as Japanese colonies that were used as ricebaskets to meet Japan's growing food requirements. By 1940, Japanese technical assistance and infrastructure development had already raised rice yields in these countries well above typical Asian levels. Postwar progress thus took off from a base of substantial accomplishments in earlier decades.

In South Korea, the first important post-1945 development was the sale of former Japanese-owned estates to Korean smallholders. Tenancy was forbidden on this land, and the maximum size of each holding was set at 7.5 acres. This helped to confirm a pattern of owner-operated farming, in which the average size of a holding is only 2.2 acres and only 12 percent of the cultivated land is operated by tenants. Next in importance has been the steady expansion of irrigation facilities. By 1972, 74 percent of all rice land was fully irrigated and an additional 20 percent partially irrigated. Foreign exchange has been made available for fertilizer imports, and fertilizer use per acre is now approaching Japanese levels. There is an active research and extension program, with U.S. technical support. Over the past decade, rice yields have been rising at about 3 percent a year, wheat and other food crops at about 2 percent. There has also been a doubling of beef and pork output and a phenomenal increase in the production of poultry, eggs, and milk. But Korean per capita income has been rising so fast that, despite this strong output performance, food imports have also been rising rapidly. Given the country's resource endowments—scarce land, ample labor—it will probably prove efficient for Korea to trade manufactured exports for food imports on an increasing scale in the future.

In Taiwan, too, the first major step in the postwar period was a land reform program comprising: (1) a rent ceiling of 37.5 percent of the main crop; (2) sale of former Japanese lands, amounting to about

20 percent of the cultivated area, to smallholders; and (3) forced sale of landholdings in excess of 2.9 hectares to small farmers. This program both improved the situation of tenants and greatly reduced their number. The proportion of land farmed by tenants, 59 percent in 1939, had fallen to 17 percent by 1953. Building on this base, the government followed an agricultural policy that Ho terms "developmental and extractive."[6] Agriculture was called on to make, and did make, substantial transfers of foodstuffs, labor, and finance. But there was clear recognition that this required a rapidly expanding production base. Government pursued an active and comprehensive development policy involving improvement of rural health and education, development of agricultural research and extension,[7] expansion of irrigation facilities, development of farmers' self-help organizations and government financial institutions, and provision of growing amounts of intermediate inputs. From 1953 to 1967, use of these new inputs grew at the remarkable rate of 6 percent per year. With virtually no increase in cultivated acreage (though cropped acreage rose 0.9 percent per year due to growth of irrigation and double cropping), crop output grew at 4.6 percent a year and livestock output at 5.9 percent.

Mexico has achieved a high growth rate of agricultural output from 1940 onward. Food output has increased a good deal faster than population, and there has been a balanced expansion of agriculture and industry that is perhaps unique in Latin America. The foundation for this growth, Clark Reynolds concludes,[8] was laid by the Mexican Revolution, which broke up the large haciendas and created a class of small farmers, with nonalienable holdings averaging 7–8 hectares. A second component was unusually heavy and systematic investment in road building, irrigation works, and other rural infrastructure. Investment in irrigation and roads alone, as a percentage of total federal government investment, rose from 22 percent during 1925–29 to a peak of 45 percent during 1935–39 before declining gradually to 20 percent during 1960–65 (while continuing to rise in absolute terms). There has been an active research and development program,

6. Samuel P. Ho, *Economic Development of Taiwan, 1890–1970* (New Haven: Yale University Press, 1977), chap. 9. This is the most thorough analysis available of Taiwanese agricultural development in both the colonial and the post-1945 periods.

7. Taiwan has more agricultural research workers per 100 farmers than any country in the world; and only Japan exceeds it in number of extension workers.

8. Clark Reynolds, *The Mexican Economy: Twentieth-Century Structure and Growth* (New Haven: Yale University Press, 1970).

notably a wheat research center that has developed and disseminated improved Mexican wheat varieties to many other countries. In addition to favorable government policies, the rapid growth of the domestic market plus the close proximity of northern Mexico to the American market have stimulated agricultural expansion from the demand side.

In West Malaysia (the former Federated Malay States), the most important feature of agriculture is the strong predominance of export crops. The acreage devoted to rubber alone is more than five times that devoted to rice. In rubber, the major trends have included a steady decline in the proportion of output coming from large foreign-owned estates as compared with that produced by Malay smallholders. This results from a policy of reserving new land cleared by the government for allocation to smallholders, with preference given to landless laborers. The rubber acreage under smallholder cultivation is now about double the estate acreage. A second trend is that, although total acreage has not increased very much, rubber output per acre has increased since 1955 at about 5 percent per year. This is due to massive replanting of improved tree varieties on both estates and smallholdings, with a view to keeping Malayan rubber competitive with synthetics and with rubber exports from other countries. The Rubber Research Institute of Malaya is the world center for basic research in rubber cultivation. Rubber replanting has typically amounted to between 15 and 20 percent of government development expenditure.

In food production, an important consideration is that a large majority of farmers are Malays, while the bulk of businessmen and other city dwellers are Chinese. A pro-Malay policy (which the Malay-dominated government might be expected to prefer) thus tends to be synonymous with a proagriculture policy.[9] Public investment has been strongly oriented toward food production as well as export agriculture. Large amounts have been spent on land clearing and settlement, feeder-road construction, irrigation, and rural electrification. It is hoped that these efforts will both raise the living standards of Malay country dwellers and check migration to the cities. In rice, much the most important food crop, acreage grew between 1955 and 1971 at an annual rate of 2.6 percent, and output per acre rose at 1.6 percent.

Before World War II, Thailand could have been characterized as;

9. This point, and the consequences that follow from it, are well documented in Douglas Paauw and John C. H. Fei, *The Transition in Open Dualistic Economies*, chap. 9.

(1) an open-frontier economy, in which population was spreading out gradually from the rich Central Plain to other parts of the country (the area planted to rice increased sixfold between 1850 and 1950);[10] (2) a one-crop economy, in which 95 percent of cultivated acreage was devoted to rice; (3) a government almost entirely inert in economic affairs. After 1950, however, government became considerably more active in economic development. The highway network was increased from 760 miles in 1949 to almost 10,000 miles in 1969, opening many new areas to external markets. The irrigated area increased almost fourfold, from 3.8 million rai in 1949 to 14.0 million in 1969 (out of a total of 42 million rai planted in rice.) There have been systematic efforts to adapt International Rice Research Institute (IRRI) rice strains to Thai growing conditions. Fertilizer is readily imported in this quite open economy, and its use is rising rapidly, though from a base much below the Taiwan-Korea level. Another favorable feature is that Thailand is a country of small owner-operators, in which tenancy is of minor importance. On the unfavorable side, the government levies an export tax on rice, usually in the range of 25–35 percent, which serves to depress farmers' returns below the world price level by roughly this amount. Despite this, rice acreage continued to rise at about 2 percent per year during 1950–70, and yields per acre have also been rising at about 2 percent. With speeded-up population growth, estimated at more than 3 percent annually, domestic rice conumption has been rising faster than output, and the export surplus is declining.

The most striking development since 1950, however, has been a marked diversification into nonrice production, partly for export (corn, kenaf, cassava, and rubber) and partly for domestic use (cotton, coconuts, sugarcane, fruits and vegetables, and livestock products). Although rice acreage was rising between 1950 and 1970 from 35 million rai to 46 million, the area planted to other crops rose from 5 to 22 million rai. This seems to have occurred as a spontaneous small-holder response to relative prices and profitability.[11] Yields per acre have also risen considerably faster in the nonrice sector, particularly for rubber, corn, soybeans, kenaf, and cassava.

10. For historical background as well as recent developments, see James C. Ingram, *Economic Change in Thailand, 1850–1970* (Stanford: Stanford University Press, 1971).

11. Ingram, on the basis of research by Behrman and others, reports that during 1965–67 the average value yielded by various crops (in bahts per rai) was as follows: rice, 291; corn, 325; cassava, 611; sugarcane, 606; cotton, 501; kenaf, 569; rubber, 377; vegetables 852.

The theoretical literature poses several additional questions about agricultural-sector behavior. How are the gains from productivity growth divided among different groups in the population—large farmers, small farmers, landless laborers? Has rural-urban migration been large enough to prevent rising underemployment in agriculture? Has agriculture made a net contribution of finance as well as labor to the urban sectors? The literature on the economies in our sample does not provide definitive answers to these questions, partly because the underlying data on wage rates, incomes, labor force, and employment are weak. But we can make some surmises that may suggest useful lines of research.

Dualistic Agriculture and Income Distribution

Dualistic structure is not characteristic of all LDC agriculture. Dualism is not prominent in Africa or in East and Southeast Asia; but it is a major fact of life in Latin America, South Asia, and the Middle East.

In Nigeria and the Ivory Coast, and probably in most other African countries, farmers cultivate family-sized plots allocated by the village authorities. They have the right of use, but not of ownership. In Taiwan and South Korea, the postwar land reforms established a pattern of smallholder proprietorship, with tenancy a minor feature. Thailand is also a nation of peasant proprietors, though some families have accumulated larger land holdings than others. Small owner-operator farming also dominates food production in Malaya, although a good deal of rubber and palm oil production comes from large estates.

Dualism reaches its peak in Latin America and is prominent in all four Latin countries in our sample. Quite often, large and small farms differ in product mix. Thus in Colombia, as Berry points out, there are at least four distinct "agricultures": coffee growing for export, which is done by both large and small farmers; livestock production, which is typically large scale; commercial farming by relatively large and mechanized farms, producing corn, wheat, sugarcane, cotton, and other field crops; and small-scale, low-income farming producing beans, potatoes, cassava, plantain and other traditional food crops. As in dualistic systems generally, the large farms differ from the small ones in having smaller labor inputs per acre (a more extensive cultivation pattern), larger capital inputs per acre, higher productivity per worker but lower productivity per acre, much higher income per owner family, much larger percentage of output marketed, and more rapid rate of productivity increase. The reasons for these differences were examined in some detail in chapter 4.

Several other countries in our sample have a markedly dualistic pattern. In the Philippines, which can be regarded as an honorary member of the Latin American group, large holdings dominate the sugar sector and are important also in food crops. A recent survey estimates that the top 5 percent of landowners own almost half the total land.[12] In Pakistan, large farmers dominate wheat growing in the Punjab. In Iran, much land belonged traditionally to the Shah and the leading families. Although this pattern was somewhat eroded by the land reforms of the 1960s, there remains a class of relatively large and rich farmers, particularly prominent in the four northernmost provinces where good soil and congenial climate permit the growing of luxury crops such as oranges, rice, tea, and tobacco. In Turkey, too, much of the more fertile and desirable land along the Aegean and Mediterranean seas is occupied by large farmers growing industrial and export crops, while smallholders are confined primarily to cereal growing in the drier interior provinces. Kenya, perhaps partly as a carryover from the days of European settlement, also shows a marked dualism between some 3,200 farms of more than twenty hectares apiece and 1,200,000 small holdings averaging two hectares each. The bottom 50 percent of landholdings—those below two hectares in size —occupy only 4 percent of the cultivated area, and one-sixth of the rural population has no direct access to land.

There does not seem to be any close relation between agricultural structure and rate of increase in crop yields or total agricultural output. Several of the more egalitarian countries have achieved rapid increases in yields, but others have not; and there is a similar variation among the dualistic economies. One cannot say, then, that either type of structure is a prerequisite for agricultural progress; but structure does influence the distribution of the income gains from such progress.

There is some evidence, as we suggested in chapter 4, that under dualistic agriculture the distribution of gains is heavily weighted toward the larger farms. This is partly because, having superior access to

12. ILO, *Sharing in Development: A Programme of Employment, Equity, and Growth in the Philippines*, 1973, vol. 2, paper 3.

capital and technology, the larger farmers tend to make larger productivity gains; partly because income gains are imputed mainly to scarce capital and land, rather than to labor, and hence are distributed in proportion to *ownership;* and partly because the gains are realized through commercial marketings, which make up a higher proportion of output on large farms than they do on small ones. Less clear is the question of whether one can expect a "trickle-down" effect to the smaller, more subsistence-oriented farmers. To the extent that large and small farmers are growing similar crops (which is often *not* the case), one might expect a gradual diffusion of improved technology to smaller units, with a consequent rise in productivity and incomes. Further, expansion of output on the large farms may require larger inputs of hired labor, thus setting up a suction within the rural labor market that will benefit landless laborers and may also draw some labor from smallholdings, raising per capita output and income there. In some of the dualistic economies, however, one observes quite rapid mechanization on large farms, which usually is privately profitable even though its social profitability may be questioned. Thus, increases in output may actually be accompanied by a *reduction* in employment through dismissal of hired labor and/or dismissal of tenants so that the land can be farmed in the large, consolidated units that the new technology has made profitable.

Even though smallholders and landless laborers may benefit, their benefits are likely to be relatively small; and it seems virtually certain that the first impact of improved technology is to increase the inequality of rural-income distribution. But information with which to test this hypothesis is fragmentary. In the secondary literature, one finds statements that rural living standards in Iran increased very little up to 1970 and that the real wage level in Philippine agriculture has not increased materially over time. In Colombia, on the other hand, Berry concludes that the real wage level of farm workers did rise substantially from 1945 to 1965. For most countries, however, the literature is virtually silent.

In the more egalitarian agricultural economies, one would predict a more equal distribution of the gains from progress. Particularly where output increases have come from rising yields per acre, one would expect a widely diffused increase in per capita income within farm families and a consequent rise in the supply price of hired labor for either farm or nonfarm employment. Particularly in Taiwan, South Korea, Malaysia, and Thailand, there is evidence of a continuing rise in per capita farm incomes and in real wage rates for hired agricultural workers. The income-distribution data for Taiwan, which are unusually good and will be examined in some detail in chapter 14, show a gradual decline of inequality in incomes derived from agriculture and a quite low Gini coefficient (about 0.30) at the present time.

Labor Force and Employment

In most countries in our sample, the rural population has been growing at more than 1 percent a year, and in several at more than 2 percent (table 5). Not all rural people are engaged in agriculture, of course, nor does population growth correspond exactly with labor-force growth. But one can still conclude that, almost everywhere, a growing number of people are seeking agricultural employment.

The amount of work done in agriculture has also been increasing. In many countries, new land is being settled on the extensive margin of cultivation. Intensification of yields also usually involves an increase in labor inputs per acre. We would naturally like to know whether increasing demand for labor from these sources has kept up with labor supply—that is, whether rural underemployment is increasing or decreasing. Unfortunately, there are few countries for which we can

Table 5. Average Annual Growth Rates of Rural and Urban Population,
1950–1960 and 1960–1970
(Percent)

Country	Rural Population		Urban Population	
	1950–60	*1960–70*	*1950–60*	*1960–70*
Brazil	1.43	0.54	7.35	6.28
Colombia	0.78	1.78	6.81	6.29
Iran	2.22	1.17	6.49	8.69
Ivory Coast	n.a.	n.a.	n.a.	n.a.
Kenya	0.75	2.32	9.00	14.42
Korea, South	1.77	1.76	8.28	7.51
Malaysia	0.41	0.89	17.20	8.82
Mexico	1.87	1.57	6.12	6.46
Nigeria	n.a.	−0.61	n.a.	5.79
Pakistan	2.37	2.19	5.18	6.24
Philippines	2.43	1.93	5.87	5.26
Taiwan	2.63	0.42	5.26	5.17
Thailand	2.89	2.71	10.00	6.25
Turkey	2.44	1.27	5.48	9.14
Venezuela	1.02	0.64	5.60	6.90

Source: UN, *Demographic Yearbook*.

answer this question with any assurance. In addition to the conceptual difficulty of estimating underemployment in agriculture, there is the complication that part of the labor time of farm family members is devoted to handicrafts, petty trade, and other nonagricultural activities. Thus, whether rural underemployment rises or falls depends partly on the expansion rate of these other activities.

That this is not a minor qualification may be illustrated by evidence from Nigeria and the Philippines. In Nigeria, a recent Labor Force Survey indicated that only 66 percent of rural Nigerian families report farming as their main occupation. Another 8.5 percent regard business as their primary activity, while 23 percent combine business and agriculture. Moreover, even those engaged mainly in agriculture usually have one or more side occupations. Thus, in the Sokoto and Zaria areas of Northern Nigeria, 85 percent of families reported such side occupations, and about 40 percent of total working days per year were devoted to them.[13]

The recent International Labor Organization (ILO) Employment Report on the Philippines found that, in general, rural families have more diversified sources of income than urban families. This is due partly to seasonal underemployment and partly to low returns from agriculture, which lead family members to supplement farm income from other sources. In 1971, 47 percent of rural families reported earnings from farm operation as their main source of income, while another 14 percent relied mainly on wage labor in agriculture. This leaves 39 percent who derived most of their income from other sources. What these people were doing is suggested by the following percentage distribution of rural workers in 1972:[14]

	Males	*Females*	*Both Sexes*
Agriculture	80.1	52.0	72.0
Manufacturing	4.8	17.1	8.7
Commerce	3.5	19.2	6.9
Services	4.2	10.9	6.2
Other	6.6	0.9	4.5

13. Reported in IBRD Country Mission Report 416a-UNI, August 5, 1974. A good deal is known about the use of rural labor time in Nigeria through research by Professor Carl Eicher and colleagues at Michigan State University, and through a Zaria-based agricultural research center affiliated with Kansas State University. Their studies confirm the large amount of labor time devoted to off-farm employment, particularly during the slack season in agriculture.

14. ILO, *Sharing in Development*, vol. 2, paper 6.

Because of this complex interpenetration of agricultural and non-agricultural activities, and because of the importance of rural-urban migration, the question of whether underemployment is increasing or decreasing should really be addressed to the economy as a whole rather than specifically to the agricultural sector. To answer the question would require sample household surveys at intervals over an extended period, and few LDCs have this kind of data. Scattered data on full-time urban unemployment shows such unemployment rising in most countries; but this does not necessarily indicate that underemployment, which is quantitatively more important, is also increasing.

The only two countries in our sample that have reached a condition of labor scarcity are Taiwan and South Korea. In these countries, because of an unusually rapid growth of industrial output and GNP during the 1960s, the rural labor reservoir had by 1970 been substantially exhausted. In Taiwan, open unemployment declined from 3.4 percent of the labor force in 1965 to 1.5 percent in 1974, and part-time unemployment went down from 3 percent to 0.8 percent. As one would expect, labor scarcity led to a rapid increase in both urban and rural wage rates and also stimulated farm mechanization.

Intersectoral Financial Transfers

A financial transfer from agriculture to nonagriculture is a common feature of development models, and it is interesting to inquire whether such a transfer has occurred in this group of economies. The question is difficult to answer because, as we indicated in chapter 6, the potential transfer mechanisms are numerous and complex. The simplest is saving by farmers and landowners for investment in the urban sector. Transfers in either direction can occur through the fiscal system, depending on whether the direct and indirect taxes derived from the rural population exceed the total of government investment in and current services provided to the rural population. Income transfers occur also through changes in the rural-urban terms of trade, which may be "natural" in the sense of reflecting demand and cost trends or "artificial" in that they result mainly from government price policies.

Except for Taiwan, where a large net transfer from agriculture has been documented by T. H. Lee,[15] one finds only scattered references, which do not warrant a firm conclusion. A careful reading of the country literature, however, suggests two hypotheses: that a net outflow from agriculture has been the typical pattern since 1950; and that this has mainly resulted, not from private saving and investment decisions, but from actions of government, including policy-induced changes in the internal terms of trade and heavy taxation of agricultural exports.

In most countries, import-substitution policies involving tariff protection, import controls, overvalued exchange rates, and exchange rationing have raised the domestic price of manufactures substantially above the world level, while reducing real returns from agricultural exports. This hits the farmer as consumer, buyer of agricultural inputs, and exporter. In addition, there have sometimes been ceilings on the domestic price of foodgrains, as in Kenya and Pakistan. In other countries, such as Malaysia, free import of foodstuffs has served as a price-regulating device, reducing pressure on the money-wage level for the benefit of industrialists and plantation owners.

Land taxes are notoriously difficult to assess and collect, and their small size may yield an impression that agriculture is lightly taxed. But this is misleading because of the major importance of indirect taxes in LDC fiscal systems. Agricultural exports are usually subject to a substantial tax, either directly (as in Thailand), via government marketing boards (as in the West African countries), or via the overvalued exchange rate. Sales, excise, and value-added taxes also form a large part of government revenue. These are regressive and fall on agriculturalists in proportion to their consumption of industrial products. On the expenditure side of the budget, agriculture typically receives small allocations relative to its contribution to national output. This point will be documented in chapter 13, where we present data on government current and capital expenditures by economic sectors.

The evidence suggests that agriculture is normally milked for the benefit of other sectors. But there are several doubtful cases in which the net transfer may have been in the other direction. These are Mexico, Malaysia, Iran, and Turkey. Mexico has allocated an un-

15. Teng-Hui Lee, *Intersectoral Capital Flows in the Economic Development of Taiwan, 1895–1960* (Ithaca: Cornell University Press, 1971).

usually large share of public investment to roads, irrigation, and other forms of rural infrastructure. Clark Reynolds concludes that "public transfers of investable funds from industry to agriculture have more than offset the flow of private savings from rural to urban areas...."[16] In Malaysia, too, the pro-Malay policy has led the government to invest large amounts in land clearance, irrigation, and agricultural development. Iran is unusual in that large oil revenues reduce the need for domestic taxation, although agriculture has received a substantial share of development expenditure, usually in the neighborhood of 25 percent. Turkey has also invested heavily in agriculture and has maintained support prices for key foodgrains at a substantial fiscal loss.

A Summary Word

Agricultural performance in these countries has been superior to that in the LDC world in general, and this has been an important factor in their overall economic success. Domestic output, supplemented in some countries by food imports, has been sufficient to meet rising demand, as indicated by the general stability of the internal terms of trade. In some countries, there has been a marked price rise for animal products, relative to both cereals and manufactured goods. Only one country, the Philippines, shows signs of having encountered a general food bottleneck.

The actual course of events in agriculture has not closely resembled the predictions of any of the models found in the literature. There is nothing resembling the Fei-Ranis model, in which food and labor are simply reallocated to the urban sector with no increase in food output. Rising food output per capita has characterized our sample countries; without it, their post-1950 growth would surely have been retarded. In few countries has agricultural expansion followed either the purely extensive course visualized in land-surplus models or the purely intensive course imposed by land scarcity. Both elements have normally been blended in varying proportions. Technical progress has been important in most countries and dominant in some.

The growth of total agricultural output has made possible sizable rural-urban transfers. Large food transfers can be inferred from the fact that urban populations have grown rapidly with no deterioration,

16. Clark Reynolds, *The Mexican Economy*, pp. 143–44.

and in some cases an improvement, in diet. The rapid growth of urban populations also implies substantial rural-urban migration. This has not been large enough, however, to prevent a continued increase in the rural population. Whether rural underemployment has also increased is unclear and could be estimated only by more intensive country-by-country investigation. In most countries, there appear to have been substantial financial transfers out of agriculture, resulting mainly from government policies rather than from the operation of private markets. Several countries, however, might turn out, on close examination, to be counterexamples, in which there has been a net transfer to agriculture. The transfers that have occurred—regardless of direction—have not involved a high degree of economic calculation and may well have been far from optimal in their effect on national output.

12

The Industrial Sector

Particular interest attaches to the industrial sector, first because it is often regarded as the spearhead of economic development, and second because we are well supplied with hypotheses about industrial growth. These stem largely from the work of Kuznets,[1] Hoffman,[2] and Chenery[3]—the first two working with time series for the older industrial countries over the past century, Chenery using mainly post-1945 cross-section data for samples covering virturally all non-Communist countries.

HYPOTHESES ABOUT INDUSTRIAL GROWTH

Industry in the broad sense of Kuznets's I sector includes manufacturing, mining, transport, power, communications, and construction. Over the past century, in the mature economies that he analyzes, the weight of this sector has risen typically by 20 or more percent, tending to level off at about 50 percent of national product. This rise has been offset by a steady decline in the percentage of output originating in agriculture. The behavior of the services sector is less regular. In some countries, the S proportion of output has remained almost stable, and occasionally it has declined; but in other countries, and particularly in the richest countries such as the United States, it has tended to increase.

Kuznets finds also that the I share of the labor force rose less rapidly than its share of output, indicating that output per worker

1. Simon Kuznets, *Modern Economic Growth.* A Publication of the Economic Growth Center, Yale University (New Haven: Yale University Press, 1966), esp. chap. 3.

2. Walther G. Hoffman, *The Growth of Industrial Economies* (Manchester: University of Manchester Press, 1958).

3. Hollis B. Chenery, "Patterns of Industrial Growth," *American Economic Review* (September 1960) Hollis B. Chenery and Lance Taylor, "Development Patterns: Among Countries and Over Time," *Review of Economics and Statistics* (November 1968): 391–416.

rose more rapidly in this sector than in the economy as a whole. The *S* sector shows an opposite behavior: the labor force share rose faster than the output share, indicating subnormal productivity growth. In most of Kuznets's countries, the rate of productivity increase in agriculture was close to the economy-wide average.

Manufacturing is the largest component of the *I* sector, accounting in the mature economies for 60 to 65 percent of industrial output. In the long-term growth of these economies, the manufacturing share of GNP rises quite rapidly at first and then tapers off to a plateau level of 25–30 percent, though in a few industry-oriented countries with large manufactured exports it has risen as high as 40 percent. The reasons for this rising share of manufactures in GNP are well known. First, organized manufacturing tends to supersede household and handicraft production, so that the *reported* share of manufacturing rises faster than the actual share. Second, at low income levels, most manufactured goods have relatively high income elasticities of demand. Third, because of import substitution induced by growth of the domestic market, domestic output rises considerably faster than domestic consumption. Chenery's (1960) cross-section analysis yields "growth elasticities" with respect to per capita income of 1.31 for consumer goods, 1.50 for intermediate goods, and 2.16 for capital goods. These represent the combined effects of income elasticities of demand and import substitution. Import substitution accounts for most of the relative increase in output of investment goods and intermediate goods. For consumer goods, on the other hand, growth of final demand is the dominant factor.

Chenery and Taylor (1968) find different growth patterns for three groups of countries: (1) "large" countries, defined as those with a population of at least 15 million. Cross-section analysis of this group shows the typical Kuznets pattern, the industry share rising with income but eventually tapering off to a plateau; (2) small countries with an industrial orientation. Here trade enters as an important variable. Unusual success in exporting manufactures can raise the industry share above what would be predicted from the country's income level; (3) small countries with a primary export orientation. Here, favorable conditions for primary exports at first retard the decline of the primary share and the rise of the industry share. But eventually, at higher income levels, the industry share traces an accelerating path (as in Australia or Denmark) rather than the tapering-off pattern of the large-country group.

There is also a systematic relation between the size of the national market and the composition of manufacturing output. Hoffman, using long time series for the mature economies, found a steady rise in the heavy-industry share, which now constitutes well over half of manufacturing output in such industrial leaders as the United States, Germany, and Japan. Chenery and Taylor (1968) broke down manufacturing output in their large-country group to the two-digit level and concluded, from cross-section analysis, that industries can be divided into: (1) "early industries," such as food processing, leather goods, and textiles, whose share of GNP ceases to rise above a per capita income level of $200 or so; (2) "middle industries," such as rubber, wood products, chemicals, petroleum refining, and nonmetallic minerals, whose percentage of GNP continues to rise up to a per capita income of about $500; and (3) "late industries," whose share of GNP rises indefinitely and which contribute about 80 percent of the increase in the total manufacturing share from an income level of $300 upward. In addition to the metals-machinery-transport equipment complex, this group includes printing and paper plus some consumer durables with high income elasticities of demand.

The reasons for this changing composition of output are complex. They include differing income elasticities of demand for final output, a rising ratio of capital and intermediate goods to final output, and import substitution, which occurs earlier in some industries than in others because of differences in the minimum efficient scale of plant.

THE SIZE AND COMPOSITION OF MANUFACTURING OUTPUT

Turning to our sample of developing countries, the first task is to examine the record of industrial growth since 1950. We shall then consider selected aspects of this growth: changes in the relative importance of large-scale and small-scale industry; relative importance of the public and private sectors; sources of capital and entrepreneurship; behavior of manufacturing wage rates and employment; and possible ways of increasing the rate of labor absorption.

The importance of industry in the broad sense was shown in chapter 10, table 8. In every country, the *I* sector increased as a proportion of GNP between 1950 and 1973, typically by 5 to 10 percentage points. In several countries (Pakistan, Taiwan, Thailand, Turkey), the increase was some 15 percentage points, and in South Korea it was a remarkable 23 points. As of the early 1970s the *I* percentage for most

Table 1. Manufacturing Share of National Output and Employment

Country	Manufacturing as Percentage of Gross National Product[a]			Manufacturing Labor Force as Percentage of Total Labor Force 1970[b]
	1949–51 *(1)*	*1959–61* *(2)*	*1971–73* *(3)*	
Brazil	20.6	21.6	24.3	17.8
Colombia	13.92	16.62	19.67	12.8
Iran	n.a.	10.7	n.a.	
Ivory Coast	n.a.	n.a.	15.0	
Kenya	10.0	9.7	12.67	
Korea, South	7.5	9.3	14.67	13.2
Malaysia	n.a.	8.90	13.67	8.7
Mexico	23.41	26.25	23.0	16.7
Nigeria	2.77	4.79	6.67	
Pakistan	7.67	9.89	14.0	9.5
Philippines	12.28	18.66	16.67	11.4
Taiwan	11.89	16.97	22.93	
Thailand	10.50	12.50	16.67	3.4
Turkey	16.6	16.0	20.0	7.1
Venezuela	9.04	12.91	17.67	

[a] Data from UN, *Yearbook of National Accounts Statistics*, 1974. Three-year averages were used to smooth out the effect of fluctuations in agricultural output. Data for the precise periods shown in the table were not available for every country, in which cases the nearest three-year period was used.

[b] Data are from D. Morawetz, "Employment Implications of Industrialisation in Developing Countries: A Survey," *Economic Journal* 84, no. 335 (September 1974): 491–542.

of our countries lay in a range of 25 to 35 percent. We noted earlier that, in the mature economies, the *I* sector typically contributes about 50 percent of national output. Judged by this norm, most of the countries in our sample are well along on the path of industrialization.

Turning to manufacturing proper, the estimates shown in table 1 are not completely reliable. Although most countries prepare national accounts every year, and are thereby obliged to enter a figure for manufacturing, actual censuses of manufacturing are sporadic. Moreover, these censuses usually cover only establishments above a certain size—say those with ten or more employees. Production by households, self-employed handicraft workers, and workers in small shops is estimated rather than counted—and may well be underestimated. This introduces possible error at each point in time. There is also likely to be error in comparisons over time because, if large-scale production is growing more rapidly than small-scale production, censuses of manufacturing will yield too high an estimate of the growth rate of total manufacturing output.

We can nevertheless conclude that, in every country in our sample, manufacturing has increased in relative importance. In a few countries, which either were quite industrialized in 1950 (Brazil, Mexico) or are still at an early stage of industrialization (Kenya, Malaysia), manufacturing as a percentage of GNP has risen over the past generation by only a few percentage points. But in most countries, it has risen by 5 to 10 percent and, in the exceptional case of Taiwan, by more than this. Structural change has been more rapid than in nineteenth-century developing economies; but this is not surprising, since the rates of increase in per capita income have also been higher.

Moreover, this relative expansion of manufacturing has occurred in countries that were following rather different trade-development strategies: in highly protectionist countries such as Pakistan, the Philippines, and the Latin American countries; in moderately protectionist countries such as Iran, Kenya, and Nigeria; in relatively open economies such as Thailand and Malaysia; and in countries that changed course dramatically within the period, such as South Korea and Taiwan. This does not demonstrate that industrial-promotion policies were without effect; but it does suggest that the dominant influences over the long run are sheer increases in population and per capita income.

Looking down the 1971–73 column of table 1, it is clear that our countries stand at different stages of manufacturing development. In general, the Latin American countries have the highest manufacturing —GNP ratios, the African countries have the lowest such ratios, and most Asian countries are in an intermediate position. The final column of table 1 highlights the familiar fact that the contribution of manufacturing to employment is usually below its contribution to output, which is another way of saying that output per worker in manufacturing is above the economy-wide average.

This same phenomenon appears from a different standpoint in table 2, which compares rates of increase in manufacturing output and employment over the decade 1960–69. The rate of increase of employment is typically well below that of output, indicating a substantial increase in output per worker. Note, however, that there is considerable intercountry variation, which can be explained only by further analysis. The low rate of productivity increase in Iran and Malaysia

Table 2. Average Annual Percentage Increase in Gross Manufacturing
Output and Employment, *1960–1969*

Country	Gross Output	Employment
Brazil	6.5	1.1
Colombia	5.9	2.8
Iran	11.2	9.8[a]
Korea, South	18.4	13.0
Malaysia	8.6	8.1[b]
Mexico	8.7	n.a.
Nigeria	14.1	5.7[a]
Pakistan	12.3	2.6[a]
Philippines	6.1	4.8
Taiwan	16.8	13.3[b]
Thailand	10.7	n.a.
Turkey	14.5	5.2[c]
Venezuela	6.2	n.a.

Source: D. Morawetz, "Employment Implications of Industrialisation in Developing Countries," *Economic Journal* 84, no. 335 (September 1974): 492–95.
[a] 1963–68.
[b] 1966–69
[c] 1960–68

may be related to the fact that, even in 1970, manufacturing in these countries was still relatively small scale, consumer-goods oriented, and undercapitalized. The results for Taiwan and South Korea are influenced by the fact that these countries were adept at capital-stretching expedients, which will be described in a later section. The unusually wide gap between output and employment increase in Pakistan and Brazil may arise partly from the low rate of plant utilization that existed in these countries as of 1960, which permitted output to be increased subsequently with little increase in employment.

A word, finally, about the composition of manufacturing output, where historical evidence from the mature economies would lead us to expect substantial change. It is clear from table 3 that such changes have occurred. At the beginning of modern development, food processing, beverages, and tobacco often constitute 40 to 50 percent of manufacturing output. Although this group of industries continues to expand in absolute terms, its growth rate is limited by relatively low income elasticity of demand, and so its percentage contribution declines.

We are accustomed to thinking of textiles as the showpiece of early industrialization; and in about half the countries in our group, the

Table 3. Changes in the Composition of Manufacturing Output,
approximately 1950 and 1970
(Percent)

Country[a]	Food and Beverages		Textiles and Clothing		Other Light Industry		Heavy Industry	
	Beg. Year	End Year	Beg. Year	End Year	Beg. Year	End Year	Beg. Year	End Year
Brazil	26.1	17.0	24.2	12.9	15.8	11.7	31.8	55.7
Colombia	44.6	33.3	24.4	18.4	10.5	11.4	19.3	35.0
Iran	31.2	29.6	29.8	28.1	12.3	7.7	25.5	32.6
Ivory Coast	n.a.	n.a.	n.a.	n.a.	n.a.	n.a.	n.a.	n.a.
Kenya	31.9	30.9	6.3	9.1	22.1	11.7	39.7	47.3
Korea, South	20.2	23.4	31.4	19.9	16.3	11.8	30.1	42.7
Malaysia	25.4	23.0	1.9	2.5	37.3	23.1	29.9	32.7
Mexico	29.5	30.6	17.5	5.4	11.6	15.1	40.5	47.9
Nigeria	52.9	38.3	0.3	18.1	25.0	10.9	21.8	26.7
Pakistan	11.7	28.3	57.2	32.0	6.2	6.4	23.3	32.4
Philippines	48.4	40.7	11.8	8.2	14.3	13.8	25.1	36.6
Taiwan	41.8	18.8	16.1	13.4	10.9	11.5	29.9	54.3
Thailand	56.6	41.5	5.6	7.8	14.2	16.1	17.2	33.0
Turkey	44.8	33.4	27.8	14.5	6.5	5.9	20.5	45.7
Venezuela	41.6	32.4	15.4	8.3	16.5	11.0	24.7	48.3

Source: UNIDO, *Growth of World Industry*, vol. 2, 1973.

Note: Food includes, food, beverages, and tobacco. Textiles includes textiles, clothing, and footwear. Other light industry includes leather and fur, wood products, furniture, paper printing, and rubber. Heavy industry includes chemicals, petroleum refining, plastic products, nonmetallic mineral products, metal products, machinery, electrical apparatus, and transport equipment.

[a] Beginning and end years for individual countries are as follows:

Brazil: 1949, 1969	Colombia: 1953, 1967–69	Iran: 1963–64, 1967–68
Kenya: 1954, 1967–69	Korea, S.: 1958, 1967–69	Malaysia: 1963, 1968–69
Mexico: 1950, 1967–68	Nigeria: 1950, 1967–68	(includes West Malaysia
Pakistan: 1955, 1967–68	Philippines: 1956, 1968–70	only)
Thailand: 1963, 1967–69	Turkey: 1950, 1967–69	Taiwan: 1954, 1967–69
Venezuela: 1953, 1971		

textiles-clothing-footwear group did provide one-quarter or more of industrial output in 1950. Note, however, that the British colonies (Kenya, Nigeria, and Malaysia), which were accustomed to importing British textiles, had little indigenous development in this area. This was also true of the very open Thai economy. In these countries, and particularly in Nigeria, this branch of manufacturing expanded relatively over the next twenty years. In most countries, however, the textile-clothing group declined in relative importance along with food processing.

The last two columns of table 3 include more than heavy industry proper.[4] In addition to metal products, machinery, electrical apparatus, and transport equipment, they include chemicals, petroleum refining, plastics, and nonmetallic mineral products. They thus include consumer goods and some lines of production that are relatively small scale and labor-intensive, such as electronics assembly. The bulk of output in this category, however, consists of intermediate and capital goods from relatively large-scale production units. Most of the industries included are, in Chenery's schema, either "middle industries" (chemicals and petroleum) or "late industries" (the metals-machinery-transport equipment complex).

We would expect a shift in favor of these industries in the course of economic growth; but the speed of the shift over this twenty-year period is striking. In more than half the countries, the heavy-industry group gained in relative importance by more than 10 percentage points, and in several countries (Brazil, Taiwan, Turkey, Venezuela) the increase was a remarkable 25 percent. By 1970, these industries were producing one-third or more of manufacturing output in every country except Nigeria and (probably) the Ivory Coast, and in seven countries the proportion was close to a half.

These shifts in the composition of manufacturing output follow, in general, the Chenery-Taylor sequence. As the domestic market grows, manufacturing expansion initially takes the form of consumer-goods production, which is relatively small scale, labor-using, and often based on local materials. This expansion reflects both growth in the size of the domestic market and replacement of imports by domestic production. In the older industrial countries in our group, notably Mexico and Brazil, import substitution in consumer goods had been substantially completed by 1950. In other countries, including Pakistan and the Philippines, it was substantially complete (that is, imports were less than 10 percent of domestic consumption) by 1960. By 1970, this phase of import substitution was largely completed throughout our sample except for the Ivory Coast, Kenya, Malaysia, and Thailand, which were late starters in the industrialization parade. In

4. The S.I.T.C. two-digit categories that are most readily available in the international sources do not provide a neat separation between capital and consumer-goods production. To obtain this would have involved further disaggregation, which it did not seem worthwhile to undertake.

Kenya, imports still constituted 28 percent of consumer-goods availability in 1970, and in Thailand the proportion was 32 percent in 1968.

The main thrust of contemporary import substitution, then, is in capital goods and intermediates. Only in Brazil is this phase also substantially complete—by 1965, imports of intermediate and capital goods had fallen below 10 percent of total supply. In most countries of our sample, imports still provide one-third to two-thirds of the supply of capital goods. For example, in 1970 the proportion of capital goods imported was about one-third in Turkey, one-half in Mexico, 60 percent in Pakistan, three-quarters in Colombia, and still higher in late industrializers such as Malaysia, Thailand, and the African countries.

MANUFACTURING DUALISM: LARGE AND SMALL PRODUCERS

During the early decades of growth acceleration in England and Japan, most of manufacturing output still came from households and small workshops, often rural-based and employing farm family labor. Replacement of these producers by larger factory units was a gradual process extending over many decades. In today's developing economies, however, one might expect a less leisurely tempo of change. Large production units have become standard in the mature economies, and transfer of machinery and know-how from more to less developed economies is faster than it was a century ago. One might expect, therefore, that new industries in the developing economies would be of larger scale from the outset and that displacement of household and handicraft production would proceed more rapidly.

Information in this area is scanty. Censuses of manufacturing are recent, sporadic, and usually omit small plants as well as handicraft and household production. Country monographs, however, contain information that enables us to say something about the size distribution of manufacturing establishments, the rate of decline in the importance of small producers, and typical differences in factor proportions and productivity by size classes.

The size distribution of manufacturing establishments is extremely skewed. The great majority of establishments are very small; and these provide the bulk of manufacturing employment, though not of value added. This is true especially of countries at an early stage of industrialization, such as Malaysia, Nigeria, the Ivory Coast, and pre-1970 Iran.

We noted in chapter 11 that about one-third of Nigerian rural households are engaged in nonagricultural market activity. Although much of this is petty trade, a good deal of it involves manufacturing. It is estimated that, as of 1965, the industrial sector included some 900,000 households engaged in rural cottage industry, producing textiles and clothing, processing foodstuffs, extracting palm oil, and making household utensils and other small metal products. Urban small-scale industry, defined as shops with less than ten workers, employed at this time some 100,000 people. Employment in plants with ten or more employees totaled 76,000.[5] These urban establishments, like the rural workshops, were engaged almost entirely in consumer-goods production.

In Malaya, as of 1957, about 45,000 of the 135,000 workers engaged in manufacturing were self-employed. Of establishments with employees, about half had only one to four workers. Only 600 plants, or about 13 percent of the total, had twenty or more employees.[6] Although census data are not available for the Ivory Coast, narrative accounts describe production units as very small scale and engaged mainly in processing agricultural and forestry products. The first large-scale textile plant was scheduled for completion in 1974. Iran is reported to have a large stock of skilled handicraft workers, in numbers probably exceeding the total of factory employment. In the organized manufacturing sector, as of 1967, 97 percent of the establishments had less than ten employees. These establishments employed 67 percent of manufacturing workers, though they produced only 36 percent of value added.[7]

It is more surprising to find handicraft and small-scale industry still important in such semi-industrialized countries as Colombia and the Philippines. In Colombia, handicraft employment in 1964 was estimated at 355,000 workers, compared with about 300,000 in the organized manufacturing sector. Within the organized sector, however, there is a more even spread of employment over the size classes and a higher percentage in the larger establishments than in the

5. Peter Kilby, *Industrialization in an Open Economy: Nigeria, 1945–66* (London: Cambridge University Press, 1969), chap. 1.

6. E. L. Wheelwright, "Industrialization in Malaya," in *Thailand: Social and Economic Studies in Development*, ed. Thomas H. Silcock (Canberra: Australian National University Press, 1967).

7. J. Bharier, *Economic Development in Iran, 1900–1970* (New York: Oxford University Press, 1971), p. 111.

early-industrializing economies. As of 1967, about half the manufacturing employees were in plants with more than 100 workers, only
15 percent in those with less than twenty workers.[8] In the Philippines,
as late as 1971, about one million workers were engaged in household
and workshop manufacturing, comprising 70 percent of all manufacturing employment. More than half of these were unpaid family
workers. In the organized manufacturing sector, establishments tend
to be very small or quite large, with the intermediate size classes rather
hollow. More than half the workers in this sector are in plants with
200 or more employees, while another 17 percent are in plants with
fewer than twenty workers.[9]

As atypical cases, in which large-scale manufacturing became
dominant at an early stage, we may note Pakistan and South Korea.
In South Korea as of the 1960s, Kuznets found that the distribution
of manufacturing establishments by employee size classes was very
similar to that for the United States.[10] There are many small establishments in clothing, footwear, furniture, and other consumer-goods
industries. But textile plants are large, and so are those for chemicals,
petroleum products, and metal working, perhaps partly because these
are also "new" industries. In Pakistan, too, which had been almost
entirely agricultural before the partition of the subcontinent, industry
had to be started from scratch, using largely imported technology.
Thus, plants were large from the outset. But this pattern, which one
might have hypothesized as typical of today's developing economies,
is in fact unusual.

The wide variation of establishment sizes in most countries raises
many questions. To what extent are different-sized firms producing
different goods for different markets? To the extent that they are
competing in the same market, how do very small firms manage to
stay in competition over the long run? Or do they mange? Perhaps
they are squeezed out gradually by the pressure of larger competitors.
Again, the data permit only surmises rather than firm conclusions.

There are large interindustry differences in optimum scale of plant.
Thus, one finds large establishments clustered in industries where their

8. John Todd, "Plant Size, Factor Proportions and Efficiency in Colombian Industry,"
in *Essays on Colombian Industrialization* ed. R. A. Berry (forthcoming).

9. ILO, *Sharing in Development: A Programme of Employment, Equity, and Growth
in the Philippines*, 1973, vol. 2, paper 9.

10. Paul W. Kuznets, *Economic Growth and Structure in the Republic of Korea*. A
Publication of the Economic Growth Center, Yale University (New Haven: Yale University Press, 1977), chap. 6.

comparative advantage is greatest. This is partly, but by no means entirely, a consumer-goods versus capital-goods division. In Iran, for example, the industries with a high percentage of value added coming from small establishments include machinery, electrical equipment, and metal products. On the other hand, the industries with very little output from small establishments include tobacco, beverages, printing, rubber, and plastic products.

There is market segmentation also in two other dimensions: location and product quality. In a large country with limited infrastructure, such as Nigeria, transport and information costs give the small producer in the interior some protection against the larger urban manufacturer. The small man may also be offering a less expensive substitute, such as sandals cut out of old tires instead of leather shoes. Finally, the small shop may function as a subcontractor for a larger assembly firm. Japanese experience emphasizes the possibility of a symbiotic relationship between large and small producers along these lines.

Where competition is direct and unavoidable, the small producer has a partial escape by adjusting his factor proportions and factor returns, as will be documented in a moment. But even so, he may not escape fully or permanently. The small-scale sector of LDC manu-facturing seems to operate in the way that Marshall visualized as typical for competitive industries. It is a testing ground from which some well-managed enterprises emerge and grow to larger size, while the majority vanish from the scene. Over time, too, the weight of this sector diminishes gradually relative to that of large-scale industry.

We cannot say much about the speed of this transformation, because the data are fragmentary and our time period is short; and what we can say relates mainly to tendencies within the organized manufacturing sector. Todd's data for Colombia show the percentage of workers in establishments with more than 200 employees rising from 46 percent in 1956 to 55 percent in 1967, with the proportion in the below-20-employees category falling from 15 percent to 11 percent. In the Philippines, the ILO Employment Report shows the following percentage increases in employment between 1965 and 1971: house-hold and workshop production, 30 percent; plants with 5–19 workers, 16 percent; plants with 20 or more workers, 30 percent.[11] This suggests that, although large establishments were gaining relative to small ones within organized manufacturing, the number of very small handicraft

11. ILO, *Sharing in Development*, vol. 2, paper 9.

workshops was growing about as fast. In Iran, Bharier's data for the 1960s show output growing faster in the larger establishments but employment growing faster in the small-scale sector. For Pakistan, Falcon and Stern[12] show the output of large industrial plants growing faster than total manufacturing output: 10.7 percent per year compared with 7.4 percent per year over the period 1954/55–1968/69. Thus, while small-plant output continued to rise in absolute terms, its share of total output fell from more than half in 1955 to about one-quarter by 1970.

The data suggest that, except for a few of the most highly industrialized countries, handicraft and small-shop workers constitute a majority of all manufacturing workers in the countries of our sample and that employment in this sector has continued to rise absolutely while declining relatively. The larger plants seem to have been increasing their share of output faster than their share of employment, suggesting a growing divergence of productivity levels. This is related, of course, to the fact that the composition of manufacturing output is shifting gradually toward heavy industries, which tend to have larger optimum scale, higher capital-labor ratios, and higher labor productivity. It is not clear, however, that displacement of smaller by larger production units is occurring rapidly within narrowly defined product groups.

Turning to the evidence on factor proportions, productivity, and profitability, it would be desirable to have information on plants of differing size producing an identical product; but such material is rare, even for the mature economies. What we usually have is either aggregative data for all manufacturing or data for two-digit industries, each of which embraces a wide variety of product lines.[13] The observed differences, then, arise from a blend of: (1) differing products with different production functions; (2) the possibility of nonhomogeneous production functions for the same or similar products—"technological dualism"; (3) differing factor proportions chosen as a response to

12. Walter P. Falcon and Joseph J. Stern, "Pakistan's Development: An Introductory Perspective," in *Development Policy II: The Pakistan Experience*, ed. Walter P. Falcon and Gustav Papanek (Cambridge: Harvard University Press, 1971).

13. For example, in Colombian manufacturing, "To a considerable degree these two groups produced different products. Within the so-called metal-products industry, the craft firms produced pots and pans; the more modern firms produced some parts for, and assembled, washing machines and refrigerators." Richard R. Nelson, T. Paul Schultz, and Robert L. Slighton, *Structural Change in a Developing Economy* (Princeton: Princeton University Press, 1971), p. 115.

different factor price ratios confronting large and small firms; and (4) economies of scale. To sort out these influences statistically is difficult.

The analysis done in a few countries[14] suggests several hypotheses:

1. There are large differences in the factor price ratios confronting large and small producers. With regard to labor, in Colombia in the mid-1960s, earnings per worker within a two-digit industry were typically two to three times as high in plants with 200 or more workers as in plants with less than ten employees. This does not necessarily measure the relative price of *identical* labor. The larger plants probably had a somewhat superior skill mix, and their higher wage level may have enabled them to attract higher-quality workers and reduce labor turnover. With reasonable allowance for these factors, however, there was still a wide wage gap among the different size classes, a gap that is hard to explain on profit-maximizing assumptions.

While data on capital costs are less plentiful, it is usually thought that larger firms have a distinct advantage. They usually have preferential access to government lending agencies or private commercial banks—at regulated interest rates that are below the marginal productivity of capital and that may even be negative under inflationary conditions. To the extent that capital equipment is imported, preferential access to import licenses is also important. The small firm, whose collateral may be judged unsatisfactory by commercial banks, has to depend mainly on family savings and/or resort to the unorganized money market at relatively high interest rates.

2. The capital-labor ratio rises steeply with plant size. In the Philippines, for example, plants with 500 or more employees have abour four times as much fixed capital per worker as plants with 5–19 employees. How far this is due simply to factor price ratios, how far to differential access to imported equipment and technology, and how far to differing production functions is hard to determine; but a consistent difference in factor proportions is well established.

3. It follows that output per worker rises with plant size. The data for Colombia suggest that the gap in value added per worker between large and small establishments is somewhat wider than the wage gap,

14. For Colombia, in addition to the Nelson-Schultz-Slighton study, see John Todd, "Plant Size," in *Essays*, ed. Berry. On the Philippines, see *Sharing in Development*, vol. 2, paper 9. Bharier's study of Iran contains some information on productivity differences by size. There is also a substantial literature, noted in chap. 9, on dualism in Japanese manufacturing.

so that the large establishments have lower unit labor costs and a smaller labor share of value added. Todd found that the ratio of wages-plus-fringe-benefits to value added was 40–42 percent in the smaller establishments, while in the largest size classes it was 26–33 percent. The large plants, of course, have heavier outlays for capital and perhaps for other inputs; so it does not necessarily follow that profit margins were wider in the largest plants. Large-scale industry in Colombia was very profitable at this time, the rate of return on capital ranging from 30 to 40 percent; but since comparable data are not available for small plants, we cannot say whether their returns were lower.

4. While the partial productivity of labor is lower in the small establishments, the partial productivity of capital is distinctly higher. The evidence from different countries is quite consistent, indicating a strong inverse relation between the output-capital ratio and establishment size. A few such ratios may be cited.[15] *Colombia* (1967): plants with 0–15 workers, 1.17; plants with 200 or more workers, 0.48. *Mexico* (1965): plants with 1–5 workers, 1.17; plants with 500 or more workers, 0.47. *Pakistan* (1960): plants with 0–9 workers, 1.16; plants with 100 or more workers, 0.28. *Japan* (1961): plants with 4–9 workers, 2.50; plants with 300–1,000 workers, 0.85. *India* (1965): "small" (fixed capital less than $100,000), 1.16; "large" (fixed capital above $350,000), 0.29.

If capital is scarce and (unskilled) labor abundant, one is tempted to conclude that the smallest plant sizes are socially most efficient and should be encouraged at the expense of larger producers. But several cautions are in order. Management and skilled labor are usually as scarce as capital. Imported raw materials and other inputs are also scarce and, depending on exchange-rate policy, their shadow and market prices may be quite different. Even unskilled labor is not socially costless, though the small-firm wage level may be closer to social cost than the large-scale level. So numerous adjustments, involving judgment as well as hard data, are required to arrive at estimates of relative social efficiency. There are also dynamic considerations, including skill improvement, rates of productivity increase, and externalities. The Nelson-Schultz-Slighton study found that the rate of productivity improvement in Colombian manufacturing

15. Data for Colombia are from Todd, "Plant Size," in *Essays*, ed. Berry; data for other countries are cited and footnoted in *Sharing in Development*.

firms between 1958 and 1964 rose steeply by firm size; and they considered this an important reason for the gradual shift of gravity in the manufacturing sector from smaller to larger producers.

Todd, also using Colombian data, attempted an estimate of static social efficiency, which admittedly could not capture all relevant factors but which did deflate the wage level of large firms to the craft level and also took account of the shadow price of imported materials. The results, which are averages for the period 1956–67, indicate marked superiority for the smaller establishments. The estimate of net social benefit per unit of capital is 0.87 for plants with 0–14 employees, 0.83 for those with 15–49, 0.67 for those with 50–199 employees, and 0.40 for those with 200 or more workers.

FACTORS IN INDUSTRIAL GROWTH: CAPITAL, ENTREPRENEURSHIP, PUBLIC POLICY

New manufacturing industries may be inaugurated under differing auspices: government, indigenous private concerns, foreign enterprises. In general, for our group of countries, local private investment has been dominant. But the other two sources of investment have been important at some times and places.

Public Investment and Foreign Investment

In several countries, particularly those with a statist tradition, such as Iran and Turkey, state factories were dominant at an early stage but have declined in relative importance over time. In Iran as of 1946, about half of all factory workers were employed in government factories, most of which lost money consistently. Partly on this account, state enterprise was deemphasized, and virtually all plants established after 1960 were privately owned. Most recently, however, with large oil revenues that flow in the first instance into the state treasury, there has once more been substantial investment in government-owned oil refining, petrochemical, and steel facilities.

In Turkey in 1950, about 45 percent of value added in the relatively small industrial sector came from state enterprises. This emphasis on the public sector continued during the 1950s, which was a period of intensified import substitution. Since the early 1960s, however, there has been increasing concern over the inefficiency of state enterprises and the need to move from import substitution to export promotion. The share of manufacturing output produced by state enterprises has now fallen below 40 percent, but the state retains a virtual monopoly in steel, oil refining, fertilizers, petrochemicals, and pulp and paper.

In Thailand, there was considerable government investment in manufacturing in the early 1950s, partly with a view to keeping industry in Thai rather than Chinese hands. These enterprises proved a heavy drain on the budget, however, and fear of government competition also discouraged private investment. By the late 1950s, policy had shifted to encouraging private businesses, often managed by a Chinese with a "silent partner" in the Thai government. In Pakistan, many new industries were initiated through government investment bodies such as the Pakistan Industrial Development Corporation, but most of these were later sold to private inestors.

South Korea is unusual in that government continues to play a large role in manufacturing, particularly in heavy industry. As of the late 1960s, two government fertilizer companies were producing virtually all the output of fertilizer; another government company had a monopoly of oil refining; a government shipbuilding company had two-thirds of the output in that area; and government enterprises were prominent in metal refining and heavy machinery. The other unusual feature is that government enterprises in South Korea are typically profitable. Kuznets reports profits-sales ratios varying from 1 to 20 percent and generally rivaling with those of private enterprises in similar industries.[16]

Government-owned or mixed public-private enterprises are of some importance in the Latin American countries, particularly in metals and oil refining, but they typically produce only a small percentage of value added in manufacturing. In Brazil, for example, government enterprises dominate oil refining, mine 80 percent of the iron ore, have 70 percent of steel ingot capacity and 45 percent of aluminum-refining capacity, produce a sizable share of the autos and trucks, and have a small portion of production in shipbuilding, lead refining, electrical equipment, and pulp and paper.[17] Overall, however, the government percentage of value added in manufacturing is below 10 percent; and only about 10 percent of public-sector investment funds are allocated to industry.

16. P. Kuznets, *Economic Growth and Structure*, chap. 6.

17. Joel Bergsman, *Industrialization and Trade Policies in Brazil* (Oxford University Press, for the OECD, 1970).

In Mexico, government operates to a large extent through powerful financial institutions such as the Nacional Financiera. It is the majority stockholder in numerous manufacturing enterprises, particularly in heavy industry, including the national steel, automobile, railroad car, and textile companies. An important function of these companies is to establish cost and price yardsticks in oligopolistic industries where private operators might otherwise engage in joint profit maximization. Their leverage in the economy is thus greater than their modest contribution to GNP might suggest.

In sum, in only three countries of our sample (Iran, Turkey, and South Korea) do government enterprises produce a large share of manufacturing output. Where government is important, it is typically in heavy manufacturing, light industry being mainly in private hands. The managerial and financial difficulties that afflict government manufacturing enterprises are well known; but the experience in South Korea suggests that these difficulties are not insuperable. The mixed industrial enterprises in Mexico and Brazil function quite satisfactorily, perhaps because of their semiautonomous character. Moreover, failure of a public enterprise to earn profit is not necessarily an indication of poor social performance. In Turkey, for example, public manufacturing concerns are used for a variety of objectives: to contribute to regional development by setting up in locations that appear unprofitable to private business; to serve as model employers; to provide low-cost inputs to agriculture; and to restrain inflation by holding their sales prices below what the market would permit. Performance on these fronts should be weighed along with financial returns.

Concerning foreign private investment in manufacturing, our countries can be divided into three groups. In the three African countries, foreign investment still predominates, and their manufacturing sectors are in a sense still in colonial status. At the other pole are countries such as Turkey, in which foreign investment is viewed with great suspicion and is virtually excluded. Finally, the most common situation is one in which foreign investment is admitted, but with restrictions that have tended to increase over the course of time. A common requirement, particularly in Latin America, is 51 percent local participation. Other regulations involve use of local materials and components, ratio of foreign to indigenous personnel, and limits on the repatriation of profits and capital.

In addition to the three African countries, foreign private investment is of considerable importance in Brazil (Europe, United States), Mexico

(United States), Thailand (Japan, United States, Taiwan), and South Korea (United States, Japan). It is quantitatively small in Iran but important in some high-technology areas. In the remaining countries of our group, it is quite small. Overall, for our sample, the contribution of foreign private capital to manufacturing investment is smaller than one might have expected in view of current controversies over the role of multinational corporations. The world of the multinationals is still largely the world of the mature economies.

Domestic Entrepreneurship

We come back, then, to the indigenous private businessman—usually a small businessman in the first instance—as the main agent of industrial development. It is striking that, in the country literature we surveyed as background for this study, there are virtually no complaints about the "shortage of entrepreneurship" that bulked large in writings on economic development during the 1950s. Potential industrialists seem to have been in good supply everywhere. In some cases the lead was taken by migrant groups—the Chinese in West Malaysia and Thailand; the mainland Chinese who moved to Taiwan after 1949; Moslems who migrated to Pakistan from India or East Africa after partition; and English, French, and other expatriate businessmen in the African countries. But in other countries, the entrepreneurs were people who had always been there and who either shifted to manufacturing or expanded the scale of their manufacturing operations.

Who these people were and what they were doing previously has not been thoroughly studied. For Pakistan, there has been some investigation by Gustav Papanek[18] and Stephen Lewis.[19] Lewis's tabulation of the occupations of fathers and grandfathers of Pakistani entrepreneurs shows "traders and merchants" as the largest single source, but farmers and industrialists are also prominent. With regard to the entrepreneurs' own first occupation, about 40 percent had been in manufacturing from the outset, while 20 percent had started out as traders and another 20 percent as skilled craftsmen. Papanek finds that the schooling level of the new industrialists was relatively low (though they had had extensive informal training in family businesses); nor was there any significant

18. Gustav F. Papanek, "Pakistan's Industrial Entrepreneurs," in *Development Policy II*, ed. Falcon and Rapanek.
19. Stephen R. Lewis, Jr., *Pakistan: Industrialization and Trade Policies* (Oxford University Press, for the OECD, 1970), esp. pp. 45–50.

relation between educational level and business success. This suggests that a supply of entrepreneurs is not contingent on development of a large educated class.

Trading experience and a profit orientation, however, are not sufficient conditions for success in industry. The government of Nigeria has tried to encourage small-scale, indigenous enterprises by means of planned industrial estates, government lending agencies, and other promotional devices; but results have been disappointing. The main reason, Kilby concludes, is limited absorptive capacity, which "can be restated as the problem of deficient entrepreneurial capabilities."[20] This shows up in poor maintenance of equipment, poor supervision of plant employees, unwillingness to delegate authority, and erosion of profits through pilfering and embezzling by the clerical staff. The problem seems to lie, not in deficiences of education, but in deep-rooted cultural attitudes. Wealth commands high status, but efficient managerial performance does not. On the contrary, the "big man" gains status by a display of conspicuous leisure. Similar complaints are not unknown in other countries. Witness descriptions of the traditional Puerto Rican factory owner as compared with the U.S.-trained branch plant executive.[21]

Capital Supply

With regard to capital supply, the story is thoroughly classical and could almost be transcribed from English or Japanese experience. Virtually all small businesses and many larger businesses are family concerns, even though they may use the corporate form. In many countries, business law is not well developed and property rights are not effectively enforceable. A businessman accordingly trusts only those over whom he has at least a moral claim, that is, family members. Initial capital for manufacturing is accumulated from profits in trading or other family businesses. Papanek, in his analysis of a sample of Pakistani industrialists, found that 75 percent of their initial capital had been assembled in this way. Government banks, commercial banks, and outside shareholders had contributed only 25 percent.

From that point on, capital accumulates mainly through reinvest-

20. Kilby, *Industrialization*, chap. 10.
21. Lloyd G. Reynolds and Peter Gregory, *Wages, Productivity, and Industrialization in Puerto Rico*. A Publication of the Economic Growth Center, Yale University (Homewood, Ill.: Richard D. Irwin, Inc., 1965).

ment of earnings. Papanek found that, of the increase in capital between the founding of the business and the date of the survey, 70 percent had come from plowing back of profits. This is supported by Lewis's estimate that gross corporate saving (including depreciation) was about 50 percent of pretax gross income in the mid-1960s and amounted to about 70 percent of gross profit after taxes. Kuznets reports similar findings for South Korea. In the year he analyzed, 1967, profits of manufacturing concerns constituted 26 percent of value added. The total of profits plus depreciation was slightly above the total of fixed capital formation—69 billion won compared with 64 billion. In spite of this, manufacturers were raising substantial amounts of money through short-term borrowing and security issues. The reason is partly that, in an inflationary environment where real interest rates are often negative, it pays to be in debt. Further, there are profitable uses for funds other than fixed capital formation, notably inventory accumulation and land speculation.

Monopoly or oligopoly is the standard situation in manufacturing, and profit rates are high. (In Britain, the United States, and Japan, profit rates were also much higher in the early decades of industrialization than they are today. In this as in other respects, today's developing countries are reliving the past.) Rates of return on capital of 20, 30, even 40 percent are commonly reported. These high rates provide both an incentive to, and a major source of funds for, continued investment.

Self-finance is the main source of capital accumulation, but important supplementary sources are private commercial banks and government development banks. Commercial banking is an old and familiar story; but government development banks are mainly a post-1945 development. They are prominent in virtually every country in our sample. They often draw a substantial part of their funds from abroad, the balance coming from domestic borrowing and budget allocations. They serve as a source of both initial and supplemental capital for government-owned infrastructure industries as well as for large-scale manufacturing concerns, public and private. In relatively industrialized countries with a substantial financial sector, such as Mexico or Brazil, one finds specialized government banks serving particular industries.

One of the oldest and largest of such organizations, the Nacional Financiera of Mexico, may serve as an example.[22] The N.F., whose

22. For a detailed discussion, see Calvin P. Blair, "Nacional Financiera," in *Public Policy and Private Enterprise in Mexico*, ed. Raymond T. Vernon (Cambridge: Harvard University Press, 1964).

creditworthiness is well established, gets about half its funds by placing its own securities in New York and other foreign markets. In addition to borrowing and relending on its own account, it plays an important role in guaranteeing direct foreign loans to Mexican corporations. More than half its lending operations are in power, railroads, irrigation, and other infrastructure industries. Another 20 percent goes to heavy manufacturing industries in which the N.F. is a majority stockholder. It furnishes credit to private concerns mainly through bond purchases, medium-term loans, and loan guarantees rather than through equity participation. Representatives of the N.F. sit on the boards of many private companies, and private industrialists sit on its board. It is an interesting, Zaibatsu-like organization, technically competent and entrepreneurially oriented, overlapping the private and public sectors (the interrelations of which, in Mexico, are both complex and pragmatic).

In Mexico as elsewhere, however, the bulk of private investment is internally financed, and only a minor part of private savings are transferred through the financial system. Brothers and Solis estimate that 10–20 percent of private saving is transferred to private investment via financial intermediaries, while another 5–10 percent is transferred to the public sector. This would leave 70–80 percent being reinvested directly by businesses. Long-term debt and equity instruments are underdeveloped, and the stock market is of limited importance.[23] Underdevelopment of long-term capital markets, indeed, is characteristic of all the countries in our sample. This suggests that development of such institutions is not a precondition of accelerated industrial growth; but there is no doubt that it can play an important facilitating role.[24]

Industrial Promotion: Benefits and Costs

Especially before 1960, but in some measure to the present day, government policy in most developing countries has been strongly

23. Dwight S. Brothers and Leopoldo Solis M., *Mexican Financial Development* (Austin: University of Texas Press, 1966). See also R. L. Bennett, *The Financial Sector and Economic Development: The Mexican Case* (Baltimore: Johns Hopkins Press, 1965).

24. See in this connection Ronald I. McKinnon, *Money and Capital in Economic Development* (Washington: Brookings Institution, 1973). For an account of recent Brazilian experiments, including "indexing" of security yields, see Walter L. Ness, Jr., "Financial Markets Innovations as a Development Strategy: Initial Results From the Brazilian Experience," *Economic Development and Cultural Change* 22 (April 1974): 453–72.

proindustry. The devices used for industrial promotion are familiar:
(1) high rates of effective protection, operating through quantitative
restrictions as well as tariff rates; (2) preferential treatment in imports
of raw materials, machinery, and intermediate goods; (3) preferential
access to capital through government lending institutions; (4) pegging
of interest rates in the organized money market at artificially low, even
negative, levels; (5) a variety of tax holidays and tax rebates for new
industries; and (6) in recent years, with increasing attention in some
countries to export promotion, a variety of financial incentives for
manufactured exports.

These policies have succeeded in the sense that, in most developing
economies, manufacturing has grown rapidly and has yielded high rates
of private profit. At the same time, they have been criticized as leading
to resource misallocation and production of manufactured goods at
excessive cost. We cannot go into this controversy in depth; but several
impressions stand out from the country literature.

1. The first is some doubt about the importance of promotional
policies as against market size and other economic variables. The
countries in our sample, over the period 1950–70, were following rather
different trade-industrial strategies. Some were outward-looking,
export-oriented economies; some had moderate rates of protection
for domestic industry; some were highly protectionist; and some made
one or more changes of course within the period. Yet if one did not
know this in advance and were simply presented with the evidence in
tables 1, 2, and 3, it would be hard to sort countries into these "strategy
boxes." The developmental tendencies seem broadly similar and in
accord with hypotheses derived from earlier growth acceleration in
the mature economies.

2. Within the manufacturing sector, some industries received more
protection and encouragement than others. But again, there is the
question of how far this was responsible for differential rates of industrial growth. From a regression analysis of industry growth rates in
Pakistan, Lewis concluded that the most important single determinant
was the extent to which an industry relied on domestic rather than
imported raw materials. Local jute and cotton, for example, were
increasingly exported as cloth rather than in raw form. Market size
was also a major determinant. By 1965, the structure of Pakistani
manufacturing was approaching the Chenery "normal," though it was
still somewhat low on most intermediate and capital goods. All this,
Lewis concludes, is consistent with a finding that the development of

Pakistan's manufacturing structure was based on "real" consideration and that economic policies that attempted to distort the relative price structure did not have as much effect on investment patterns as might have been anticipated.

3. There is no doubt that the highly protectionist policies of some countries imposed cost on the economy by diverting resources toward unpromising "infants." Some indication of this can be obtained by comparing the domestic price with the price of duty-free imports. In Colombia, for example, the domestic price-import price ratio for most manufactures is in the range of 1.0–1.5; but for trucks it is 2.5, and for automobiles, 4.0. In Brazil, Winpenny found[25] that unit production cost for manufactured items was typically above the U.S. level, an advantage in unit labor cost being more than offset by other items, particularly higher unit cost of raw materials and adminstration. The percentage by which the Brazilian price exceeded the import price was correlated with the rate of effective protection. Not surprisingly, the Brazilian goods that are least protected and least overpriced are those that have done best in export markets. A similar variation in the relative efficiency of specific branches of manufacturing has been reported by Stephen Lewis[26] for Pakistan. At the extreme, there are cases in which value added to the domestic economy is negative when calculated at world prices. For Mexico, King reports[27] that the domestic price of manufactures is typically 20 to 30 percent above the world level, but with substantial interindustry variation. Thus, the Mexican price is 50 percent higher for cars, but only 9 percent higher for fertilizer and petroleum.

Overprotection, that is, a tariff higher than required to cover the inherent difference in production costs, is also a common situation. Excess protection permits varying combinations of production inefficiency, that is, operation above the technically feasible cost curves; above-normal profits; and unused protection space, that is, a domestic price-world price gap smaller than the tariff would permit. The actual combination varies among countries and industries. In Brazil, Bergsman concludes that overprotection of consumer goods, where import

25. I. T. Winpenny, *Manufactured Exports and Government Policy: Brazil's Experience Since 1939* (Hove, Sussex: Hove Printing Co., 1972).

26. Stephen R. Lewis, Jr., *Pakistan: Industrialization and Trade Policies* (New York: Oxford University Press, 1970.)

27. Timothy King, *Mexico: Industrialization and Trade Policies Since 1940* (New York: Oxford University Press, 1970).

substitution is now virtually complete, has contributed to a general lowering of efficiency, with the antiquated and noncompetitive textile industry a particularly glaring example. In Pakistan, Lewis finds that "... it seems that a substantial amount of the protection received by various industries came in the form of high profits, rather than in the form of major inefficiencies."[28] In Mexico, King finds that most manufacturing industries have unused protection space. This could result from a lag in reducing tariffs as domestic industries succeed in reducing costs and prices relative to world levels.

There is some evidence to support the protectionist argument that new industries, even if relatively inefficient at the outset, will make subsequent improvements through a learning process. Thus, in Pakistan Lewis found that the import-substituting industries that were established earliest gradually improved their efficiency, as evidenced by cost declines ranging from 5 to 60 percent over the period 1955–65. The industries with the largest drop in costs and relative prices were edible oils, cigarettes, cotton textiles, soap, matches, pharmaceuticals, and metal products. By the early 1960s some of these industries had begun to export. In Colombia, using data for twenty-five three-digit metal manufacturing industries, Dudley found learning to be a major factor in productivity improvement.[29] He also concluded that learning by both workers and firms was important and that learning was a function of both cumulative output and passage of time.

The fact that some countries in the group are now substantial exporters of manufactures might also be regarded as supporting the argument that infants do grow up. South Korea and Taiwan are the best-known examples; but we shall see in chapter 13 that manufactured exports are now a significant share of total exports in several other countries and are growing rapidly in percentage terms from a small initial base.

28. Joel Bergsman, *Brazil: Industrialization and Trade Policies* (New York: Oxford University Press, 1970), p. 91.

29. "... The effect of learning would appear to be considerably more important than the effects of increased capital per worker or larger scale. Learning from experience alone would seem capable of explaining annual productivity increases of from two to three percent in the metal-products sector as a whole, with considerably higher rates in individual industries.... The production functions with learning provide a better explanation of productivity change in Colombian metal products than a simple neoclassical production function with either disembodied or capital-embodied technical change." Leonard Dudley, "The Effects of Learning on Productivity in the Colombian Metal Products Sector," in *Essays*, ed. Berry.

INDUSTRIAL WAGES AND EMPLOYMENT

In this important area we must deal mainly in hypotheses, which cannot yet be tested adequately because of scarcity and low quality of the data. The consumer price indexes needed to convert money wage movements to real terms are usually unsatisfactory. Wage data are limited and frequently consist only of establishment-wide averages, the movement of which is influenced by changes in skill mix as well as changes in rates for narrowly defined labor grades. Data on labor and capital shares of income produced are fragmentary.

Perhaps the best-documented hypothesis is that the real wage level in the modern sector rises over time, even under conditions of labor surplus. Turner and Jackson found this to be true of real wages in manufacturing in a sample of 35 less developed economies.[30] Over the decade 1955–65, money wages rose on average by 8.6 percent per year, consumer prices went up 5.3 percent, and real wages increased 3.3 percent. Excluding three notably inflationary economies (Argentina, Brazil, and Chile) reduces the money wage and price increase figures, but it does not alter the average rate of increase in real wages. The 3.3 percent LDC average for real wages, in fact, was identical with the average for a sample of nineteen advanced "market" economies.

These results confirm our impression from the country literature. In only two of our fifteen countries is there any indication of the wage stability posited by the Lewis and Fei-Ranis models. For Pakistan, Lewis notes that up to 1965 "the industrial sector did not experience rising real wage rates, despite the rapid increase in the demand for industrial workers."[31] For the Philippines, the real wage rate for common laborers in Manila rose and fell intermittently over the period 1951–72 but exhibited no clear upward trend.[32] For the remaining countries, however, one encounters repeated statements, often supported by quantitative estimates, that the real industrial wage level has been rising.

This coexistence of surplus labor and rising industrial wages is still poorly understood. Before seeking institutional explanations, one might ask whether there are plausible economic explanations for the phenomenon. There are several possibilities: (1) hypotheses about the

---

30. H. A. Turner and D. A. S. Jackson, "On the Determination of the General Wage Level—A World Analysis: or 'Unlimited Labour Forever'," *Economic Journal* 80 (December 1970): 827–49.

31. Lewis, *Pakistan*, chap. 3.

32. ILO, *Sharing in Development*, vol. 2, paper 2.

rural-urban wage gap relate implicitly to unskilled labor, while industry employs workers over a wide skill range. There are indications, moreover, that occupational wage differentials tend to widen in the early years of development because skilled labor is in short supply. Thus, a plant's *average* wage level might rise, because of widening skill differentials and possibly an enrichment of its skill mix, even if its rate for unskilled labor did not change; (2) the workers attracted to and accepted by industrial employers may be of higher quality than those remaining in traditional occupations; (3) even if not initially of higher quality, they become so over time by learning both specific skills and the general habit of factory work—and also because the higher industrial wage allows them to improve their nutrition and health; (4) experienced factory workers thus become less and less interchangeable with potential new recruits. The fact that replacing them would involve substantial costs warrants a wage above the supply price of new workers. Wage theorists in mature economies have recently come to rely on this as a partial explanation for interemployer wage differences in the same local labor market.

It seems unlikely, however, that the large modern-traditional wage gap can be explained entirely on these grounds; and it is widely believed that political mechanisms are also at work. Government is itself a major employer, in public corporations as well as in general government; and the industrial labor force is concentrated in the capital city and other urban centers, where it can make things difficult for government by strikes and public demonstrations. Kilby describes the operation of this mechanism in Nigeria,[33] where real wages in the "organized" sector have been rising at more than twice the rate of per capita product in the economy as a whole. A key factor is the government wage scale, which is above the supply price of labor but is also sluggish, being adjusted only intermittently to take account of inflation. Large private employers use the government scale as a guideline but adjust wages more frequently, so that they are sometimes ahead of the government and sometimes behind. The wage structure is underpinned also by a legal minimum wage, effectively applicable only to the larger employers. Trade unions make wage gains, not through collective bargaining, but by pressuring government to raise the minimum wage, raise government wage scales, and bring government pressure to bear on large private employers. As of 1965,

33. Kilby, *Industrialization.*

Table 4. Wage Bill as Percent of Value Added in Manufacturing

Country	Initial Period	Terminal Period
Brazil	27.7 (1949)	25.3 (1967–69)
Colombia	27.9 (1953)	23.8 (1971)
Iran	22.2 (1963)	25.6 (1969)
Kenya	42.0 (1954)	50.3 (1971)
Korea, South	36.6 (1958)	23.6 (1972)
Malaysia (West)	36.5 (1963)	28.0 (1971)
Mexico	30.9 (1950)	37.0 (1972)
Nigeria	25.7 (1962–63)	20.9 (1972)
Pakistan	34.6 (1955)	20.5 (1970)
Philippines	34.7 (1956)	19.3 (1972)
Taiwan	23.6 (1954)	31.4 (1967–69)
Thailand	20.0 (1963)	16.6 (1967–69)
Turkey	32.1 (1950)	19.2 (1970)
Venezuela	37.6 (1953)	13.2 (1971)

Source: UNIDO, *Growth of World Industry*, vol. 1, 1973, country tables.

wage rates in the organized sector were roughly double those in small-scale manufacturing.

Although industrial workers are doing well in absolute terms, there are indications that, in many countries, labor's share of value added has been falling, producing a distributional shift toward profits à la Lewis. The United Nations Industrial Development Organization (UNIDO) yearbook on Growth of World Industry contains data that permit a calculation of the wage bill as a percentage of value added in manufacturing. These data (table 4) are not highly reliable but can be taken as indicating rough orders of magnitude. In ten of the fourteen countries, the wage share of value added fell between the initial and terminal periods, in five cases by ten or more percentage points. The other striking impression from the table is the small size of the labor share as of the late 1960s. The median for the group is only about 24 percent, compared with the 60 percent or more that would be normal in the mature economies.

The fact that labor's share has fallen is not conclusive evidence that the product wage (the money wage deflated by the product price) has also fallen. If W is the wage rate, L is employment, Q is output, and P is the product price, then labor's share is

$$\frac{W \cdot L}{P \cdot Q} \text{ or } \frac{W}{P} \cdot \frac{L}{Q}$$

Labor's share could fall because of a fall in W/P; but it could also fall because an increase in W/P is more than offset by a decline in L/Q. We know that L/Q has been falling, that is, that output per worker has been rising, due among other things to an increase in capital per worker, induced by a continuing rise in wage costs relative to capital costs. What has happened to W/P thus cannot be inferred directly from table 4 but would required more detailed investigation.

So much as been written on the behavior of manufacturing employment that little need be added here.[34] In a particular country, over a specified time period, the rate of growth of manufacturing employment depends on: (1) the growth rate of aggregate industrial output, which, apart from the temporary booster shot that can be obtained from accelerated import substitution, depends on the growth of the domestic market plus (eventually) growing competitiveness in exports; (2) shifts in the product composition of manufacturing output, which are important because some products are inherently more labor-using than others; (3) shifts in the size mix of production units for a given output, which are important because of the characteristic differences in factor proportions described in an earlier section; and (4) capital accumulation, capital-labor substitution, and technical progress within production units.

Clearly, there are steps that government can take under each of these categories. It can attempt to enlarge the domestic market, affect the product composition of output, increase the viability of small and labor-intensive production units, and influence choice of techniques within units. On this last point, there may have been some tendency to overstate the inflexibility of equipment imported from advanced economies. Microeconomic inquiry suggests a variety of capital-stretching possibilities: judicious importation of slightly antiquated equipment; the running of machinery at higher speeds; multiple-shift rather than single-shift operation; assignment of more workers per machine; use of labor-intensive methods for machine repair and servicing; use of labor-intensive methods for materials handling and other supplementary operations; subcontracting to small enterprises and even "putting out" some activities to farmers' sheds; and international subcontracting in which a country performs one labor-

34. For a review of the issues and the literature, see D. Morawetz, "Employment Implications of Industrialisation in Developing Countries: A Survey," *Economic Journal* 84 (September 1974): 491–542.

intensive phase of a multistage production operation. Such capital-stretching devices were important in early Japanese manufacturing development, and Ranis has found widespread use of them in contemporary South Korea and Taiwan,[35] which may help to explain the unusual success of those countries in raising both industrial output and employment.

A Summary Word

The main features of industrial development that stand out from the data are:

1. Manufacturing development has been rapid—remarkably so in Taiwan and South Korea. In most countries the manufacturing share of GNP has risen since 1950 by 5 to 10 percent.

2. The composition of manufacturing output has shifted from light toward heavy industry, following the normal sequence analyzed by Chenery and others.

3. The structure of manufacturing industry is strongly dualistic. In many countries small workshops, with relatively low capital-labor and capital-output ratios, still provide more than half of manufacturing employment, though less than that share of manufacturing output. The small-industry share is diminishing gradually, as happened in Japan and elsewhere at an earlier stage.

4. Although government enterprise and foreign private enterprise have been of substantial importance in some countries, the domestic private entrepreneur has usually been dominant. There is little indication of the shortage of entrepreneurship that has been so widely discussed. Capital accumulation has proceeded in classical fashion, with initial family savings being augmented by reinvestment of earnings.

5. There has typically been an excess supply of labor for new industries, though in Taiwan and South Korea the labor reservoir had been substantially exhausted by 1970. Despite a labor surplus, the real wage level in large-scale industry has risen substantially in most countries, for reasons which are by no means clear. This has been accompanied by capital deepening in manufacturing, rather than the capital shallowing that might have been preferable in the circumstances.

35. Gustav Ranis, "Industrial Sector Labor Absorption," *Economic Development and Cultural Change* 21 (April 1973): 387–408.

6. Manufacturing employment has risen a good deal less rapidly than output and has not made a major contribution to the absorption of the rapidly growing labor force. The rate of labor absorption, however, is not independent of policy. Taiwan and South Korea, in particular, have made effective use of capital-stretching devices.

13

The Government and Foreign Sectors

By government, I mean what in fiscal analysis is termed *general government*. Public and mixed corporations engaged in manufacturing, transport, power, and infrastructure industries I treat as part of the industrial sector, though I shall depart from this rule in discussing the allocation of capital budgets. In principle, all levels of government should be included; but in some countries only data on central government operations are available.

The development literature provides a picture of what should be happening in a successfully developing economy. The current revenue —GNP ratio should be rising. An increasing proportion of current revenue should come from income-elastic tax sources, notably personal and corporate income taxation. A high proportion of this revenue should be allocated to growth-promoting expenditures. Current expenditures, however, should be held below the rising revenues, to provide a surplus that can be used for capital expenditure. Government capital formation should be rising as a percentage of GNP, and this capital formation should also be developmental in character. Power plants and irrigation systems should be preferred over pyramid-building. To the extent that government capital formation cannot be financed from budget surpluses, it should be financed by domestic nonbank borrowing or by foreign borrowing. Heavy reliance on the central bank, with consequent inflationary pressure, is usually taken to indicate mismanagement.

These normative principles sound reasonable. But to what extent are they followed? Does failure to follow them act as a brake on development? How important is the government sector anyway in the growth process?

CURRENT REVENUE: SIZE AND COMPOSITION

The current revenue–GNP ratio is usually termed the *tax ratio*. There is a substantial literature[1] on the determinants of intercountry variations in this ratio. Independent variables that have been used with some success include: per capita GNP, which is positively related to the tax ratio for countries above a threshold level of income, though not for the poorest stratum of countries; openness of the economy, which is also positively related to the tax ratio because of the importance of export and import duties in LDC fiscal systems; and degree of monetization, as indicated by per capita money supply, which also shows a significant positive relation. The best regressions to date, however, yield only low R^2's, so that a large part of the variance remains unexplained. The political orientation of government— "welfare statist" or "free enterprise"—and its efficiency in tax collection must be important; but these variables are difficult to incorporate into statistical analyses.[2]

Data on the tax ratio in our sample of countries are presented in table 1. A limitation of these data, which there is no ready means of overcoming, is that they usually cover only central government revenue; revenue collected at lower levels is excluded. For large countries with a federal structure, this is an important limitation. For what they are worth, however, the data show little relation between tax ratio and per capita income. Some higher-income countries (Brazil, Turkey) have relatively high tax ratios, but others (Mexico, Colombia) do not. The same is true of low-income countries. Malaysia, Kenya, and the Ivory Coast have much higher tax ratios than South Korea, the Philippines, and Thailand. Scatter diagrams relating the 1973 tax ratio to 1973 GNP per capita, or to the 1965–73 rate of increase in GNP per capita, show no visible relation.

1. See in particular Alison Martin and W. Arthur Lewis, "Patterns of Public Revenue and Expenditure," *Manchester School* 24 (1956): 203–44; Jeffrey G. Williamson, "Public Expenditure and Revenue: An International Comparison," *Manchester School* 29 (1961): 43–56; Harley H. Hinrichs, "Determinants of Government Revenue Shares Among Less Developed Countries," *Economic Journal* 75 (1965): 546–56; Jorgen R. Lotz and Elliott R. Morss, "Measuring Tax Effort in Developing Countries," *IMF Staff Papers* 14, 1967, pp. 478–99; Richard S. Thorn, "The Evolution of Public Finances During Economic Development," *Manchester School* 35 (1967): 19–53; Richard A. Musgrave, *Fiscal Systems* (New Haven: Yale University Press, 1969); Raja J. Chelliah, "Trends in Taxation in Developing Countries," *IMF Staff Papers* July 1971, pp. 254–331.

2. For one important effort to do this, however, see Fredric L. Pryor, *Public Expenditures in Communist and Capitalist Nations* (Homewood, Ill.: Richard D. Irwin, Inc., 1968).

Table 1. Current Revenue as Percentage of GNP at Current Prices,
1950–1951 and 1971–1973

Country	1950–51[a]	1971–73[b]
Brazil	9.7	15.7
Colombia	7.1	8.7
Iran	10.7	23.5
Ivory Coast	17.1	20.6
Kenya	15.9	19.1
Korea, South	19.8	15.9
Malaysia	—	22.8
Mexico	10.4	8.6
Nigeria	7.5	21.8
Pakistan	5.7	13.9
Philippines	6.4	10.2
Taiwan	—	20.5
Thailand	9.4	13.6
Turkey	13.5	20.8
Venezuela	19.4	20.8

[a] Average of 1950 and 1951, with the following exceptions: Iran, 1959–60; Ivory Coast, 1962; Kenya, 1964; South Korea, 1961–62; Nigeria, 1951–52; Pakistan, 1959–60; Thailand, 1952; Turkey, 1952.
[b] Average of 1971–73, except for the Ivory Coast, where data are for 1971–72 only.

Trends over time are somewhat obscured by the fact that 1971–73 was a boom period for primary exports, which tended to swell government revenues because of the prominence of export and import taxes in most countries' fiscal systems. Even after taking account of this, however, there was a significant rise in the tax ratio in most countries, as one would expect. In only two countries did the tax ratio decline between 1950–51 and 1971–73.

The tax ratio, of course, does not necessarily reflect the country's *tax effort*. A country's tax ratio should be compared with what would be normal given its per capita income, degree of monetization, foreign trade ratio, and so on. Two studies have evaluated tax effort in terms of the ratio of actual to expected tax collections.[3] Chelliah's study, for the period 1966–68, covers fifty-two LDC's, including twelve of our fifteen countries. On the basis of the actual-expected index, our countries fall into three groups: (1) countries with superior tax performance, that is, Brazil (1.78), Turkey (1.16), Kenya (1.16), and Taiwan (1.12). Brazil ranks first among all LDCs in both this study

3. Lotz and Morss, "Measuring Tax Effort," *IMF Staff Papers*; and Chelliah, "Trends in Taxation," *IMF Staff Papers*.

and the Lotz-Morss study; (2) countries with average tax effort, that is, Malaysia (1.02), Thailand (1.00), Iran (0.97), Korea (0.97), and Venezuela (0.97); and (3) countries with substandard tax performance, that is, Mexico (0.77), the Philippines (0.77), and Pakistan (0.75). These three countries rank near the bottom of the list, the only sizable countries with lower indexes being Bolivia and Indonesia.

With regard to tax effort, then, our countries cover the entire spectrum. As a group, they seem neither superior nor inferior to LDCs in general. Thus, one cannot say that high tax effort is essential to rapid economic growth. But should it in any case be regarded as helpful? Rising tax revenues *permit* government to direct more resources toward growth acceleration; but they do not *ensure* that resources will be directed in this way. On the negative side, almost every tax may have a net disincentive effect, depending on whether the income effect or the substitution effect predominates.

One could argue that a country aiming to develop via the capitalist route should maintain a low tax ratio, such as existed in the older capitalist nations during their growth acceleration periods; and one can point to contemporary developing economies that have followed this course. Mexico has the smallest general government sector of any Latin American country—about half of what would be normal for its size and per capita income. Several other countries have government sectors constituting less than one-tenth of GNP: Colombia, South Korea, Nigeria, Pakistan, the Philippines. In several successful countries—Taiwan, South Korea, Mexico—the ratio of current government exhaustive expenditures to GNP has been falling rather than rising over time. The statistical explanation is an unusually rapid expansion of the private sector, which has outpaced a moderate increase in government expenditures.

Turning to the sources of current revenue, table 2 shows the percentage distribution as of about 1950 (period I) and in 1973 (period II). Although we believe that the orders of magnitude in the table are correct, some deficiencies in the data should be noted. For some countries, 1950 data were not available, and period I refers to later years. The 1973 data are not completely comparable with those for period I. State and local revenues are generally excluded, an important omission for large countries with a federal structure. The figures are somewhat influenced by institutional differences. Thus, in Venezuela and Nigeria, where in 1973 petroleum revenue accrued to government mainly through taxes on private companies, this revenue goes to

Table 2. Sources of Current Revenue, 1950 and 1973
(Percent)

Country[a]		Export & Import Duties	Commodity & Transactions Taxes	Taxes on Income & Wealth	Other[b]
Brazil	I	11.1	57.3	31.7	—
	II	4.9	41.2	22.8	31.2
Colombia	I	28.1	16.7	42.6	12.6
	II	30.8	19.1	43.3	6.8
Iran	I	29.1	7.8	10.1	53.0
	II	15.0	4.8	10.6	64.2
Ivory Coast	I	54.4	26.2	9.2	6.8
	II	51.4	23.5	16.7	8.3
Kenya	I	24.8	17.0	24.7	34.0
	II	19.0	19.2	32.2	29.6
Korea, South	I	18.9	24.7	28.6	27.8
	II	8.9	31.9	26.2	33.0
Malaysia	I	37.7	20.9	25.3	16.0
	II	26.2	16.5	24.7	22.3
Mexico	I	28.4	30.7	23.4	18.0
	II	9.6	27.9	47.3	15.6
Nigeria	I				
	II	13.1	8.9	59.3	18.7
Pakistan	I	47.7	20.6	13.0	20.6
	II	29.3	31.6	11.6	27.4
Philippines	I	10.2	32.4	38.1	19.1
	II	23.7	26.5	26.8	23.0
Taiwan	I	13.3	27.0	18.5	41.2
	II	19.4	22.5	8.4	49.6
Thailand	I	46.0	30.9	6.4	16.7
	II	27.5	36.7	12.1	23.7
Turkey	I	26.8	32.3	37.5	8.9
	II	8.4	32.6	32.8	26.3
Venezuela	I				
	II	3.9	6.8	59.9	28.7
Unweighted average	I	30.3	26.5	24.2	21.2
	II	18.1	21.3	29.0	27.5

[a] Period I data are for either the fiscal year 1949–50 or 1950–51, with the following exceptions: Ivory Coast, 1962; Kenya, 1963–64; South Korea, 1965; Malaysia, 1966–67; Taiwan, 1952; Turkey, 1962–63. Period II data are for 1973.

[b] Includes property taxes, other business taxes and fees, local taxes remitted to central government, profits of fiscal monopolies, receipts from government enterprises, other nontax income, and (for Iran, Nigeria, and Venezuela) petroleum income.

swell the income tax percentage; but in Iran, where the oil industry was nationalized in the 1950s, petroleum revenue appears in the "other" column. In some countries, profits of government enterprises remitted to the central government are an important component of 1973 revenue, as in Brazil (21.2 percent), South Korea (17.5 percent), and Taiwan (23.2 percent).

There is considerable diversity among countries with regard to the composition of current revenue. Several countries with large primary export sectors still derive close to a third of their revenue from taxes on foreign trade. Brazil has developed heavy dependence on a value added tax and other internal commodity taxes; and a half-dozen other countries get 30 percent or so of their revenue from this source. Finally, and surprisingly in view of the common complaint that LDCs cannot levy direct taxes, half the countries in the sample draw a quarter or more of their revenue from taxes on income and wealth. The main source is usually taxes on business profits; but several countries also make substantial use of personal income taxes, including Mexico (19 percent of revenue), South Korea (25 percent), and Turkey (29 percent). On average, for the group as a whole, income taxes are now the largest revenue source, followed by the miscellaneous "other revenue" category. The growth in the relative importance of this last category suggests some diversification of revenue sources in many countries since 1950.

GOVERNMENT EXPENDITURE: SIZE, COMPOSITION, FINANCING

Current Expenditure

What does the government sector look like in production terms? Information on the percentage composition of current expenditure is assembled in table 3. For ten countries, it was possible to obtain a detailed breakdown from country budget sources for years around 1970. This was supplemented for the remaining five countries by information on several major expenditure categories from the 1973 IBRD *World Data Book*. As in the case of table 2, the data refer to central government expenditures only; and for some countries the "other" category is regrettably large.

There is substantial intercountry variation in budget allocations. But there is also a typical distribution of expenditure among major categories. More than a third (in a few countries, more than half) of

Table 3. Current Government Expenditure, by Purpose, 1969–1970
(Percent)

Country[a]	Admin.	Defense	Education	Health	Other Soc.	Agriculture	Infra-structure	Other Economic	Other[c]
Brazil[b]		13.7	4.3	1.7		2.1	40.7	4.5	9.1
Colombia	5.5	3.1	7.2	4.1	12.7	13.1	4.4	6.5	9.1
Iran	9.6	45.4	16.0	4.9	n.a.	4.1	6.4	7.3	7.1
Ivory Coast	31.1	6.7	22.2	8.9	6.6	3.7	3.3	4.8	30.1
Kenya	25.5	6.5	13.3	5.9	4.8	5.8	2.1	3.9	19.5
Korea, South	13.9	30.7	17.3	0.8	6.9	4.9			20.9
Malaysia	10.7	22.7	21.3	7.7	9.3	2.4	5.0	n.a.	14.3
Mexico	14.5	4.0	12.5	2.5	13.5	6.0	20.2	12.5	
Nigeria[b]		33.3	1.1	1.8		1.4			
Pakistan[b]		51.7	0.8	0.8		2.8			
Philippines	18.2	11.4	32.1	5.8	1.6	4.9	8.8	3.9	13.3
Taiwan[b]	10.0	56.5	20.6	2.1	3.0	2.6	2.0	n.a.	3.1
Thailand	19.8	33.8	17.2	3.7	3.1	6.0	4.4	1.2	10.6
Turkey	n.a.	30.0	19.3	5.3	n.a.	3.7	5.2	n.a.	37.5
Venezuela[b]		14.6	25.6	9.6		3.3			

[a] For most countries, averages are for the fiscal years 1969 and 1970; in a few cases, averages are for 1970 and 1971.

[b] Data for these countries are for 1973.

[c] Includes interest on public debt, transfer payments to individuals, and other transfer payments.

the current budget usually goes for general administration and defense. The reasons for heavy military expenditure are apparent in some cases, not so obvious in others. Next most important, usually taking a quarter or more of the budget, are education, health, and "other social" (primarily housing and urban development) expenditures. The typically heavy outlay for education is explained by high population-growth rates and a large school-age component in the population, and by the fact that universal primary education is in most countries a high-priority objective. Note, however, the wide intercountry variation in the importance attached to health and education expenditures.

Economic expenditures typically take about one-fifth of the current budget. On the average, and excluding the atypical distribution in Colombia and Mexico, this amount is distributed fairly equally among agriculture, infrastructure (including roads and public works), and other economic purposes. These allocations, and particularly the amounts devoted to agriculture, may seem low for countries aiming at economic development. But we must remember that capital expenditures, which are heavily economic in character, have still to be considered. There are limits to the feasibility of current expenditure, which is mainly expenditure on labor services, even in a field as important as agriculture.

Having considered current revenue and current expenditure, it might seem logical to look next at the current budget surplus (or deficit). Let us instead look at government's capital expenditures and then return to budget surpluses as one source of finance for such expenditures.

Public-sector Capital Formation

Most LDCs prepare, along with the current budget, a capital or "development" budget. In countries with good planning procedures, this budget is usually projected for several years ahead and constitutes the hard core of the national economic plan. Unfortunately, the definitions of current and capital expenditures vary from country to country and do not correspond precisely to economic concepts of capital formation. Budget-making procedures and availability of funds have considerable influence. If the development budget is fatter than the current budget at a particular time, there may be a tendency to allocate to it part of what is in fact current expenditure. For example, if the development budget contains an allocation for new school construction, it may be stretched to include the salaries of teachers required to staff the new schools. There is nothing we can do about this, however, short of a laborious job of budget reclassification; so we must take the figures as we find them.

How important is government capital formation as a percentage of national capital formation? Is it higher in today's developing economies than it was in the mature economies during their growth acceleration period? In considering these questions, it is desirable to look beyond general government to public corporations and enterprises and to speak of *public-sector* capital formation. Unfortunately, we cannot simply abstract the necessary data from the UN *Yearbook of National Account Statistics*. The reason is the variable treatment of public corporations, which in some countries are lumped with general government and in other countries are combined with private corporations. For still other countries, there is no breakdown of capital formation by institutional form.

For the countries in our sample, however, we have estimates from country monographs and other sources that permit general conclusions. For almost all these countries, gross public-sector capital formation as a proportion of gross domestic capital formation falls in the range of 30 to 50 percent. Countries toward the low end of the range are of two sorts: (1) Latin American countries that are semi-industrialized and have a vigorous private sector. Thus, the PSCF-GDCF ratio is about 30 percent in Mexico and Colombia and about 35 percent in Brazil. (In Mexico, however, it was higher in earlier times, reaching a peak of more than 50 percent during 1940–45 and declining gradually since that time. The Mexican experience, indeed, resembles one standard scenario for economic development—heavy infrastructure investment by government at an early stage, followed by a burst of private investment in manufacturing, agriculture, and other "directly productive activities";) (2) other countries with a strong private enterprise orientation, such as South Korea and Thailand, where the PSCF-GDCF ratio is also about 30 percent.

Countries at the high end of the range include Turkey (50 percent), whose strong statist tradition has already been noted; Ivory Coast (50 percent), where manufacturing and other private nonagricultural activities are little developed; and Iran (60 percent), where the large oil revenues flow in the first instance into government channels.

In most countries, the PSCF-GDCF ratio rose somewhat over the period 1950–73. Private investment usually increased its share of

GNP. But public investment rose even faster as governments succeeded in mobilizing investment funds and enlarging their project-planning capacity.

The relative importance of public-sector capital formation in these countries is much greater than it was in the mature economies at a comparable stage of development.[4] In Canada, the United States, the United Kingdom, and Sweden, the PSCF-GDCF ratio in the mid-nineteenth century was below 10 percent, though it was above this in several other European countries. The only two countries in which the ratio approached contemporary levels were Japan, where (even if one excludes the substantial military investment) it fluctuated in the range of 30 to 40 percent over the period 1880–1940; and Australia, where it was 40 percent from 1860 to 1880 and 45 percent from 1880 to 1910. This unusually high ratio is explained partly by the continental scope of the economy and the heavy cost of linking scattered population centers by rail, road, and communications media.

There are several reasons for the greater prominence of public-sector investment in modern times:

1. Concepts of the appropriate scope of the public sector have expanded over time. Today, roads and railroads, power facilities, natural resource industries, communications media, and often heavy manufacturing industries are regarded as within the normal ambit of government activity.

2. LDC fiscal systems, though they capture a smaller percentage of national income than the mature economies are able to do today, do capture a higher percentage than those countries did a century ago, thus providing larger resources for investment as well as current expenditure. Public sector corporations can also earn and invest profits, so that the Lewis reinvestment mechanism is no longer a purely capitalist mechanism.

3. Foreign funds for long-term investment now flow mainly through public rather than private channels. Bilateral and multilateral lending agencies operate on a scale unknown before 1940, while private lending is mainly short-term rather than long-term in character.

4. Modern manufacturing, trade, and service activities, which are prime areas for private investment, are at an early stage of develop-

4. For a survey of long-term trends in the PSCF-GDCF ratio in the mature economies, see L. G. Reynolds, "Public Sector Saving and Capital Formation," in *Government and Economic Development*, ed. Gustav Ranis (New Haven: Yale University Press, 1971), pp. 516–52.

ment in most Asian and African countries. As these activities increase in relative importance, one might expect the public-sector share of capital formation to decline gradually toward the Latin American level.

Turning to the composition of public-sector investment, the estimates in table 4 are not as complete and dependable as the current-expenditure data in table 3, nor are they fully comparable among

Table 4. Public Sector Capital Expenditures, by Purpose, 1969–1970
(Percent)

Country	Education	Agriculture, Irrigation, Natural Resources	Transportation	Power	Other Industry	Other
Brazil	5.6	0.8	28.5	24.8	12.5	27.8
Colombia	7.7	14.7	30.3	8.7	3.9	34.7[a]
Iran[b]		23.0	←41.0→		8.0	28.0
Ivory Coast[c]	7.0	76.1	n.a.	n.a.	n.a.	16.9
Kenya	4.8	12.9	n.a.	8.4	9.7	64.2[d]
Korea, South	13.8	17.2	26.5	5.8	9.4	27.3[e]
Malaysia	7.4	24.1	←18.8→		20.3	29.4[f]
Mexico	n.a.	13.1	21.3	←38.4→		18.2[g]
Nigeria[c]	7.5	12.4	31.0	←19.2→		29.9
Pakistan[c]	n.a.	34.5	9.7	n.a.	n.a.	55.9
Philippines	5.8	15.8	46.5	←9.4→		22.5
Taiwan	—	8.5	31.6	24.1	17.5	18.3
Thailand	15.2	19.6	28.0	1.2	0.2	35.8[h]
Turkey[i]	8.6	13.3	22.0	15.0	26.2	0.9
Venezuela	7.4	18.9	38.1	n.a.	n.a.	35.6[j]

[a] Of which, "other social" equals 28.8 percent; includes housing, urban facilities, public buildings.
[b] Data relate to the third plan period, 1962–67, and are from J. Amuzegar, *Iran: Economic Development under Dualistic Conditions*, Chicago: University of Chicago Press, 1971.
[c] Data for these countries are for 1973.
[d] Of which, general administration equals 7.7 percent; other social services, including housing, 9.0 percent; community services, including roads, 31.0 percent.
[e] Of which, general administration equals 5.3 percent; community services, 14.2 percent.
[f] Of which, general administration equals 2.3 percent; defense and security, 22.0 percent.
[g] Of which, "social" equals 25.8 percent; presumably includes education, health, housing, urban facilities.
[h] Of which, other social equals 11.4 percent; transfers to local governments and state enterprises, 20.2 percent.
[i] Data are averages for the fiscal years 1968–72.
[j] Of which, defense equals 10.0 percent; other social, 12.8 percent.

countries.[5] The breakdown by purposes is not as fine or as uniform as one would wish. In some countries, major-expenditure items are lost in the "other" category, though we have tried to sort these out where possible in the table footnotes.

Not all the capital budget is available for economic purposes. If we define these as including expenditures for agriculture and natural resources, transport, power, and other industry (mining, manufacturing, commerce), they seem never to get more than 70 percent of the capital budget and sometimes as little as 55 percent. The balance goes for public buildings, military installations, schools and hospitals, housing, streets and sewerage, and other urban facilities. We have separated out education to indicate that it is a large item of capital as well as current expenditure, taking usually from 5 to 15 percent of the capital budget.

Among economic purposes, transportation usually gets the largest allocation, amounting to 25 to 35 percent of capital budget. Agriculture typically gets 15 to 20 percent, though its treatment varies considerably among countries. Note the very low allocation in Brazil and the unusually high allocation in the Ivory Coast. Electric power is also a substantial claimant on capital funds, while manufacturing, trade, and other sectors are relatively minor claimants.

The data do not allow us to say much about trends over time. In the countries for which time series are available, the shifts in sector allocations have been gradual and moderate, representing mainly increased attention to sectors that had been neglected in earlier years. In Mexico, for example, the early emphasis was on infrastructure, agriculture, and irrigation; but manufacturing grew in relative importance from the 1950s onward. Only recently has education begun to get a reasonable share of allocations, and human capital is still underdeveloped relative to most other Latin American countries. In Iran, where in the 1950s there had been a swing away from government investment in light manufacturing, the late 1960s and early 1970s brought a flood of oil revenue that found an outlet partly in heavy

5. The main source for table 4 is the statistical appendix to the most recent IBRD Mission Report on the countries in question, except for a few countries where other sources were used as noted in the footnotes. The percentages are usually averages for the fiscal years 1969 and 1970, though in a few cases the average is for 1970 and 1971. Expenditures are normally those for central government plus public corporations, but there is some intercountry variation on this point. In addition, some countries count defense installations as capital formation; others do not. No adequate source was discovered for Taiwan; and for the Ivory Coast, Nigeria, and Pakistan, we were able to get only an incomplete breakdown for 1973 from the IBRD *World Data Book*.

manufacturing investment. The share of the capital budget going to manufacturing, mining, and infrastructure rose, but agriculture, education, housing, and social programs decreased in relative importance.

Financing Public-sector Capital Formation

There are three potential sources of finance for public-sector capital formation: (1) government saving out of current revenue plus saving by public enterprises; (2) borrowing from private domestic savers or from abroad; and (3) monetary expansion, commonly in the form of borrowing from the central bank.

In the less developed world generally, public-sector saving contributes less than one might hope. Although current government revenue usually rises faster than GNP, current expenditure has tended to rise even faster. There is a pressing need for expenditure on health, education, urban facilities, and economic development. There is upward pressure on the government wage scale, which often serves as the wage leader for the economy; and because of substantial unemployment, there is also pressure for overstaffing. Centralized budget-making machinery is often too weak to contain upward pressure on the current budget.[6] Thus, in many countries the current budget surplus has tended to shrink and even vanish over time. Public corporations, too, often fail to cover their investment needs and may even require current operating subsidies. There is strong political pressure for low and stable selling prices, high and rising wages, and overstaffing. An IMF study of a sample of sixty-four public corporations in all parts of the world over the years 1955–65 found that, even if depreciation was not counted as a cost, their surplus of revenue over cost averaged only 4 percent of revenue. Including depreciation in costs turned this into a deficit of 8 percent. This operating deficit, plus all net investment, had to be covered by outside funds, of which about half came from the general government budget.[7]

6. Central control of expenditure during the budget year is also often defective, leading to ex post results that differ substantially from ex ante allocations. For a good discussion of these matters, see Aaron Wildavsky and Naomi Caiden, *Planning and Budgeting in Poor Countries* (New York: John Wiley & Sons, 1974).

7. Andrew H. Gault and Guiseppe Dutto, "Financial Performance of Government-Owned Corporations in Less Developed Countries," *IMF Staff Papers*, March 1968, pp. 102–42. Operating results, however, varied substantially by type of industry and region of the world. Electric power and petroleum enterprises almost always make money, but railroads and other transport enterprises typically lose. The average performance of public corporations is substantially better in Africa and Asia than in Latin America, which is unusually deficit-prone.

The feasibility of domestic borrowing depends on the level of private savings and on the existence of financial institutions that enable government to tap these savings. Experience in Japan and elsewhere suggests that an ingenious government can create appropriate institutional forms even in a very low income country. The feasibility of foreign borrowing depends somewhat on advantageous political factors; but it also depends heavily on the creditworthiness of a country in the eyes of major lenders and on the country's ability to develop and present bankable projects. Here success breeds success; loan funds flow most readily to countries that are least in need of them.

The last resort is commercial bank and central bank borrowing. In an increasingly monetized economy, a moderate rate of monetary expansion, which can be roughly estimated, is feasible without inflationary pressure. Beyond this, however, there is pressure on the price level; and persistent deficit financing tends to be associated with persistent inflation. On the question of whether inflation has adverse effects on economic development, there is still a wide difference of opinion. The Lewis model of constructive, self-liquidating inflation (which resembles the earlier models of Hayek and Schumpeter) appears plausible; but it assumes that the borrowed funds are invested in producing enterprises and result in an increased flow of marketable products within a reasonable period. Statistical efforts to relate country growth rates to inflation rates typically yield inconclusive results; but this may prove only that foolish questions deserve foolish answers. In any event, bankers and aidgivers regard strong and persistent inflation (especially when accompanied by failure to adjust exchange rates proportionately) as an unfavorable symptom. And in a world where LDC borrowers are somewhat dependent on foreign lenders, this view carries weight independent of its economic merit.

The proportion in which these sources of finance are used by a given country in a given year is not easy to discover. Capital formation is carried out by different levels of government and by a variety of public enterprises. Cash flows are complicated, and comprehensive flow-of-funds accounts are rare. There are no standard international sources on which one can draw. The estimates in table 5 are thus only approximate. The fiscal year in question is usually 1972, though in a few cases an adjacent year was chosen when the 1972 figures were clearly untypical. The data normally relate to central governments only, though for a few countries (Brazil, Mexico, Venezuela, and Malaysia) they cover the entire public sector. Totals are not always equal to 100 percent because of changes in cash surpluses and other minor items.

Table 5. Financing of Government Investment, 1972
(Percent)

Country	Government Saving	Foreign Borrowing (net)	Domestic Borrowing (net)
Brazil	88	9	3
Colombia	56	39	5
Iran	58	8	34
Ivory Coast	76	− 10	33
Kenya	39	16	45
Korea, South	100	—	—
Malaysia	25	25	50
Mexico	58	14	27
Nigeria	n.a.	n.a.	n.a.
Pakistan	2	63	35
Philippines	15	14	60
Taiwan	84	← 16 →	
Thailand	18	15	67
Turkey	39	3	58
Venezuela	79	5	16

Source: Statistical appendixes of IBRD Mission Reports for individual countries, of 1973 and 1974 vintage, and IBRD, *World Data Book*, 1975.

It appears that nine of the fifteen countries secured more than half their investment finance from government saving. One would expect this of the three oil economies. In the early 1970s, Venezuela was already financing four-fifths of its investment from government saving. Nigeria has depended traditionally on tax revenues and marketing board surpluses, supplemented by U.K. loans and grants. More recently, with sharply rising oil revenues, the budget surplus has risen faster than the government's ability to plan and execute capital projects; and today we could safely enter a figure of 100 percent in the first column of table 5.

In Iran, oil revenues rose rapidly after the oil nationalization of 1950 and the subsequent 1954 agreement with the private oil companies, which sharply increased government's share of the value of output. Current expenditure rose even faster than current revenue, however, and capital expenditure also rose with inordinate speed. Thus, as of 1970 Iran was still borrowing abroad on a substantial scale. During 1973–75, oil revenues reached a level more than sufficient to cover current and capital budgets; but by 1976 Iran was once more a net borrower.

Six of the nonoil countries (South Korea, Taiwan, Brazil, Colombia, Mexico, and the Ivory Coast) have also managed to finance most of their public investment from government saving. Colombia, a fiscally conservative country, runs a consistent budget surplus that covers about half of government investment. Most of the balance comes from foreign borrowing, and resort to the banking system is minor. In South Korea, transfers from the United States were a major source of current revenue until the mid-1960s. As Korean economic growth accelerated, however, domestic current revenue rose above current expenditure by 1963, and the surplus grew rapidly thereafter. By the late 1960s, government saving was more than sufficient to cover government capital formation, and government increasingly became a net lender to public corporations and private enterprise. The cycle of events in Taiwan has been similar. U.S. aid was a major prop of the fiscal system during the 1950s, but then it tapered off and ended in 1965. Domestic public-sector saving, slightly negative in the 1950s, grew rapidly after 1960 and took over the task of financing public-sector investment. By 1966–69, net public-sector saving (including saving by public enterprises), was already about 30 percent of net national saving, and by 1973 this figure had risen to 50 percent.

In Mexico, there were substantial injections of deficit finance until the mid-1950s. Since that time, however, there has been an effort to bring the budget under better control and develop government securities that private investors will be willing to hold. There is also moderate foreign borrowing through the Nacional Financera and other government financial institutions. Brazil, which has traditionally had a high rate of inflation fueled by public-sector deficits, also underwent a sharp change of course in the mid-1960s. There was a determined effort to bring both public enterprise and general government budgets under firmer control, and by the early 1970s public-sector saving had risen to the point where it covered the bulk of public investment. In consequence, the inflation rate, which had reached 90 percent in 1964, fell to 20 percent by 1969 and has since remained near that level.

In general, foreign funds are not a major source of finance for public investment, and their importance has declined over time. Foreign finance was important in Taiwan until the mid-1960s, and in South Korea and Iran until the late 1960s, but it is small in those countries today. The only countries in our group where it is still of substantial importance are: (1) Malaysia and the Ivory Coast, which are quite open economies with booming export trades that make them eminently creditworthy; (2) Colombia, also a stable and creditworthy country, which attracts substantial funds from the United States, the IBRD, and elsewhere; and (3) Pakistan, in which foreign funds are less important as a percentage of GNP than they were during the heyday of aid in the 1960s, but which still depends rather heavily on outside support.

It is usually impossible from published sources to separate domestic borrowing into bank and nonbank components; but where this can be done, bank borrowing typically predominates. In few countries are financial institutions sufficiently developed to allow government to tap voluntary private savings on a significant scale. Mexico is almost the only case in our sample, though Brazil is moving in this direction. In Malaysia and the Philippines, the domestic borrowing figure includes borrowing from pension and other government trust funds. (In most countries such funds are not separated out from the general budget and so would be included in the government savings column of table 5.)

Only a few countries in our sample still resort to the banking system on a substantial scale. An indirect indication of monetary restraint is the marked price stability in most countries in our sample. Their median inflation rate since 1960 is no higher than that of the mature economies. The most inflationary member of the group is Brazil, where, even after the anti-inflation campaign of the mid-1960s, prices continued to rise at about 20 percent a year.

Regarding financing of public investment, then, the record of these countries is relatively good: a substantial share financed through government saving; moderate foreign borrowing, mainly by creditworthy countries; and limited resort to inflationary finance. Only in the development of financial institutions and instruments for mobilization of private savings can most of these countries be regarded as laggards.

THE FOREIGN SECTOR

A country's exports, imports, and capital movements form an interdependent system. A wide trade gap may indicate a need for capital inflow; but it may also indicate the availability of foreign capital, without which import behavior would have been different. Indeed, the foreign sector is interdependent with agriculture, manufacturing, and other domestic sectors. Thus, anything less than a general equilibrium view is oversimplified. We shall focus separately on exports, imports, and capital flows, but their actual interdependence should be remembered.

Table 6. Merchandise Exports and Imports as a Percentage of GDP
(Three-year averages)

Country	Exports			Imports			Export Surplus (+) or Deficit (−), 1971–73
	1950–52	1960–62	1971–73	1950–52	1960–62	1971–73	
Brazil	3.9	6.0	7.0	4.2	7.0	8.7	− 1.7
Colombia	13.2	13.7	13.7	12.2	14.7	14.7	− 1.0
Iran	n.a.	19.2	20.4	n.a.	14.7	16.0	− 4.4
Ivory Coast	n.a.	34.5	32.3	27.8	29.3	28.3	+ 4.0
Kenya	13.9	13.8	27.3	n.a.	20.0	30.7	− 3.3
Korea, South	n.a.	3.7	23.7	n.a.	15.0	26.0	− 2.3
Malaysia[a]	58.0	52.3	40.3	50.0	41.0	35.0	+ 5.3
Mexico	11.2	10.3	8.6	14.1	11.7	9.3	− 0.7
Nigeria	10.3	14.3	22.0	16.9	18.7	17.7	+ 4.3
Pakistan	7.2	6.7	12.3	8.6	10.0	14.7	− 2.3
Philippines	12.6	12.3	19.0	14.8	14.3	18.7	+ 0.3
Taiwan	9.9	9.6	19.1	8.9	17.8	21.9	− 2.8
Thailand	13.3	17.7	19.7	14.9	19.0	21.3	− 1.7
Turkey	9.6	5.8	6.7	12.8	8.2	10.3	− 3.7
Venezuela	34.6	33.7	29.0	17.2	19.7	20.3	+ 8.7

Source: UN, International Accounts Year Book, 1974, vol. 3. Data for the precise periods shown in the table were not available for every country, in which cases the nearest three-year period was used.

[a] Data for 1950–52 not strictly comparable; includes Federated Malay States plus Singapore.

Export Behavior

The importance of merchandise exports relative to national output differs from country to country. Table 6 indicates that in ten countries of our sample exports are highly important, with export-GDP ratios in the range of 20 to 30 percent. The main commodities involved are oil in Iran, Venezuela, and Nigeria; rubber and tin in Malaysia; coffee, cocoa, and timber in the Ivory Coast; a variety of agricultural products in Kenya and Thailand; labor-intensive manufactures in Taiwan and South Korea; and a diversity of exports in Mexico, among which agricultural products are increasingly important. There are five countries—Brazil, Colombia, Pakistan, the Philippines, and Turkey—with relatively low export percentages. Even in these cases, however, export earnings have usually at least kept up with the growth of GNP.

Table 7 focuses on growth rates of exports and imports rather than on their absolute size; and it includes services as well as merchandise

Table 7. Growth Rate of Exports and Imports, 1950–1960, 1960–1970, and 1965–1973
(Percent)

	Exports			Imports		
	1950–60	*1960–70*	*1965–73*	*1950–60*	*1960–70*	*1965–73*
Brazil	−2.0	7.2	8.8	−1.2	6.2	9.2
Colombia	0.4	3.6	13.5	1.2	4.0	14.4
Iran	36.3[a]	12.0	22.7	15.4	12.5	17.5
Ivory Coast	10.8	21.4	40.4	19.5	20.6	38.3
Kenya	6.5	6.3	29.0	5.0	7.8	30.6
Korea, South	1.4	39.6	19.3	17.2	21.3	27.4
Malaysia	0.6	4.7	43.4	3.2	4.0	39.5
Mexico	3.4	6.2	6.9	6.2	8.0	8.0
Nigeria	4.1	8.3	21.5	10.9	3.0	19.0
Pakistan[b]	−6.1	7.6	n.a.	−0.1	5.6	n.a.
Philippines	4.5	7.2	17.8	3.7	8.2	18.1
Taiwan	6.2	23.2	34.7	6.7	18.6	32.4
Thailand	1.5	5.8	18.8	6.6	12.5	21.4
Turkey	0.0	6.0	8.9	0.2	5.3	9.6
Venezuela	8.1	1.5	28.6	8.9	6.2	20.5

Source: UNCTAD, *Handbook of International Trade and Development Statistics*, tables 1.5 and 1.6.
[a] Abnormal, in that it reflects the shutdown of oil producing facilities during the 1950 nationalization dispute. The 1960–70 figure for Venezuela is low on similar grounds.
[b] Data for 1965 and 1973 not comparable because of change in territorial boundaries in 1971.

items. The export columns of table 7 thus provide the best indication of the rate of increase in foreign exchange earnings. In almost every country, exports rose faster in the 1960s than in the 1950s, and the rate of increase was still higher from 1965 to 1973. The figures for this last period are influenced by the sharp increase in primary product prices in the early 1970s, but performance was also good in quantity terms.

There was, however, considerable diversity of country experience. The most spectacular growth of exports has been in Taiwan, South Korea, the Ivory Coast, and the three oil economies. Growth rates have been more modest in a number of other countries, including Brazil, Colombia, Mexico, Pakistan, and Turkey. Note also that the high export growth rates of 1965–73 were accompanied in most countries by an equivalent spurt in imports.

In chapter 7 we noted studies that suggest that successful export performance tends to be accompanied by diversification of the export list. This was generally true of the countries in our sample. It shows up in two ways. First, there are shifts over time in the percentage dis-

Table 8. Composition of Merchandise Exports, 1950–1952 and 1970–1972
(Percent)

Country	Foodstuffs		Other Primary Products		Manufactures	
	1950–52	1970–72	1950–52	1970–72	1950–52	1970–72
Brazil	73.1	55.7	19.5	26.2	0.7	18.0
Colombia	82.3	69.0	15.6	20.3	0.2	10.7
Iran	21.1	2.3	43.3	92.6	8.7	5.1
Ivory Coast	81.2	62.9	17.5	31.8	1.3	5.3
Kenya	60.0	58.6	31.5	30.0	0.0	11.3
Korea, South	26.2	6.8	57.5	11.2	8.7	81.9
Malaysia	3.5	5.6	77.7	60.2	12.4	34.1
Mexico	21.9	38.1	39.4	19.4	32.7	42.4
Nigeria	26.1	16.9	70.2	78.1	1.0	4.9
Pakistan	4.0	11.6	91.3	31.4	0.2	56.9
Philippines	24.1	25.3	64.6	66.8	2.8	7.8
Taiwan	88.6	7.2	4.4	0.8	0.9	92.0
Thailand	45.5	49.4	49.4	27.5	1.2	28.0
Turkey	33.8	26.3	60.5	50.9	5.3	22.7
Venezuela	2.4	1.2	95.8	97.0	0.0	1.3

Note: Figures are average for 1970–72, with the following exceptions: Colombia, 1969–71; the Ivory Coast, Malaysia, Nigeria, the Philippines, and Venezuela, 1971; Brazil, 1972. The initial period is 1959–61 rather than 1950–52 for Ivory Coast, Kenya, South Korea, Malaysia, Nigeria, and Thailand.

tribution of exports among major commodity categories (table 8). Exports of foodstuffs, usually regarded as unpromising because of low demand elasticities, declined relatively in most countries. Exports of other primary products also tended to decline in relative terms. On the other hand, in almost every country manufactured products increased their share of the export bill, often quite sharply. This was true not only in the well-publicized cases of Taiwan and South Korea but also in Mexico and Pakistan—and even in Thailand, Turkey, and Brazil. (The high figure for Malaysia is misleading in that it represents mainly initial processing of domestic raw materials, sufficient to push them into the manufactured category in the S.I.T.C. classification.)

A second development, which shows up only in a finer commodity classification, is diversification of exports *within* the primary products group. A few examples may be cited. In Brazil, coffee, which formed 72 percent of all exports in 1925–29, has now fallen to less than 25 percent, while other agricultural products (cotton, cocoa, sugar, tobacco, sisal) have risen to 40 percent. There has been diversification also into manganese, iron ore, and other mineral products. In Colombia, coffee has fallen from three-quarters of the total in 1950 to only half today, while there has been a relative rise in exports of manufactures, semimanufactures, and other primary products (cattle, cotton, bananas, hides and skins, sugar, tobacco, minerals.) In the Ivory Coast, the traditional "big three" (cocoa, coffee, and timber) are now down to 75 percent of exports, and still falling. In Malaysia, tin and rubber have fallen from 65 percent to 50 percent, the slack being taken up by palm oil, timber, petroleum, and manufactured exports. In Mexico, the traditional oil and mineral exports have now fallen to minor proportions. There has been rapid diversification into agricultural and livestock products, manufactured exports, and tourism. In Thailand, the rice share of exports fell from 48 percent in 1950 to 20 percent in 1970. Meanwhile, there has been a rapid rise in the share of other agricultural products (hard maize for animal food, kenaf, cassava, and rubber) as well as of light manufactures.

This good export performance is all the more surprising in view of the typical antiexport bias of public policy. Exporters have been penalized through overvalued exchange rates, open or hidden export taxes, and high prices for their inputs as a result of protectionist policies. In a number of countries, however, policies have been revised in a pro-export direction since about 1960. The Taiwan export drive dates from about 1960. (During the 1950s Taiwan had followed all the "bad" policies for which import-substituting countries are criticized.) The Pakistan liberalization program, with the export bonus voucher scheme as its central feature, was adopted at about the same time. The Philippines also devalued the peso and liberalized exchange controls, though this failed to give any permanent lift to exports. The South Korean export drive, with its array of tax exemptions and subsidies, began in 1962. Colombia made a sharp shift toward export promotion in 1967, when the exchange rate was floated and a variety of tax concessions were introduced. Its export performance since that time has been much better than it was before 1967. In Mexico, the strong performance of agricultural exports arises partly from prior and continuing agricultural investment by government. By the early 1970s, there were only a few countries—Brazil, the Philippines, possibly Thailand—in which adverse public policies could be regarded as drags on export performance.

Import Behavior

There is a well-established doctrine that a developing economy passes through a "normal" debtor-creditor cycle. It is expected to be a borrower in the early decades of accelerated growth. Imports run ahead of exports, with the deficit possibly widening for a considerable time before it begins to shrink and (eventually) turns into a surplus.

It is worth noting, therefore, that our sample contains a number of foreign-exchange-rich countries: the Ivory Coast, Iran, Malaysia, Venezuela, and (since the late 1960s) Nigeria. Malaysia and the Ivory Coast are consistent capital exporters, though Iran has usually managed to more than spend its available foreign exchange on virtually unrestricted imports. If we look only at the other ten countries, however, the normal expectation is realized. The import-GDP ratio is usually above the export-GDP ratio, and in several countries—Pakistan, Thailand, and Turkey—the gap is wide.

More interesting than sheer size of the import bill is its composition, which indicates the degree of import substitution. As Paauw and Fei point out, import substitution can be defined in either an *exchange allocation sense*—as the percentage distribution of merchandise imports among consumer goods, capital goods, and so on—or in a *domestic market sense*—as the percentage of available supply in a particular commodity category coming from foreign sources.

In a developing economy, import substitution proceeds in a regular sequence. It begins with nondurable consumer goods, where at an

Table 9. Composition of Merchandise Imports, 1950–1952 and 1970–1972
(Percent)

Country	Foodstuffs[a]		Other Primary[b]		Heavy Manufacturing[c]		Other Manufacturing[d]	
	1950–52	1970–72	1950–52	1970–72	1950–52	1970–72	1950–52	1970–72
Brazil	13.5	7.9	14.4	17.0	36.0	49.6	36.1	25.4
Colombia	6.3	5.5	15.5	9.5	33.8	58.0	43.9	27.0
Iran	35.3	7.0	0.5	7.0	10.1	61.8	37.8	24.1
Ivory Coast[a]	19.1	12.4	17.0	9.5	44.1	44.0	23.5	32.4
Kenya[a]	9.9	5.8	15.8	12.9	24.1	45.4	50.2	35.9
Korea, South[a]	9.0	15.6	30.4	28.0	12.7	37.9	37.4	18.4
Malaysia[a]	27.5	19.0	26.1	17.8	14.7	36.1	29.7	27.0
Mexico	8.1	5.9	12.8	12.3	40.4	35.0	34.0	26.7
Nigeria	10.7	2.9	8.8	5.1	17.7	49.9	62.9	42.1
Pakistan[e]	0.7	14.1	19.3	17.8	9.3	31.8	66.2	36.0
Philippines	15.2	11.8	14.8	18.8	30.4	34.0	39.6	35.9
Taiwan[e]	18.3	8.6	15.9	16.1	7.0	34.9	25.7	29.0
Thailand[a]	8.6	3.9	13.6	17.7	24.7	46.0	52.5	32.3
Turkey	3.9	2.9	16.0	15.5	36.8	55.2	43.2	26.3
Venezuela	13.2	7.8	5.8	5.8	37.1	57.6	43.5	28.7

Source: UN, Yearbook of International Trade Statistics.
[a]S.I.T.C. 0; [b]S.I.T.C. 1 + 2 + 3 + 4; [c]S.I.T.C. 7 + 67 + 68 + 69; [d]S.I.T.C. 5 + 6 + 8 (−67 −68 −69).
[e]Figures are for 1968–70.

early stage the percentage of exchange allocated to such goods approaches zero while the ratio of domestic production to total supply approaches 100 percent. In durable consumer goods, which involve more complex technology and usually a larger optimum scale of plant, import substitution moves more slowly. But here, too, the ratio of imports to consumption falls gradually toward zero, and the country reaches a stage at which imports of capital goods, industrial raw materials, fuels, and other intermediate products comprise 80 or 90 percent of imports. The "fat" (if consumer requirements can be so regarded!) has been squeezed out of the import bill. Beyond this point, there is import substitution in intermediates through the spread of backward linkages, followed or accompanied by import substitution in light machinery and finally succeeded by import substitution in basic metals, heavy machinery, transport equipment, and other industries of large optimum scale. As the industrial sector matures, the imports-total supply ratio falls gradually even in capital goods, though it usually remains well above zero.

This sequence is observable in our sample of countries. Table 9 shows the changing composition of imports in terms of major S.I.T.C. categories. "Heavy manufacturing" includes metals, machinery, and transport equipment. The "other primary" category includes fuels and industrial raw materials and can also be regarded as destined to support industrialization. The "other manufacturing" category is heterogeneous, including chemicals, petroleum refining, and some other intermediate products along with finished consumer goods.

In a developing economy, the metals-machinery-transport-equipment group tends to increase in relative importance and to form one-third to one-half of the import bill. The older industrial countries in our sample—the four Latin American countries and Turkey—had already reached the one-third proportion by 1950; and all the others had done so by 1970. Fuels and industrial raw materials, included in the "other primary" category, also often increase in relative weight. Food imports have declined in relative importance in most countries, another indication of good agricultural performance. The "other manufacturing" category also typically shows a sharp decline and, within this category, there has been a relative decline of finished consumer-goods imports and an increase in intermediate products.

The fact that foodstuffs appear in the import bill may appear odd, since most of these countries are also agricultural exporters. In a few cases, it indicates lagging agricultural capacity (Pakistan) or a shift

Table 10. Import Substitution: Foreign Exchange Allocation Sense
(Imports as a percentage of total imports)

Country and Year		Capital Goods	Fuels, Materials, Intermediates	Consumer Goods	
				Durable	Nondurable
Colombia[a]					
Iran[b]	1960	40.3	35.5	[2]	19.6
	1969	46.1	41.5	[2]	12.0
Malaysia[c]	1957			←31.9→	
	1967			31.0	
Philippines[d]	1949	9.9	52.7	2.5	34.8
	1967–69	19.9	67.8	1.1	11.1
Taiwan[e]	1952	13.1	74.2	12.7	
	1968	35.2	57.4	7.4	
Thailand[f]	1950	25.1	15.9	59.0	
	1969	46.5	27.7	25.8	
Turkey[g]	1950	46.0	33.4	20.6	
	1973	47.8	47.9	4.3	
Venezuela	1972	47.6	34.1	18.3	

[a] IBRD, *Economic Growth of Colombia*, statistical annex.
[b] Looney, p. 97; consumer durables included with capital goods.
[c] Paauw and Fei, p. 276.
[d] Power and Sicat, p. 39.
[e] Hsing, p. 80.
[f] Ingram, chap. 12.
[g] IBRD Report 376a-Tu, 1974, table 3.1.

toward a comparative advantage in manufacturing (South Korea). But more commonly, it simply indicates specialization along lines of comparative advantage within the diversified agricultural industry. Moreover, the imports are partly exotic products—sugar, coffee, tea— which countries in an easy foreign exchange situation, such as Iran, South Korea, or Malaysia, are well able to afford.

The S.I.T.C. categories do not yield what one would really like, that is, a clear separation among consumer-goods, capital-goods, and intermediate-goods imports. The commodity disaggregation required for this is laborious; but some country monographs have attempted the task. Thus, although we cannot give a comprehensive tabulation for the entire sample, we can assemble fragments of evidence. Table 10 presents evidence on the commodity composition of imports (import

Table 11. Import Substitution: Domestic Market Sense
(Imports as percentage of domestic supply)

Country and Years		Capital Goods	Fuels, Materials, Intermediates	Consumer Goods Durable	Consumer Goods Nondurable
Brazil[a]	1949	59.0	25.9	60.1	3.7
	1966	13.7	6.8	1.0	1.6
Iran[b]	1960	82.7	62.7	[2]	6.2
	1969	57.5	45.1	[2]	0.6
Kenya[c]	1970	67.0	60.0	←28.0→	
Malaysia[d]	1960			59.0	
	1967			47.0	
Mexico[e]	1939	92.0	56.0		22.0
	1950	74.0	42.0	[5]	7.0
	1970	51.0	22.0		5.0
Pakistan[f]	1951	76.3	73.2	77.5	
	1965	62.3	15.0	11.4	
Philippines[g]	1950			40.4	
	1965			20.6	
Taiwan[g]	1951			37.7	
	1966			18.5	
Thailand[g]	1952			41.5	
	1967			29.8	
Turkey[h]	1972	35	15	Near zero	

[a] 1949, Baer
  1966, Baer and Kerstenetzky in Ellis, ed.
[b] Looney, p. 98; consumer durables included with capital goods.
[c] IBRD Report 201-KE, 1974.
[d] Paauw and Fei, p. 275.
[e] Rene Villareal, unpublished thesis; consumer durables included with capital goods.
[f] Lewis, p. 11.
[g] Paauw and Fei, p. 275.
[h] IBRD Report 376a-TU, 1974.

substitution in the exchange allocation sense), while table 11 shows imports as a percentage of total supply (import substitution in the domestic market sense).

Two things stand out from these tables. Almost every country has moved in the expected direction, in terms of the import-substitution sequence outlined above. But it is clear also that they stand at different points in this sequence. In some countries, consumer goods have been virtually eliminated from the import bill. In others, they still constitute 20 percent or more of imports and form a substantial proportion of domestic supply. What makes the difference? Econometric investigation is needed. But simple inspection of the data suggests that the important factors include: (1) age of the industrial sector. In countries that have been industrializing for a half-century, such as Brazil, Mexico, or Turkey, import substitution is farther along than in countries where modern industry appeared only in the 1950s; (2) size of the domestic market, as measured by total GNP. Countries with large markets tend to be more self-contained in consumer goods, and increasingly also in capital goods, than smaller countries; (3) balance-of-payments position. Countries that have a high rate of export growth, and that are consequently under little pressure to restrict imports, have moved more slowly in import substitution than those with chronic balance-of-payments difficulties. Good export performance, of course, is not independent of policy and tends to be associated with an outward-looking development strategy.

Capital Movements

Most countries in our sample are dependent in some measure on capital inflows. A crude but useful indicator of such dependence is the current-account deficit. If we assume that changes in reserves balance out over long periods, the current-account deficit indicates the gap that must be covered by foreign loans or grants.

Under the "two-gap" reasoning discussed in chapter 8, capital inflows may either make up a deficiency of foreign exchange or a deficiency of domestic saving. In table 12 we show the relative importance of foreign and domestic saving in the finance of domestic investment over the years 1965–73. Note that several countries—Taiwan, Malaysia, Iran, and Venezuela—had a current-account surplus. Most of the other countries in the sample show only moderate dependence on foreign capital. The main exceptions are Pakistan and South Korea, where U.S. government and other transfers are still of substantial importance.

The sources of foreign capital also vary substantially from country to country. The largest source in most cases is public medium- and long-term loans, supplemented on occasion by IMF and commercial bank short-term credit. But two-thirds of the countries in the sample also have a substantial, and in most cases a growing, amount of foreign

Table 12. Sources of Finance for Domestic Investment, 1965–1973
(Percent)

Country	1960–73			1965–73		
	Public Saving (gross)	Private Saving (gross)	Current Account Deficit	Public Saving (gross)	Private Saving (gross)	Current Account Deficit
Brazil	11.8	77.6	−10.6	12.1	77.0	−10.9
Colombia	22.8	62.3	−14.9	23.9	61.0	−15.1
Iran	47.8	39.8	12.3	46.4	39.4	14.2
Ivory Coast	12.4	71.6	−16.0	9.3	70.0	−20.7
Kenya	—	—	−14.8	—	—	−17.5
Korea, South	18.9	45.0	−33.4	20.2	45.4	−31.8
Malaysia	20.1	50.5	11.5	16.3	49.3	11.1
Mexico	13.5	74.8	−11.7	14.2	73.3	−12.5
Nigeria	30.4	49.2	−20.4	33.2	50.1	−16.7
Pakistan	13.6	55.4	−30.0	5.3	75.9	−26.6
Philippines	5.8	86.8	−7.4	6.3	86.8	−7.0
Taiwan	22.0	64.6	6.4	24.5	65.9	10.7
Thailand	6.4	41.8	−10.7	7.7	50.5	−10.8
Turkey	40.0	51.4	−4.7	44.6	53.6	−1.8
Venezuela	33.9	75.3	9.2	29.9	71.9	1.9

Source: IBRD, *World Data Book*, 1975.

private investment. This group includes Brazil, Iran, Kenya, South Korea, Mexico, Nigeria, Taiwan, Thailand, and Turkey. These economies are vigorous and stable enough to attract a continuing flow of private funds. Outright grants and grant-like transfers are now of minor importance.

Our measurements say nothing about the growth contribution of foreign capital.[8] Some revisionist writers have argued that the contribution may be zero, foreign capital simply displacing an equivalent amount of domestic saving, and that in any event, because of the discouraging effect on saving, a dollar of foreign capital contributes less than a full dollar to aggregate saving and investment. My intuitive impression is that capital inflows, where they have occurred, have been helpful to the countries in our sample. But rarely, and even then only temporarily, have they been of major importance. Domestic effort, and ability to use resources, have been the critical growth ingredients.

8. For a bibliography and critique of this literature, see G. F. Papanek, "The Effect of Aid and Other Resource Transfers on Savings and Growth in Less Developed Countries," *Economic Journal* 82 (September 1972): 934–50.

14

Patterns of Development:
Growth, Employment, and Distribution

This chapter will round out the discussion of today's developing economies in three directions. First, the analysis in chapters 11–13 pulled economic sectors out of their setting in the total economy. This destroys the integrated view of each economy as a historical individual. It seems useful, therefore, to reconstruct the growth pattern of some representative countries.

Second, we must reconsider the typology issue. Are the growth experiences of our fifteen countries essentially similar? Or can they be sorted into different analytical boxes?

Third, it is now commonplace to say that employment and income distribution are significant criteria of success in development. It is often asserted that the poor have not shared proportionately in the rise of per capita income, or even that their situation has deteriorated absolutely. What has been the experience of our countries in this respect?

SOME COUNTRY CASES

Taiwan

Taiwan shares with Korea the advantages of having first been a colony of Japan and later a close associate of the United States. Though indigenous effort was no doubt decisive, association with these two powerful economies was certainly helpful.

The Japanese took economic development as a high-priority objective, not just for Japan, but for the overseas territories that were viewed as auxiliary arms of the Japanese economy. Initially, Taiwan was viewed as a rice basket, whose main function was to supplement lagging home production. The colonial authorities set about stimulating agriculture in ways that had worked earlier in Japan; and by 1940 Taiwanese rice yields were already well above the level of other Asian

363

countries, though still below that of Japan. In the 1930s, as the wartime vulnerability of the home islands became increasingly apparent, a good deal of military-hardware production was shifted to Taiwan and Korea, laying a foundation for later industrialization.

The large influx of mainland Chinese in 1949–50, although initially disorganizing to the economy, brought in many educated entrepreneurs and administrators who were to dominate both the private and public sectors over the next generation. The confrontation with the mainland made the government conscious of the need to build a strong economy as a base for political and military power. The American presence from the 1950s onward was helpful, not just in terms of financial aid, but also in terms of technical assistance. The institutional reforms of the 1950s, including the land reform program, were worked out in close collaboration with American advisers.

Land reform was part of a systematic and successful effort at agricultural development. Picking up where Japan had left off, Taiwan raised yields to levels exceeded only by Japan itself. The agricultural effort paid off in large transfers of food and finance to nonagriculture and in large agricultural exports, which were the main source of foreign exchange in the 1950s. The agricultural sector effectively performed the functions attributed to it in growth models.

A decisive development was the successful shift from import substitution in the 1950s to industrial export promotion in the 1960s. By 1960, import substitution in consumer goods was substantially completed, and the limits of the domestic market were apparent. At this point, industrial development might well have gotten stuck, as seems to have happened in the Philippines. But by a well-designed package of export incentives, Taiwan managed to turn its industry in an outward-looking direction. The institutional innovations included the ingenious "export processing zones," which are essentially a way of marketing Taiwanese labor, all other components coming from the outside—to which the product also returns. The export drive was aided by wage and price stability, which in turn rested on labor surplus—a rate of progress in agriculture sufficient to release large amounts of labor to industry. Ties with U.S. and Japanese markets were important, and so was the smallness of Taiwan relative to its trading partners. One can imagine the outcry from U.S. consumer-goods industries if India suddenly began to export on a scale—relative to its GNP—as large as that of Taiwan.

Labor surplus ended around 1970, and as of the mid-1970s Taiwan

has clearly entered a new growth phase, including such things as improved incentives to farmers, to maintain food self-sufficiency, and
farm mechanization on the Japanese pattern to permit continued labor
transfer; a gradual shift to more capital-intensive industries, since
Taiwan's rising wage level is reducing its competitiveness in labor-
intensive fields; and large-scale government investment in infrastructure and heavy manufacturing. Taiwan is close to graduating into the
mature-economy category, if it has not already done so.

South Korea

The parallels between Taiwanese and South Korean experience are
apparent: a Japanese heritage, including emphasis on primary education, agricultural development, and the beginnings of industrialization;
confrontation with a powerful neighbor, which made economic success
a condition of survival; a large, educated group of indigenous entrepreneurs; a thoroughgoing land reform early in the postwar period; a
labor surplus situation conducive to development of labor-intensive
manufactures; large-scale U.S. aid; and close trade ties with the U.S.
and Japanese economies.

The main difference lies in the less-satisfactory performance of
South Korea's agricultural sector. The Japanese-created agricultural
infrastructure was less extensive in Korea than in Taiwan; and the
postwar South Korean government was less active and successful in
raising agricultural productivity. As a result, South Korea never
achieved a significant agricultural export capacity and, indeed, fell
increasingly behind in meeting domestic food requirements. In Taiwan,
foreign exchange earnings from agricultural exports served to finance
necessary imports of capital goods and intermediate products. South
Korea, on the other hand, had to depend on industrial exports heavily
supplemented by foreign capital inflows. U.S. grants and soft loans
were the dominant source of finance for imports through the early
1960s. As Korea's export drive gained momentum in the mid-1960s,
however, export earnings took over more of the burden. In addition,
the booming state of the economy attracted an increasing flow of
foreign private investment and also enabled South Korea to borrow on
hard-loan terms from the IBRD, Japan, and elsewhere.

A key feature of South Korea's economic success has been a spectacular growth of manufactured exports from the early 1960s onward.
From 1961 to 1973, the annual growth rate of manufactured exports

fluctuated in the range of 40 to 80 percent. By 1972, Korea's exports as a percentage of GDP were double the norm for a country of her size and per capita income. Through most of the 1960s, too, manufacturing employment rose almost as fast as output, with only a modest increase in labor productivity. An important reason was that government allowed wages to be set by competitive forces, with little unionization and no minimum wage system. Real wages in manufacturing were almost constant during 1957–67 and only slightly above the level of earnings in agriculture.

Eventually, as in Taiwan, the labor surplus reservoir ran dry. The farm population reached a peak in 1967 and began to decline. The unemployment rate reached a peak of 8.3 percent in 1962 but had fallen to 4.5 percent by 1970. Real wages in manufacturing rose sharply from 1967 onward. The growth rate of manufacturing employment dropped from 9.6 percent in 1957–67 to 7.2 percent in 1967–72, while the rate of increase in labor productivity shot up from 2.6 percent to 11.9 percent.

Although rapid growth was facilitated by large-scale foreign aid, the vigor of Korean entrepreneurship, and the high educational level of the population, credit must also be given to the pragmatic economic policies of the government. In addition to the competitive-wage policy already noted, these included: (1) an interest-rate reform in 1965 that sharply raised the real interest rate on savings. As a consequence, household savings, which had been negligible up to that time, increased five-fold between 1965 and 1969; (2) an exchange-rate policy that offset domestic inflation by allowing the won to fall at a rate corresponding to its purchasing-power parity; (3) a liberal trade regime, with an average level of nominal protection on manufactures that averaged only 10.7 percent in 1968 and is even lower today. By allowing the structure of domestic prices to correspond closely to that of world prices, the South Koreans steered their economy toward efficient specialization in labor-intensive goods, while capital-intensive products continued to be imported; (4) a remarkably wide array of export incentives, introduced mainly between 1964 and 1966. These are supported by moral suasion, public honors for successful exporters, and informal assurances that exporters who find themselves in trouble can draw on government credit.[1]

1. For documentation of these points, see Charles R. Frank, Jr., Kwang Suk Kim, and Larry Westphal, *Foreign Trade Regimes and Economic Development* (New York: National Bureau of Economic Research, 1975).

Malaysia

From two remarkably successful exporters of manufactures we turn to two remarkably successful exporters of primary products: Malaysia and the Ivory Coast. In so doing, we turn also from densely populated countries with a limited resource base to thinly populated countries rich in natural resources. In both Malaysia and the Ivory Coast, exports form more than 30 percent of GDP, and primary products dominate the export list. Moreover, both countries consistently have a balance-of-payments surplus.

Malaysia is not without its problems. The guerilla insurgency of the 1950s occasionally threatens to reappear. There is an ethnic cleavage between the Malays, who predominate in the countryside and dominate the government, and the Chinese, who form the bulk of the merchants, industrialists, and urban wage earners. But outbreaks of racial violence have been rare. Government has been stable, moderate, growth-oriented, and administratively competent. Here, as in other ex-British colonies, the British left a tradition of honesty and efficiency in the civil service.

The traditional mainstays of the export trade were tin and rubber, which in colonial days formed more than 90 percent of Malayan exports. These industries have not been neglected. Malaysia is still the world's largest tin producer and leader of the cartel that controls tin prices and marketings. In rubber, which requires continuing investment because the aging of trees brings a decline in yields, there has been massive replanting of trees on both large estates and smallholdings. Between 1960 and 1970, rubber yields per acre rose 5 percent a year, helping reduce costs and keep crude rubber competitive with synthetics.

Even more significant however, has been diversification into new export lines. There has been a large government program of clearing virgin lands, which are then resold to Malay smallholders. Some of this new land has been put into rubber, but a great deal has been put into oil palms, using new, high-yield palm varieties. Between 1970 and 1975, palm oil production tripled, and it is expected to double again by 1980. There has also been a sharp rise in timber exports, the beginning of petroleum exports, and a doubling in the relative importance of manufactured exports. Tin and rubber now make up less than half the export total.

Government revenues have been buoyant. There has been no need to resort to inflationary finance, and the price level has been stable. Tax collections are now close to 25 percent of GNP, and, although taxes on foreign trade are the largest single source, taxes on income and wealth contribute 30 percent of the total. The current budget emphasizes education and public health, which get 30 percent of the total. Government also finances about 40 percent of Malaysian capital formation. Agriculture gets one-quarter of this—the highest proportion for any country in our sample—with transport and power getting about 20 percent and industry another 20 percent. Most of the financing of industry, however, is left to the private sector.

Great emphasis has been placed on agricultural development, partly because the rural Malays are the poorest group in the population, and there is a desire both to improve their condition and to check excessive migration to the city. Malaysian agriculture is unusual in that about 80 percent of the acreage is devoted to export crops. More than four million acres are in rubber and more than a million in palm oil, compared with less than a million in rice. Although the main emphasis has been on export crops, the domestic food-growing sector has not been neglected. There has been a marked increase in irrigation and double-cropping, and since 1960 rice output has grown at about 6 percent per year. A substantial part of domestic rice consumption, however, is still imported.

Manufacturing development has been encouraged in a variety of ways: a moderate level of tariff protection, averaging about 14 percent on all manufactures but 25 percent on finished consumer goods; a package of tax advantages to "pioneer industries" producing new products; expansion of government long-term lending facilities to supplement finance from private banks; development of industrial estates, of which fifteen were in operation by 1973; and limited development of export processing zones.

In general, Malaysia has followed outward-looking policies rather than policies of accelerated import substitution. With export receipts buoyant, there was no urgent need for import substitution; and political considerations were also important. Protecting industry would have meant benefiting Chinese businessmen at the expense of consumers. In addition, by raising consumer prices, it would have put upward pressure on money wages, a development that would have been harmful to the rubber planters and other estate operators who employ large amounts of wage labor.

The manufacturing sector nevertheless expanded during the 1950s and 1960s because of a variety of favorable circumstances. These included the rapid growth of consumer demand; stable and relatively low wage rates and a low level of union organization; high educational level of the population and good infrastructure facilities, developed through public expenditure in these directions; and free capital movements, which permitted foreign concerns to repatriate profits as desired. The manufacturing sector grew from 8 percent of GDP in 1961 to 15 percent in 1970. Because of the openness of the economy, new manufacturing industries have had to be relatively efficient from the outset—and so have considerable export potential. As of 1970, about 20 percent of manufacturing output was being exported. Of the total growth of manufacturing output between 1963 and 1970, about one-third is attributable to export expansion, one-third to import substitution, and one-third to growth of the domestic market.[2]

The Ivory Coast

This economy, like that of Malaysia, shows a rapid and sustained rise in exports.[3] From 1946 to 1970, export proceeds rose 9 percent per year. This was largely a quantity increase since the terms of trade, though fluctuating in the short run, show no appreciable trend over the period. Exports of cocoa and coffee rose more than five times, and timber increased more than twenty times to become the largest single export product. Moreover, a number of new export crops, such as palm oil, have grown from zero to sizable proportions. As a result of this diversification, the export share of the three major products, formerly close to 100 percent, is now below 75 percent and falling steadily.

As in Nigeria and Ghana, cocoa and coffee production were expanded by peasant farmers putting more land into cultivation and expending additional labor time on top of the small amount of time required for food production. (Timber production, on the other hand, is mainly in the hands of European companies and is highly mechanized.) The Ivory Coast is still a land-surplus economy, though good

2. Lutz Hoffman and S. E. Tan, "Employment Creation Through Export Growth: A Case Study of West Malaysia's Manufacturing Industries," in *The International Division of Labour*, ed. Herbert Giersch (Tübingen: I. C. B. Mohr, for the Kiel Institute of World Economics, 1974).
3. The following discussion draws in part on J. Dirck Stryker, "Exports and Growth in the Ivory Coast: Timber, Cocoa, and Coffee," mimeographed (New Haven: Yale Economic Growth Center, 1972), Discussion Paper no. 147.

land is less available today than it was a generation ago. There is also an unlimited supply of labor because, though Ivoirians are quite fully employed, the labor supply is supplemented by large-scale migration from Mali, Upper Volta, and other poorer countries to the north.

The rapid growth of exports has been paralleled by a rapid growth of imports, including foodstuffs, which form about 20 percent of the import bill. Even so, there is a consistent surplus on merchandise account. The country is highly creditworthy and able to afford free movement of capital. Foreign residents and foreign companies can remit earnings to France and elsewhere without restriction. In the other direction, there is a substantial inflow of both private investment funds and government borrowing from France, the World Bank, and elsewhere.

The expansion of export industries has had linkage effects on the rest of the economy. Perhaps the most important of these is on government revenue. Export taxes and proceeds of the cocoa and coffee stabilization funds provide a sizable share of current revenue, and another sizable share comes from import duties. Government revenues have been buoyant, running around 25 percent of GNP. Government consumption expenditures run about 20 percent of GNP, leaving a large current surplus. This surplus, plus surpluses from the usually profitable public enterprises, finances about 80 percent of government capital expenditure, the remainder coming mainly from foreign borrowings. Gross national capital formation is about 20 percent of GNP, and about half of this is in the public sector.

Backward linkages in production have not been very important, except for the road building and other infrastructure development required to move export products to the ports. Nor is there as yet much forward linkage via processing of primary products. The main stimulative effect of the incomes generated in export production, apart from the fiscal effect, is via growth of final consumer demand. Rapid growth of demand has stimulated the manufacturing sector, which, though still relatively small, is growing rapidly in percentage terms. Government has encouraged this through a program of investment incentives, including free repatriation of profits. Tariff protection is low, which enforces efficiency in the new industries; and the environment seems favorable to eventual development of industrial export capacity.

The government has been stable. It is a one-party government, and there has been only one president since independence was achieved in

1960. There is still substantial French influence and technical assistance in both the public and private sector. Government has been strongly proagriculture. It is symbolic that the president, himself a large farmer, requires each of his cabinet members to own at least 12.5 acres of farmland, and each member of parliament must own 7.5 acres. Through research and extension, credit facilities, and model government plantations, government has encouraged diversification into palm oil, sugarcane, cotton, bananas, pineapples, coconuts, and additional food crops such as rice and corn. Government has also been an active investor in roads, railroads, port development, and power generation, which together form about 45 percent of public-sector capital formation. At the same time, manufacturing development, largely in private hands is gradually turning the economy in a less-export-dependent direction.

Brazil

Brazil is a middle-aged, middle-income economy, long independent of colonial rule. It has been growing in an extensive way since at least the mid-nineteenth century. Nineteenth- and early twentieth-century growth, however, was erratic and much influenced by fluctuations in world demand for primary products. As recently as 1940, coffee was still preeminent, and two-thirds of the people were engaged in agriculture. Growth acceleration, accompanied by institutional modernization and rapid structural change, set in only after 1940. From 1947 to 1975, GNP grew at an annual compound rate of 7.1 percent, and since 1967 the growth rate has been about 10 percent.

Brazil's growth record is rather surprising, because over most of this period economic policy has not been very tidy. Deficits have been endemic, both in the general government budget and in the budgets of public enterprises. Inflation has been chronic, ranging from 20 to 80 percent per year. Import substitution policies have involved considerable resource waste. Agriculture has been relatively neglected. Yet the economy has grown. The lesson may be that a country with rich resources, an open frontier, a vigorous private sector, and some centers of entrepreneurship in the public sector can survive erratic and even erroneous policies.

The agricultural sector has been not merely neglected but exploited by policies of accelerated import substitution. Primary exports have been penalized by the exchange-rate regime; and the substitution of high-cost domestic sources of supply for cheaper imports has hurt farmers as buyers of both consumer goods and agricultural inputs. Government has spent little on agricultural research and extension, and this is reflected in failure of crop yields to improve substantially. There has been extensive road building, which has facilitated settlement of the frontier in the southwestern states. But only the existence of the frontier has enabled food output to keep pace with demand.

The methods used to promote manufacturing have been described in many places, and there is nothing very original about them. Exchange controls, quantitative import restrictions, high tariff rates, the use of government development banks for financing, interest ceilings on private bank lending, and direct government investment have all played a part. Foreign investment has been welcomed; and large government enterprises have been established in iron-ore mining, steel production, petroleum, petrochemicals, and several other areas. A 1974 study of the 5,113 largest nonfinancial enterprises in Brazil showed that public enterprises owned 20 percent of manufacturing assets; foreign enterprises, 29 percent; and domestic private enterprises, 51 percent. (Inclusion of smaller manufacturing enterprises, of course, would raise the domestic private share). Import substitution, which was almost complete in consumer goods by 1960, is now largely complete in capital goods and intermediates as well.

This forced growth of manufacturing has involved considerable inefficiency, as Bergsman and others have documented. Brazilian prices are above import prices by varying amounts, the gap being correlated with the rate of effective protection. Capital goods, which have not been as highly protected as consumer goods, are not so seriously overpriced; and it is not surprising that this is the first area in which Brazil has been able to develop export capacity.

Perhaps partly because domestic demand has been rising so rapidly, Brazilian manufacturers are very inward-oriented, tending to regard exports as only a "vent for surplus" when domestic demand slackens. In addition, until recently, exports of manufactures and other goods were penalized by the exchange-rate regime. The situation was improved in 1964, however, and again in 1968 by the adoption of a "crawling peg" system. By 1973, manufactured exports had risen to 22 percent of the export total, mainly through export of capital goods to other Latin American countries. There has also been a marked diversification of primary-product exports into cotton, cocoa, sugar, tobacco, sisal, manganese, and iron ore. Coffee, which comprised more than 70 percent of all exports in the 1920s, is below 20 percent today.

Future growth was placed on a firmer basis by a series of financial reforms instituted by the military government that took power in 1964. Tax revenue has been raised substantially, and prices of transport and other public enterprises have been increased sufficiently to put them on a profitable basis. As deficit finance has declined, the inflation rate has been brought down from 80 percent to less than 20 percent, which is moderate by Brazilian historical standards. Adoption of a gliding exchange rate has already been mentioned. Real interest rates, often negative in the past, have been raised to a positive level. Interest payments on government bonds and on some private bonds have been indexed to prevent erosion through inflation. New intermediaries for medium-term lending have been created. Improved tax treatment has been given to corporate dividend payments and to corporate depreciation allowances, which can now be based on replacement cost. All this has produced a sharp upswing in both private savings and business investment.

There is little doubt that the gains of progress have thus far been unequally distributed—regionally, where discrepancies between São Paolo and the northeastern states remain remarkably wide, and by occupational level, where real wages seem to have risen little for unskilled labor but substantially for skilled and white-collar workers. Continuation of growth at anything like recent rates, however, should soon produce a general labor-shortage situation. There are already complaints of this in São Paolo state, the center of industrial growth.

Mexico

Mexico, like Brazil, is historically a land-surplus economy, long independent. It experienced a raw-materials-based growth from the 1870s onward, but its growth has accelerated markedly since 1940. Mexico differs from Brazil, however, in having made a strong and successful effort in agriculture before the onset of industrialization.

An important conditioning factor in Mexican development has been the stability of government since the Mexican Revolution. Leadership is passed down from one president to the next through a single governing party, which has a strong base of popular support and regularly wins open elections. The six-year presidential term provides continuity in economic strategy. There is a good supply of able economists, many of whom occupy important positions in government.

Transformation of agriculture began with the revolution, which broke the power of the former landowning class. This was followed by large-scale land redistribution, mainly between 1925 and 1940, which created individual nonalienable *ejidos* averaging seven to eight hectares, and collective *ejidos*, where former plantation-type operations were placed under collective management to preserve economies of scale. This creation of a smallholder class enabled farmers to earn an assured, though low, standard of living and reduced the necessity of migration to the cities; it also increased political stability along the lines of Jeffersonian democracy.

Mexico has not, up to now, been a land-scarce economy. Between 1929 and 1959, the amount of land under cultivation increased 92 percent while labor inputs increased only 69 percent, so that the man-land ratio decreased. New land was drawn into cultivation through heavy government investment in rural infrastructure. The proportion of federal government investment going into roads and irrigation has been above 20 percent for fifty years and reached a peak of 45 percent during 1935–39. Much of the post-1940 increase in agricultural output can be interpreted as a lagged response to this investment, which called forth a large amount of complementary private investment. In the process, a new class of large-scale commercial farmers has grown up, particularly on irrigated land in the northern states. Although this has contributed to output, including large agricultural exports to the United States, it has also intensified agricultural dualism.

Rapid industrial growth has been facilitated by: (1) the ability of agriculture to provide ample labor and food at stable prices; (2) government policies that reduced investment risks and raised returns, including low, controlled interest rates and the establishment of a wide array of government lending institutions. Tariff protection has been more moderate than in many other countries, the average effective rate on manufactures being presently about 25 percent. This has held down the world price-Mexican price gap and increased the likelihood that Mexican industry will attain export capacity; (3) a lag of wage rates behind productivity increases, with a consequent shift to profits and heavy reinvestment of profits à la Lewis; and (4) an active new group of Mexican entrepreneurs, who have taken over industrial leadership in the post-1945 period. Foreign investment in manufacturing is permitted under strict controls, usually involving at least 51 percent Mexican ownership; but only about 10 percent of manufacturing capital is foreign-owned.

The main dynamic of postwar growth has been internal. Exports have tended to decline as a percentage of GDP, while at the same time becoming more diversified. In lieu of the pre-1940 dependence on minerals, petroleum, gold, and silver, two-thirds of exports now come from a diversified array of agricultural products. Manufactured exports, although still relatively small, are rising rapidly; and export of tourist services has also risen rapidly. There is normally a substantial deficit in the current balance of payments, which is offset mainly by official borrowing and private capital inflow.

Mexican fiscal capacity has never been high. The current expenditure-GDP ratio is among the lowest in Latin America. Investment expenditures by government and public enterprises, however, form a substantial share of national investment. Because of the great upsurge in private investment, the public-sector share has fallen from about 50 percent in 1940–45 to about 30 percent today, although public investment has continued to grow in absolute size. The emphasis has shifted from period to period: large allocations to agriculture through the 1940s, heavy emphasis on industry and infrastructure in the 1950s and 1960s, and currently an increased emphasis on education and other social expenditures, which in the past have been relatively neglected. Until about 1955, public investment was financed partly by inflationary methods. As private saving capacity has grown, however, it has become increasingly possible to finance deficits through domestic nonbank borrowing. Since 1960, about 90 percent of the federal government deficit has been financed in this way.

Proximity to the United States has probably on balance been advantageous to the economy. Three-quarters of Mexico's trade relations are with the United States. The string of "border factories," which process imported materials for reexport to the United States, allows Mexico to export labor at wages that are good by Mexican standards though low by U.S. standards. There is also large-scale export of labor for agricultural and other work in the United States.

In spite of rapid economic expansion, Mexico still has surplus labor, a large number of rural people living at the subsistence level, and a highly unequal distribution of income.

PATTERNS OF ECONOMIC DEVELOPMENT?

There have been two major comparative analyses of long-term economic growth. The first, by Kuznets, used long time series for fourteen presently mature economies, whose growth acceleration began during or before the nineteenth century.[4] The second, by Chenery, used post-1945 cross-section data for a hundred or so countries, interpreting different current levels of per capita income (measured in U.S. dollars) as analogous to different points along a historical growth path.[5] The difficulties of this approach, and the reasons for preferring time-series methods, were noted in chapter 1. The structural changes that occur during long-term growth are sufficiently striking, however, that they stand out in both Chenery and Kuznets and warrant our speaking of a "standard" growth pattern. The stylized facts of this pattern are so well known that they need not be repeated here.

At the same time, individual countries always deviate in some respects from the standard pattern. Are these deviations to be interpreted as entirely idiosyncratic, or stochastic? Or do certain groups of countries show deviations sufficiently similar to give them a family resemblance? This is the typology problem that we considered briefly in chapter 5—but on which we must now bring our country experience to bear.

The Development Pattern in Our Sample

The experiences of our fifteen countries confirm the conventional picture of countries passing through a broadly similar development process. At an empirical level, there are strong similarities of observed behavior. We shall also argue that a single analytical schema can be used to interpret the historical experience of apparently diverse economies.

At the level of empirical generalization we note, first, that few of our countries were democratically governed, in the sense of having a multiparty political system. They were, however, firmly governed and cannot be listed among Myrdal's "soft states." There was continuity of leadership personnel and a marked interest by the political leaders in economic development. There was also usually a capable group of policymakers, technocrats if you will, among whom economists were often prominent.

4. Simon Kuznets's work has appeared in numerous forms and places; but we refer here primarily to the summary statement in his *Modern Economic Growth* (New Haven: Yale University Press, 1966).

5. Chenery has also made a variety of contributions, mainly in article form, which will be found in the bibliography. We refer here mainly to Hollis Chenery and Moises Syrquin, *Patterns of Development, 1950–1970* (New York: Oxford University Press, for the World Bank, 1975).

Governments were not notably welfaristic, the general government sector remaining relatively small and transfer payments usually minor. There was some modernization of tax structures, some rise in tax revenues as a percentage of GNP, and a general ability to finance public-sector capital formation from current surpluses and domestic nonbank borrowing. The GDCF-GNP ratio rose substantially in most cases, with public-sector capital formation usually increasing in relative importance and now constituting one-half to one-third of total capital formation. Tax and other policies were generally favorable to private investment.

Agricultural performance was typically good, with food output rising at least as rapidly as domestic demand. This was done partly by bringing new land under cultivation, though technical progress was important in most countries and dominant in some. A few countries, which have dependable nonagricultural exports, have continued to import food on a substantial scale. In the standard situation, however, agriculture not merely meets domestic food requirements but is a major source of exports, which include both foodstuffs and nonfood products (rubber, palm oil, kenaf, cotton, and so on).

In all countries the industrial sector has grown in relative importance, with output composition shifting gradually from light toward heavy industry. There is marked dualism within industry, and in some countries handicraft and small-shop employment still exceeds foctory employment. Domestic private entrepreneurship has been dominant in manufacturing, though government enterprises and foreign private investment have sometimes played substantial roles. Capital accumulation has occurred mainly through reinvestment of earnings. The growth rate of (large-scale) industrial employment has been disappointingly low. Few of our countries have reached the labor-shortage point, and most are probably no nearer this point today than they were in 1950.

Rates of export growth have been above average for third-world countries. While primary exports are still dominant in most cases, there has been a healthy diversification of the export list, so that one-crop or two-crop dependence has diminished markedly. Manufactured exports are increasing at a high percentage rate, though from a small initial base. On the import side, finished consumer goods have diminished greatly and in some countries almost vanished from the import list; capital goods, raw materials and intermediates now dominate that list.

These and other common features of development can be visualized more readily with the aid of a flow diagram (figure 1). Rural activities

Figure 1. Simplified View of Intersectoral Commodity Flows

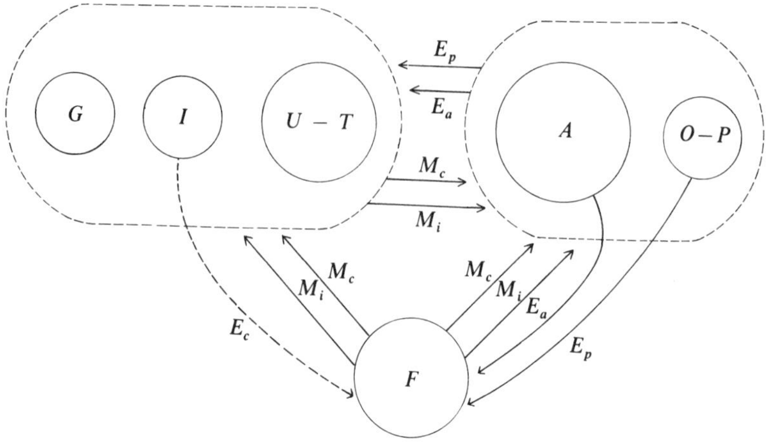

Meaning of Symbols

A	Agriculture	E_a	Export of agricultural products
O–P	Other primary	E_p	Export of other primary products
U–T	Urban traditional	E_c	Export of consumer goods
I	Industry	M_c	Import of consumer goods
G	General government	M_i	Import of production inputs
F	Foreign		(capital goods and materials)

appear at the right of the diagram, urban activities at the left. The size of the circles can be varied to indicate the relative output of various sectors. The arrows indicate intersectoral flows of commodities and services; and in a realistic application, the width of the arrows could be varied to show size of flows. Financial flows could be diagramed by reversing the direction of the arrows and by adding unrequited flows, such as tax payments and foreign borrowing. The diagram is simplified in that exchanges of goods within the rural and urban economies are not shown explicitly; but these could readily be added.

This diagram is sufficiently flexible, we believe, to depict the situation in any of our countries at a given point in time merely by making appropriate changes in size of circles and width of arrows; and it can also be used to trace structural changes in a particular economy over the course of time.

In a typical economy at the beginning of growth acceleration, the two largest sectors are agriculture and the urban traditional sector. (We neglect, for simplicity, the fact that a good deal of traditional production is physically located in rural areas). The interchange of foodstuffs and raw materials for services and handicrafts—Adam Smith's "great commerce" between town and country—is the hub of the economy. The government and (modern) industrial sectors are small at the outset. The "other primary" sector, which includes minerals, petroleum, timber, and other nonagricultural primary products, may be virtually absent (as in Thailand) or very large (as in Iran). The foreign trade flows also vary in relative importance, depending on the size and resource richness of the country, from 5 percent of national output in some cases to 30 percent in others.

We have not divided the agricultural sector into "traditional" and "export" agriculture, as sometimes is done.[6] There are cases in which agricultural exports come from specialized, capitalistic plantations using wage labor. More common, however, is the case of peasant export production, in which the family produces both for home use and off-farm sale. The export product may be identical to the subsistence product, as in the case of wheat, rice, and other food grains; or it may be added onto subsistence production, as in the cases of cocoa and coffee. Peasant production predominates in West Africa and in South and Southeast Asia. In Latin America there is more differentiation between the products, techniques, and markets served by larger and smaller farmers; but even the large commercial farms usually supply domestic as well as export markets.

The agricultural sector exports its products both to the domestic urban market and to foreign buyers; and it imports consumer goods and production inputs from both sources. The domestic urban sectors export goods and services to the agricultural area (in addition to a substantial circulation of such goods within the urban economy, similar to the large volume of subsistence production within the rural economy), and they import consumer goods and production inputs from abroad.

Let us consider now how figure 1 can be used to trace the changes that occur during the decades of growth acceleration. To do this, one would need a series of diagrams at successive points in time, with appropriate changes in the circles and arrows; or even better, a motion

6. For example, Douglas Paauw and John C. H. Fei, *The Transition in Open Dualistic Economies*. A Publication of the Economic Growth Center, Yale University (New Haven: Yale University Press, 1973), p. 4, figure 1.1.

picture, in which one minute of running time might correspond to five years of growth. Lacking such equipment, let us suggest the main directions of change, leaving it to the reader to translate these into visual terms. Remember, too, that we are concerned only with what happens in a "success case," leaving the ultimate sources of success or failure unexplained.

1. All sectors expand in absolute size. This would be required in any case by population growth, and still more where output per capita is also rising.

2. The rate of increase, however, differs among sectors, thus graddually changing the production structure of the economy. Agriculture grows at, say, 5 percent per year, to meet domestic food requirements and to keep its export contribution rising in absolute terms. The industrial sector grows a good deal faster—say, at 10 percent per year—partly in response to relatively high income elasticities of demand, partly by encroaching on household production of Z-goods, and partly by replacing imports. The output of general government is sluggish, and its share of GNP rises only gradually if at all (which is not inconsistent with an active development policy). The urban traditional sector remains large, perhaps growing at about the same rate as total output. Schematically, then, one might visualize something like these annual percentage rates of change:

Industry	10
Government	7–8
Urban traditional	7
Agriculture	5
GNP	7
Population	3
GNP per capita	4

3. The trade arrows connecting the rural and urban branches of the economy increase in size faster than output in the two branches. In the case of agricultural sales, this increase represents the food transfers required by rapid urbanization of population plus growing industrial needs for raw materials. In the case of agricultural purchases, it arises from higher agricultural incomes, replacement of household Z-goods by factory production, and increased agricultural inputs needed to support higher production levels. This growth of monetary transactions, accompanied by a growing willingness to hold cash and other intangible assets, is what we mean by "monetization."

4. Export flows increase at least as rapidly as GNP, and even more rapidly in resource-rich economies. Although one cannot specify any minimum rate of increase as essential to sustained growth, a higher rate of increase is clearly better than a lower one, because a higher rate directly facilitates imports and indirectly increases the country's creditworthiness in the eyes of foreign lenders.

5. Except in a few resource-rich countries, imports tend to exceed exports, the difference being covered by capital inflows. Net borrowing is normal for a country at this stage and, if domestic output and exports are rising fast enough, can continue for a long time without raising the debt service ratio to a burdensome level.

6. There is a gradual shift in the composition of the import bill, which will occur in any event but can be accelerated by protectionist measures. Even at an early stage, imports consist largely of capital goods, fuels, raw materials, and intermediate products. Later, many of these products are import-substituted, and the import list shrinks to fuels and materials not available at home plus finished manufactures for which optimum plant size is very large.

7. The opposite side of this coin is a shift in the composition of domestic industrial output toward capital goods and consumer durables and a decline in the relative importance of food, textiles, and clothing. This arises partly from import substitution, but mainly from the growing size of the domestic market. The percentage of finished manufactures supplied from domestic sources rises steadily, while the imported share falls toward zero.

8. As the country gains experience and increases efficiency in manufacturing, it will develop an export capacity in some products. Thus, a new arrow—export of manufactures—appears on the flow diagram. We show this as a broken rather than a solid line to indicate that, in the early stages, it is potential rather than actual. The growth of this flow to substantial size indicates a late stage of successful development.

A Growth Typology?

At any point in time, and in any economic dimension one wants to measure, there will be intercountry differences within the universe of LDCs and also within the smaller universe of developing economies. There will be differences in degree of labor surplus, in the presence and amount of surplus land, in richness of other natural resources, in extent and pattern of trade participation, and so on.

Such static or point-of-time differences, however, do not provide a useful basis for country classification. Whatever economic characteristic one may measure will be subject to change over time—and typically to one-way change in a predictable direction. In success cases, one can predict a shrinkage and eventual disappearance of labor surplus, an eventual disappearance of surplus land, a gradual shift in the composition of export and import flows, a change from early-debtor to mature-debtor status, and so on.

Put differently, even though developing economies may be on a similar growth path, some will be farther along on the path than others, because their growth acceleration began earlier or because their subsequent growth rate was higher. Cross-sectionally, therefore, they will look rather different. But this does not indicate a basic difference in growth pattern. A significant typology should relate, not to cross-sectional differences, but to differences in long-term growth behavior.

Efforts to develop a typology in the latter sense usually involve differential behavior of the foreign sector. Leading examples are the Fei-Paauw and Chenery-Syrquin classifications. The Fei-Paauw schema distinguishes between (1) continued reliance on growth of primary exports, which they term a neocolonial growth pattern; (2) import substitution policies aimed at accelerating the growth of the industrial sector; and (3) "export substitution," in which manufactured goods increasingly replace primary products in the export bill.

Instead of viewing these as alternative long-run growth patterns, however, one might better regard them as successive stages in a normal historical sequence. Any LDC will export primary products in the first instance, because such products dominate its production pattern. A sustained rise in primary exports, however, will raise total and per capita income and enlarge domestic demand for manufactures. The industrial sector then grows in relative size through the normal import substitution sequence outlined in chapter 12; and the import bill is correspondingly restructured. This restructuring can be accelerated by import substitution policies, which can be applied with varying degrees of severity, ranging from moderate tariff protection to a more complex and restrictive set of import controls. It is not clear, however, that a specific degree of restriction warrants placing a country in a separate import substitution category, especially in view of the likelihood of policy shifts over time. Many countries that followed restrictionist, inward-looking policies for a decade or two after 1945 concluded eventually that continued growth of the industrial sector required development of an export capacity in manufactures, aided by a more outward-looking policy stance.

A country with a developed industrial base that decides to push industrial exports usually has no difficulty raising such exports at a rapid rate. World demand for manufactures has a higher income elasticity than that for primary products. There is the possibility of taking over a larger share of the rich-country market, particularly in standardized, labor-intensive goods for which the low-wage countries have a potential comparative advantage. There is also a large potential for exchange of manufactures among the LDCs. In a successfully growing LDC, it is normal for the manufactured share of exports to rise and the primary product share to fall. Taiwan and South Korea are merely the most dramatic examples of this general tendency.

A successful LDC, then, tends to move through the three Fei-Paauw stages in sequence, ending up with a large component of manufactured exports. There are, however, intercountry differences in the tempo of movement through the sequence. These stem partly from differences in the richness and variety of the resource base. The most significant measures of resource richness are perhaps agricultural indicators, such as cultivated land per capita and average crop yields. A good agricultural base, plus in some cases oil, mineral, or forestry resources, may enable a country to enjoy a strong competitive position in a diversified array of primary products. Given this, a country can afford to be more leisurely about manufacturing development, which will occur in any event unless thwarted by obtuse policies. It need not resort to highly restrictionist measures that impose serious resource costs on the economy. Primary exports may not carry an economy forever; but they can carry it for a long time and help it reach a high level of per capita income, as the cases of Denmark and New Zealand suggest.

Size of country is also a major consideration. Increasing size of country means, *ceteris paribus*, a larger domestic market. It thus tends to hasten the rate of industrialization and broaden its pattern, so that even "late" industries arrive fairly soon. In a small country, these would appear tardily or not at all (or perhaps prematurely at very high cost).

The large country-small country dimension and the rich resources-poor resources one yield a four-box classification of countries that could prove useful. The growth experiences, and especially the industrialization experiences, of countries in different boxes probably differ in a systematic way. The most difficult situation is that of a small country with a poor resource base. It is almost bound to depend heavily in the first instance on foreign loans and grants; and, depending on the competence of government and the skills of the population, these may or may not be sufficient to induce growth. Given favorable internal circumstances, temporary foreign aid may enable the country to move directly into development of domestic industry and labor-based manufactured exports, without ever passing through the primary export stage. This is somewhat the postwar experience of South Korea and Puerto Rico.

The Chenery-Syrquin typology also rests heavily on foreign-sector performance. They start from the "normal" pattern of production and trade for a country of a certain size and per capita income and then measure the extent to which a particular country deviates from these standards. On this basis they divide countries into those exhibiting: (1) primary specialization. These countries have an abnormally high primary product share of exports, an abnormally high primary product share of domestic output and (usually) an export level above normal. These tend to be resource-rich economies such as Malaysia, the Ivory Coast, and Venezuela; (2) balanced production and trade— countries close to the norm with regard to composition of exports and domestic output. Thailand, the Philippines, Peru, and Ghana fall in this group; (3) import substitution. These countries have a production pattern that is not primary-oriented, an export pattern that *is* primary-oriented, and an abnormally low ratio of exports to GNP. This group includes Mexico, Brazil, Colombia, Chile, Argentina, Turkey, and India; (4) industry specialization. These are countries with an abnormally high industrial share of both output and exports. This group has such obvious members as Taiwan, South Korea, Pakistan, Puerto Rico, and Israel and, less obviously, Kenya. Groups 3 and 4 are further subdivided into countries with normal capital inflow and countries with high capital inflow.

Chenery and Syrquin interpret these categories as indicative of differing development strategies; but this view is open to question. It is doubtful how far one can observe a unified and persistent economic strategy in most LDCs. Policy making tends to be disaggregated and incremental rather than centralized and coherent; and there are substantial changes of direction from time to time. Indeed, the authors recognize that some features of these economies represent failure of policy rather than its fulfillment. For example, the import substitution countries in group 3 would have liked to raise manufactured exports substantially, and some of them took policy steps in this direction. Had they succeeded, they would have been classified as members of group 2; so it is failure of policy that consigns them to a separate category.

Further, despite the dynamic tone conveyed by the terms *development strategy* and *development pattern*, the classification actually rests on a cross-sectional comparison of 1965 output and trade data. But as we argued earlier, the features that show up in a cross-sectional comparison may be quite transitory. Import substitution is a phase rather than a permanent condition. Foreign capital inflow may be substantial for some time but then, if it serves its intended purpose (or even if it does not), it may taper off and decline.

As we argued with respect to the similar Fei-Paauw classification, the Chenery-Syrquin categories are best regarded as successive stages in a temporal sequence rather than as alternative growth paths. The tempo of movement through this sequence is affected by resource richness on one hand, and by economic size on the other. Their group 1 countries are cases of leisurely industrialization, permitted by a strong natural-resource base. Their group 4 consists mainly of countries that, because of limited resources and small economic size, had to move into manufactured exports at an early stage in order to grow at all.

GROWTH, EMPLOYMENT, AND DISTRIBUTION

It is now accepted that success in development cannot be judged solely by the rate of increase in per capita output. Employment is important not only because it yields output and income but also because of its contribution to personal dignity and sense of social participation. It is also important *who gets* the increments of income that accrue in the course of economic growth and whether income disparities narrow or widen in the process.

These subjects have not been prominent in earlier chapters, largely because of lack of information. But we should now say what little can be said.

Employment

A handful of countries, including several of those in our sample, have survey material on unemployment rates among former or would-be wage and salary earners in urban areas. In appraising the significance of this information, it is important to look at the characteristics of the unemployed. The ILO study of Colombia,[7] for example, found that about 60 percent of the urban unemployed were less than 25 years old. The unemployment rate for people aged 15–24 was 26.5 percent, compared with 7.5 percent for those aged 35–64. (This discrepancy in age-specific unemployment rates is found also in the United States, though in less extreme form.) A substantial proportion of those reporting themselves as unemployed were first-time jobseekers. Of these, 60 percent were looking for professional, clerical, or sales jobs, and another 23 percent were seeking jobs as skilled craftsmen. Another interesting finding was that the unemployment rate among people born in the eight major cities studied was typically 50 percent or more above the rate among those who had migrated from elsewhere.

These findings suggest that a substantial proportion of the urban unemployed are young, city-born people with above-average educations, whose families can afford to support them while they wait for the white-collar openings they prefer. These people are by no means the worst off in the population. As Berry comments, "One might conclude ... that with an overall urban unemployment rate of 10 percent, perhaps 3 to 5 percent of the labor force is unemployed *and* in bad straits. This is much smaller than the group which is *employed* and in bad straits. In short, unemployment may well be considered an indication of the price people are willing to pay in terms of waiting to avoid unsatisfactory jobs."[8] The worst off are those who, lacking educational and skill qualifications and having abandoned hope of modern-sector jobs, have squeezed into petty trade, service, and other "spongy" sectors that yield very low earnings.

There is similar evidence from the Philippines. A 1972 household survey found an unemployment rate of 26.9 percent among urban males aged 15–24, but only 7.8 percent among those 25 and over. The ILO report comments, "This concentration at young ages probably reflects their access to support from their families while they are looking for their first job."[9]

---

7. ILO, *Towards Full Employment: a Programme for Colombia*, 1970.
8. R. Albert Berry, "A Review of Development in Colombia Since World War II," mimeographed (New Haven: Yale Economic Growth Center), p. 40.
9. ILO, *Sharing in Development: A Programme of Employment, Equity and Growth for the Philippines*, 1973, p. 4.

Turning to trends over time, the countries in our sample have done quite well in reducing, or at least containing, open unemployment. In Taiwan, the unemployment rate, never high, had fallen to 0.9 percent by 1972. In South Korea, the rate first rose to a peak of 8.3 percent in 1962, then declined steadily to 4.5 percent in 1972. In Mexico, the open unemployment rate was only 3.7 percent in 1970, and growing labor scarcity was signaled by a sharp rise in industrial wage rates. In the Ivory Coast, labor scarcity is sufficiently severe that the economy absorbs hundreds of thousands of migrants from poorer neighboring countries. For Colombia, Berry concludes that the unemployment rate has fluctuated about a level trend line. For the Philippines, the ILO report concludes that measures of open unemployment over the previous fifteen years have fluctuated between 5 and 10 percent, with a stable or slightly declining trend. Bharier reports that open unemployment in urban areas of Iran rose from 4 percent in 1956 to 5 percent in 1966, but this trend has probably been reversed by the boom of the 1970s. For Turkey, unemployment figures do not reflect the domestic demand situation, since Turkey is linked to the EEC labor market and sends large numbers of migrant workers to Europe. This is true also of Mexico vis-à-vis the United States.

The experience of our countries is consistent with the results of Turnham's broader survey.[10] He also found that, for the limited number of countries with data, the urban unemployment rate was typically in the range of 5 to 10 percent, there was no marked trend in most countries over the period 1957–68, unemployment rates for young workers were much higher than those for older workers, and the unemployed were above average in education and job expectations. The unemployment rate seems to rise with education through the level of high school graduation, then drops substantially for college graduates.

Failure of the open unemployment rate to rise, of course, does not prove that there has been no deterioration in the employment situation. Only those actively seeking work are counted as unemployed. If the number of workseekers is rising faster than the number of available jobs, and if jobs are consequently becoming harder to find, some people may respond by ceasing to seek work—the discouraged-worker effect.

10. David Turnham, *The Employment Problem in Less Developed Countries* (Paris: OECD, 1971), especially chap. 3.

This will show up as a decline in labor force participation rates. There are signs of this in some of the countries that have been studied intensively. Thus, in Colombia the participation rate for urban males aged 15–19 dropped from 71.6 percent in 1951 to 47.6 percent in 1964, and the rate for urban males aged 20–24 went from 91.8 percent to 83.5 percent.[11] In the Philippines, the overall labor force participation rate seems to have fallen by from 5 to 8 points between 1957 and 1972.[12]

The meaning of these trends, however, is not self-evident. Durand, using cross-sectional evidence from a large number of countries, finds a general tendency for participation rates of both young male workers and older male workers to fall with rising level of development.[13] One obvious reason is increasing years of school attendance by young people. Another is growing urbanization of the population, since age-specific participation rates are typically lower in urban than in rural areas. The discouraged-worker effect may also play some part in the secular decline within a particular country; but there is little basis for estimating its quantitative significance.

Still more difficult statistical problems arise from the large number of people who are either self-employed or unpaid family workers and who function as part of household production units. By convention, family members share in the work and the resulting income. No one is wholly unemployed, but there may still be unutilized productive capacity—underemployment. This is difficult to define or measure precisely.

One should distinguish here between the rural and urban sectors. In agriculture, underutilization of family labor is associated with small farm sizes and with seasonality.[14] The evidence presented in chapters 3 and 4 is relevant here. For a given crop and technology,

11. Berry, "A Review of Development in Colombia," p. 44. Data originally from DANE, Population Census of Colombia, 1951, and from unpublished 1964 census data.

12. ILO, *Sharing in Development*, vol. 2, paper 1.

13. John D. Durand, *The Labor Force in Economic Development* (Princeton: Princeton University Press, 1975.)

14. For good analytical discussion, see Anthony Y. C. Koo, *The Role of Land Reform in Economic Development* (New York: Frederick A. Praeger, 1968); Amartya Sen, *Employment, Technology, and Development* (New York: Oxford University Press, 1975); Bent Hansen, "Employment and Wages in Rural Egypt," *American Economic Review* (June 1969): 298–313; Warren C. Robinson, "Disguised Unemployment Once Again: East Pakistan, 1951–61," *American Journal of Agricultural Economics* (August 1969): 592–604; Robinsons, "Disguised Unemployment: A Survey," in Carl K. *Agriculture in Economic Development*, ed. Carl K. Eicher and Lawrence W. Witt (New York: McGraw-Hill, 1964), pp. 129–44.

one can determine roughly how many acres are required to provide full employment for a farm family of a given size. This might be 1,000 acres for a wheat farmer in Kansas, eight acres for a rice grower in Taiwan. As actual acreage decreases below the full-employment level, the family typically adjusts in several ways. Some members may leave the family. Koo found that, in Taiwan, farms with five acres averaged about 50 percent more family members than farms with one acre. In addition, labor inputs per acre may increase. This does not necessarily mean working farther down the same schedule of marginal productivity of labor; rather, it may involve a shift to more labor-using crops, expenditure of labor on irrigation and drainage, and greater use of multiple cropping. Finally, more labor may be hired out for off-farm work. In the smallest size classes, time worked off the farm may exceed that worked on the farm.

Despite these adjustments, as farm size falls, income per family member also falls, and the amount of unutilized labor time rises. Koo, on the admittedly arbitrary assumption that family members on eight-to-nine-acre rice farms were working as much as they wanted to, concluded that there was involuntary unemployment of 35 percent on farms of less than one acre.

At the same time, on farms larger than "family size," there often seem to be unutilized opportunities for employment, that is, the amount of labor employed seems to be less than would be optimal at existing farm wage levels. Possible explanations of this phenomenon, which has been observed particularly in Latin America, were considered in chapter 4. Where it exists, the amount of labor time used might be increased considerably by subdivision of large farms into smaller units.

Whatever may be the waste of labor time in these respects, seasonal fluctuations in labor demand are even more important. Even on quite small farms, family members may be fully employed at the peaks of planting and harvesting. But in the intervening months, the amount of work required drops off sharply; and this is not fully offset by opportunities for off-farm work. The significant feature of seasonal underemployment is that it does not make labor available for permanent transfer to the city. Seasonal underemployment has to be absorbed either by smoothing out seasonal labor requirements in agriculture through such things as multiple cropping and diversification into livestock or by creating nearby employment opportunities in small-scale rural industries, construction of roads and other forms of rural infrastructure, and so on.

Whether underemployment in agriculture has increased or decreased over the past generation in our sample of countries is impossible to say. One would need comparable farm survey data at different points in time, and little such material is available. With some hesitation, I would hazard a judgment that the employment situation in most of these countries has *not* deteriorated over time. Rates of net increase in rural population have been moderate. On the demand side, there has been substantial expansion of cultivated acreage in some countries; and in others, increasing yields have been achieved partly by larger labor inputs per acre. In the cases of Taiwan and South Korea, the suction of labor into urban activities has been strong enough so that labor is now scarce in both country and city.

What about traditional, low-wage activities in the cities? Here, those who are not qualified, or cannot afford to wait, for modern-sector jobs have the option of squeezing into petty trade, handicraft, or service activities. If the rate of increase of workers in this sector exceeds the rate of increase in demand for their services, then output and income per worker must fall. Some indication of what is happening might be obtained by looking at the movement of intersectoral relative productivity ratios; but the data are admittedly weak. In the simplest three-way classification of activities, "services" includes some modern-sector jobs in government, finance, foreign trade, and so forth, along with traditional activities; and the output of those in traditional activities is usually estimated rather than measured.

Estimates from the employment study in the Philippines suggest that employment deterioration in a productivity sense is a realistic possibility. Between 1960 and 1971, relative value added per worker fell in the commerce sector from 1.94 to 1.15 and in the services sector from 1.74 to 1.23. In agriculture, on the other hand, there was a moderate increase from 0.55 to 0.72.[15]

Income Distribution

Although data on income distribution are fragmentary and imprecise, it is clear that inequality is substantially greater in the LDC's than in the mature economies. In a recent survey, Chenery and Ahluwalia classified countries according to the share of income received by the lowest 40 percent, middle 40 percent, and top 20 percent of the population.[16] Eleven of our fifteen countries show a high degree

15. ILO, *Sharing in Development*, chap. 1.
16. Hollis Chenery and others, *Redistribution with Growth* (New York: Oxford University Press, 1974), chap. 1.

of inequality. The income share of the bottom 40 percent of the population in these countries is typically 10 to 12 percent, while the top 20 percent receive 60 to 70 percent of the income. In the United States, the United Kingdom, Canada, Australia, and Japan, on the other hand, the bottom 40 percent receive about 20 percent of the income, and the top 20 percent receive about 40 percent.

Four of our countries show substantially greater equality than the others. The income shares of the bottom 40 percent and top 20 percent in these countries are as follows: Pakistan, 17.5 and 45.0; Thailand, 17.0 and 45.5; South Korea, 18.0 and 45.0; and Taiwan, 20.4 and 40.1. Taiwanese income distribution is as equal as that in the United States or Britain.

What determines the degree of income inequality in an LDC? A pioneer investigation by Irma Adelman and Cynthia Taft Morris concluded that the income share of the lowest 60 percent of income recipients is related statistically to the extent of socioeconomic dualism, the level of social and economic modernization, and the coverage of secondary and higher education. The income share of the bottom group is relatively high under two quite different circumstances: where there is pervasive underdevelopment marked by the presence of small-scale or communal subsistence agriculture; and where there is substantial development associated with major efforts to improve human resources. On the other hand, the income share of the bottom group is relatively low "where a sharply dualistic development process has been initiated by well-entrenched expatriate or military elites."[17]

It is useful, where the data permit, to distinguish between the rural and urban populations. The median income in the rural sector is usually well below that in the urban sector, and most of the poorest people are in the countryside. Chenery found that in Mexico some 63 percent of the poorest group in the income distribution were involved in agriculture. The corresponding percentage for Chile was 70 percent and for Malaysia, 71 percent. In terms of employment status, the poor were predominantly self-employed rather than wage earners.

The determinants of size distribution in the two sectors are also different. It is possible for income inequality to be increasing in

17. Irma Adelman and Cynthia Taft Morris, *Economic Growth and Social Equity in Developing Countries* (Stanford: Stanford University Press, 1973), especially chapter 4. There is a parallel analysis of the conditions under which the income share of the top 5 percent of income recipients tends to be high or low. The authors are careful to point out that statistical association does not reveal the chain of causation, and that the cross-section data used in their analysis cannot be interpreted as equivalent to time trends.

agriculture but decreasing in urban areas, or vice versa, in which case a finding that the economywide Gini coefficient is stable is not very informative.

In the rural sector, the most important income determinant is the distribution of property ownership. Labor being relatively abundant and land and capital relatively scarce, the property share of agricultural income is higher than in the mature economies. In Colombia as of 1964, Berry and Urrutia conclude that about 62 percent of farm income was attributable to land and capital (including the human capital of farm operators) and that the "pure labor share" was only 38 percent.[18] Moreover, land and capital ownership is highly skewed and accounts for most of the income of the top income recipients—about 87 percent for those in the top decile of the distribution. Even the labor share is somewhat skewed by unequal division of land because, as farm size decreases, family members are not able to work as many hours per year on the farm. Thus, even if the hourly return to labor were equal across farm sizes, the small farmer would earn less; and this is not fully offset by opportunities for off-farm employment.

The urban income distribution is influenced by the relative numbers attached to the modern and urban traditional sectors and by the size of the earnings gap between these sectors. Within the modern sector, distribution is influenced by the size of the property share, the concentration of property ownership, and the size of wage-salary differentials. In each of these respects, LDC conditions typically produce greater inequality than prevails in the mature economies. In LDCs, the white-collar blue-collar gap is wider, the gap between skilled craftsmen and laborers is wider, the property share of value added is higher, and property ownership is more highly concentrated.

Regarding trends over time, two questions are pertinent. First, in the countries of our sample, has economic growth been accompanied by an absolute decline in per capita income for the poorest groups in the population? Second, even if the lowest incomes have been rising absolutely, have the incomes of the better off been rising faster, so that income inequality has increased? Kuznets has hypothesized that, in the course of economic growth, income inequality tends initially to increase and later to diminish. Adelman and Morris also surmise that

18. R. Albert Berry and Miguel Urrutia, *Income Distribution in Colombia.* A Publication of the Economic Growth Center, Yale University (New Haven: Yale University Press, 1976), p. 62.

the benefits of early economic growth go disproportionately to the middle-income groups in the population and that the incomes of the poorest groups may even fall absolutely.

The first question, we believe, can be answered in the negative. In none of the country studies we have examined is there evidence of an absolute deterioration in the condition of the poor. This is also the impression yielded by the Chenery-Ahluwalia study. For eighteen countries, they were able to chart[19] the growth rate of GNP against the growth rate of income of the lowest 40 percent over periods of a decade or so. For two countries, Peru and Panama, the annual growth rate of total income for the lowest 40 percent was only 3 percent, implying approximate stagnation in per capita terms. In all other cases, however, per capita income rose for even the poorest groups.

But even though the poorest have gained absolutely, the better off may have gained even more. For most of the countries in our sample, there is too little information to warrant any conclusion on this point. We can say something, however, about Colombia, the Philippines, South Korea, and Taiwan.

In Colombia, Berry and Urrutia reach different conclusions for the rural and urban sectors. They find a secular increase of inequality in agriculture between the 1930s and the 1960s, related to a decline in the labor share of agricultural output. This may stem partly from a shift toward less-labor-intensive commercial and export crops, plus an increase in mechanization on the larger farms, which has reduced demand for farm labor. The combination of sluggish labor demand and rapid population growth has slowed the rise of real wages in agriculture, which has been well below the rate of increase in output per capita.

In the urban sector, income distribution seems to have worsened from 1935 to 1955, but it appears to have improved since that time. In the earlier period, white-collar earnings rose much faster than blue-collar earnings, but more recently the reverse has been true. In the earlier period, too, returns to capital were inflated by import substitution policies.

The ILO employment mission report on the Philippines finds that the evidence on income distribution there is complex and somewhat conflicting.[20] There is a clear indication of growing inequality in the rural sector. The income share received by the poorest 20 percent of

19. Chenery and others, *Redistribution With Growth*, p. 14, fig. 1.1.
20. ILO, *Sharing in Development*, chap. 1.

rural Philippine households fell from 7.0 percent in 1956 to 4.4 percent in 1971, while the share of the top 10 percent rose from 30.1 to 34.4 percent. The rural Gini coefficient rose from 0.38 to 0.46. This agrees with evidence from other sources that large farmers have adopted new agricultural technology and raised yields faster than smaller farmers. Regionally, the poorest agricultural regions have had the lowest rate of increase in median income.

The situation in urban areas is less clear. There are some indications of worsening distribution—a tendency toward decline of real wages for both industrial workers and government employees during the 1960s, and an increase in the share of GNP going to undistributed corporate profits plus depreciation from 10.1 percent in 1961 to 16.2 in 1971. On the other hand, household surveys showed a slight increase between 1956 and 1971 in the income share of the bottom 40 percent of the urban population and a slight decline in the share of the top 20 percent.

Finally, there was a modest narrowing of the urban-rural gap. The median urban income was 2.45 times the median rural income in 1956 but only 2.08 times in 1971. The report suggests that this "was partly the result of incomes in nonagricultural rural activities—services, craftsmen, and transport workers—moving up to the urban levels, and partly the result of changes in the internal terms of trade, with agricultural products becoming relatively more expensive."

Taiwan has an unusually good series of household surveys, and the period 1964–72 has been analyzed intensively by Gustav Ranis and John Fei.[21] These surveys identify households by rural or urban location and income by source—wages, property income, or income from agriculture—so that one can calculate "factor Ginis" as well as the overall Gini for both rural and urban households.

In both rural and urban sectors, there was a marked trend toward greater equality over the period, but the reasons for the trend were varied. As farm families increasingly provided labor to nearby industrial activities, the percentage of rural income derived from wages rose steeply, until by 1972 it slightly exceeded the share derived from agriculture. Since wage income is more equally distributed than income from property or from agriculture, its growing importance tended to reduce the overall rural Gini. In addition, the Gini for income derived

21. Most of this material is unpublished at the date of writing, but the authors have kindly given me access to it.

from agriculture fell from .35 in 1966 to .30 in 1972, indicating a broadly based process of agricultural improvement that benefited farms of all sizes. These two developments account for a drop in the Gini coefficient for rural households from .31 in 1966 to .28 in 1972.

In urban areas, on the other hand, there was little change in factor shares. Wage income rose from 57 to 63 percent of the total between 1964 and 1972, and property income fell from 32 to 30 percent. The significant development was that *both* labor and property income became more equally distributed, as indicated by a decline in both factor Ginis. The overall Gini for urban households thus fell from .33 in 1964 to .28 in 1972. These trends, of course, are related to the rapid growth of labor-intensive industrial exports, the shift from a labor-surplus to a labor-scarce economy, and the rapid rise in real wages.

An unusual feature of the Taiwan case is the smallness of the rural-urban gap. As of 1964, the average urban family had an income only 15 percent above that of the average rural family. Thus, the economy-wide Gini is close to the rural and urban Ginis, which themselves are virtually equal.

For South Korea,[22] we know that the income distribution as of 1970 was one of the most equal in the less-developed world, though we cannot say exactly when this equality came about. The factors responsible are similar to those that were operative in Taiwan: a land reform program that created a large number of small family farms; a great expansion of education, which raised the literacy rate from 30 percent in 1953 to 80 percent in 1963, by which time South Korea's human-resource development had exceeded the norm for a country with three times its per capita GNP; and a successful shift into labor-intensive exports, which rapidly exhausted the surplus labor reservoir. Between 1964 and 1970, real wage rates of production workers in manufacturing rose by more than 85 percent, while those of wage earners in agriculture doubled. The lowest income groups seem to have shared at least proportionately in the general rise of per capita incomes.

The number of countries for which detailed information is available is small, and the time period is short. It would thus be hazardous to draw general conclusions. The material assembled by Chenery and Ahluwalia suggests marked diversity of country experience. Countries in our sample for which they report improvement in income distribution

22. See Irma Adelman, Annex 4, "South Korea," in Chenery and Ahluwalia, *Redistribution With Growth*, pp. 280–85.

during the 1960s are Taiwan, Iran, and Colombia. On the other hand, inequality appears to have increased in Mexico, Brazil, the Philippines, and Venezuela. Interestingly, their scatter diagram of GNP growth rate against income growth rate for the poorest 40 percent shows no visible relation. In some high-growth economies (Taiwan) distribution improved, while in others (Brazil, Mexico) it worsened; and the same was true of low-growth economies. It does not seem to be true, as is sometimes asserted, that a high growth rate per se makes for a worsening of income distribution.

15

Growth Acceleration under Socialism

By *socialist* I mean a country in which productive enterprises (with the exception of farms in some countries) are state-owned and managed. I am concerned here with a subset of such countries: those that have embarked on sustained growth since 1945 from a low-income, heavily agricultural base. This does not include the Soviet Union, which was already semi-industrialized in 1917; or East Germany and Czechoslovakia, which were quite heavily industrialized in 1940.

What does this leave? First and preeminently China, which is the largest LDC in the world and by far the largest socialist LDC. Second, there are three East European countries—Bulgaria, Rumania, and Yugoslavia—that were heavily agricultural in 1945. I count Yugoslavia in the socialist group despite its idiosyncratic institutional structure. I shall not discuss Cuba, where per capita output seems to have fallen during the 1960s, or North Vietnam, whose economy was devastated by bombing during the Vietnam War. North Korea has made rapid economic progress since the end of the Korean War in 1952; but the amount of information available in English is still limited.

Hungary and Poland can be considered as fringe members of the socialist LDC group. In income level, degree of industrialization, and most other respects, they fall somewhere between the Balkan countries on one hand and East Germany and Czechoslovakia on the other. I shall normally include these semideveloped economies in my comparative statistical tabulations, but the discussion will focus on the LDCs proper.

A basic question at the outset is whether socialist economic organization facilitates economic development from a low-income level. Is there any a priori reason to expect growth to be faster (or slower) under socialist than nonsocialist conditions? After examining this issue in general terms, I proceed to a review of the evidence on growth rates and growth patterns.

DOES SOCIALIST ORGANIZATION FACILITATE GROWTH?

Doctrinaire Marxists and anti-Marxists are quite willing to give definite, though opposite, answers to this question; but an objective approach suggests numerous pros and cons.

There are certainly ways in which socialist organization might facilitate growth acceleration. Four in particular deserve attention:

1. Absorption of resource slack. In earlier chapters I emphasized that an LDC usually has considerable resource slack at the beginning of growth acceleration. There was much resource slack in the East European countries in 1945 and in China in 1949. Thus, apart from efforts to increase resource supplies, much can be accomplished in the early years by fuller use of resources already there.

The kinds of resources available, and the way in which they can be reoriented for growth purposes, may be illustrated from Montias's analysis of Rumania.[1] The most obvious surplus in 1945 was under-utilized labor, particularly in the rural sector. Part of ths labor was diverted into manufacturing, particularly light manufacturing, where ample labor supplies served to counterbalance limited capital allocations. Labor was also directed into construction, expansion of public services, and other activities.

Rumania also inherited from the past a good deal of fixed capital, which in the short run could be used more intensively without expansion or even full maintenance. The economy could "coast on the depreciation fund" for a time. Thus, the rail network and the rolling stock were used more intensively than before. More people were crowded into existing housing, with little new construction. Plants that had been working one shift were converted to multipleshift operation.

There was a potential surplus also in the foreign sector, in the sense that exports of cereals, petroleum, timber, cement, and other materials could be stepped up by repressing domestic consumption. The rise in exports, plus virtual cessation of imports of consumer goods, permitted

---

1. John M. Montias, *Economic Development in Communist Rumania* (Cambridge: M.I.T. Press, 1967).

a large increase in imports of machinery and industrial raw materials for accelerated industrialization.

Only in terms of a forced draft on preexisting resources can one explain the fact that the Rumanian economy, which had been growing quite slowly up to 1940, suddenly began in the late 1940s to grow at one of the highest rates of any European country.

2. Removal of demand constraints. The organization of a socialist economy precludes any problem of deficient demand. On the contrary, socialist economies are normally excess-demand economies, with persistent inflationary pressure. The effort to repress inflation through controlled prices leads to shortages throughout the economy. Kornai has aptly labeled this pervasive sellers' market a *suction economy*.[2]

There are several reasons for chronic excess demand. Labor is scarce, as are other inputs. In a tight labor market, socialist managers, like capitalist managers, compete for workers by overclassifying jobs and permitting loose piece rates. The wage bill thus tends to rise faster than the money value of available consumer goods. With fixed prices this leads to queuing, informal rationing, and disappointment of consumers' buying plans.

There is also a tendency to set higher output targets than can be attained with available plant capacity and input supplies. This is often termed *planning tension*, or a tendency toward *taut plans*. Enterprises straining toward these targets find themselves chronically short of basic materials and intermediate products. This produces a sellers' market for everything from raw materials to finished goods.

Although chronic excess demand creates administrative problems and is unfavorable to management efficiency, it does encourage full employment of resources. In socialist economies, one does not see large numbers of workers standing idle or plants shut down for lack of orders.

3. Built-in capital accumulation. In physical terms, the production plans direct a large share of resources toward manufacturing facilities and economic infrastructure. In financial terms, funds are accumulated in the government budget from enterprise profits, excise taxes, and other sources, and the surplus over current expenditure is allocated to investment. Effective mechanisms for government saving make it unnecessary to coax out private saving. Household saving is normally

2. Janos Kornai, *Anti-Equilibrium* (Amsterdam: North-Holland Publishing Co., 1971).

permitted, with interest paid by the savings banks, but this forms only a small part of national saving.

The opposite side of accelerated capital formation is a drop in the proportion of national output going to consumption. The growth rate of per capita consumption is well below that of national output. A Communist government has sufficient political control to enforce austerity in the present for the sake of a more or less distant future.

4. Emphasis on human capital formation. The socialization of an LDC is normally accompanied by rapid educational expansion. Primary education becomes available (and free) to all. Even in China, with its enormous and far-flung population, primary education is now universal in the cities and rapidly becoming so in the countryside. The capacity of secondary and higher educational institutions—technical institutes as well as universities—is also enlarged and given a strongly vocational direction. Humanistic studies are downgraded. Science, engineering, medicine, agriculture, pedagogy, and other skills are emphasized at the university level, and specific skills plus work experience are emphasized at the secondary level. The problem of the unemployed arts graduate in India, or the unemployed "school leaver" in Nigeria, does not exist in socialist economies.

This impressive list of advantages seems to make the productive superiority of socialism almost self-evident. But there is a counterlist of disadvantages, of which the most serious are:

1. Poor performance of agriculture. In socialist LDCs, as in others, agriculture is initially the largest production sector. Yet it is precisely in this sector that socialist performance is poorest. Output tends to lag behind consumer demand for foodstuffs. Countries that were once food exporters tend to become food importers. Whatever its potential advantages, large-scale collective farming has in practice proved less favorable than private family farming to effort, innovation, and efficiency.[3] In addition, in some socialist countries, there has been an antiagricultural bias in public policy. Both agriculture itself, and supporting facilities such as farm-machinery plants and fertilizer factories, receive skimpy allocations of investment funds. Pricing and procurement policies for farm products, plus wide price-cost margins

3. For analysis of possible reasons for this result, see Z. Kozlowski, "Agriculture in the Economic Growth of the East European Socialist Countries," in *Agriculture in Development Theory*, ed. L. G. Reynolds (New Haven: Yale University Press, 1975).

for manufactured consumer goods, turn the internal terms of trade against agriculture. Agriculture is treated as an exploitable, backward, nonpreferred sector, and so it remains backward.

2. Lack of microefficiency. The socialist economies depart widely from the Paretian requirements for microefficiency, probably more widely than do nonsocialist LDCs. Resource prices are not scarcity prices, and so nominal costs of production may depart widely from opportunity costs. Greatly varying price-cost margins for consumer goods, plus the chronic state of excess demand, interfere with transmission of consumer preferences to producing units. The cumbersome, bureaucratic apparatus of production planning makes it difficult for enterprises to respond to markets signals. The pervasive sellers' market, the attitude that "buyers must take what they can get," reduces attention to quality and also discourages product and process innovations.

In such countries as Hungary, this is less true today than it was before the "economic reform" movement of the 1960s; but it is still largely true. In consequence, the output of socialist economies is less than it should be, given the degree of resource mobilization. At any point in time, less is available for consumption or capital formation than could be available with more efficient organization. One might also expect a low rate of productivity improvement over time, because of the weakness of economic incentives for such improvement at the enterprise level and the limited extent to which improvement can be compelled by administrative supervision. The evidence on actual rates of productivity change will be reviewed in a later section.

3. Low trade ratios and inefficient international specialization. Foreign trade, even with other socialist countries, is attended by several difficulties that combine to create an antitrade bias. The fact that foreign demand is less predictable than domestic demand presents difficulties for a planning system in which predictability and control are of the essence. Arbitrary pricing creates difficulties in foreign as well as domestic trade. The East European currencies are not freely convertible, even with each other. Trade thus takes the form of bilateral negotiation among pairs of countries, with an effort to achieve balance on an annual basis—a cumbersome and intrinsically inefficient procedure. Persistent excess demand creates strong pressure for imports plus a reluctance to export goods that could be used advantageously at home—the reverse of the preference system in

capitalist countries. A socialist producing enterprise has no incentive to export, since it sells to the foreign trade organization at the domestic price—and in any event can usually market its full output at home.

In view of all this, it is not surprising that the trade ratios of the socialist countries are disproportionately low for their economic size. With regard to the East European countries, Pryor has estimated that in 1928 their trade ratios did not differ significantly from those of comparable West European countries. But in the 1950s, after the change in regime, the ratios were only 50 to 60 percent as high as those of Western countries of similar size and income level.[4] This situation seems to have continued through the 1960s.

Socialism does not eliminate nationalism. There are strong national aspirations toward across-the-board industrialization as a basis of economic and military power; these aspirations are voiced in China or Rumania in much the same terms as they are in nonsocialist LDCs. Like many other LDCs, the socialist countries seem to prefer home production over imports, manufacturing over agriculture, heavy industry over light industry. Rumania does not want to remain a hewer of wood and drawer of water for the Czechs and East Germans, any more than Brazil wants to occupy this position vis-à-vis the United States. Chinese leaders have also complained that the Soviet Union desires a division of labor that would retard China's industrial development; and this must have been an important factor contributing to the breakdown of relations in 1960.[5]

Although this preference pattern is understandable, it must—especially in the relatively small economies of Eastern Europe—entail

4. Frederic L. Pryor, "Discussion," in *International Trade and Central Planning*, ed. Alan Brown and Egon Neuberger (Berkeley and Los Angeles: University of California Press, 1968). Compare, however, the contrasting opinion of P. J. D. Wiles (*Communist International Economics*, [New York: Frederick A. Praeger, 1968] chap. 15) that East European trade ratios were not out of line in the early 1960s.

5. "You constantly accuse us of 'going it alone' and claim that you stand for extensive economic ties and division of labor among the socialist countries. But what is your actual record in this respect?

"You infringe the independence and sovereignty of fraternal countries and oppose their efforts to develop their economy on an independent basis in accordance with their own needs and potentialities.

"You bully those fraternal countries whose economies are less advanced and oppose their policy of industrialization and try to force them to remain agricultural countries and serve as your sources of raw material and as outlets for your goods." Letter from Communist Party of China to Communist Party of the USSR, cited in Alexander Eckstein, Walter Galenson, and T. C. Liu, *Economic Trends in Communist China* (Chicago: Wdine Publishing Co., 1968), p. 554.

resource costs similar to those ascribed to accelerated import substitution in nonsocialist LDCs.

The conflicting considerations in the previous section do not warrant any a priori expectation that socialist LDCs will grow faster than nonsocialist ones. But why speculate in an area where we can hope to measure? Before looking at the evidence, we should note that socialist-nonsocialist growth comparisons are inherently treacherous. First, socialist calculations based on material product omit most of the service sector. Since service outputs have grown less rapidly than commodity outputs in the socialist countries, an adjustment to Western GNP definitions reduces the growth rate below that shown by official statistics. Further, the wide divergence of sectoral growth rates in the socialist countries reduces the significance of the average. Typically, the growth rate of heavy industry and electric power is very high (from a low base), while the growth rate of light industry is much lower but still above average, and the growth of agricultural and service outputs is lower still. Thus, it is even more misleading in socialist than in nonsocialist countries to interpret the aggregate growth rate as a welfare indicator.

The East European countries, like the West European ones, have low rates of population growth, which distinguishes them sharply from other LDCs. Moreover, the population growth rate today is lower than it was before 1940. Comparing 1938 with 1967, the crude death rate has fallen from around 14 to 8 or 9. But crude birth rates have fallen from around 25 to 15. Thus, the rate of natural increase has fallen below 1 percent—in Hungary, it is only 0.4 percent. How far the decline in birth rates reflects specific characteristics of a socialist society, and how far it simply reflects urbanization and rising per capita incomes, can only be surmised.

Chinese population data are conjectural, even within China, but the rate of natural increase is usually estimated at about 2 percent per year—lower in the cities, higher in the countryside. There is evidence, however, that this rate is being gradually reduced by energetic promotion of family planning. The announced objective is to reduce the population growth rate to 1 percent by the year 2000.

Table 1 presents estimates of growth rates in five East European countries, adjusted to Western GNP concepts. The estimates for

Table 1. Average Annual Rate of Increase in GNP
per Capita, Selected Periods, 1950–1972

	1950–55	*1955–60*	*1960–72*
Bulgaria	5.4	6.3	5.9
Hungary	4.4	3.5	3.9
Poland	2.6	2.9	3.7
Rumania	6.0	3.1	5.3
Yugoslavia	2.9	6.2	4.5
Unweighted Average	4.3	4.4	4.7

Bulgaria, Hungary, Poland, and Rumania, prepared by Thad P. Alton, result from a large-scale research project at Columbia University[6] and can be taken as the most accurate presently available. For the 1960–72 period in Yugoslavia, not included in the Alton study, we have used IBRD data.[7]

Over the years 1950–72, GNP per capita in these countries rose at about 4.5 percent per year. With population growing at about 1 percent, the growth rate of total output was about 5.5 percent. Note that the lowest-income countries (Bulgaria, Rumania, and Yugoslavia) grew somewhat faster than the middle-income countries (Hungary and Poland). The highest-income countries of Eastern Europe, East Germany and Czechoslovakia, grew still more slowly—at 3.4 percent per year over the period 1960–72.

In China, total GNP seems to have grown since 1949 at about 5 percent per year on the average, but with substantial short-term fluctuations. These arise partly from weather variations in a still heavily agricultural economy; but they are due also to periods of political turbulence, which produce temporary slowdowns in growth. From 1952 to 1957, when the economy was absorbing the large amount of economic slack existing at the time of the revolution, output is estimated to have grown at 8 percent per year. The confusion of the Great Leap Forward campaign produced a drop in output during 1958–60, followed by recovery during 1961–66, a deceleration

6. See Thad P. Alton, "Economic Structure and Growth in Eastern Europe," in *Economic Developments in Countries of Eastern Europe* (Washington: Government Printing Office, for the Joint Economic Committee, 91st Cong., 2 sess., 1970) and idem, "Economic Growth and Resource Allocation in Eastern Europe," in *Reorientations and Commercial Relations of the Economies of Eastern Europe* (Washington: Government Printing Office, for the Joint Economic Committee, 93rd Cong., 2d sess., 1974).

7. *World Bank Atlas: Population, Per Capita Product, and Growth Rates* (Washington: IBRD, 1973), p. 10.

of growth during the Cultural Revolution of 1966–69, and recovery to normal growth rates from 1970 onward. Although no official statistics have been published since 1957, Perkins has estimated[8] that over the period 1957–72, GNP rose at an average annual rate of about 5 percent. If the 2-percent estimate of the population growth rate is roughly correct, this would mean a growth of 3 percent per year in per capita terms.

How do these growth rates compare with those of nonsocialist LDCs? The answer depends on whether one compares with LDCs in general or with our sample of the more successful LDCs—and on whether one compares growth rates of *total* or *per capita* output. For nonsocialist LDCs as a whole, UN sources report an average annual growth rate over the period 1950–68 of 4.7 percent in total output, 2.4 percent in population, and 2.2 percent in output per capita. For reasons explained in chapter 10, however, these estimates contain an upward bias. Kuznets's reworking of the data yields an estimate of 1.1 percent for the average annual increase in per capita output.[9] Western reestimates of GNP growth in the socialist LDCs may not have succeeded entirely in eliminating upward bias from those data. Even so, one can reasonably conclude that China and the Balkan countries did substantially better than the LDC world in general.

For our sample of fifteen success cases, the conclusion is rather different. It will be recalled from chapter 10, table 5, that the median rate of GNP increase in these countries was 6.3 percent during 1950–60 and 6.6 percent during 1960–70. Even allowing for some upward bias, this is in line with the 5.0–5.5 percent performance of the socialist LDCs. The main difference between the two groups is that population was growing faster in the countries of our sample, at about 3.0 percent during 1960–70. This reduces the median growth rate of per capita output for the decade to 3.6 percent, which is intermediate between the Chinese 3.0 percent and the East European 4.5 percent.

The moral appears to be that accelerated economic growth is attainable by either socialist or nonsocialist routes. The socialist LDCs did manage to lift themselves above the general run of LDCs and

8. Dwight H. Perkins, "Looking Inside China: An Economic Reappraisal," *Problems of Communism* 22 (May–June 1973): 1–13. For estimates for the 1950s, see Eckstein et al., *Economic Trends in Communist China* (Chicago: Aldine Publishing Co., 1968).

9. Simon Kuznets, "Problems in Comparing Recent Growth Rates for Developed and Less Developed Countries," *Economic Development and Cultural Change* 20 (January 1972): 185–209.

Table 2. Composition of Gross National Product by Industrial Origin
(at factor cost, constant prices)

Country and Period	Agriculture and Forestry	Industry and Handicrafts	Construction	Transport and Communications	Trade	Housing	Government and Other Services
Bulgaria:							
Prewar	55.1	9.5	3.0	2.5	6.9	14.4	8.6
1950	39.4	18.1	5.6	5.9	4.8	15.3	10.9
1972	21.1	39.0	7.5	8.2	6.7	8.8	8.7
Hungary:							
Prewar	37.3	20.7	4.3	5.0	6.7	11.6	14.1
1950	29.7	25.3	6.2	9.5	6.2	12.0	11.1
1972	17.1	37.3	8.7	11.5	9.5	6.1	9.8
Poland:							
Prewar	36.6	18.9	4.0	3.4	12.3	11.7	13.1
1950	36.9	22.0	4.5	5.7	6.2	12.9	11.8
1972	19.6	29.3	7.7	9.2	7.7	8.4	8.2
Rumania:							
1950	31.3	19.2	4.1	6.6	7.4	13.8	17.7
1972	24.5	41.8	9.0	9.0	6.8	4.6	4.3
Yugoslavia:							
1950	27.6	22.7	5.9	8.6	5.2	12.2	17.8
1967	22.6	37.2	3.4	10.2	7.9	7.7	11.0

clearly deserve to be regarded as success cases. But they did not do any better than our sample of nonsocialist success cases.

CHANGES IN THE COMPOSITION OF OUTPUT

Sector growth rates differ in any developing economy, but in the socialist economies the differences are unusually large. This arises from a preference for material output over services and for manufacturing and infrastructure industries over agriculture. The main policy instrument is investment allocations; but industry, especially heavy industry, is also favored in labor recruitment.

Output by Sector of Origin

Aggressive pursuit of such policies can produce large shifts in output composition in a relatively short time. Table 2 compares the output pattern of the East European countries in 1972 with that in 1950 and, for some countries, with the prewar pattern.[10] The picture is quite consistent from country to country. In these once heavily agricultural countries, the proportion of output coming from agriculture had fallen by 1972 to less than one-quarter. The share of the manufacturing-construction-utilities complex had risen sharply, forming more than half of national output in all the countries except Poland. The housing and service sectors fell sharply in relative importance, indicating their low priority in national plans, while the share of trade stagnated or declined.

The sector composition of employment, also available in the Alton study,[11] shows characteristic differences from the output table. Agriculture's share of employment is typically larger than its share of output; the reverse is true in industry. From this, following Kuznets, we can compute intersectoral productivity differences (table 3). The productivity gap is narrower in medium-income Hungary than in the four lower-income countries. In most of the countries, it has narrowed considerably since 1950, confirming Kuznets's hypothesis about the convergence of sectoral productivity levels in the course of long-term

10. Alton, "Economic Structure," in *Economic Developments*, pp. 54–55; idem, "Economic Growth," in *Reorientations*, p. 256.

11. Alton, "Economic Structure," in *Economic Developments*, pp. 58–59; and idem, "Economic Growth," in *Reorientations*, pp. 256, 263. For Yugoslavia, not included in the second Alton study, the second figure is for 1967 rather than for 1972.

Table 3. Output per Worker, Agriculture and Industry, as a
Percent of Total Output per Worker, 1950 and 1967

Year	Bulgaria		Hungary		Poland		Rumania		Yugoslavia	
	Ag.	Ind.	Ag.	Ind.	Ag.	Ind.	Ag.	Ind.	Ag.	Ind.
1950	48	230	59	128	69	106	42	160	35	244
1972	59	125	84	99	57	99	55	160	40	190

growth. On the average, for the five countries, the gap is narrower
than for the typical nonsocialist LDC. The main reason may be that,
in the socialist economies, the strong suction of labor from the
countryside into urban activities pulls up the average output of the
remaining agricultural workers. East European agriculture is also
superior to that in most LDCs with respect to use of fertilizer,
machinery, and other modern inputs.

For China, Liu has estimated[12] the composition of national output
by major sectors in a prewar base year and in the immediate post-
revolutionary period. The impact of the industrialization drive
launched by the new regime during the 1950s is apparent from table
4. Note the sharp drop in the agricultural sector, offset by a sharp rise
in the importance of industry broadly defined. Although official data
are not available for more recent years, it seems certain that these
general tendencies have continued. Perkins estimates[13] that, over the
period 1957–72, industrial output grew at the rate of 8 to 9 percent
per year, agricultural output at 3 percent per year. If this is correct,
and if we assume that services have continued to grow only in proportion to NNP, the agricultural share of output has by now fallen
below 30 percent while the industrial share is approaching 50 percent.
This is still not as high as the industrial share in the East European
countries, but it is remarkably high for a country at such a low income
level.

A comparison of structural shifts in these economies with those in
our sample of nonsocialist economies (table 6, chapter 10) reveals the
same direction of movement but a considerable difference in tempo.
In the nonsocialist group, over the period 1950–70, the industrial
share of output typically rose by 5 to 10 percent. In the socialist LDCs,

12. T. C. Liu, "Quantitative Trends in the Economy," in Eckstein, Galenson, and Liu,
Economic Trends.
13. Dwight Perkins, "Looking Inside China: An Economic Reappraisal," *Problems
of Communism* 22 (May–June 1973): 1–13.

Table 4. Shares of Major Sectors in Net National Product,
China, 1933, 1952, and 1957
(Percent)

	Agriculture	Industry	Services
1933	56.9	22.0	21.1
1952	46.1	29.0	24.9
1957	38.6	37.9	23.5

on the other hand, the increase was of the order of 20 points. In consequence, by 1970, industry bulked considerably larger in the output mix of the socialist LDCs—typically above 50 percent, compared with 25 to 35 percent in the nonsocialist group. The other striking difference is in the relative size of the service sector. The median size of this sector in the nonsocialist LDCs is about 40 percent of national output, compared with 20 to 25 percent in the socialist countries. This difference doubtless arises partly from socialist de-emphasis of personal, repair, and business services. But it may also be due partly to the fact that, in the nonsocialist LDCs, this "spongy" sector absorbs a good deal of the pervasive underemployment. In the labor-scarce socialist economies, on the other hand, labor tends to be sucked out of both services and agriculture to permit rapid expansion of industrial employment.

Output by End Uses

Estimates on this point are less precise than those for output by sector of origin. Alton reports GCF-GNP ratios of about 30 percent for Poland and Hungary in the early 1970s.[14] The UN Economic Commission for Europe estimates that, for the years 1965–68, the GCF-GNP ratio averaged 32 percent in Bulgaria and Hungary.[15] Ernst gives estimates of 27 percent for Hungary, 28 percent for Poland, and 41 percent for Bulgaria for the years 1960–63.[16] Montias presents a figure of 34 percent for Rumania as early as 1953,[17] with indications that the rate was higher in subsequent years.

These differing estimates may reflect different definitions of capital

14. Alton, "Economic Growth," in *Reorientations*, p. 259.

15. United Nations, *Economic Survey of Europe, 1968*, 1969, pp. 144–45.

16. Maurice Ernst, "Postwar Economic Growth in Eastern Europe," in *New Currents in Soviet-type Economies*, ed. George R. Feiwel (Scranton, Pa.: International Textbook Company), p. 93.

17. Montias, *Economic Development*, p. 27.

formation as well as data inadequacies. One can still conclude, how-ever that capital formation rates were much higher by 1970 than they had been twenty years earlier—and much higher also than the 15-to-20-percent rates prevailing in our sample of successful nonsocialist LDCs. For that matter, the East European rates are above the general level of those for the mature capitalist economies, which averaged 23 percent over the decade 1955–65.[18] Considering that the East Euro-pean countries have a lower income level than the capitalist economies, one might expect them to also have lower capital formation rates. The fact that their rates are actually a good deal higher testifies to both the importance they attach to capital formation and the effectiveness of their mechanisms for achieving it.

There is, however, something of a puzzle here. The East European countries have been investing a substantially higher proportion of national output than either the mature capitalist countries or the suc-cessful nonsocialist LDCs. Yet on average they have not achieved a higher rate of GNP increase. As a matter of arithmetic, this means that the ICOR has been higher in Eastern Europe. Ernst has calcu-lated,[19] for example, that over the period 1951–64 the ICOR averaged 5.0 in Poland, 5.1 in Bulgaria, 5.3 in Hungary, 6.1 in East Germany, and 6.7 in Czechoslovakia. This compares with 3.9 in Italy, 4.1 in France, and 4.6 in West Germany. Moreover, ICORs in Eastern Europe in the 1960s were higher than those in the 1950s, indicating diminishing returns to investment.

Such calculations do not reveal *why* the socialist LDCs have gotten relatively low returns on their investment. One can surmise that continuing year after year to pump most of the new capital into already capital-rich industries will yield lower returns than would a more balanced allocation. One must also consider that supplies of the main complementary factor, labor, have been rising at a decreasing rate because of the combination of slow population growth and progressive exhaustion of the agricultural reservior. In addition, the kinds of microinefficiency noted early are not favorable to high returns on investment. So, although these economies are capable of mounting a massive capital-accumulation effort, they do not reap the returns that such an effort would seem to warrant.

With the capital-formation proportion rising, consumption must

18. Calculations by the author from the UN *Yearbook of National Accounts Statistics.*
19. Ernst, "Postwar Economic Growth," in *New Currents*, ed. Feiwel, p. 95.

decline in relative importance. It is interesting that this appears to be true of collective consumption as well as of personal consumption. Output of public goods does not seem to have risen more rapidly than that of private consumer goods. Relative decline in consumption, of course, it almost a definition of economic growth; but in the socialist LDCs, this decline has been unusually rapid, and the consumption share of GNP is well below that in our group of successful nonsocialist LDCs.

The relative decline of personal consumption under socialism reflects, first, the disappearance of small-scale service, repair, and handicraft enterprises that provide an important part of personal consumption in nonsocialist countries. These are regarded as relics of capitalism and so are usually abolished. Their functions could conceivably be carried on by small-scale socialist enterprises, but this would run counter to the ideological bias against service outputs and to the preference for large production units that are more easily fitted into the framework of a centrally planned economy. A second factor is the relatively slow growth of agriculture and, within agriculture, a preference for industrial raw materials and export products over domestic foodstuffs. Finally, the small allocations of new capital to consumer-goods industries, even if partially offset by larger allocations of labor, mean a slower rate of expansion than would occur in a market economy in response to income elasticities of demand.

Where total output is rising rapidly, however, shrinkage of the personal-consumption share is quite compatible with rising consumption levels. It seems clear that per capita consumption in Eastern Europe by the late 1960s was well above the level of 1950 or of 1938.[20] Concretely, this increase has shown up in a higher proportion of calories derived from animal sources and decreased importance of potatoes and other starchy food in the diet; increased per capita supplies of cloth and clothing; a rapid increase in per capita supplies of radios, television sets, refrigerators, washing machines, and other consumer durables; and substantial improvement in health and educational facilities.

The course of events in China has been broadly similar. There, too,

20. In the Joint Economic Committee, 1970, report on Eastern Europe, in addition to the Alton article see Terence E. Byrne, "Levels of Consumption in Eastern Europe," pp. 297–316. The Montias study of Rumania contains information not only on Rumanian living standards but on per capita consumption of selected consumer goods in the other East European countries (Montias, *Economic Development*, pp. 49–51).

the capital formation rate jumped sharply after 1949. Yeh estimates[21] that the GDCF-GNP ratio, measured in constant 1957 prices, averaged 7.4 percent during 1931–36 and 24.0 percent during 1952–57. Ishikawa's estimates for the 1950s are also in the 20–25-percent range.[22] Comparable data for more recent years are not available. But Perkins estimates that, from 1957 to 1972, the output of heavy industry rose at about 10 percent a year, compared with 4 percent a year for consumer-goods manufacturing, and that the share of heavy industry in GNP was twice as high in 1972 as in 1957. Granted that part of this increased output went for military purposes and that the output of heavy industry does not measure construction and other components of capital formation, the data suggest that the capital formation rate today is probably even higher than it was in the 1950s.

In China, too, shrinkage of the consumption share of output has not meant a decline in living standards. On the contrary, a slow but perceptible improvement is evident, taking the same general forms as in Eastern Europe: rapid expansion of educational facilities; marked improvement of health services in rural as well as urban areas; some diversification of diet in the direction of fruits, vegetables, and animal products; improvement in the availability and variety of clothing; provision of low-cost mass transportation; and an increase in supplies of such consumer durables as watches, radios, and bicycles.

SECTOR PERFORMANCE: AGRICULTURE AND INDUSTRY

Agriculture

Gregor Lazarcik, as part of the East European project at Columbia University, has assembled a variety of output measures: total agricultural output, including fodder and other intermediate goods put back into agriculture; output of agricultural end products for consumption or industrial use; value added in agriculture after deducting production expenses; and net value added after allowing for depreciation.[23] These show somewhat different results. Inputs of fertilizer, machinery, pesti-

21. See his paper "Capital Formation" in *Economic Trends*, ed. Eckstein, Galenson and Liu (Chicago: Aldine Publishing Co., 1968).

22. Shigeru Ishikawa, *National Income and Capital Formation in Mainland China* (Tokyo: Institute of Asian Economic Affairs, 1965).

23. For a detailed discussion, see Gregor Lazarcik, "Agricultural Output and Productivity in Eastern Europe," in *Reorientations*, pp. 328–93.

Table 5. Average Annual Growth Rates of Final Product in Agriculture, Selected East European Countries, 1950–1972
(Percent)

	Bulgaria		Hungary		Poland		Rumania		Yugoslavia	
	Crops	Animal prods.	Crops	Animal prods.	Crops	Animal prods.	Crops	Animal prods.	Crops	Animal prods.
Output	3.6	4.9	2.1	3.3	2.8	2.8	2.9	3.9	3.5	4.1
Output per hectare of agricultural land	3.3	4.6	2.5	3.6	3.0	3.1	2.6	3.6	3.4	4.0
Output per worker employed in agriculture	7.2		5.8		2.7		5.1		5.5	

cides, and so on have risen a good deal faster since 1948 than has output of agricultural end products. Thus, the average annual rate of increase in value added, country by country, runs about one percentage point below the rate of increase in end products. We nevertheless select the latter figure as most indicative of the adequacy of agricultural supplies for consumption or industrial use.

In interpreting the data in table 5, one should bear in mind that the rate of increase in food output for domestic consumption is somewhat below that of total output. Part of crop output consists of industrial raw materials, which have increased with disproportionate speed. Moreover, these countries have continued to be important food exporters, foodstuffs comprising 20 to 35 percent of total exports as of the mid-1960s. Even so, consumable supplies have increased at rates well above the typical 1 percent population growth rate. Reports of food shortages in Eastern Europe do not necessarily indicate physical inadequacy of supplies. Rather, as Kozlowski argues,[24] they result from the excess of money demand characteristic of socialist economies, which, given the limited supply of manufactured consumer goods and the system of fixed retail prices, tends to show up as excess demand for foodstuffs.

The rate of output growth has varied among countries. Low-income Bulgaria and Rumania raised output faster than higher-income Hungary. (Czechoslovakia and East Germany, not shown here, had markedly lower growth rates for agricultural output and traded manufactured exports for food imports on a substantial scale.) There is no striking difference between socialist countries with collectivized agriculture and those (Poland, Yugoslavia) that continued to rely mainly on private agriculture. The latter group, however, shows a markedly lower growth rate for material inputs to agriculture; so in terms of value added their performance is somewhat superior.

There was little change in agricultural acreage in these countries, and output increases reflect almost entirely higher yields per hectare. By 1972, yields of most crops, particularly wheat and sugar beets, were well above the 1934–38 level, though they remained below the current level of more advanced economies such as West Germany.[25] The fact that output per worker rose faster than yields reflects a marked shrink-

24. Z. Kozlowski, "Agriculture in the Economic Growth of the East European Solcialist Countries," in *Agriculture in Development Theory*, ed. Reynolds, pp. 411–50.
25. Lazarcik, in Joint Economic Committee, 1970, pp. 502–03.

age of the agricultural labor force under the pressure of intense labor demand in industry. Compared with 1938, employment in agriculture in 1972 had fallen by 25 percent in Rumania, 30 percent in Poland, 40 percent in Yugoslavia, 46 percent in Hungary, and 51 percent in Bulgaria.

China differs widely from Eastern Europe in agricultural traditions and resource endowments. Although the land area is vast, only about 11 percent of this area is suitable for crop cultivation; and much of that land does not have the level topography, soil characteristics, and controlled water supply needed for high agricultural yields. Population pressure is severe, and the rate of natural increase is double the European level. Thus, despite rapid industrialization, the agricultural population of working age has continued to increase. Between 1949 and 1960 it is estimated to have risen from 257 million to 293 million,[26] and it must be substantially larger today. This has meant increasing labor inputs per hectare, with consequent downward pressure on the marginal productivity of labor. Modern inputs to agriculture are also much scarcer than in Eastern Europe or the Soviet Union.

Even under these difficult conditions, China has managed to raise agricultural output somewhat faster than its population has grown. Output growth has been erratic, because of political disturbances and policy shifts as well as normal weather variations.[27] The Great Leap Forward resulted in the establishment of a good many communes of excessive size, produced what turned out to be an overcentralization of production decisions in the hands of top commune officials, abolished farmers' private plots, and diverted much effort to ill-advised rural industries (along with more promising ones that have survived). There was a marked drop in agricultural output from 1958 to 1961, which, accentuated by bad weather, had a ripple effect on consumer-goods industries using agricultural raw materials.

The Chinese leadership responded by a marked shift to the policy of "walking on two legs," Under this policy, some of the largest communes were dissolved into smaller units, production decisions were returned to the village (or "production team") level, private plots were reinstituted, and more investment was allocated to agriculture. By 1963, output had regained the 1958 level and has continued to

26. Eckstein, Galenson, and Liu, *Economic Trends*, p. 345.
27. For a good historical review, see Alva L. Erisman, "China: Agricultural Development, 1949–71," in *Reorientations*, pp. 112–46.

grow at a moderate rate, agriculture having apparently been shielded from the Cultural Revolution, whose impact was felt mainly in the cities.

On the average, agricultural output since 1949 has risen at about 2.5 percent per year. Compared with a population growth rate of 2 percent, this has allowed a modest margin for dietary improvement— some diversification into fruits and vegetables, a slow increase in availability of animal proteins. Increased output has not come from any one dramatic breakthrough but rather from gradual progress in a variety of directions.

(1) There has been an extension of irrigation and water-control systems, partly from river sources but also through pumping systems on individual farms. The area rated as "stable, high-yield farmland" was about doubled between 1957 and 1971, amounting in the latter year to about 12 percent of national acreage.

(2) Controlled irrigation has permitted both intensification of cultivation and an increase in multiple cropping. Thus, although cultivated acreage in China has increased little, there has been a substantial increase in cropped acreage.

(3) Considerable effort has been put into seed selection and simple crossing experiments by peasant farmers, leading to improved indigenous varieties. There has also been an effort to exchange improved varieties among regions, rather reminiscent of Japan during 1880–1910.

(4) Supplies of modern inputs have risen at a rapid percentage rate, though from a small base. There have been large imports of fertilizers, and more recently of turnkey fertilizer factories, mainly from Japan. There is also widespread production of fertilizer in small-scale plants on individual communes. Perkins estimates this at about 60 percent of China's total fertilizer output in 1971.

Since the early 1960s, too, government policies toward agriculture have been markedly more favorable than in the 1950s—and distinctly more favorable than traditional Soviet policies. Procurement prices for grain and other major crops have been raised moderately since 1960, while prices of manufactures have tended downward, so that agriculture's terms of trade have been improving. Direct taxation of agriculture is moderate, currently taking about 6 percent of gross agricultural output. This percentage has declined over time because assessments, which are based on "normal yields," lag behind the growth of output capacity. For nonkey products (vegetables, fruits, poultry, eggs, pigs, milk, fish, forestry products), the communes have a high degree of autonomy. Delivery contracts are made directly with municipal trading authorities in nearby cities, at locally negotiated prices. Produce from private plots can also be traded at local farmers' markets. This favorable policy stance must have contributed to the rise in farm output.

With regard to agriculture's contributions to economic development, the system has generated a sufficient food surplus to feed the growing urban population. There has probably been some financial transfer out of agriculture, but on a more moderate scale than in other socialist economies. The labor transfer has also been moderate, as we shall explain when we consider the employment situation.

How does the agricultural performance of the socialist LDCs compare with that of the successful nonsocialist group? It will be recalled from chapter 11 (table 1) that, during the 1960s, the median rate of increase in food output in the nonsocialist group was about 6 percent per year. The data in table 6 of this chapter are not precisely comparable, because they include industrial crops as well as food crops, and because we do not have weights for animal versus crop outputs. Nevertheless, they still warrant a judgment that food output in the East European group grew at between 3 and 4 percent per year. We must remember, however, that in most of the nonsocialist LDCs the increase in output came partly (in some countries primarily) from expansion of acreage, whereas the East European countries had to rely on increases in yields. Thus, the performance of the East European nation is not prima facie inferior. We should remember also that population in the nonsocialist LDCs was growing at close to 3 percent per year, compared with 1 percent in the socialist countries. Thus, food availability per capita was growing at a comparable rate in the two groups.

In China, on the other hand, food availability per capita grew at a rate distinctly below that of either the East European countries or the successful nonsocialist countries—a rate closer to that of India, which has somewhat similar characteristics of ancient agricultural practices, dense settlement, low income level, and still-limited availability of modern inputs.

Industry

We have already noted the strong bias of the socialist LDCs toward industrial development, leading to a GNP composition in which the industrial sector bulks relatively larger than it does in nonsocialist

countries of comparable size and per capita income. Within the industrial sector, there is a tendency to push heavy industry in preference to
light industry, leading to a rapid increase in its relative weight. This is
rationalized by a supposed "natural law of socialist development,"
emphasized by Stalin as a policy guide, which holds that balanced
growth requires the output of Marx's department I (capital goods) to
rise at a higher rate than that of department II (consumer goods).

This tendency stands out clearly in Montias's data for Rumania
(table 6).[28] The output of power, metals, machinery, chemicals, and
building materials grew very rapidly. Since these industries were
expanding from a small base, the high percentage rates of increase do
not necessarily indicate heavy weight in the economy. Other tables in
the Montias study, however, indicate that, as early as 1955, the first
seven industries in table 6 (roughly, "heavy industry") provided more
than half of all industrial employment and owned about three-quarters
of all fixed assets in industry.[29]

It is of course natural for heavy industry to grow faster than light
industry in an industrializing economy. This normal pattern of industrialization has been examined by Hoffman and, more recently, by
Chenery and others.[30] Paul Gregory has analyzed output patterns in
the Soviet Union and the East European countries as of the early
1960s to see how far they deviate from average behavior in nonsocialist
countries.[31] For the East European countries, he finds that (excluding
East Germany) the manufacturing share of GNP is, on the average,
about 5 percent higher than one would expect for countries of this
size and income level. (In East Germany, the manufacturing share is
a remarkable 24 percent above normal.) When the manufacturing
sector is decomposed, the heavy manufacturing-total manufacturing
ratio is 10 to 15 percent above normal. These economies might thus be
characterized as "prematurely heavy-industry oriented." Gregory finds
that they are also abnormally autarchic, confirming Pryor's earlier
findings.

The deviations of the East European economies from the standard
pattern are strikingly similar to those for the Soviet Union, confirming

28. Montias, *Economic Development*, p. 13.

29. Ibid., p. 34.

30. See in particular Hollis B. Chenery, "Patterns of Industrial Growth," *American
Economic Review* (September 1960): 624–54.

31. Paul Gregory, *Socialist and Nonsocialist Industrialization Patterns: A Comparative
Appraisal* (New York: Frederick A. Praeger, 1970).

Table 6. Output Indices for Rumanian Manufacturing, 1938, 1948, and 1963
(1938 = 100)

Branch	Output Index	
	1948	*1963*
Electric power	133	1,034
Fuel	78	245
Ferrous metallurgy	107	876
Nonferrous metallurgy	68	809
Machine building, metal working	87	1,063
Chemicals	117	2,060
Building materials	119	825
Lumber and woodworking	84	374
Cellulose and paper	118	486
Glass and ceramics	141	705
Textiles	86	393
Leather and hides	128	848
Food	82	434
Soap and cosmetics	89	422
Clothing	123	1,000
Printing and bookbinding	131	822
All industries	90	575

that they have followed a similar development strategy despite their much smaller economic size. Further, neither time-series nor cross-section analysis reveals any tendency for convergence toward the non-socialist output pattern. The deviations seem to represent, not just the drastic shifts that might be expected during an initial "big push" in the industrial sector, but a continuing difference in growth strategy.

There are two other interesting features of socialist manufacturing development. The first is the virtual absence of a small-scale industrial sector. Private handicraft workshops are (except in Yugoslavia) prohibited as remnants of capitalism. The design of socialist enterprises seems to reflect a belief that long-run average total cost curves slope downward indefinitely, so that, from a production standpoint, bigger is always better.

But although there is no dualism in scale, there is dualism with respect to the factor proportions characteristic of heavy and light industry. We noted earlier the tendency for capital to be channeled into heavy manufacturing and power, with consumer-goods manufacturing kept on short rations. Heavy industry is also favored in labor recruitment, through higher wage scales and priority in the placement of school leavers and workers passing through state employment

Table 7. Chinese Industrial Production by Sector, 1952 and 1970

	1952	1970
Index:		
Total industrial production	100	388–449
Fuels and power	100	567–655
Industrial materials	100	669–773
Machinery	100	570–659
Light industry	100	202–234
Relative shares:		
Total industrial production	100	100
Fuels and power	12	17
Industrial materials	20	34
Machinery	13	20
Light industry	56	29

agencies. But labor is (relatively) not as scarce as capital, and so light industry does not suffer as seriously in labor as in capital allocations. The result, as Montias points out in the Rumania case, is a difference in capital-labor ratios that tends to widen over time.

The capital-to-labor ratios of industries that were relatively capital intensive, such as power, petroleum, mining, and nonferrous metals tended to rise. The capital-to-labor ratios of labor-intensive industries, such as machine building, lumber, and textiles, fell even below their previous levels.[32]

Chinese industrialization policy has been orthodox with regard to emphasis on heavy industry, but it has been innovative in several other respects. The unusually rapid growth of heavy industry over the period 1952–70 is apparent from table 7, which gives the distribution of industrial output by major sectors.[33] Innovation is apparent in the regional distribution of production, the relatively great decentralization of production planning and control, and the emphasis on small-scale, rural-based industries managed by the people's communes.

32. Montias, *Economic Development*, p. 35.
33. These estimates are from Robert M. Field, "Chinese Industrial Development, 1949–70," in *People's Republic of China: An Economic Assessment* (Washington: Joint Economic Committee, 92nd Cong., 2 sess., May 1972). See also Kang Chao, "Policies and Performance in Industry," in Eckstein, Galenson, and Liu, *Economic Trends*, pp. 549–96.

   Pre-1949 industrialization was carried out in good measure under foreign auspices and centered on a few treaty ports, particularly Tientsin, Shanghai, and Canton. As of 1949, about three-quarters of all industrial output came from seven coastal provinces. The new regime considered this economically disadvantageous, since domestic raw materials (and markets) were more widely dispersed and both materials and products had to travel long distances on an overloaded transportation network. The danger of military invasion, which in the 1950s was thought to come mainly from the sea, also suggested the wisdom of dispersing industry toward the interior provinces. Since the early 1950s, then, more than half of new industrial investment has been allocated to the interior, and this has gradually altered the geographic distribution of output. By 1970, the proportion of industrial output coming from the coastal provinces had fallen to about 55 percent.

   The initial organization of industry was quite centralized, in traditional Soviet fashion, with most industries grouped under ministries located in Peking. But during 1957–58, a sweeping decentralization was carried out that, despite subsequent zigzags of policy, has persisted in broad outline to the present time. Only a few industries, mainly those producing military end products, remain under direct Peking control. The great majority of industrial enterprises operate under provincial and county governments, guided by plans drafted at those levels. Central plans are concerned mainly with balancing interprovincial commodity flows.

   The most original feature of Chinese economic organization is the people's commune, which is simultaneously an agricultural production unit, an industrial production unit, and (under the county) the basic unit of local government. Although the vision of backyard iron smelters in every village has understandably abated, there has been substantial development of industries that can operate efficiently on a relatively small scale. These rural industries produce partly for farm use—tractor and implement repair shops, small hand tools, fertilizer, bricks, cement, power generating units, electric motors, water pumps. Perkins estimates that in the early 1970s about 60 percent of China's chemical fertilizer output, and close to half its cement output, came from these small enterprises. In addition, they turn out consumer goods for off-farm sale and even for export.

   In this emphasis on small-scale, labor-intensive industries, China differs sharply from Soviet-East European practice and comes closer to the pattern of Japan from 1880 to 1910 or of many nonsocialist LDCs today.

INCOME DISTRIBUTION AND EMPLOYMENT

Growth analysis tends to emphasize output. But I should not conclude without a word on employment and income distribution, which in the 1970s have been increasingly emphasized as criteria of successful development. Here I shall emphasize particularly the experience of China, which in income level is most nearly comparable to the nonsocialist LDCs and which, because of its already dense population, might be considered to have the most severe employment problem.[34]

Income Distribution

It is not easy to compare personal income distribution in socialist and nonsocialist economies. In the socialist economies, a wider range of basic-consumption items are provided either free or at controlled and subsidized prices, so that the distribution of money incomes is not a reliable guide to real-income distribution. Further, income taxes are either low or (as in the case of China) nonexistent, while in the nonsocialist economies the pretax and posttax distributions are distinctly different. Finally, for the socialist countries we have very little of the household survey information on which conclusions about personal distribution usually rely.

The UN Economic Commission for Europe has assembled data for a number of East and West European countries, which make possible a rough comparison of the distribution of urban wage-salary incomes only.[35] The percentage of all (pretax) wage and salary income received by the top 5 percent of households was as follows: United Kingdom, 13.2 percent; West Germany, 13.6 percent; Netherlands, 18.8 percent; France, 19.0 percent; Sweden, 16.2 percent; Hungary, 10.4 percent; Czechoslovakia, 9.8 percent; East Germany, 9.0 percent; Poland, 12.0 percent.

34. The comments on China draw on my article, "China as a Less Developed Economy," *American Economic Review*, (June 1975): 418–28.
35. United Nations, Economic Commission for Europe, *Incomes in Postwar Europe*, Geneva, 1967, chap. 6, p. 21 and chap. 9, pp. 23–26. Data are not for the same year for every country but relate to years in the late 1950s and early 1960s.

The Chenery-Ahluwalia study, on the other hand, emphasizes the income share received by the lowest 40 percent of the population.[36] The percentages for selected countries were as follows: Sweden, 14.0; West Germany, 15.4 percent; United Kingdom, 18.8 percent; United States, 19.7 percent; Japan, 20.7 percent; Poland, 23.4 percent; Hungary, 24.0 percent; Bulgaria, 26.8 percent; Czechoslovakia, 27.6 percent.

A look at either the top or the bottom of the distribution, therefore, suggests that income distribution is distinctly more equal in the socialist countries than it is in the mature capitalist economies; and it would follow that it is more equal than in the nonsocialist LDCs.

Concerning China, only fragments of information are available; but it appears that, despite the egalitarian outlook of the political leadership, substantial income differences remain. There are wide differences in per capita income among the rural communes, which are related to differences in soil fertility, water availability, climate, distance to urban markets, and other factors. Perkins reports a 1965 survey of thirteen communes that revealed that income per worker in the richest commune was 3.4 times as high as in the poorest. The average level of rural incomes is substantially below that of urban incomes. Within the urban sector, monthly incomes range from 30 to 40 yuan a month for an unskilled factory worker to 110 yuan for a skilled worker and as much as 400 yuan for a top civil servant for university professor.

The Chinese have succeeded, however, in cutting off the extreme "tails" of the income distribution. There are no longer any rich people —no large houses, private automobiles, staffs of servants, expensive foreign vacations, conspicuous displays of luxury. Nor are there any beggars or destitute people. No one is allowed to fall below a minimum level of living. Abolition of poverty in this sense, in a still poor and backward economy, is surely a major accomplishment.

The devices used for poverty elimination include: (1) free education and virtually free medical care; (2) a pricing system that discriminates in favor of basic food and clothing items, apartment rents, public utility services, public transportation, and other essential items and that is reinforced by rationing of food grains, vegetable oils, cloth, and housing space; (3) an incomes policy that involves raising the lowest wage rates from time to time while leaving higher rates un-

36. Hollis Chenery and others, *Redistribution With Growth*, (New York: Oxford University Press, 1974), pp. 8–9.

changed; (4) high demand for labor plus elimination of sex discrimination in employment, which means that city families are usually two-income families whose combined earnings are sufficient to buy the minimum bundle of necessities; and (5) special provision for the aged, including a retirement pension equal to 70 percent of previous earnings plus old people's homes for those unable to live with children. The traditional Chinese family system, under which young people live with the family and contribute to its income until marriage, and old people remain within the family unit, is also helpful in solving the familiar American problem of the isolated, impoverished individual.

Although inequalities above the minimum remain substantial, the thrust of government policy is toward whittling down these inequalities gradually over the years. The continuing increase in farm procurement prices is intended to reduce the rural-urban income gap. Wage adjustments in the city typically involve raising rates for the lowest two or three labor grades without raising the top of the structure, thus compressing occupational differentials. Gradual expansion of the supply of subsidized necessities works in the direction of equalizing real incomes.

Employment

In the socialist economies, under excess-demand conditions, the demand for labor is consistently high. This tends to raise labor force participation rates, particularly for women;[37] reduce unemployment to a low, frictional level; and suck labor out of agriculture at an accelerated rate, reducing labor slack and raising output per worker in that sector. In Bulgaria, Hungary, Poland, and Rumania between 1950 and 1968, the economically active population increased by about 8 million people; but the number employed in agriculture fell by more than 3 million. Thus, about 11 million workers were available for redeployment, of whom about half went into industry and about half into other nonagricultural activities.

Particularly interesting is the case of China. In 1949, China was already a densely populated country with much open unemployment and widespread rural underemployment. Since 1949, population and

---

37. For data on labor force participation in the East European countries, see United Nations, *Incomes in Postwar Europe*, chap. 8; United Nations, *Economic Survey of Europe, 1968*, chap. 3; and U.S. Congress, Joint Economic Committee, *Economic Developments in Countries of Eastern Europe* (Washington: Government Printing Office, 1970), pp. 197–200.

the labor force have continued to increase at about 2 percent per year. Yet, Chinese leaders today assert that labor in China is scarce and fully employed. Is this claim correct, and, if so, what have been the main sources of additional employment?

Unlike the nonsocialist LDCs, China has effective control over excessive rural-urban migration. The policy instruments employed in the cities are: (1) control of hiring. Enterprises may not recruit workers directly but must apply to a municipal employment bureau. If an enterprise asks for additional labor, the first response is to urge it to get more output from its present labor force. Second, the bureau tries to make sure that the potential labor supply from the existing urban population is being fully utilized. Only as a last resort will new workers be accepted from the countryside; (2) control of housing allocations. A would-be migrant from the country who applies for an apartment in the city is asked, "Do you have a job?" If the answer is no, he is back to square one; (3) the food and clothing rationing system. Every citizen has a "ration book location." To change this requires lengthy paperwork, and permission is given only for good cause. This network of controls makes it almost impossible to be unemployed in the city.

Not only are there restraints on rural-urban migration, but the flow of labor is sometimes in the other direction. There have been years recently in which the number of new jobs available in Canton or Shanghai was insufficient to accommodate all the school leavers. In such a situation, the labor surplus is simply dispatched to the country for farm work.

The effectiveness of migration policy is suggested by the fact that the proportion of Chinese population living in rural areas has been holding steady at about 80 percent, instead of falling as one might expect in the course of economic growth.

But does not the damming up of population in the countryside mean simply that full employment in the city is achieved at the cost of growing rural underemployment? In many less developed countries, such underemployment is a chronic and growing problem. The Chinese assert that, on the contrary, their rural labor force is fully employed and that labor is scarce. If the Chinese claim is correct, the number of man-hours being worked in the rural sector today must be much larger than in 1949.

It appears that there has indeed been a major increase in rural employment since 1949. The main sources of additional employment have been:

1. A marked increase in the labor time devoted to infrastructure activities such as reforestation and the building of roads, water-control and irrigation systems, land terraces, schools, hospitals, public buildings, and housing. These activities are organized mainly by a commune; but large-scale projects may be planned at higher levels and draw labor from several communes. The work is done mainly in the off-season and helps reduce seasonal underemployment.

2. These infrastructure activities, especially improved water control, have allowed a considerable shift of acreage from single to double cropping. They also make possible greater use of fertilizer and more sophisticated input packages, which substantially increase crop yields. All this requires more labor.

3. Particularly in areas near city markets, there has been a diversification of production into fruits and vegetables, poultry, eggs, milk, and meat. These products are more labor-intensive than grain.

4. As already noted, the communes are industrial as well as agricultural producing units. As much as 20 percent of the available labor time in some communes near large cities is devoted to industrial activities, though the average for the country as a whole is probably closer to 5 percent. At seasonal peaks of harvest activity, most of these industrial workers go into the fields; but their main activity is factory work, which helps fill in the seasonal valleys in the agricultural production cycle.

5. The expansion of education, health, and other public services in the rural areas absorbs substantial amounts of labor. Education is very labor-intensive, using the time of students as well as teachers. Medical and paramedical personnel in a typical commune run into the dozens. Administrative staffs, which perform local-government as well as production-management functions, are also substantial, though all except a few of the top commune officials also engage regularly in farm labor.

All in all, it appears that the claims of full employment in the rural sector are valid. Some of this employment, to be sure, has a low marginal yield per man-hour—for example, creating new farmland by carrying baskets of earth from some other area. The available labor time is apparently regarded as a fixed factor, and any small addition it can make to output is considered worthwhile. Until there is more demand for labor in urban industries, its use in low-productivity rural activities is sound social policy.

A SUMMARY WORD

What conclusions emerge from a comparison of socialist and nonsocialist success cases?

1. The socialist LDCs have managed to raise their GNP at about the same rate as the successful nonsocialist LDCs. This underscores what should by now be a widely accepted conclusion: that growth acceleration is feasible (though not guaranteed) along either socialist or capitalist lines. A political preference for one or the other of these routes should not lead one to deny the existence of a viable alternative.

2. Although the directions of structural change are similar in the two groups, the tempo of change is faster in the socialist LDCs, leading quickly to a characteristically different pattern of national output. The capital formation rate is raised to levels well above those prevailing in nonsocialist LDCs. The industrial sector swells up with unusual speed and with a strong bias toward capital as against consumer goods. The socialist growth pattern is also strongly inward-looking, leading to disproportionately low participation in foreign trade. Cases of export-led growth do not occur.

3. Considering the massive effort in the socialist countries to mobilize human resources and accumulate physical capital, one would a priori expect their growth rate to be higher than it is. Why is this not so? The answer has to be substantial inefficiency in resource use, arising from such things as misallocation of capital among economic sectors; overcentralization of decision making, leading to bureaucratic slowness and mismanagement; arbitrary pricing, lack of accurate cost calculations, and overreliance on physical targets; weak efficiency incentives for lower-level management; difficulties in building technical progress, innovation, and quality improvement into a planned (and excess-demand) economy; antiagriculture bias; and antitrade bias, leading to loss of potential gains from specialization and exchange. Socialist performance on these fronts, however, does not need to be as bad as it sometimes has been in the past; and as socialist planners and managers learn from experience, one should expect improvement in microefficiency over time. Nor do I mean to imply that microefficiency is high in the nonsocialist LDCs, where it ranges from rather good in the more successful countries to quite bad in many of the stagnant economies.

4. The socialist LDCs have a superior record with respect to

employment and income distribution. Everyone who can work is able to work. All citizens are assured of a (low) minimum level of living; and inequality above the minimum can be expected to diminish over time.

5. One should be cautious about generalizing for all socialist LDCs, just as for all nonsocialist ones. Chinese leaders would object strongly to being classified with the "revisionists" of Eastern Europe and the Soviet Union; and they have a certain point. In addition to differences of culture and ideology, I have noted substantial differences in economic strategy appropriate to China's great size, population density, and heavily agrarian structure. In its emphasis on agricultural development and small-scale, rural-based industry, China's recent development appears closer to that of Japan from 1880 to 1910 than to East European development from 1950 to 1975.

16

Reflections on Development Policy

Is it not strange to get around to policy only at the end of the road? Should the whole book not have been organized around policy objectives and the means of attaining them? Many books on economic development are organized in this way, reflecting a view that the main thrust of the subject is toward policy prescription.

I do not share this view. Rather, I believe that the relationship of economic research to policy does not differ between developing and mature economies. For poor as well as rich countries, there is merit in Keynes's dictum that "the theory of economics does not furnish a body of settled conclusions immediately applicable to policy. It is a method rather than a doctrine, an apparatus of the mind, a technique of thinking. . . ." Policy advice is a spin-off from an understanding of the economic mechanism. The fact that economic policy in the LDCs is often erratic or misguided stems partly from defects of governmental structure; but it also reflects gaps in our knowledge of how these economies operate. The first duty of the economist is to repair these deficiencies in knowledge, not to tell governments what to do.

Another common misconception is to identify development policy with preparation of a multiyear economic plan. This can be a useful exercise, though its usefulness may be rather different from what appears on the surface. But to do only this is to do very little. Under modern conditions, government's influence is felt throughout the economy, and the range of policy decisions is enormously varied. Most of these decisions are sector-specific or market-specific, though there are also important macro decisions on trade strategy, exchange rates, wage and interest levels, monetary expansion, and other matters. It is not clear that there is a useful distinction between development policy and economic policy in general.

What can be said in a few pages about such a wide range of policy issues? We can try to sort out priorities and distinguish issues that are likely to be of prime importance in a typical developing economy. It will also be useful to say something about institutional development.

Some might say that this is not economics; but the point is arguable. Why should economists not take an interest in the design of economic institutions—in economic engineering, if you will—as well as in analyzing behavior within a given institutional framework? In a formative LDC economy, institutional change is important; and we should follow important questions wherever they may lead.

INSTITUTION BUILDING

This phrase in itself implies a paradox. Who is the builder? Presumably, the government. But government *is* the primary economic institution, which may itself be seriously flawed. Who will guard the guardians? Let us solve this problem after the manner of the economist who, stranded on a desert island with a case of canned food, assumed a can opener. Let us assume a government—unified, growth-minded, reasonably efficient—fill in the specifications as you wish. What should this orderly and well-intentioned government do?

Let us be clear that we are discussing a development path that is capitalist in the sense that most productive resources are privately owned and managed. A country may, of course, choose comprehensive state ownership, in which case it will face the opportunities and difficulties examined in chapter 15. But the discussion here will be limited to countries that have opted for the other path.

Is the idea of capitalist development implausible, out of date, even self-contradictory? Alongside the mainstream development literature runs a current of writing by Marxists and other "radical" economists, who contend that development along capitalist lines has done and can do little to increase welfare for the mass of the population. Many countries with a high GNP growth rate continue to face massive underemployment and a highly unequal, even worsening, distribution of personal income. Government, usually dictatorial in form, represents mainly the interests of the richer groups in society; and the rising national income has been distributed disproportionately to those groups.

The argument is often overstated, and usually poorly documented, partly because of the inadequacy of employment and income statistics. But granting it some degree of validity, the question is where does it lead in terms of policy conclusions. An orthodox Marxist might conclude that one cannot speak seriously of improving the condition of the poor within the existing institutional framework. Progress must wait on a revolution, which will bring a Communist party to power.

But many others, including many socialists (in the Western social democratic rather than the Communist tradition), take a gradualist view. They argue that structural reform and welfare improvement are possible without the drastic surgery implied by the revolutionary position. This view, which the writer shares, rests necessarily on judgment, and perhaps partly on hope, rather than on scientific demonstration.

In a mixed economy with a predominant private sector, the higher-income groups will usually have disproportionate influence on government; but their voice need not be as dominant as it has been in the past. The mass of the population can exercise increasing influence, and the instruments of government can be bent toward employment-creating and income-equalizing policies. Looking at economies as diverse as Sweden and Taiwan, it is difficult to justify the Marxist view that a non-communist government *must* act as an agent for oppression of the poor.

If the gradualist view is accepted, it follows that one should try to strengthen the capitalist engine of growth, not as an end in itself, but in order to generate more employment and higher incomes. Over a period of decades, the potential gains to the poor from output growth are much larger than from redistribution alone. An LDC government is well advised to lay out a strategy for stimulating private investment and enterprise, with an eye on the remarkable success story of Japan. In urging this, one can even claim to be true to the spirit of Marx, as distinct from his latter-day exponents. Marx believed that the capitalist stage of development served the necessary historical function of developing large-scale economic organization and high productive capacity so that, on the day of the revolution, there would be something to be socialized. One can share this view even while remaining agnostic about the revolution itself.

Some requirements for development via capitalism were outlined by John Stuart Mill (*Principles*, 1848) in a passage that is not entirely out of date:

> ... The desideration for such a [less developed] country, economically considered, is an increase of industry and of the effective desire of accumulation. The means are, first, a better government; more complete security of property; moderate taxes, and freedom from arbitrary exaction under the name of taxes; a more permanent and more advantageous tenure of land, securing to the cultivator as far as possible the undivided benefits of the industry, skill, and

economy he may exert. Secondly, improvement of the public intel-
ligence. . . . Thirdly, the introduction of foreign arts, which raise
the returns derivable from additional capital . . . and the importation
of foreign capital, which renders the increase of production no
longer exclusively dependent on the thrift or providence of the
inhabitants themselves . . . and by instilling new ideas and breaking
the chains of habit . . . tends to create in them new wants, increased
ambition, and greater thought for the future. These considerations
apply more or less to all the Asiatic populations, and to the less
civilized and industrious parts of Europe, as Russia, Turkey, Spain,
and Ireland.

No contemporary LDC, of course, would wish to be as purely
capitalistic as Britain in 1800 or Japan in 1880. There is now a general
preference for public enterprises in transport and power, in natural-
resource industries, and sometimes in other sensitive or quasi-mono-
polistic areas. But in the sectors where private initiative is allowed to
prevail, government should establish the conditions needed to stimulate
private initiative. These conditions include a legal framework that
protects property, enforces contracts, and permits large-scale corporate
organization. They include attention to the structure of markets, which
cannot be counted on to spring up and improve themselves spontane-
ously. They include allowing markets to function without interference
with market results, except in clear cases of public injury. They include
freedom from excessive taxation, and sudden or arbitrary changes in
the tax system, and freedom from other forms of intervention that
make profits uncertain or precarious.

Such consistency of policy is rare in practice. More commonly,
there is nominal acceptance of private ownership in most sectors; but
this is combined with a shifting maze of regulations that not merely
reduce profits ex post but, more importantly, introduce uncertainty
into estimates of future profit and induce a short time-horizon in
business planning. Capitalists are allowed to exist, but they are not
allowed to realize their economic potential. This is then rationalized
as "shortage of entrepreneurship." Thus, the economy remains on
dead center, with no strong push from either public or private enterprise.

Two particularly important sets of institutions are the landholding
system and the financial structure. Most of the successfully developing
countries have undergone a major land reform (or, as in Mexico, a
revolution) at some point. Though these reforms differ in detail, they

typically involve some combination of: (1) the subdivision of large, often absentee-managed, landholdings into smaller, family-sized farm units; (2) the provision for tenants to become farm owners through long-term government financing; and (3) an arrangement for giving the tenants who remain greater security of tenure, a larger share of output, better access to credit, and greater economic independence. Some countries may be fortunate enough to already have an agrarian structure based on owner-operated units. But where this is not the case, a restructuring of ownership is usually needed for sustained growth of farm productivity and hence for economic development in general.

The importance of financial institutions is dramatized by the case of Japan, where a modern financial structure was created almost *de novo* in a short span of years. A developing country does not need an instant Wall Street. But it does need a central bank; a system of commercial banks that will lend at flexible, market-determined rates; facilities for long-term investment finance, usually including a government development bank; a system of savings institutions providing security and attractive rates of return; and a public market for government securities, which can gradually be extended to cover high-grade private securities.

Another important institution is the government's own budget-making machinery. Government usually produces 10 to 15 percent of national output, and it often accounts for 30 to 40 percent of gross capital formation. We tend to assume that, whatever may be happening in the private sector, the resources flowing through government channels will be allocated rationally. But this cannot be taken for granted. It is quite possible for the allocation to be whimsical, unstable, even corrupt. The critical factor here is the character of the top political leadership. Bad leadership cannot be remedied by any redrawing of organizational charts. But given reasonable competence and continuity of leadership, one can design budget procedures that will aid rational decision making.

POLICY OBJECTIVES: COMPLEMENTARY OR CONFLICTING?

It is now widely accepted that a country's growth performance should be judged not only by the rate of increase in output but also by the rate of increase in employment and by changes in the distribution of personal income. The heavy emphasis on output that prevailed until about 1965 has been replaced by a trinity of objectives: output, employment, and income distribution.

The tradition in Western economics has been to treat these objectives as separable. In one part of a principles text, we examine the requirements for efficient allocation and use of resources, for operating on the production frontier. In another part, we try to remedy lapses from full employment. In still another, we explain the income distribution that emerges from the market economy and then consider—on a second round, as it were—how this distribution can be improved through the fiscal system.

For a developing economy this procedure is not very satisfactory. Underemployment is a continuing rather than a cyclical phenomenon. The problem is to increase the slope of the employment trend line rather than to iron out fluctuations around the trend. Fiscal systems are too weak to perform the redistributional function that they achieve to some extent in the mature economies. If income distribution is to improve at all, it must improve as an integral part of the growth process rather than through adjustments after the fact.

But this poses a problem. Can one define a growth path that will dominate other potential paths with regard to *all three* objectives? Or are we in a trade-off situation that forces a choice between more rapid growth of output or of employment, or between more rapid output growth and more equal distribution of income? If this were an easy question, it would already have been answered; but explorations in this area are still at an early stage. My intuition is that the three objectives are largely complementary and that employment is the key to success on the other two fronts. If one can find ways of absorbing more labor time in productive uses, this will tend to both increase output and equalize income distribution.

By employment, of course, I do not mean digging holes and filling them up again or overstaffing government offices with people who add nothing to output. I mean using additional man-hours in ways that will yield a positive marginal product. The measures commonly suggested to create employment—land redistribution, technical progress in agriculture, development of rural infrastructure, encouragement of small and/or rural-based industries, use of capital-shallowing techniques in large-scale manufacturing, encouragement of labor-intensive exports—will at the same time add to national output.

In a completely aggregative model one can show that, beyond a certain point, efforts to combine more labor with a given capital stock will reduce output rather than increase it. But a less developed economy is not fully integrated, nor is capital completely fungible. Some of the employment-increasing measures listed above involve land use, mobilization of idle labor time, and better organization rather than increased allocations of capital. The traditional argument is relevant mainly to manufacturing; and even within that sector, most LDCs are currently so far to the capital-intensive side of the maximum-output point that they can be advised to pursue capital shallowing with little risk of overshooting.

There is also a complementary relation between employment and income distribution. The poorest groups in these economies are poor because they have no work, little work, or work that yields little output. Anything that enables people to work more, or to work more productively, will help pull up the bottom of the income distribution. This is not all that needs to be done. Expansion of education, which broadens the ownership of human capital and tends to erode wage differentials; restructuring of government tax and expenditure systems; improvement of financial markets, so that the credit system no longer subsidizes only those who are already well off, are also helpful. But a rapid increase in demand for labor is crucial. This will in time push the economy into the labor-scarce category, with the income-equalizing results that follow.

In an employment-oriented program, the agricultural sector is of central importance. First, there are large possibilities for absorption of additional labor time in agriculture—through adoption of higher-yielding plant varieties and the associated input packages, through an increase in irrigation and multiple cropping, through a shift toward more labor-intensive products (such as fruits and vegetables, milk, eggs and poultry), and through construction of agricultural infrastructure. Second, the higher incomes arising from increased agricultural employment will raise demand for outputs of the industry and service sectors, generating a second round of employment in those sectors. Third, given consumption patterns and income elasticities of demand in the lower-income groups, most of the increased income of the newly employed will be spent on foodstuffs, which again requires higher agricultural output. This view of the primacy of agriculture has been argued cogently by John Mellor.[1] Although his discussion relates

1. "Agriculture will dominate an employment-oriented strategy of development because it contains over two-thirds of the labor force, including the bulk of the reserve army of low-productivity labor, produces the principal consumer goods needed to sustain rapid increases in incomes of the newly employed, and may provide a major net stimulus to demand for the output of other sectors." John W. Mellor, *The New Economics of Growth* (Ithaca: Cornell University Press, 1976), p. 22.

specifically to India, the reasoning is applicable to a wide range of developing economies.

The Taiwanese case suggests that a development path can simultaneously yield a high rate of output growth, the elimination of surplus labor, and a growing equality of personal incomes. It also suggests some of the features of such a path: land redistribution to achieve greater equality of ownership, technical assistance to agriculture to reduce the rural-urban income gap, diffusion of industry throughout rural areas, widespread educational opportunities, and an outward-looking policy stance favorable to labor-intensive exports.

MICROECONOMIC POLICIES

There are many more markets in an economy than there are significant economic aggregates. In consequence, the number of microeconomic decisions greatly exceeds the number of macroeconomic decisions. Even decisions conventionally classified as macroeconomic often rest, or at least should rest, on a substructure of micro analysis. Efficient allocation of government expenditure among sectors and purposes requires detailed cost-benefit estimates. Encouragement of industrial growth through tariff protection and other measures requires selectivity among industries, based on detailed estimates of probable competitiveness.

In a developing mixed economy, markets perform, albeit imperfectly, the same functions they perform in a mature economy. Faced with indications of malfunctioning, and in a second- or third-best world, it does not necessarily follow that government should intervene. A micro decision can be negative, a decision to abstain from action. If the decision is to intervene, there is a strategy choice between overriding the market through administrative decisions and redesigning the market to ensure better results. An activist government does not necessarily imply an ever-growing array of detailed regulations, though this often is the result in practice. A substantial body of opinion—and not merely neoliberal opinion—holds that LDC governments tend to overregulate, given the fragility of their administrative structures. Myrdal, certainly not a conventional free-market economist, has made a richly documented argument on this point. In discussing individual policy areas, then, we should be sensitive to possibilities of achieving desired results through markets rather than by superseding them.

Agriculture

I need scarcely reiterate that the food–population balance is the most basic concern of any developing economy. Every country needs to achieve sustained increases in food output. This is true even of successful manufacturing exporters such as Britain and Japan (historically) or Taiwan and South Korea (currently). Even here, holding down food imports through increases in domestic agricultural productivity leaves room for larger imports of capital goods and industrial materials without straining the balance of payments.

The progress of agriculture is affected by a wide array of government actions. A strategic decision that "agriculture matters" is needed as a starting point; but making this meaningful requires oversight and coordination of specific policy decisions, which otherwise may work against each other. Important ingredients of the policy mix include: reform of land tenure systems; pricing of farm outputs; supply and pricing of modern agricultural inputs, notably fertilizers; availability and cost of farm credit; extent and forms of agricultural taxation, including implicit taxes via export duties or the exchange rate system; development of agricultural research and experiment-station systems; adequacy of agricultural extension staffs; development of irrigation works and other water-control systems; improvement of roads, transport facilities, and crop-storage facilities.

Two things are of prime importance: strengthening agricultural research and maintaining income incentives for farmers. One might think that improved agricultural technology could readily be borrowed from the mature economies or from international research centers such as IRRI; but borrowing is a complicated process. Technology always needs to be adapted to specific soil-rainfall-sunshine configurations within countries, regions, and districts. Effective borrowing and adaptation thus depends on a strong local network of research centers and experiment stations. Evenson and others have done cross-sectional analyses of countries and of individual states within India; these analyses suggest a strong relation between agricultural research activity and rates of increase in agricultural productivity. Rates of return to research expenditure are typically very high, suggesting that research is usually underfinanced.

Farmers are capitalists par excellence. Perhaps in no other sector does one find such a predictable response to economic incentives. To call forth a sustained rise in output requires a configuration of infra-structure investment policies, farm input and output price policies, credit policies, and tax policies that permit higher output to be reflected in higher posttax incomes. This often implies simply nonintervention in the market—for example, *not* setting price ceilings on farm output in the interest of urban wage earners, or *not* subjecting agricultural exports to abnormally high rates of taxation. Rising farm output, stimulated by income incentives, provides the best assurance of an increasing flow of tax revenues, rural savings, and food supplies to the cities at stable terms of trade. On the other hand, policies designed simply to squeeze agriculture may lead farmers to take their revenge by reducing their market participation.

Population

Many LDCs still have reserves of unexploited land, which permits them, for the time being, to follow a pattern of extensive growth with minimal improvement of yields per acre. They are, of course, living on borrowed time and will eventually reach the fully settled state that Egypt, India, Bangladesh, Java, and other areas have already reached. In the fully settled countries, continued high rates of population growth pose an urgent problem of food supply, and some countries are threatened with famine and starvation in poor crop years. Even in countries with land reserves, more rapid population growth probably retards increases in income per capita, because a larger fraction of investment in material and human capital is needed just to maintain existing per capita stocks.

The social determinants of fertility are still far from thoroughly explored. In the United States, the popularity of "the new home economics" has stimulated research on fertility behavior. Economic models incorporating the costs and benefits of child production have turned out to have considerable predictive power. Much less work of this sort has been done in the LDCs. But there, too, some research results suggest that large numbers of births may, in part, represent rational calculation rather than lack of contraceptive information or religious taboos. Where infant mortality rates are high, so that ten births may be needed to ensure five surviving children; where children can begin contributing to farm output or earn cash wages at an early age; where the opportunity cost of mothers' time is low because of restricted employment opportunities; where social security systems are undeveloped and parents eventually become dependent on children for support—under such circumstances an economic model might well predict high *desired* birth rates.

The moral is, first, that additional research on LDC fertility behavior would have a high payoff. Second, to the extent that people have large families because they want to have them, provision of contraceptive information and supplies is a necessary but not a sufficient condition for marked reduction in fertility. Changes in the status, education, and employment opportunities of women; growth of school attendance and a rise in the school-leaving age; urbanization; development of old-age pension systems; and other things that change the incentive structure may be of dominant importance over the long run. These are normal accompaniments of economic growth; and a country that can keep its head above water in the short run may eventually enter a demographic transition. A few LDCs have already done so, and further research on their experience would be useful. How far is the decline in birth rates explainable in incentive terms? Is there evidence that it was accelerated appreciably by government population policy?

Industrial Development

In a developing economy, the manufacturing sector is bound to grow in relative importance, but its rate of growth and its commodity composition can be influenced by public policy. The main policy prescription here is selectivity by industries and products to avoid favoring those that require very high effective protection or other subsidies and that are unlikely to develop comparative advantage.

There is a wide variety of specific policies bearing on industrial development. They involve such issues as: whether to admit foreign private investment, and on what terms; the choice of public enterprise versus domestic private enterprise; explicit or implicit policies toward small-scale as against large-scale enterprise; how far to second-guess the market by selecting specific industries as especially worthy of encouragement; the choice of specific promotional instruments— foreign exchange allocations, preferential exchange rates, tariff protection, export bonuses, industrial licensing, preferential credit arrangements; business taxation; and intervention in industrial wage determination, either directly or via policies toward union organization.

To comment on each of these policy areas would carry me far beyond my space limits. Perhaps most important is some sense of overall strategy, some effort to coordinate the numerous government actions that influence industrial growth. In practice, one often finds a confusing mixture of policies that encourage industrial expansion and others that hamper it or seriously distort its direction.

Output of Public Goods

Government faces a problem of allocating current expenditures among general administration, defense and policing, economic purposes such as agricultural and industrial development, and quasi-economic purposes such as education and public health. In some areas, returns are sufficiently intangible that clear economic criteria for allocation are lacking. Actual allocations are influenced by the relative power of cabinet ministers and other noneconomic considerations. Although there is usually some central budgeting machinery, its operation is imperfect. Preparation of budget estimates, allocation decisions, and subsequent expenditure controls do not approach the level of sophistication found in mature economies.

Most countries profess an objective of holding current expenditure below current revenue, thus providing a margin of public saving that can be devoted to investment. Although some countries have done well in this respect, many have not. Upward pressure on the government wage level, often accentuated by pressure for overstaffing, is a major problem.

The larger LDCs face the problem, familiar in the United States, of how to divide production of public goods among central, state, and local governments. There is usually an overcentralization of revenue collection. The revenues thus pulled into the center may be reallocated in part to lower levels of government, or they may not. Fiscal advisers from the mature economies tend to advise collection of a larger percentage of government revenues at the local level, which would permit more of the public works, educational facilities, and other activities to be planned and executed at that level. Ursula Hicks's well-known *Development from Below*[2] gives the rationale of this approach. Such decentralization could increase both the efficiency of decision-making and the citizens' sense of participation in government.

A parallel set of allocation problems arises in the capital budget, which often finances a third or more of national investment. Ideally, a good capital budgeting system should embrace: cost-benefit analysis

2. Ursula K. Hicks, *Development From Below* (Oxford: Clarendon Press, 1961).

of proposed investment projects by a staff of skilled analysts; accurate information on the present degree of completion of ongoing projects; multiyear projections of future capital resources and requirements; the channeling of allocation recommendations through a central authority—a budget bureau, planning board, cabinet office, or whatever; strong presidential leadership capable of enforcing consistency and rationality in allocation decisions; and follow-up controls to ensure consistency of expenditures with budget allocations.

No LDC has such a budget system, and most fall well short of it. Wildavsky's investigations in this area are both discouraging and instructive.[3] But procedures are gradually being improved. The training programs in project evaluation that have been carried on for many years by the IBRD and by regional agencies of the UN have strengthened government staffs in this respect; and overall allocations are based increasingly on a substructure of project analysis.

Tax Structures

The issues here are familiar and not very different from those that arise in the mature economies. How heavily, and by what means, can farmers be taxed without undue reduction of production incentives? How can one develop an enforceable system of personal income taxes, and what is a proper degree of progressivity in the rate structure? What is an optimal level of corporate income taxation, taking into account the impact on investment incentives and resources? Should export taxes be avoided as interfering with a desirable rate of export expansion? And so on and on.

The impact of specific taxes on labor supplies, business saving and investment, and other economic variables can be analyzed in qualitative terms by using standard micro tools. But even in the mature economies, it has proven difficult to translate this analysis into clear quantitative predictions. On many important practical questions—the effect of a progressive income tax on work incentives, the incidence of a payroll tax, or the establishment of a corporate income tax—the authorities speak with an ambiguous voice. The wisdom available for transfer to the LDCs is less than one would wish.

"Taxes" should be interpreted to include transfer payments, or

3. Naomi Caiden and Aaron Wildavsky, *Planning and Budgeting in Poor Countries* (New York: John Wiley & Sons, 1974).

negative taxes. The tax-transfer system, in addition to its incentive and output effects, alters the distribution of income. In mature economies, the fiscal system usually serves to make the distribution of household incomes after taxes and transfers considerably more equal than the pretax distribution.

In the LDCs, however, with their limited ability to collect taxes on income and wealth and their limited development of transfer programs, the fiscal system cannot be expected to make a major contribution to income equality. A reduction in inequality has to be accomplished mainly by steering the economy onto a different growth path. As we argued earlier in the chapter, an employment-oriented growth strategy can lead to greater income equality than would prevail otherwise, and with no sacrifice of output. Beyond this, the most powerful instrument for reducing inequality is the allocation of government expenditure. Heavy allocations to agriculture, education, and health can do much to reduce disparities in real economic welfare between rural and urban families as well as within each sector.

MACROECONOMIC POLICIES

What is a macroeconomic decision? A set of micro decisions may produce additive effects that can be summarized in an economic aggregate; but this does not alter their micro character. For example, government revenues and expenditures can be summarized in budget totals; but this does not alter the fact that tax and expenditure decisions are microeconomic and that analysis of them involves applications of micro theory.

The domain of macroeconomic policy, then, is limited to: (1) policy toward prices that have a pervasive influence throughout the economy, such as the exchange rate, the interest rate, and the industrial wage rate, the rate of monetary expansion also belongs in this category; (2) policies affecting an entire economic sector, such as manufacturing, agriculture, or foreign trade; (3) comprehensive multiyear economic plans intended as a framework for the evolution of the economy over the period in question.

Sectoral Policies

Trade-industrialization strategy is the leading issue in this area. As we have noted in earlier chapters, strategies are conventionally divided into import-substitution and export-promotion types; and these can be regarded as forming a sequence, logically as well as chronologically. A country first develops a strong manufacturing base behind a protective wall, serving the domestic market. Later on, some industries become internationally competitive and begin to export part of their output. This plausible scenario, however, glosses over the question of whether forced import substitution is a necessary prelude to development of export capacity in manufactures. May not excessive protection produce weak, high-cost infants rather than sturdy ones? May not a country get stuck in midstream, with high-cost industries that never achieve export capacity? Why not emphasize production for export from the outset?

The foreign sector is fertile in other problems that, while micro in character, have important macro implications. One such issue, now prominent in international discussion, is the pricing of raw-material exports. Fluctuations in prices (as well as in quantities) can produce sharp fluctuations in an LDC's capacity to import, setting off economic cycles not unlike those set off by investment fluctuations in the mature economies. The remedy usually urged is price stabilization through an international commodity agreement. Space limits prevent our entering into the controversies over the merit and forms of such agreements, on which there is a large literature. They clearly affect resource allocation and income distribution within and between countries; they also affect economic stability and growth.

A similar issue is how an LDC can operate most effectively in the international capital market. A foreign loan brings in real resources, often in specific form and for a specific purpose, and it usually requires eventual repayment in real resources. Although a particular loan transaction can be analyzed in cost-benefit terms, the totality of such transactions affects the balance of payments, the national capital formation rate, and hence the output growth rate. Efficient debtmanship, as I suggested in chapter 8, thus stands high on the list of policy problems confronting an LDC government.

The Exchange Rate

Exchange-rate strategy is closely linked with trade strategy. Maintenance of an overvalued exchange rate taxes exports and subsidizes imports, and it has been a familiar device for transferring income from rural primary producers to the urban sector. Differential exchange rates, and systems of exchange rationing, can serve along with or in lieu of tariff protection as part of an import substitution program.

Any LDC faces a choice of exchange-rate regimes: fixed rates, usually accompanied by occasional devaluations; fixed rates with more frequent—weekly or even daily—devaluations; rates tied to the dollar or some other major currency; managed floats; completely free floats; and other possible variants. In addition to these variations in the way the exchange rate is determined, there are different degrees of intervention and control in the foreign exchange *market*, varying from tight rationing systems to virtually free markets. There is a large literature on the mechanics of exchange control systems and on how they affect trade and domestic production.

Perhaps the most common pattern historically has been maintenance of a fixed rate that, particularly in countries with high inflation rates, becomes increasingly overvalued with the passage of time. This eventually leads to devaluation, after which the cycle is repeated. Devaluation to a realistic exchange rate is often accompanied by liberalization of the foreign exchange market, with the IMF or some other outside agency lending sufficient international reserves to cushion the transition. Such a liberalization package typically has a stimulating effect on exports, including manufactured exports. A recent development has been the adoption by some countries, including Brazil and Colombia, of continuous devaluation or a "gliding peg." This may be partly responsible for recent improvement in the export performance of these countries.

The Interest Rate

The key stylized fact here is that, in the organized money market, lending rates are usually pegged below the shadow rate of interest. This has been true especially in some of the Latin American countries, where inflation rates are so high that the real rate of interest is often negative. Interest rates paid to savers are typically lower than bank lending rates, leading again to negative real rates in some countries. Meanwhile, in the unorganized money market, farmers and small businessmen borrow at very high rates. The adverse effects of this situation have been much discussed: discouragement of saving, credit rationing leading to misallocation of resources, a favored position for the large businessman or farmer relative to the small producer, and a bias toward capital-intensive production methods.

In principle, these distortions are not difficult to correct. Such correction requires raising, or preferably abandoning, legal ceilings on both rates paid to savers and lending rates to business; a simultaneous strengthening of commercial banks and nonbank lending institutions; and liberalization and unification of the money market, leaving credit allocation to be determined by market competition. McKinnon and others argue that development economists, in their concentration on real economic processes, have neglected the growth-promoting potential of an improved financial structure. Countries such as South Korea and Brazil have already done a good deal in this direction.

The Modern Sector Wage Level

Here, the stylized facts run in the opposite direction. Labor employed in factory manufacturing and government is paid substantially more than labor in traditional urban activities or agriculture; and in many countries the industrial real wage has been rising over time despite substantial underemployment.

Labor, of course, is heterogeneous. The high modern-sector wage level produces a long queue of applicants and enables employers to sort out workers of superior education, experience, physique, and motivation. The wage gap in terms of efficiency units of labor is smaller than the crude wage gap. Further, on-the-job training and experience makes the worker increasingly valuable to the employer and raises the cost of turnover. It is now familiar in labor market theory that a high-wage strategy may be offset wholly or partly by a reduction in recruitment, selection, and training costs. Finally, in the presence of a union, high wages—in effect, some sharing with employees of monopoly or oligopoly profits—may be a calculated effort to minimize potential output and profit losses from strikes. On such grounds, one can argue that an apparently large wage gap is not incompatible with rational profit maximization.

All such qualifications aside, however, overpricing of industrial labor seems a common phenomenon; and it has predictable adverse effects: bias toward capital-intensive production methods; reduction of employment opportunities in the modern sector; overstimulation of rural-urban migration and a higher equilibrium level of urban unemployment; and a worsening of income distribution through creation of a small, highly paid elite. All this contrasts unfavorably with early capitalist (and early Soviet) development, which was marked by low real wage levels and a lag of real wages behind productivity increases. Minimum wages were unheard of, and union organization was forbidden or sufficiently discouraged to limit its impact on wages.

There is some question about how much LDC governments can do about the modern-sector wage level; but they are not entirely without instruments. Government is usually a large employer and sometimes even serves as a wage leader for the private sector. Restraint in government's own wage policy can thus do more than anything else to prevent excessive increases in wages. Beyond this, government can contribute by not doing certain things, such as establishing minimum wage systems, whose effect at this stage of development is even more harmful than it would be in the mature economies. And is it reactionary to suggest that trade unions, if not actually prohibited, should at any rate not be actively encouraged?

Money Supply and the Price Level

In an economy that is becoming increasingly monetized, some degree of monetary expansion is not incompatible with price stability. Many LDCs, however, tend to exceed this warranted rate, which leads to chronically high rates of price increase. This tends to be associated with fiscal indiscipline—large deficits in the current government budget and often also in the accounts of public corporations, which are closed in part by monetary expansion.

Efforts to demonstrate that inflation must have a negative effect on growth have not been very successful. The most obvious adverse effect, that on international transactions, can be countered by the gliding-peg device. Simple correlation of national growth rates with inflation rates shows little relation. It is still intuitively plausible that the social friction and increased "noise" in the economic mechanism generated by high inflation can scarcely be helpful to development. In any event, choice of an inflation rate is another important item on the economic agenda of an LDC government.

Multiyear Macroeconomic Planning

The catalog of policy issues already examined should suffice to warrant my initial statement that economic planning and development policy are far from identical. Adoption of a planning document does not resolve the detailed issues of economic management that must be handled successfully if economic stagnation is to be avoided. Conversely, a country that is able to handle these issues can get along without an overall plan, as some LDCs have done with notable success.

This is not to deny that macroeconomic projections or "development plans," commonly covering a five-year future period, can serve a useful purpose. Pressure for such plans has come partly from lending institutions in the mature economies, which prefer to view an LDC's loan requests against the background of the country's overall resource availabilities and use. Such plans are typically quite aggregative, focusing on projections of public and private investment, domestic saving, exports, imports, and the balance-of payments; but they may be supported by varying degrees of sectoral detail, particularly with regard to government budget allocations.

The control power of such plans should not be overstated. The public sector, which is most nearly subject to central control, is still small in most LDCs. In the private sector, one can set targets; but the instruments available to steer the economy in the direction of these targets are often weak. It is not surprising, therefore, that ex post analysis of a five-year planning period typically reveals considerable divergence between events and expectations.

But this does not mean that the planning exercise is useless. In the first place, it typically stimulates improvement of basic economic information and better reporting of current government operations. Since absence or inaccuracy of data is one of the major obstacles to improved economic management, this is a distinct contribution. Further, the "hard" part of the plan relates to the public sector and is essentially a multiyear budget, embracing current as well as capital expenditures, which serves as a guide for preparation of annual budgets. This directs attention to long-run priorities rather than simply to immediate pressures. It requires each department of government to document its budget requests more fully and to relate each year's budget more systematically to budgets for preceding and following years. This can scarcely fail to improve resource allocation.

Probably the most direct contribution of an economic planning board or commission is to strengthen the central budget-review procedures, which are often quite defective. Among other things, it can exert pressure on departments to support their requests for capital allocations with cost-benefit analyses of individual projects. Despite much effort, ex ante project evaluations and careful checks on project execution remain the weakest links in the budgeting chain.

Quite different, and in my judgment less useful, are the dynamic optimizing models that occupy considerable space in the literature. These models, which rely heavily on input-output analysis, are usually structured in the following manner. The value of each output is given, usually at existing market prices. Capital and current input coefficients are given and constant. There are no returns to scale, no choices of technology, no technical progress. The problem then is, in the simplest models, to maximize consumption in some future year subject to resource supply constraints, a terminal capital-stock constraint to provide for years beyond the planning period, and a constraint on consumption over the intervening years—say, a provision that per capita consumption may at no time fall below its level in the base year.[4] Solution of the model yields not only the menu of outputs but a shadow price for each factor, which will be zero for any factor (such as, possibly, unskilled labor) that is in excess supply.

The results of such exercises might seem potentially useful in a socialist economy. Yet, for a variety of reasons familiar to students of socialist planning, they have not actually been used. The barriers to application are not just informational and technical; they are rooted in the nature of political decision making, which is pluralistic rather than monistic, incremental rather than synoptic. Even in a socialist economy there is no supreme optimizer, capable of turning computer printouts into binding orders. Decisions are reached by struggle and compromise among proponents of different growth strategies, different economic sectors, and different regions of the country.

All this is even more true in a nonsocialist developing country with a relatively small public sector, a limited span of control over the private sector, and limited competence in economic management.

In conclusion, I return to two points made at the beginning of this chapter. First, development policy should be conceived broadly as including the multitude of ways in which government action (or, in some cases, carefully calculated inaction) impinges on the economy. A macroeconomic plan can serve useful purposes, notably improved resource allocation within the public sector. But it is no substitute for a battery of policies bearing on agricultural output, population growth, industrial investment, trade relations, and other issues.

Second, the importance of strength and continuity in the political leadership and competence in economic administration cannot be

4. There are also more complex variants of the problem, all of which require the same basic information and involve the same methodology. Thus, one can maximize consumption over the planning period rather than in the terminal year; or one can maximize for several future planning periods; or one can work with a moving time horizon that is always, say, five years in the future.

overstated. It is more important to be able to do something than to know precisely what to do. Mistakes are bound to be made; but a competent government will learn from experience, and gross errors will be corrected. But if government itself is the missing ingredient, the country's development prospects are dim.

Appendix to Chapters 5 and 6:
Model of a Labor-Surplus Economy
with Government and a Price System

JAMES A. M. ELLIOTT*

The sector division is as follows:

1. Industry
2. Agriculture
3. Government
4. Traditional nonagriculture.

Subscripts in the variables and equations below refer to these sectors. Thus, D_1 = demand for industrial goods; L_1 = industrial employment; and so on.

1. *Endogenous Variables* (27)

1	Q_1	supply of industrial output
2	Q_2	supply of agricultural output
3	Q_4	supply of output of traditional nonagricultural sector
4	P	price of industrial goods in terms of agricultural goods $\left(\dfrac{P_1}{P_2} \text{ where } P_1, P_2 \text{ are the respective money prices} \right)$
5	π	price of traditional, nonagricultural sector goods in terms of agricultural goods $\left(\dfrac{P_4}{P_2} \text{ where } P_4 \text{ and } P_2 \text{ are the respective money prices} \right)$
6	W_1	wage rate (in terms of the agricultural good) in industry (sector 1) and government (sector 3)

*Assistant Professor of Economics, Georgetown University. Most of this work was done while the author was associated with the Center for Research on Economic Development, University of Michigan.

7	W_2	per capita income in agriculture (sector 2) and in traditional nonagriculture (sector 4)
8	r	after-tax rate of return on capital
9	$D_{1_{HW}}$	consumption demand for industrial goods by high-income workers (industry and government)
10	$D_{1_{LW}}$	consumption demand for industrial goods by low-income workers (agriculture and traditional nonagriculture)
11	$D_{2_{HW}}$ ⎫	demands for agricultural goods
12	$D_{2_{LW}}$ ⎭	
13	$D_{4_{HW}}$ ⎫	demands for output of traditional nonagriculture
14	$D_{4_{LW}}$ ⎭	
15	I	investment in capital goods in industry (sector 1)
16	Q_{21}	quantity of agricultural (sector 2) goods used as inputs in sector 1 (industrial) production
17	L_1	labor employed in industry
18	L_2	potential labor supply in agriculture (working-age population)
19	$L_{2_{cp}}$	agricultural labor engaged in current production (full man-year equivalents)
20	L_{2_I}	agricultural labor engaged in land improvement
21	H_{cp}	man-hour inputs to current production in agriculture
22	H_I	man-hour input by peasant families to land improvements in agriculture
23	L_{3_A}	labor employed by government for agricultural improvements
24	$L_{3_{NA}}$	labor employed by government for nonagricultural purposes
25	L_S	surplus labor in the agricultural sector
26	L_4	labor employed in traditional nonagriculture
27	R	government revenue

2. *Exogenous, Predetermined, and Policy Variables* (19)

1	η_L	rate of natural increase of population (and labor force)
2	x	capital technical progress variable
3	y	labor technical progress variable
4	z	land technical progress variable
5	η_{w_1}	rate of increase in the industrial wage
6	τ_1	tax rate on industrial output
7	τ_2	tax rate on agricultural output
8	τ_3	tax rate on industrial profits

9 λ percent of government revenue allocated to agricultural improvement

10 μ farmers' investment response coefficient (additional unpaid man-hours of farmers' time devoted to agricultural improvement per additional government-paid man-hour)

11 u input-output coefficient technical progress variable

12 δ_1 rate at which capital depreciates

13 δ_2 rate at which improvements due to peasant-family labor investment depreciate

14 δ_3 rate at which improvements due to labor investment by government-hired workers depreciate

15 K capital stock in industry at beginning of the period

16 J_1 stock of improvements in agriculture due to labor investment by peasant families in previous periods and allowing for depreciation, at beginning of the period.

17 J_2 stock of improvements in agriculture at beginning of the period, due to labor investment by government-hired workers in previous periods, allowing for depreciation.

18 L labor force at beginning of the period

19 T land endowment of the peasant sector

3. Key Parameters

$\beta_1, \beta_2, (1 - \beta_1 - \beta_2)$ Engels coefficients of supernumerary ("discretionary") income

γ minimum required amount of foodstuff consumption

θ the (constant) marginal rate of substitution between leisure and farm income for peasant families

h some standard number of hours of work per fully employed worker

4. Initial Conditions

These include the initial capital stock in industry, the initial stock of improvements in agriculture inherited from previous periods, the size of the labor force, and the level of the wage rate in industry and government in the initial period.

ALGEBRAIC SUMMARY OF THE MODEL

5. Static Version of the Model

Production:
$$Q_1 = F^1[xK, yL_1, uQ_{21}] \tag{1}$$

$$Q_2 = F^2[yH_{cp}, z \, \phi \, (J_1, J_2)T] \qquad 2$$
$$Q_4 = aL_4 \qquad 3$$

Consumption demand:

$$D_{1_{HW}} = \beta_1 \frac{[W_1 - \gamma]}{P} [L_1 + L_3] \qquad 4$$

$$D_{1_{LW}} = \beta_1 \frac{[W_2 - \gamma]}{P} [L_2 + L_4] \qquad 5$$

$$D_{2_{HW}} = [\beta_2(W_1 - \gamma) + \gamma][L_1 + L_3] \qquad 6$$

$$D_{2_{LW}} = [\beta_2(W_2 - \gamma) + \gamma][L_2 + L_4] \qquad 7$$

$$D_{4_{HW}} = (1 - \beta_1 - \beta_2)\frac{[W_1 - \gamma]}{\pi} [L_1 + L_3] \qquad 8$$

$$D_{4_{LW}} = (1 - \beta_1 - \beta_2)\frac{[W_2 - \gamma]}{\pi} [L_2 + L_4] \qquad 9$$

Investment:
$$I \quad = rK \qquad 10$$

Factor demand and supply; factor incomes:

$$W_1 \quad = P(1 - \tau_1)\frac{\partial Q_1}{\partial L} \qquad 11$$

$$W_1 \quad = W_1(0) \, e^{\eta w_1 t} \qquad 12$$

$$W_2 \quad = \frac{Q_2(1 - \tau_2)}{L_2} \qquad 13$$

$$L_{3A} \quad = \lambda \frac{R}{W_1} \qquad 14$$

$$L_{3_{NA}} = (1 - \lambda)\frac{R}{W_1} \qquad 15$$

$$H_I \quad = \delta_2 J_1 + \mu[L_{3_A} - \delta_3 J_2] \qquad 16$$

$\dfrac{\partial Q_2}{\partial H_{cp}} = \theta$ where θ is the constant marginal rate of substitution between leisure and farm income. The volume of labor involved in current production activity in the agricultural sector, H_{cp}, is determined by this equality. Note that $\theta \neq W_2$. (See example using the Cobb Douglas function.) 17

$r \quad = (1 - \tau_1)(1 - \tau_3)\dfrac{\partial Q_1}{\partial K}$ (after-tax rate of return to capital in sector 1, in terms of the industrial good) 18

$$\pi a \quad = W_2 \tag{19}$$

$$\frac{1}{P(1 - \tau_1)} = \frac{\partial Q_1}{\partial Q_{21}} \tag{20}$$

Labor-balancing equations:

$$L_{2_{cp}} = \frac{H_{cp}}{h} \tag{21}$$

$$L_{2_I} = \frac{H_I}{h} \text{ where } h \text{ is some standard number of manhours per fully employed worker} \tag{22}$$

$$L_S = L_2 - L_{2_{cp}} - L_{2_I} \quad \text{(surplus labor equation)} \tag{23}$$

$$\bar{L} = L_1 + L_2 + L_{3_A} + L_{3_{NA}} + L_4 \tag{24}$$

Government revenue:

$$R \quad = P\tau_1 Q_1 + \tau_2 Q_2 + \frac{\tau_3}{1 - \tau_3} PrK \tag{25}$$

Market-balancing equations:

$$Q_1 = D_{1_{HW}} + D_{1_{LW}} + I \tag{26}$$

$$Q_2 = D_{2_{HW}} + D_{2_{LW}} + Q_{21} \tag{27}$$

$$Q_4 = D_{4_{HW}} + D_{4_{LW}} \tag{28}$$

Comment: Only two of the market-balancing equations are independent—so the number of independent equations is 27.

Commentary on static version of the model:

Comments on equations 1–3.

Production of the modern industrial good is a function of labor and capital inputs, input of the agricultural good, Q_{21}, and of factor augmenting technical progress, x, y, u, where

$$x = x(0)e^{\eta_x t}$$
$$y = y(0)e^{\eta_y t}$$
$$u = u(0)e^{\eta_u t}$$

Production of the agricultural good is a function of current labor input—man-hours in current agricultural production activity H_{cp}—land (T), z where z is autonomously occurring land-augmenting technical progress, and the joint contribution of improvements, which is a function of cumulative labor investment in improvements by the peasant families themselves, J_1, which depreciates at rate δ_2,

$$J_1 = \sum_{\tau=1}^{t} (1 - \delta_2)^{t-\tau} H_I(\tau - 1)$$

and cumulative labor investment in improvements by government-hired workers, J_2, which depreciates at rate δ_3,

$$J_2 = \sum_{\tau=1}^{t} (1 - \delta_3)^{t-\tau} L_{3_A}(\tau - 1)$$

Output of the traditional nonagricultural sector 4 is a simple function of labor input (L_4).

Comments on equations 4–9.

The consumption demand functions are Stone Geary demand functions, which can be derived from constrained maximization of utility functions of the form

$$u = q_{1_c}^{\beta_1}(q_{2_c} - \gamma)^{\beta_2} q_{4_c}^{\beta_4}, q_{2_c} \geq \gamma$$

where q_{1_c} = individual's consumption of modern-sector good

q_{2_c} = individual's consumption of agricultural-sector good

q_{4_c} = individual's consumption of sector 4 good

γ = individual's minimum required consumption of the agricultural-sector good.

Per capita income, in terms of the agricultural good, (W_1) and relative prices (P, π) are taken as parameters over which the individual has no control.

This poses difficulties so far as the theoretical interpretation of peasant-household decisions is concerned. To get surplus-labor behavior along the lines postulated by Sen and Ishikawa (and also postulated for this model), we have to suppose that the peasant household freely chooses the number of hours it works—hence its members' per capita incomes. So that for it, per capita income is *not* really a parameter, though its leisure-farm output transformation *schedule* is a given.

Surplus labor will exist in the agricultural sector a la Sen-Ishikawa in the simple case where there are only two goods, leisure (L) and "income" (y), if the individual's utility function in L and y is of a form such that the marginal rate of substitution between leisure and income is constant.

Such a utility function would be

$$u = AL + By$$

The reader can easily verify that in this case

$$-\frac{dy}{dL}\bigg|_{u=const.} = \frac{\dfrac{\partial u}{\partial L}}{\dfrac{\partial u}{\partial y}} = \frac{A}{B}$$

That is, indifference curves between leisure and income are straight lines and the equilibrium labor-leisure choice is given by the point of tangency of one of these to the income-leisure transformation curve.

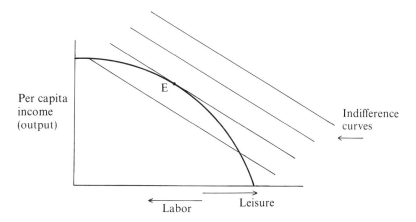

It seems, though, that the multiple-good case is complicating— one either has to assume that the peasant family chooses an optimum labor-leisure combination, then allocates the resulting farm income among Q_1, Q_2, and Q_4 consumption following a Stone Geary scheme, or one can try to justify this assertion by supposing utility functions to be of the form, say

$$u = AL + B(q_{1_c})^{\beta_1}(q_{2_c} - \gamma)^{\beta_2}(q_{4_c})^{1-\beta_1-\beta_2}$$

It is supposed that everyone has utility functions, hence demand functions, of the same type—with the same values for the coefficients. But outside agriculture, people are not free to choose their hours of work.

In what follows, an approach reconciling the assumption of a constant marginal rate of substitution between farm income and leisure, with specification of a Stone Geary commodity demand system, is proposed.

Each period is divided into two subperiods. In the first, the peasant family trades off leisure (L) against farm output (Q_2), some of which is to be consumed in subperiod 2, some to buy Q_1 and Q_4. In the first subperiod, the prices that will prevail for the second subperiod are not known; but peasant families have definite price expectations. Their production decisions aim to maximize expected utility on the basis of expected values P^* and π^* of P and π. These expectations are based on past experience.

In the second subperiod, with farm output (Q_2), and hence per capita farm output (q_2), now a given, and with P and π known, the individual's consumption basket

$$\{q_{1_c}, q_{2_c}, q_{4_c}\}$$

is chosen to maximize the utility function

$$u_2 = B(q_{1_c})^{\beta_1} (q_{2_c} - \gamma)^{\beta_2} (q_{4_c})^{1 - \beta_1 - \beta_2}$$

subject to the budget constraint

$$Pq_{1_c} + q_{2_c} + \pi q_{4_c} = q_2, \text{ where } q_2 \text{ is per capita farm output.}$$

If total utility is given by $u = u_1 + u_2 = AL + Bq_{1_c}{}^{\beta_1} (q_{2_c} - \gamma)^{\beta_2} q_{4_c}^{1 - \beta_1 - \beta_2}$, and P^* and π^* are the relative prices *anticipated* for subperiod w, then we conclude that anticipated utility-maximizing quantities for subperiod 2, as a function of q_2, are:

$$q_{1_c}^* = \beta_1 \frac{(q_2 - \gamma)}{P^*}$$

$$q_{2_c}^* = \beta_2(q_2 - \gamma) + \gamma$$

$$q_{4_c}^* = \frac{(1 - \beta_1 - \beta_2)(q_2 - \gamma)}{\pi^*}$$

where P^* and π^* are *anticipated* values of P and π and there is no excise tax on Q_2.

Therefore, anticipated utility from consumption of commodities in this subperiod can be written as a function of q_2 and price anticipations only. (It is assumed that there is no uncertainty about Q_2 once H_{cp} has been chosen.)

$$u_2^* = (q_{12}^*)^{\beta_1} (q_{22}^* - \gamma)^{\beta_2} (q_{42}^*)^{1-\beta_1-\beta_2}$$

$$u_2^* = \left[\beta_1 \left(\frac{q_2 - \gamma}{P^*} \right) \right]^{\beta_1} \left[\beta_2 (q_2 - \gamma) + \gamma - \gamma \right]^{\beta_2}$$

$$\left[\frac{(1 - \beta_1 - \beta_2)(q_2 - \gamma_2)}{\pi^*} \right]^{1-\beta_1-\beta_2}$$

Obviously this can be simplified as follows:

$$u_2^* = \frac{\beta_1{}^{\beta_1} \beta_2{}^{\beta_2} (1 - \beta_1 - \beta_2)^{1-\beta_1-\beta_2}}{P^{*\beta_1} \pi^{*(1-\beta_1-\beta_2)}} (q_2 - \gamma)$$

Therefore, clearly,

$$\frac{\partial u^*}{\partial q_2} = constant \text{---which will be higher, the lower } P^* \text{ and } \pi^* \text{ are.}$$

If $\dfrac{\partial u_1}{\partial \text{ Leisure}} = A$,

then it is correct to write

$$\frac{\partial Q_2}{\partial H_{cp}} = \theta$$

where θ is a function of β_1, β_2, and price anticipations, which are revised in the light of past experience.

So, we can write simply that in subperiod 1

$$u^* = u_1^* + u_2^*$$

$$= AL + B \left[\left(\frac{\beta_1}{P^*} \right)^{\beta_1} \beta_2{}^{\beta_2} \left[\frac{1 - \beta_1 - \beta_2}{\pi^*} \right]^{1-\beta_1-\beta_2} \right] [q_2 - \gamma]$$

and it is clear that

$$\frac{\dfrac{\partial u^*}{\partial L}}{\dfrac{\partial u^*}{\partial q_2}} = \frac{dq_2}{dL} \bigg|_{u^* = const.}$$

$$= \frac{A/B}{\left(\dfrac{\beta_1}{P^*} \right)^{\beta_1} (\beta_2)^{\beta_2} \left[\dfrac{1 - \beta_1 - \beta_2}{\pi^*} \right]^{1-\beta_1-\beta_2}}$$

This, then, is the value of θ used in equation 16.

Upon inspection, one can see that θ will be lower, the lower P^* and π^* are. Therefore, lower anticipated values of P^* and π^* lead to increased peasant labor input into current production activities.

Comment on equation 10.
All sector 1 profits are reinvested in sector 1.

Comments on equations 11–20.
The wage rate in the modern part of the economy, W_1, for industry (sector 1) and government (sector 3) is determined exogenously—here by its initial value and a time trend.

Sector 1 employers, given this exogenously determined wage rate (note that it is given in terms of the agricultural good) and the relative price of their product, P, determine the volume of employment by hiring labor up to the point where the value of labor's marginal product (after payment of the turnover tax, which is paid in the first instance by producer-sellers) in terms of agricultural goods equals W_1.

The volume of sector 1 employment is thus influenced by:

1. P —endogenously determined within the period
2. W_1 —predetermined
3. technical progress—values of x and y at time t—predetermined.

Government pays a wage rate equal to W_1, and the volume of its employment is a simple function of its revenue (determined elsewhere in the model) and W_1. From equations 14 and 15 we have

$$L_{3A} + L_{3NA} = \frac{R}{W_1}$$

The volume of peasant labor input to improvements activity is a function of government-hired labor input to improvements activity (equations 14 and 16). The constant term in equation 16 represents labor input required to make good wear and tear (of which the magnitude is given by the depreciation coefficient δ_2 in equation 2) and perhaps something over this to close a gap that may exist between the actual and the desired level of improvements stock as perceived by the peasant families.

This formulation can be improved by specification of a land-improvements function, postulating that a peasant family calculates an optimal level of improvements that is a function of (among other things) the level of labor investment in the agricultural sector by the government, which the family can realize within a single period. Making good depreciation requires a certain amount of maintenance investment from period to period; further labor investment by the government raises the optimal level of peasant labor investment—in addition to contributing independently to an outward shift in peasant families' leisure-farm output transformation curves. (The resulting equation would be somewhat similar to equation 16.)

Comments on equations 21–25.

Labor in all sectors must add up to the working-age population $\bar{L}$ which is a predetermined variable ($\bar{L} = \bar{L}(0)e^{nLt}$).

Surplus labor in agriculture is calculated on an essentially arbitrary but intuitively satisfying basis—as the difference between the number of working-age, full-time worker equivalents in the agricultural sector and the number of full-time equivalent workers corresponding to the number of man-hours actually devoted to current production and improvements activity in agriculture (equations 23, 21 and 22).

Alternative form of equation 16:

$$H_{I_t} = \delta_2 \sum_{\tau=0}^{t-1} H_{I_\tau}(1 - \delta_2)^{t-\tau-1} + \mu \left[L_{3A_t} - \delta_3 \sum_{\tau=0}^{t-1} L_{3A_\tau}(1 - \delta_3)^{t-\tau-1} \right]$$

In this formulation, peasant households' labor investment in the current period depends on investment in past periods, the rate at which improvements deteriorate (replacement needs), and the current rate of *net* labor investment in improvements financed by the government. If the government invests less than is required to make good depreciation on its past investment, the effect on peasant households' labor investment is negative. Implicit in this is the notion that peasant households are trying to maintain a desired level of improvements investment, which can be shifted by the government's decisions on its own rate of net investment in the agricultural sector.

Note: Supply of man-hours in agriculture; surplus labor specification (equation 16) example using a Cobb Douglas production function

In the surplus labor phase, the utility functions of peasant family members are such that the ratio of the marginal utility of leisure to that of income is constant, so that man-hour input into current production activity, H_{cp}, is determined by equalization of the first derivative of Q_2 with respect to H_{cp} to this [constant] ratio, θ.

$$\frac{\partial Q_2}{\partial H_{cp}} = \frac{\dfrac{\partial u}{\partial \, Leisure}}{\dfrac{\partial u}{\partial Q_2}} = \frac{dQ_2}{d \, Leisure}\bigg|\, u = const. = \theta$$

Hence $H_{cp} = \phi(\theta)$ where θ is a constant.

With a Cobb Douglas production function,

$$Q_2 = A_2(yH_{cp})^{\alpha_2}(zT)^{1-\alpha_2}$$

$$\frac{\partial Q_2}{\partial H_{cp}} = \alpha_2 A_2(yH_{cp})^{\alpha_2-1} y(zT)^{1-\alpha_2} = \theta$$

Hence,

$$H_{cp} = \frac{\alpha_2^{\frac{1}{1-\alpha_2}} A_2^{\frac{1}{1-\alpha_2}} y^{\frac{\alpha_2}{1-\alpha_2}} zT}{\dfrac{1}{\theta^{1-\alpha_2}}}$$

A shift in equilibrium can be produced by variations in technological side parameters

$$A_2, y, z \text{ or } \alpha_2$$

$\left(\text{recall that } \alpha_2 = \dfrac{H_{cp}}{Q_2}\dfrac{\partial Q_2}{\partial H_{cp}}\right)$ or by a shift in θ (leisure-income preferences).

6. *Dynamic Properties of the Model*

$$
\begin{aligned}
x(t) &= x(0)e^{(\eta_x)t} & &1\\
y(t) &= y(0)e^{(\eta_y)t} & &2\\
z(t) &= z(0)e^{(\eta_z)t} & &3\\
u(t) &= u(0)e^{(\eta_u)t} & &4\\
J_1(t) &= H_I(t-1) + (1-\delta_2)J_1(t-1) & &5\\
J_2(t) &= L_{3_A}(t-1) + (1-\delta_3)J_2(t-1) & &6\\
K(t) &= K(t-1) + (1-\delta_1)K(t-1) & &7\\
L(t) &= L(0)e^{(\eta_L)t} & &8
\end{aligned}
$$

7. *Financial Flows and Net Resource Transfers between Agriculture and Nonagriculture*

Starting from the constraint that a spending unit's total expenditures must equal its disposable income after taxes, borrowings, and so forth, it can easily be shown that the sectoral export surplus, $E - M$, must equal the excess of savings over investment, $S - I$, within the sector and that both must equal the net flow of financial transfers to the rest of the economy, on private and public current and capital accounts, $V + K$, when savings and investment are properly defined. This expenditure constraint is automatically built into a system with Stone-Geary demand functions and constant returns to scale in production.

In the model as presented, consumption of the sector-2 good by laborers hired by the government to engage in improvements activity in this sector must be regarded as consumption internal to sector 2 rather than as exports to nonagriculture. The rationale for this is that the activity of these government workers, by expanding the stock of improvements in agriculture, benefits members of the agricultural sector, in the first instance at least. Similarly, consumption of the output of sectors 1 and 4 by these workers must be counted as imports on sector 2's account. With this interpretation, the relations discussed in the chapter, $E_A - M_A = S_A - I_A = V + K$, clearly hold, with E_A representing exports to nonagriculture less consumption of the sector 2 good by government-hired workers engaged in agricultural improvements activity; M_A, imports from nonagriculture for consumption by sector 2 members and government-hired workers engaged in agricultural improvements activity; S_A, the sum of forced savings in the form of taxes levied on sector 2, $\tau_2 Q_2$, plus voluntary savings, which we may consider to be identically equal to the value of labor investment by peasant families in improvements activity; I_A, the sum of the value of the labor of government-hired workers engaged in improvements activity (measured by government expenditure on their wages, λR) and that of labor investment by peasant families in improvements activity; V equal to tax revenues, $\tau_2 Q_2$, K equal to the flow of payments from the government sector to finance improvements activities (λR). (This latter is basically a grant-financing capital expenditure).

Let

E_2 exports of agricultural sector, defined in terms of the agricultural good

M_2 imports of agricultural sector, defined in terms of the agricultural good

S_2 savings of agricultural sector

I_2 investment in agricultural sector

V net financial transfers on current account from agriculture to nonagriculture ($= \tau_2 Q_2$)

K net financial transfers on capital account from agriculture to nonagriculture $(= -\lambda R)$

D_{12} consumption demand by peasant families in the agricultural sector for output of sector 1

D_{22} consumption demand by peasant families for output of their own sector

D_{42} consumption demand by peasant families for output of sector 4.

$D_{1_{3_A}}$ consumption demand by government-hired workers engaged in agricultural improvements activity for output of sector 1

$D_{2_{3_A}}$ consumption demand by government-hired workers engaged in agricultural improvements for output of the agricultural sector

$D_{4_{3_A}}$ consumption demand by government-hired workers engaged in agricultural improvements for output of sector 4

W_2 after-tax income per capita of peasant families

W_1 income per capita of government-hired workers $= \lambda R/L_{3_A}$

Exports and imports can be written, respectively:

$$E_2 = Q_2 - D_{22} - D_{2_{3_A}}$$
$$M_2 = PD_{12} + \pi D_{42} + PD_{1_{3_A}} + \pi D_{4_{3_A}}$$

Hence, the export surplus is

$$E_2 - M_2 = Q_2 - D_{22} - D_{2_{3_A}} - PD_{12} - \pi D_{42} - PD_{1_{3_A}} - \pi D_{4_{3_A}}$$

$$\begin{aligned}
E_2 - M_2 = {} & Q_2 - \beta_1 \left[(1 - \tau_2)Q_2 - \gamma L_2\right] - \beta_1 \left[\lambda R - \gamma L_{3_A}\right] \\
& - \{\beta_2 \left[(1 - \tau_2)Q_2 - \gamma L_2\right] + \gamma L_2\} \\
& - (1 - \beta_1 - \beta_2) \left[(1 - \tau_2)Q_2 - \gamma L_2\right] \\
& - \{\beta_2 \left[\lambda R - \gamma L_{3_A}\right] + \gamma L_{3_A}\} \\
& - (1 - \beta_1 - \beta_2) \left[\lambda R - \gamma L_{3_A}\right] \\
= {} & Q_2 - \{(\beta_1 + \beta_2) + (1 - \beta_1 - \beta_2)\} \left[(1 - \tau_2)Q_2\right. \\
& \left. - \gamma L_2\right] + \gamma L_2 - \{(\beta_1 + \beta_2) + (1 - \beta_1 - \beta_2)\} \\
& \left[\lambda R - \gamma L_{3_A}\right] + \gamma L_{3_A}
\end{aligned}$$

$$\begin{aligned}
E_2 - M_2 &= \tau_2 Q_2 - \lambda R \\
&= V + K
\end{aligned}$$

Looking at the savings-investment side, and recognizing that, for accounting purposes, voluntary savings, S_{V_2}, by peasant families are equal to the opportunity cost of their voluntary labor investment in improvements activity, I_{22}, (S_{V_2} represents potential consumption in the present period forgone as a result of labor's being directed to improvements activity), we have:

$$S_2 = Q_2 - PD_{12} - D_{22} - \pi D_{42} + S_{V_2}$$
$$I_2 = I_{22} + \lambda R$$
$$S_{V_2} = I_{22}$$
$$\begin{aligned}S_2 - I_2 &= Q_2 - PD_{12} - D_{22} - \pi D_{42} - \lambda R\\&= Q_2 - \beta_1 \left[(1 - \tau_2)Q_2 - \gamma L_2\right]\\&\quad - \{\beta_2 \left[(1 - \tau_2)Q_2 - \gamma L_2\right] + \gamma L_2\}\\&\quad - (1 - \beta_1 - \beta_2)\left[(1 - \tau_2)Q_2 - \gamma L_2\right] - \lambda R\\&= \tau_2 Q_2 - \lambda R\end{aligned}$$

Thus far, net resource transfers occur only through the fiscal mechanism, since, in the formulation of the model in section 5, it was assumed that capital is employed only in sector 1 (the modern industrial sector) and that recipients of income from other sources do not voluntarily save in the conventional sense. It will be noted that, depending on the relative sizes of $\tau_2 Q_2$ and λR, the net resource transfer between agriculture and nonagriculture can go either way.

The model can easily be modified to permit the inclusion of financial transfers on private capital account and the corresponding flows on current account to which these give rise. For example, it can be assumed that peasant families save a fixed proportion of their incomes, which they use to acquire claims to capital stock in the first sector. With investment in the conventional sense not possible in sector 2, the net flow of private savings is necessarily from agriculture to industry, unless sector-1 individuals are assumed to make consumption loans to sector-2 people, acquiring claims on future agricultural output without corresponding income-producing physical assets being created, on a large enough scale.

To encompass resource transfers on private capital account in either direction corresponding to conventional investment in physical capital, the model can be expanded to include capital as a factor of production in agriculture as well as in industry. This involves introducing four new endogenous variables, K_1 (capital employed in sector 1), K_2 (capital employed in sector 2), r_1 (rate of return on capital in sector 1), and r_2 (rate of return on capital in sector 2), and four new equations:

$$K_1 + K_2 = K \quad \text{(full employment of the capital stock)} \qquad 1$$

$$(1 - \tau_2)(1 - \tau_3)\frac{\partial Q_2}{\partial K} = r_2 \quad \text{(value of marginal product of capital net of tax equals the rate of return on capital in sector 2)} \qquad 2$$

$r_1 = r$ (after-tax rate of return on capital is equalized between
sectors 1 and 2)   3

$r_2 = r$ 4

Between any two periods, investment in sector 1 by capitalists, $I_1^K(t - 1)$, is equal to

$$K_1(t) - (1 - \delta_1)K_1(t - 1)$$

while savings out of sector 1 capital income, $S_1^K(t - 1)$, is equal to

$$r_1(t - 1)K_1(t - 1).$$

Hence, as of period t, the difference between savings and investment by capitalists in period $t - 1$ can be calculated ex post facto.

$$S_1^K(t - 1) - I_1^K(t - 1) = r_1(t - 1)K_1(t - 1) - K_1(t)$$
$$+ (1 - \delta_1)K_1(t - 1)$$
$$S_2^K(t - 1) - I_2^K(t - 1) = r_2(t - 1)K_2(t - 1) - K_2(t)$$
$$+ (1 - \delta_1)K_2(t - 1)$$

From equation 1 in section 5, $I_1^K + I_2^K = rK$, so that $S_1^K - I_1^K = I_2^K - S_2^K$ must hold.

The direction of the savings-investment on private account flow between agriculture and nonagriculture depends on the magnitude and direction of capital reallocation between sectors from period to period. This depends on a host of factors; although the presumption is in favor of a net flow from agriculture to nonagriculture, it seems evident that the flow can go in either direction.

8. *The Open Economy*

The model can readily be modified to fit the open-economy case. This requires the addition of two more endogenous variables and two more equations plus the modification of three equations (25, 26, 27). Equations 26 and 27 are modified as follows:

$$Q_1 + M = D_{1_{HW}} + D_{1_{LW}} + I \qquad\qquad 26'$$
$$Q_2 - E = D_{2_{HW}} + D_{2_{LW}} + Q_{21} \qquad\qquad 27'$$

where M equals imports of sector 1's good; E equals exports of sector 2's good. (This is assuming that sector 1's good is an importable, sector 2's good is an exportable, and sector 4's good is not tradeable externally.)

Balance of payments equilibrium must obtain:

$$(P_w)M = E + F \qquad\qquad 29$$

where P_w is the world price ratio for commodities 1 and 2 and F is foreign capital inflow (exogenous variables).

Finally, the link between P and P_w is given by the following equation:

$$P = (1 + \tau_4)P_w \qquad\qquad 30$$

where τ_4 is the tariff rate, another policy variable.

Government revenue (equation 25) now becomes:

$$R = P\tau_1 Q + \tau_2 Q_2 + \frac{\tau_3}{1 - \tau_3} PrK + \tau_4 M \qquad\qquad 25'$$

A Selected Bibliography of
Development Economics

This listing is limited to items that I regard as useful reading for a graduate student or teacher of development economics. It excludes items of secondary interest, ones that have become dated since they appeared, or ones that are mainly policy-oriented. Those marked with an asterisk (*) are high-priority items.

The classification system is necessarily somewhat arbitrary. Where an item overlaps two or more categories, I have tried to assign it on the basis of its primary relevance. Undoubtedly, too, some good pieces of work have been overlooked, and I apologize in advance to authors whose work has inadvertently been omitted.

1. General References

Baran, Paul. *The Political Economy of Growth*. New York: Monthly Review Press, 1967.
Bauer, P. T., and Yamey, B. S. *The Economics of Underdeveloped Countries*. Chicago: University of Chicago Press, 1957.
*Kuznets, Simon. *Modern Economic Growth*. New Haven: Yale University Press, 1966.
Lewis, W. A. *The Theory of Economic Growth*. Homewood, Ill.: Richard D. Irwin, Inc., 1955.
*Myint, Hla. *Economic Theory and the Underdeveloped Countries*. London and New York: Oxford University Press, 1971.
*————. *The Economics of the Developing Countries*. London: Hutchinson and Company, 1964.
*Rostow, W. W. "The Take-Off into Self-Sustained Growth." *Economic Journal* 66 (March 1956): 25–48.

2. Development Theory: The Classical Period

*Adelman, Irma. *Theories of Economic Growth and Development*. Stanford: Stanford University Press, 1961.
Marshall, Alfred. *Principles of Economics*. Book 4, chaps. 7–13; Book 6, chaps. 12, 13.
*Marx, Karl. *Capital*. Vol. 1, part 8.
Mill, John Stuart. *Principles of Political Economy*. Book 4, chaps. 1–5.
*Ricardo, David. *Principles of Political Economy and Taxation*. Chaps. 5, 6, 31.

Robbins, Lionel. *The Theory of Economic Development in the History of Economic Thought.* New York: St. Martin's Press, 1968.

Robinson, Joan. *An Essay on Marxian Economics.* London: Macmillan, 1947.

Schumpeter, Joseph. *Capitalism, Socialism, and Democracy,* part one.

―――. *History of Economic Analysis.* New York: Oxford University Press, 1954. Portions of pts. 2 and 3.

*Smith, Adam. *The Wealth of Nations.* Book 1, chaps. 1, 2, 3, 8, 9; Book 2, chaps. 1–5; Book 3, chaps. 1–4.

3. Development Theory: Closed-economy Models

Adelman, I., and Thorbecke, E., eds. *The Theory and Design of Economic Development.* Baltimore: Johns Hopkins Press, 1966.

Berry, R. A., and Soligo, R. "Rural-Urban Migration, Agricultural Output, and the Supply-Price of Labor in a Labor-Surplus Economy." *Oxford Economic Papers* 20 (July 1968): 230–49.

*Fei, John C. H., and Ranis, Gustav. *Development of the Labor-Surplus Economy: Theory and Policy.* A Publication of the Economic Growth Center, Yale University. Homewood, Ill.: Richard D. Irwin, Inc., 1964.

Hahn, F. H., and Matthews, R. C. O. "The Theory of Economic Growth: A Survey." *Economic Journal* 74 (December 1964): 779–902. Reprinted in American Economic Association and Royal Economic Society *Surveys of Economic Theory.* Vol. 2. New York: St. Martin's Press, 1965.

*Helleiner, Gerald K. "Typology in Development Theory: The Land Surplus Economy (Nigeria)," *Food Research Institute Studies* 6 (1966): 181–94.

*Hymer, S., and Resnick, S. "A model of an Agrarian Economy With Non-Agricultural Activities." *American Economic Review* 59 (September 1969): 493–506.

*Ishikawa, Shigeru. *Economic Development in Asian Perspective.* Tokyo: Kinokuniya Bookstore, Ltd., 1967.

Islam, Nurul. "Development of the Labour Surplus Economy" (review of Fei-Ranis). *Pakistan Development Review* 5 (Summer 1965): 271–94.

Jorgenson, Dale. "Development of the Dual Economy." *Economic Journal* 71 (June 1961): 309–34.

Kelley, Allen C.; Williamson, Jeffrey G.; and Cheatham, Russell. *Dualistic Economic Development.* Chicago: University of Chicago Press, 1972.

*Lewis, W. Arthur. "Economic Development with Unlimited Supplies of Labor." *Manchester School* 22 (May 1954): 139–91.

*―――. "Reflections on Unlimited Labor." In *International Economics and Economic Development.* New York and London: Academic Press, Inc., 1972.

*―――. "Unlimited Supplies of Labor: Further Notes." *Manchester School* 26 (January 1958): 1–32.

Mellor, John W., and Lele, Uma J. "A Labor Supply Theory of Economic Development." Ithaca, N.Y.: Cornell Agricultural Economics Staff Paper no. 34, June 1971.

Minami, R. *The Turning Point in Economic Development: Japan's Experience.* Tokyo: Kinokuniya Bookstore, 1973.

Paglin, M. "Surplus Agricultural Labor and Development: Facts and Theories." *American Economic Review* 55 (September 1965): 815–33.

Reynolds, L. G. "Economic Development with Surplus Labor: Some Complications." *Oxford Economic Papers* 21 (March 1969): 89–103.

*Sen, A. K. "Peasants and Dualism With or Without Surplus Labor." *Journal of Political Economy* 74 (October 1966): 425–50.

Zarembka, Paul. *Toward a Theory of Economic Development*. San Francisco: Holden-Day, Inc., 1972.

4. Factor Supplies: Labor (including employment and underemployment, migration, training and education, wages)

Bowles, S. *Planning Educational Systems for Economic Growth*. Cambridge: Harvard University Press, 1969.

Durand, John D. *The Labor Force in Economic Development*. Princeton: Princeton University Press, 1975.

Farooq, Ghazi M. "An Aggregative Model of Labor Force Participation in Pakistan." *The Developing Economies* 10 (September 1972): 267–89.

Frank, C. R. "Urban Unemployment and Economic Growth in Africa." *Oxford Economic Papers* 20 (July 1968): 250–74.

*Hansen, Bent. "Employment and Wages in Rural Egypt." *American Economic Review* 59 (June 1969): 298–313.

*———. "Marginal Productivity Wage Theory and Subsistence Wage Theory in Egyptian Agriculture." *Journal of Development Studies* 2 (July 1966): 367–99.

*Harris, J. R., and Todaro, M. "Migration, Unemployment and Development: A two-Sector Analysis." *American Economic Review* 60 (March 1970): 126–42.

Isbister, John. "Urban Unemployment and Wages in a Developing Economy: The Case of Mexico." *Economic Development and Cultural Change* 20 (October 1971): 24–46.

Jolly, Richard. *Planning Education for African Development*. Nairobi: East African Publishing House, for the Makerere Institute of Social Research, 1969.

Knight, J. B. "Earnings, Employment, Education, and Income Distribution in Uganda." *Bulletin of the Oxford Institute of Economics and Statistics* 30 (November 1968): 267–97.

Mathur, A. "The Anatomy of Disguised Unemployment." *Oxford Economic Papers* 16 (July 1964): 161–93.

*Morawetz, D. "Employment Implications of Industrialisation in Developing Countries: A Survey." *Economic Journal* 84 (September 1974): 491–542.

Moses, L. N.; Beals, R. E.; and Levy, M. B. "Rationality and Migration in Ghana." *Review of Economics and Statistics* 49 (November 1967): 480–86.

Norman, D. W. "Labor Inputs of Farmers: A Case Study of the Zaria Province of the North-Central State of Nigeria." *Nigerian Journal of Economic and Social Studies* 11 (1969): 3–14.

*Ranis, Gustav. "Industrial Sector Labor Absorption." *Economic Development and Cultural Change* 21 (April 1973): 387–408.

Robinson, Warren C. "Disguised Unemployment Once Again: East Pakistan 1951–1961." *American Journal of Agricultural Economics* 51 (August 1969): 592–604.

Sahota, Gian S. "An Economic Analysis of Internal Migration in Brazil." *Journal of Political Economy* 76 (March/April 1968): 218–45.

*Sen, Amartya. *Employment, Technology, and Development*. New York: Oxford University Press, 1975.

————. *The Choice of Techniques*. 3rd ed. Oxford: Blackwell, 1968.

*Todaro, Michael. "A Model of Labor Migration and Urban Unemployment in less Developed Countries." *American Economic Review* 59 (March 1969): 138–48.

————. "Income Expectations, Rural-Urban Migration, and Employment in Africa." *International Labor Review* 104 (November 1971): 387–414.

*Turner, H. A., and Jackson, D. A. S. "On the Determination of the General Wage Level—A World Analysis: or 'Unlimited Labour Forever'." *Economic Journal* 80 (December 1970): 827–49.

Turnham, David. *The Employment Problem in Less Developed Countries*. Paris: OECD, 1971.

5. *Factor Supplies: Capital* (including domestic saving, financial institutions, interest rates)

Baer, W., and Kerstenetzky, I., eds. *Inflation and Growth in Latin America*. A Publication of the Economic Growth Center, Yale University. Homewood, Ill.: Richard D. Irwin, Inc., 1964.

Baumol, W. J. "On the Social Rate of Discount." *American Economic Review* 58 (September 1968): 788–802.

Ezekiel, H. "Monetary Expansion and Economic Development." *IMF Staff Papers* 14 (March 1967): 80–87.

Gantt, Andrew H., and Dutto, Giuseppe. "Financial Performance of Government-Owned Corporations in Less Developed Countries." *IMF Staff Papers* 15 (March 1968): 102–42.

*Mckinnon, Ronald I. *Money and Capital in Economic Development*. Washington Brookings Institution, 1973.

*Mikesell, R. F., and Zinser, J. E. "The Nature of the Savings Function in Developing Countries: A Survey of the Theoretical and Empirical Literature." *Journal of Economic Literature* 11 (March 1973): 1–26.

Ness, Walter L., Jr. "Financial Markets Innovations as a Development Strategy: Initial Results from the Brazilian Experience." *Economic Development and Cultural Change* 22 (April 1974): 453–72.

Robinson, E. A. G., ed. *Problems in Economic Development*. New York: St. Martin's Press, 1965.

Schatz, Sayre P. "The Capital Shortage Illusion: Government Lending in Nigeria." *Oxford Economic Papers* 17 (July 1965): 309–16.

Sen, A. K. "On Optimising the Rate of Saving." *Economic Journal* 71 (September 1961): 479–95.

Wai, U Tun, and Patrick, Hugh T. "Stock and Bond Issues and Capital Markets in Less Developed Countries." *IMF Staff Papers* 20 (July 1973): 253–317.

Williamson, J. G. "Personal Saving in Developing Nations: An Intertemporal Cross-Section from Asia." *Economic Record* 44 (June 1968): 194–210.

6. Population Growth

*Becker, Gary S. "An Economic Analysis of Fertility." In *Demographic and Economic Change in Developed Countries*. Universities-National Bureau Conference Series, no. 11. Princeton: Princeton University Press, 1960.

Berg, Alan. *The Nutrition Factor: Its Role in National Development*. Washington: Brookings Institution, 1973.

Blandy, R. "The Welfare Analysis of Fertility Reduction." *Economic Journal* 84 (March 1974): 109–29.

Boserup, Ester. *Women's Role in Economic Development*. New York: St. Martin's Press, 1970.

Coale, A., and Hoover, E. M. *Population Growth and Economic Development in Low-Income Countries*. Princeton: Princeton University Press, 1958.

*Kuznets, Simon. "Fertility Differentials Between Less Developed and Developed Regions: Components and Implications." *Proceedings of the American Philosophical Society* 119, no. 5 (October 1975): 363–96.

———. *Population, Capital and Growth*. New York: W. W. Norton, 1973.

*Ohlin, Göran. *Population Control and Economic Development*. Paris: OECD, 1967.

Rosenzweig, M., and Evenson, R. E. "Fertility, Schooling, and the Economic Contribution of Children in Rural India." Yale Economic Growth Center Discussion Paper no. 239, 1975.

*Schultz, T. Paul. "An Economic Model of Family Planning and Fertility." *Journal of Political Economy* 77 (March/April 1969): 153–80.

*———. "An Economic Perspective on Population Growth." In *Rapid Population Growth: Consequences and Policy Applications*. Baltimore: Johns Hopkins Press, for the National Academy of Sciences, 1972.

———. *Evaluation of Population Policies*. Santa Monica: Rand Corporation, R–643, 1971.

*Schultz, T. W., ed. *Economics of the Family: Marriage, Children, and Human Capital*. (Chicago: University of Chicago Press, 1974. Also in *Journal of Political Economy Supplement* 81 (March/April 1973): S1–S299.

7. The Agricultural Sector (including agricultural organization, farmers' economic responses, technology generation and transfer)

Ady, Peter. "Supply Functions in Tropical Agriculture." *Bulletin of the Oxford Institute of Economics and Statistics* 30 (May 1968): 157–88.

Bardhan, P. K. "Size, Productivity, and Returns to Scale: An Analysis of Farm-level Data on Indian Agriculture." *Journal of Political Economy* 81 (November/December 1973): 1370–86.

Bardhan, P. K., and Srinavasan, T. N. "Cropsharing Tenancy in Agriculture: A Theoretical and Empirical Analysis." *American Economic Review* 61 (March 1971): 48–64.

Behrman, J. R. *Supply Response in Underdeveloped Agriculture*. Amsterdam: North-Holland Publishing Co., 1968.

Berry, R. Albert. "Farm Size Distribution, Income Distribution, and the Efficiency of Agricultural Production: Colombia." *American Economic Review* 62 (May 1972): 403–08.

*Bhagwati, J. N., and Chakravarty, S. "Contributions to Indian Economic Analysis: A Survey." *American Economic Review* 59, pt. 2 (September 1969): 2–73.

Boserup, Ester. *The Conditions of Agricultural Growth*. London: Allen and Unwin; Chicago: Aldine Publishing Co., 1964.

*Bottomley, Anthony. *Factor Pricing and Economic Growth in Underdeveloped Rural Areas*. London: Crosby, Lockwood and Son, 1971.

Cheung, Steven N. S. *The Theory of Share Tenancy*. Chicago: University of Chicago Press, 1969.

Cheung, Steven N. S. "Transaction Costs, Risk Aversion, and the Choice of Contractual Arrangements." *Journal of Law and Economics* 12 (April 1969): 23–42.

Cline, William R. *Economic Consequences of a Land Reform in Brazil*. Amsterdam: North-Holland Publishing Co., 1970.

Dean, Edwin R. "Economic Analysis and African Responses to Price." *Journal of Farm Economics* 47 (May 1965): 402–09.

*Evenson, Robert, and Kislev, Yoav. *Agricultural Research and Productivity*. A Publication of the Economic Growth Center, Yale University. New Haven: Yale University Press, 1975.

Falcon, Walter. "Farmer Response to Price in a Subsistence Economy: The Case of West Pakistan." *American Economic Review* 54 (May 1964): 580–91.

*Hayami, Y., and Ruttan, V. W. *Agricultural Development: An International Perspective*. Baltimore: Johns Hopkins Press, 1971.

Johnston, Bruce F., and Cownie, J. "The Seed-Fertilizer Revolution and the Labor Force Absorption Problem." *American Economic Review* 59 (September 1969): 569–82.

Johnston, Bruce F., and Kilby, Peter. *Agriculture and Structural Transformation: Economic Strategies in Late-Developing Countries*. New York: Oxford University Press, 1975.

Koo, Anthony Y. C. *The Role of Land Reform in Economic Development*. New York: Frederick A. Praeger, 1968.

Krishna, Raj. "Farm Supply Responses in India-Pakistan: A Case Study of the Punjab Region." *Economic Journal* 73 (September 1963): 447–87.

*Lipton, Michael. "The Theory of the Optimising Peasant." *Journal of Development Studies* 4 (April 1968): 327–51.

Mangahas, M.; Recto, E.; and Ruttan, V. "Price and Market Relationships for Rice and Corn in the Philippines." *Journal of Farm Economics* 48 (August 1966): 685–703.

Mazumdar, D. "Size of Farm and Productivity: A Problem of Indian Agriculture." *Economics* 32 (May 1965): 161–73.

*Mellor, John W. "Accelerated Growth in Agricultural Production and the Intersectoral Transfer of Resources." *Economic Development and Cultural Change* 22 (October 1973): 1–16.

———. *The Economics of Agricultural Development*. Ithaca: Cornell University Press, 1966.

————. *The New Economics of Growth*. Ithaca: Cornell University Press, for The Twentieth Century Fund, 1976.

————. "The Uses and Productivity of Farm Family Labor in Early Stages of Economic Development." *Journal of Farm Economics* 45 (August 1963): 517–34.

Nicholls, W. "An 'Agricultural Surplus' as a Factor in Economic Development." *Journal of Political Economy* 71 (February 1963): 1–29.

Nowshirvani, Vahid. "Land Allocation Under Uncertainty in Subsistence Agriculture." *Oxford Economic Papers* 23 (November 1971): 445–55.

————. "The Regional and Crop-Wise Pattern of the Growth of Per Acre Output in India." *Bulletin of the Oxford Institute of Economics and Statistics* 32 (February 1970): 59–79.

*Raj, K. N. "Some Questions Concerning Growth, Transformation, and Planning in Agriculture in Developing Countries." *Journal of Development Planning*, no. 1 (Department of Economic and Social Affairs, UN, 1969): 15–38.

*Reynolds, Lloyd G., ed. *Agriculture in Development Theory*. A Publication of the Economic Growth Center, Yale University. New Haven: Yale University Press, 1975.

*Schultz, T. W. *Transforming Traditional Agriculture*. New Haven: Yale University Press, 1964.

Wellisz, S. et al. "Resource Allocation in Traditional Agriculture: A Study of Andhra Pradesh." *Journal of Political Economy* 78 (July/August 1970): 655–84.

*Wharton, Clifford, ed. *Subsistence Agriculture and Economic Development*. Chicago: Aldine Publishing Co., 1969.

8. *The Industrial Sector* (including organization, productivity, technology choice, technology transfer; see also references under 11. Foreign Trade)

Berry, R. Albert, ed. *Essays on Colombian Industrialization*. Forthcoming.

*Chenery, Hollis B. "Patterns of Industrial Growth." *American Economic Review* 50 (September 1960): 624–54.

*Chenery, Hollis B., and Taylor, Lance. "Development Patterns: Among Countries and Over Time." *Review of Economics and Statistics* 50 (November 1968): 391–416.

Clague, C. "An International Comparison of Industrial Efficiency: Peru and the U.S." *Review of Economics and Statistics* 49 (November 1967): 487–93.

Daniels, M. R. "Differences in Efficiency Among Industries in Developing Countries." *American Economic Review* 59 (March 1969): 159–71.

Hoffman, Walther G. *The Growth of Industrial Economies*. Manchester: University of Manchester Press, 1958.

Kilby, Peter. *Industrialization in an Open Economy: Nigeria, 1945–66*. London: Cambridge University Press, 1969.

Kim, Y. C. "Sectoral Output-Capital Ratios and Levels of Economic Development: A Cross-Sectional Comparison of Manufacturing Industry." *Review of Economics and Statistics* 51 (November 1969): 453–58.

Little, I. M. D., and Mirrless, J. A. *Project Appraisal and Planning for Develop-

ing Countries. New York: Basic Books, 1974.

Mehta, B. V. "Size and Capital Intensity in Indian Industry." *Bulletin of the Oxford Institute of Economics and Statistics* 31 (August 1969): 189–204.

Nelson, R. R. "A 'Diffusion' Model of International Productivity Differences." *American Economic Review* 58 (December 1968): 1219–48.

Prest, A. R., and Turvey, R. "Cost-Benefit Analysis: A Survey." *Economic Journal* 75 (December 1965): 683–735.

Reynolds, Lloyd G., and Gregory, Peter. *Wages Productivity, and Industrialization in Puerto Rico.* A Publication of Economic Growth Center Yale University. Homewood, Ill.: Richard D. Irwin, Inc., 1965.

Suzuki, N., ed. *Asian Industrial Development.* Tokyo: Institute of Developing Economies, 1975.

Winston, G. C. "Capital Utilization in Economic Development." *Economic Journal* 81 (March 1971): 36–60.

9. *The Public Sector* (including taxation, budgeting, and development planning)

Bird, Richard M. *Taxation and Development: Lessons from Colombian Experience.* Cambridge: Harvard University Press, 1970.

————. *Taxing Agricultural Land in Developing Countries.* Cambridge: Harvard University Press, 1974.

*Chelliah, Raja. "Trends in Taxation in Developing Countries." *IMF Staff Papers* 18 (July 1971): 254–331.

Due, John. *Indirect Taxation in Developing Economies.* Baltimore: Johns Hopkins Press, 1970.

Hagen, E., ed. *Planning Economic Development.* Homewood, Ill.: Richard D. Irwin, Inc., 1963.

*Haq, Mahbubul. *The Strategy of Economic Planning: A Case Study of Pakistan.* Karachi: Pakistan Branch, Oxford University Press, 1963.

Hicks, Ursula K. *Development Finance: Planning and Control.* New York: Oxford University Press, 1965.

————. *Development From Below.* Oxford: Clarendon Press, 1961.

Hinrichs, Harley H. "Determinants of Government Revenue Shares Among Less-Developed Countries." *Economic Journal* 75 (September 1965): 546–56.

Khalid, R. O. "Fiscal Policy, Development Planning, and Annual Budgeting." *IMF Staff Papers* 16 (March 1969): 53–84.

*Lewis, W. A. *Development Planning.* London: Allen and Unwin, 1966.

Lewis, W. Arthur, and Martin, Alison. "Patterns of Public Revenue and Expenditure." *Manchester School* 24 (September 1956): 203–44.

Lotz, Jorgen R., and Morss, Elliott R. "Measuring 'Tax Effort' in Developing Countries." *IMF Staff Papers* 14 (November 1967): 478–99.

Musgrave, Richard A. *Fiscal Systems.* New Haven: Yale University Press, 1969.

Prest, Alan. *Public Finance in Underdeveloped Countries.* London: Weidenfeld and Nicholson, 1962.

Pryor, Frederic L. *Public Expenditure in Communist and Capitalist Nations.*

A Publication of the Economic Growth Center, Yale University. Homewood, Ill.: Richard D. Irwin, Inc., 1968.

Ranis, Gustav, ed. *Government and Economic Development.* A Publication of
the Economic Growth Center, Yale University. New Haven: Yale University
Press, 1971.

Stolper, W. A. *Planning Without Facts.* Cambridge: Harvard University Press,
1966.

Thorn, Richard S. "The Evolution of Public Finances During Economic
Development." *Manchester School* 35 (January 1967): 19–53.

Waterston, A. *Development Planning: Lessons of Experience.* Baltimore: Johns
Hopkins Press, for the IBRD, 1965.

*Wildavsky, Aaron, and Caiden, Naomi. *Planning and Budgeting in Poor
Countries.* New York: John Wiley & Sons, 1974.

Williamson, Jeffrey G. "Public Expenditure and Revenue: An International
Comparison." *Manchester School* 29 (January 1961): 43–56.

10. The Distribution of Income

*Adelman, Irma, and Morris, Cynthia Taft. *Economic Growth and Social
Equity in Developing Countries.* Stanford: Stanford University Press, 1973.

Berry, R. Albert, and Urrutia, Miguel. *Income Distribution in Colombia.*
A Publication of the Economic Growth Center, Yale University. New
Haven: Yale University Press, 1976.

*Chenery, Hollis; Ahluwalia, Montek S.; and others. *Redistribution With
Growth.* New York: Oxford University Press for the IBRD, 1974.

11. Foreign Trade (including models of trade and growth, problems of primary exports, the import-substitution controversy, and alternative foreign trade and payments regimes)

Balassa, Bela. "Growth Strategies in Semi-Industrial Countries." *Quarterly
Journal of Economics* 84 (February 1970): 24–47.

———. "Industrial Policies in Taiwan and Korea." *Weltwirtschaftliches Archiv*
106 (1971): 55–76.

———. "Trade Policies in Developing Countries." *American Economic
Review* 61 (May 1971): 178–87.

Balassa, Bela, and others. *The Structure of Protection in Developing Countries.*
Baltimore: Johns Hopkins Press, 1971.

Baldwin, R. *Economic Development and Export Growth: A Study of Northern
Rhodesia, 1920–1960.* Berkeley and Los Angeles: University of California
Press, 1966.

*Baldwin, R. E., ed. *International Trade and Finance: Readings.* Boston: Little,
Brown, 1974.

*Bhagwati, J., ed. *International Trade: Selected Readings.* Harmondsworth:
Penguin, 1969.

Bhagwati, J., and other, eds. *Trade, Balance of Payments and Growth.* Amsterdam: North-Holland Publishing Co., 1971.

*Bhagwati, J. N. *Anatomy and Consequences of Exchange Control Regimes.* New

York: Columbia University Press, for the NBER, 1977.

———. "The Theory of Comparative Advantage in the Context of Under-development and Growth." *Pakistan Development Review* 2 (Autumn 1962): 339–53.

Birnberg, Thomas, and Resnick, Stephen A. *Colonial Development*. A Publication of the Economic Growth Center, Yale University. New Haven: Yale University Press, 1975.

Bruton, Henry. "Productivity Growth in Latin America." *American Economic Review* 57 (December 1967): 1099–116.

———. "The Import Substitution Strategy of Economic Development." *Pakistan Development Review* 10 (Summer 1970): 123–46.

*Caves, R. E., and Johnson, H., eds. *Readings in International Economics*. Homewood, Ill.: Richard D. Irwin, Inc., for the AEA, 1968.

*Chenery, Hollis B. "Comparative Advantage and Development Policy." *American Economic Review* 51 (March 1961): 18–51.

Cohen, B. J. *The Question of Imperialism: The Political Economy of Dominance and Dependence*. New York: Basic Books, 1973.

Cooper, R. "Growth and Trade: Some Hypotheses About Long Run Trends." *Journal of Economic History* 24 (December 1964): 609–28.

———. *Currency Devaluation in Developing Countries*. Princeton: Princeton Essays in International Finance, no. 86. 1971.

Diaz Alejandro, Carlos. "On the Import Intensity of Import Substitution." *Kyklos* 17 (1965): 495–509.

———. "Some Characteristics of Recent Export Expansion in Latin America." In *The International Division of Labor: Problems and Perspectives*, edited by H. Giersch. Tübingen: Mohr, 1974.

———. "Trade Policies and Economic Development." In Peter B. Kenen, ed. *International Trade and Finance*. New York: Cambridge University Press, 1975.

Donges, J. B. "From an Autarchic Toward a Cautiously Outward-Looking Development Policy: The Case of Spain." *Weltwirtschaftliches Archiv* 107 (1971): 33–72.

Giersch, H., ed. *The international Division of Labor: Problems and Perspectives*. Tübingen: Mohr, 1974.

Harrod, R., and Hague, D. C., eds. *International Trade Theory in a Developing World*. London: Macmillan, 1963.

Helleiner, G. *International Trade and Economic Development*. Harmondsworth: Penguin, 1972.

———. "Manufactured Exports from Less Developed Countries and Multi-national Firms." *Economic Journal* 83 (March 1973): 21–48.

*Johnson, Harry. "Comparative Cost and Commercial Policy Theory in a Developing World Economy." *Pakistan Development Review* 9, supp. (Spring 1969): 1–33. Wicksell Lectures, 1968.

———. *Economic Policies Toward Less Developed Countries*. Washington. The Brookings Institution, 1967.

Kindleberger, C. P. *Foreign Trade and the National Economy*. New Haven: Yale University Press, 1962.

———. *The Terms of Trade: A European Case Study*. Cambridge: M.I.T. Press, 1956.

Kravis, Irving B. "International Commodity Agreements to Promote Aid and Efficiency: The Case of Coffee." *Canadian Journal of Economics* 1 (May 1968): 295–317.

———. "Trade as a Handmaiden of Growth: Similarities Between the Nineteenth and Twentieth Centuries." *Economic Journal* 80 (December 1970): 850–72.

Krueger, Anne O. *Liberalization Attempts and Consequences.* New York: Columbia University Press, for the NBER, 1977.

———. "Evaluating Restrictionist Trade Regions: Theory and Measurement." *Journal of Political Economy* 80 (Jan./Feb. 1972b): 48–62.

———. "Some Economic Costs of Exchange Control: The Turkish Case." *Journal of Political Economy* 74 (October 1966): 466–80.

*Lewis, W. Arthur. *Aspects of Tropical Trade, 1883–1965.* Stockholm: Almquist and Wiksell, 1969.

*Little, Ian; Scitovsky, Tibor; and Scott, Maurice. *Industry and Trade in Some Developing Countries.* New York: Oxford University Press, for the OECD, 1970.

MacBean, A. *Export Instability and Economic Development.* Cambridge: Harvard University Press, 1966.

Maizels, Alfred. *Exports and Economic Growth of Developing Countries.* London: Cambridge University Press, 1968.

*Meier, Gerald. *The International Economics of Development.* New York: Harper and Row, 1968.

*Nurkse, R. *Equilibrium and Growth in the World Economy.* Cambridge: Harvard University Press, 1962.

———. *Patterns of Trade and Development.* Stockholm: Almquist and Wiksell, 1959.

———. *Problems of Capital Formation in Underdeveloped Countries.* New York: Oxford University Press, 1953.

Paauw, Douglas, and Fei, John C. H. *The Trasition in Open Dualistic Economies.* A Publication of the Economic Growth Center, Yale University. New Haven: Yale University Press, 1973.

*Prebisch, R. "Commercial Policy in the Underdeveloped Countries." *American Economic Review* 49 (May 1959): 251–73.

Resnick, Stephen A. "The Decline of Rural Industry Under Export Expansion: A Comparison Among Burma, Philippines, and Thailand, 1870–1938." *Journal of Economic History* 30 (March 1970): 51–73.

Reynolds, Clark, and Mamalakis, Markos. *Essays on the Chilean Economy.* A Publication of the Economic Growth Center, Yale University. Homewood, Ill.: Richard D. Irwin, Inc., 1965.

Rodriguez, Carlos A. "Trade in Technological Knowledge and the National Advantage." *Journal of Political Economy* 83 (February 1975): 121–35.

12. *International Factor Movements* (including official capital transfers, private investment, multinational corporations, brain drain)

Adams, W., ed. *The Brain Drain.* New York: Macmillan, 1968.

Bhagwati, J., and Hamada, K. "The Brain Drain, International Integration of Markets for Professionals, and Unemployment." *Journal of Development*

Economics 1 (June 1974): 19–42.

Caves, R. E. *International Trade, International Investment, and Imperfect Markets*. Special Papers in International Economics. Princeton: International Finance Section, Princeton University, 1974.

————. "International Corporations: The Industrial Economics of Foreign Investment." *Economica* 38 (February 1971): 1–27.

Chenery, Hollis, and Bruno, Michael. "Development Alternatives in an Open Economy: The Case of Israel." *Economic Journal* 72 (March 1962): 79–103.

*Chenery, Hollis, and Strout, Alan. "Foreign Assistance and Economic Development." *American Economic Review* 56 (September 1966): 679–733.

Cohen, Benjamin. *Multinational Firms and Asian Exports*. A Publication of the Economic Growth Center, Yale University. New Haven: Yale University Press, 1975.

Hymer, S. "The Efficiency Contradictions of Multinational Corporations." *American Economic Review* 60 (May 1970): 441–48.

Kindleberger, Charles, ed. *The International Corporation*. Cambridge: M.I.T. Press, 1970.

Little, I., and Clifford, J. M. *International Aid*. Chicago: Aldine Publishing Co., 1968.

*MacDougall, G. D. A. "The Benefits and Costs of Private Investment From Abroad: A Theoretical Approach." *Economic Record* 36, special issue (March 1960): 13–35. Reprinted in Bhagwati, J., ed. *International Trade: Selected Readings*. Baltimore: Penguin Books, 1969.

*McKinnon, R. W. "Foreign Exchange Constraints in Development and Efficient Aid." *Economic Journal* 74 (June 1964): 388–409.

*Ohlin, Göran. *Foreign Aid Policies Reconsidered*. Paris: OECD, 1966.

Pincus, John A. *Economic Aid and International Cost Sharing*. Baltimore: Johns Hopkins Press, 1965.

Ranis, Gustav, ed. *The Gap Between Rich and Poor Nations*. New York: St. Martin's Press, 1972.

Vernon, R. *Sovereignty at Bay: The Multinational Spread of U.S. Enterprises*. New York: Basic Books, 1971.

13. *Development Experience: Britain and Europe*

Ashton, T. W. *An Economic History of England. Vol. 3, The Eighteenth Century*. New York: Barnes and Noble, 1955.

*Ashton, T. S. *The Industrial Revolution, 1760–1830*. New York: Oxford University Press, 1970.

Cipolla, Carlo M., ed. *The Fontana Economic History of Europe*. 3 vol. London: Collins/Fontana Books, 1973.

*Deane, Phyllis. *The First Industrial Revolution*. Cambridge: Cambridge University Press, 1965.

*Deane, Phyllis, and Cole, W. A. *British Economic Growth, 1688–1959*. Cambridge: Cambridge University Press, 1962.

Gerschenkron, A. *Economic Backwardness in Historical Perspective*. Cambridge: Belknap Press of Harvard University Press, 1962.

Milward, A., and Saul, S. B. *The Economic Development of Continental Europe, 1780–1870*. London: Allen and Unwin, 1973.

*Rostow, W. W., ed. *The Economics of the Takeoff.* New York: St. Martin's Press, 1964.

Supple, Barry E., ed. *The Experience of Economic Growth.* Pt. 1, secs. A–D. New York: Random House, 1963.

*Youngson, A. J. *Possibilities of Economic Progress.* Cambridge: Cambridge University Press, 1959.

Youngson, A. J., ed. *Economic Development in the Long Run.* London: Allen and Unwin, 1972.

14. Development Experience: Japan

Emi, Koichi. *Government Fiscal Activity and Economic Growth in Japan.* Tokyo: Kinokuniya Bookstore, 1963.

Hayami, Yujiro, and others. *A Century of Agricultural Growth in Japan.* Minneapolis: University of Minnesota Press, 1975.

*Klein, Lawrence, and Ohkawa, Kazushi, eds. *Economic Growth: The Japanese Experience Since the Meiji Era.* A Publication of the Economic Growth Center, Yale University. Homewood, Ill.: Richard D. Irwin, Inc., 1968.

Lockwood, W. W. *The Economic Development of Japan.* Princeton: Princeton University Press, 1954.

Lockwood, W. W., ed. *The State and Economic Enterprise in Japan.* Princeton: Princeton University Press, 1965.

Minami, R. *The Turning Point in Economic Development: Japan's Experience.* Tokyo: Kinokuniya Bookstore, 1973.

Ohara, Keiji. *Japanese Trade and Industry in the Meiji-Taisho Era.* Tokyo: Obunsha, 1957.

Ohkawa, Kazushi. *Differential Structure and Agriculture.* Tokyo: Kinokuniya Bookstore, 1972.

———. *The Growth Rate of the Japanese Economy Since 1878.* Tokyo: Kinokuniya Bookstore, 1957.

*Ohkawa, Kazushi, and Rosovsky, Henry. *Japanese Economic Growth.* Stanford: Stanford University Press, 1973.

*Ohkawa, K.; Johnston, B. F.; and Kaneda, H., eds. *Agriculture and Economic Growth: Japan's Experience.* Tokyo: Tokyo University Press, and Princeton: Princeton University Press, 1969.

Rosovsky, Henry. *Capital Formation in Japan, 1868–1940.* New York: Free Press, 1961.

Rosovsky, Henry, ed. *Industrialization in Two Systems.* New York: John Wiley & Sons, 1966.

Shinohara, M. *Structural Change in Japan's Economic Development.* Tokyo: Kato Bummeisha Printing Co., 1970.

15. Contemporary Development: Mixed Economies (This is not a comprehensive listing of the country-specific literature but is limited mainly to the countries analyzed in chapters 10–14.)

Adelman, Irma, and Morris, Cynthia Taft. *Society, Politics, and Economic Development: A Quantitative Approach.* Baltimore: Johns Hopkins Press, 1967.

Amuzegar, Jahangir. *Iran: Economic Development Under Dualistic Conditions.* London and Chicago: University of Chicago Press, 1971.

Avramovic, V. *Economic Growth of Colombia.* Baltimore: Johns Hopkins Press, for the IBRD, 1972.

Baer, Werner. *Industrialization and Economic Development in Brazil.* A Publication of the Economic Growth Center, Yale University. Homewood, Ill.: Richard D. Irwin, Inc., 1965.

*Balassa, Bela. "Industrial Policies in Taiwan and Korea." *Weltwirtschaftliches Archiv* 106 (1971): 55–76.

*Baldwin, Robert E. *Foreign Trade Regimes and Economic Development: The Philippines.* New York: Columbia University Press, for the NBER, 1975.

Behrman, Jere R. *Foreign Trade Regimes and Economic Development: Chile.* New York: Columbia University Press, for the NBER, 1976.

* Bergsman, Joel. *Industrialization and Trade Policies in Brazil.* Oxford: Oxford University Press, for the OECD, 1970).

*Bhagwati, J., and Desai, P. *India, Planning for Industrialization: Industrial and Trade Politicies Since 1951.* London: Oxford University Press, 1970.

*Bhagwati, J., and Srinavasan, T. N. *Foreign Trade Regimes and Economic Development: India.* New York: Columbia University Press, for the NBER, 1976.

Bharier, J. *Economic Development in Iran, 1900–1970.* New York: Oxford University Press, 1971.

*Chenery, Hollis, and Syrquin, Moises. *Patterns of Development, 1950–1970.* New York: Oxford University Press, for the IBRD, 1975.

*Chenery, Hollis, and Taylor, Lance. "Development Patterns: Among Countries and Over Time." *Review of Economics and Statistics* 50 (November 1968): 391–417.

*Diaz Alejandro, Carlos. *Essays on the Economic History of the Argentine Republic.* A Publication of the Economic Growth Center, Yale University. New Haven: Yale University Press, 1970.

*———. *Foreign Trade Regimes and Economic Development: Colombia.* New York: Columbia University Press, for the NBER, 1976.

Ellis, Howard S., ed. *The Economy of Brazil.* Berkeley: University of California Press, 1969.

*Fishlow, Albert. *Foreign Trade Regimes and Economic Development: Brazil.* New York: Columbia University Press, for the NBER, 1976.

*Frank, Charles R., Jr.; Kim, Kwang Suk; and Westphal, Larry. *Foreign Trade Regimes and Economic Development (South Korea).* New York: NBER, 1975.

*Helleiner, Gerald. *Peasant Agriculture, Government and Economic Growth in Nigeria.* A Publication of the Economic Growth Center, Yale University. Homewood, Ill.: Richard D. Irwin, Inc., 1966.

*Ho, Samuel P. *Economic Development of Taiwan, 1890–1970.* A Publication of the Economic Growth Center, Yale University. New Haven: Yale University Press, 1977.

Ho, Y. M. "Development with Surplus Population—the Case of Taiwan: A Critique of the Classical Two-Sector Model a la Lewis." *Economic Development and Cultural Change* 20 (January 1972): 210–34.

*Hsing, M.; Power, J.; and Sicat, G. P. *Taiwan and the Philippines: Industrialization and Trade Policies.* New York: Oxford University Press, 1970.

Ingram, James C. *Economic Change in Thailand, 1850–1970.* Stanford: Stanford University Press, 1971.

*International Labor Organization. *Sharing in Development: A Program of Employment, Equity, and Growth in the Philippines.* Geneva: ILO, 1973.

———. *Towards Full Employment: A Program for Colombia.* Geneva: ILO, 1970.

Kasper, W. *Malaysia: A Study in Successful Economic Development.* Washington: American Enterprise Institute, 1974.

*Kilby, Peter. *Industrializations in an Open Economy: Nigeria, 1945–66.* New York: Cambridge University Press, 1967.

*King, Timothy. *Mexico: Industrialization and Trade Policies Since 1940.* Oxford: Oxford University Press, for the OECD, 1970.

*Krueger, Anne O. *Foreign Trade Regimes and Economic Development: Turkey.* New York: Columbia University Press, for the NBER, 1975.

Kuznets, Paul W. *Economic Growth and Structure in the Republic of Korea.* A Publication of the Economic Growth Center, Yale University. New Haven: Yale University Press, 1976.

*Kuznets, Simon. "Problems in Comparing Recent Growth Rates for Developed and Less Developed Countries." *Economic Development and Cultural Change* 20 (January 1972): 185–209.

Lee, Teng-Hui. *Intersectoral Capital Flows in the Economic Development of Taiwan, 1895–1960.* Ithaca: Cornell University Press, 1971.

Lewis, S. R. *Economic Policy and Industrial Growth in Pakistan.* Cambridge: M.I.T. Press, 1969.

*———. *Pakistan: Industrialization and Trade Policies.* Oxford: Oxford University Press, for the OECD, 1970.

Mamalakis, M. *The Chilean Economy: From Independence to Allende.* A Publication of the Economic Growth Center, Yale University. New Haven: Yale University Press, 1977.

Nelson, Richard R.; Schultz, T. Paul; and Slighton, Robert L. *Structural Change in a Developing Economy (Colombia).* Princeton: Princeton University Press, 1971.

Pack, Howard. *The Development of the Economy of Israel.* A Publication of the Economic Growth Center, Yale University. New Haven: Yale University Press, 1970.

*Reynolds, Clark. *The Mexican Economy: Twentieth-Century Structure and Growth.* A Publication of the Economic Growth Center, Yale University. New Haven: Yale University Press, 1970.

Silcock, T., ed. *Thailand: Economic and Social Studies in Development.* Canberra: Australian National University Press, 1967.

Stryker, J. Dirck. "Exports and Growth in the Ivory Coast: Timber, Cocoa, and Coffee." Yale Economic Growth Center Discussion Paper no. 147. 1972. Mimeographed.

Vernon, Raymond T., ed. *Public Policy and Private Enterprise in Mexico.* Cambridge: Harvard University Press, 1964.

Winpenny, J. *Brazil: Manufacturing Exports and Government Policy.* London:

Latin American Publication Fund, distributed by Grant & Cutler, 1972.

16. Contemporary Development: Socialist Economies

Chung, I. S. *The North Korean Economy: Structure and Development.* Stanford: Hoover Institution Press, 1974.

Dubey, V. *Yugoslavia: Development with Decentralization.* Baltimore: Johns Hopkins University Press, 1975.

Eckstein, Alexander. *China's Economic Revolution.* Cambridge: Cambridge University Press, 1977.

Eckstein, Alexander; Galenson, Walter; and Liu, Ta-Chung. *Economic Trends in Communist China.* Chicago: Aldine Publishing Co., 1968.

*Gregory, Paul. *Socialist and Nonsocialist Industrialization Patterns: A Comparative Appraisal.* New York: Frederick A. Praeger, 1970.

*Kornai, Janos. *Anti-Equilibrium.* Amsterdam: North-Holland Publishing Co., 1971.

Mesa-Lago, Carmelo. *Cuba in the 1970s.* Albuquerque: University of New Mexico Press, 1974.

Mesa-Lago, Carmelo, ed. *Revolutionary Change in Cuba.* Pittsburgh: University of Pittsburgh Press, 1971.

*Montias, John M. *Economic Development in Communist Rumania.* Cambridge: M.I.T. Press, 1967.

*Perkins, Dwight H. "Looking Inside China: An Economic Reappraisal." *Problems of Communism* 22 (May/June 1973): 1–13.

Reynolds, Lloyd G. "China as a Less Developed Country." *American Economic Review* 65 (June 1975): 418–28.

―――. *The Three Worlds of Economics.* New Haven: Yale University Press, 1971.

*U.S., Congress, Joint Economic Committee. *China: A Reassessment of the Economy* (Washington: Government Printing Office, for the Joint Economic Committee, 1975.

―――. *Economic Developments in Countries of Eastern Europe* (Washington: Government Printing Office, for the Joint Economic Committee, 1970).

―――. *People's Republic of China: An Economic Assessment* (Washington: Government Printing Office, for the Joint Economic Committee, 1972).

*―――. *Reorientations and Commercial Relations of the Economies of Eastern Europe* (Washington: Government Printing Office, for the Joint Economic Committee, 1974).

Index

Absorptive capacity for investment, 195, 197, 199
Adelman, Irma, 16, 256, 257, 261, 391, 392
Ady, Peter, 76
Africa: agriculture in, 63, 64, 96, 107; colonialism in, 159, 160, 161; growth classification of, 6; land surplus in, 86; migrant labor in, 64, 81–82, 180
Aged, 424
Agricultural sector: Brazilian, 371–372; capital formation and, 74; Chinese, 409, 426, 428; classical economics on, 32; constraints on adjustment in, 70–74; development patterns in, 13, 377, 379; dualism in, 101, 295–98; employment and, 435–36; exports and, 173, 175, 353, 355; as family-based enterprise, 55; financial transfers and, 300–02; food output and availability in, 281–87; growth acceleration and, 11, 216, 218; in developing economies, 280–303; East European, 408; government expenditures on, 342, 346, 347; income distribution and, 295–98, 442; industrial sector and, 134, 140; Japanese, 221, 222, 225, 226, 227–32, 249; labor market and, 73–74, 116–20, 141–42, 298–300; land as key factor in, 56, 73; Malaysian, 368; man-land ratio in, 85–91; market development in, 59–65; Marxian theory on, 30–31; Mexican, 373–74; microeconomic policies for, 37, 437–38; models on, 22, 23–24, 41, 44–52, 65–69, 131; motivation in, 70–71; nonland inputs and, 56–57; open economy and, 171–72; output increase and, 273–74, 287–94; physiocratic policy on, 21, 22; prices and, 71–72, 74–85; production unit in, 54–91, 135–38; productivity gap in, 59; resources

and, 115–22, 143–46; scale economies in, 57–58; socialist economies and, 412–17; South Korean, 365; static equilibrium in, 69–70; supporting activities in, 58; surplus food in, 120; surplus saving in, 120–21; taxation increases in, 83–85; technical change in, 58, 61, 92, 102–14, 147–48; unemployment and, 388–90, 400–01; wages in, 81–83, 114; yields in. *See* Yields, agricultural
Ahluwalia, Martek S., 390, 393, 395, 423
Aid. *See* Foreign aid
Alcan, 164
Aligarh District (India), 112
Alton, Thad R., 404, 409
Argentina, 7*n*, 184, 191, 329, 384
Artisans, 139
Asia: agriculture in, 92, 96, 107, 108, 110, 135; growth classification of, 6
Australia: capital formation in, 205, 242, 344; income distribution in, 391; industry in, 202, 305; loans from, 193
Austria, 193

Baba, Masao, 245, 246
Balanced growth concept, 181, 182
Balance of payments: export development and, 182, 188; Japanese growth acceleration and, 248; multinational corporations and, 205
Balassa, Bela, 184
Baldwin, R. E., 175
Bangladesh, 170, 438
Banks, 361: borrowing from, 347, 348, 351; Japanese development of, 433
Baran, Paul, 156
Becker, Gary S., 203
Belgian Congo, 162
Bergsman, Joel, 327–28, 372
Berry, R. Albert, 66, 82, 98, 101, 121, 295, 297, 386, 387, 392, 393

485

Economic Growth Center Book Publications

Werner Baer, *Industrialization and Economic Development in Brazil* (1965).

Werner Baer and Isaac Kerstenetzky, eds., *Inflation and Growth in Latin America* (1964).

Bela A. Balassa, *Trade Prospects for Developing Countries* (1964). Out of print.

Albert Berry and Miguel Urrutia, *Income Distribution in Columbia* (1976).

Thomas B. Birnberg and Stephen A. Resnick, *Colonial Development: An Econometric Study* (1975).

Benjamin I. Cohen, *Multinational Firms and Asian Exports* (1975).

Carlos F. D´ıaz Alejandro, *Essays on the Economic History of the Argentine Republic* (1970).

Robert Evenson and Yoav Kislev, *Agricultural Research and Productivity* (1975).

John C. H. Fei and Gustav Ranis, *Development of Labor Surplus Economy: Theory and Policy* (1964).

Gerald K. Helleiner, *Peasant Agriculture, Government, and Economic Growth in Nigeria* (1966).

Lawrence R. Klein and Kazushi Ohkawa, eds., *Economic Growth: The Japanese Experience since the Meiji Era* (1968).

Paul W. Kuznets, *Economic Growth and Structure in the Republic of Korea* (1977).

A. Lamfalussy, *The United Kingdom and the Six* (1963). Out of print.

Markos J. Mamalakis, *The Growth and Structure of the Chilean Economy: From Independence to Allende* (1976).

Markos J. Mamalakis and Clark W. Reynolds, *Essays on the Chilean Economy* (1965).

Donald C. Mead, *Growth and Structural Change in the Egyptian Economy* (1967).

Richard Moorsteen and Raymond P. Powell, *The Soviet Capital Stock* (1966).

Douglas S. Paauw and John C. H. Fei, *The Transition in Open Dualistic Economies: Theory and Southeast Asian Experience* (1973).

Howard Pack, *Structural Change and Economic Policy in Israel* (1971).

Frederick L. Pryor, *Public Expenditures in Communist and Capitalist Nations* (1968).

Gustav Ranis, ed., *Government and Economic Development* (1971).

Clark W. Reynolds, *The Mexican Economy: Twentieth-Century Structure and Growth* (1970).

Lloyd G. Reynolds, *Image and Reality in Economic Development* (1977).

Lloyd G. Reynolds, ed., *Agriculture in Development Theory* (1975).

Lloyd G. Reynolds and Peter Gregory, *Wages, Productivity, and Industrialization in Puerto Rico* (1965).

Donald R. Snodgrass, *Ceylon: An Export Economy in Transition* (1966).